THE ROUGH GUIDE TO

The Dordogne
& the Lot

There are more than two hundred Rough Guide titles
covering destinations from Alaska to Zimbabwe
and subjects from Acoustic Guitar to Travel Health

Forthcoming travel guides include
Madeira • Malta & Gozo • Tenerife
Thai Beaches & Islands • US Rockies

Forthcoming reference guides include
Children's Books • Online Travel • Videogaming • Weather

Rough Guides Online
www.roughguides.com

ROUGH GUIDE CREDITS

Text editors: Sam Thorne and Andrew Tomicic
Series editor: Mark Ellingham
Editorial: Martin Dunford, Jonathan Buckley, Jo
Mead, Kate Berens, Ann-Marie Shaw, Paul Gray,
Helena Smith, Judith Bamber, Orla Duane, Olivia
Eccleshall, Ruth Blackmore, Geoff Howard, Claire
Saunders, Gavin Thomas, Alexander Mark Rogers,
Polly Thomas, Joe Staines, Richard Lim, Duncan Clark,
Peter Buckley, Lucy Ratcliffe, Clifton Wilkinson, David
Glen, Alison Murchie, Matthew Teller, Andrew Dickson
(UK); Andrew Rosenberg, Stephen Timblin, Yuki
Takagaki, Richard Koss (US)
Production: Susanne Hillen, Andy Hilliard, Link Hall,
Helen Prior, Julia Bovis, Michelle Draycott, Katie

Pringle, Mike Hancock, Zoë Nobes, Rachel Holmes,
Andy Turner
Cartography: Melissa Baker, Maxine Repath, Ed Wright,
Katie Lloyd-Jones
Picture research: Louise Boulton, Sharon Martins
Online: Kelly Cross, Anja Mutić-Blessing, Jennifer Gold,
Audra Epstein, Suzanne Welles (US)
Finance: John Fisher, Gary Singh, Edward Downey,
Mark Hall, Tim Bill
Marketing & Publicity: Richard Trillo, Niki Smith,
David Wearn, Chloë Roberts, Claire Southern (UK);
Simon Carloss, David Wechsler, Kathleen Rushforth (US)
Administration: Tania Hummel, Demelza Dallow, Julie
Sanderson

ACKNOWLEDGEMENTS

This book is dedicated to Erica.

Jan Dodd would like to thank Pauline & Paul
Carpenter in Bordeaux, Helen Goossens in Nérac,
Sally Gosheron in Montcabrier and Sophie Bacou in
Montcuq for their help, advice and encouragement.
Thanks are also due to Joelle Savary for rugby
coaching, Miranda Neame of *The News*, Gavin Dick
and Howard Newman for answering my questions,
and to Audrey and David Connelly for their hospitality

in Figeac. As ever, I am heavily indebted to the Wa
Dodd for sleuthing esoteric facts and out-of-print
books, and to Steve for his unfailing support and for
helping to keep in mind the big picture. Last but by
no means least, a big thank you to everyone at
Rough Guides, especially Andrew Tomicic and Sam
Thorne for their work in editing the book, Andy
Turner for typesetting, Maxine Repath and Katie
Lloyd-Jones for maps, Sharon Martins for picture
research and David Price for proofreading.

PUBLISHING INFORMATION

This first edition published July 2001 by
  Rough Guides Ltd, 62–70 Shorts Gardens,
  London WC2H 9AH.
Distributed by the Penguin Group:
Penguin Books Ltd, 27 Wrights Lane, London W8 5TZ
Penguin Putnam, Inc. 375 Hudson Street, New York 10014,
  USA
Penguin Books Australia Ltd, 487 Maroondah Highway,
  PO Box 257, Ringwood, Victoria 3134, Australia
Penguin Books Canada Ltd, 10 Alcorn Avenue, Toronto,
  Ontario, Canada M4V 1E4
Penguin Books (NZ) Ltd, 182–190 Wairau Road,
  Auckland 10, New Zealand
Typeset in Linotron Univers and Century Old Style to an
  original design by Andrew Oliver.
Printed by Clays Ltd St Ives PLC
Illustrations in Part One and Part Three by Edward Briant.

THE ROUGH GUIDE TO

The Dordogne & the Lot

written and researched by

Jan Dodd

ROUGH GUIDES

THE ROUGH GUIDES

TRAVEL GUIDES • PHRASEBOOKS • MUSIC AND REFERENCE GUIDES

 We set out to do something different when the first Rough Guide was published in 1982. Mark Ellingham, just out of university, was travelling in Greece. He brought along the popular guides of the day, but found they were all lacking in some way. They were either strong on ruins and museums but went on for pages without mentioning a beach or taverna. Or they were so conscious of the need to save money that they lost sight of Greece's cultural and historical significance. Also, none of the books told him anything about Greece's contemporary life – its politics, its culture, its people, and how they lived.

So with no job in prospect, Mark decided to write his own guidebook, one which aimed to provide practical information that was second to none, detailing the best beaches and the hottest clubs and restaurants, while also giving hard-hitting accounts of every sight, both famous and obscure, and providing up-to-the-minute information on contemporary culture. It was a guide that encouraged independent travellers to find the best of Greece, and was a great success, getting shortlisted for the Thomas Cook travel guide award,

and encouraging Mark, along with three friends, to expand the series.

The Rough Guide list grew rapidly and the letters flooded in, indicating a much broader readership than had been anticipated, but one which uniformly appreciated the Rough Guide mix of practical detail and humour, irreverence and enthusiasm. Things haven't changed. The same four friends who began the series are still the caretakers of the Rough Guide mission today: to provide the most reliable, up-to-date and entertaining information to independent-minded travellers of all ages, on all budgets.

We now publish more than 150 titles and have offices in London and New York. The travel guides are written and researched by a dedicated team of more than 100 authors, based in Britain, Europe, the USA and Australia. We have also created a unique series of phrasebooks to accompany the travel series, along with an acclaimed series of music guides, and a best-selling pocket guide to the Internet and World Wide Web. We also publish comprehensive travel information on our Web site:

www.roughguides.com

HELP US UPDATE

We've gone to a lot of effort to ensure that the first edition of *The Rough Guide to the Dordogne & the Lot* is accurate and up to date. However, things change — places get "discovered", opening hours are notoriously fickle, restaurants and rooms raise prices or lower standards. If you feel we've got it wrong or left something out, we'd like to know, and if you can remember the address, the price, the time, the phone number, so much the better.

We'll credit all contributions, and send a copy of the next edition (or any other Rough Guide if you prefer) for the best letters. Please mark letters: "Rough Guide Dordogne, & the Lot Update" and send to:
Rough Guides, 62–70 Shorts Gardens, London WC2H 9AH, or Rough Guides, 4th Floor, 345 Hudson St, New York, NY 10014.
Or send email to: mail@roughguides.co.uk
Online updates about this book can be found on Rough Guides' Web site at www.roughguides.com

THE AUTHOR

Jan Dodd (*www.jandodd.com*) arrived in southwest France by accident in 1992 and has been there every since, eager to ascertain whether duck fat, red wine and garlic really are the key to longevity. She has written several guidebooks and provides European and Asian coverage for books, magazines, newspapers and Web sites. As well as contributing regularly to *The Rough Guide to France*, Jan is co-author of *The Rough Guide to Vietnam* and *The Rough Guide to Japan*.

CONTENTS

Introduction ix

 **PART THREE** CONTEXTS **351**

LIST OF MAPS

MAP SYMBOLS

----	International boundary	♖	Castle
--- ·	Chapter division border	▲	Tower
▬▬	Motorway	▂▪▂	Fortifications
▮ ▬ ▬ ▮	Motorway under construction	∴	Ruin
===	Main road	♱	Church (regional maps)
===	Minor road	⌂	Abbey
⊪⊪⊪⊪⊪	Steps	⚘	Gardens
-----	Footpath	✈	Airport
━━━	Railway	℗	Parking
━━━━	Tourist train	ⓘ	Tourist office
———	River	⊠	Post office
— · —	Ferry route	⊞	Hospital
♦	Point of interest	▨	Building
⊠—⊠	Gate	✛	Church (town maps)
◠	Cave	⊹⊹⊹	Cemetery
⁂	Cliffs	▨	Park
�	Viewpoint	▨	National Park
🏛	Château		

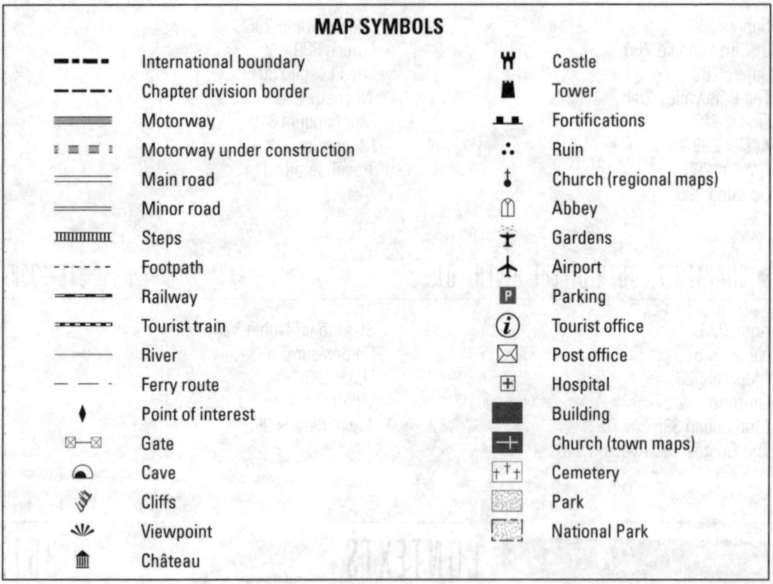

INTRODUCTION

History started with a bang in the **Dordogne and Lot** region. It was here, along its green, secretive valleys, that prehistoric people first started chiselling away at statues of round-hipped fertility figures. It was here, too, that they penetrated deep into the limestone caves to paint the world's earliest masterpieces of pot-bellied, prancing ponies, mammoths and muscular bison by the light of flickering oil lamps. Later occupants of the area expressed their faith in the Romanesque churches to be found, uncomplicated and enduring, on many a sun-drenched hilltop, and in the array of abbeys, cloisters and towering cathedrals. The legacy of a more bellicose era lies in the medieval fortresses perched on airy pinnacles of rock and in the feudal villages held snug within their ramparts, while an altogether more intimate link with the past is recorded among the ancient farmhouses tucked into the landscape's folds.

In addition to this richly layered history, the Dordogne and Lot is also endowed with a tremendous variety of **scenery**, from the dry limestone plateaux of the *causses*, sliced through with narrow gorges, to the lushly wooded valleys of the Périgord Noir and the Bordeaux vineyards' serried ranks. Through these landscapes slide the great **rivers** that unify and define the region: the **Dordogne**, which flows 500km from the Massif Central west to the Atlantic coast, and its more modest tributary, the **Isle**; and further south the **Lot**, writhing across country on its way to join the **Garonne**, which, along with its tributaries, the **Tarn** and **Aveyron**, marks this region's southern border.

Within this riverine framework each area possesses its own local character, marked by subtle shifts in architectural styles, in the hue of the building stone, the crops grown and in the cuisine. It is a region best savoured at its own unhurried pace; there is always something to catch the eye, some forgotten corner to stumble upon, a market or a village *fête*, where even today older folk use dialects whose origins date back to Roman times. This isn't to say the region is undiscovered – indeed, certain of its sights number amongst the most visited in France – but its heartland is still steeped in what the French call the *douceur de vivre*, the gentle way of life.

The **food and wine** are the other great inducements to bring you to the region. This is the land of duck and goose, of foie gras and truffles, of succulent lamb, smoky-sweet goats' cheeses and a rainbow array of fruits and vegetables to be sampled in simple country inns or in elegant dining rooms dedicated to *haute cuisine*. The choice of wines is no less intoxicating, from rich, ruby Cahors to the velvety sweet whites of Sauternes and Monbazillac; wandering the region's highways and byways, sampling these and other local offerings, is a pleasure not to be missed.

There is also endless scope for **outdoor activities**. In summer all the major rivers are flecked with canoes in colourful gaggles, while the Lot is now also open for navigation by houseboats. Walkers and cyclists are well served with a skein of well-marked tracks. Trekking is widely popular, and potholing and rock-climbing are also on offer in certain locations.

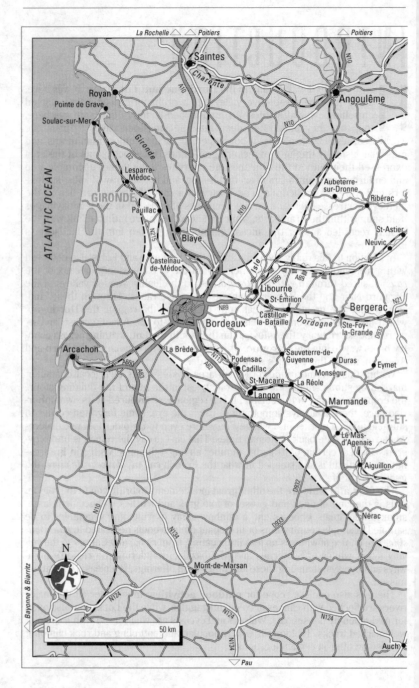

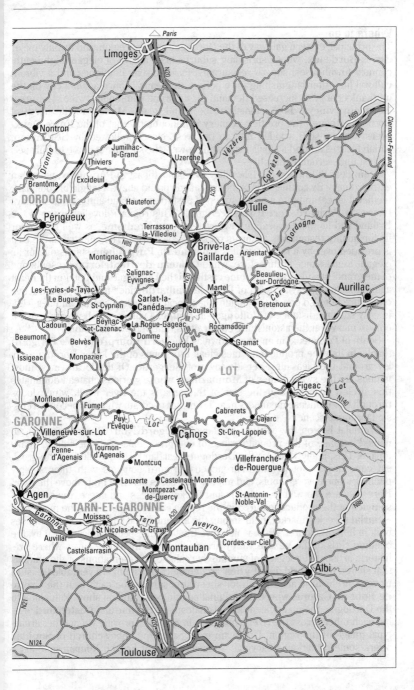

Where to go

The principal, eastern gateway to the Dordogne and Lot region, and its only major city, is **Bordeaux**, whose sprawling suburbs belie a core of elegant eighteenth-century townhouses, superb restaurants, Parisian-style boutiques and a vibrant cultural life. After languishing for a period, Bordeaux is once again a city on the up thanks partly to increased demand for its prime commodity, wine. The great **Bordeaux vineyards** are mostly to be found in the **Médoc**, to the north of Bordeaux, though the prettiest scenery is undoubtedly that of the **Entre-Deux-Mers** with its soft, wooded hills to the west, closely followed by **St-Émilion**, which focuses around a small, captivating town – the surprising home to Europe's largest underground church.

From near St-Émilion the Isle valley heads northeast to **Périgueux**, where an extraordinary Byzantine-style cathedral stands proud above a tangle of cool, dark medieval lanes, and into a broad sweep of pasture, woodland and intimate valleys known as **Périgord Vert** (Green Périgord). This region's loveliest river is the Dronne and its most appealing town water-bound **Brantôme**, as well known for its top-quality restaurants as for its rock-cut sanctuaries. The country to the east is presided over by a rash of castles: **Château de Puyguilhem** stands out for its elegant Renaissance architecture, while **Château de Hautefort** represents one of the grandest and most handsome castles in the Dordogne and Lot. Further east again, the rugby-playing town of **Brive-la-Gaillarde** hides not only an attractive old centre but also one of the region's best local history museums, and lies within easy striking distance of **Collonges-la-Rouge**, a village which merits a visit if only to marvel at the astonishing colour of its rich, red building stone.

South of Périgueux, in an area known as **Périgord Pourpre** (Purple Périgord) thanks to its wine production, vines cloak the slopes of the lower Dordogne valley around the pleasant, riverside town of **Bergerac**. Of the local wines, most famous are the sweet whites of **Monbazillac**, whose glorious château dominates this stretch of valley. But the star of this area is the river itself, which loops through two immense meanders near **Trémolat** to create what has become a classic Dordogne scene.

Trémolat lies on the western border of **Périgord Noir** (Black Périgord), so named because of the preponderance of evergreen oaks with their dark, dense foliage. This, if anywhere, is the Dordogne heartland. Here you'll find the greatest concentration of geranium-drenched Périgord cottages with their steeply pitched, stone-covered roofs, and mighty fortresses perched high above the river. Here, too, are the walnut orchards and flocks of ducks and geese, the source of so much of the produce featured in the region's markets. Of these the most vivid is **Sarlat**'s weekly market, held among the fine medieval and Renaissance houses built in honey-coloured stone which give the town its special allure. Close by, the beetling cliffs of the **Vézère valley** are riddled with limestone caves where prehistoric artists left a legacy of stunningly realistic representations of the animals that shared their world. **Les Eyzies**' archeological museum is a veritable treasure trove of prehistoric art, though for sheer atmosphere you can't beat the **Grotte de Font-de-Gaume**, where the original paintings are still on show. Returning to the Dordogne, the magnificent feudal châteaux of **Beynac** and **Castelnaud**, eyeing each other across the river from their dizzy eyries, provide yet another archetypal image of the region. Upstream from Sarlat the abbey-church of **Souillac** offers some remarkable carvings – masterpieces of French Romanesque art –

while the nearby pilgrimage town of **Rocamadour** is equally compelling thanks to its unrivalled setting halfway up a cliff-face. Further east, it's the castles that steal the show once again: **Château de Castelnau**, a supreme example of medieval military architecture, and the Renaissance **Château de Montal** with its exquisite ornamental detailing.

Shadowing the Dordogne to the south, the River Lot flows through comparatively wild and empty country where, even in high summer, it's possible to find quiet corners. Even the departmental capital, **Cahors**, is an appealingly unassuming town, despite the fact that it's home to France's best surviving fortified medieval bridge and one of its oldest cathedrals. Upstream, the perched village of **St-Cirq-Lapopie** provides the valley's most dramatic sight, while the nearby **Grotte de Pech-Merle** comes close with its dazzling display of prehistoric cave-art. From here the Célé valley, pretty and untamed, cuts northeast to the beguiling town of **Figeac**, which, apart from a well-restored core of medieval streets, also boasts a highly rewarding museum dedicated to the man who unravelled the mystery of hieroglyphics. In the high country west of Cahors, on the other hand, the atmospheric villages of **Monflanquin** and **Monpazier** represent outstanding examples of *bastides*, the "new towns" of the Middle Ages, built on a grid plan around arcaded central squares.

Though the flat Garonne valley, to the south of the Lot, is visually less exciting, it hides an ace up its sleeve: **Moissac**. The town itself is unspectacular, but the Romanesque carvings of its abbey-church are among the finest of their kind. Further east, **Montauban**, a sunny southern town built in warm, pink brick, sits on the banks of the Tarn not far from the **Gorges de l'Aveyron**. These narrow defiles are at their most dramatic around the attractive old town of **St-Antonin-Noble-Val** and **Najac**, where a semi-ruined fortress commands the valley, but it's worth continuing on to **Villefranche-de-Rouergue**. This *bastide* town springs into life on market days when stalls fill its superb central square – a scene that, in essence, has changed little for centuries.

When to go

To a certain extent, the **climate** of the Dordogne and Lot region need not be a major consideration. Under the influence of the Atlantic weather systems, the winters are wet and mild, with very few days of snow or frost – when the sun does appear, it is possible to sit outside at midday even in deepest December. Spring can be very changeable: some years see glorious sunny weather, while in others it is cold and wet. Temperatures begin to pick up around May and can climb into the 40s in July and August, though more usually hover around the mid-20s. Typical summer weather sees the heat and humidity building up into spectacular thunderstorms, after which the air clears, temperatures drop and the cycle starts over again. Autumn is similar to spring, though on the whole tends to bring slightly more reliable sunshine.

Rather than the climate, the single most important factor in deciding when to visit is the **holiday seasons**. During July and August it seems as though the whole of northern France heads southwards en masse, their ranks swelled by an invasion of north Europeans, most notably British, Dutch and Germans. By far the worst period is from mid-July to the end of August, with August itself being the peak, when hotels and campsites are bursting at the seams, the roads crowded and the top-rank sights absolutely heaving. If you have to come in summer, make sure you book your accommodation well in advance – which means several months ahead for the most popular places. Conversely, in the dead, winter season from October to April many sights, hotels and restaurants close down completely; in general, Easter marks the start of the tourist season. Which means that, overall, the **best time to visit** the Dordogne and Lot region is during September and early October, with May and June coming a close second.

	Jan	Feb	March	April	May	June	July	Aug	Sept	Oct	Nov	Dec
AVERAGE TEMPERATURES (°C) AND MONTHLY RAINFALL (MM)												
Agen												
max	9	11	14	16	20	24	27	26	24	19	13	9
min	2	3	4	6	9	13	15	14	12	9	5	2
rainfall	64	63	58	60	79	60	50	58	48	59	58	61
Bordeaux												
max	9	11	14	16	20	23	26	26	24	19	13	10
min	2	3	4	6	10	12	14	14	12	9	5	3
rainfall	100	84	78	75	79	58	48	57	76	85	88	100
Sarlat												
max	8	10	13	16	19	23	26	25	23	18	12	9
min	1	2	3	6	9	11	14	13	12	9	4	2
rainfall	78	78	76	80	92	78	59	64	65	79	78	79

PART ONE

THE
BASICS

GETTING THERE FROM BRITAIN

The quickest and most cost-effective way of reaching the Dordogne and Lot from most parts of Britain is by air, though in the southeast of England this is now rivalled closely by the Channel Tunnel rail link, from where you can connect to the fast and efficient TGV services south from Lille and Paris. The standard rail or road-and-sea routes are generally more affordable, but can be uncomfortable and tiring – and if you're just going for a short break, the journey time can significantly eat into your holiday.

BY AIR

Flying can represent a considerable saving in time compared to other methods of getting to the Dordogne: you can fly into Bordeaux or nearby Toulouse in less than two hours from London, for example. Direct flights from British regional airports also exist, and prices are not unfavourable compared with London fares. However, as often as not, if you live outside London, you'll find it pays to go to the capital and fly on to France from there: scheduled return flights from London to Bordeaux are available for as little as £80 and to Toulouse for around £120. To find the best deals you should shop around, ideally a month or so before you plan to leave.

Predictably, Air France and British Airways are the main carriers to France from Britain, offering **scheduled flights** and Apex fares which must be reserved one or two weeks in advance (depending on the route taken), and must include one Saturday night. Your return date must be fixed when purchasing, and no subsequent changes are allowed. The most basic return to Bordeaux starts at £175. A couple of **low-cost airlines** also offer scheduled flights into the region – or hubs within easy striking distance of it – namely Ryanair and Buzz. There are no advance purchase conditions with these airlines, but obviously the earlier you book your seat the greater chance you have of taking advantage of special offers and availability.

Air France fly from Heathrow at least once daily direct to Bordeaux and Toulouse, and to Paris Charles de Gaulle (from where you can make onward connections to both gateways) around ten times daily; they also fly four times daily from London City (Mon–Fri) to Paris CDG, and daily from Manchester, Birmingham, Edinburgh and Glasgow. **British Airways** fly three times daily from Gatwick to Bordeaux and Toulouse; they also fly to Paris CDG three times daily from Gatwick, eight times daily from Heathrow and at least once daily from Birmingham, Manchester, Newcastle, Aberdeen, Edinburgh and Glasgow.

There are a few direct flights into the region – mostly out of the London airports – with the new breed of low-cost airlines; these companies also offer a more frequent service into Paris, from where you could connect to internal flights or TGV trains south. **Buzz**, for example, currently fly daily from Stansted to Bordeaux for as little as £40 each way, as well as three times daily to Paris CDG; while **Ryanair** fly from Stansted to Biarritz– some 100km south of Bordeaux – for around £100.

A good place to look for **discount fares** from London to France is the classified travel sections of papers such as the *Independent* and the *Daily Telegraph* (Saturday editions), the *Observer*, *Sunday Times* and *Independent on Sunday*, where agents advertise special deals; if you're in London, check the back pages of the listings magazine *Time Out*, the *Evening Standard* or the free travel mag *TNT*, found outside main-line train stations. Independent travel specialists such as STA Travel and Campus Travel do deals for students and anyone under 26, or can simply sell a scheduled ticket at a discount price. Bear in mind that any travel agent can sell you a **package deal** with a tour operator (see p.8) and these can often offer exceptional bargain travel; sometimes it's possible to just buy the ticket for the **charter flight** – in theory supposed to be sold in

AIRLINES AND TRAVEL AGENTS IN BRITAIN

AIRLINES

Air France ☎0845/084 5111, www.airfrance.fr.

British Airways ☎0845/773 3377, www.britishairways.com.

British Midland ☎0870/6070 555, www.britishmidland.co.uk.

Buzz ☎0870/240 7070, www.buzzaway.com.

Ryanair direct sales ☎0541/569 569, www.ryanair.com.

TRAVEL AGENTS

Campus Travel (www.campustravel.co.uk), 52 Grosvenor Gardens, London SW1W 0AG (☎0870/240 1010). There are also branches in Birmingham (☎0121/414 1848); Brighton (☎01273/570 226); Bristol (☎0117/929 2494); Cambridge (☎01223/324 283); Edinburgh (☎0131/668 3303); Glasgow (☎0141/553 1818); Manchester (☎0161/273 1721); and Oxford (☎01865/242 067). Student/youth travel specialists, with branches also in YHA shops and on university campuses all over Britain.

Flightbookers, 177–178 Tottenham Court Rd, London W1P 0LX (☎020/7757 2000, ebookers.com); Gatwick Airport, South Terminal inside the British Rail Station (☎01293/568 300). Low fares on a wide selection of scheduled flights.

North South Travel, Moulsham Mill Centre, Parkway, Chelmsford, Essex CM2 7PX (☎01245/608 291). Friendly, competitive travel agency, offering discounted fares to most destinations – profits are used to support projects in the developing world, especially the promotion of sustainable tourism.

STA Travel (www.statravel.co.uk), London: 86 Old Brompton Rd, SW7 3LH; 117 Euston Rd, NW1 2SX; 38 Store St, WC1E 7BZ; and 11 Goodge St, W1P 2SX (☎020/7361 6161). There

are also branches in Brighton (☎01273/728 282); Bristol (☎0117/929 4399); Cambridge (☎01223/366 966); Manchester (☎0161/834 0668); Leeds (☎0113/244 9212); Liverpool (☎0151/707 1223); Newcastle-upon-Tyne (☎0191/233 2111); Oxford (☎01865/792 800); Aberdeen (☎0122/465 8222); Edinburgh (☎0131/226 7747); and Glasgow (☎0141/338 6000); and on university campuses throughout Britain. Worldwide specialists in low-cost flights and tours for students and under-26s.

Thomas Cook, 45 Berkeley St, London W1X 5AE; and high streets across London and the UK (nationwide ☎0870/5666 222; Flights Direct ☎0870/5101 520; www.tch.thomascook.com). Long-established travel agency for package holidays and scheduled flights, with bureau de change (issuing Thomas Cook traveller's cheques), own travel insurance and car rental.

Trailfinders (www.trailfinders.com), London: 1 Threadneedle St, EC2R 8JX (☎020/7628 7628); 215 Kensington High St, W6 6BD (☎020/7937 5400). There are also branches in Birmingham (☎0121/236 1234); Bristol (☎0117/929 9000); Manchester (☎0161/839 6969); Glasgow (☎0141/353 2224). One of the best-informed and most efficient agents for independent travellers.

conjunction with accommodation – at a discount. It's also worth keeping an eye on **Web sites** such as www.lastminute.com, www.cheapflights.co.uk, www.deckchair.com and www.travelocity.com, which can offer some of the best discounted fares and last-minute deals available.

BY TRAIN

The Channel Tunnel has slashed travelling time by **train** to France and has also led to a multitude of cut-rate deals on regular train and ferry or hovercraft fares via Calais, Boulogne and Dieppe (see p.7). Crossing the Channel by sea and making onward connections to the Dordogne and Lot by train can work out to be slightly cheaper than

using the Channel Tunnel, but you should note that it does take considerably longer, and is generally less convenient.

Eurostar operate high-speed passenger trains daily from London Waterloo to the Continent via Ashford in Kent and the Channel Tunnel. There are nine trains daily direct to **Lille** (2hr) in northern France, from where you can connect at the same station with the high-speed **TGV network** to Bordeaux (approx. 6hr) and Toulouse (approx. 8hr) for £100–140. There are also at least thirteen Eurostar trains daily from London to Paris Gare du Nord (3hr).

Standard-class return **fares** from London to Lille range from £60 with the "Leisure Apex 14", which must be bought up to fourteen days before departure and must include a Saturday night, with fixed outward and return dates and no refunds. There are other cheap deals – such as the "Leisure Flexi", which can be purchased up to thirty minutes before departure for £110 – but for a high-season ticket with changeable departure and return times, bought close to your departure date, you're looking at £220. Youth-fare **concessions** are available on all the routes (student discounted tickets are only available from STA and USIT Campus Travel, not directly from Eurostar) – there are concessions also for over-60s, and for holders of an international rail pass.

You can also get **through-ticketing** – including the tube journey to Waterloo International – from other main-line stations in Britain; a typical add-on price for a return ticket to Lille from Edinburgh or Glasgow is £30, from Manchester £20 and Birmingham £10. However, there is still no sign of the promised direct high-speed Eurostar services from the Midlands, the north of England and Scotland, which means that add-on time to your journey is around four to six hours if you're travelling from the north of England or southern Scotland.

Tickets can be bought directly over the phone from Eurostar, from most travel agents, from all main train stations in Britain, and from the Waterloo International and Ashford ticket offices.

TRAIN PASSES

If you plan to use the rail network to travel more widely than in just the Dordogne and Lot region, there are several **train passes** you might consider buying before you leave.

The **Euro Domino Pass**, available from Rail Europe (SNCF) and USIT Campus, offers unlimited rail travel through France for any three (£99), four (£119), five (£139), six (£159), seven (£178) or eight (£198) days within a calendar month; passengers under 25 pay £79, £95, £111, £127, £143 and £159 respectively. Children under 4 travel free, and those aged between 4 and 11 are charged half the adult price.

InterRail passes cover eight European "zones" and are available for either 22-day or one-month periods; you must have been resident in Europe for at least six months before you can buy the pass. The passes for those over 26 have now been extended to cover the same territory as for those under 26 and the only difference now is the price. France is in the zone including Belgium, the Netherlands and Luxembourg. A 22-day pass to travel this area is £159 for under-26s £229 for over-26s, a two-zone pass valid for a month is £209/279, a three-zone £229/309, and an all-zones pass £259/349. The pass is available from the same outlets as the Euro Domino (see above) and from STA Travel.

Note that InterRail passes do not include travel between Britain and the Continent. Both the Euro Domino and InterRail passes entitle you to a discount on the Eurostar service, and on rail-ferry links to France.

BY BUS

Eurolines run regular bus-ferry services from London Victoria to over sixty French cities. Prices are very much lower than for the same journey by train, with adult return fares at the time of writing just £89 for Bordeaux, with a journey-time of roughly nineteen hours. Regional return fares from the rest of England and from Wales are available, as are student and youth discounts. Again, prices are very much lower than for the same journey by train. As well as ordinary tickets on its scheduled coach services to an extensive list of European cities, Eurolines offers a pass for Europe-wide travel, for either thirty days (over-26s £245, youth pass and over-60s £195) or sixty days (£283/£227). **Tickets** are available directly from the company, from National Express agents and from most high-street travel agents.

USEFUL TRAIN CONTACTS

Campus Travel (see opposite).

Eurolines, 52 Grosvenor Gardens, London SW1W 0AU (bookings and enquiries ☎020/7730 8235 or 01582/404 511, *www.gobycoach.com*). Tickets can also be purchased from any National Express agent (☎0870/5808 080).

Eurostar, Eurostar House, Waterloo Station, London SE1 8SE (☎0870/5186 186, *www.eurostar.com*).

Eurotunnel, Customer Services Centre, PO Box 300, Dept 302, Folkestone, Kent CT19 4QD (information and bookings ☎0870/5353 535, *www.eurotunnel.com*).

Rail Europe, 179 Piccadilly, London W1V 0BA (☎0870/584 8848, *www.raileurope.co.uk*).

Rail Pass Express *www.railpass.com*

BY CAR: EUROTUNNEL AND MOTORAIL

It's a long drive south to the Dordogne and Lot from the north coast of France, but if you do want to take your **car** with you – and don't fancy a long sea journey and a short drive into the region from northern Spain (see opposite) – then you might wish to consider using the **Channel Tunnel**, which will whisk you under the Channel in just 35 minutes, depositing you at Coquelles on the French side, near Calais. The Channel Tunnel entrance is off the M20 at junction 11A, just outside Folkestone, and the sole operator, **Eurotunnel**, offers a frequent, daily service. Because of the frequency of the service, you don't have to buy a ticket in advance (though this might be advisable in midsummer and during other school holidays), but you must arrive at least thirty minutes before departure; the target loading time is just ten minutes. Inside the carriages, you can get out of your car to stretch your legs during the crossing. Tickets are available through Eurotunnel's Customer Service Centre, on the Internet or from your local travel agent. Fares are calculated per car, regardless of the number of passengers, and rates depend on the time of year, time of day and length of stay (the cheapest ticket is for a day-trip, followed by a five-day return); it's cheaper to travel between 10pm and 6am, while the highest fares are reserved for weekend departures and returns in July and August. As an example, a five-day trip at an off-peak time starts at £95 (passengers included) in the low season and goes up to £135 in the peak period.

If you don't want to drive far when you've reached France, you can take advantage of SNCF's **motorail**, which you can book through Rail Europe, putting your car on the train in either Calais or Paris for the journey south to Brive and Toulouse. This is a relatively expensive option though: for four people travelling from Calais to Brive, for example, the return price ranges from £520 to £940, dependent on the time of year.

BY FERRY, HOVERCRAFT AND CATAMARAN

Though undoubtedly slower than travelling by plane or via the Channel Tunnel by train, **ferry**, **hovercraft and catamaran services** can work out to be much the cheapest way of getting to the Dordogne and Lot, especially if you are travelling in a group, or are planning on hitching overland. The most frequent crossings are between Dover and Calais, and Folkestone and Boulogne; while the services out of Portsmouth to St-Malo, Cherbourg,

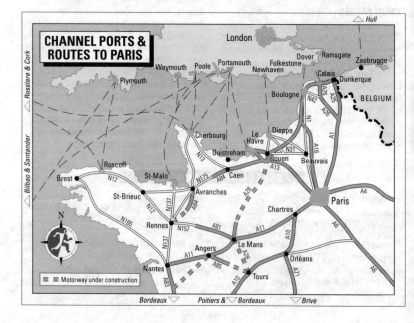

CHANNEL PORTS & ROUTES TO PARIS

SEA CROSSINGS

The following services are ferry crossings, unless otherwise stated.

Route	Operator	Crossing Time	Frequency	One-Way Fares Small car + 2 adults	Foot passengers
BRITTANY					
Portsmouth–St-Malo	Brittany Ferries	8hr 45min–11hr	7 weekly	£97–203	£24–47
Poole–St-Malo (via Jersey and Guernsey)	Condor Ferries	5hr 25min	1 daily	£95–187	£26
Plymouth–Roscoff	Brittany Ferries	6hr–7hr 30min	2–12 weekly	£110–189	£27–48
Weymouth–St-Malo (via Jersey and Guernsey)	Condor Ferries	5hr	May–Oct 1 daily	£95–187	£27
NORMANDY					
Newhaven–Dieppe (catamaran)	Hoverspeed	2hr	1–3 daily	£139–£195	£28
CHERBOURG					
Portsmouth–Cherbourg	P&O Portsmouth	2hr 45min–7hr 30min	1–7 daily	£95–178	£20–41
Poole–Cherbourg	Brittany Ferries	4hr 15min–5hr 45min	1–2 daily	£100–171	£21–42
Portsmouth–Caen	Brittany Ferries	6hr	2–3 daily	£80–185 .	£19–43
Portsmouth–Le Havre	P&O Portsmouth	5hr 30min–7hr 30min	2–3 daily	£95–178	£20–41
PAS-DE-CALAIS					
Folkestone–Boulogne (catamaran)	Hoverspeed	55min	4 daily	£115–155	£24
Dover–Calais	P&O Stena	1hr 15min	30–35 daily	£105–123	£24
Dover–Calais	Sea France	1hr 30min	15 daily	£118–163	£15
BELGIUM					
Hull–Zeebrugge	P&O North Sea Ferries	13hr 15min	1 daily	£152–188	£37–46
SPAIN					
Plymouth–Santander	Brittany Ferries	24hr	2 weekly	£238–£1144	£66–£376
Portsmouth–Bilbao	P&O Portsmouth	36hr	2 weekly	£264–£468	£96–£158

RELEVANT FERRY COMPANIES IN BRITAIN

Brittany Ferries ☎0870/901 2400, *www.brittany-ferries.co.uk*
Condor Ferries ☎01305/761551, *www.condorferries.co.uk*
Hoverspeed ☎0870/524 0241, *www.hoverspeed.co.uk*

P&O North Sea Ferries ☎01482/377177, *www.ponsf.com*
P&O Portsmouth ☎0870/242 4999, *www.poportsmouth.com*
P&O Stena ☎087/0600 0600, *www.posl.com*
Sea France ☎0870/571 1711, *www.seafrance.com*

Caen and Le Havre are amongst the most competitively priced. If you're coming from the north of England or Scotland, you should consider the Hull–Zeebrugge (Belgium) overnight crossing with P&O North Sea Ferries. One other option worth considering is taking a long cruise south to one of two north-Spanish ports: Santander and Bilbao. Crossing times are long (see box), but prices to both are competitive, and the route north into the Dordogne, by car or train, is a relatively short one – it's roughly 200km from Bilbao to Bordeaux.

Ferry **prices** are seasonal and, for motorists, depend on the size of your vehicle. The popular Dover–Calais routeing costs from £105 one-way for a car and two adults; from Plymouth to Santander prices start at £238. Note that return prices are substantially cheaper than one-way fares, but generally need to be booked in advance

TOUR OPERATORS AND VILLA AGENCIES IN THE UK

Allez France, 27–31 West St, Storrington, West Sussex RH20 4DZ (☎01903/742 345, *www.greatescapes.co.uk*). Self-drive and fly-drive accommodation packages (cottages, villas, hotels and caravans) throughout the Dordogne and Lot. Also offers help organizing camping trips.

Belle France, 15 East St, Rye TN31 7JY (☎01797/223777, *www.bellefrance.co.uk*). Offers walking and cycling holidays in the Dordogne.

Bike Tours, Victoria Works, Lambridge Mews, Larkhall, Bath BA1 6QE (☎01225/310 859, *www.biketours.co.uk*). Biking through the region.

Canvas Holidays, 12 Abbey Park Place, Dunfermline Fife, KY12 7PD (☎08709/022022, *www.canvas.co.uk*). Offers caravan as well as canvas holidays throughout the Dordogne region.

Dominique's Villas, 25 Thames House, 140 Battersea Park Rd, London SW11 4NB (☎020/7738 8772, *www.dominiquesvillas.com*). Small, upmarket agency with a diverse and tempting range of mostly older properties (some quite historic). Most are for large groups, sleeping six to eight or more.

French Country Cruises, 54 High St East, Rutland LE15 9PZ (☎01572/821 330). Offers a comprehensive range of cruises throughout France as well as offering boat rental for those who'd sooner go it alone.

Gîtes de France Ltd. The UK operation of this French Government letting service was taken over in 1997 by Brittany Ferries (☎0870/901 2400, *www.brittany-ferries.co.uk*), although you can still deal directly with Gîtes de France (see p.38). Comprehensive list of houses, cottages and *gîtes* throughout the Dordogne; ferry crossings extra.

Holiday in France, Model Farm, Rattlesden, Suffolk IP30 0SY (☎01449/737 664). Off-the-beaten-track specialists, with a variety of villas and some very attractive *chambres d'hôte* in châteaux and farmhouses. Also golf, horse-riding and boating holidays.

Susie Madron's Cycling for Softies, 2 & 4 Birch Polygon, Manchester M14 5HX (☎0161/248 8282, *www.cycling-for-softies.co.uk*). An easy-going cycle holiday operator. Although luggage transfer is not included in the deals, this can be arranged for an additional fee.

Voyages Ilena, 1 Old Garden House, The Lanterns, Bridge Lane, London SW11 3AD (☎020/7924 4440). Specializing in self-catering villas, this helpful and friendly agency can also arrange accommodation in luxury hotels; flights, fly-drives and tailor-made holidays.

Winetrails, Greenways, Vann Lake, Ockley, Dorking RH5 5NT (☎01306/712111, *www.wine-trails.co.uk*). Walking, cycling and gourmet holidays.

– details of routes, companies and current fares are given in the box on p.7. You can either contact the companies direct to reserve space in advance – essential in peak season if you're intending to drive – or any travel agent in the UK or France will do it for you. All ferry companies also offer foot-passenger fares only, from £20 one-way; accompanying bicycles can usually be carried free, at least in the low season, and for a charge of around £5 one-way in mid- and high seasons.

The ferry companies will often offer **special deals** on three-, five- and ten-day returns, or discounts for regular users who own a property abroad. The tour operator **Eurodrive** (☎020/8324 4007, *www.eurodrive.co.uk*) can also arrange discounts on ferry crossings for people taking their cars across the Channel.

PACKAGE TOURS

Any travel agent will be able to provide details of the many operators running **package tours** to the Dordogne and Lot (see box above), which can be a competitively priced way of travelling. Some deals are straightforward travel-plus-hotel affairs, while others offer tandem touring, air-and-rail packages and stays in country cottages. If your trip is geared around specific interests – like cycling or self-catering in the countryside – packages can work out much cheaper than the same arrangements made on arrival. Packages can also be a good idea if you are on a tight schedule, as these deals often include free transfers to your hotel and guided tours as well as flights and accommodation, leaving you more time to enjoy your holiday.

In addition to the addresses in the box above, bear in mind that most of the ferry companies and flight operators (see p.4) also offer their own travel and accommodation deals. The **French Holiday Service** at 178 Piccadilly, London W1V 0AL (☎020/7355 4747), can book an especially large range. A complete list of package operators is available from the **French Government Tourist Office**, also at 178 Piccadilly, London W1V 0AL (☎0906/824 4123).

GETTING THERE FROM IRELAND

By far the fastest – though often not the cheapest – way of getting to the south of France from Ireland is by plane. There are good deals out of the regional airports direct to the south of France as well as out of Dublin via Paris and London; you can also fly via these two cities from Belfast, but the costs are generally much higher and the

number of flights far fewer. It is possible, too, to sail to northern France from Cork and Rosslare, and from there head south by car or train. However, the journey time is long (sea crossings are around 15hr) and the costs are not significantly lower than the flight deals out of the regional airports – but for families, or other groups travelling by car, and for those for whom cost is a bigger consideration than time, the ferries are an attractive option.

BY AIR

By far the most convenient way to fly from the **Irish Republic** to the Dordogne and Lot is with Go Holidays, who arrange charter flights in high season (April–Sept) from Shannon, Cork and Dublin to Toulouse from IR£179/€227.28 return. Other options include flying with Aer Lingus, direct from Dublin and most other regional airports, to Paris CDG for around IR£199/€253, and continuing by air or overland from there; or with

---

AIRLINES, AGENTS AND TOUR OPERATORS IN IRELAND

AIRLINES

Aer Lingus Republic: ☎01/705 3333; Northern Ireland: ☎0845/973 7747; *www.aerlingus.ie*.

British Airways Republic: ☎1800/626 747; Northern Ireland: ☎0845/722 2111; *www.british-airways.com*.

Ryanair Republic: ☎01/609 7800; Northern Ireland ☎0870/156 9569; *www.ryanair.com*.

TRAVEL AGENTS

Joe Walsh Tours, 69 Upper O'Connell St, Dublin 2 (☎01/872 2555); 8–11 Baggot St, Dublin 2 (☎01/676 3053); 117 St Patrick St, Cork (☎021/277 959). Discounted flight agent.

Thomas Cook, 118 Grafton St, Dublin 2 (☎01/677 0469); 11 Donegall Place, Belfast (☎028/9055 0232 or 554 455). Package holiday and flight agent who can also arrange traveller's cheques, insurance and car rental.

Trailfinders, 4–5 Dawson St, Dublin 2 (☎01/677 7888, *www.trailfinders.ie*). Competitive fares out of all Irish airports, as well as deals on hotels, insurance, tours and car rental.

USIT (*www.usitnow.ie*), 19 Aston Quay, Dublin 2 (☎01/602 1777 or 677 8117; Fountain Centre, College St, Belfast (☎028/9032 4073); plus branches in Cork, Galway, Limerick, Waterford and Derry. Student and youth specialists for flights and trains.

TOUR OPERATORS

Go Holidays, 28 North Great George St, Dublin 1 (☎01/874 4126). French holiday specialists offering city-breaks, fly-drive packages and charter flights to regional destinations.

Irish Ferries, 2–4 Merrion Row, Dublin 2 (☎1890/313 131, *www.irishferries.ie*). Self-drive self-catering package holidays – camping, mobile homes, apartments – to all coastal regions.

Ryanair, who have two flights daily from Dublin to Beauvais Tillé airport outside Paris for IR£97.50/€124, as well as frequent flights to London Stansted, from where you can make onward connections to Biarritz (see p.3).

In **Northern Ireland**, British Airways fly direct from Belfast City Airport to Paris CDG, but prices are generally much higher than taking a routeing through London or Amsterdam – for example, Ryanair fly out of Derry Airport to London Stansted for around £60, from where you can pick up their onward flight to Biarritz. The French Holiday Service (see p.8) can arrange package deals including flights from Belfast.

BY FERRY

The cheapest way of getting to France from Ireland – though far from the quickest – is by **ferry** from Cork or Rosslare outside Wexford to Cherbourg or Roscoff, in Brittany. From here you

can head south by car or continue your journey by train – any of the ferry operators detailed in the box below should be able to arrange an **onward train ticket** when you book your ferry crossing direct with them.

Ferry **prices** vary according to season and, for motorists, the size of their car; note that return prices are substantially cheaper but generally need to be booked in advance. Services are run by Brittany Ferries and Irish Ferries, and prices are around IR£140/€178 to IR£330/€419 for a small car and two adults one-way; P&O Irish Sea offer a slightly cheaper service for cars with no passengers. Foot passengers will pay between IR£45/€57 and IR£85/€108. Often ferry companies will offer special deals on return fares for a specified period, so check first. You can either contact the companies direct to reserve space in advance (essential at peak season if you're driving), or any competent travel agent at home can do it for you.

FERRY ROUTES AND PRICES

Route	Operator	Crossing Time	Frequency	One-Way Fares (Small car + 2 adults) (Foot passenger)
Cork–Roscoff	Brittany Ferries	14hr	April–Sept 1 weekly	IR£140–330/€177.76–419 IR£45–85/€57.14–107.93
Rosslare–Cherbourg	Irish Ferries	16hr	March–Oct 2–3 weekly	IR£140–330/€177.6–149 IR£45–85/€57.14–107.93
Rosslare–Cherbourg	P&O Irish Sea	18hr	3 weekly	IR£110–260/€139.67–330 not allowed
Rosslare–Roscoff	Irish Ferries	15hr	April–Sept 1–3 weekly	IR£140–330/€177.76–149 IR£45–85/€57.14–107.93

ADDRESSES IN IRELAND

Brittany Ferries Republic: ☎021/277801; Northern Ireland: 0870/536 0360; *www.birttany-ferries.com*

Irish Ferries 24hr information: ☎1890/313131, *www.irishferries.ie*

P&O Irish Ferries Republic: ☎1800/409049; Northern Ireland: 0870/598 0777; *www.poirishsea.com*

GETTING THERE FROM NORTH AMERICA

Getting to the Dordogne and Lot region from North America is straightforward; there are direct flights from over thirty major cities to Paris, from where you can take a domestic flight or transfer to the rail network. Nearly a dozen different scheduled airlines operate flights from North America to Paris, making it one of the cheapest destinations in Europe. If the Dordogne and Lot is part of a longer European trip, a Eurail train pass may be a useful option (see box on p.14).

SHOPPING FOR TICKETS

Barring special offers, the cheapest fare is usually an **Apex** ticket, although this will carry certain restrictions: you have to book – and pay – at least 21 days before departure, spend at least seven days abroad (maximum stay three months), and you tend to get penalized if you change your schedule. On transatlantic routes there are also winter **Super Apex** tickets, sometimes known as "Eurosavers" – slightly cheaper than an ordinary Apex, but limiting your stay to between seven and 21 days. Some airlines also issue **Special Apex** tickets to people younger than 24, often extending the maximum stay to a year. Many airlines offer youth or student fares to **under-25s**; a passport or driving licence are sufficient proof of age, though these tickets are subject to availability and can have eccentric booking conditions. It's worth remembering that most cheap return fares involve spending at least one Saturday night

away and that many will only give a percentage refund if you need to cancel or alter your journey, so make sure you check the restrictions carefully before buying a ticket.

You can normally cut costs further by going through a specialist flight agent – either a **consolidator**, who buys up blocks of tickets from the airlines and sells them at a discount, or a **discount agent**, who deals in blocks of tickets offloaded by the airlines, and often offers special student and youth fares and a range of other travel-related services such as travel insurance, rail passes, car rental, tours and the like. Bear in mind, though, that penalties for changing your plans can be stiff, and that these companies make their money by dealing in bulk – don't expect them to answer lots of questions. Some agents specialize in **charter flights**, which may be cheaper than anything available on a scheduled flight, but again departure dates are fixed and withdrawal penalties are high (check the refund policy). If you travel a lot, **discount travel clubs** are another option – the annual membership fee may be worth it for benefits such as cut-price air tickets and car rental. The Internet is also a useful resource; check out the **Web sites** *www.cheaptickets.com*, *www.travelocity.com* and *www.lastminute.com* to compare prices.

A further possibility is to see if you can arrange a **courier flight**, although the hit-or-miss nature of these makes them most suitable for a single traveller who travels light and has a very flexible schedule. In return for shepherding a parcel through customs and possibly giving up your baggage allowance, you can expect to get a deeply discounted ticket. For more options, consult *Courier Bargains: How to Travel Worldwide for Next to Nothing* by Kelly Monaghan (US$17.50, postpaid, from The Intrepid Traveler, PO Box 438, New York, NY 10034). Flights are issued on a first-come, first-served basis, and there's no guarantee that the Paris route will be available at the time you want. Round-trip fares cost from around US$350, with last-minute specials as low as US$150 for flights booked within three days of departure.

Don't automatically assume that tickets purchased through a travel specialist will be the cheapest – once you get a quote, check with the airlines and you may turn up an even better deal. Be advised also that the pool of travel companies is swimming with sharks – exercise caution and never deal with a company that demands cash up front or refuses to accept payment by credit card.

Note that fares are heavily dependent on **season**, and are highest from around early June to the end of August; they drop during the "shoulder" seasons (Sept–Oct & April–May) and you'll get the best deals during the low season

---

AIRLINES AND TRAVEL AGENTS IN NORTH AMERICA

AIRLINES

Air Canada in US ☎1-800/776 3000; in Canada ☎1-800/555 1212; *www.aircanada.ca.*

Air France in US ☎1-800/237 2747; in Canada ☎1-800/667 2747; *www.airfrance.fr.*

American Airlines ☎1-800/433 7300, *www.aa.com.*

AOM French Airlines ☎1-800/892 9136, *www.aom.com.*

Canadian Airlines in US ☎1-800/426 7000; in Canada ☎1-800/665 1177; *www.cdnair.com.*

Continental Airlines ☎1-800/231 0856, *www.flycontinental.com.*

Delta Airlines ☎1-800/241 4141, *www.delta-air.com.*

Iceland Air ☎1-800/223 5500, *www.icelandair.com.*

Northwest Airlines ☎1-800/225 2525, *www.nwa.com.*

TWA ☎1-800/892 4141, *www.twa.com.*

United Airlines ☎1-800/538 2929, *www.ual.com.*

US Air ☎1-800/622 1015, *www.usairways.com.*

DISCOUNT TRAVEL AGENTS

Air Brokers International, 150 Post St, Suite 620, San Francisco, CA 94108 (☎1-800/883 3273, *www.airbrokers.com*). Consolidator.

Air Courier Association, 15000 W 6th Ave, Suite 203, Golden, CO 80401 (☎1-800/282 1202, *www.aircourier.com*). Courier-flight broker.

Airhitch, 2641 Broadway, New York, NY 10025 (☎1-800/326 2009 or 212/864 2000, *www.airhitch.org*). Standby-seat broker: for a set price, they guarantee to get you on a flight as close to your preferred destination as possible, within a week.

Airtreks.com, 442 Post St, Suite 400, San Francisco, CA 94102 (☎1-800/428 8735, *www.airtreks.com*). Travel company with a highly recommended interactive Web site.

Council Travel, 205 E 42nd St, New York, NY 10017 (☎1-800/226 8624, *www.counciltravel.com*). Nationwide US student travel organization with branches in (among others) San Francisco, Washington DC, Boston, Austin, Seattle, Chicago, Minneapolis.

Flight Centre, 3030 Granville St, Vancouver, BC V6H 3J9 (☎1-604/739 9539, *www.flightcentre.com*). Discount air fares from Canadian cities.

Last Minute Travel Club, 100 Sylvan Rd, Suite 600, Woburn, MA 01801 (☎1-800/LAST MIN). Travel club specializing in standby deals.

New Frontiers/Nouvelles Frontières, 12 E 33rd St, New York, NY 10016 (☎1-800/366 6387 or 514/526 8444, *www.newfrontiers.com*). French discount-travel firm; also markets charters to Paris and Lyon. Branches in New York, Montréal, Los Angeles, San Francisco and Québec City.

STA Travel, 10 Downing St, New York, NY 10014 (☎1-800/777 0112, *www.sta-travel.com*). Worldwide specialist in independent travel with branches in the Los Angeles, San Francisco and Boston areas.

Travac, 989 6th Ave, 16th Floor, New York, NY 10018 (☎1-800/872 8800, *www.thetravelsite.com*). Consolidator and charter broker; branches in New York and Orlando.

Travel Avenue, 10 S Riverside Plaza, Suite 1404, Chicago, IL 60606 (☎1-800/333 3335, *www.travelavenue.com*). Discount travel agent.

Travel Cuts, 187 College St, Toronto, ON M5T 1P7 (☎1-800/667-2887 or 416/979 2406, *www.travelcuts.com*). Canadian specialist student and discount travel organization with branches all over the country.

Travelers Advantage, 3033 S Parker Rd, Suite 1000, Aurora, CO 80014 (☎1-800/548 1116, *www.travelersadvantage.com*). Discount travel club.

Worldtek Travel, 111 Water St, New Haven, CT 06511 (☎1-800/243 1723, *www.worldtek.com*). Discount travel agency.

TOUR OPERATORS IN NORTH AMERICA

Adventure Center, 1311 63rd St, Suite 200, Emeryville, CA 94608 (☎1-800/227-8747, www.adventurecenter.com). Small-group hiking or cycling tours. The eight-day "Dordogne and Discovery" includes a bit of hiking, boating, walking and cycling; starting at US$375, land only.

Abercrombie & Kent, 1520 Kensington Rd, Oak Brook, IL (☎1-800/323-7308, www.abercrombieandkent.com). Deluxe hiking, biking, rail and canal journeys, including a 6-night "Walking in the Dordogne Valley" tour starting at US$2950, excluding air fare.

Back Door Travel, 130 4th Ave North, Edmonds, WA 98020 (☎425/771 8303, www.ricksteves.com). Off-the-beaten path, small-group travel with budget travel guru Rick Steves and his enthusiastic guides.

Backroads, 1516 Fifth St, Suite L101, Berkeley, CA 94710 (☎1-800/462-2848, www.backroads.com). Upmarket bike tours; a five-night tour of the Dordogne and Bordeaux, staying in châteaux accommodation, costs US$2698 excluding air fare.

Butterfield and Robinson, 70 Bond St, Toronto, ON M5B 1X3 (☎1-800/678-1147, www.butterfield.com). Walking and hiking tours with first-class accommodation throughout France, including a four-night "Bordeaux Getaway" and a seven-night "Walking in Dordogne" starting at CDN$2690 and CDN$3975 respectively.

Euro-Bike Tours, PO Box 990, DeKalb, IL 60115 (☎1-800/321-6060, www.eurobike.com). Eight-day bike tours around Bordeaux and in the Dordogne, overnighting in luxury hotels, for US$2495, excluding air fare.

The French Experience, 370 Lexington Ave, # 812, New York, NY 10017 (☎1-800/28-FRANCE, www.frenchexperince.com). Four-day, self-drive tours of Bordeaux and the Dordogne including good hotels and rental car pick-up anywhere in France.

Globus and Cosmos Tourama, 5301 S Federal Circle, Littleton, CO 80123-2980 (☎1-800/221 0090; www.globusandcosmos.com). Travel club offering tours in the region and throughout France.

Himalayan Travel, 110 Prospect St, Stamford, CT 06901 (☎1-800/225-2380, www.gorp.com). Hiking and cycling tours in the Dordogne; an eight-day hiking tour starts at US$1095, a ten-day cycling tour at US$1125.

Interhome, 1990 NE 163rd St, N Miami Beach, FL 33162 (☎305/940-2299, www.interhome.com). Short-term house and villa rentals in the Bordeaux, Dordogne and Lot regions.

Saga International Holidays, 222 Berkeley St, Boston, MA 02116 (☎1-800/343 0273, www.sagaholidays.com). Specialist in group travel for 50s plus.

Vacances en Campagne, PO Box 299, Elkton, VA 22827 (☎1-800/327-6097, www.britishtravel.com). Châteaux and country houses for rent in the Bordeaux, Dordogne and Lot regions.

(Nov–March, excluding Christmas). Note that Friday, Saturday and Sunday travel tends to carry a premium, and that one-way fares are generally slightly more than half the round-trip.

   Air passes, coupons and discounts on further flights within Europe vary with airlines, but the basic rules are that they must be pre-booked with the main ticket, are valid for three months, and are available only with a return fare with the one airline – for example, you have to fly to France with KLM alone to be eligible for their air-pass deals. Air France offers a Euroflyer for use in France and Europe at US$99 each flight (min 3, max 9). KLM's Passport to Europe uses coupons for single flights within Europe at US$100 each (min 4, max 12). Lufthansa's start at US$89 (max 12) during the low season up to US$159 in the high season per coupon. British Airways have a

"One World: Visit Europe" programme that offers flights within Europe from US$92 to US$145 depending on the destination (min 2, max 12).

FLIGHTS FROM THE USA

Transatlantic fares to France from the USA are very reasonable, thanks to intense competition. Any local travel agent should be able to access airlines' up-to-the-minute fares, although they may not have time to research all the possibilities, and you could call the airlines direct. The lowest discounted scheduled fares you're likely to get in low and high season flying midweek to Paris are US$448/966 from Chicago, US$468/876 from Houston, US$498/1116 from Los Angeles, US$368/866 from New York and US$408/635 from Washington DC.

EUROPEAN TRAIN PASSES FOR AMERICANS, AUSTRALIANS AND NEW ZEALANDERS

There are a number of European **train passes** that can only be purchased before leaving home, though consider carefully how much travelling you are going to be doing: these all-encompassing passes only really begin to pay for themselves if you intend to travel widely beyond the Dordogne and Lot region.

The best-known and most flexible is the **Eurail Youthpass** (for under-26s), which costs US$388/A$733 for fifteen days, and there are also one-month and two-month versions; if you're 26 or over you'll have to buy a first-class **Eurail** pass, which costs US$554/A$1046 for the fifteen-day option. You stand a better chance of getting your money's worth out of a **Eurail Flexipass**, which is good for a certain number of travel days in a two-month period. This, too, comes in under-26/first-class versions: ten days for under-26s costs US$458/A$865, for over-26s US$654/A$1234; and for fifteen days US$599/A$1131 and US$862/A$1627.

A scaled-down version of the Flexipass, the **Europass** allows travel in France, Germany, Italy, Switzerland and Spain for US$233/A$440 and US$348/A$657 for five days in two months, on up to US$513/A$968 and US$728/A$1374 for fifteen days in two months; there are also cheaper three- and four-country combinations, as well as the option of adding adjacent "associate" countries. In addition to the passes outlined above, you can buy **more specific passes** valid for travel in France only. The **France Railpass** provides three days' unlimited travel in a one-month period for US$180/A$340, or, if travelling in groups of two or more, US$146/A$276 per person. Up to six additional days of travel may be purchased for US$30/A$57 per day. For under-26s, the **France Youthpass** provides four days of unlimited travel in a two-month period for US$164/A$310; up to six additional days may be purchased for US$20/A$38 per day. All passes must be purchased before departure and are available through travel agents or with rail specialists (see p.5).

In addition, the SNCF has a range of other reductions and passes, which can be purchased once in France: details of these can be found in "Getting around", p.32.

RAIL CONTACTS IN NORTH AMERICA

CIT Rail, 15 W 44th St, 10th Floor, New York, NY 10036 (☎1-800/223 7987; www.fs-on-line.com). Eurail passes only.

Rail Europe, 226 Westchester Ave, White Plains, NY 10604 (☎1-800/438 7245; www.raileurope.com). Official Eurail pass agent in North America; also sells the widest range of European regional and individual country passes.

ScanTours, 3439 Wade St, Los Angeles, CA 90066 (☎1-800/223 7226 or 310/636 4656; www.scantours.com). Eurail, and many other European country passes.

RAIL CONTACTS IN AUSTRALIA AND NEW ZEALAND

CIT World Travel, see p.17.

Rail Plus, Level 3, 459 Little Collins St, Melbourne, Australia (☎03/9642 8644 or 1300/555 003; info@railplus.com.au); Level 2, 60 Parnell Rd, Auckland, New Zealand (☎09/303 2484).

Thomas Cook, see p.17.

Most airlines use Paris as the transatlantic gateway to France. Of nearly a dozen different **scheduled** airlines operating flights to Paris, Air France has the most frequent and convenient service, but their fares tend to be on the expensive side. Other airlines offering nonstop services to Paris from a variety of US cities are United, daily from Chicago, San Francisco and Washington DC; Delta, daily from Cincinnati, Atlanta and New York; TWA, daily from New York and St Louis; and AOM French Airlines from Los Angeles three to five times a week, depending on the season. For the best fares, check the ads in Sunday newspaper travel sections and book with a discount agent or consolidator. It's also worth considering **charter flights**, which operate from late spring to early autumn. New Frontiers, a Canadian discount travel agency, has summer nonstop charters from Los Angeles to Paris on Corsair from US$800 round-trip.

FLIGHTS FROM CANADA

The strong links between France and Québec's Francophone community ensure regular air services from **Canada to Paris**. The main route is Vancouver–Toronto–Montréal–Paris Charles de Gaulle, although most departures originate in Toronto.

Air France and Air Canada offer nonstop services to Paris from the major Canadian cities. There are also some excellent charter deals. Travel Cuts is a good source of general information on flights. The lowest discounted scheduled **fares** for midweek travel to Paris in low/high season will be around CDN$976/1316 from Montréal, CDN$976/1316 from Toronto, CDN$1360/1728 from Vancouver, and CDN$1008/1258 from Halifax on Iceland Air.

PACKAGE TOURS

A tour is inevitably more confining than independent travel, but it can be efficient if time is tight; a tour can also ensure a worry-free first few days of a trip, and time to find your feet. Hundreds of tour operators specialize in travel to France, and many can put together very **flexible deals**, sometimes amounting to no more than a flight plus car or train pass and accommodation. If you're planning to travel in moderate or luxury style, and especially if your trip is geared around special interests, such packages can work out cheaper than the same arrangements made on arrival.

Of greater interest are the **package-tour operators** that help you explore the country's unique points: many organize walking or cycling trips, boat trips along canals, and any number of theme tours based around history, art, wine and so on. The box on p.13 mentions a few of the possibilities, and a travel agent will be able to point out others.

Many **airlines** have reasonably priced packages including round-trip air fare, hotel, some sightseeing tours and, in the case of fly-drive packages, a rental car. Delta offers a seven-day fly-drive package to Paris starting at US$599 for New York departures. American Airlines offer a seven-day England–France fly-drive package, including Channel Tunnel crossing, from around US$900 per person for hotel, breakfast, rental car and Channel tickets.

GETTING THERE FROM AUSTRALIA & NEW ZEALAND

Many people travelling to France from Australia and New Zealand will choose to travel via London although there are scheduled flights to Paris from Sydney, Melbourne, Brisbane, Cairns, Perth and Auckland. Most airlines can add on a Paris **(or any other major French destination) leg to any Australia/New Zealand–Europe ticket. Travelling time is around 22 hours via Asia and 30 hours via the USA – not counting time spent on stopovers. From Paris you can get onward flights to Bordeaux and other regional airports.**

Fares to France vary according to the **season** and the carrier. In general, low season lasts from mid-January to the end of February, and from the beginning of October to mid-November; high season is from mid-May to the end of August, and from the beginning of December to mid-January.

SHOPPING FOR TICKETS

Tickets purchased direct from the airlines tend to be expensive; the **discount agents** listed in the box below offer much better deals, and have the latest information on limited special offers. Some of the best discounts are offered by companies such as Flight Centres, STA and Trailfinders (see box on pp.16–17); they can also help with visas, travel insurance and tours. You might also want to have a look on the **Internet**: *www.travel.com.au* and *www.sydneytravel.com* offer discounted fares online.

If you intend to travel more extensively outside the Dordogne and Lot and have only limited time, it's worth considering an **air pass**. Air passes, coupons and discounts on further flights within Europe vary with airlines, but the basic rules are that they must be pre-booked with the main ticket, are valid for three months, and are available only with a return fare with the one airline – for example, you have to fly to France with British Airways alone to be eligible for their air-pass deals. Air France offers a Euroflyer for use in France and Europe at A\$200 each flight (minimum 3, maximum 9). British Airways have a zone system: around A\$140 for each flight within France, A\$210 each for single flights to and around Germany, Italy and Belgium, although you may originally have to travel via London, from where it will cost an extra A\$170 to get to France (min 3, max 12).

AIRLINES, TRAVEL AGENTS AND TOUR OPERATORS IN AUSTRALIA AND NEW ZEALAND

AIRLINES

Air France in Australia ☎02/9244 2100; in New Zealand ☎09/308 3352; *www.airfrance.fr*.

British Airways in Australia ☎02/8904 8800; in New Zealand ☎09/356 8690; *www.british-airways.com*.

Canadian Airlines in Australia ☎1300/655 767; in New Zealand ☎09/309 9159; *www.cdnair.ca*.

Cathay Pacific in Australia ☎13/1747 or 02/9931 5500; in New Zealand ☎09/379 0861; *www.cathaypacific.com*.

Garuda in Australia ☎1300/365 330; in New Zealand ☎09/366 1855 or 1800/128 510.

Japan Airlines (JAL) in Australia ☎02/9272 1111; in New Zealand ☎09/379 9906; *www.japanair.com*.

KLM in Australia ☎1300/303 747; in New Zealand ☎09/302 1452; *www.klm.com*.

Lauda Air in Australia ☎02/9251 6155 or 1800/642 438; *www.lauda-air.com*.

Lufthansa in Australia ☎1300/655 727 or 02/9367 3887; in New Zealand ☎09/303 1529 or 008/945 220; *www.lufthansa.com*.

Malaysian Airlines in Australia ☎13/2627; in New Zealand ☎09/373 2741 or 008/657 472; *www.malaysiaair.com*.

Olympic Airways in Australia ☎02/9251 2044 or 1800 221 663; *www.olympic-airways.com*.

Qantas in Australia ☎13/1313; in New Zealand ☎09/357 8900 or 0800/808 767; *www.qantas.com*.

Singapore Airlines in Australia ☎02/9350 0262 or 13/1011; in New Zealand ☎09/303 2129 or 0800/808 909; *www.singaporeair.com*.

Sri Lankan Airlines in Australia ☎02/9244 2234; in New Zealand ☎09/308 3353.

Thai Airways in Australia ☎1300/651 960; in New Zealand ☎09/377 3886; *www.thaiair.com*.

United Airlines in Australia ☎13/1777; in New Zealand ☎09/379 3800; *www.ual.com*.

TRAVEL AGENTS

All the agents listed below offer competitive discounts on air fares as well as a good selection of packaged holidays and tours, and can also arrange car rental.

Budget Travel, 16 Fort St, Auckland (☎09/366 0061 or 0800/808 040, *www.budgettravel.co.nz*); plus branches around the city.

Flight Centre (*www.flightcentre.com*) Australia: 82 Elizabeth St, Sydney (☎02/9235 3522); plus branches nationwide (for the nearest branch call ☎13/1600). New Zealand: 350 Queen St, Auckland (☎09/358 4310 or 0800/354 448); plus branches nationwide.

Northern Gateway, 22 Cavenagh St, Darwin (☎08/8941 1394; *oztravel@norgate.com.au*).

STA Travel (*www.statravel.com*) Australia: 855 George St, Sydney; 256 Flinders St, Melbourne; other offices in state capitals and major universities (for nearest branch call ☎13/1776; telesales ☎1300/360 960). New Zealand: 10 High St, Auckland (☎09/309 0458); other offices in major cities and university campuses (for nearest branch call ☎0800/874 773; telesales ☎09/366 6673). Fare discounts for students and those under 26, as well as student cards.

Student Uni Travel, 92 Pitt St, Sydney (☎02/9232 8444; *sydney@backpackers.net*); plus branches in

If you're planning to visit the Dordogne and Lot as part of an extensive European trip, it's also worth looking into a variety of **rail passes**. Details of these and rail contacts in Australia and New Zealand are given in the box on p.14.

Finally, if you wish to travel in style, and especially if your visit is going to be geared around special interests, such as walking, cycling, art or wine, you may want to consider one of the **package tours** offered by the operators in the box below. Though these tours are inevitably more restrictive than independent travel, they may work out cheaper than making the same arrangements on arrival in France and can save time if you're on a tight schedule.

FLIGHTS FROM AUSTRALIA

Airfares **from east-coast gateways** are common rated, with Ansett and Qantas providing a shuttle service to the point of international departure. **From Perth and Darwin** they're around

---

Brisbane, Cairns, Darwin, Melbourne and Perth. Student/youth discounts and travel advice.

Thomas Cook Australia (*www. thomascook.com.au*): 175 Pitt St, Sydney (☎02/9231 2877); 257 Collins St, Melbourne (☎03/9282 0222); plus branches in other state capitals (for nearest branch call ☎13/1771; telesales ☎1800/801 002). New Zealand (*www.thomascook.co.nz*): 191 Queen St, Auckland (☎09/379 3920).

Trailfinders (*www.travel.com.au*), 8 Spring St, Sydney (☎02/9247 7666); 91 Elizabeth St, Brisbane (☎07/3229 0887); Hides Corner, Shield St, Cairns (☎07/4041 1199).

Usit Beyond (*www.usitbeyond.co.nz*), cnr Shortland St & Jean Batten Place, Auckland (☎09/379 4224 or 0800/788 336); plus branches in major cities. Student/youth travel specialists.

TOUR OPERATORS

Adventure Specialists, 69 Liverpool St, Sydney (☎02/9261 2927). Offer a good selection of adventure and specialist holidays in the region.

Adventure World Australia: 73 Walker St, North Sydney (☎02/9956 7766 or 1300/363 055); plus branches in Adelaide, Brisbane, Melbourne and Perth. New Zealand: 101 Great South Rd, Remuera, Auckland (☎09/524 5118; *www. adventureworld.co.nz*). Agents for a vast array of international adventure travel companies that operate small group tours in France.

CIT, 2/263 Clarence St, Sydney (☎02/9267 1255, *www.cittravel.com.au*); plus offices in Melbourne, Brisbane, Adelaide and Perth. Specialize in city tours and accommodation packages, plus bus and rail passes and car rental.

European Travel Office (ETO), 122 Rosslyn St, West Melbourne (☎03/9329 8844); Suite 410/368 Sussex St, Sydney (☎02/9267 7714); 407 Great South Rd, Auckland (☎09/525 3074). Offer a wide selection of tours and accommodation, from hotels to country inns, palaces and monasteries.

France Unlimited, 16 Goldsmith St, Elwood, Melbourne (☎03/9531 8787). All French travel arrangements, individually tailored holidays and guided walking and cycling holidays.

French Cottages and Travel, 674 High St, E Kew, Melbourne (☎03/9859 4944). International

and domestic travel, independent tours and cottage rental throughout the region.

French Travel Connection, Level 6, 33 Chandos St, Sydney (☎02/9966 8600). Offers a good selection of country cottages in the region.

Peregrine, 258 Lonsdale St, Melbourne (☎03/9662 2700 or 1300/655 433; *www. peregrine.net.au*); plus offices in Brisbane, Sydney, Adelaide and Perth. Agents for Headwater's guided and independent walking and cycling trips through the region.

The Adventure Travel Company, 164 Parnell Rd, Parnell, Auckland (☎09/379 9755, *advakl@hot.co.nz*). The NZ agent for Peregrine (see above).

Travel Notions, 136 Bridge Rd, Glebe, Sydney (☎02/9552 2852). Agents for the leisurely "Cycling for Softies" tours through the region.

Walkabout Gourmet Adventures, PO Box 52, Dinner Plain, Victoria (☎03/5159 6556, *www.reho.com/walkabout*). All-inclusive four-teen-day food-and-wine walking trip through the Dordogne.

Yalla Tours, 661 Glen Huntley Rd, Caulfield, Melbourne (☎1300/362 844, *www. yallatours.com.au*). Self-skippered canal and river cruises along the River Lot.

A\$100–300 less via Asia, and A\$400 more via the USA. There's a host of airlines operating a service between major cities in Australia – with either a transfer or overnight stop in their home ports – to Paris.

Flights **via Southeast Asia**, with either a transfer or overnight stop in the airlines' home ports, are generally the cheaper option. The lowest fares are with Sri Lankan Airways and Garuda for A\$1400 in the low season rising to A\$2400 in the high season, while Alitalia/Qantas, Olympic Airways and JAL are A\$1500 low season to A\$2600 high season. Mid-range fares are with KLM, Malaysian Airlines, Lauda Air, Thai International, Air France (on to 87 destinations within France), Cathay Pacific and Lufthansa, all costing A\$1600–2600. Qantas/Air France, British Airways and Singapore Airlines are higher still at A\$1900–2800.

Generally flights to Paris cost more **via the US**, with the best deals offered by United Airlines (via LA, Miami and Washington), from A\$2100 to 3000; Canadian Airlines (via Toronto or Vancouver) are more expensive at A\$2200 low season and A\$3000 high season.

FLIGHTS FROM NEW ZEALAND

From New Zealand, there are also a good range of airlines flying to Paris with either a transfer or overnight stop in their home ports. The best discounted deals to Paris from Auckland are **via Southeast Asia** with Garuda at NZ\$1800 low season to NZ\$2400 high season. Mid-range fares are with Japanese Airlines, Thai International, Malaysia Airlines, Cathay Pacific and Singapore Airlines, all costing NZ\$2000–2400. Most of these airlines also include a **side-trip** within Europe in their fare.

As with Australia, flights **via the US** are more expensive, the best deals being with United Airlines (via LA, Miami and Washington) for NZ\$2200 and NZ\$3000. Fares with British Airways (via LA and London) and Canadian Airlines (via Vancouver or Toronto) cost NZ\$2399 to NZ\$3000.

VISAS AND RED TAPE

Citizens of EU (European Union) countries can travel freely in France. Citizens of Australia, Canada, the United States and

New Zealand, among other countries, do not need any sort of visa to enter France, and can stay for up to ninety days. However, the situation can change and it is advisable to check with your embassy or consulate before departure. Note that the British Visitor's Passport is no longer available.

EU citizens (or other non-visa citizens) who **stay longer than three months** are officially supposed to apply for a **Carte de Séjour**, for which you'll have to show proof of income at least equal to the minimum wage (at least 6700F/€1021 per month). However, EU passports are rarely stamped, so there is no evidence of how long you've been in the country. If your passport does get stamped, you can cross the border and re-enter for another ninety days legitimately.

FRENCH EMBASSIES AND CONSULATES OVERSEAS

BRITAIN
Embassy: 58 Knightsbridge, London SW1X 7JT (☎020/7201 1004, *www.ambafrance.org.uk*).

IRELAND
Embassy: 36 Ailesbury Road, Ballsbridge, Dublin 4 (☎01/260 1666, *www.ambafrance.ie*).

USA
Embassy: 4101 Reservoir Rd NW, Washington DC 20007 (☎202/944 6195, *www.info-france usa.org*).
Consulates: Prominence in Buckhead, Suite 1840, 3475 Piedmont Rd NE, Atlanta, GA 30305 (☎404/495 1660, *www.consulatfranceatlanta.org*); 31 St James Ave, Park Square Building, Suite 750, Boston, MA 02116 (☎617/542 7374, *www.france-boston.com*); 737 North Michigan Ave, Suite 2020, Chicago, IL 60611 (☎312/787 5360, *www.france-consulat.org/chicago*); 777 Post Oak Blvd, Suite 600, Houston, TX 77056 (☎713/572 2799, *www.consulatfrancehouston.org*); 10990 Wilshire Blvd, Suite 300, Los Angeles, CA 90024 (☎310/235 3200, *www.etats-unis.com/consulat-la*); One Biscayne Tower, 17th Floor, South Biscayne Blvd, Miami, FL 33131 (☎305/372 9799, *www.info-france-usa.org/miami*); 1340 Poydras St, Amoco Building, Suite 1710, New Orleans, LA 70112 (☎504/523 5772, *www.consulfrance-nouvelleorleans.org*); 934 Fifth Ave, New York, NY 10021 (☎212/606

3689, *www.franceconsulatny.org*); 540 Bush St, San Francisco, CA 94108 (☎415/397 4330, *www.accueil-sfo.org*).

CANADA
Embassy: 42 Sussex Drive, Ottawa, ON K1M 2C9 (☎613/789 1795, *www.amba-ottawa.fr*).
Consulates: 777 Main St, Suite 800, Moncton, NB E1C 1E9 (☎506/857 4191, *www.moncton.consulfrance.org*); 1 place Ville Marie Bureau 2601, Montréal, QC H3B 4S3 (☎514/878 4385, *www.montreal.consulatfrance.org*); 25 rue St-Louis, Québec, QC G1R 3Y8 (☎418/694 2294, *www.quebec.consulatfrance.org*); 130 Bloor St West, Suite 400, Toronto, ON M5S 1N5 (☎416/925 8044, *www.toronto.consulatfrance.org*); 1100–1130 West Pender St, Vancouver, BC V6E 4A4 (☎604/681 4345, *www.vancouver. consulatfrance.org*).

AUSTRALIA
Consulates (*www.france.net.au*): 492 St Kilda Rd, Melbourne, VIC 3001 (☎03/9820 0921); 31 Market St, Sydney, NSW 2000 (☎02/9261 5779).

NEW ZEALAND
Embassy: 34–42 Manners St, PO Box 11-343, Wellington (☎04/384 2555, *www.ambafrance. net.nz*).

COSTS, MONEY AND BANKS

Until the euro is introduced in January 2002 (see box opposite), the French unit of currency is the franc (F or FF), divided into 100 centimes. Notes are available in denominations of 500, 100, 50 and 20F, while coins come in values of 20, 10, 5, 2 and 1F, and 50, 20, 10 and 5 centimes. In early 2001 the exchange rate hovered around 10.40F to the pound, 7.20F to the US dollar, 4.70F to the Canadian dollar, 3.80F to the Australian dollar, and 3.10F to the New Zealand dollar. For the most up-to-date exchange rates, consult Yahoo's currency converter at *quote.yahoo.com/m3* or the Oanda site *www.oanda.com*.

COSTS

Because of the relatively low **cost** of accommodation and eating out, at least by northern European standards, the Dordogne and Lot region may not seem an outrageously expensive place to visit, though this will depend on the relative strength of your own country's currency. When you travel also makes a difference: in prime tourist spots accommodation prices can go up by a third during July and August. For a reasonably comfortable existence, including a hotel room for two, a light restaurant lunch and a proper restaurant dinner plus moving around, café stops and museum visits, you need to allow at least 600F/€91.47 a day per person. But by counting the pennies, staying at cheap **hostels** and the cheapest hotels, limiting yourself to one inexpensive restaurant meal a day and being strong-

willed about extra cups of coffee and doses of culture, you can just about squeeze by on a daily budget of 250F/€38.11 (or 300F/€45.73 if you're travelling singly and therefore not splitting hotel charges) – less if you opt for **camping** and your eating is limited to street snacks or market food.

For two or more people, **hotel accommodation** may be cheaper and is nearly always better value than hostels, which are generally only worth it if you're by yourself. A sensible average estimate for a double room would be around 280F/€42.69, though adequate but simple doubles can be had for 180F/€27.44 or less. Single-rated and -sized rooms are sometimes available, beginning from 150F/€22.87 in the cheapest hotels, though often you'll simply be given the cheapest double. **Breakfast** at hotels is normally at least an extra 30F/€4.50 for coffee, croissant or bread and orange juice – about the same as you'd pay in a – more agreeable – bar.

As for other **food**, there are large numbers of reasonable **restaurants** with three- or four-course menus for between 65F/€9.91 and 120F/€18.29; the lunchtime menu is nearly always cheaper. **Picnic fare**, obviously, is much less costly, especially when you buy in the markets and cheap supermarket chains, and take-away baguette sandwiches from cafés are not extortionate. **Wine** and **beer** are both very cheap in supermarkets, though buying wine from the barrel (*en vrac*) at village co-op cellars will give you the best value for money. The mark-up on wine in restaurants is high, though the house wine in cheaper establishments is still very good value. **Drinks** in cafés and bars are what really set you back: black coffee, wine and draught lager are the cheapest drinks to order; glasses of tap water are free; and remember that it's cheaper to stand and drink at the bar than to sit at a table.

Transport will inevitably be a large item of expenditure if you move around a lot, which makes some kind of train pass a good idea, although French trains are in any case good value, with many discounts available – two sample one-way full fares are Paris to Bordeaux 360F/€54.88, and Bordeaux to Périgueux 100F/€15.24. Though prices vary enormously from one operator to another, buses are cheaper;

THE EURO

France is one of twelve European Union countries who have changed over to a single currency, the **euro** (€). The transition period, which began on January 1, 1999, is however lengthy: euro notes and coins are not scheduled to be issued until January 1, 2002, with francs remaining in place for **cash transactions**, at a **fixed rate** of 6.55957 francs to one euro, until they are scrapped entirely on February 17, 2002. Up until June 30 it will still be possible to exchange francs at high-street banks.

Even before euro cash appears in 2002, you can opt to pay in euros by **credit card** and you can get **traveller's cheques** in euros – you should not be charged commission for changing them in any of the twelve countries in the euro zone (also known as "Euroland"), nor for changing

from any of the old Euroland currencies to any other (Italian lira to francs, for example). However, note that some banks charge a handling fee of up to 50F/€7.62 for each transaction.

All **prices** in this book are given in francs and the exact equivalent in euros, with the exception of accommodation price codes and sums over 1000F, when the euro equivalent is rounded up to the nearest whole unit. When the new currency takes over completely, prices are likely to be rounded off – and if decimalization in the UK is anything to go by, rounded up.

Euro notes will be issued in denominations of 5, 10, 20, 50, 100, 200 and 500 euros, and coins in denominations of 1, 2, 5, 10, 20 and 50 cents and 1 and 2 euros.

a one-way bus ticket from Périgueux to Sarlat, for example, costs 50F/€7.62, as against around 75F/€11.43 by train. Bicycles cost about 80F/€12.20 per day to rent. Petrol prices shot up in late 2000, and at the time of writing are around 7F/€1.07 a litre for unleaded (*sans plomb*), 7.50F/€1.14 a litre for *super*, and 5.50F/€8.40 a litre for diesel; there are 3.8 litres to the US gallon. Most *autoroutes* have tolls: rates vary, but to give you an idea, travelling only by motorway from Calais to Bordeaux (850km on the *autoroute*) would cost you 370F/€56.41.

Museums and monuments can also prove a major expense. Reduced admission is often available for those over 60 and under 18 (for which you'll need your passport as proof of age) and for students under 26 (for which you'll need an International Student Identity Card, or ISIC). Many museums and monuments are free for children under 12, and nearly always for kids under 4. Anyone under 26 can also get a free **youth card**, or Carte Jeune, available in France from youth travel agencies like USIT and from main tourist offices (120F/€18.29; valid for a year), which entitles you to further reductions.

CHANGING MONEY

Standard **banking hours** are 9am to 4pm or 5pm. All banks close on Sundays, public holidays and on either Saturday morning or Monday; some also close at midday (noon/12.30pm–2/2.30pm). They

will have a notice on the door if they offer currency exchange. **Rates and commission** vary from bank to bank, so it's worth shopping around; the usual procedure is a 2–3 percent commission (with a minimum flat fee of anything between 25F/€3.81 and 50F/€7.62 on changing traveller's cheques and cash. Be wary of banks claiming to charge no commission at all; often they are merely adjusting the exchange rate to their own advantage. There are **money-exchange counters** (*bureaux de change*) at Bordeaux airport and in the city centre (see p.91), and very occasionally in local tourist offices, but rates are usually poor.

TRAVELLER'S CHEQUES AND THE VISA TRAVELMONEY CARD

Traveller's cheques are one of the safest ways of carrying your money. Worldwide, they're available from almost any major bank and from special American Express or Thomas Cook offices, usually for a service charge of one percent on the amount purchased. Banks may charge more, but check first as some offer cheques free of charge to customers meeting certain criteria. The most widely recognized brands of traveller's cheques are Visa, Thomas Cook and American Express, which most banks will change; American Express traveller's cheques can also be cashed at post offices.

French franc traveller's cheques can be worthwhile: they may often be used as cash, and you should get the face value of the cheques when you change them, so commission is only paid on purchase. Banks being banks, however, this is not always the case.

The latest way of carrying your money abroad is with a **Visa TravelMoney Card** (VTM), a sort of electronic traveller's cheque. The temporary disposable debit card is "loaded up" with an amount between £100 and £5000 and can then be used in any ATM carrying the Visa sign. When your funds are depleted, you simply throw the card away. It's recommended you buy at least a second card as back up in case your first is lost or stolen, though like traveller's cheques the cards can be replaced if such mishaps occur. Up to nine cards can be bought to access the same funds – useful for couples or families travelling together. Charges are two percent commission with a minimum charge of £3, or the equivalent. The card is available from, among other places, Citicorp and Thomas Cook. For further information, call your nearest 24hr toll-free Visa Global customer service centre (UK ☎0800/963 833; US & Canada ☎1-800/847-2399; Australia ☎1-800/125-161; New Zealand ☎0800/449 149), or check out their Web site at *www.visa.com*.

CREDIT AND DEBIT CARDS

Credit and debit cards are widely accepted; just look for the window stickers. Visa – known as Carte Bleue in France – is almost universally recognized; MasterCard (often called EuroCard) followed by American Express rank a bit lower. It's worth bearing in mind that some smaller places either don't accept cards, or only for sums above a certain threshold. Be aware, also, that French cards have a smart chip, and machines may reject cards with a magnetic strip even if they are valid.

You can also use credit and debit cards for **cash advances** at banks and in ATMs (*DAB* or *distributeur automatique de billets*) bearing the

---

LOSS OR THEFT OF CREDIT CARDS

If your credit or debit card is lost or stolen, you should ring the appropriate credit card company to cancel it immediately, since few cashiers even glance at the signature. The emergency numbers below are all available 24hr and should have English-speaking staff on call; the ☎08.00 numbers are toll-free.

MasterCard ☎08.00.90.13.87.
Visa ☎08.00.90.11.79.
American Express lost or stolen cards ☎01.47.77.72.00; lost or stolen travellers' cheques ☎08.00.90.86.00.
Diners Club ☎08.00.22.20.73.

---

appropriate network symbol; all ATMs give you the choice of instructions in French or English. On the whole, this is the cheapest way to obtain francs, but before you leave home check with your bank or credit agency to find what charges they levy on ATM transactions abroad. Since in most cases it's either a flat fee or a sliding scale above a minimum charge, it's cheaper to make a few reasonably large withdrawals rather than lots of small ones.

It's also a good idea to check your PIN number before you leave home since the majority of French ATMs expect a four-digit number and the key-pads don't allow for letters. Also, because French credit cards are smart cards, some ATMs baulk at foreign plastic and tell you that your request for money has been denied. If that happens, ask in the bank or try the post office, which will give cash advances on Visa cards if they won't work in ATMs.

Given these potential difficulties, it's advisable to carry at least two cards in different networks, and never rely entirely on your plastic. Always have some spare currency or traveller's cheques as a backup.

HEALTH AND INSURANCE

Citizens of all EU countries are entitled to take advantage of French health services under the same terms as residents as long as they have the correct documentation. British citizens need form E111, available from post offices. All non-EU citizens have to pay for most medical attention and are strongly advised to take out some form of travel insurance.

Under the French health system, every hospital visit, doctor's consultation, prescribed medicine and even ambulance call-out incurs a charge, which you have to pay upfront. EU citizens carrying the correct documents are entitled to a refund of 70–75 percent of any medical and dental expenses they incur, providing the doctor is a *médecin conventionné* (recognized under the government health service). This can still leave a

hefty shortfall, especially after a stay in hospital, and obtaining refunds can be complicated, so it's still worth considering taking out travel insurance with medical cover, which generally allows full reimbursement, minus the excess, and also covers the cost of repatriation.

In the Guide we give the phone numbers and addresses of **hospitals**, along with the number for the local police station, which can provide details of doctors on call and of pharmacies open after hours. To find a **doctor** in smaller towns, stop at any pharmacy and ask for an address, or look under "Médecins" in the Yellow Pages of the phone directory. An average consultation fee falls between 150F/€22.87 and 180F/€27.44. You will be given a *Feuille de Soins* ("Statement of Treatment") for later documentation of insurance claims. Prescriptions should be taken to a **pharmacie**, signalled by an illuminated green cross. In addition to dispensing medicine, all pharmacies are equipped, and obliged, to give first aid on request – for a charge.

In serious **medical emergencies** you will always be admitted to the nearest general hospital (*Centre Hospitalier*), either under your own power or by ambulance. The national number for calling an **ambulance** is ☎15, though many people call ☎18 for the *pompiers* (fire brigade), who are also trained for such circumstances.

TRAVEL INSURANCE

A typical **travel insurance** policy usually provides cover for the loss of baggage, tickets and –

ROUGH GUIDES TRAVEL INSURANCE

Rough Guides now offer their own **travel insurance**, customized for our readers by a leading UK broker and backed by a Lloyds underwriter. It's available for anyone of any nationality travelling anywhere in the world. There are two main plans: **Essential**, for effective, no-frills cover, starting at £10 for two weeks; and **Premier** – more expensive but with more generous and extensive benefits. Both offer European or Worldwide cover, and can be supplemented with a "Hazardous Activities Premium" if you plan to indulge in sports considered dangerous, such as skiing, scuba diving or trekking. Unlike many

policies, the Rough Guides schemes are calculated by the day, so if you're travelling for 27 days rather than a month, that's all you pay for. Alternatively, you can take out annual **multi-trip insurance**, which covers you for all your travel throughout the year (with a maximum of sixty days for any one trip).

For a **policy quote**, call the Rough Guides Insurance Line on UK freefone ☎0800/015 0906, or, if you're calling from outside Britain on ☎(+44) 1243/621 046. Alternatively, get an online quote or buy a policy direct at *www.roughguides.com/insurance*.

up to a certain limit – cash or cheques, as well as cancellation or curtailment of your journey. Most of them exclude so-called **dangerous sports** unless an extra premium is paid. Read the small print and benefits tables of prospective policies carefully; coverage can vary wildly for roughly similar premiums. Many policies can be chopped and changed to exclude coverage you don't need – for example, sickness and accident benefits can often be excluded or included at will. If you do take **medical coverage**, ascertain whether benefits will be paid as treatment proceeds or only after return home, and whether there is a 24-hour medical emergency number. When securing baggage cover, make sure that the per-article limit – typically under £500 equivalent – will cover your most valuable possession. If you need to make a claim, you should keep receipts for medicines and medical treatment, and in the event you have anything stolen, you must obtain an official statement from the police.

British bank and credit cards often have certain levels of medical or other insurance included

and you may automatically get travel insurance if you use a major credit card to pay for your trip. If you have a good all-risks home insurance policy it may cover your possessions against loss or theft even when overseas. Many private medical schemes such as BUPA or PPP also offer coverage plans for abroad, including baggage loss, cancellation or curtailment and cash replacement as well as sickness or accident.

Americans and **Canadians** should also check that they're not already covered. Canadian provincial health plans usually provide partial cover for medical mishaps overseas. Holders of official student/teacher/youth cards are entitled to meagre accident coverage and hospital in-patient benefits. Students will often find that their student health coverage extends during the vacations and for one term beyond the date of last enrolment. Homeowners' or renters' insurance often covers theft or loss of documents, money and valuables while overseas, though conditions and maximum amounts vary from company to company.

TRAVELLERS WITH DISABILITIES

France has no special reputation for providing facilities for disabled travellers. For people in wheelchairs, the haphazard parking habits and stepped village streets are serious obstacles, and public toilets with disabled access are rare. However, the situation is improving, especially in major cities like Bordeaux, where ramps and other forms of access are gradually being added to hotels, museums and some theatres and concert halls, and as all but the oldest hotels are required to adapt at least one room to be wheelchair accessible. APF, the French paraplegic organization, which has offices in each *département* (see box opposite), will be the most reliable source of information.

Public **transport** is becoming more wheelchair-friendly, and many train stations now have ramps to enable wheelchair-users to board and descend from carriages; at others it is still up to the guards to carry the chair. The high-speed **TGVs** (including Eurostar) all have places for

wheelchairs in the First Class saloon coach, which you must book in advance, though no higher fee is charged; on other trains, a wheelchair symbol within the timetable denotes whether that service offers special features (though it's best to doublecheck when booking), and you and your companion will again be upgraded to first class with no extra charge. The *Guide du Voyageur à Mobilité Réduite*, available free at main train stations, details all facilities. **Taxis** are obliged by law to carry you and to help you into the vehicle, also to carry your guide dog if you are blind. For self-drive, Hertz can provide automatic cars and those with hand controls at Bordeaux and other towns on request (central reservations ☎01.39.38.38.38; Bordeaux airport ☎05.56.34.59.59).

Up-to-date information about handicap accessibility, special programmes and discounts is best obtained from organizations at home before you leave or from the French disability organizations listed opposite. Some tourist offices have information but, again, it is not always very reliable. The Holiday Care Service has an information sheet on accessible **accommodation** in France, while guides produced by Gîtes de France (see p.38) indicate places with specially adapted rooms.

CONTACTS FOR TRAVELLERS WITH DISABILITIES

FRANCE

APF (Association des Paralysés de France), 17 bd Auguste-Blanqui, 75013 Paris (☎01.40.78.69.00, fax 01.45.89.40.57, *www.apf.asso.fr*). National association which can answer general enquiries, and put you in touch with their departmental offices.

Association France-Handicaps, 9 rue Luce-de-Lancival, 77340 Pontault-Combault (☎ & fax 01.60.28.50.12). Produces the French-language

Guide Rousseau (150F/€22.87 including postage) detailing accessible hotels, museums and other tourist sites.

CNRH (Comité National Français de Liaison pour la Réadaptation des Handicapés), 236bis rue de Tolbiac, 75013 Paris (☎01.53.80.66.66, *www.handitel.org*). Information service mostly concentrating on Paris, but which can also provide advice on regional accommodation and transport.

BRITAIN

Access Travel, 6 The Hillock, Astley, Lancashire M29 7GW (☎01942/888 844, fax 891 811, *www.access-travel.co.uk*). Tour operator that can arrange flights, transfers and accommodation. This is a small business, personally checking out places before recommendation. Established 1991; ATOL bonded.

Disability Action Group, Portside Business Park, 189 Airport Rd West, Belfast BT3 9ED (☎028/9029 7880, fax 9029 7881, *www.disabilityaction.org*). Can provide general information about holidays and accommodation suitable for disabled travellers, as well as a wide range of useful publications.

Holiday Care, 2nd floor, Imperial Building, Victoria Rd, Horley, Surrey RH6 7PZ (☎01293/774 535, fax 784 647, Minicom 01293/776 943, *www.holidaycare.org.uk*). Publishes a useful

France information sheet covering transport, accommodation and tour operators. Another sheet gives details of financial assistance available for holidays. Both cost £1, requested in stamps.

Mobility Information Service, Unit 2 Atcham Estate, Shrewsbury, Shropshire SY4 4UG (☎01743/761 889, fax 761 181, *www.mis.org.uk*). Can provide general advice on driving in France, including recommended routes.

Tripscope, Alexandra House, Albany Rd, Brentford, Middlesex TW8 0NE (☎0845/758 5641, fax 020/8580 7022, *www.justmobility.co.uk/tripscope*). Registered charity providing a phone-in travel information service that offers free advice on transport for those with a mobility problem.

IRELAND

Irish Wheelchair Association, Blackheath Drive, Clontarf, Dublin 3 (☎01/833 8241, fax

3873, *iwa@iol.ie*). Offers information about travel and access for disabled travellers abroad.

USA

Access First Travel, 239 Commercial St, Malden, MA 02148 (☎1-800/557 2047). Offers up-to-date information for disabled travellers.

Directions Unlimited, 123 Green Lane, Bedford Hills, NY 10507 (☎1-800/533 5343). Tour operator specializing in customized tours for people with disabilities.

Jewish Rehabilitation Hospital, 3205 Place Alton Goldbloom, Chomedy Laval, PQ H7V 1R2

(☎450/688 9550, ext 226). Provides guidebooks and travel information.

Mobility International USA, PO Box 10767, Eugene, OR 97440 (☎541/343 1284 voice & TDD, *www.miusa.com*). Offers information and referral services, access guides, tours and exchange programmes. Annual membership $25 (includes quarterly newsletter).

continued overleaf...

USA continued

Society for the Advancement of Travel for the Handicapped (SATH), 347 Fifth Ave, Suite 610, New York, NY 10016 (☎212/447 7284, *www.sath.org*). Non-profit-making travel industry referral service that passes queries on to its members as appropriate.

Travel Information Service (☎215/456-9600). Telephone-only information and referral service for disabled travellers.

Wheels Up!, PO Box 5197, Plant City, FL 33564-5197 (☎1-888/389 4335, *www.wheelsup.com*). Provides discounted air fares, tour and cruise prices for disabled travellers, as well as publishing a free monthly newsletter. Their Web site is comprehensive.

CANADA

Twin Peaks Press, Box 129, Vancouver, WA 98666 (☎360/694 2462 or 1-800/637 2256, *www.pacifier.com/twinpeak*). Publisher of the *Directory of Travel Agencies for the Disabled* ($19.95), listing more than 370 agencies world-wide; *Travel for the Disabled* ($19.95); the *Directory of Accessible Van Rentals* ($9.95); and *Wheelchair Vagabond* ($14.95), which is loaded with personal tips.

AUSTRALIA

ACROD (Australian Council for Rehabilitation of the Disabled), PO Box 60, Curtin, ACT 2605 (☎02/6282 4333); 24 Cabarita Rd, Cabarita, NSW 2137 (☎02/9743 2699). Provides lists of travel agencies and tour operators for people with disabilities.

Barrier Free Travel, 36 Wheatley St, North Bellingen, NSW 2454 (☎02/6655 1733). Independent consultant – draws up individual itineraries for people with disabilities for a fee.

NEW ZEALAND

Disabled Persons Assembly, PO Box 10, 138 The Terrace, Wellington (☎04/472 2626, *www.dpa.org.nz*). Provides details of tour opera-tors and travel agencies for people with disabilities.

INFORMATION AND MAPS

The French Government Tourist Office gives away maps and brochures for the Dordogne and Lot region, including lists of hotels and campsites. Some of these – like the maps of the inland waterways or footpaths, lists of festivals and so on – can be useful; others not. Before leaving home you could also try writing to the regional or departmental tourist offices (see below) which offer similarly useful practical information. And, of course, there's also the vast, if not always reliable, reservoir of information available on the Internet.

FRENCH GOVERNMENT TOURIST OFFICES ABROAD

The official French Government Tourist Office, La Maison de France, is on the Web at *www.franceguide.com*. You'll find a full list of their offices round the world at *www.franceguide.com/gb/maisonfrance/bureaux.cfm*.

Britain 178 Piccadilly, London W1V 0AL (☎0906/824 4123, 60p per min, fax 020/7493 6594).

Ireland 10 Suffolk St, Dublin 2 (☎01/679 0813, fax 0814).

USA 444 Madison Ave, 16th floor, New York, NY 10022 (☎410/286 8310, fax 838 7855); 676 North Michigan Ave, Suite 3360, Chicago, IL 60611-2819 (☎312/751 7800, fax 337 6339); 9454 Wilshire Blvd, Suite 715, Beverly Hills, CA

90212-2967 (☎310/271 6665, fax 276 2835); 1 Biscayne Tower, suite 1750, 2 South Biscayne Blvd, Miami, FL 33131 (☎305/373 8177, fax 5828).

Canada 1981 Ave McGill College, Suite 490, Montreal, QUE H3A 2W9 (☎514/876 9881, fax 845 4868).

Australia 25 Bligh St, Level 22, Sydney, NSW 2000 (☎02/9231 5244, fax 9221).

New Zealand contact the Australian office.

REGIONAL AND DEPARTMENTAL TOURIST OFFICES

Aquitaine Tourisme d'Aquitaine, Cité Mondiale, 23 parvis des Chartrons, 33074 Bordeaux (☎05.56.01.70.00, fax 05.56.01.70.07, *tourisme@crt.cr-acquitaine.fr*).

Aveyron Comité Départemental du Tourisme, BP 831, 12008 Rodez (☎05.65.75.55.75, fax 05.65.75.55.71, *aveyron-tourisme-cdt @wanadoo.fr*).

Corrèze Comité Départemental du Tourisme de la Corrèze, Quai Baluze, 19000 Tulle (☎05.55.29.98.78, fax 05.55.29.98.79, *www.cg19.fr*).

Dordogne Comité Départemental du Tourisme de la Dordogne, 25 rue Wilson, 24009 Périgueux (☎05.53.35.50.24, fax 05.53.09.51.41, *www.perigord.tm.fr*).

Gironde Maison du Tourisme de la Gironde, 21 Cours de l'Intendance, 33000 Bordeaux

(☎05.56.52.61.40, fax 05.56.81.09.99, *www.tourisme-gironde.cg33.fr*).

Lot Comité Départemental du Tourisme du Lot, 107 quai Cavaignac, BP7, 46001 Cahors (☎05.65.35.07.09, fax 05.65.23.92.76, *www.tourisme-lot.com*).

Lot-et-Garonne Comité Départemental du Tourisme du Lot-et-Garonne, 4 rue André-Chénier, BP158, 47005 Agen (☎05.53.66.14.14, fax 05.53.68.25.42, *www.lot-et-garonne.com*).

Midi-Pyrénées Comité Régional du Tourisme, 54 bvd de l'Embouchure, BP 2166, 31022 Toulouse (☎05.34.25.05.05, fax 05.34.25.05.09, *www.tourisme-midi-pyrenees.com*).

Tarn-et-Garonne Comité Départemental du Tourisme du Tarn-et-Garonne, BP 534, 82005 Montauban (☎05.63.63.31.40, fax 05.63.66.80.36, *cdt82@wanadoo.fr*).

MAP OUTLETS

BRITAIN

Bristol Stanfords, 29 Corn St, BS1 1HT (☎0117/929 9966, *www.stanfords.co.uk*).

Cambridge Heffers Map and Travel, 20 Trinity St, CB2 1TJ (☎01223/586 586, *www.heffers.co.uk*; mail order available).

Glasgow John Smith and Sons, 26 Colquhoun Ave, G52 4PJ (☎0141/221 7472, *www.johnsmith.co.uk*; mail order available).

Inverness James Thin Melven's Bookshop, 29 Union St, IV1 1QA (☎01463/233 500, *www.jthin.co.uk*; mail order available).

London Daunt Books, 83 Marylebone High St, W1M 3DE (☎020/7224 2295), and 193 Haverstock Hill, NW3 4QL (☎020/7794 4006); National Map Centre, 22–24 Caxton St, SW1H 0QU (☎020/7222 2466, *www.mapsnmc.co.uk*); Stanfords, 12–14 Long Acre, WC2E 9LP

(☎020/7836 1321, *www.stanfords.co.uk*; maps by mail or phone order are available on this number and via email), and within the British Airways offices at 156 Regent St, W1R 5TA (☎020/7434 4744); The Travel Bookshop, 13–15 Blenheim Crescent, W11 2EE (☎020/7229 5260, *www.thetravelbookshop.co.uk*).

Manchester Waterstone's, 91 Deansgate, M3 2BW (☎0161/837 3000, *www.waterstonesbooks.co.uk*).

Newcastle Newcastle Map Centre, 55 Grey St, NE1 6EF (☎0191/261 5622, *www.newtraveller.com*).

Oxford Blackwell's Map and Travel Shop, 53 Broad St, OX1 3BQ (☎01865/792 792, *bookshop.blackwell.co.uk*).

IRELAND

Belfast Waterstone's, Queens Bldg, 8 Royal Ave, Belfast BT1 1DA (☎01232/247 355, *www.waterstonesbooks.co.uk*).

Cork Waterstone's, 69 Patrick St (☎021/276 522).

Dublin Easons Bookshop, 40 O'Connell St, 1 (☎01/873 3811; mail order available;

www.eason.ie); Fred Hanna's Bookshop, 27–29 Nassau St, 2 (☎01/677 1255, *www.hannas.ie*); Hodges Figgis Bookshop, 56–58 Dawson St, 2 (☎01/677 4754, *www.hodgesfiggis.ie*); Waterstone's, 7 Dawson St, 2 (☎01/679 1415).

TOURIST OFFICES

In the Dordogne and Lot region you'll find a **tourist office** – usually an Office du Tourisme (OT) but sometimes a Syndicat d'Initiative (SI) – in practically every town and many villages (addresses, contact details and opening hours are detailed throughout the Guide). For the practical purposes of visitors, there is little difference between them; sometimes they share premises and call themselves an OTSI. In small villages where there is no OT or SI, try the *mairie* (mayoral office), often located in the town hall.

All these offices can provide specific local information, including listings of hotels and restaurants, leisure activities, car and bike rental, bus timetables, laundries and countless other things; many can also book accommodation for you. If asked, most offices will provide a free town plan (though some places charge a nominal sum), and will have maps and local walking guides on sale. In Bordeaux and the larger towns you can usually also pick up free *What's On* guides or at least a list of summer festivals, while those in and around Bordeaux will additionally provide information on local vineyards, and in peak season may conduct vineyard tours.

INTERNET RESOURCES

Though France has been slow to catch on to the **Internet**, information about practically every aspect of travel and French culture can now be accessed online. Many local tourist offices are now hooked up, and hotels and restaurants are also coming to realize the importance of an online presence. Web or email addresses are given where available throughout the Guide, while a selection

USA

Rand McNally has more than twenty stores across the US; call ☎1-800/333 0136 (ext 2111), or go to *www.randmcnally.com* for the address of your nearest store, or for **direct mail** maps.

Chicago Rand McNally, 444 N Michigan Ave, IL 60611 (☎312/321 1751).

Corte Madera Book Passage, 51 Tamal Vista Blvd, CA 94925 (☎415/927 0960, *www.bookpassage.com*).

New York The Complete Traveler Bookstore, 199 Madison Ave, NY 10016 (☎212/685 9007,); Rand McNally, 150 E 52nd St, NY 10022 (☎212/758 7488); Traveler's Choice Bookstore, 2 Wooster St, NY 10013 (☎212/941 1535, *tvl-choice@aol.com*).

Palo Alto Phileas Fogg's Books & Maps, #87 Stanford Shopping Center, CA 94304 (☎1-800/533-FOGG,

CANADA

Montreal Ulysses Travel Bookshop, 4176 St-Denis, QUE H2W 2M5 (☎514/843 9447, *www.ulyssesguides.com*).

Toronto Open Air Books and Maps, 25 Toronto St, ON M5R 2C1 (☎416/363 0719).

Vancouver International Travel Maps and Books, 552 Seymour St, BC V6B 3J5 (☎604/687 3320, *www.itmb.com*).

AUSTRALIA

Adelaide The Map Shop, 16a Peel St (☎08/8231 2033, *www.mapshop.net.au*).

Brisbane Worldwide Maps and Guides, 187 George St (☎07/3221 4330).

Melbourne Map Land, 372 Little Burke St (☎03/9670 4383, *mapland@lexicon.net*).

Perth Perth Map Centre, 884 Hay St (☎08/9322 5733, *www.perthmap.co.au*).

Sydney Travel Bookshop, Shop 3, 175 Liverpool St, 2000 (☎02/9261 8200).

NEW ZEALAND

Auckland Specialty Maps, 58 Albert St (☎09/307 2217).

Christchurch Mapworld, 173 Gloucester St (☎03/374 5399, *www.mapworld.co.nz*).

of the most useful and important sites are listed in the box below. As anywhere on the Net, persistent combing of links pages and use of search engines (among the best are *www.google.com*, *www.dogpile.com* and the French *www.yahoo.fr*) will almost certainly get you the information you are looking for. If not, try posting a message on the *rec.travel.europe* newsgroup.

MAPS

In addition to the various free leaflets – and the maps in this Guide – the one extra map you'll probably want is a reasonable **road map** of France. The Michelin (*www.michelin-travel.com*) yellow series (1:200,000) is the best for the motorist, though you'll need four maps to cover the entire area encompassed by the Guide, or you can get the whole series in one large spiral-bound *Atlas*

Routier. While there are no decent single maps of the whole area, Euromap's 1:300,000 series is good and covers it in two: *The Dordogne* (no. 6) and *Languedoc* (no. 7). Otherwise, the IGN (Institut Géographique National; *www.ign.fr*) Top 250 "red" maps of Bordelais/Périgord and Auvergne (nos. 110 and 111 respectively; 1:250,000) give you all but the extreme southeast corner. A useful free map for car drivers, obtainable from filling stations and traffic information kiosks, is the Bison Futé map, showing alternative back routes to the main roads, clearly signposted on the ground by special green Bison Futé road signs.

If you're planning to **walk or cycle**, check the more detailed IGN maps published under the "green" (1:100,000; Top 100), "orange" (1:50,000; Top 50) and blue (1:25,000; Top 25) series. The IGN 1:100,000 is recommended for cyclists.

FRANCE ON THE NET

TOURISM AND RECREATION

www.franceguide.com
The official site of the French Government Tourist Office, with news, information on local festivals and useful links.

www.info-france-usa.org
Well-designed site run by the French Embassy in Washington, with useful links to other French embassies, government offices, media and sports sites.

www.tourisme.fr
Searchable database run by the national tourist office association (FNOTSI), giving a brief overview of all French towns and cities.

www.monuments.fr
Well worth accessing for information on France's national monuments and museums, including news on special events.

NEWS AND INFORMATION

www.lemonde.fr
The French-language Web version of one of France's most reputable daily newspapers. Includes national and international news, culture and sports.

www.france2.fr/cyber
France TV 2's daily Web page has the latest news, weather, and road conditions as well as listings and reviews of cultural events. Also has a youth section.

www.sudouest.com
The online version of the *Sud Ouest* daily paper is all in French, but gives some information about what's on in the area in addition to its local, national and international news coverage.

ARTS AND CULTURE

web.culture.fr
French Ministry of Culture's page, with information on everything from monuments to exhibitions and also comprehensive lists of links to organizations related to the whole gamut of artistic media.

www.zeroennui.com
Database of selected arts and cultural events around the region, from jumble sales to classical music concerts.

www.vins-bordeaux.fr
A good introduction to Bordeaux and its vineyards, including tips on tasting and buying wines.

www.truffe-perigord-noir.com
Everything you could possibly want to know about truffles at this bilingual site run by the village of Ste-Alvère, "the first village to put its truffle market on the Net". You can even buy them online.

GETTING AROUND

France has the most extensive train network in western Europe, and rail provides the best way of moving between the main towns in the Dordogne and Lot. The nationally owned French train company, the SNCF (Société Nationale des Chemins de Fer), runs fast, modern trains. In rural areas where branch lines have been closed, routes (such as Agen–Villeneuve-sur-Lot) are covered by buses operated by the SNCF or in partnership with independent lines. It's an integrated service, with buses timed to meet trains and the same ticket covering both.

The private **bus** services that supplement the SNCF services can be confusing and unco-ordinated. A few areas, such as around Bordeaux and Brive, are reasonably well served, but throughout the rest of the region services are often extremely sporadic and usually cater to schoolchildren or locals heading for the weekly markets, and so not greatly useful to visitors. Where they do exist, approximate journey times and frequencies can be found in the "Travel Details" at the end of each chapter.

For truly independent transport, by **car** or **bicycle**, you'll need to be aware of a number of French road rules and peculiarities. **Hitching** is also an option, but is not easy and is becoming less and less popular. For information about **walking**, **trekking** and **canoeing**, as well as other activities, see "Sports and outdoor activities", p.55.

TRAINS

The SNCF has pioneered one of the most efficient, comfortable and user-friendly railway systems in the world. Its staff are, with a few exceptions, courteous and helpful, and its trains – for the most part, fast, clean and frequent – serve much of the Dordogne, though the Lot valley is less well covered. The region's principal rail corridors run north–south (Paris–Bordeaux, Limoges–Périgueux–Agen and Paris–Brive–Toulouse), with the important exception of the main line cutting southeast from Bordeaux via Agen and Montauban to Toulouse. From Bordeaux, three cross-country lines strike out northeast and east: Limoges via Périgueux; Brive via Périgueux; and along the Dordogne valley to Bergerac and Sarlat. For national train **information**, you can either phone (☎08.36.35.35.35; 2.23F/€0.34 per minute) or check on the Internet at *www.sncf.fr*; it is also possible to purchase tickets by credit card through these two services.

SNCF's pride and joy is the high-speed **TGVs** (*trains à grande vitesse*), capable of 300kph, and their offspring Eurostar. The region's principal stations served by the TGV are Bordeaux (approximately 3hr from Paris), Agen (4hr), and Montauban (5hr). The only difference between TGV and other train fares is that you pay a compulsory reservation charge (from 20F/€3.05), plus a supplement on certain peak-hour trains. It is easiest to use the counter service for buying tickets, though the touch-screen system available in most stations can be read in English and is a good way to check fares and times.

All **tickets** – but not passes (see below) – must be validated in the orange machines beside the entrance to the platforms, and it is an offence not to follow the instruction *Compostez votre billet* ("Validate your ticket"). Train journeys may be broken any time, anywhere, for as long as the ticket is valid (usually two months), but after a break of 24 hours you must revalidate your ticket when you resume your journey. On night trains an extra 100F/€15.24 or so will buy you a couchette.

After a spate of terrorist bombings in the late 1990s most train stations closed their **luggage lockers** (*consignes automatiques*); these days a few have reopened, and larger stations have a manned luggage check-in, usually with limited hours, while occasionally the ticket office will keep luggage for you for a short period (facilities are noted in the Guide).

Regional **timetables** and leaflets covering particular lines are available free at stations. *Autocar* (often abbreviated to *car*) at the top of a column means it's an SNCF bus service, on which rail tickets and passes are valid.

Aside from the regular lines, in summer there are three special **tourist trains**. The *Autorail Espérance* runs along the Dordogne valley between Sarlat and Bergerac (see p.205 & p.178 respectively), while the Chemin de Fer Touristique de Haut Quercy operates on a disused line between Martel and St-Denis (see p.251). Quercyrail does likewise between Capdenac, near Figeac, and Cahors (see p.278). None of these is covered by normal rail passes.

DISCOUNTS AND RAIL PASSES

There are several **passes** offering unlimited travel on the French network; most must be bought before you leave for France and are detailed on p.5 and the box on p.14. In addition, SNCF itself offers a whole range of **discounted fares** within France on *période bleue* (blue period) and *période blanche* (white period) days, depending on exactly what time you want to travel. A leaflet showing the blue, white (smaller discount) and red (peak) periods is given out at *gares*.

There is also a range of special **reductions** for which no pass is required. Any two people travelling together (*à deux*), or a small group of up to five people – whether a married couple, friends, family, whatever – are entitled to a 25 percent discount on return tickets on TGVs, subject to availability, or on other trains if they start their journey on a blue-period day; the same reduction applies to a group of up to four people travelling with a child under 12, to under 26-year-olds, over-60s, and for anyone who books a return journey of at least 200km in distance, including a Saturday night away (this latter is called the *séjour*).

In addition, there are several other train passes which can be purchased through most travel agents in France or from main stations and are valid for one year. Over-60s can get the **Carte Senior**, which costs 285F/€43.45 for unlimited travel. It offers up to fifty percent off tickets on TGVs, subject to availability, or other journeys starting in blue periods, a 25 percent reduction on white-period journeys, as well as a thirty-percent

reduction on through international journeys involving most countries in western and central Europe. The same percentage reductions are available for under-26s with a **Carte 12–25** pass, which costs 270F/€41.16. Under-12s can obtain the same advantages for themselves and up to four travelling companions of any age by purchasing the **Carte Enfant Plus** (350F/€53.36).

BUSES

The most convenient **bus services** are those run as an extension of rail links by SNCF, which always run to and from the train station and reach areas not accessible by rail. In addition to SNCF buses, private, municipal and departmental buses can be useful for local and some cross-country journeys, though be prepared for some early starts and careful planning if you want to see much outside the main towns. There's a frustrating lack of co-ordinated departure information for buses around the Dordogne (where you'll have to rely on local tourist offices for help), but the Conseils Généraux of the Gironde, Lot, Lot-et-Garonne and Corrèze, on the other hand, produce comprehensive **timetables** – or, in the case of the Gironde, a map and individual leaflets – detailing all the routes in the *département*; you can get copies by writing to the departmental tourist offices (see box on p.27), or in person from tourist offices in the main towns.

Larger towns usually have a **gare routière** (bus station), often next to the gare SNCF. However, the private bus companies don't always work together and you'll frequently find them leaving from an array of different points (the local tourist office will help locate them).

DRIVING

Driving in the Dordogne and Lot can be a real pleasure – and is often the only practical means of reaching the more remote sights. At present there are two **autoroutes** in the area: the A62 runs along the Garonne from Bordeaux to Toulouse, while the A20 – still under construction – cuts south from Limoges to Toulouse. The latter is due for completion in 2003; for the moment there's a 70km stretch missing from Souillac south to Cahors, causing tremendous bottlenecks during the peak holiday migrations – most notoriously, weekends in July and August – where motorway traffic has to join the old N20. Another *autoroute*, the A89, is also being built, linking

Clermont-Ferrand in the northeast with Brive, Périgueux and Bordeaux, due for completion in 2004 at the earliest. Motorway **tolls** are payable in cash or by credit card at the frequent toll gates (*péages*). For an idea of the costs involved, the trip from Calais to Bordeaux (850km) adds up to 370F/€56.41, while from Bordeaux to Agen (128km) would be 48F/€7.32. Outside the busiest periods and if you're in a hurry, it is well worth paying this to avoid the slow and congested free national roads.

Across country, the older trunk roads or **routes nationales** (marked N21 or RN21, for example, on signs and maps) and particularly the smaller **routes départementales** (marked with a D) are generally uncongested and make for a more scenic drive, though may occasionally be in relatively poor condition.

Of course, there are times when it is wiser not to drive, most obviously in Bordeaux, where parking can be difficult and expensive; if you're renting a car here, it's better to do so at the airport.

The region's other towns and cities are all of a manageable size – just follow signs for *centre ville* or the tourist office and you'll normally find a car park nearby. **Congestion** can be a problem throughout the region in July and August, most notably around major towns and tourist spots, including the most scenic stretches of the Dordogne, Lot and Aveyron valleys. The high cost of **fuel** can also be a discouraging factor; you'll find the cheapest petrol (*essence*) or diesel fuel (*gasoil*) at out-of-town hypermarkets (see p.21 for a rough idea of prices). Four-star is *super*, unleaded is *sans plomb*. Note that in rural areas most petrol stations close in the evening, on Sundays and bank holidays, while some also don't open on Mondays.

If you run into **mechanical difficulties** you'll find garages and service stations in the Yellow Pages of the phone book under "Garages d'automobiles"; for **breakdowns**, look under "Dépannages". If you have an accident or break-in, you should contact the local police – keeping a

---

CAR RENTAL AGENCIES

BRITAIN AND IRELAND

Autos Abroad (in the UK ☎020/7287 6000, *www.autosabroad.co.uk*).

Avis (in Britain ☎0870/606 0100; Northern Ireland ☎0870/590 0500; Irish Republic ☎01/874 5844; *www.avis.com*).

Budget (in the UK ☎0800/181 181; Irish Republic ☎0800/973 159; *www.budgetrentacar.com*).

Europcar (in the UK ☎0845/722 2525; Irish Republic ☎01/874 5844; *www.europcar.com*).

Hertz (in Britain ☎0870/844 8844; Northern Ireland ☎0870/599 6699; Irish Republic ☎01/676 7476; *www.hertz.com*).

Holiday Autos (in Britain ☎0870/400 0011; Northern Ireland ☎0870/530 0400; Irish Republic ☎01/872 9366; *www.kemwel.com*).

National Car Rental (in the UK ☎01895/233 300, *www.nationalcar.com*).

Thrifty (in the UK ☎01494/442 110, *www.thrifty.com*).

USA AND CANADA

Auto Europe (☎1-800/223 5555, *www.autoeurope.com*).

Avis (☎1-800/331 1084).

Budget (☎1-800/527 0700).

Europe by Car (☎1-800/223 1516, *www.europebycar.com*).

Hertz (in US ☎1-800/654 3001; in Canada ☎1-800/263 0600).

Holiday Autos (☎1-800/422 7737)

National (☎1-800/CAR-RENT).

Thrifty (☎1-800/367 2277).

AUSTRALIA AND NEW ZEALAND

Avis (in Australia ☎13/6333; in New Zealand ☎09/526 5231 or 0800/655 111)

Budget (in Australia ☎1300/362 848; in New Zealand ☎0800/ 652 227 or 09/375 2270)

Fly and Drive Holidays New Zealand ☎09/529 3709.

Hertz (in Australia ☎1800/550 067; in New Zealand ☎09/309 0989 or 0800/655 955)

Renault Eurodrive Australia ☎02/9299 3344.

copy of their report – in order to file an insurance claim. Within Europe, most car insurance policies cover taking your car to France; check with your insurer. However, you're advised to take out extra cover for motoring assistance in case your car breaks down; an average policy costs around £45 for seven days – contact your local Automobile Association to see what deals they offer.

RULES OF THE ROAD

British, Irish, Australian, Canadian, New Zealand and US **driving licences** are valid in France, though an International Driver's Licence makes life easier. If the vehicle is rented, its registration document (*carte grise*) and the insurance papers must be carried. Coming from Britain, GB stickers are, by law, meant to be displayed, and a Green Card, though not a legal requirement, might save some hassle. If your car is right-hand drive, you must have your headlight dip adjusted to the right before you go – it's a legal requirement – and as a courtesy paint them yellow or stick on black glare deflectors. Remember also that you have to be eighteen years of age to drive in France, regardless of whether you hold a licence in your own country.

The law of *priorité à droite* – **giving way** to traffic coming from your right, even when it is coming from a minor road – is being phased out as it is a major cause of accidents. However, it still applies on some roads in built-up areas and the occasional roundabout, so it pays to be vigilant at junctions, especially in rural areas where old habits die hard. A sign showing a yellow diamond on a white background gives you right of way, while the same sign with an oblique black slash indicates priority goes to vehicles emerging from the right. *Stop* signs mean stop completely; *Cédez le passage* means "Give way".

Fines of up to 2500F/€381 for driving violations are exacted on the spot, and only cash is accepted; you should be given a receipt. The fines for exceeding the speed limit by 1–30kph (1–18mph) range from 900F/€137 to 5000F/€762, and if you're caught exceeding the limit by 40kmph (25mph) or over the police will take away your licence then and there. Speed limits are: 130kph (80mph) on *autoroutes*; 110kph (68mph) on dual carriageways; 90kph (55mph) on other roads; and 50kph (31mph) in towns. In wet weather, and for drivers with less than two years' experience, the limits for the first three types of road are 110kph (68mph), 100kph (62mph), and 80kph (50mph) respectively, while the town limit

remains constant. Random breath tests are common, and the legal blood alcohol limit (0.05 percent alcohol) is lower than in the UK and North America; fines range from 900F/€137 to 30,000F/€4574.

CAR RENTAL

Car rental in France costs upwards of 2000F/€305 a week (from around 290F/€44.21 a day), but can be cheaper if arranged before you leave home. You'll find the big firms at airports and in most major towns and cities, with addresses detailed throughout the Guide. Rental from airports normally includes a surcharge. Local firms can be cheaper but you need to check the small print and be sure of where the car can be returned to. It's normal to pay an indemnity of around 2000F/€305 against any damage to the car – they will take your credit card number rather than cash. You should return the car with a full tank of fuel. The cost of car rental includes the basic legally required car insurance. North Americans and Australians in particular should be forewarned that it is very difficult to arrange the rental of a car with **automatic** transmission; if you can't drive a manual you should try to book an automatic well in advance, and be prepared to pay a much higher price for it.

Most rental companies will only deal with people over 25 unless an extra insurance premium, typically around 130–150F/€19.82–22.87 per day, is paid (but you still must be over 21 and have driven for at least one year). OTU Voyage (Paris office ☎01.40.29.12.12), the student travel agency, can arrange car rental for young drivers, with prices beginning at 459F/€69.97 for three days, insurance extra.

MOPED AND MOTORBIKE RENTAL

Mopeds and scooters are relatively easy to find, and though they're not built for long-distance travel, are ideal for shooting around the local area. Places that rent out bicycles often also rent out mopeds; you can expect to pay 175F/€26.68 a day for a 50cc Suzuki. No licence is needed for bikes 50cc and under, but for anything larger you'll need a valid **motorbike** licence. Rental prices are around 220F/€33.54 a day for an 80cc motorbike, 300F/€45.73 for a 125cc; also expect to leave a hefty deposit by cash or credit card – 6000F/€915 is not unusual – which you may lose in the event of damage or theft. Crash helmets are now compulsory on all mopeds and motorbikes.

HITCHING

If you're intent on **hitching**, you'll have to rely almost exclusively on car drivers, as lorries very rarely give lifts. Even so, it won't be easy. Experience suggests that hitching the less-frequented D-roads is much quicker, while in rural areas a rucksack and hiking gear will help procure a lift from fellow aficionados.

Autoroutes are a special case. Hitching on the *autoroute* itself is strictly illegal, but you can make excellent time going from one service station to another. It helps to have the *Guide des Autoroutes*, published by Michelin, which shows all the rest stops, service stations, tollbooths (*péages*), exits, etc. The tollbooths are a second best (and legal) option; ordinary approach roads can be disastrous.

For long-distance rides, and for a greater sense of safety, you might consider using the national **hitching organization**, Allostop Provoya, 8 rue Rochambeau (on square Montholon), 17009 Paris (☎01.53.20.42.42, fax 01.53.20.42.44, *pcb.ecritel .fr/allostop/welcome*). The cost comprises a registration fee (30–70F/€4.57–10.67 depending on journey length). Alternatively, you can buy a 180F/€27.44 membership card which is good for eight trips over two years), plus a charge of 22 centimes for every kilometre of the journey.

BICYCLES

Bicycles (*vélos*) have high status in France, where cyclists are given respect both on the roads and as customers at restaurants and hotels. In addition local authorities are actively promoting cycling, not only with city cycle lanes, but comprehensive networks linking rural areas (frequently utilizing disused roads and railways). Hotels along the way are nearly always obliging about looking after your bike, even to the point of allowing it into your room. Most towns have well-stocked retail and **repair shops**, where parts are normally cheaper than in Britain or the US. However, if you're using a foreign-made bike with nonstandard metric wheels, it's a good idea to carry spare tyres.

The **train** network runs various schemes for cyclists, all of them covered by the free bilingual leaflet *Guide Train et Vélo*, available from all main stations. Trains marked with a bicycle in the timetable and a few TGV trains (listed in the above booklet) allow you to take a bike free in the luggage van as long as there's space. Otherwise, you can take your dismantled bike, packed in a carrier, on TGVs and other trains with sufficiently large luggage racks. The other alternative is to send it parcelled up as registered luggage for a fee of 195F/€29.73. It's supposed to arrive in two

---

A CYCLING VOCABULARY

to adjust	*régler*	loose	*déserré*
axle	*l'axe*	to lower	*baisser*
ball-bearing	*le roulement à billes*	mudguard	*le garde-boue*
battery	*la pile*	pannier	*le pannier*
bent	*tordu*	pedal	*le pédale*
bicycle	*le vélo*	pump	*la pompe*
bottom bracket	*le logement du pédalier*	puncture	*la crevaison*
brake cable	*le cable*	rack	*le porte-bagages*
brakes	*les freins*	to raise	*remonter*
broken	*cassé*	to repair	*réparer*
bulb	*l'ampoule*	saddle	*la selle*
chain	*la chaîne*	to screw	*visser/serrer*
cotter pin	*la clavette*	spanner	*la clef*
to deflate	*dégonfler*	spoke	*le rayon*
derailleur	*le dérailleur*	to straighten	*redresser*
frame	*le cadre*	stuck	*coincé*
gears	*les vitesses*	tight	*serré*
grease	*la graisse*	toe clips	*les cale-pieds*
handlebars	*le guidon*	tyre	*le pneu*
to inflate	*gonfler*	wheel	*la roue*
inner tube	*la chambre à air*		

days, but may well take longer; and you do hear stories of bicycles disappearing altogether.

Eurostar allow you to take your bicycle as part of your baggage allowance provided it is dismantled and stored in a special bike bag, and the dimensions don't exceed 120cm by 90cm. Otherwise it needs to be sent unaccompanied, with a guaranteed arrival of 24 hours (you can register it up to ten days in advance; book through Esprit Europe ☎0800/186 186); the fee is £20 one way. **Ferries** either take bikes free or charge a maximum of £5 one way, while **airlines** such as British Airways and Air France also carry bikes free – contact the airlines first however.

Bikes – usually mountain bikes – are often available to **rent** from campsites and hostels, as well as from specialist cycle shops and some tourist offices for around 80F/€12.20 per day. You may be asked for a deposit of at least 1000F/€153 – make sure you get a receipt – and since the bikes are often not insured, you will have to pay for its replacement if it's stolen or damaged; check your insurance policy for cover.

As for **maps**, a minimum requirement is the IGN 1:100,000 series – the smallest scale that carries contours. In the UK, the Cyclists' Touring Club, Cotterell House, 68 Meadrow, Godalming, Surrey GU7 3HS (☎01483/417 217, fax 426 994, *cycling@ctc.org.uk*), will suggest routes and supply advice for members. Companies running specialist bike touring holidays are listed on pp.8, 13 and 17.

ACCOMMODATION

At most times of the year, you can turn up in any town in the Dordogne and Lot region and

find a room, or space in a campsite. Booking a couple of nights in advance can be reassuring, however, as it saves you the effort of trudging round and ensures that you know what you'll be paying; many hoteliers, campsite managers and hostel managers speak at least a little English. In most towns, you'll be able to get a simple double from around 180F/€27.44, though expect to pay between 200F/€30.49 and 300F/€45.73 for a reasonable level of comfort. We've detailed a selection of hotels throughout the Guide, and given a price range for each (see box); as a general rule the areas around train stations have the highest density of cheap hotels.

Problems arise mainly between mid-July and the end of August, when the French take their own

ACCOMMODATION PRICE CODES

All the hotels and guesthouses listed in this book have been price-coded according to the following scale, and though costs will rise slightly overall with the life of this edition, the relative comparisons should at least remain valid. The prices quoted are for the **cheapest available double room in high season**, although remember that many of the cheap places will have more expensive rooms with en-suite facilities.

① Under 160F/€24
② 160–220F/€24–34
③ 220–300F/€34–46

④ 300–400F/€46–61
⑤ 400–500F/€61–76
⑥ 500–600F/€76–91

⑦ 600–700F/€91–107
⑧ 700–800F/€107–122
⑨ Over 800F/€122

vacations en masse. During this period, hotel and hostel accommodation can be hard to come by and you may find yourself falling back on local tourist offices for help. Some offer a **booking service**, though they cannot guarantee rooms at a particular price, while all tourist offices can provide lists of hotels, campsites, bed-and-breakfast possibilities and any hostels. With **campsites**, you can be more relaxed about finding an empty space in summer, unless you're touring with a caravan or camper van. Note that some hotels ask for a deposit or, more rarely, a credit card number as surety, especially if you book a long time in advance.

HOTELS

Most French hotels are **graded** from zero to five stars. The price more or less corresponds to the number of stars, though the system is a little haphazard, having more to do with ratios of bathrooms-per-guest and so forth than genuine quality, and some nonclassified and single-star hotels can be very good. What you get for your money varies enormously between establishments. For under 180F/€27.44, the bed is likely to be old and sagging, there won't be soundproofing and showers (*douches*) and toilets (*WC* or *toilettes*) may be communal. However, you should have your own bidet and washbasin (*lavabo*), sometimes partitioned off from the rest of the room in what's known as a *cabinet de toilette*. The shared showers down the hall are occasionally free but usually cost between 10F/€1.52 and 20F/€3.05 per shower; if there is more than one of you, it might be cheaper to upgrade to an en-suite room. Over 250F/€38.11 should get you a room with its own shower and toilet, and, though the decor may not be anything to write home about, comfortable furniture. For around 300F/€45.73 you should expect a proper, separate bathroom (*salle de bain*) and TV, while at over 450F/€68.60 you'll find something approaching luxury. Hotels with one star or above have a telephone in the rooms, though some phones can only receive calls. **Single rooms** – if the hotel has any – are only marginally cheaper than doubles, so sharing always slashes costs, especially since most hotels willingly provide rooms with **extra beds** for three or more people at good discounts.

Breakfast is not normally included and can add at least 25–35F/€3.81–5.34 per person to a bill – though there is no obligation to take it. The cost of eating **dinner** in a hotel's restaurant can be a more important factor to bear in mind when picking a place to stay. Officially, it is illegal for hotels to insist on your taking half-board (*demi-pension*), though a few do during the summer peak. This is not always a bad thing, since you can sometimes get a real bargain.

Note that many family-run hotels close for two or three weeks a year. In small towns and villages they may also close for one or two nights a week, usually Sunday or Monday. Details are given where relevant in the Guide, but dates change from year to year and in the off season some hotels will close for a few days if they have no bookings. The best precaution is to phone ahead to be sure.

A very useful option, especially if it's late at night, is the **motel chains** located by motorway exits and on the outskirts of major towns. They may be soulless but you can count on a decent and reliable standard. Among the cheapest (around 150F/€22.87 for a three-person room with toilets and showers on the corridor) and biggest is the one-star **Formule 1** chain (brochures available from Accor central reservation service: ☎08.03.88.00.00, 0.99F/€0.15 per min; *www.hotelformule1.com/formule1/index.html*). Other budget chains include the slightly more upmarket Première Classe (☎08.36.68.81.23; 2.23F/€0.34 per min; *www.premiereclasse.fr*) and Etap Hôtel (☎08.36.68.89.00; 2.23F/€0.34 per min; *www.etaphotel.com*). More comfortable but still affordable chains are **Ibis** (☎08.03.88.00.00, 0.99F/€0.15 per min; *www.ibis.fr*) and **Campanile** (☎08.25.00.30.03, 0.98F/€0.15 per min; *www.campanile.fr*), where en-suite rooms with cable TV and direct dial phones cost 270–320F/€41.16–48.78.

Aside from the chains, there are number of **hotel federations** in France. The biggest of these is **Logis de France**, an association of some 3600 hotels nationwide. They have a central reservation service (☎01.45.84.83.84, fax 01.45.83.59.66) and Web site (*www.logis-de-france.fr*), which you can contact to obtain their free annual guide (or write to 83 av d'Italie, 75013 Paris). Two other, more upmarket federations worth mentioning are Châteaux & Hôtels de France (12 rue Auber, 75009 Paris; ☎01.40.07.00.20, fax 01.40.07.00.30, *www.chateauxhotels.com*) and the Relais du Silence (17, rue d'Ouessant 75015 Paris; ☎01.44.49.79.00, fax 01.44.49.79.01, *www.silencehotel.com*).

BED-AND-BREAKFAST AND SELF-CATERING ACCOMMODATION

In country areas, in addition to standard hotels, you will come across *chambres d'hôtes* **bed-and-breakfast accommodation** in someone's house, château or farm. Though the quality varies widely, on the whole standards have increased dramatically in recent years and the best *chambres d'hôtes* now offer greater value for money than an equivalently priced hotel. In addition, they usually have far more local character and, if you're lucky, may be good sources of traditional home-cooking and French company. Prices range between about 250F/€38.11 and 350F/€53.36 for two people including breakfast; note that payment is almost always expected in cash. Some offer meals on request (*tables d'hôtes*), usually evenings only, while others are attached to *fermes auberges*, farm-restaurants serving local produce (see p.42 for more). Again, we've listed a number of *chambres d'hôtes* throughout the Guide.

If you are planning to stay a week or more in any one place it will be worth considering renting **self-catering accommodation**. You can do this by checking adverts from the innumerable foreign-owned private homes in British Sunday newspapers (*Observer* and *Sunday Times*, mainly), or by trying one of the holiday firms that market accommodation/travel packages (see the boxes on pp.8, 13 and 17 for a brief selection of these).

Alternatively, contact **Gîtes de France**, 59 rue St-Lazare, 75439 Paris (Mon–Fri 10am–6.30pm, Sat 10am–1pm & 2–6.30pm; ☎01.49.70.75.75,

fax 01.42.81.28.53, *www.gites-de-france.fr*), a government-funded agency which promotes and manages a range of *chambres d'hôtes* and self-contained country cottages, known as **gîtes** or *gîtes ruraux*. Further details can be found in their very useful national guides, including *Chambres et Tables d'Hôtes* and *Chambres d'Hôtes de Prestige et Gîtes de Charme* in English and French (both 140F/€21.34 including postage), which are usually on sale in bookstores and tourist offices. The national guides, however, are not exhaustive; for complete listings (with photos) you need to buy the relevant departmental guide (around 60–70F/€9.15–10.67 including postage), either from the Paris headquarters or their departmental offices (see box), or from a local bookstore.

HOSTELS, FOYERS AND GÎTES D'ÉTAPE

There aren't that many **hostels** – *auberges de jeunesse* – in the Dordogne and Lot region, but at between 50F/€7.62 and 100F/€15.24 per night for a dormitory bed, sometimes with breakfast thrown in, they are invaluable for single travellers on a budget; **per-person prices** of dorm beds are given throughout the Guide. Some hostels now offer rooms for couples or families, with en-suite showers, but they don't necessarily work out cheaper than hotels – particularly if you've had to pay a bus fare to reach them. However, one or two, notably the hostel at Cadouin (see p.194), are beautifully sited, and allow you to cut costs by preparing your own food in their kitchens, or eating in their cheap canteens.

Hostels in the Dordogne and Lot region, all detailed in the Guide, are run by the municipality

---

DEPARTMENTAL OFFICES OF GÎTES DE FRANCE

Aveyron: 17 rue Aristide-Briand, BP 831, 12008 Rodez Cedex (☎05.65.75.55.60, fax 05.65.75.55.61, *gites.de.france.aveyron@wanadoo.fr*).

Corrèze: Immeuble Consulaire, Le Puy Pinçon - Tulle Est, BP 30, 19001 Tulle Cedex (☎05.55.21.55.61, fax 05.55.21.55.88, *gites.de.france.correze@wanadoo.fr*).

Dordogne: 25 rue Wilson, 24009 Périgueux (☎05.53.35.50.24, fax 05.53.09.51.41, *dordogne.perigord.tourisme@wanadoo.fr*).

Gironde: 21 cours de l'Intendance, 33000 Bordeaux (☎05.56.81.54.23, fax 05.56.51.67.13, *gites-de-france-gironde@fr.st*).

Lot: pl François Mitterand - B.P. 162, 46003 Cahors Cedex 9 (☎05.65.53.20.75, fax 05.65.53.20.79; *gites.de.france.lot@wanadoo.fr*).

Lot-et-Garonne: 4 rue André-Chénier, 47000 Agen (☎05.53.47.80.87, fax 05.53.66.88.29, *gites-de-france.47@wanadoo.fr*).

Tarn-et-Garonne: Hôtel des Intendants, pl Maréchal Foch, 82000 Montauban (☎05.63.93.59.15, fax 05.63.03.41.95, *cdt82@wanadoo.fr*).

HOSTELLING ASSOCIATIONS

FRANCE

Fédération Unie des Auberges de Jeunesse (FUAJ), 27 rue Pajol, 75018 Paris (☎01.44.89.87.27, *www.fuaj.org*).

Ligue Française pour les Auberges de Jeunesse (LFAJ), Batiment K, 67 rue Verjneaud, 75013 Paris (☎01.44.16.78.78, *www. auberges-de-jeunesse.com*).

BRITAIN AND IRELAND

Youth Hostel Association (YHA), Trevelyan House, 8 St Stephen's Hill, St Albans, Herts AL1 2DY (☎0870/870 8808, *www.yha.org.uk*); London membership desk and booking office: 14 Southampton St, London WC2 7HY (☎020/7836 8541). Annual membership £12.

Scottish Youth Hostel Association, 7 Glebe Crescent, Stirling FK8 2JA (☎01786/891 400, *www.syha.org.uk*). Annual membership £6.

Youth Hostel Association of Northern Ireland 22 Donegall Rd, Belfast BT12 5JN (☎028/9031 5435, *www.hini.org.uk*). Annual membership £8.

An Oige, 61 Mountjoy St, Dublin 7 (☎01/830 4555, *www.irelandyha.org*); annual membership IR£10/€12.70.

USA AND CANADA

Hostelling International-American Youth Hostels (HI-AYH), 733 15th St NW, Suite 840, Washington DC 20005 (☎1-800/444-6111 or 202/783 6161, *www.hiayh.org*).

Hostelling International Canada, Room 400, 205 Catherine St, Ottawa, ON K2P 1C3 (☎1-800/663 5777 or 613/237 7884, *www. hostellingintl.ca*).

AUSTRALIA AND NEW ZEALAND

YHA Australia, 422 Kent St, Sydney (☎02/9261 1111, www.*yha.com.au*).

YHA New Zealand, Level 3, 193 Cashel St, PO Box 436, Christchurch (☎03/379 9970, *www.yha.org.nz*).

or by one of two French **hostelling associations**: the Fédération Unie des Auberges de Jeunesse (FUAJ), or the much smaller Ligue Française pour les Auberges de Jeunesse (LFAJ) which runs the hostel in Bordeaux; see box for contact details. Normally, to stay at FUAJ or LFAJ hostels you must have a current HI (Hostelling International) **membership card**. It's usually cheaper and easier to join before you leave home, provided your national Youth Hostel association (see box) is a full member of HI. Alternatively, you can purchase an HI card in certain French hostels for 114F/€17.38, or buy individual "welcome stamps" at a rate of 19F/€2.90 per night; after six nights you are entitled to the HI card.

One or two larger towns, such as Villefranche-de-Rouergue and Périgueux, provide hostel accommodation in Foyers des Jeunes Travailleurs, **residential hostels** for young workers and students, where you can usually get a private room

for around 60F/€9.15. On the whole they are more luxurious than youth hostels and normally have a good cafeteria or canteen.

In the countryside, another hostel-style alternative exists: **gîtes d'étape**. Aimed primarily at hikers and long-distance bikers, *gîtes d'étape* are often run by the local village or municipality and are less formal than hostels. They provide bunk beds and primitive kitchen and washing facilities from around 40F/€6.10, and are marked on the large-scale IGN walkers' maps and listed in the individual GR *Topo-guides* (see p.57). More information can be found in the Gîtes de France booklet *Gîtes d'Étapes et de Séjours* (60F/€9.15 inc. postage), and in *Gîtes d'Étape et Refuges*, published by Guides La Cadole, available in French bookshops for 110F/€16.77.

CAMPING

Practically every village and town in France has at least one **campsite** to cater for the thousands of people who spend their holiday under canvas. The vast majority of sites are graded into **four categories**, from one to four stars, by the Fédération Française de Camping et Caravaning (78, rue de Rivoli, 75004 Paris; ☎01.42.72.84.08, fax 01.42.72.70.21, *www.campingfrance.com*), who also publish useful guides. **One- and two-star sites** are very basic, with toilets, showers (not necessarily with hot water) and public phones but little else; prices start at around 30F/€4.57 per person per night. Many in the first category are either municipal sites, usually conveniently located on the outskirts of towns, or those right out in the sticks; standards of cleanliness are not always brilliant. At the other extreme, **four-star sites** are far more spacious, have hot-water showers and electrical hook-ups. Most will have a swimming pool, sometimes heated, washing machines, a shop and sports facilities and will provide refreshments or meals in high season. At **three-star sites** you can expect a selection of these facilities and less spacious plots. A family of four with a tent and car should expect to pay around 150F/€22.87 per day at a one-star site, rising to 250F/€38.11 at a four-star. In peak season and if you plan to spend a week or more at one site, it's wise to book ahead, and note that many of the big sites now have caravans and even chalet bungalows for rent.

As with hotels, the above grading system reflects the facilities on offer rather than the real quality of a site, though it does give a rough idea of what to expect. In answer to this shortcoming, the designation **Camping Qualité** has been introduced to indicate those campsites with particularly high standards of hygiene, service and privacy. For those who really like to get away from it all, **camping à la ferme** – on somebody's farm – is another good, simple option. Lists of sites are available at local tourist offices and in the guide *Campings et Campings à la Ferme* (70F/€10.67 including postage) published by Gîtes de France (see p.38).

If you're planning to do a lot of camping, an **international camping carnet** is a good investment. The carnet serves as useful identification, covers you for third party insurance when camping, and helps you get ten-percent reductions at campsites listed in the CCI information booklet that comes with your carnet. It is available in the UK from the AA, the RAC and the Carefree Travel Service (☎024/7642 2024, *www.bccscotland. freeserve.co.uk/nation.html*), who also book inspected campsites and arrange ferry crossings; in the US and Canada from Family Campers and RVers (FCRV; *www.fcrv.org*).

A number of companies also specialize in selling **camping holidays**, including Allez France (see box, p.8), Canvas Holidays (☎08709/022022, *www.canvas.co.uk*), Keycamp (☎0870/700 0123, *www.keycamp.co.uk*) and Sunsites (☎01606/787 555, *www.sunsites.co.uk*).

Lastly, a word of **caution**: never camp rough (*camping sauvage*, as the French call it) on anyone's land without first asking permission. If the dogs don't get you, the guns might – farmers have been known to shoot first, and ask later. On the other hand, a politely phrased request for permission will as often as not get positive results. Camping on public land is not officially permitted, but is widely practised by the French, and if you are discreet you will likely not meet with problems.

EATING AND DRINKING

The Dordogne region – generally referred to as the Périgord when it comes to food – is home to one of the great traditions of French cuisine. This is by no means *haute cuisine*, but at heart country cooking (*cuisine de terroir*) plain and simple, revolving around duck and goose, garlic, a host of mushrooms, walnuts and whatever else the land has to offer. It's the sort of cuisine best sampled in little family-run places, where it's still possible to eat for well under 100F/€15.24. That said, every restaurant worth its salt offers a *menu du terroir*, featuring local specialities – indeed, it sometimes seems hard to find anything else, and in summer especially you'll be craving less hearty fare. Relief is at hand, however, in the more adventurous – and expensive – *gastronomique* restaurants found throughout the region, and most mid-priced establishments now offer at least a smattering of fish dishes. But real fish and seafood fanatics should head for Bordeaux – a city famed for the range and quality of its restaurants – and the towns and villages along the Gironde estuary. On the whole, the Dordogne and Lot region has fared better than many other parts of France when it comes to the encroachment of the processed, boil-in-the-bag and microwaved school of cooking. That said, the uniformity of middle-of-the-road restaurant menus can become tiring, and be prepared for some disappointments in prime tourist spots.

Vegetarians can expect a lean time in this region – the very concept is alien to most local chefs. There are very few specifically vegetarian restaurants, though *crêperies* and pizzerias can be good standbys. Otherwise the best you can hope for is an omelette, salad or plate of vegetables – often tinned – at an ordinary restaurant. Sometimes they'll be willing to replace a meat dish on the *menu fixe*; at other times you'll have to pick your way through the *carte*. Remember the phrase "Je suis végétarien(ne); est-ce qu'il y a quelques plats sans viande?" (I'm a vegetarian; are there any non-meat dishes?). **Vegans**, however, should probably forget about eating in restaurants and stick to self-catering.

With the exception of Bordeaux and the larger towns, the Dordogne and Lot is also not well provided with restaurants serving **foreign cuisine**. The most likely – and usually good value for money – are Vietnamese, Chinese or North African outlets.

In the rarefied world of **haute cuisine**, where the top chefs are national celebrities, a battle is raging between traditionalists and those who experiment with different flavours from around the world to create novel combinations. At this level, French food is still brilliant – in both camps – and the good news is that prices are continuing to come down. Many gourmet palaces offer weekday lunchtime menus where you can sample culinary genius for under 300F/€45.73.

BREAKFAST AND SNACKS

A croissant, *pain au chocolat* (a chocolate-filled light pastry) or a sandwich in a bar or café, with hot chocolate or coffee, is generally the best way to eat **breakfast** – at a fraction of the cost charged by most hotels, where the standard breakfast comprises bread, jam and a jug of coffee or tea, orange juice if you're lucky, for around 30F/€4.57 or more. Croissants are displayed on bar counters until around 9.30am or 10am; if you stand – cheaper than sitting down – you just help yourself to these with your coffee; the waiter keeps an eye on how many you've eaten and bills you accordingly. And if they've run out, it's perfectly acceptable to go and buy your own at the local baker or *pâtisserie*.

At **lunchtime**, and sometimes in the evening, you'll find places offering a *plat du jour* (daily special) at between 40F/€6.10 and 75F/€11.43, or *formules*, a limited or no-choice menu. *Croques-monsieur* or *croques-madame* (variations on the toasted-cheese sandwich) are on sale at cafés, brasseries and many street stands, along with *frites* (potato fries), *crêpes*, *gauffres* (waffles), *glaces* (ice creams) and all kinds of fresh-filled baguettes (these substantial sandwiches usually cost between 18F/€2.74 and 28F/€4.27 to take away).

Crêpes, or pancakes with fillings, served up at ubiquitous *crêperies*, are popular lunchtime food. The savoury buckwheat variety (*galettes*) provide the main course; sweet white-flour *crêpes* are dessert. They can be very tasty, but are usually poor value in comparison with a restaurant meal. **Pizzerias**, usually *au feu du bois* (wood-fire-baked), are also very common. They are somewhat better value than *crêperies*, but quality and quantity vary greatly.

For **picnics**, the local outdoor market or supermarket will provide you with almost everything you need. Cooked meat, prepared snacks, ready-made dishes and assorted salads can be bought at *charcuteries* (delicatessens), which you'll find even in some villages, and in most supermarkets. You purchase by weight, or you can ask for *une tranche* (a slice), *une barquette* (a carton) or *une part* (a portion).

MEALS

There's no difference between **restaurants** (or *auberges* or *relais* as they sometimes call themselves) and **brasseries** in terms of quality or price range. The distinction is that brasseries, which resemble cafés, serve quicker meals at most hours of the day, while restaurants tend to stick to the traditional meal times of noon to 2pm, and 7pm to 9pm or 9.30pm, sometimes later in larger towns and during the summer months. In touristy areas in high season, and for all the more upmarket places, it's wise to make reservations – easily done on the same day. In small towns it may be impossible to get anything other than a bar sandwich after 10pm or even earlier; in Bordeaux, town-centre brasseries will serve until 11pm or midnight and some places stay open all night.

When hunting for places to eat, don't forget that **hotel restaurants** are open to nonresidents, and are often very good value. Indeed, in many small towns and villages, you'll find these are the only restaurants, but in the countryside keep an eye out for **fermes auberges**, farm restaurants where the majority of ingredients have to be produced on the farm itself. These are often the best places to sample really traditional local cuisine at very reasonable prices; a four-course meal for around 100–150F/€15.24–22.87 is the norm, including an apéritif and wine; reservations are a must. Since restaurants change hands frequently and have their ups and downs, it's always worth asking locals for recommendations; this will usually elicit strong views and sound advice.

Prices, and what you get for them, are posted outside. Normally there's a choice between one or more *menus fixes* – where the number of courses has already been determined and the choice is limited – and choosing individually from the *carte* (menu). **Menus fixes**, often referred to simply as *menus*, are normally the cheapest option. At the bottom end of the price range, they revolve around standard dishes such as steak and chips (*steak frites*), chicken and chips (*poulet frites*) and various stews (such as *daubes*). But further up the scale they can be much the best-value way of sampling regional specialities, sometimes running to five or more courses. Going **à la carte** offers greater choice and, in the better restaurants, unlimited access to the chef's inventiveness – though you'll pay for the privilege.

In the French **sequence of courses**, any salad (sometimes vegetables, too) comes separate from the main dish, and cheese precedes a dessert. You will be offered coffee, which is always extra, to finish off the meal.

In the vast majority of restaurants a **service charge** of around fifteen percent is included in prices listed on the menu – check that it says *service compris* (*s.c.*). *Service non compris* (*s.n.c.*) or *servis en sus* means that the charge will be added to the bill. **Wine** (*vin*) or a **drink** (*boisson*) is occasionally included in the cost of a *menu fixe*. When ordering house wine, the cheapest option, ask for *un quart* (0.25 litre), *un demi-litre* (0.5 litre) or *une carafe* (1 litre). If you're worried about the cost ask for *vin ordinaire* or the *vin de table*. In the Guide the lowest price menu, or sometimes the range of menus, is given. Note that the evening menus – and often those served at weekends – are in general slightly more expensive than the standard weekday lunchtime menu. This may amount to an extra 20F/€3.05 to 40F/€6.10 in a run-of-the-mill place, but where the discrepancy is large we quote prices for both lunch and evening/weekend menus. Where average à la carte prices are given it assumes you'll have three courses, but excludes wine.

The French are extremely well disposed towards **children** in restaurants. Not only do they offer reduced-price children's menus but also create an atmosphere – even in otherwise fairly snooty establishments – that positively welcomes kids; some even provide games and toys.

One final note is that you should always call the waiter or waitress *Monsieur* or *Madame* (*Mademoiselle* if a young woman), never *Garçon*.

REGIONAL SPECIALITIES

The mainstay of Périgord cuisine, and spreading further south into the Quercy, is duck and goose. Most famously in the form of **foie gras** (see p.154), the fattened liver of either fowl whose rich and buttery taste is an experience not to be missed. Though best eaten on its own in succulent slabs, foie gras is often combined with the region's other great culinary star, **truffles**, or *truffes* (see p.157). These hugely expensive earthy black fungi crop up in all sorts of local dishes, from rich *périgordin* sauces to the humble omelette.

In addition to the livers, almost every bit of the **duck** and **goose** is used. The meat is cooked and preserved in its own thick yellow grease to make succulent *confit*, which is either served on its own or goes into the preparation of other dishes, such as soups and cassoulet, a no-nonsense concoction of *confit*, Toulouse sausage and haricot beans. Duck gizzards preserved in the same way are sliced and served warm on lettuce in a popular starter, *salade du gésiers*, while another delicacy is *cou farci*, goose neck stuffed with sausage meat, foie gras and truffles – both far more tasty than they sound. The thick juicy steaks of grilled duck breast known as *magrets* are more instantly appealing and appear on practically every restaurant menu, in fancier places accompanied by a truffle, pepper or fruit-based sauce. Both duck and goose meat go into a coarse local pâté called *rillettes*, and their fat is used in the cooking of everything from omelettes to *pommes sarladaise*, a dish originating in Sarlat in which sliced potatoes are fried with lashings of garlic and parsley. The fat is also used to brown the garlic in *tourin* (or *tourain*), the region's traditional soup, served with an egg over thick country bread. Not even the car-

casses go to waste: duck carcasses (*demoiselles*) are roasted over a wood fire after which you pick off the remaining morsels of meat.

It's not all duck and goose, however. You'll also find *poulet confit* and other **chicken** dishes, while **pork** features strongly too. In more traditional restaurants, look out for *enchaud périgordin*, sliced slow-roasted pork loin stuffed with garlic and, in fancier versions, with truffles as well; it's usually eaten cold. In the Quercy region, tender **lamb** raised on the scrubland of the *causses* is most frequently served roasted as *gigot* (leg), while towards the north and east, the excellent Limousin **beef** begins to feature more strongly. In season more upmarket restaurants offer *pigeonneau*, young pigeon, and hare (*lièvre*) among other types of **game**.

By contrast, this is not a rewarding region for **cheese** connoisseurs. There are some good farm cheeses to be had in the markets, but the only local speciality cheese is *cabécou* (also known as *Rocamadour*), a little flat disc of goat's cheese from the Quercy. It's often served soft and fresh as a cheese course, or grilled as a starter on a bed of lettuce with walnut oil. The best *cabécou* come from around Rocamadour, where they have their own AOC label.

Though it was once despised as poor people's food, these days you'll occasionally see *miques* on a restaurant menu. These maize- and wheat-flour **dumplings** are usually served in a thick soup as a substitute for bread, but they can also be doused in egg, fried and served with sugar or honey. Other more common **desserts** include a thin apple tart topped with almost transparent crinkled pastry and a hint of alcohol called *pastis*, and *clafoutis*, which has spread here from the Limousin – it's a sort of toad-in-the-hole made with cherries, pears or any other fruit. Walnut cakes and puddings are popular nowadays, as are strawberries from around Bretenoux and to the south of Périgueux. Agen, further south again, is famous for its prunes and all sorts of derived goodies.

The main exception to the cuisine described above is the area around Bordeaux and along the banks of the Garonne, where **fish and seafood** hold sway. Salmon, eel, whelk, prawns, smelt, oysters and even farmed sturgeon can all be sampled in local restaurants according to the season. Young fried elvers (*pibales*) are expensive but popular along the estuary in January and February, while further inland *alose* (shad) is

A FOOD GLOSSARY

BASIC TERMS

l'addition	bill/check	*cuit*	cooked	*œuf*	egg	*sucre*	sugar
beurre	butter	*à emporter*	takeaway	*offert*	free	*sucré*	sweet
bouteille	bottle	*fourchette*	fork	*pain*	bread	*table*	table
chauffé	heated	*fumé*	smoked	*poivre*	pepper	*verre*	glass
couteau	knife	*huile*	oil	*salé*	salted/	*vinaigre*	vinegar
cru	raw	*lait*	milk		spicy		
cuillère	spoon	*moutarde*	mustard	*sel*	salt		

SNACKS

un sandwich/	**a sandwich**	*tartine*	buttered bread or open
une baguette			sandwich
au jambon	with ham		
au fromage	with cheese	**œufs**	**eggs**
au saucisson	with sausage	*au plat*	fried
à l'ail	with garlic	*à la coque*	boiled
au poivre	with pepper	*durs*	hard-boiled
au pâté (de campagne)	with pâté (country-	*brouillés*	scrambled
	style)	*pochés*	poached
croque-monsieur	grilled cheese and ham		
	sandwich	**omelette**	**omelette**
croque-madame	grilled cheese and	*nature*	plain
	bacon, sausage, chicken	*aux fines herbes*	with herbs
	or egg sandwich	*au fromage*	with cheese
panini	toasted Italian sandwich	*aux truffes*	with truffles

PASTA (PÂTES), PANCAKES (CRÊPES) AND FLANS (TARTES)

nouilles	noodles	*pissaladière*	tart of fried onions with
pâtes fraîches	fresh pasta		anchovies and black
crêpe au sucre/	pancake with sugar		olives
aux œufs	/eggs	*tarte flambée*	thin pizza-like pastry
galette (de sarrasin)	buckwheat pancake		topped with onion,
			cream and bacon or
			other combinations

SOUPS (SOUPES)

bisque	shellfish soup	*soupe à l'oignon*	onion soup with a
bouillabaisse	Mediterranean fish soup		chunk of toasted
bouillon	broth or stock		bread and melted
consommé	clear soup		cheese topping
garbure	potato, cabbage and	*tourain, tourin*	garlic soup made with
	meat soup		duck or goose fat
potée	thick vegetable and		served over bread
	meat soup		topped with cheese
potage	thick soup, usually		
	vegetable		

STARTERS (HORS D'ŒUVRES)

assiette anglaise	plate of cold meats	*hors d'œuvres*	combination of the above
crudités	raw vegetables with	*variés*	plus smoked or
	dressings		marinated fish

FISH (POISSON), SEAFOOD (FRUITS DE MER) AND SHELLFISH (CRUSTACES OR COQUILLAGES)

alose	shad	crabe	crab	lotte de mer	monkfish
anchois	anchovies	crevettes grises	shrimp	loup de mer	sea bass
anguilles	eels	crevettes roses	prawns	maquereau	mackerel
bigourneaux	periwinkles	daurade	sea bream	merlan	whiting
brandade de	puréed, salted	écrevisses	freshwater	moules	mussels (with
morue	cod with oil,		crayfish	(marinière)	shallots in
	milk, garlic	éperlan	smelt		white wine
	and mashed	escargots	snails		sauce)
	potato	esturgeon	sturgeon	raie	skate
brème	bream	flétan	halibut	rascasse	scorpion fish
bulot	whelk	gambas	king prawns	rouget	red mullet
cabillaud	cod	hareng	herring	saumon	salmon
calmar	squid	homard	lobster	sole	sole
carrelet	plaice	huîtres	oysters	thon	tuna
colin	hake	lamproie	lamprey	truite	trout
coques	cockles	langoustines	saltwater	turbot	turbot
coquilles	scallops		crayfish		
St-Jacques		limande	lemon sole		

FISH DISHES AND TERMS

aïoli	garlic mayon-	frit	fried	mousse/	mousse
	naise served	friture	deep-fried	mousseline	
	with salt cod		small fish	pané	breaded
	and other fish	fumé	smoked	quenelles	light dumplings
arête	fish bone	grillé	grilled	thermidor	lobster grilled
assiette de	assorted fish	hollandaise	butter and		in its shell with
pêcheur			vinegar sauce		cream sauce
beignet	fritter	à la meunière	in a butter,		
darne	fillet or steak		lemon and		
la douzaine	a dozen		parsley sauce		

MEAT (VIANDE) AND POULTRY (VOLAILLE)

agneau (de	lamb (grazed	gibier	game	poitrine	breast
pré-salé)	on salt	gigot (d'agneau)	leg (of lamb)	porc	pork
	marshes)	grenouilles		poulet	chicken
andouille,		(cuisses de)	frogs (legs)	ris	sweetbreads
andouillette	tripe sausage	grillade	grilled meat	rognons	kidneys, usually
bifteck	steak	hâchis	chopped meat		lamb's
bœuf	beef		or mince	rognons blancs	testicles
boudin blanc	sausage of		hamburger	sanglier	wild boar
	white meats	langue	tongue	steak	steak
boudin noir	black pudding	lapin, lapereau	rabbit, young	tête de veau	calf's head (in
caille	quail		rabbit		jelly)
canard	duck	lard, lardons	bacon, diced	tournedos	thick slices of
caneton	duckling		bacon		fillet
contrefilet	sirloin roast	lièvre	hare	tripes	tripe
dinde, dindon	turkey	merguez	spicy, red	tripoux	mutton tripe
entrecôte	rib steak		sausage	veau	veal
faux filet	sirloin steak	mouton	mutton	venaison	venison
foie	liver	oie	goose	volaille	poultry
foie gras	(duck/goose)	onglet	cut of beef		
	liver	os	bone		

MEAT AND POULTRY DISHES AND TERMS

aiguillettes	thin, tender pieces of duck	*cuisse*	thigh or leg
aile	wing	*épaule*	shoulder
au feu de bois	cooked over wood fire	*en croûte*	in pastry
au four	baked	*farci*	stuffed
blanquette, daube,		*garni*	with vegetables
estouffade, navarin,		*gésier*	gizzard
ragoût	types of stew	*gigot (d'agneau)*	leg (of lamb)
blanquette	veal in cream and mushroom	*grillade*	grilled meat
de veau	sauce	*grillé*	grilled
bœuf bourguignon	beef stew with Burgundy,	*hâchis*	chopped meat or mince
	onions and mushrooms		hamburger
brochette	kebab	*magret de canard*	duck breast
canard à l'orange	roast duck with an orange	*marmite*	casserole
	and wine sauce	*médaillon*	round piece
canard de	roast duck with prunes, pâté	*noisettes*	small, round fillets
périgourdin	foie gras and truffles	*pavé*	thick slice
carré	best end of neck, chop or	*poêlé*	pan-fried
	cutlet	*poule au pot*	chicken simmered with
cassoulet	casserole of beans, duck and		vegetables
	sausage	*rôti*	roast
choucroute	pickled cabbage with	*sauté*	lightly cooked in butter
	peppercorns, sausages,	*steak au poivre*	steak in a black (green/red)
	bacon and salami	*(vert/rouge)*	peppercorn sauce
civet	game stew	*steak tartare*	raw chopped beef, topped
confit	meat preserve		with a raw egg yolk
côte	chop, cutlet or rib	*tournedos rossini*	beef fillet with foie gras and
cou	neck		truffles
coq au vin	chicken cooked until it falls	*viennoise*	fried in egg and breadcrumbs
	off the bone with wine,		
	onions and mushrooms		

TERMS FOR STEAKS

bleu	almost raw	*bien cuit*	well done
saignant	rare	*très bien cuit*	very well done
à point	medium		

GARNISHES AND SAUCES

américaine	white wine, cognac and	*chasseur*	white wine, mushrooms and
	tomato		shallots
au porto	in port	*diable*	strong mustard seasoning
béarnaise	sauce of egg yolks,	*forestière*	with bacon and mushroom
	white wine,	*fricassée*	rich, creamy sauce
	shallots and vinegar	*mornay*	cheese sauce
beurre blanc	sauce of white wine and	*périgourdine,*	with Madeira wine
	shallots, with butter	*périqueux*	and truffles
bonne femme	with mushroom, bacon,	*provençale*	tomatoes, garlic, olive oil
	potato and onions		and herbs
bordelaise	in a red wine, shallot and	*savoyarde*	with Gruyère cheese
	bone-marrow sauce	*véronique*	grapes, wine and cream

VEGETABLES (LÉGUMES), HERBS (HERBES) AND SPICES (ÉPICES)

ail	garlic	*ciboulette*	chives	*menthe*	mint
artichaut	artichoke	*concombre*	cucumber	*moutarde*	mustard
asperge	asparagus	*cornichon*	gherkin	*oignon*	onion
avocat	avocado	*echalotes*	shallots	*persil*	parsley
basilic	basil	*endive*	chicory	*piment*	pimento
betterave	beetroot	*épinard*	spinach	*poireau*	leek
capre	caper	*estragon*	tarragon	*pois, petits pois*	peas
carotte	carrot	*fenouil*	fennel	*poivron (vert,*	sweet pepper
céleri	celery	*fèves*	broad beans	*rouge)*	(green, red)
champignon,	types of	*flageolets*	white beans	*pommes de*	
cèpe,	mushrooms	*haricots (verts,*	beans (French/	*terre*	potatoes
chanterelle,		*rouges,*	string, kidney,	*radis*	radish
girolle,		*beurres)*	butter)	*riz*	rice
morille		*lentilles*	lentils	*salade verte*	green salad
chou (rouge)	(red) cabbage	*maïs*	corn	*tomate*	tomato
choufleur	cauliflower	*mange-tout*	snow peas	*truffes*	truffles

VEGETABLE DISHES AND TERMS

à l'anglaise	boiled	*à la grecque*	cooked in oil	*pimenté*	peppery hot
beignet	fritter		and lemon	*piquant*	spicy
biologique	organic	*jardinière*	with mixed	*pistou*	ground basil,
duxelles	fried mushrooms		diced		olive oil, garlic
	and shallots		vegetables		and parmesan
	with cream	*mousseline*	mashed potato	*râpée*	grated or
farci	stuffed		with cream		shredded
feuille	leaf		and eggs	*sauté*	lightly fried in
fines herbes	mixture of	*à la parisienne*	potatoes		butter
	tarragon,		sautéed in	*à la vapeur*	steamed
	parsley and		butter; with	*en verdure*	garnished
	chives		white wine		with green
gratiné	browned with		sauce and		vegetables
	cheese or		shallots		
	butter	*parmentier*	with potatoes		

FRUIT (FRUIT) AND NUTS (NOIX)

abricot	apricot	*framboise*	raspberry	*noisette*	hazelnut
amande	almond	*fruit de la passion*	passion fruit	*noix*	nuts, walnuts
ananas	pineapple	*grenade*	pomegranate	*orange*	orange
banane	banana	*groseille*		*pamplemousse*	grapefruit
brugnon,	nectarine	*rouge/blanche*	red/white	*pastèque*	watermelon
nectarine			currant	*pêche*	peach
cacahouète	peanut	*kaki*	persimmon	*pistache*	pistachio
cassis	blackcurrant	*mangue*	mango	*poire*	pear
cérise	cherry	*marron*	chestnut	*pomme*	apple
citron	lemon	*melon*	melon	*prune*	plum
citron vert	lime	*mirabelle*	small yellow	*pruneau*	prune
figue	fig		plum	*raisin*	grape
fraise	strawberry	*mûre*	blackberry	*reine-claude*	greengage
(de bois)	(wild)	*myrtille*	bilberry		

FRUIT DISHES AND TERMS

beignet	fritter	*flambé*	set aflame in alcohol
compôte	stewed fruit	*frappé*	iced
coulis	sauce of puréed fruit	*macédoine*	fruit salad
crème de marrons	chestnut purée		

DESSERTS (DESSERTS OR ENTREMETS), PASTRIES (PÂTISSERIE) AND RELATED TERMS

barquette	small boat-shaped flan	*fromage blanc*	cream cheese
bavarois	refers to the mould, could be a mousse or custard	*gaufre*	waffle
		gênoise	rich sponge cake
		glace	ice cream
bombe	moulded ice-cream dessert	*île flottante/ œufs à la neige*	soft meringues floating on custard
brioche	sweet, high-yeast breakfast roll	*macaron*	macaroon
		madeleine	small sponge cake
		mousse au chocolat	chocolate mousse
charlotte	custard and fruit in lining of almond fingers	*omelette norvégienne*	baked Alaska
clafoutis	heavy custard and fruit tart	*parfait*	frozen mousse, sometimes ice cream
		pâte	pastry or dough
coupe	a serving of ice cream	*petit-suisse*	a smooth mixture of cream and curds
crème à l'anglaise	custard		
crème Chantilly	vanilla-flavoured and sweetened whipped cream	*poires belle hélène*	pears and ice cream in chocolate sauce
		sablé	shortbread biscuit
crème fraîche	sour cream	*savarin*	a filled, ring-shaped cake
crème pâtissière	thick, eggy pastry-filling		
crêpe	pancake	*tarte*	tart
crêpe suzette	thin pancake with orange juice and liqueur	*tartelette*	small tart
		tarte tatin	upside-down apple tart
		yaourt, yogourt	yoghurt

often grilled over vine clippings. The least savoury of the local delicacies is lamprey (*lamproie*). An ugly, eel-like creature, the lamprey is bled while still alive and then marinated and poached in a sauce comprising Sauternes wine, leeks, onions, smoked ham and its own blood. More appetizing is the area's one non-fish speciality, Pauillac lamb, raised on the salt marshes of the Médoc.

DRINKING

Wherever you can eat you can invariably drink, and vice versa. **Drinking** is done at a leisurely pace whether it's a prelude to food (*apéritif*), or a sequel (*digestif*), and cafés are the standard places to do it. Every bar or café has to display its full price list, including service charges, with the cheapest drinks at the bar (*au comptoir*), and progressively increasing prices for sitting at a table

inside (*la salle*), or outside (*la terrasse*). You pay when you leave, and it's perfectly acceptable to sit for hours over just one cup of coffee, though a tip of a franc or two will always be appreciated.

Wine (*vin*) is drunk at just about every meal or social occasion. Red is *rouge*, white *blanc* and rosé *rosé*. *Vin de table* or *vin ordinaire* – table wine – is generally drinkable and always cheap, although it may be disguised and priced-up as the house wine, or *cuvée*. The price of AOC (*appellation d'origine contrôlée*) wines can vary from 10F/€1.52 to 100F/€15.24 and over, and that's the vineyard price. You can buy a very decent bottle of wine for under 30F/€4.57, while 60F/€9.15 and over will get you something worth savouring. By the time restaurants have added their considerable mark-up, wine can constitute an alarming proportion of the bill.

The basic **wine terms** are: *brut*, very dry; *sec*, dry; *demi-sec*, sweet; *doux*, very sweet;

mousseux, sparkling; *méthode champenoise*, mature and sparkling. There are grape varieties as well, but the complexities of the subject take up volumes. A glass of wine is simply *un verre du rouge, rosé* or *blanc. Un pichet* (a pitcher) is normally a quarter-litre, but you may need to specify the size: a quatre litre (*un quart*), a half (*un demi*). A glass of wine in a bar will cost around 20–30F/€3.05–4.57.

The best way of **buying wine** is directly from the producers (*vignerons*), either at vineyards, at Maisons or Syndicats du Vin (representing a group of wine-producers), or at Coopératifs Vinicoles (wine-producer co-ops). At all these places you can usually sample the wines first. It's best to make clear at the start how much you want to buy (particularly if it's only one or two bottles) and you will not be popular if you drink several glasses and then fail to make a purchase. The most interesting option is to visit the vineyard itself, where the owner will often include a tour of the *chais* in which the wine is produced and aged; see p.94 for more on vineyard visits. The most economical

method is to buy *en vrac*, which you can also do at some wine shops (*caves*), filling an easily obtainable plastic five- or ten-litre container (usually sold on the premises) straight from the barrel.

Familiar light Belgian and German brands, plus French brands from Alsace, account for most of the **beer** you'll find. Draught beer (*à la pression*) – usually Kronenbourg – is the cheapest drink you can have next to coffee and wine; ask for *un pression* or *un demi* (0.33 litre). A *demi* costs around 17F/€2.59. For a wider choice of draught and bottled beer you need to go to the special beer-drinking establishments or English- and Irish-style pubs found in larger towns and cities. A small bottle at one of these places will cost at least twice as much as a *demi* in a café. In supermarkets, however, bottled or canned beer is exceptionally cheap.

Strong alcohol is consumed from as early as 5am as a pre-work fortifier, and then at any time through the day according to circumstance, though the national reputation for drunkenness has lost much of its truth. Brandies and the dozens of *eaux-de-vie* (spirits) and liqueurs are

WINES OF THE REGION

The area around **Bordeaux** comprises one of the world's great wine-producing regions. The Bordelais vineyards stretch over 100km north–south and 130km east–west, divided among 57 different *appellations* and thousands of individual châteaux. The vast majority produce red wines, most famously those of the **Médoc** and **St-Émilion**, for example, but the area also produces quality white wines – the dry **Graves** and the velvety sweet **Sauternes** being the most notable. And don't overlook the lesser-known Bordeaux wines, such as Côtes de Bourg and Côtes de Blaye, and Entre-Deux-Mers, where you can still find very drinkable wines at much lower prices.

The same goes for the vineyards further inland. Around **Bergerac**, the sweet, white Monbazillac is the star, though the aromatic whites of Montravel and the reds of Pécharmant are also worth looking out for. There are also some very palatable Côtes de Bergerac and Côtes de Castillon, the best of which resemble the neighbouring St-Émilion wines but for half the price. In similar vein are the wines of **Duras** and **Buzet** to the south. Further east, the fine dark, almost peppery reds from **Cahors** provide one of the region's most distinctive tastes.

The quality of the local *vins de pays*, though very variable, can still be exceptional for the price, but for better quality vintages you need to concentrate on the **AOC wines**. It's worth noting, however, that within each *appellation* there is enormous diversity generated by the different types of soil, the lie of the land, the type of grape grown, the ability of the wine to age, and – last but by no means least – the individual skills of the viticulturist.

It's an extremely complex business and it's not difficult to feel intimidated by the seemingly innate expertise of all French people. Many individual wines and *appellations* are mentioned in the text, but trusting your own taste is the most important thing. Knowing the grape types that you particularly like (or dislike), whether you prefer wines fruity, dry, light or heavy, is all useful when you are discussing your choice with a waiter, wine merchant or the producer themselves. The more interest you show, the more helpful advice you are likely to receive.

For more on the region's major wine-producing areas see p.74 for Bordeaux, p.173 for Bergerac, and p.270 for Cahors.

always available, including locally-made walnut liqueurs (*vins de noix*). Pastis – the generic name for aniseed drinks such as Pernod or Ricard – is served diluted with water and ice (*glaçons*). It's very refreshing and not expensive. Among less familiar names, try Poire William (pear brandy), or Marc (a spirit distilled from grape pulp). Measures are generous, but they don't come cheap: the same applies for imported spirits like whisky (*Scotch*). Two drinks designed to stimulate the appetite – *un apéritif* – are Pineau (cognac and grape juice) and Kir (white wine with a dash of Cassis – blackcurrant liquor, or with champagne instead of wine for a Kir Royal). For a post-meal *digestif*, don't miss out on armagnac, oak-aged brandy from the south of the Garonne but available in bars and restaurants throughout the region. **Cocktails** are served at most late-night bars, discos and clubs, as well as at upmarket hotel bars; they usually cost at least 45F/€6.86.

On the **soft drink** front, you can buy cartons of unsweetened fruit juice in supermarkets, although in the cafés the bottled (sweetened) nectars such as apricot (*jus d'abricot*) and blackcurrant (*cassis*) still hold sway. Fresh orange or lemon juice (*orange/citron pressé*) is a refreshing choice on a hot day – the juice is served in the bottom of a long ice-filled glass, with a jug of water and a sugar bowl to sweeten it to your taste. Other soft drinks to try are syrups (*sirops*) of

mint, grenadine or other flavours mixed with water. The standard fizzy drinks of lemonade (*limonade*), Coke (*coca*) and so forth are all available. Bottles of **mineral water** (*eau minérale*) and spring water (*eau de source*) – either sparkling (*gazeuse*) or still (*eau plate*) – abound, from the big brand names to the most obscure spa product. But there's not much wrong with the tap water (*l'eau de robinet*) which will always be brought free to your table if you ask for it.

Coffee is invariably espresso – small, black and very strong. *Un café* or *un express* is the regular; *un crème* is with milk; *un grand café* or *un grand crème* are large cups. In the morning you could also ask for *un café au lait* – espresso in a large cup or bowl filled up with hot milk. *Un déca* is decaffeinated, now widely available. Ordinary **tea** (*thé*) is Lipton's nine times out of ten and is normally served black, and you can usually have a slice of lemon (*limon*) with it if you want; to have milk with it, ask for *un peu de lait frais* (some fresh milk). *Chocolat chaud* – **hot chocolate** – unlike tea, lives up to the high standards of French food and drink and can be had in any café. After eating, **herb teas** (*infusions* or *tisanes*), offered by most restaurants, can be soothing. The more common ones are *verveine* (verbena), *tilleul* (lime blossom), *menthe* (mint) and *camomille* (camomile).

COMMUNICATIONS, THE INTERNET AND THE MEDIA

With France's efficient postal system you should have no problem keeping in contact

with people at home while you are in the Dordogne and Lot region. The Internet is becoming more widely accessible and, should you need to use the phone, you can use cheap pre-paid phone cards or access home-country operators via free numbers.

French **newspapers** (not to mention **radio** and **television**) will be of less interest if you are not a reader (or speaker) of French. There are some local English-language magazines, but you will probably find yourself reaching for an international edition of a British or American newspaper or an international news magazine to keep up on current events. These are available in larger towns and tourist centres.

MAIL

French **post offices** (*bureaux de poste* or *PTT*s) – look for bright yellow-and-blue La Poste signs – are generally open 9am to 7pm Monday to Friday, and 9am to noon on Saturday. However, don't depend on these hours: in smaller towns and villages offices may close earlier and for lunch.

You can receive mail at the central post offices of all towns. It should be addressed (preferably with the surname first and in capitals) "**Poste Restante**, Poste Centrale", followed by the name of the town and its postcode, detailed in the Guide for all the main towns. To collect your mail you need a passport or other convincing ID and there may be a charge of a few francs. You should ask for all your names to be checked, as filing systems are not always brilliant, and note that they usually only hold letters for fifteen days.

For sending letters, remember that you can buy **stamps** (*timbres*) with less queueing from *tabacs* and newsagents. Standard letters (20g or less) and postcards within France and to EU countries cost 3F/€0.46, to North America 4.40F/€0.67 and to Australia and New Zealand 5.20F/€0.79. Inside larger post offices you will find a row of yellow-coloured *guichet automatiques* – automatic ticket machines with instructions available in English with which you can weigh packages and buy the appropriate stamps; sticky labels and tape are also dispensed.

You can also use Minitel (see below) at post offices, change money, make photocopies and send faxes. To post your letter on the street, look for the bright yellow **postboxes**.

PHONES AND FAXES

You can make domestic and international **phone calls** from any telephone box (*cabine*) and can also receive calls – look for the number in the top right-hand corner of the information panel. A 50-unit (40.60F/€6.19) or 120-unit (97.50F/€14.86) phone card (called a *télécarte*) is essential, since coin boxes are being phased out; **phone cards** are available from *tabacs* and newsagents as well as post offices, tourist offices and some train station ticket offices. You can also use **credit cards** in many call boxes. Coin-only boxes still exist in cafés, bars, hotel foyers and rural areas; they take 50 centimes, 1F, 5F or 10F pieces. France Télécom's rates and charging structures are not only horribly complicated but change frequently – fortunately in the downward direction. At the time of writing, peak rate **local calls** from public phones are charged at around 1F/€0.15 for three minutes; long-distance calls within France cost up to roughly 6F/€0.91 for three minutes depending on the distance. You'll pay less when calling from a private phone and usually much more from a hotel one. **Off-peak rates** (roughly 30–40 percent cheaper) apply on weekdays between 7pm and 8am and all day Saturday and Sunday.

TELEPHONE CODES

PHONING FRANCE FROM ABROAD

Dial your international access code (UK ☎00; US ☎011; Canada ☎011; Australia ☎0011; New Zealand ☎00), plus the country code (☎33), plus the area code minus the initial zero, plus the subscriber number.

PHONING ABROAD FROM FRANCE

Dial the international access code (☎00), followed by the country code (UK ☎44; US ☎1; Canada ☎1; Australia ☎61; New Zealand ☎64), plus the area code minus the initial zero, plus the subscriber number. For **international directory enquiries**, call ☎32.12, but be prepared to pay 19.70F/€3 per two requests.

INTERNATIONAL OPERATOR-ASSISTED CALLS

You can use the relevant toll-free **Pays Direct** service below to speak with an operator in your home country. You will also find alternative networks for each country listed in the France Télécom phone directory. UK ☎0800/990 044; US ☎0-800/991-011; Canada ☎0-800/990-016; Australia ☎0-800/990-061; New Zealand ☎0-800/990 064.

For calls **within France** – local or long-distance – simply dial all ten digits of the number. Numbers beginning with ☎08.00 are free-dial numbers; those beginning with ☎08.36 are premium-rate (typically charged at 2.23F/€0.34 per minute), and those beginning with ☎06 are mobile and therefore also expensive to call. For French **directory enquiries**, call ☎12 (around 5F/€0.76 per two requests). The major international calling codes are given in the box on p.51.

When **phoning abroad**, cheap rates (a reduction of between 20 and 45 percent depending on the country) also apply on weekdays between 7pm and 8am and all day Saturday and Sunday. At the time of writing it costs approximately 3F/€0.46 for a one-minute call to the UK (*Royaume-Uni*) from a public phone at peak rates; 4.50F/€0.69 to the US (*États-Unis*) and Canada; and 12.50F/€1.91 to Australia and New Zealand.

By far the most convenient way of making international calls is to use a **calling card**, which means opening an account before you leave home; calls will be billed monthly to your credit card, to your phone bill if you are already a customer or to your home address. However, the rates per minute of these cards are many times higher than the cost of calling from a public phone in France, with flat rates only. Since they're free to obtain though, you might want to consider one for emergencies. Several companies now offer cheap-rated phone cards. France Télécom's **Ticket de Téléphone International**, for example, gives you 80 minutes to Britain, America or Canada for 100F/€15.24 at off-peak rates whether you call from a public or private phone. Cards are available from France Télécom agencies, *tabacs* and newsagents. For the same price **Carte Intercall Monde** (☎08.00.51.79.43), also available from *tabacs* and newsagents, gives you slightly longer, but only if calling from a private phone.

To avoid payment altogether, you can, of course, make a reverse charge or **collect call** – known in French as *téléphoner en PCV* – by contacting the international operator (see box on p.51).

British **mobile phones** will work in France as long as they are equipped with GSM. You'd also need to check that your network provider has an arrangement with a French network which you can access.

Faxes can be sent from all main post offices and many high-street photocopy stores: the offi-cial French word is *télécopie*, but people also use the word fax. A typical rate for sending a fax within France is 25F/€3.81 for the first and 6F/€0.91 for subsequent pages.

EMAIL, THE INTERNET AND MINITEL

France has been rather slow to adopt **email** and the **Internet**, but is catching up fast as the nation comes online. Having said that, while you'll find several **cybercafés** in Bordeaux, in the rural heartland of the Dordogne and Lot they are still few and far between. We've detailed those that do exist in the Guide, but things are changing rapidly, so check in local tourist offices for the latest situation; you can expect to pay anything between 15F/€2.29 and 60F/€9.15 per hour. The alternative is to head for a main post office, most of which now have public Internet terminals, operated with a prepaid card (50F/€7.62 for the first hour, 30F/€4.57 per hour thereafter; *www.cyberpost.com*). This means it's possible to browse the Web while on the road and email people at home. For the latter you'll want to open an account with a free Web-based email service, such as Hotmail or Yahoo! Mail: head for *www.hotmail.com* or *www.yahoo.com* to find out how.

One of the reasons for the Internet's slow start in France is the presence of **Minitel**, a dinosaurial communications system which allows access to directories, databases, chat lines, etc. While it is gradually being elbowed out by the Internet, you'll still find Minitel terminals in every post office. Most organizations have a code consisting of four digits usually followed by a key-word, which you can call up for information, to leave messages, make reservations and so forth. You dial the number on the phone, wait for a fax-type tone, then type the letters on the keyboard and, when you've finished, press *Connexion Fin*. If you're at all computer-literate and can understand basic keyboard terms in French (*retour* – return, *envoi* – enter, etc), you shouldn't find them hard to use. Be warned that most services cost more than phone rates, though for directory enquiries (☎3611) the first three minutes are free.

NEWSPAPERS AND MAGAZINES

English-language newspapers, such as the *Times*, the *Washington Post* and the

International Herald Tribune, are on sale on the day of publication in Bordeaux, and the day after in larger towns in the rest of the Dordogne and Lot region. Of the **French daily papers**, *Le Monde* is the most intellectual; it is widely respected, but somewhat austere. *Libération* is moderately left-wing, independent and more colloquial, with good, if choosy, coverage, while rigorous left-wing criticism of the French government comes from *L'Humanité*, the Communist Party paper. The other nationals are all firmly right-wing in their politics: *Le Figaro* is the most respected. The top-selling national is *L'Équipe*, which is dedicated to sports coverage, while *Paris-Turf* focuses on horse-racing. The widest circulations are enjoyed by the **regional dailies**; in this area, *Sud Ouest* and *La Dépêche* based in Bordeaux and Toulouse respectively. For visitors, they are mainly of interest for their listings, and for their free supplements covering events in the area during July and August.

Weeklies of the *Newsweek/Time* model include the wide-ranging and socialist-inclined *Le Nouvel Observateur*, its right-wing counterpart *L'Express*, the boringly centrist *L'Évenement de Jeudi* and the newcomer with a bite, *Marianne*. **Monthlies** include the young and trendy – and cheap – *Nova*, which has excellent listings of cultural events, and *Actuel*, which is good for current events. With so many Brits now living in the Dordogne, it's not surprising to find a local English-language monthly, *The News*, catering primarily to the expat community but also running general background stories; you can also read it online at *www.french-news.com*.

TV AND RADIO

French TV has six channels: three public (France 2, Arté/La Cinquième and FR3); one subscription (Canal Plus – with some unencrypted programmes); and two commercial open broadcasts (TF1 and M6). In addition there are the **cable** networks, which include France Infos, CNN, the BBC World Service, BBC Prime, MTV, Planète, which specializes in documentaries, Paris Première (lots of French-dubbed films), and Canal Jimmy (*Friends* and the like in French). There are two music channels: the American MTV and the French-run MCM.

Arté/La Cinquième is a joint Franco-German cultural venture that transmits simultaneously in French and German: offerings include highbrow programmes, daily documentaries, art criticism, serious French and German movies and complete operas. During the day (6am–7pm), La Cinquième uses the frequency to broadcast educational programmes. **Canal Plus** is the main **movie channel**, with repeats of foreign films usually shown at least once in the original language. **FR3** screens a fair selection of serious movies, with its *Cinéma de Minuit* slot late on Sunday nights good for foreign, undubbed films. The main French **news broadcasts** are at 8pm on F2 and TF1 and 7.50pm on Arté.

If you've got a **radio**, you can tune into English-language news on the BBC World Service on 648kHz AM or 198kHz long wave from midnight to 5am (and Radio 4 during the day). The Voice of America transmits on 90.5, 98.8 and 102.4 FM. For radio **news in French**, there's the state-run France Inter (87.8 FM), Europe 1 (104.7 FM) or round-the-clock news on France Infos (105.5 FM).

OPENING HOURS, PUBLIC HOLIDAYS AND FESTIVALS

Basic hours of business are 8 or 9am to noon or 1pm, and 2pm or 3pm to 6.30pm or 7.30pm. In Bordeaux shops and other businesses stay open throughout the day, while in July and August most tourist offices and museums throughout the region are open without interruption. Otherwise almost everything closes for a couple of hours at midday, sometimes longer. Small food shops often don't reopen till halfway through the afternoon, closing around 7.30pm or 8pm just before the evening meal.

The standard **closing days** are Sunday and/or Monday, with shops taking turns to close with their neighbours; many food shops such as *boulangeries* (bakeries) that open on Sunday will do so in the morning only. In small towns you'll find everything except the odd *boulangerie* or minimarket shut on both days. **Banks** are usually open Monday to Friday from 9am to 4pm or 5pm, though some may close on Mondays and open on Saturday morning instead. Restaurants and cafés also often close on a Sunday or Monday, but will generally open every day in peak season.

Museums tend to open between 9am and 10am, close for lunch at noon until 2pm or 3pm, and then run through to 5pm or 6pm, although some stay open all day. **Closing days** are usually Monday or Tuesday, sometimes both. **Admission charges** can be very off-putting, though many state-owned museums have one day of the week (often Sun) when they're free or half-price, and you can often get reductions if you're a full-time student (with ISIC card), under 26 or over 60. **Cathedrals** are almost always open all day every day, with charges only for the crypt, treasuries or cloister and little fuss about how you're dressed. **Church** opening hours are often more restricted; on Sunday mornings (or at other times which you'll see posted up on the door) you may have to attend Mass to take a look. In small towns and villages, however, getting the key is not difficult – ask anyone nearby or seek out the priest, whose house is known as the *presbytère*.

FESTIVALS AND MARKETS

It's hard to beat the experience of arriving in a small French village, expecting no more than a bed for the night, to discover the streets decked out with flags and streamers, a band playing in the square and the entire population out celebrating the feast of their patron saint. Apart from Fête de St-Jean (around June 21, the summer solstice,

---

PUBLIC HOLIDAYS

There are thirteen national holidays (*jours fériés*), when most shops and businesses (though not necessarily restaurants), and some museums, are closed. May in particular is a big month for holidays: as well as Labour Day and Victory Day, Ascension Day normally falls then, as sometimes does Pentecost.

January 1 New Year's Day
Easter Sunday
Easter Monday
Ascension Day (forty days after Easter)
Pentecost or Whitsun (seventh Sunday after Easter), plus the Monday
May 1 Labour Day

May 8 Victory in Europe Day
July 14 Bastille Day
August 15 Assumption of the Virgin Mary
November 1 All Saints' Day
November 11 1918 Armistice Day
December 25 Christmas Day

and Bastille Day (July 14), both celebrated with fireworks and other events in every town and village throughout the region, there are any number of **festivals** – both traditional and of more recent origin – throughout the Dordogne and Lot.

In such dedicated **wine** country, there are inevitably festivals coinciding with the grape harvest, when each village stages its own celebrations. The biggest wine jamboree, however, is Bordeaux's Fête du Vin, which takes place in alternate years, while St-Émilion's Jurade hosts a more stately procession in spring to announce the judging of the new wines and in autumn to kick off the harvest.

The region's cathedrals, churches and châteaux make superb venues for festivals of **music** and **theatre**. All the major towns, and many of the smaller, put on at least one such festival a year, usually in summer, when you can often catch free performances in the streets. Anyone interested in contemporary theatre should make a beeline for Périgueux in early August, when international **mime** artists gather for Mimos, one of France's most exciting and innovative new festivals.

Popular local culture is celebrated in the **Félibrée**, a festival established in 1903 to promote and safeguard the local *occitan* (or *oc*) language and culture. The Félibrée takes place on the first Sunday in July, when there is a procession, an *occitan* Mass and – of course – a blowout Périgordin meal. Nowadays the celebrations also continue for around ten days either side of the Félibrée itself in the form of folk concerts, crafts demonstrations, theatre and so forth. It's a peripatetic festival which takes place in a different town in the Dordogne *département* each year; contact the Bournat de Périgueux (☎05.53.07.12.12) for the latest information.

More recent introductions are the **historical spectaculars** held at places such as Périgueux, Castelnaud and Castillon-de-Bataille, where the final battle of the Hundred Years' War is re-enacted by hundreds of local thespians. Such events may be touristy, but the atmosphere – most are held at night – and general enthusiasm more than compensate.

More traditional are the innumerable weekly **markets**, some of which have been held on the same day for centuries. One of the region's biggest and best is that at Sarlat, but the competition is fierce and it's worth including several market days in your itinerary. In winter time, you'll also find most towns in the Dordogne and Lot hold *marchés aux gras* when whole fattened livers of duck and goose are put up for sale alongside the other edible bits of the fowl. Often these events double up as truffle markets.

For details of the region's most important and interesting festivals and markets, see the boxes at the beginning of each chapter of the Guide.

SPORTS AND OUTDOOR ACTIVITIES

The Dordogne and Lot region offers a wide range of sports – both spectator and participatory. Although you can watch local teams play big league sports such as football, you'll find that locally popular games like rugby are more worthwhile to seek out. You also have the choice of a variety of outdoor activities, including hiking, cycling, trekking and water-borne diversions such as canoeing.

SPECTATOR SPORTS

Although Bordeaux boasts a major-league **football** team, which has regularly produced national players, the sport that raises the most passion in this region is **rugby**. Southwest France has a rich rugby heritage and local teams are renowned for their style and the spirit of adventure with which they play. At a local, everyday level, the rather less gripping game of **boules** is the sport of choice, played in every town and village.

FOOTBALL AND RUGBY

By far the most prominent **football** team in the region is Bordeaux's – **FC Girondins** (*www.fc-girondins-bordeaux.com*). Top-rank players such as Zidane, Deschamps, Wiltord and Lizarazu – all members of France's 1998 World Cup squad – have all played for Bordeaux at one time or another. Founded in 1881, the club dropped briefly out of the First Division in 1991, before staging a comeback to reach the final of the European Cup in 1996. They lost to Bayern-Munich and then continued through a frustrating run of near misses in national and European competitions, until in 1999 they returned home victorious from the final of the French Championship, having beaten Paris St-Germain in the Parc des Princes. Though they haven't reached the same heights since, the team remains at the top of the First Division. Their home ground is Stade Lescure, in Bordeaux's southwestern suburbs.

Despite the influence of France's World Cup victory, **rugby** remains the most important and closely followed field game throughout the region. Virtually every town worth its salt boasts a team and if you go along to a match you'll soon get swept up in the camaraderie. If you're here in season (mid-September to mid-May), it's well worth going along; tickets, costing around 80F/€12.20, are easy to buy at the gate. The top teams to look out for are Agen, Brive and, again, Bordeaux, this time represented by CA Bègles-Bordeaux Gironde (*www.cabbg.fr*). All these teams are in the First Divison and attract a number of foreign players, but there's a big shake-up going on as French rugby becomes increasingly professional; the region's fourth élite team, Périgueux, looks set to drop down to the Second Division. Both Agen (*www.sua-rugby.com*) and Brive (*www.cabc.fr*) have also lost some of their best players, but still consistently make it to the final rounds of the championships. The high point in local rugby in recent years was when Brive won the European Cup in 1997.

BOULES

Once the preserve of elderly men in berets, recently **boules**, or *pétanque*, has seen a surge in popularity and a broadening of appeal to include more young people and women. The game is similar to English bowls. Two equally numbered teams (from one to three persons) find a space of hard, compact ground and throw a *cochonnet* (jack) six to ten metres. From a fixed spot each player then proceeds in turns to launch a total of three balls (two in a six-person match), aiming to place their metal *boules* closest to the *cochonnet* at the end of the exchange. A point is gained for each ball that is closer than the nearest ball of the opposing team. The jack is then thrown again and play continues until one side scores 13. Matches invariably draw a crowd of onlookers, and you will

not be considered rude if you stop to observe. The best times to watch are during village *fêtes*, which invariably include a tournament, drawing out the best players. If you want to hone your *boules* skills, sets of varying degrees of quality are available in sports shops and hypermarkets throughout the region.

OUTDOOR ACTIVITIES

As with much of rural France, the Dordogne and Lot region provides a fantastically wide range of **outdoor activities**. One of the most popular – and highly recommended – is **walking**, taking advantage of the extensive network of footpaths, including several long-distance routes. **Cycling** is also a great way to get about as long as you stick to the quieter back roads, while the more leisurely pursuit of **canoeing** has an extremely high profile in this region in the summer months. Details of these and other activities are outlined throughout the Guide, and local and departmental tourist offices (see box on p.27) will also provide in-depth information about activities in their area. Alternatively, contact the appropriate national federation (see box opposite) who can put you in touch with their regional or departmental offices.

HIKING AND BIKING

Hiking is without doubt the best way to enjoy this region of France. Well-maintained long-distance paths known as *sentiers de grande randonnée*, or simply **GRs**, cut across country, signed with red and white waymarkers and punctuated with campsites and *gîtes d'étapes* – walkers' hostels – at convenient distances. Some of the main routes in the region are the GR6, linking Ste-Foy-la-Grande in the west to Figeac; the GR36, which wanders southeast from Périgueux via Les Eyzies to the Gorges de l'Aveyron; and the GR65, the great pilgrimage route passing through Figeac, Cahors and Moissac on the way to Santiago de Compostela in Spain.

WEATHER INFORMATION

To check on the **weather** outlook, call ☎08.36.68.02 plus the number of the *département*: Aveyron 12; Corrèze 19; Dordogne 24; Gironde 33; Lot 46; Lot-et-Garonne 47; Tarn-et-Garonne 82. Météo France (*www.meteo.fr/temps*) provides the most reliable online forecasts.

NATIONAL SPORTS FEDERATIONS

Canoeing Fédération Française de Canoë Kayak, 87 quai de la Marne, BP 58, 94344 Joinville-le-Pont (☎01.45.11.08.50, fax 01.48.86.13.25, *www.ifrance.com/ffck-cel*).

Caving Fédération Française de Spéléologie, 130 rue St-Maur, 75011 Paris (☎01.43.57.56.54, fax 01.49.23.00.95, *www.ffspeleo.fr*).

Cycling Fédération Française de Cyclotourisme, 8 rue Jean-Marie-Jégo, 75013 Paris (☎01.44.16.88.88, fax 01.44.16.88.99, *www.ffct.org*).

Riding Délégation Nationale du Tourisme Équestre (DNTE), 30 av d'Iéna, 75116 Paris (☎01.53.67.44.44, fax 01.53.67.44.22, *dnte@magic.fr*).

Rock climbing Fédération Française de la Montagne et de l'Escalade, 8–10 quai de la Marne, 75019 Paris ☎01.40.18.75.50, fax 01.40.18.75.59, *www.ffme.fr*).

Walking Fédération Française de la Randonnée Pédestre, 14 rue Riquet, 75019 Paris (☎01.44.89.93.93, fax 01.40.35.85.67, *www.montagnes.com/us/ffrp*).

Each path is described in a **Topoguide** (available outside France in good travel bookshops) which gives a detailed account of the route, including maps, campsites, refuges, sources of provisions, etc. In France, the guides are available from bookshops and some tourist offices, or direct from the principal French walkers' organization, the Fédération Française de la Randonnée Pédestre (see box for details); prices range from 50–100F/€7.62–15.24.

In addition, many tourist offices can provide guides to their local footpaths. Particularly noteworthy are the guides produced by Sarlat tourist office detailing walks in the Périgord Noir, the series *Promenades et Randonnées* produced by the Comité Départemental du Tourisme du Lot, and the free pamphlets describing various options in the Gironde. For recommendations on walking **maps**, see p.29; **guidebooks** to look out for are listed on p.363 & 364.

While there are no specifically demarcated **cycling** routes in the Dordogne and Lot, the area's minor roads provide plentiful alternatives; it's best to avoid the main ones if you want to enjoy yourself, particularly in the high season. The exception is in the Gironde *département*, around Bordeaux, where disused railways have been converted into cycle – and walking – routes stretching all the way to the coast. Bordeaux itself is becoming more cycle-friendly with the increased provision of cycle lanes. For more on cycling in France, see p.35.

CANOEING AND BOATING

Canoeing is hugely popular in the Dordogne and Lot region, and in the summer months every navi-

gable river has outfits renting canoes and organizing excursions. Most popular is the Dordogne itself, particularly the stretch between La Roque-Gageac and Beynac, where you pass beneath some of the region's most dramatic castles. The Vézère on the other hand is quieter and shallower – ideal for beginners – and you can stop off at various points to visit the valley's prehistoric sights. Other options include the River Lot, through the Aveyron gorges and the smaller Dronne, Dropt and Célé rivers. The upper reaches of the Célé in particular offer more exciting canoeing through wilder country.

You can **rent** two-to-three-person canoes and single-seater kayaks on all these rivers, as detailed in the Guide; every tourist office also stocks lists of local operators. Although it's possible to rent by the hour, it's best to take at least a half-day and simply cruise downstream. The company you book through will provide transport as required. Prices vary according to what's on offer, but you can expect to pay 80–120F/€12.20–18.29 for a day's rental.

On the Dordogne and Lot rivers you can make **longer excursions** of up to two weeks, either accompanied or on your own, sometimes in combination with cycling or walking. Various tour operators offer canoeing packages (see pp.8, 13 & 17), or you can book direct with the local company. The two biggest and most geographically widespread are Safaraid (☎05.65.30.74.47, fax 05.65.30.74.48, *www.canoe-dordogne.com*) which covers the rivers Dordogne, Lot and Célé, and Copeyre Canoë (☎05.65.37.33.51, fax 05.65.37.31.71, *canoe@mail.netsource.fr*) with 13 bases on the Dordogne from Argentat to Beynac. As an example, you can expect to pay around

600–700F/€91.47–106.71 for a seven-day outing – plenty of time to paddle the most interesting stretch from Beaulieu to Limeuil (220km) – and see a few sights on the way; rates include transport, tent and waterproof containers.

The length of the canoeing **season** depends on the weather and the water levels. Most operators function daily in July and August, on demand in May, June and September, and close between October and April when the rivers are too high for inexperienced canoeists, though one or two stay open throughout the year. All companies are obliged to equip you with lifejackets (*gilets*) and teach you basic safety procedures. You must be able to swim.

From April to October the River Lot is navigable for **house boats** from St-Cirq-Lapopie downstream to Luzech (65km), and from Villeneuve-sur-Lot down to its confluence with the Garonne (40km); there are plans to open up more of the river over the next few years. The other option is to potter along the Canal latéral which tracks the River Garonne eastwards from Langon to Toulouse, where it joins the Canal du Midi. The main operators in both cases are detailed in chapters 6 and 7 of the Guide. Boats are usually rented by the week, though shorter periods are also available outside the July and August peak. No licence is required, but you'll receive instruction before taking the controls. The going rate for a four- to six-person boat is between 5000F/€762 and 10,000F/€1525 per week depending on the season and level of comfort.

If you're bringing **your own boat** to France, for information on maximum dimensions, documentation, regulations and so forth, ask at a French Government Tourist Office for their booklet *Boating on the Waterways*, or contact Voies Navigables de France, 175 rue Ludovic-Boutleux, 62408 Bethune (☎03.21.63.24.24, fax 03.21.63. 24.42, *www.vnf.fr*).

OTHER ACTIVITIES

Horse-riding is another excellent way of enjoying the countryside. Practically every town in the Dordogne and Lot, and many farms, have equestrian centres (*centres équestres*) where you can ride with a guide or unaccompanied – depending on your level of experience – on marked riding trails that span the region. Local and departmental tourist offices can provide details, or you can contact the Délégation Nationale du Tourisme Équestre (see box on p.57).

In the limestone regions of the Dordogne and Lot **rock climbing** (*escalade*) and **caving** (*spéléologie*) are popular activities. Several local canoe rental outfits, such as Couleurs Périgord (see p.229), offer beginners courses and half-day or full-day outings. Again, further information is available from tourist offices or the appropriate national federation.

More placid activities include **fishing** – local tourist offices will assist you in obtaining a licence – and **swimming**. There are many river beaches along the Dordogne and Lot rivers, usually well signposted, and on smaller rivers such as the Célé. An alternative is to head for one of the real and artificial lakes which pepper the region. Many have leisure centres (*Bases de plein airs*) at which you can rent pedaloes, windsurfers and dinghies, as well as larger boats and jet-skis (on the bigger reservoirs). It's worth noting, however, that in high summer, when the water is at its lowest, pollution warnings have been issued on rivers and lakes in the Dordogne *département*. Check with local tourist authorities for the current situation.

THE POLICE AND TROUBLE

In the more rural parts of the Dordogne and Lot region crime is not a problem. However, petty theft is endemic in Bordeaux and, to a lesser extent, in other major towns. In urban areas, cars with foreign number plates also face a high risk of break-ins. Vehicles are rarely stolen, but car radios and luggage make tempting targets.

There are two main types of **police** in France – the Police Nationale and the Gendarmerie Nationale. The former deals with all crime, parking and traffic affairs within large and mid-sized towns, where you will find them in the Commissariat de Police. The Gendarmerie Nationale covers everything else, in other words, small towns and rural areas. Addresses of commissariats are given in the Guide for all major towns; in smaller towns, ask for the Gendarmerie.

It obviously makes sense to take the normal **precautions** to avoid getting into trouble: not flashing wads of notes or traveller's cheques around; carrying your bag or wallet securely; never letting cameras and other valuables out of your sight; and parking your car overnight in an attended garage or within sight of a police station. But the best security is having a good insurance policy, keeping a separate record of cheque numbers, credit card numbers and the phone numbers for cancelling them (see p.22), and the relevant details of all your valuables.

If you need to **report a theft**, go along to the local Commissariat de Police, where they will fill out a *constat de vol*. The first thing they'll ask for is your passport, and vehicle documents if relevant. Although the police are not always as co-operative as they might be, it is their duty to assist you if you've lost your passport or all your money.

RACISM IN THE DORDOGNE AND LOT

Racism can be a problem in Bordeaux, particularly if you are Arab or look as if you might be, but is less of an issue in the rest of the region. It generally takes the form of hotels claiming to be booked up and police demanding your papers. In addition, even entering France can be difficult, with customs and immigration officers being obstructive and malicious. The clampdown on illegal immigration (and much tougher laws) have resulted in a significant increase in police stop-and-search operations in Bordeaux and the larger towns such as Périgueux and Montauban.

Carrying your passport at all times is a good idea.

If you suffer a **racial assault**, you're likely to get a much more sympathetic hearing from your consulate than from the police. There are many anti-racism organizations which will offer support (though they may not have English-speakers): SOS Racism (*www.sos-racisme.org*) have an office in Bordeaux (29 rue Bergeret, 33000 Bordeaux; ☎05.56.31.94.62), while the Mouvement contre le Racisme et pour l'Amitié entre les Peuples (MRAP; *www.mrap.asso.fr*) is based in Ribérac (BP 48, 24600 Ribérac, ☎05.53.90.53.40).

If you have an **accident** while driving, you must fill in and sign a *constat à l'aimable* (jointly agreed statement); car insurers are supposed to give you this with the policy, though in practice few seem to have heard of it. For **non-criminal driving offences** such as speeding, the police can impose on-the-spot fines or even take away your licence.

People caught smuggling or possessing **drugs**, even a few grams of marijuana, are liable to find themselves in jail, and consulates will not be sympathetic.

Should you be **arrested** on any charge, you have the right to contact your consulate (addresses are given on p.91).

GAY AND LESBIAN ISSUES

France is more liberal on homosexuality than most other European countries; the legal age of consent is sixteen. In the Dordogne and Lot region there's a thriving gay and lesbian community in Bordeaux and smaller groups in the other towns and cities. You'll find details of local and national information resources in the box below.

In general, the French consider sexuality to be a private matter and homophobic assaults are very rare. On the whole, gays tend to be discreet outside specific gay venues, parades and the prime gay areas of Bordeaux. Lesbians tend to be extremely discreet.

Hedonistic lifestyles have changed, here as elsewhere, since the advent of **AIDS** (SIDA in French). The resulting homophobia, though not as extreme as in most parts of the world, has nevertheless increased the suffering among gay men. Lesbian organizations fight alongside gays on the general issue of anti-homosexuality, while also lobbying for womens' rights.

GAY AND LESBIAN CONTACTS AND INFORMATION SOURCES

Centre Gai et Lesbien, Maison de l'Homosocialité, 30/32 rue Paul-Bert, 33000 Bordeaux (☎ & fax 05.56.01.12.03, *m.homo@netcourrier.com*). This is the main hub of Bordeaux's gay and lesbian community. They run a lively bar and organize lots of social activities (Tues, Thurs & Fri 6–11pm), and also provide information and advice (Mon–Fri 6–9pm). They can also provide contact details of other groups and meeting places around the region.

DykeplaNET *www.dykeplanet.com*. Another good resource with a directory of lesbian and mixed bars, clubs and cafés throughout France. Also produces the *DykeGuide 2000* (59F/€8.99), containing 180 pages of addresses, articles and information; you can buy it online, or at FNAC music stores.

Fréquence Gaie (FG), 98.2 FM. 24-hour gay and lesbian radio station with music, news, chats, information on groups and events, etc.

Guide GaiPied. The most comprehensive gay guide to France (79F/€12.05), published annually and carrying a good selection of lesbian and gay addresses, with an English section; available in newsagents and bookshops in main towns and cities. You can also consult their bilingual Web site at *www.gaipied.fr*.

La France Gaie et Lesbienne
www.france.qrd.org. Useful Internet information resource, with a directory of local groups, media, news and so forth at
www.france.qrd.org/assocs/index.html.

Lesbia. The most widely available lesbian publication, available from most newsagents. Each monthly issue features a wide range of articles, listings, reviews, lonely hearts and contacts.

Spartacus International Gay Guide. Guidebook in English focusing mainly on gay travel in Europe with an extensive section on France. Geared mostly towards males but with some info for lesbians. Available around the world at travel and gay bookshops.

Têtu. Highly-rated monthly gay/lesbian magazine (30F/€4.57) with a good "what's on" section and lots of useful addresses. Available in main towns and cities, or through their Web site (*www.tetu.com*), which is also worth a look, notably for its well-organized and up-to-date links pages.

WORK AND STUDY

Specialists aside, most British citizens, North Americans, Australians and Kiwis who manage to survive for long periods of time in France do it on luck, brazenness and willingness to live in pretty basic conditions. In Bordeaux and the larger towns, bar and club work, teaching English, translating or working as an au pair are some of the ways people scrape by; in the countryside, the options come down to seasonal fruit- or grape-picking, teaching English, busking or DIY oddjobbing. Remember that unemployment in France is high. The current rate in Bordeaux stands at around 13 percent, dropping to between nine and ten percent in the rest of the region, in line with the national average.

Anyone staying in France for over three months must have a *carte de séjour*, or residency permit – in theory, citizens of the EU are entitled to one automatically, though the bureaucratic hoops you may be required to jump through can drive you to distraction. France has a **minimum wage** – the SMIC – Salaire Minimum Interprofessional de Croissance), indexed to the cost of living; it's currently around 40F/€6.10 an hour (for a maximum 169-hour month). Employers, however, are likely to pay lower wages to temporary foreign workers who don't have easy legal resources, and make them work longer hours. By law, however, all EU nationals are entitled to exactly the same pay, conditions and trade union rights as French nationals.

If you're looking for something secure, it's important to plan well in advance. A few books which might be worth consulting are *Work Your Way Around the World* by Susan Griffiths (Vacation Work), *A Year Between* and *Working Holidays* (both Central Bureau) and *Living and Working in France* by Victoria Pybus, published by Vacation Work 1998. **In France**, check out the "Offres d'Emploi" (Job Offers) in *Le Monde, Le Figaro* and the *International Herald Tribune*; and try the youth information agency CIDJ (Centre d'Information et de Documentation Jeunesse), 101 quai Branly, 75015 Paris, or the Centre d'Information Jeunesse Aquitaine in Bordeaux (see p.92), which has information about temporary jobs in the region. The national employment agency, ANPE (Agence Nationale pour l'Emploi), with offices all over France, advertises temporary jobs in all fields, but is not renowned for its helpfulness to foreigners; non-EU citizens will have to show a work permit to apply for any of their jobs. Vac-Job, 46 av Réné-Coty, 17014 Paris (☎01.43.20.70.51), publishes the annual *Emplois d'Été en France* ("Summer Jobs in France"), which may be useful.

Finding a job in a **French language school** is also best done in advance. In Britain, jobs are often advertised in the *Guardian*'s "Education" section (every Tues), or in the weekly *Times Educational Supplement*. You don't need fluent French to get a post, but a degree and a TEFL (Teaching English as a Foreign Language) qualification are normally required. The annual *ELT Guide* gives a thorough breakdown of TEFL courses available; the booklet is produced by EFL Ltd, 1 Malet St, London WC1E 7JA (☎020/7255 1969), and the same company publishes the monthly *ELT Gazette* which is filled with job advertisements. If you apply for jobs from home, most schools will fix up the necessary papers for you. It's just feasible to find a teaching job when you're in France, but you may have to accept semi-official status and no job security. For the addresses of schools, look under "Écoles de Langues" in the local phone book. Offering **private lessons**, you'll have lots of competition, but it's always worth a try.

Au pair work is usually arranged through one of a dozen agencies, listed in Vacation Work's guide (see above). In Britain, *The Lady* is the magazine for classified adverts for au pairs. As initial numbers to ring, try Avalon Au Pairs (☎01344/778 246, *www.city2000.com/avalonaupairs/top*) in

Britain, the American Institute for Foreign Study (☎203/869 9090, *www.aifs.com*) in the US, or Accueil Familial des Jeunes Étrangers (☎01.42.22.50.34; 690F/€105.23 joining fee) in Paris; these have positions for female au pairs only; you shouldn't get paid less than 1650F/€252 a month (on top of board and lodging and some sort of travel pass). It is wise to have a ticket home in case you find the conditions intolerable and your employers insufferable. It may be better to apply once in France, where you can at least meet the family first and check things out.

Temporary jobs in the **travel industry** revolve around courier work – supervising and working on bus tours or summer campsites. You'll need good French and should preferably write to tour operators in early Spring. In Britain, ads occasionally appear in the *Guardian*'s "Media" section (every Mon), as they do in travel magazines like *Wanderlust*. Getting work as a courier on a campsite is slightly easier. It usually involves putting up tents at the beginning of the season, taking them down again at the end, and general maintenance and troubleshooting work in the months between; Canvas Holidays (see box, p.8) are worth approaching.

STUDYING IN FRANCE

It's relatively easy to be a **student** in the Dordogne and Lot region, specifically Bordeaux, which boasts one of France's major universities (see p.92 for contact details). Foreigners pay no more than French nationals to enrol for a course, and the only problem then is to support yourself. Your *carte de séjour* and – if you're an EU citizen – social security will be assured, and you'll be eligible for subsidized accommodation, meals and all the student reductions. In general, French universities are much less formal than British ones but there are strict entry requirements, including an exam in French, for undergraduate degrees, but not for postgraduate courses. For full **details and prospectuses**, contact the Cultural Service of any French embassy or consulate (see p.19). In Britain, the embassy will refer you to the French Institute, 17 Queensbury Place, London SW7 2DT (☎020/7838 2148), a cultural centre where you can pick up a list of language courses in France (library hours Tues–Fri noon–7pm & Sat noon–6pm); otherwise send a letter requesting the list accompanied by a self-addressed envelope. The embassies and consulates can also give details of **language courses** at French universities and colleges, which are often combined with lectures on French "civilization" and usually very costly. You'll find ads for lesser language courses advertised all over the place.

It's also worth noting that if you're a full-time non-EU student in France, you can get a non-EU **work permit** for the following summer so long as your visa is still valid.

DIRECTORY

CAMERAS AND FILM Film is not particularly cheap in France, so stock up before travelling. If you're bringing a video camcorder, make sure any tapes you purchase in France will be compatible.

CHILDREN AND BABIES Kids are generally welcome everywhere, including most bars and restaurants. Hotels charge by the room, with a small supplement for an additional bed or cot, and family-run places will usually babysit or offer a listening service while you eat or go out. Almost every restaurant offers children's menus – usually of the chips and ice cream variety – or may cook simple food on request. You'll have no difficulty finding disposable nappies (*couches à jeter*), but nearly all baby foods have added sugar and salt, and French milk powders are very rich indeed. SNCF charge nothing on trains and buses for under-4s, and half-fare for 4–11s (see p.32 for other reductions). In most museums under-4s are free and it's usually half-price for under-18s, while entry to many monuments is free for under-12s. Most local tourist offices have details of specific activities for children, and almost every town has a children's playground with a good selection of activities. Most parks have a children's play area; unfortunately the majority of parks are gravelled rather than grassed.

CONTRACEPTIVES Condoms (*préservatifs* or *capotes*) are available at all pharmacies, as well as from many clubs and street dispensers (10F/€1.52 for 3–4 condoms). You can also get spermicidal cream and jelly (*dose contraceptive*), plus the suppositories (*ovules, suppositoires*), a diaphragm (*le diaphragme*) or IUD (*le sterilet*) and the Pill (*la pillule*), the last only available on prescription. Test sticks (*tests réactifs*) for the Persona monitor are readily available in pharmacies for 95F/€14.48 per packet.

ELECTRICITY This is almost always 220V, using plugs with two round pins. If you haven't bought the appropriate transformer before leaving home, the best place in France to find the right one is the electrical section of a department store, where someone is also more likely to speak English; cost is around 60F/€9.15.

LAUNDRY Laundries are common in French towns – just ask in your hotel, or the tourist office, or look in the phone book under "Laveries Automatiques". They are often unattended, so come armed with small change. Machines are graded in different wash sizes, costing between 12F/€1.83 and 20F/€3.05 or more. Dryers are around 2F/€0.30 a pop. If you're doing your own washing in hotels, keep quantities small as most forbid doing any laundry in your room.

PEDESTRIANS French drivers pay no heed to pedestrian/zebra crossings marked with horizontal white stripes on roads. It is very dangerous to step out onto one and assume drivers will stop as in Australia and Britain. Take just as great care as you would crossing at any other point.

SWIMMING POOLS Swimming pools (*piscines*) are well signposted in most French towns and rea-sonably priced, usually around 16F/€2.44 per person. You may be requested to wear a bathing cap, whether you are male or female, so come prepared.

TIME France is one hour ahead of the UK, six hours ahead of Eastern Standard Time, and nine hours ahead of Pacific Standard Time. This also applies during daylight savings seasons, which are observed in France from the end of March through to the end of September.

TIPPING Since restaurants add a service charge to your bill, you only need to leave an additional cash tip if you feel you have received service out of the ordinary. It is customary to tip porters between 5F/€0.76 and 10F/€1.52 and taxi drivers – for example 2–5F/€0.30–0.76 for a journey costing 40–70F/€6.10–10.67.

TOILETS Ask for *les toilettes* or look for signs for the WC (pronounced "vay say"); when reading the details of facilities outside hotels, don't confuse *lavabo*, which means wash-basin, with lavatory. Usually found downstairs along with the phone, French toilets in bars are still often of the hole-in-the-ground squatting variety, and tend to lack toilet paper. Standards of cleanliness are often poor, and men shouldn't expect much privacy in the urinal, which often won't have a door. Both bar and restaurant toilets are usually free, as are toilets in museums, though those in railway stations and department stores commonly charge a small sum. Some have coin-operated locks, so always keep 50 centimes and one-and-two franc pieces handy for these and for the frequent Tardis-like public toilets found on the streets. These have automatic doors which open when you insert coins to the value of two francs, and are cleaned automatically once you exit. Children under ten aren't allowed in on their own.

PART TWO

THE

GUIDE

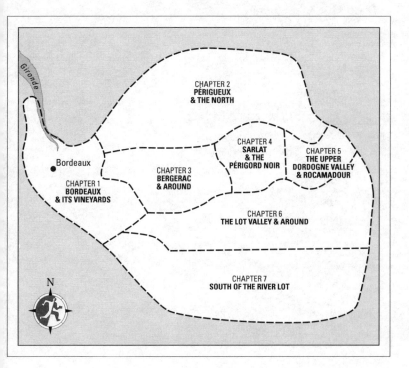

CHAPTER ONE

BORDEAUX AND ITS VINEYARDS

rance's second largest Atlantic port, **Bordeaux**, lying on the west bank of the River Garonne shortly before it flows into the Gironde estuary, is at heart a trading city, built on revenues from exporting wine and also, in the eighteenth century, from the expansion of colonial trade. The legacy of this wealth is a city centre dignified by grand avenues, civic monuments and graceful rows of town houses, and for many the architecture alone provides sufficient attraction, but Bordeaux also boasts several rewarding museums, any number of superb restaurants and a thriving cultural and nightlife scene. It is also the area's principal administrative centre – capital of both the Aquitaine *région* and the Gironde *département* – and, with its European air services and good train connections, a major gateway to the Dordogne and Lot region.

Before setting off into the Dordogne heartland, however, there are the Bordeaux **vineyards** – one of the world's foremost wine-producing regions – to explore. Neatly tended rows of vines stretch from the Médoc peninsula in the north and then south and east of Bordeaux along the Garonne and Dordogne valleys for more than fifty kilometres. The northern peninsula is the place to start. The countryside may not be the most enticing – the **Médoc** vineyards are flat and monotonous – but the chateaux – Margaux, Palmer, Mouton-Rothschild and Lafite – are world-famous, though there are also any number of lesser-known producers to visit. Some have established wine-related museums as an added attraction. Médoc wines are mostly reds, while to the southeast of Bordeaux the **Graves** is known for its dry white wines and the **Sauternes** for sweet, golden-coloured whites, some of which, such as those of Château d'Yquem, are amongst the most highly sought-after wines in the world. There are, however, a couple of non-wine-related diversions in the region as well: the

---

ACCOMMODATION PRICE CODES

All the hotels and *chambres d'hôtes* listed in this book have been price-coded according to the following scale. The prices quoted are for the **cheapest available double room in high season**, although remember that many of the cheap places will have more expensive rooms with en-suite facilities.

① Under 160F/€24
② 160–220F/€24–34
③ 220–300F/€34–46

④ 300–400F/€46–61
⑤ 400–500F/€61–76
⑥ 500–600F/€76–91

⑦ 600–700F/€91–107
⑧ 700–800F/€107–122
⑨ Over 800F/€122

moated fourteenth-century **Château de la Brède**, home of the philosopher Montesquieu, and in the very south of the region the **Château de Roquetaillade**. Although dating from the same period, the latter is of particular interest for its exuberant late-nineteenth-century make-over by architect Viollet-le-Duc.

Heading north across the Garonne from the Sauternes, the **Entre-Deux-Mers** may not be the most prestigious but it is by far and away the prettiest of

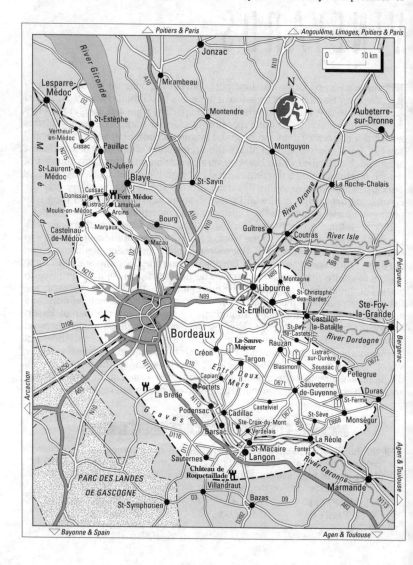

Bordeaux's wine regions. The vineyards here are interspersed with pasture, orchards and woodland across rolling hills topped with sun-warmed villages. Many of these settlements, such as the well-preserved **Sauveterre-de-Guyenne** and **Monségur**, are *bastides*, medieval new-towns built on a strict grid-pattern around a central market square (see box on p.310). The Entre-Deux-Mers is also home to a number of once-wealthy abbeys in various states of ruin. Best is the twelfth-century **La Sauve-Majeure**, in the west of the region, where fragments of wall shelter the most beautiful array of carved capitals.

Religion and wine come together again in **St-Émilion**, north of the Entre-Deux-Mers, where they combine to produce the region's most enchanting wine-town. It sits on a south-facing slope overlooking the Dordogne valley, a huddle of grey-white houses, towers and spires encircled by vines; in 1999 both town and vine-yards were inscribed on UNESCO's World Heritage list. St-Émilion largely owes its existence – and certainly its name – to an eighth-century hermit whose cave, and the vast subterranean church next door, now provide the town's most compelling sights. Not forgetting, of course, the surrounding wine châteaux. This combination of historical monuments, fine wine and attractive countryside make St-Émilion a perfect place to spend a couple of days.

The Bordeaux region is relatively well covered by **public transport**. There are train services along the Garonne and Dordogne valleys, though the latter is rather sporadic, and a branch line north through the Médoc. Rather more comprehensive are the buses. Though some routes duplicate the train services, others cut across country to places such as Sauveterre-de-Guyenne, Monségur and La Sauve. If you intend to use the buses a lot, pick up a Trans-Gironde route-map and the relevant timetables from the Bordeaux tourist office. That said, to make the most of the region, and particularly when it comes to visiting the vineyards, you will need your own transport. Renting a car is the obvious solution, but **cycling** is also an option. Out of Bordeaux, the back roads are pleasant to cycle on and the departmental authorities have established a number of dedicated cycle paths, of which the most useful is that from Bordeaux to Sauveterre in the Entre-Deux-Mers.

Bordeaux

Big and obviously wealthy, with a population of over half a million, **BORDEAUX** is very much an Atlantic city, characterized by a monumental, Parisian-style grandeur and sophistication, as opposed to the Mediterranean warmth of its local rival, Toulouse. The French novelist Stendhal called it "the most beautiful town in France". That's perhaps overstating it a bit, but Bordeaux has undergone a transformation in the last few years and it's possible once again to see what he meant. Many of the magnificent, eighteenth-century buildings have been cleaned of their grime – the place de la Bourse in particular looks absolutely stunning – and the river-front is, after years of debate, being reclaimed for pedestrians.

Especially attractive is the relatively compact and unusually homogeneous eighteenth-century centre, paid for by the expansion of colonial trade. Its main interest lies in its **architecture**, notably the marvellous ironwork and sculptural embellishments found on more bourgeois residences. Here and there rem-

FESTIVALS, EVENTS AND MARKETS

As you might imagine, the majority of **festivals** and **events** in the Bordeaux region revolve around wine. Nearly all the different *appellations* have a *portes ouvertes*, when you can visit participating châteaux without an appointment and sample some of their wares for free; we list the two most important such events below. Then in autumn, most villages celebrate the end of the grape harvest with a *fête des vendanges* in mid- to late-October. This normally takes the form of a big meal (to which members of the public are welcome, though you'll have to reserve in advance) and some form of entertainment, followed by dancing. Where we haven't given a specific information number contact the relevant tourist office.

Late March and early April Médoc: Les Portes Ouvertes dans les Châteaux. Some eighty châteaux and wine co-operatives representing the Médoc's eight *appellations* offer free tastings over two weekends. Other events include beginners' wine-tasting courses organized by Pauillac tourist office.

MAY
Early May Pauillac: Fête de l'Agneau. A weekend dedicated to Pauillac lamb, raised on the surrounding salty meadows. Events include sheep-dog trials and organized walks as well as special restaurant menus.
Early May St-Émilion: Journées Portes Ouvertes (☎05.57.55.50.55). Just twenty châteaux open their *chais* and offer free tastings over a weekend.

JUNE
Late June Bordeaux: Fête du Vin (*www.bordeaux-fete-le-vin.com*). In even-numbered years the city celebrates its wine heritage with a jamboree lasting three days. In addition to sampling the wines, there are introductory tasting lessons, concerts, street performers and a wine auction, amongst other events. The festival culminates in a spectacular fireworks display over the river. In odd-numbered years there's a more modest Fête du Fleuve with wine and food stalls along the quays.
Third Sunday St-Émilion: Fête de Printemps. Members of the Jurade dust off their finery for a procession through the town. They then announce the evaluation of the new vintage from the top of the Tour du Roi.

nants of an older city survive, including a few fragments of what the Romans called Burdigala and some fine churches, of which **Cathédrale St-André**, recently inscribed on UNESCO's World Heritage List, is by far the most outstanding. There's also a clutch of engaging **museums** detailing the history of the city and its region. All this, in addition to some fabulous restaurants and plenty of reasonably priced hotels, makes Bordeaux well worth a couple of days' stopover.

Some history

Bordeaux was founded by the Bituriges Vivisci, a local Gaulish tribe, some time around the third century BC. In 56 BC it was absorbed peacefully into the Roman empire as the capital of the Aquitania adminstrative region. Successive Germanic invasions in the third century AD prompted the construction of stout defensive

JULY, AUGUST AND SEPTEMBER

Early July to mid-Sept St-Macaire: Les Nuits Macariennes. Comprises a variety of cultural events, from concerts in the church and plays in its cloister to folk music and outdoor cinema. There are also wine-tasting opportunities and candlelight walks through the town.

First weekend in July Monségur: 24 Heures du Swing (☎05.56.61.60.12, *www. swing-monsegur.com*). The whole of central Monségur is closed off for its jazz festival (entry by ticket only) featuring French and international artists. Concerts take place in the cafés, the streets and under the market hall.

Mid-July Fort Médoc: Festival du Jazz (☎05.56.58.91.30). Weekend festival hosting big-name international acts in the semi-ruined fort; the audience sits on hay-bales. There are local wines on sale and oysters from Arcachon, or full meals (reservations required), and a firework display on the last night.

Late July Pauillac: Fête du Vin et du Terroir. Three days of tastings (featuring around forty local producers), concerts and open-air restaurants along the riverfront.

Mid-Aug Pauillac: Jazz, Wine and Cinema. More tastings of Médoc wines, a jazz concert and an open-air film show on the banks of the Garonne. One-day festival.

First weekend in Sept Langon: Foire aux Vins, Fromages et Pains. Over 150 wine and cheese producers from throughout France as well as displays of traditional crafts.

Early Sept Pauillac: Marathon des Châteaux du Médoc. Some 10,000 runners descend on the Médoc, many in fancy-dress, to be serenaded by musicians as they run through the vineyards.

Third Sun in Sept St-Émilion: Ban des Vendanges. Following their spring outing (see opposite), the Jurade once again process through the town. This time they also induct new members of the Jurade and attend mass in the collegiate church before announcing the start of the harvest from the Tour du Roi.

December Bordeaux: Grand marché de Noël. From early December stalls selling Christmas goodies set up along the allées de Tourny.

walls, following the route of present-day cours de l'Intendance, rue des Remparts and cours d'Alsace-Lorraine, but the city nevertheless fell to the Visigoths in 409. After peace was finally re-established in the tenth century, Bordeaux came into the hands of the Counts of Poitou, later titled the **Dukes of Aquitaine**, who ruled a vast area stretching from the Loire to the Pyrenees. In 1152 the then Duchess Eleanor of Aquitaine (see box on p.356) married Count Henry of Anjou, and when he was crowned King Henry II of England two years later, Bordeaux began three centuries under **English rule**. Though the local lords – an unruly lot – initially balked at the takeover, they were soon assuaged when they found themselves at the heart of a very profitable business exporting wine to England.

This was Bordeaux's **first golden age**. In the thirteenth and fourteenth centuries a succession of new walls had to be built to encompass the expanding city – some of the stones were brought as ballast in ships returning home from the

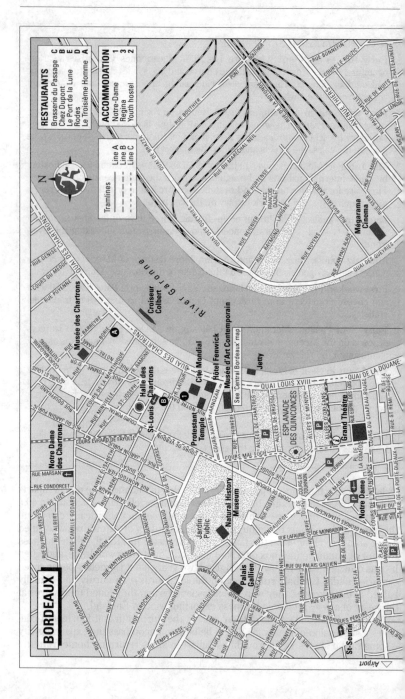

BORDEAUX

RESTAURANTS
Brasserie du Passage C
Chez Dupont B
Le Port de la Lune E
Rodès D
Le Troisième Homme A

ACCOMMODATION
Notre-Dame 1
Regina 3
Youth hostel 2

Tramlines
Line A
Line B
Line C

N

River Garonne

Croiseur Colbert

Megarama Cinema

Notre Dame des Chartrons

Musée des Chartrons

Cité Mondial

Hôtel Fenwick

Musée d'Art Contemporain

Jetty

Halle des Chartrons

St-Louis

Protestant Temple

See 'Central Bordeaux' map

QUAI LOUIS XVIII

QUAI DE LA DOUANE

ESPLANADE DES QUINCONCES

Grand Théâtre

Natural History Museum

Jardin Public

Palais Gallien

Notre Dame

St-Seurin

Airport

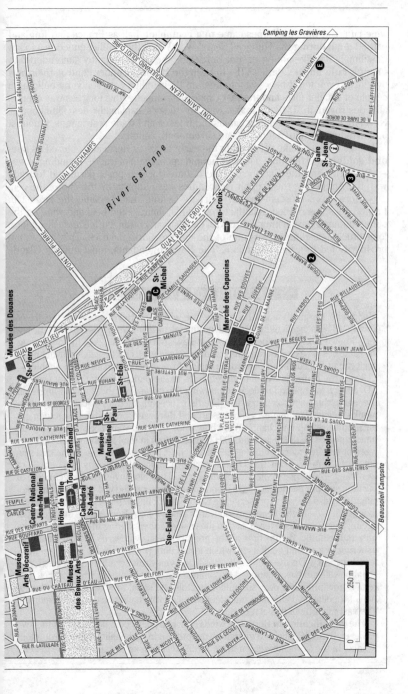

Camping les Gravières △

River Garonne

Musée des Douanes
St-Pierre
QUAI RICHELIEU
St-Éloi
St-Paul
Centre National Jean-Moulin
Tour Pey-Berland
Musée d'Aquitaine
Hôtel de Ville
Cathédral St-André
Ste-Eulalie
Musée des Beaux Arts
Musée Arts Décoratif

St-Michel
Marché des Capucins
Ste-Croix

Gare St-Jean

St-Nicolas

PLACE DE LA VICTOIRE

▷ Beausoleil Campsite

250 m

0

wine run. But the good times came to a grumbling halt as France and England battled it out during the Hundred Years' War. When the conflict ended in 1453 at Castillon-la-Bataille, not far east of Bordeaux, the city reluctantly surrendered to **French rule** under Charles VII – to keep the Bordelais under control, their new overlords even felt it necessary to beef up their military presence by building a couple of smaller forts and the vast Château Trompette; this fortress was eventually destroyed in 1818 to make way for today's esplanade des Quinconces. Nevertheless, local rebellions against high taxes and trade restrictions, amongst other things, continued into the late seventeenth century.

Things began to take off again in the early 1700s as Bordeaux entered its **second golden age**, this time based on a rapid opening up of trade – including slaves – with Africa and the Caribbean. One of only thirteen ports permitted to trade with the Antilles, as the French West Indies were known, by the end of the century Bordeaux's crescent-shaped "port de la lune" had become the largest in France. Its ships carried manufactured goods, flour, salted beef and wine on the outward journey, returning home with cane sugar, cotton, coffee and cacao; for a long time sugar-refining was one of the city's major industries. This new-found prosperity led to a building boom. The Royal Intendants, most notably Claude

THE WINES OF BORDEAUX

Along with Burgundy and Champagne, the **wines of Bordeaux** form the "Holy Trinity" of French viticulture. Despite producing as many whites as reds, it is the latter – known as claret to the British – that have graced the tables of the discerning for centuries. The countryside that produces them encircles the city, enjoying near-perfect climatic conditions and soils ranging from limestone to sand and pebbles.

It was the **Romans** who introduced vines to the region during the first century AD. After a long period of decline following the collapse of the Roman Empire, in the early thirteenth century the **English**, accompanied by local Benedictine monks, began planting new vineyards around Bordeaux, precipitating a golden era for producers and merchants. Wine bound for England went tax-free and the volume exported in 1307 – around 700,000 hectolitres in total for the whole region – was not reached again until the 1950s. The next great boost came in the mid-seventeenth century when the **Dutch** started draining the marshy land north of Bordeaux, giving rise to the Médoc vineyards. They also invented the technique of burning sulphur inside barrels to disinfect and preserve the wood and which, coincidentally, also helped to preserve the wine. Since it no longer deteriorated after six months or so – to the benefit of vineyards further from Bordeaux – the merits of ageing were soon discovered, first in the cask and then, during the eighteenth century, in the bottle. By this time all the great Bordelais vineyards had been planted, ushering in a second golden age which lasted until **phylloxera** hit in the late nineteenth century. On the whole, the Bordeaux vineyards weathered the crisis reasonably well and have continued to dominate the world's quality wine market. The region now produces over six million hectolitres, equal to 800 million bottles, of AOC (Appellation d'Origine Contrôlée) wines, of which about a third are exported. The vast majority of this is red wine.

The **classification** of Bordeaux wines is an extremely complex affair. At the lowest level, the AOC label is a guarantee of both origin and quality found throughout France. In the Bordeaux region there are 57 *appellations*, starting with the general

Boucher (1720–43) and his successor the **Marquis de Tourny** (1743–57; see p.80), began knocking down the city's medieval walls, replacing them with the grand boulevards and triumphal arches we see today, and the wealthy merchants quickly developed a taste for luxury, erecting fine mansions furnished with exotic woods. Strangely enough, despite all this construction, there was no attempt to bridge the Garonne – this wasn't achieved until Napoléon stopped here on his way to Spain in 1808 and ordered the construction of the Pont de Pierre.

Even today, central Bordeaux only boasts two bridges, and the **modern city** remains concentrated on the river's west bank, though all this may be set to change if the present mayor and deputy, the ex-Prime Minister Alain Juppé gets his way. Since 1995 he has succeeded in reinvigorating the city, creating new public spaces and giving some of the more important landmarks a much-needed spring-clean – its long-neglected riverfront in particular has benefited, now the scene for the hugely successful Fête du Vin (see box on p.70). Other works in progress include a tram line linking central Bordeaux with its eastern suburbs and a network of gardens, footpaths and cycle-paths along the Garonne. Some of these projects may never see the light of day – much depends on whether Juppé remains in office – but for the moment there's a definite touch of dynamism in the Bordeaux air.

Bordeaux and Bordeaux Supérieur, which can come from anywhere in the Gironde *département*. Within this broad category, districts producing better wines, such as Graves and Haut-Médoc, are entitled to use their more specific *appellation*. Finally, come the villages and communes known for the very finest wines – Margaux, Pauillac and Sauternes, to name but a few.

Then, on top of this, individual vineyards around Bordeaux were classified in 1855. What were then considered the region's best wines were graded into five **grands crus**, or "great growths", based largely on the prices the wines had fetched over the previous century. Of the reds, only the Médoc wines and a single wine from the Graves (Haut-Brion), were deemed worthy of consideration and of these, just four were voted Premiers Grands Crus Classés: Margaux, Lafitte, Latour and Haut-Brion. Of the sweet Sauternes wines, which were classified at the same time, Château d'Yquem alone merited the title Premier Cru Supérieur. With the exception of Château Mouton-Rothschild, which moved up a class to become the Médoc's fifth Premier Cru in 1973, there have been no official changes since, so divisions between the Grands Crus should not be taken too seriously. Since then, additional categories, such as Crus Bourgeois and Crus Artisans, have been devised, both of which include some excellent wines. Rather unjustly, St-Émilion wines were not classified until 1955.

Nearly all Bordeaux wines are blended, in other words contain at least two, and usually three, **grape varieties**. To a large extent the type of grapes grown depends on local soil conditions, after which there is enormous skill in deciding the exact proportions required – which varies from year to year and is almost always done after vinification – to bring out the best in the wines. Bordeaux reds comprise a blend of Cabernet Sauvignon, the oldest of the Bordeaux grapes, Cabernet Franc, Merlot and, in smaller proportions – if at all – Malbec and Petit-Verdot. The whites, on the other hand, can only contain Sémillon, Sauvignon and Muscadelle grapes.

For more on Bordeaux's most important individual wine regions see the following: **Médoc** p.93; **Graves** p.102; **Sauternes** p.104; **St-Émilion** p.121. Tips on visiting the vineyards appear on p.94.

Arrival, information and city transport

Bordeaux's **airport** lies 12km west of the city centre. Its facilities include a Travelex **bureau de change** (Mon–Fri 6am–9.30pm, Sat & Sun 6am–9pm), as well as a branch of Banque Populaire with a 24hr ATM and counter facilities; offices of all the major **car rental** companies are also represented (see "Listings", p.91). From the airport a shuttle bus into town (every 30–45min; 37F/€5.64) takes around thirty to 45 minutes, with stops on place Gambetta and place de la Comédie near the tourist office. Alternatively, a taxi will cost 100–180F/€15.24–27.44.

Arriving by train, you'll find yourself at the **gare St-Jean**, with its own small tourist office (May–Oct Mon–Sat 9am–noon & 1–7pm, Sun 10am–noon & 1–6pm; Nov–April Mon–Sat 9am–noon & 1–6pm; ☎05.56.91.64.70), and **left-luggage** lockers, in which you can leave your bags for up to 72 hours at a cost of 15–30F/€2.29–4.57, depending on the size of the locker. The *gare* is at the heart of a somewhat insalubrious area, nearly 3km south of the centre; buses #7 or #8, both of which stop on place Gambetta and place de la Comédie, will save you the hike – there's an "Info Bus" outside the station.

There's no central **gare routière** in Bordeaux; for the moment most regional bus services terminate at the park on the north side of the esplanade des Quinconces, just a couple of minutes' walk from place de la Comédie. It is possible, however, that the bus park may be relocated as work gets going on the new tramway (see below). Eurolines buses, on the other hand, stop outside the gare St-Jean. If you're arriving **by car**, there's a big car park on both sides of the esplanade des Quinconces (25F/€3.81 per day), but at night it's advisable to use one of the underground car parks, such as those under the allées de Tourny or place des Grands-Hommes (8pm–8am 30–40F/€4.57–6.10). Bear in mind too that central Bordeaux – the area of streets between place Gambetta, the Jardin Public and the river – is closed to traffic on the first Sunday of each month from 10am to 7pm.

Bordeaux's main **tourist office**, 12 cours du 30-juillet (May–Oct Mon–Sat 9am–8pm, Sun 9am–7pm; Nov–April Mon–Sat 9am–7pm, Sun 9.45am–4.30pm; ☎05.56.00.66.00, fax 05.56.00.66.01, *www.bordeaux-tourisme.com*), can book accommodation free of charge and stocks masses of useful maps and information leaflets; ask for their "Heritage Tour Map", a recommended walking tour of the city centre, and the free magazine *Bordeaux Tourisme* which details special exhibitions and other events. The tourist office also organizes various **guided tours**, both around Bordeaux itself, and into the surrounding wine regions – these wine tours (May–Oct daily; Nov–April Wed & Sat; 160–290F/€24.39–44.21) are highly recommended, particularly if you're short of time. Opposite the tourist office the extremely helpful **Maison du Vin**, 1 cours du 30-Juillet (Mon–Thurs 8.30am–6pm, Fri 8.30am–5.30pm; late May to mid-Oct also Sat 9am–4.30pm; ☎05.56.00.22.88) provides huge amounts of detailed information on Bordeaux's wine regions, including suggestions for château visits and *dégustations*; they also offer two-hour introductory wine-tasting courses in season (see "Listings" for further details, and p.94 for more on visiting the vineyards).

Central Bordeaux is eminently walkable, but for longer journeys you might want to make use of its extensive **city bus** network. There's no one particular hub, though the majority of city-centre buses stop on place Gambetta; of these, routes

#7 and #8 are perhaps the most useful – both run from the gare SNCF in the south via place de la Victoire, place Gambetta and place de la Comédie before reaching the northerly Chartrons district. Le Bus du Soir is a **nightbus** service comprising eleven routes which operate until 12.30am; the most useful route is #S11, running from the clubland area along quai du Paludate via the *gare* to place de la Victoire, where you can change to route #S7 for place Gambetta. Day or night, single-journey tickets are available on the bus (7.50F/€1.14), but it's cheaper if you buy a carnet of ten (55.50F/€8.31) from a tobacconist or one of the "Info Bus" booths – aside from the one outside the station there's a booth in the city centre just off place Gambetta at 4 rue Georges-Bonnac. You must punch your ticket on the bus; carnet tickets are then valid for one hour, within which period you can change bus up to four times, though remember to re-punch the ticket each time.

Bordeaux's new **tramway** is currently under construction, with the first trams due to start operating at the end of 2002. There will be three lines: line A will run east–west via the pont de Pierre and place Pey-Berland; line B will cut southwest–northeast through the city centre with stops at place de la Victoire, place Gambetta and place de la Comédie; and line C will head north from the gare SNCF along the quais to place de la Comédie and the Jardin Public. Transfers between the three lines will be possible at place de la Comédie, place Pey-Berland and place de Bir-Hakeim (at the west end of the pont de Pierre). Trams will run every four to eight minutes depending on the time of day, from between 5am and 1am the following morning. The ticket prices have not yet been fixed, but will be approximately the same as for the buses, with a flat fee for a single journey, and with plans for a joint ticket system covering both trams and buses.

As for **cycling**, a short stretch of the projected riverside cycle-path (also designed for walking, jogging and other activities) is open in the centre around the esplanade des Quinconces; on completion in 2003 it will run from pont St-Jean in the south all along the riverfront to quais Bacalan and then turn inland to Bordeaux's leisure lake, Le Lac. **Bike rental** is available from Bord'eaux Vélo Loisirs (☎05.56.44.77.31; Oct–May afternoons only, closed Mon & Thurs), on quai Louis-XVIII beside the Quinconces boat dock, who rent out everything from bikes to rollerblades and baby-strollers, with the recent addition of "talking bikes" to guide you round the city. Another option is Cycles Pasteur at 42 cours Pasteur (☎05.56.92.68.20). There are 24hr **taxi** stands at the *gare SNCF* (☎05.56.91.48.11) and outside the Grand Théâtre (☎05.56.48.03.25), with other main stands on cours Clémenceau near place Gambetta (☎05.56.48.00.79) and place de la Victoire (☎05.56.91.47.05).

Accommodation

The area around the *gare SNCF* – particularly rue Charles-Domercq and cours de la Marne – has any number of one- and two-star **hotels**, though this isn't the most appealing area to stay. Better to head for the city centre, where you'll find a good range of accommodation, from the basic to the luxurious. On the whole, rooms are not difficult to come by, with the notable exception of the period of the Vinexpo trade fair and Fête du Vin (held in alternate years) in June, when Bordeaux is packed to the gunnels and you'll need to reserve well in advance. All the hotels listed below are marked on the map on p.80, apart from *Notre-Dame* and *Regina*, which are marked on pp.72–73, along with the youth hostel.

Hotels

Blayais, 17 rue Mautrec (☎05.56.48.17.87, fax 05.56.52.47.57). This small hotel just off place de la Comédie comes in at the very bottom of the price range. Rooms are functional – with chipboard furniture – but clean, fresh and of a reasonable size. All are en suite and some also have a kitchenette for longer-term guests. ③.

de la Boétie, 4 rue de la Boétie (☎05.56.81.76.68, fax 05.56.51.24.06). Surprisingly cheap for such a central location, this one-star hotel is on a quiet street between the Musée des Beaux-Arts and place Gambetta. Owned by the *Bristol*, it shares the same reception and all rooms boast phone, TV and en-suite facilities, some with just a shower cubicle, others with bath. ①.

Boulan, 28 rue Boulan (☎05.56.52.23.62, fax 05.56.44.91.65). In a quiet side-street near the cathedral, this is one of Bordeaux's most economical hotels. None of the rooms have their own toilet, nor shower at the cheaper end, but they are all spruce and some have recently been renovated. ①.

Bristol, 4 rue Bouffard (☎05.56.81.85.01, fax 05.56.51.24.06, *bristol@hotel-bordeaux.com*). Comfortable, relaxed two-star hotel just south of place Gambetta. The well-equipped, en-suite rooms are decently sized and stylishly decorated, with bold blue curtains and friezes set off against cream walls. ②.

Dauphin, 82 rue du Palais-Gallien (☎05.56.52.24.62, fax 05.56.01.10.91). Though a little out of the action, this arty, old-fashioned hotel is justifiably popular. The more spacious, top-price rooms (200F/€30.49), with their huge windows and high ceilings, offer best value for money. Closed last fortnight of Aug. ②.

de Lyon, 31 rue des Remparts (☎05.56.81.34.38, fax 05.56.52.92.82). Another budget option right in the city centre on a pedestrianized street. Basic and slightly run-down but well-priced rooms, with tiny en-suite bathrooms, are available both here and in their nearby annexe, the *Amboise* at 22 rue Vieille-Tour (same ☎ & fax). ①.

Notre-Dame, 36 rue Notre-Dame (☎05.56.52.88.24, fax 05.56.79.12.67). Quiet, refined establishment offering reasonable value for money in an area of old streets just north of esplanade des Quinconces. Air conditioning and generous bathrooms come as standard, though the decor is unexciting. The cheapest rooms are on the small side for two people. ③.

de la Presse, 6–8 rue Porte-Dijeaux (☎05.56.48.53.88, fax 05.56.01.05.82, *quality.bordeaux@wanadoo.fr*). Recently renovated, this family-run hotel in the pedestrian heart of Bordeaux represents good value for the level of service. Its light, bright rooms are well-proportioned, with big beds to match, and provide three-star comforts such as minibar and air conditioning. Closed one week at Christmas. ④.

des Quatre Sœurs, 6 cours du 30-Juillet (☎05.57.81.19.20, fax 05.56.01.04.28, *4soeurs.free.fr*). Popular, efficient and friendly hotel in an ideal spot next to the tourist office. While the narrow foyer is all nineteenth-century woodwork and mirrors, the rooms have been redecorated somewhat incongruously with cheerful, hand-painted furniture and wallpaper to match. Some are a touch boxy for the price (at the bottom of this range). ⑤.

Regina, 34 rue Charles-Domercq (☎05.56.91.66.07, fax 05.56.91.32.88). The best value for money near the train station, the *Regina* is open 24 hours, offering simple, neat rooms of a good size. The cheapest have a shower but no toilet and, while all rooms are equipped with phones, only some have TVs. Ask for a quieter room at the back. ②.

de la Tour Intendance, 14–16 rue de la Vieille-Tour (☎05.56.81.46.27, fax 05.56.81.60.90). Despite its featureless exterior, this pleasant hotel tucked into a quiet corner off place Gambetta boasts an elegant little lobby and comfortable, airy rooms – all en suite but disappointingly plain. You can also use their garage for 40F/€6.10 per night. ③.

Tulip Inn Bayonne Etche-Ona, 4 rue Martignac & 11 rue Mautrec (☎05.56.48.00.88, fax 05.56.48.41.60, *bayetche@bordeaux-hotel.com*). Now under new ownership, the old *Bayonne* and *Etche-Ona* hotels have been completely refurbished, the former in bright contemporary chic and the latter echoing its Basque roots in plush reds and greens. All mod cons and attentive service, making this one of the top options in the city centre. ⑤.

Hostel and campsites

Beausoleil, 371 cours du Général-de-Gaulle, Gradignan (☎05.56.89.17.66). Small, well-kept two-star campsite 9km southwest of the centre on the N10. Take bus #G from place de la Victoire to its terminus at Beausoleil, then walk the last 200m. Open all year.

Camping les Gravières, Villenave -d'Ornon (☎05.56.87.00.36, fax 05.56.87.24.60). A two-star site with shop and bar but no pool, 4km south of gare St-Jean in a forest near the Garonne river. By car, take exit #20 from the N230 ring road. From the station, take bus #7 or #8 to place de la Victoire, then bus #B to its terminus at Courréjean. Open all year.

Youth hostel, 22 cours Barbey (☎05.56.91.59.51, fax 05.56.94.02.98). Situated off cours de la Marne, this recently renovated hostel is a 10min walk – or a short bus ride (lines #7 & #8) – northeast from gare St-Jean. It's in a bit of a seedy area, but they've tightened up on security. All rooms (for 2, 4 or 6 people) are equipped with showers (toilets are on the corridor), and there are laundry facilities, a kitchen, restaurant and bar. HI card required; 80F/€12.20 per night.

The City

Bordeaux is reasonably spread out along the west bank of the Garonne river, with the eighteenth-century **old town** lying between the **place de la Comédie** to the north, cours d'Albret to the west and cours Victor-Hugo to the south. Cutting north–south through this district, the old Roman road, the die-straight rue Ste-Catherine, forms the city's spine and its principal shopping street. To the east of this you'll find the imposing buildings of the riverfront and **quartier St-Pierre**, its narrow streets lined with grand mansions from Bordeaux's glory days, while westwards the triple spires of the **cathedral** provide a focal point for the city's museum district. There are a couple of sights further south, namely the churches of **St-Michel** and **Ste-Croix**, before heading north across the vast, open square of the **esplanade des Quinconces** to the **quartier des Chartrons**, where Bordeaux's wine merchants once lived and worked. Finally, there are some very scant remains of the city's Roman past to be found beyond the welcome greenery of the **Jardin Public** and one last church, **St-Seurin**, which is worth a detour for its delicate alabaster carvings.

The Grand Théâtre and the Golden Triangle

The social hub of eighteenth-century Bordeaux was **place de la Comédie** and the impeccably classical **Grand Théâtre**, built on the site of a Roman temple, at the northern end of rue Ste-Catherine. Completed in 1780 by the architect Victor Louis, this lofty building is faced with an immense colonnaded portico topped by statues of the nine Muses and three Graces. Inside, a monumental stone staircase – the inspiration for Paris's Opéra Garnier and using natural light to great effect – leads to theatre itself, recently restored to its original blue, grey and gold colour scheme. Its walls and ceiling, even the fire curtain, are covered in sumptuous trompe l'oeil, lit by a massive crystal chandelier. The best way to see it is to attend one of the operas, concerts or ballets staged throughout the year (see p.90) – alternatively, sign up at the tourist office for one of their **guided tours** (1hr; 30F/€4.57), though note that these are fairly infrequent in winter.

Smart streets radiate from place de la Comédie. Ritzy **cours de l'Intendance**, whose most famous address is no. 57, where Goya spent the last years of his life

CENTRAL BORDEAUX

Tramlines
— Line A
--- Line B
- - - Line C

(1824–28), runs west to café-lined **place Gambetta**. Once a majestic space laid out in the early eighteenth century to replace a malodorous rubbish dump, the *place* is now little more than a busy roundabout. Marooned in its midst a valiant attempt at an English garden marks where the guillotine lopped off 300 heads at the time of the Revolution, while its southeastern corner is occupied by the Neoclassical **Porte Dijeaux**, one of several triumphal arches erected in the mid-1700s. From here cours Georges-Clemenceau leads northeast to place de Tourny, which commemorates the eighteenth-century administrator the **Marquis Louis Aubert de Tourny**, a prime mover of the city's "Golden Age" who supervised much of the rebuilding. Sandy, tree-lined allées de Tourny then cuts back to the place de la Comédie, enclosing an area of smart shops and attractive residential streets known as the **Golden Triangle**. Its focus is the lovely, circular **place des**

Grands-Hommes, its centre now filled with a striking ironwork market hall completed in 1900, though it feels far more recent with its clean lines and expanse of glass.

The triangle is also home to Bordeaux's only Baroque church, the late-seventeenth-century church of **Notre-Dame** (Mon 2.30–6.30pm, Tues–Fri 9am–noon & 2.30–6pm, Sat 9am–noon). Its gently curved facade comprises a pleasing arrangement of columns, friezes, scrolls and pinnacles centred on a bas-relief of the Virgin Mary presenting a rosary to St Dominic. Inside, light plays off the smooth planes of curved and arched stone, providing a perfect backdrop for typically extravagant Baroque decoration: ornate gilded ironwork, vigorous statuary and trompe l'oeil frescoes in the side chapels, where you'll also find an interesting collection of religious paintings.

Place de la Bourse, Quartier St-Pierre and the Pont de Pierre

West of place de la Comédie, cours du Chapeau-Rouge (the Red Hat), named after a venerable *auberge* once located here, leads to the banks of the Garonne and the imposing **place de la Bourse**. This superb, U-shaped classical ensemble is centred on the Grand Pavilion, in fact a relatively small building topped with a pinnacled grey-slate lantern; either side of it stretch the Palais de la Bourse, the former stock exchange, to the north and the Hôtel des Douanes, the old customs house, balancing it to the south. When the square was first laid out in the early eighteenth century, it was known as the place Royale in honour of Louis XV, and its focal point was an equestrian statue of the king. Come the Revolution, however, the statue was melted down for canon and wasn't replaced until the 1860s when the present Three Graces fountain was installed. The impressive bulk of the Hôtel des Douanes contains the **Musée des Douanes** (April–Sept Tues–Sun 10am–noon & 1–6pm; Oct–March 10am–noon & 1–5pm 20F/€3.05), detailing the city's mercantile past through the history of the French customs service. Apart from some good late-nineteenth-century engravings of Bordeaux's quays thronged with ships, the most engaging displays relate to the efforts of customs officials – wickedly caricatured in contemporary cartoons – to prevent smuggling.

Inland from place de la Bourse, **quartier St-Pierre** encompasses the area from cours du Chapeau-Rouge to cours d'Alsace-Lorraine in the south and west as far as rue Ste-Catherine. This is the heart of Bordeaux's old town, an area of narrow streets lined with typical Bordelais mansions (see box on p.83). Its residents were a mixed bunch, from merchants and members of parliament – the old parliament house once stood on place du Palais to the south – to artisans whose trades are recorded in the street names: rue des Bahutiers (chest-makers); rue des Argentiers (gold and silversmiths); and rue du Cancéra (coopers, in the local dialect). To see the best of the quarter, take rue Fernand-Philippart from behind place de la Bourse to lovely, paved **place du Parlement**. Though the surrounding buildings span more than two centuries, from 1760 on, this square remains one of Intendant Tourny's most successful creations; not rigidly uniform, and small enough to be intimate, but without the architecture losing its sense of nobility. In summer it is filled with tables spilling out of the surrounding cafés and restaurants. Nearby **place St-Pierre** is even smaller and less formal. It is dominated by the attractive fourteenth- and fifteenth-century church of St-Pierre, with its delicate arched windows and a symmetry offset by the adjacent belfry, though there's little to see inside.

Further south down rue des Argentiers, the ornate, almost fairy-tale **Porte Cailhau** – topped by an array of exaggerated pinnacles – takes its name from the stones (*cailloux*, or *cailhaux* in dialect) used as ships' ballast which were unloaded on the neighbouring quay. It is one of Bordeaux's only two remaining medieval city gates, erected in the late fifteenth century in honour of an early victory by Charles VIII in the Italian Wars (1494–1559). Crossing the river just south of here, the long, low **Pont de Pierre** – its red brick bringing a touch of Mediterranean warmth – was the city's first bridge, constructed after Napoléon struggled to ferry his troops across en route to the Spanish campaigns; its seventeen arches are said to commemorate each of his victories. Despite the traffic, the views along the riverfront from here are memorable, particularly when floodlit at night.

Cathédrale St-André and the Hôtel de Ville

Bordeaux's old town west of rue Ste-Catherine is dominated by the **Cathédrale St-André** (Mon–Sat 7.30–11.30am & 2–6pm), whose most eye-catching feature is the great upward sweep of the twin steeples over the north transept, an effect heightened by the adjacent but separate bell tower. Of the earlier eleventh-century church, in which Eleanor of Aquitaine married Louis VII in 1137, only the west wall remains. In the thirteenth and fourteenth centuries the building was almost completely remodelled, with a much higher nave and the addition of a finely carved **Royal Door**, depicting the Last Judgement, in the north wall; according to local legend, the door was closed permanently after Louis XIII and Anne of Austria, daughter of the King of Spain, passed through it on their wedding day in 1615. Unfortunately, it's badly in need of cleaning and the carving on the adjacent north door – of the Last Supper and Christ's Ascension – is much easier to make out.

The cathedral's interior holds no great interest, apart from the **choir** which provides one of the few complete examples of the florid late-Gothic style known as *Rayonnant*. Some of the **carvings** are also worth closer inspection: in the ambulatory around the choir look out for an expressive statue of the Virgin with St Anne as a child, and a very gaunt St Martial, the legendary founder of the church, fashioned out of alabaster in the fifteenth century; the capitals in the Sacrement Chapel, at the cathedral's far east end behind the altar, tell the story of the birth of Christ and the flight into Egypt in superb detail; finally, at the opposite end of the building, under the organ loft, are two powerful Renaissance-era bas-reliefs of the descent into hell and the Resurrection.

In 1440 Archbishop Pey-Berland, who also founded Bordeaux University, laid the corner stone of the cathedral bell tower, built on a separate site as was the custom at the time. It's worth climbing the fifty-metre-high **Tour Pey-Berland** (June–Sept daily 10am–6.30pm; Oct–May Tues–Sun 10am–noon & 2–5pm; 25F/€3.81) for fine views over the cathedral and the city's red-tiled roofs to the river beyond.

West of the cathedral the **Hôtel de Ville**, formerly Archbishop Rohan's palace – was completed in 1784, marking the arrival of Neoclassical architecture in Bordeaux. To see the grand stone staircase, iron balustrades and trompe-l'oeil artwork inside you have to join a one-hour **guided tour** (Wed 2pm; 10F/€1.52).

The museum district

The cream of Bordeaux's museums, all detailed on *www.mairie-bordeaux. fr/musees/indexmusees.html*, lie scattered in the streets around the cathedral.

BORDEAUX'S ARCHITECTURE

As you explore the old city centre, now a conservation area, look out for the splendid detailing of the eighteenth-century **architecture**. In addition to intricate wrought-iron balconies, balustrades, locks and door-knockers, these aristocratic facades are enlivened by sculpted animals and human faces – many are thought to be portraits of the original owners – above the doors and windows. Though such *mascarons* had been used to decorate buildings for some time, the practice reached its peak in eighteenth-century Bordeaux. Not surprisingly, bunches of grapes and the figure of Bacchus, god of wine, also feature strongly, as does Neptune, the sea god. The local, porous building-stone tends to blacken easily, but recent restoration projects have returned many of these frontages to their original gleaming white – to glorious effect.

Directly behind the Hôtel de Ville, with its entrance on cours d'Albret, the **Musée des Beaux-Arts** (Mon & Wed–Sun 11am–6pm; 20F/€3.05) offers a small but worthy selection of European painting from the fifteenth to the early twentieth century. Only a fraction of the 3000-strong collection is on view at any time, featuring works by Reynolds, Titian, Rubens, Delacroix, Matisse and Marquet (a native of the city) amongst many others. Delacroix's *La Grèce sur les ruines de Missolonghi* is probably the most famous work, but look out too for the superb play of light in Henri Gervex's *Rolla* in the museums' north wing.

Far more engaging, however, is the **Musée des Arts Décoratifs** (Mon & Wed–Fri 11am–6pm, Sat & Sun 2–6pm; 15F/€2.29), two blocks further north in rue Bouffard. It occupies the handsome Hôtel de Lalande, built in 1780 as the home of a local wine merchant; today it is in remarkably good repair, with its high-ceilinged rooms, parquet floors and plasterwork mostly intact. Some of the wall coverings, such as the attractive grey-and-white-wash paper in the first room you enter, have been relocated from other Bordelais houses, as has the extensive collection of period furniture, miniatures, paintings, clocks and glassware. The most remarkable items are the beautiful displays of mainly French porcelain and faïence, including some Oriental-inspired designs and others imitating Wedgwood. There's also an attractive *salon de thé* in the museum's courtyard, serving light meals (closed Tues & Sun).

Continuing clockwise round the cathedral brings you to the **Centre National Jean-Moulin** (Tues–Fri 11am–6pm, Sat & Sun 2–6pm; free), a moderately interesting museum dedicated to the Resistance, on place Jean-Moulin. Among all the documentation – unfortunately not translated – on the ground floor look out for a pint-size, collapsible motorbike which was dropped by parachute from British planes towards the end of the war. The second floor serves as a gallery for related works of art, while upstairs again is a mock-up of Jean Moulin's office in Nice, where he worked under cover as an art dealer while co-ordinating the Resistance movement. Arrested in 1943, he was tortured and died on the way to Germany. There's also an engaging, grainy film of Moulin doing Charlie Chaplin impressions in the snow, and several caricatures he penned under the pseudonym Romanin.

A short walk south past the Tour Pey-Berland down rue Duffour-Dubergier, the excellent **Musée d'Aquitaine** (Tues–Sun 11am–6pm; 25F/€3.81) is another of the city's top museums, in this case charting the history of Bordeaux and its region from prehistoric times to the present day, with a section devoted to artefacts brought back from around the world by local merchants, missionaries and colonial administrators. Best, though, are the ground-floor rooms covering the prehistoric and Gallo-Roman eras and containing a number of important finds; look out for the little 20,000-year-old statue of Venus carrying a crescent-shaped horn (see also p.211), and a magnificent Hercules in bronze from the second century AD.

A couple of minutes' walk east of the museum along cours Victor-Hugo, a heavy Gothic tower, the fifteenth-century **Grosse Cloche**, straddles rue St-James. A remnant of the city walls, the gate also doubles as a bell-tower for the medieval city hall. Until 1945 the start of the grape harvest and all other major events in the city were marked by peals of the single, big bell hanging between the gate's sturdy towers.

The southern districts

Bordeaux's **southern districts** were developed outside the medieval walls after the twelfth century as an artisan's quarter of coopers, carpenters and ships' chandlers, and home to the sailors and stevedores who worked the boats come to unload their cargoes at the nearby quays. It is still very much a working-class area with little to see beyond a huge, atmospheric flea market and a couple of historic churches which are worth a quick detour.

The main **flea market** takes place on Sunday mornings (see "Listings" for more) when it fills the wide square in front of the Gothic **Église St-Michel**, which you reach from cours Victor-Hugo by heading south down rue des Faures. Started in the mid-fourteenth century and not completed for another two hundred years, the church is one of Bordeaux's most famous landmarks thanks to its soaring **bell-tower** – at 114m tall, it is the highest in southern France. The original fifteenth-century spire was destroyed in a storm in the 1700s and not restored until Paul Abadie (1812–84), the architect of Paris's Sacré-Coeur, got to work on it in 1861. As with the cathedral's, it stands apart from the main body of the church, in which the only real point of interest is a charming statue of St Ursula sheltering some of her fellow virgin-martyrs – alongside a few bishops – under her outspread cloak. Find her in the first chapel on the right as you enter the church's west door.

Rue Camille-Sauvageau leads further south to the district's older and more attractive, honey-coloured **Église Ste-Croix**. This Benedictine abbey-church is said to have been founded by Clovis, the first Merovingian king (481–511) and a Christian convert, in 510 AD. It was heavily restored in the twelfth and thirteenth centuries, by which time it had become one of the region's most important religious foundations. In fact, old engravings show that the church was even better-looking before the ubiquitous Paul Abadie added the north tower and remodelled its Romanesque facade in the 1860s. Nevertheless, the irregular assembly of arches and columns provide a pleasing frame for the deep-set west door with its rhythmic carvings. By contrast the interior boasts very little decoration save a few carved capitals and faded murals. As you enter, note the sarcophagus in the first chapel on the left which holds the body of the abbot and, later, St Mommolin who was buried here in 643. Further on, to the left of the altar, there's also an unusual bald-headed representation of Christ on the Cross. It's believed that the fifteenth-century, lime-wood statue might originally have sported a wig for extra realism, as some Spanish figures do.

North into the quartier des Chartrons

Back in the centre of town, cours du 30-Juillet leads north from place de la Comédie into the bare, gravelly – and frankly unattractive – expanse of the **esplanade des Quinconces**. Said to be Europe's largest municipal square, it was laid out in the early nineteenth century on the site of the Château Trompette (see p.74). At its eastern end stand two tall columns, erected in 1829 and topped by allegorical statues of Commerce and Navigation; at the opposite end is the **Monument aux Girondins**, a glorious *fin-de-siècle* fantasy of statues and fountains built in honour of the influential local deputies to the 1789 Revolutionary Assembly, later purged by Robespierre as moderates and counter-revolutionaries (see p.359). During the last war, the occupying Germans made plans to melt the bronze statues down, only to be foiled by the local Resistance, who got there first and, under cover of darkness, dismantled them piece by piece and hid them in a barn in the Médoc for the duration of the war. It was only in 1983 that the monument was reassembled. It is, again, highly allegorical: at the top of the column Liberty breaks free from her chains; beneath her, facing the river, the French cockerel stands over three empty pedestals representing the Girondins deputies; on the opposite, west side, a trio of voluptuous nudes symbolize Bordeaux flanked by the rivers Garonne and Dordogne. The best statues by far, though, are the rescued bronze compositions in the fountains, particularly the powerful, semi-mythical horses with their webbed and clawed feet.

The district north of the esplanade is known as the **quartier des Chartrons** after the Carthusian monks who settled here in the fourteenth century and began draining the marshy land. They were followed in the next century by Dutch and other European wine merchants who avoided taxes by loading their boats outside the city walls. As business prospered in the seventeeth and eighteenth centuries they built themselves offices, as well as comfortable houses complete with stone-lined cellars, for ageing the wine. Though most of the merchants, or *négociants*, have moved on, the Chartrons district still has a gentrified feel and its quiet streets make it a pleasant area to wander.

Starting on the quayside, the first sight you come to is the Neoclassical **Hôtel Fenwick** overlooking shady cours Xavier-Arnozan. Built in 1795 to house America's first French consulate, it is a grand affair, topped with two viewing towers, presumably to enable the consul to keep an eye on happenings in the port. The maritime theme is echoed by a pair of ships' prows emerging either side of the main door. Across cours Xavier-Arnozan, with its entrance on rue Ferrère, the **Musée d'Art Contemporain** (Tues–Sun 11am–6pm; 30F/€4.57) occupies a converted early-nineteenth-century warehouse for colonial imports. The vast, arcaded hall provides a magnificent setting for the mostly post-1960 works by artists such as Daniel Buren, Richard Long and Sol LeWitt. Few pieces from the permanent collection are on display at any one time, the main space being filled by temporary exhibitions, so it's hit-and-miss as to whether you'll like what's on offer. If you're in the area around lunchtime, though, there's also a suitably chic café-restaurant on the roof.

Rue Notre-Dame, which runs north from cours Xavier-Arnozan, has become a centre for **antiques shops**. At its southern end, the bulk and austerity of the Protestant Temple, or chapel, built in the 1830s along pure Classical lines, comes as something of a shock after the fussy, bourgeois facades around, while further along, a left turn beside the church of St-Louis brings you into an attractive, café-lined square, in the middle of which stands the graceful **Halle des Chartrons**, a market hall built in 1869, now used to stage a variety of temporary exhibitions. It's worth continuing to the top of rue Notre-Dame to visit the informative **Musée des Chartrons**, at 41 rue Borie (Mon–Fri 2–6pm; May–Oct also Sat 9am–noon; 20F/€3.05). The museum, home of an Irish wine merchant in the 1720s, is full of fascinating facts and figures relating to the life of the Chartrons district and the wine trade in general; ask to borrow their unusually thorough English-language booklet taking you round the main exhibits. You start in the three ageing-cellars, of which there were originally twelve, their vaulted roofs covered with a dusty deposit left by vapours condensing on the cold stone over the last two hundred years. Displays show how barrels were made, sealed and transported and how, later, bottling took over. Upstairs, in the museum proper, the story continues with a mock-up of a bottling floor as well as various antique bottles, stencils and labels produced for local châteaux. Note the labels marked "Retour des Indes", referring to a bizarre but highly profitable practice that started sometime in the eighteenth or nineteenth century when the proprietor of Château Cos d'Estournel in the Médoc brought some wine back from India after the proposed sale fell through. He discovered that the wine had improved markedly during the long sea voyage, presumably due to the constant temperature and rocking motion. Soon everyone was shipping wines to India and back before selling them at a premium.

The Jardin Public south to St-Seurin

West of the Chartrons district, across cours de Verdun, the formal **Jardin Public** (daily: June–Aug 7am–9pm; April, May, Sept & Oct 7am–8pm; Nov–March 7am–6pm; free) represents one of the city's rare open green spaces. It began life in the mid-1700s as a tree-filled park, another of Intendant Tourny's improvements, but later had to be redesigned after serving as a parade ground in the Revolution. This second, smaller garden follows English styling in its landscaped lake and lawns. It also contains the city's botanical gardens, its 3000 species all neatly labelled, and a missable collection of fossils and stuffed animals belonging to the **Natural History Museum** (Mon & Wed–Fri 11am–6pm, Sat & Sun 2–6pm; 20F/€3.05).

Behind the garden to the southwest stretches a quiet, provincial quarter of two-storey stone houses. Concealed among the narrow streets, next to rue Dr-Albert-Barraud, a large chunk of brick and stone masonry, rather grandly titled the **Palais Gallien**, is all that remains of Roman Burdigala's arena, whose terraces could hold an estimated 15,000 spectators. Further south again, **Église St-Seurin** (Mon–Sat 8am–noon & 2–7.30pm, Sun 8am–12.30pm & 5–8pm), on place des Martyrs-de-la-Résistance, marks the site of a Gallo-Roman burial ground. Though its exterior reflects numerous remodellings since it was founded in the sixth century, the church is of interest for its collection of intricate alabaster carvings; the soft white stone was imported from England in the fourteenth and fifteenth centuries. The first group you come to, just before the altar opposite the equally ornate Gothic bishop's throne, comprises fourteen bas-relief panels portraying the lives of St Seurin, a fifth-century bishop, and St Martial, a third-century evangelizer from Limoges, in superb detail. The life of the Virgin Mary is the subject of the second group in the chapel to the left of the choir; unfortunately, these twelve panels were replaced in the wrong order after a nineteenth century clean-up.

Eating and drinking

Bordeaux is packed with a bewildering choice of **restaurants**, many of them top-notch, and because of its position close to the Atlantic coast fresh seafood features prominently on many a menu. Being a student city, there's also no shortage of **cafés** and **bars** to explore. For **picnic fare**, there's a small but select **market** in the place des Grands-Hommes (Mon–Sat 7am–7pm) while on rue Montesquieu, just off the square, Jean d'Alos runs the city's best *fromagerie*, with dozens of farm-produced cheeses. In the Grands-Hommes market you'll also find Baillardran, a confectioner specializing in the succulent little *cannelé* cakes which were once made by the Bordeaux nuns – surprising, since they are laced with rum.

Restaurants

The best single area to trawl for **restaurants** is the area around place du Parlement and place St-Pierre, where you'll find something to please all tastes and budgets. There are numerous sandwich bars and fast-food outlets at the south end of rue Ste-Catherine and spilling into studenty place de la Victoire. After a night on the town, join the workers at the marché des Capucins for a hearty **breakfast** at one of several all-night café-bars such as *Rodes* (see below). In recent summers, *guinguettes* – open-air **riverside stalls** selling shrimps, king prawns and other seafood snacks – have proved a huge success; they set up along the quai des Chartrons.

Baud et Millet, 19 rue Huguerie (☎05.56.79.05.77; see map, p.80). The ultimate cheese-and-wine feast, with dishes such as a flaky-pastry starter filled with melted Jura and a creamy chive sauce to oven-baked Gouda with smoked salmon, consumed around a few tables at the back of a wine shop. Portions are generous and this is rich fare, so one dish goes a long way. Menus start at 140F/€21.34, or you can eat well from the *carte* for around the same price. Closed Sun.

Le Bistrot d'Édouard, 16 pl du Parlement (see map, p.80). Undeniably touristy these days, but recommended for its moderate prices and position on this lovely square, with outdoor seating in summer. There's a good-value, three-course menu (60F/€9.15 at lunch; 70F/€10.67 in the evening) offering a choice of regional dishes and standard brasserie fare. If it's full, try the slightly more upmarket sister-restaurant, *L'Ombrière*, next door. Nov–Feb closed Sun afternoons.

Bistrot de l'Embarcadère, 3 rue du Pas-St-Georges (☎05.56.52.23.29; see map, p.80). Smart, popular Parisian-style brasserie specializing in fresh seafood. Best at lunchtime when there's a *formule* of a salad and *plat du jour* for 60F (€9.15). Evening menus start at 105F (€16.01) for two courses, and they also do dramatic seafood platters. Closed Sun and Mon.

Le Bistrot des Quinconces, 4 pl des Quinconces (☎05.56.52.84.56; see map, p.80). Lively bistro which doubles as a daytime café and early-evening tapas bar (7.30–8pm). In fine weather locals vie for the outdoor tables in a great spot facing the fountains. The modern, eclectic *carte* includes main dishes from around 70F/€10.67, with a three-course weekday lunch menu at 80F (€12.20). Daily 7.30am–11.30pm.

Brasserie du Passage, 14–15 pl Canteloupe (see map, pp.72–73). After strolling round the St-Michel flea market, head for this fun brasserie in an antique hall, formerly a banana-ripening warehouse, serving uninspirational but perfectly adequate food. There's a choice of two lunch menus at around the 70F/€10.67 mark, rising to 100F/€15.24 in the evening. Closed Sun afternoon and Mon.

Chez Dupont, 45 rue de Notre-Dame (☎05.56.81.49.59; see map, pp.72–73). Bustling, old-fashioned restaurant in the Chartrons district with wooden floors, Toulouse-Lautrec posters and waiters sporting stripy waistcoats. Their seasonal menus include *pot-au-feu, boudin,* foie gras and *crevettes* and prices are very reasonable, with a two-course lunch for 62F/€9.45, and full menus from 140F/€21.34. Reservations are recommended in the evening – and there's a surprise in store in the toilet.

Didier Gélineau, 26 rue Pas-St-Georges (☎05.56.52.84.25; see map, p.80). One of the high spots of Bordeaux cuisine just west of place St-Pierre, where you can eat exquisitely cooked, imaginative food at affordable prices. Seasonal dishes include foie gras, truffles, lobster and pigeon, all beautifully presented in an elegant dining room decked out in cool, muted greens. Menus 130–300F/€19.82–45.73. Closed Sat lunch & Sun.

L'Imprévu, 11 rue des Remparts (see map, p.80). At the other end of the scale, this is a good option for those on a budget. Menus around 60–70F/€9.15–10.67, with a fair choice of traditional regional dishes. Menus change daily, making it popular among locals, especially at lunchtime. Closed Sun.

Le Mably, 12 rue Mably (☎05.56.44.30.10; see map, p.80). Informal, friendly and not-surprisingly popular restaurant offering good value and a warm atmosphere among its mirrors, candles and sepia shots. Choose from a variety of *formules* starting with a *plat du jour* at 55F/€8.38 or three-course menus from 120F/€18.29. The food is plentiful and of excellent quality, using lots of fish and local produce, with dishes such as duck-breast with acacia-flower honey. Closed Sun & Mon.

Le Parlement des Graves, 9 rue du Parlement-Ste-Catherine (see map, p.80). Fresh seafood and modern takes on regional dishes served in a jolly, blue-yellow dining room festooned with pot plants. An excellent choice of local Graves wines accompany the well-priced menus: from 60F/€9.15 for a weekday lunch up to around 150F/€22.87 in the evening. June–Sept closed Sun lunchtime.

Les Plaisirs d'Ausone, 10 rue Ausone (☎05.56.79.30.30; see map, p.80). This is one of Bordeaux's top restaurants, offering exquisite food in an atmospheric, stone-vaulted dining room featuring an ornamental fountain. The cheapest menu (170F/€25.92) is available at lunch and dinner, though the next up is the *menu dégustation* at 350F/€53.36. Closed Sun and Mon & Sat lunchtime.

Le Port de la Lune, 59 quai de Paludate (☎05.56.49.15.55; see map, pp.72–73). Big, noisy brasserie with a great atmosphere out on the southern quays next to the *Comptoir du Jazz* (see p.90); the photos, the sound system and their motto – "jazz-abuse is good for your health" – give you some idea of the priority here. The food is reasonable and varied, with a three-course menu including coffee and wine at 106F/€16.16. Daily until 2am.

Rodes, 22 pl des Capucins (see map, pp.72–73). Old-style home cooking in a cheerful, red-and-white-tiled room in a corner of the Capucins marketplace. Originally catering to market workers, the restaurant is now a popular breakfast spot among clubbers. *Plat du jour* from 45F/€6.86. Open for breakfast, lunch and dinner Tues–Sat; and all night Wed, Thurs & Fri. Closed Sun lunchtime & Mon.

Le Troisième Homme, 6 rue Borie (☎05.56.51.12.47; see map, pp.72–73). Friendly Chartrons restaurant-bar with pine panelling, open fire and – of course – a poster from the film after which the place is named. The food is solid, no-nonsense meat-based fare. Weekday lunch menu at 60F/€9.15, or 90F/€13.72 in the evening, both with a choice of dishes. Reservations recommended for dinner. Open for lunch Mon–Fri; dinner Thurs–Sat. Closed Sun.

Cafés and bars

Surprisingly, Bordeaux lacks any truly grand, people-watching **cafés**. Though *Café Regent* on place Gambetta is the place to be seen, a nicer, cheaper alternative is to be found across the square at *Café Dijeaux* beside the city gate. You will, however, find a collection of young, lively **bars**, mostly around place de la Victoire, several of which offer live music and all of which are packed on Thursday nights.

There's also a clutch of English, Irish and antipodean **pubs** now in Bordeaux and a well-established **gay** scene concentrated at the south end of rue des Remparts.

Bar de l'Hôtel de Ville (BHV), 4 rue de l'Hôtel-de-Ville. Friendly little gay café-bar which stages a variety of free events every other Sunday (10.30pm). Open daily 6pm–2am.

Bodega Bodega, 4 rue des Piliers-de-Tutelle. Large wine bar with a Spanish ambience, also serving sangria and beer, and pretty authentic tapas (from 20F/€3.05 per dish) to soak it all up. Open noon–3pm & 7pm–2am. Closed Sun lunchtime.

El Bodegon Rock Café, 14 pl de la Victoire. One of the largest and most popular bars on the square where it all happens on Thursday nights. There's a happy hour (6–8pm) as well as regular promotions, theme parties, free concerts and the big matches on screen. Brasserie food available weekday lunchtimes only. Mon–Sat 7am–2am, Sun 2pm–2am.

Le Boeuf sur le Toit, 15 rue de Candale. Loud, dark rock-bar just northeast of place de la Victoire frequented by a happily rough-and-ready, university crowd. Cheap beer to 10.30pm and concerts in the stone-vaulted *cave* every Wednesday from October to June (10.30pm; 20F/€3.05). Daily 8pm–2am.

Café des Arts, 138 cours Victor-Hugo. This café-brasserie on the corner of rue Ste-Catherine is one of the city's few old-style cafés, its ambience created from 1930s faded relics. Serves reasonable food (the kitchens stay open till 1am), while twice-monthly free jazz concerts – mostly Sixties' acoustic – pack them in. Daily 9am–2am.

Calle Ocho, 24 rue des Piliers-de-Tutelle (☎05.56.48.08.68). Bordeaux's best-known and liveliest salsa bar is packed to the gunnels on Friday and Saturday nights. They serve real Cuban rum and *mojitos*, a traditional drink of mint, lemon, sugar, sparkling water and lots of rum, and the music is loud. Free salsa courses on Thursdays at 9.30pm. Open Mon–Sat 5.30pm–2am.

La Comtesse, 25 rue du Parlement-St-Pierre. More like an antiques shop than a bar, this tiny place is decked out with old paintings, chandeliers, distressed woodwork and faded sofas set off against bare, stone walls. The music is contrastingly young, and gets louder as the evening progresses. Mon–Sat 6pm–2am.

Connemara, 18 cours d'Albret. For the homesick pining for a pint of Guinness, this is Bordeaux's best Irish pub, with free concerts or some other event most nights. You can also fill up on pub grub, or eat upstairs in the suitably green restaurant (Mon–Sat only; *plat du jour* 60F/€9.15). Mon–Sat 11.45am–2am, Sun 6pm–2am.

Le Débit Rouge, pl des Capucins. Classic little café-bar, the tiles and sawdust reflecting its market-stall origins, which caters to market workers and night owls. Tues–Sat 4am–2pm.

Dick Turpin's, 72 rue du Loup. Opposite a wisteria-filled courtyard, this is a pretty good rendition of an English town pub, with a great atmosphere and a mixed clientele. There's the standard range of beers, in addition to well-priced bar meals, or tea and cakes on quieter afternoons. Happy hour 5.30–8.30pm. Open Mon–Sat 11.30am–2am, Sun 6pm–2am.

Down Under, 104 cours Aristide-Briand. Aboriginal wall-paintings, Fosters on tap – there's no mistaking the origins of this laid-back pub just off place de la Victoire. Theme parties, darts competitons and sports broadcasts draw an international crowd, especially at weekends. Happy hour from 7–9pm Monday to Saturday and all Sunday. Open daily 8pm–2am.

Golden Apple, 64 rue Pomme-d'Or. Old perennial with the ambience of a quiet British country pub which makes a good pit stop in the Chartrons district. Simple food, from chicken-and-mushroom pie to cheesecake, available on weekdays only (*plat du jour* 35F/€5.34). Happy hour 6–8pm. Open Mon–Fri 11am–3pm & 6pm–2am, Sat 6pm–2am, Sun 8pm–2am.

Le Plana, 22 pl de la Victoire. One of the more relaxed student hangouts around the square though, like everywhere else, it's jumping on Thursday nights. Free live music on Sun (jazz), Mon & Tues (various). Open daily 7am–2am.

Seven Café, 73 rue des Trois-Conils. Welcoming gay bar near the Hôtel de Ville which turns into a disco as the night wears on. Particularly popular for its DJ slots on Fridays and Saturdays; the music is mostly techno and house. Open daily 6pm–2am.

Entertainment and nightlife

Bordeaux's cultural life runs the gamut from classical theatre to avant-garde performance art and big-name rock concerts. In recent years a decent late-night scene has taken root along the southern quays, though it's still pretty low-key compared to other French cities of this size. To find out what's happening in and around Bordeaux, get hold of the regional newspaper *Sud Ouest*; or one of the fortnightly **listings** booklets: *Spectaculair 33* (3F/€0.46); the free but less comprehensive *Bordeaux Plus*; and *Clubs & Concerts*, also free, detailing the city's current favourites. To buy **tickets** for city and regional events, contact the venue direct or head for the Box Office (☎05.56.48.26.26) in the nineteenth-century Galerie Bordelaise arcade wedged between rue Ste-Catherine and rue des Piliers-de-Tutelle. Virgin Megastore (☎05.56.56.05.55) on place Gambetta also has a ticket outlet.

The city's most prestigious **theatrical events** take place in the sumptuous Grand Théâtre, which hosts a varied programme of theatre, opera, dance and classical music. So much, in fact, that performances spill over into the Théâtre Fémina, 20 rue de Grassi, and the unlovely Palais des Sport on place de la Ferme-de-Richemont, near cours Victor-Hugo; for tickets and information for all these venues contact the Grand Théâtre (☎05.56.00.85.95; prices range from 40–350F/€6.10–53.35 depending on the venue and the event). Occasional **classical concerts** (tickets 60–120F/€9.15–18.26) also take place in several churches, notably the cathedral, but also Notre-Dame, Ste-Croix and St-Seurin, which are well worth looking out for.

More informal **café-théâtre** and modern performance arts get a strong showing in venues throughout the city. A few of the more accessible include La Comédie Gallien, 20 rue Rolland (☎05.56.44.04.00; tickets 80–120F/€12.20–18.29), Théâtre des Salinières, 4 rue Bohan (☎05.56.48.86.86, *www.salinieres.com*; tickets around 110F/€16.77) and, last but not least, the *Troisième Homme* (see "Restaurants" p.88), which hosts plays and concerts – usually jazz or blues – roughly twice a month (25–50F/€3.81–7.62).

When it comes to **cinema**, the best venue, where you're also most likely to find Version Originale (V.O.) films is the Utopia on place Camille-Jullian (☎05.56.52.00.03), housed in a converted church complete with frescoes and Gothic arches, not to mention six screens. Other good options include the Trianon Jean Vigo, 6 rue Franklin (☎05.56.44.35.17), near place des Grands-Hommes, and UGC Cinécité, 13–15 rue Georges-Bonnac (☎08.36.68.68.58). For more standard fare, there's the vast, new 17-screen Mégarama (☎08.36.69.33.17) across the Pont de Pierre in the old Gare d'Orléans.

Jazz and blues fans should head for *Comptoir du Jazz* next to the *Port de la Lune* restaurant (see above) on the southern quays. Entry is free but, while it's not essential to eat, you are expected to buy at least a drink. Other options are the very laid-back *L'Avant Scène*, 36 rue Borie (☎05.57.87.55.88; closed Sun), the *Café des Arts* (see "Cafés and bars" p.89) and the more frenetic *L'Alligator*, 3 place du Général-Sarrail (☎05.56.92.78.47), which blasts out the blues on Wednesday nights. There's no shortage of more **contemporary music** either. Rock is alive and kicking at *Le Barclay*, 57 cours de l'Argonne (☎05.56.31.44.66), a music-bar near place de la Victoire, and near the station at the concert hall *Rock School Barbey*, 18 cours Barbey (☎05.56.33.66.00). *Le Jimmy*, 68 rue de Madrid

(☎05.56.98.20.83), meanwhile, is Bordeaux's most famous rock-bar, popular for its DJ nights and a programme ranging from heavy metal to techno.

Since Bordeaux's **dance clubs** are constantly changing – places often come and go within six months – it's best to ask around for the latest hot spots. There are one or two discos in the city centre, such as the *Paris-Pékin*, at 10 rue de la Merci (☎05.56.44.19.88), with a varied play list, but the majority of clubs are spread out along southerly quai du Paludate, where things don't really get going until two in the morning and continue till around four or five. Two of the district's more established venues are *La Plage* at no. 40 (☎05.56.49.02.46; Wed–Sat; free), a fun, mainstream disco in a tropical-beach setting, and the nicely tatty *Living Room*, 14 rue du Commerce (☎05.56.85.71.85; daily; free), which plays mostly house and techno. The music is pretty much the same at the *Shadow Lounge*, 5 rue Cabanac (☎05.56.49.36.93; closed Mon; free), but its decor is distinctly baroque, all classy chandeliers and velvet drapes.

Listings

Airlines Air France (☎05.56.44.05.69); Air Liberté (☎05.56.34.54.55); British Airways (☎08.25.82.54.00); Buzz (☎01.55.17.42.42); Regional Airlines (☎08.03.00.52.00).

Airport Bordeaux-Mérignac (☎05.56.34.50.50, *www.bordeaux.aeroport.fr*).

Banks and exchange Other than those offices at the airport, American Express, 14 cours de l'Intendance (Mon–Fri 8.45am–noon & 1.30–5.30pm), handles most traveller's cheques and foreign currencies, though not always at the best rates. The main banks along cours de l'Intendance and on pl de la Comédie also offer exchange facilities and 24hr ATMs.

Boat trips The *Aliénor* (☎05.56.51.27.90) offers a varied programme of cruises, from a short trip round the port (school hols only; 1hr 30min; 65F/€9.91) to a jaunt downriver (7hr return journey; cruise only 130F/€19.82; with *plat du jour* 190F/€28.97; full menu 270F/€41.16). The ticket office is located on quai Louis-XVIII near the esplanade des Quinconces, while boats leave from the Embarcadère des Quinconces, a little further north along the quay. In July and August the *Ville de Bordeaux* (☎05.56.52.88.88) leaves from the same place for a guided historical tour of the riverfront (1hr 30min; 60F/€9.15).

Books and newspapers Maison de la Presse, 61 rue Ste-Catherine and pl Gambetta, sells the main English-language papers in addition to some regional guides and maps. Bordeaux's largest bookstore, Mollat, 15 rue Vital-Carles, has a good selection of local guides and maps, and stocks a few English-language titles, though there's a better choice at helpful Bradley's Bookshop, 8 cours d'Albret (*www.bradleys-bookshop.com*).

Bus departures You can get information and tickets for buses around the region from the booth at the bus park between esplanade des Quinconces and allées de Chartres, or phone ☎05.56.99.57.83. Eurolines buses leave from outside their office opposite the *gare SNCF* at 32 rue Charles-Domercq (☎05.56.92.50.42).

Car rental Numerous rental firms are located in and around the train station, including Avis (☎05.56.91.65.50); Budget (☎05.56.31.41.40); Europcar (☎05.56.31.20.30); Hertz (☎05.57.59.05.95); and National/Citer (☎05.56.92.19.62). They all have outlets at the airport as well: Avis (☎05.56.34.38.22); Budget (☎05.56.47.84.22); Europcar (☎05.56.34.05.79); Hertz (☎05.56.34.59.59); National/Citer (☎05.56.34.20.68).

Consulates British, 353 bd du Président-Wilson (☎05.57.22.21.10). The nearest US consulate is in Toulouse: (☎05.34.41.36.50). In Paris there are embassies for Australia (☎01.40.59.33.00), Canada (☎01.44.43.29.00) and New Zealand (☎01.45.01.43.43).

Hospital Centre Hospitalier Pellegrin-Tripode, pl Amélie-Raba-Léon (☎05.56.79.56.79), to the west of central Bordeaux.

Internet access Cyberstation, 23 cours Pasteur (Mon–Sat 11am–2am, Sun 2pm–midnight; 5F/€0.76 per 5min, 40F/€6.10 per hour).

Language courses Bordeaux University is divided into four campuses. For information on language studies, apply to Bordeaux III, esplanade des Antilles (☎05.56.84.50.50). The Alliance Française, 38 rue Ferrèrre (☎05.56.79.32.80), also offers a range of courses.

Markets The main fresh-food markets are the vast marché des Capucins (Tues–Sat midnight–12.30pm) and the smaller, more upmarket marché des Grands-Hommes (Mon–Sat 7am–7pm). On Sunday mornings there's a lively food market on the quays near the retired *Colbert* gunship. The square in front of St-Michel is the venue for flea markets (Tues, Thurs, Fri and, the biggest, Sun morning) with more general fare on offer on Mondays and Saturdays.

Police Commissariat Central, 87 rue Abbé-de-l'Épée (☎05.56.99.77.77).

Post office The central post office is located at 52 rue Georges-Bonnac, 33000 Bordeaux.

Shopping Bordeaux's principal shopping streets are rue Ste-Catherine and rue Porte-Dijeaux. You'll find luxury food shops in and around place des Grands-Hommes, while antiques sellers gather at the south end of rue Notre-Dame in the Chartrons district. For wines, La Vinothèque, next to the tourist office at 8 cours du 30-Juillet, stocks a broad range, mostly from the Bordeaux region. L'Intendant, 2 allées de Tourny, specializes in Premiers Grands Crus Classés (see p.75), stored in a circular tower with the oldest vintages at the top, while Badie, 62 allées de Tourny, also offers a good range of wines and local liqueurs.

Student information CIJA (Centre d'Information Jeunesse Aquitaine), 5 rue Duffour-Dubergier (☎05.56.56.00.56), has vast amounts of information and useful notice boards. CROUS, 18 rue du Hamel (☎05.56.33.92.00, *www.crous-bordeaux.fr*), caters to university students and those in higher education. Foreign students can also call ☎05.56.33.92.38 for help and information.

Wine tasting In summer (late June to mid-Sept) the Conseil Interprofessionnel du Vin de Bordeaux, 1 cours du 30-Juillet (☎05.56.00.22.88), opposite the tourist office, holds introductory two-hour wine-tasting courses in English three afternoons per week (100F/€15.24). Reservations recommended at least a day in advance. For more serious study, their Wine School offers longer courses in various languages.

The Médoc

The landscape of the **Médoc**, a long, thin slice of land northwest of Bordeaux, wedged between the forests bordering the Atlantic coast and the Gironde estuary, is in itself rather monotonous. Its gravel plains occupying the west bank of the brown, island-spotted inlet rarely swell into anything resembling a hill, but these soils sustain Bordeaux's best vineyards, producing some of the world's finest **wines**. Until Dutch civil engineers were employed to drain the Médoc in the early seventeenth century, and thus increase the potential acreage, the area was largely marshland, good only for sheep, corn or wheat, and most transport was by water. A century later the sand and pebble ridges had been planted with vines and the area never looked back.

The D2 **wine-route**, forking off the N215 just north of Bordeaux, passes through a string of small, prosperous towns sitting in an island of vines. While none are particularly interesting in themselves, each is surrounded by an incredible concentration of top-name châteaux, many of which are open to visitors by appointment. First stop for most people is **Margaux**, home to the great Château Margaux and within easy reach of Château Palmer and many other Grands Crus Classés. From here it's a hop northwards across remnants of marsh and lesser vineyards before reaching **St-Julien** and the biggest of the wine towns, **Pauillac**. Again the châteaux come thick and fast on the waves of higher ground, led by the Rothschilds' estates and Château Latour, until the wine-route reaches its end at **St-Estèphe**.

Considering the number of visitors it attracts, the Médoc is surprisingly short of affordable places to stay and eat, perhaps because many people come on a day-trip from Bordeaux. It's worth taking a little more time, however, and spending at least one night in the region. While it's easier to explore with your own car (see

THE WINES OF THE MÉDOC

The Médoc wine area is divided into two regional *appellations*, Haut-Médoc, from Bordeaux to St-Estèphe, and Médoc (sometimes known as Bas-Médoc), the area at the northern tip of the peninsula, which in general produces lower-quality red wines. Confusingly, when people talk about Médoc wines in general, they are usually referring to the far more important Haut-Médoc. This is where you'll find the "big six" communes with their individual labels – Margaux, St-Julien, Pauillac, St-Estèphe, Moulis and Listrac – and all the region's classified vineyards.

The Médoc as a whole produces almost exclusively **red wines**, from the grape varieties of Cabernet Sauvignon, Merlot, Cabernet Franc and, to a lesser degree, Malbec, Petit Verdot and Carmenère. Tannin-rich Cabernet Sauvignon is the quintessential Médoc grape. It gives body, bouquet, colour and maturing potential to the wine, while Merlot makes it rounder and softer. In general these are more delicate, distinctive wines showing greater finesse than the heartier St-Émilion (see p.121), particularly when properly aged, but there is a certain amount of variation. In **Margaux**, for example, where the soils are more sandy, wines contain a larger proportion of Merlot. Consequently these are the most supple and feminine of the Médoc wines and can be drunk younger, though they also age extremely well. Further north a higher clay content makes for darker, fuller-bodied wines around **St-Julien**, though they still mature relatively quickly, while the very gravelly soils of **Pauillac** favour Cabernet Sauvignon – hence a high concentration of top-rank vineyards producing very individual wines which benefit from ageing. The region's most fruity, full-bodied wines, often compared to St-Émilion, come from **St-Estèphe**, on the northern border of Haut-Médoc.

The majority of Médoc vineyards date from the late-seventeenth and early-eighteenth centuries. In 1855 the most prestigious wines were ranked into five Crus Classés ("Classified Growths") by a committee of Bordeaux brokers in order that only the best should be represented at the Great Exhibition in Paris. Much has changed since then and it is now generally acknowledged that, while the Premiers Crus ("First Growths") remain valid, the lower four rankings need a complete overhaul. There are many great wines among the Crus Bourgeois – currently being classified by the Syndicat des Crus Bourgeois, due to report in two years' time – some of which are now superior to a number of Crus Classés and equal in price, and, increasingly, among the more lowly but rapidly improving Crus Artisans. Indeed, with prices rising ever higher, it's among this last group that you'll probably find the best value for money in the Médoc. As a very general rule of thumb, expect to pay from 60F/€9.15 to 200F/€30.49 for Crus Bourgeois or Crus Artisans, while classified wines start at around 200F/€30.49 a bottle and can reach over ten times that amount for the most sought-after vintages.

VINEYARD VISITS

Touring the vineyards around Bordeaux and sampling a few local wines is a pleasure not to be missed. Many of the larger producers now offer properly organized **visits** – often in English if you ring ahead – of their vinification plant and ageing cellars (*chais*), but rarely inside the château itself. They increasingly charge a fee, usually in the region of 25F/€3.81, though this generally includes two or three **tastings**. In a few cases you have to make an **appointment** several days, or even weeks, in advance, sometimes in writing. Other producers are happy for you just to roll up within specified hours. But even so it is advisable to phone ahead, especially outside the main summer season, to ensure someone will be there. And note that the majority of producers don't accept visitors during **harvest time** (generally late Sept–early Oct).

Where the **smaller vineyards** are concerned, the visits are a lot more ad hoc. Some charge, but may waive the fee if you make a purchase, while others offer them free. Nevertheless, it's worth bearing in mind that these are commercial operations and that, while there's no compulsion to buy, the purchase of just one or two bottles will be much appreciated – and seems fair recompense for the time spent showing you round.

In the Guide we recommend vineyards open to visitors in each of Bordeaux's wine regions. There are, of course, hundreds more. The local **Maison du Vin** will be able to provide you with detailed lists and will often offer advice or help make appointments. For those without their own transport, getting to most of these vineyards is hard work. In which case, the simplest thing is to take one of the Bordeaux tourist office's excellent bilingual **guided tours** covering a different region each afternoon (May–Oct daily; Nov–April Wed & Sat; 160F/€24.39). Tastings are generous and expert tuition on how to go about it is part of the deal.

p.91 for Bordeaux rental outlets), there are regular **bus services** from Bordeaux via Margaux and St-Julien to Pauillac, with a limited service on to St-Estèphe, and also a country **train** line which roughly tracks the D2 as far as Pauillac and then continues on to Soulac-sur-Mer and the Pointe-de-Grave.

Margaux and around

The small village of **MARGAUX**, some 20km north of Bordeaux on the D2, basks in the reflected glory of the surrounding châteaux, and not without reason. Château Margaux itself, arguably the prettiest in the Bordeaux region, sits right on the doorstep, while the renowned Château Palmer is within striking distance. With its helpful Maison du Vin, several restaurants and even a hotel, the village makes a natural place to start exploring the Médoc.

Unless you've already picked up information in Bordeaux (see p.76), first stop should be the **Maison du Vin** (daily: July & Aug 9am–7pm; Sept–June 9am–noon & 2–6pm; ☎05.57.88.70.82, fax 05.57.88.38.27, *syndicat.margaux@wanadoo.fr*), on the main road through the village. They don't offer tastings, but sell a selection of local wines and can advise on vineyard visits. It's necessary to book at least two weeks in advance to visit the impeccable *chais* of **Château Margaux** (☎05.57.88.83.83, *www.chateau-margaux.com*; by appointment only Mon–Fri 10am–noon & 2–4pm; closed Aug and during harvest; free), beyond the church on the east side of the village. Even without an appointment, however, it's worth approaching as far as the gates just to see its elegant Neoclassical facade. The château's wine, a classified Premier Cru and world-famous in the 1940s and 1950s, went through a rough patch in the two succeeding decades but has improved markedly since the estate was bought by a Greek family in the 1980s, and is now back as one of Bordeaux's premier wines.

Just south on the D2, with its owners' French, English and Dutch flags clearly visible across the vines, **Château Palmer** (☎05.57.88.72.72; April–Oct daily 9–11.30am & 2–5pm; Nov–March Mon–Fri same times ; free) is contrastingly welcoming to visitors. It is also Neoclassical in style, but this time with a strong hint of the Loire in its steep, grey-tiled roof and corner turrets. The very English name derives from a General Charles Palmer, from Bath, who bought the estate in 1814 only to completely mismanage it and go bankrupt. The wines were nevertheless classified in 1855 and now rank among Margaux's best. Another relatively easy place to visit is **Château Lascombes** (☎05.57.88.70.66; daily 9am–noon & 2–4.30pm; free), also a Cru Classé, on the northern outskirts of the village; it's of interest for its high-tech, computerized vinification methods.

The excellent Crus Bourgeois wines of **Château Siran** (☎05.57.88.34.04; daily 10.15am–6pm; free, tasting 25F/€3.81), a pale ruby-coloured *chartreuse* on the D209 4km southeast of Margaux, provide a good example of how the 1855 classification is in need of revision (see box on p.93). As an added attraction, since 1980 they have followed the example of Mouton-Rothschild (see p.98) in commissioning topical labels from well-known artists – most notably Joan Miró on a theme of the Football World Cup in 1982. These are reserved for their top wine under the Château Siran label, but they also produce a range of more modest wines including a Haut-Médoc and a Bordeaux-Supérieur.

Practicalities

Buses on the #705 Bordeaux–Pauillac route stop in the centre of Margaux village, while the **gare SNCF** lies less than a kilometre to the southwest. The Maison du Vin (see above), which also doubles as a **tourist office**, can provide information about **accommodation** in the area, but the choice is rather limited. Within Margaux itself, on the main road coming in from the south, there's the moderately expensive but very comfortable *Le Pavillon de Margaux* (☎05.57.88.77.54, fax 05.57.88.77.73; ⑤), with a fine restaurant (menus from 89F/€13.57; closed two weeks in Jan, also Tues & Wed out of season).

Besides the hotel, you can **eat** at Margaux's *Auberge de Savoie* (☎05.57.88.31.76; closed Sun, also Mon eve Oct–April & second half of Feb), next to the Maison du Vin, with good traditional food and menus at 85–220F/€12.96–33.54, though not always the warmest of welcomes. In spring and summer (April–Oct), however, there's nothing to beat the two *guinguettes* – casual, open-air restaurants – beside the river at **MACAU** port, 6km south of Margaux, where they serve platters of prawns, winkles, crabs and other delicacies straight from the Gironde (dishes from around 50F/€7.62).

In addition to the Maison du Vin (see above) and the châteaux themselves, another option for tasting and **buying wines** is La Cave d'Ulysse (closed Jan & Feb) in Margaux village, on the main road to the south of the centre. They stock a wide selection from all the Médoc *appellations* at very reasonable prices.

North towards St-Julien

Northwest of Margaux lie the two less-well-known Haut-Médoc *appellations*, **Moulis** and **Listrac**. At just six hundred hectares, Moulis has the smallest area under vines, while Listrac boasts the highest elevation at a grand 43m above sea level. The **wines** are full-bodied and, while there are no classified châteaux in the district, there are some notable Crus Bourgeois and Crus Artisans. To draw the tourists, a couple of châteaux have set up their own museums, which merit a look in passing, and on the coast there's also a ruined fort to provide some relief from the wine trail. If you're looking for a base in the Médoc, this area is worth considering since there are some more affordable accommodation options over to the west, particularly around Castelnau-de-Médoc.

To sample some of the best wine that **MOULIS-EN-MÉDOC** has to offer, head north on the D2 from Margaux for about 8km before turning left on the D5 to **Château Maucaillou** (☎05.56.58.01.23, *www.chateau-maucaillou.com*; daily 10am–noon & 2–6pm; 45F/€6.86). The château, constructed in 1875 in a fanciful mix of architectural styles ranging from Renaissance to railway-station, produces an elegant, fruity Cru Bourgeois as well as Haut-Médoc and Bordeaux AOC wines. Before tasting you learn all about the mysteries of modern wine production by visiting the vinification room and the *chais* and then see how things used to be in the unusually informative museum. Exhibits – mostly labelled in English – take you from planting via pruning and harvest to bottling, covering corks and cooperage on the way. The highlight, though, is a machine dispensing different aromas, such as herbs and spices, allowing you to test your sense of smell.

Pick up some picnic provisions in **LAMARQUE** village, a couple of kilometres to the east, before heading for the next stop, signed to the east a little further north off the D2 towards the river. **Fort Médoc** (May–Oct daily 9am–8pm; Nov–April Tues–Sun 10am–5.30pm; 12F/€1.83) was designed by the prolific military architect Vauban to defend the Gironde estuary, and thus Bordeaux, against British attack in the late seventeenth century. It formed the western end of a chain of three forts slung across the river, the others being Blaye and the island Fort Paté, but Fort Médoc soon began subsiding in the marshy ground and was abandoned. Though little remains of the buildings, Vauban's signature is still apparent in the moats, grassy ramparts and in the star-shaped ground-plan, and in summer the ruins have a leafy charm, marred only by a view of the nuclear power station across the river just north of Blaye. A very slow restoration project is under way, in aid of which there's an annual **jazz festival** in mid-July (see box on p.71 for details).

Like Château Maucaillou above, **Château Lanessan** (☎05.56.58.94.80; daily 9am–noon & 2–6pm; 35F/€5.34) distinguishes itself with a small museum of horse-drawn carriages in addition to its highly-rated but reasonably priced Haut-Médoc Cru Bourgeois. It's signed west off the D2 down a dirt track about 5km north of Lamarque, not long after **CUSSAC** village; note that it's the second château you come to. As with so many Médoc châteaux, Lanessan was rebuilt in the late nineteenth century, in this case by someone with a taste for neo-Tudor gables, mullions and tall skinny chimneys, and also with a passion for horses. The stable-block, where the museum is housed, was the last word in luxury: wood-lined stalls, marble water-troughs, even a tap for running water installed long before the château boasted such amenities. Not surprisingly, the carriages some of these pampered beasts pulled are also in immaculate condition. There are only ten in all, dating from 1884 to 1903, but the guide will explain what they were used for and point out their special features, such as their particular breaking, lighting or suspension systems.

Practicalities

Lamarque and Cussac are both stops on the #705 **bus** route while **trains** stop at the less convenient Listrac-Moulis station, midway between Moulis and Lamarque. Those with their own transport can cross the Gironde here on the Lamarque–Blaye **ferry** (30min; ☎05.57.42.04.49); there are at least four sailings per day in winter rising to ten during the summer peak.

As for **accommodation** in the area, the workaday town of **CASTELNAU-DE-MÉDOC**, on the main N125 Bordeaux–Pointe de Grave road 4km southwest of Moulis, has several reasonable options. In the town itself, on the junction with the D207 Carcans road, the *Hôtel Les Landes* (☎05.56.58.73.80, fax 05.56.58.11.59, *www.logis-de-france.fr*, ③) offers a clutch of simple, en-suite rooms above its popular restaurant, which serves generous, country meals (menus 60–160F/€9.15–24.39; closed Sun). Otherwise, there's a friendly **chambres d'hôtes** *Domaine de Carrat* (☎ & fax 05.56.58.24.80; ④) 500m southwest of Castelnau on the N125 and down a long drive. Its three spacious rooms, all en suite, occupy an old stable block among the pine trees; no meals, but kitchen facilities are available. Or, for something much grander, book well ahead to stay in one of four large *chambres d'hôtes* decorated with family heirlooms in *Château du Foulon* (☎05.56.58.20.18, fax 05.56.58.23.43; ⑥; closed mid-Dec to end Jan), a lovely nineteenth-century château surrounded by fifty hectares of park on the southern edge of Castelnau.

Five kilometres further north along the N125, **LISTRAC** is home to another welcoming small hotel, the *Auberge Médocaine* (☎ & fax 05.56.58.08.86; ② including breakfast); note that cheaper rooms lack toilets and showers, but the communal facilities are sufficiently clean. Its restaurant features eels in parsley sauce and *gambas* flambéed in Pineau among local dishes, and the desserts are good too (menus from 65F/€9.91). Alternatively, try the *chambres d'hôtes* at *Château Cap Léon Veyrin* (☎05.56.58.07.28, fax 05.56.58.07.50; ③), a working château 3km east of Listrac on the edge of **DONISSAN** village.

When it comes to **eating**, by far the best restaurant in the area is the *Lion d'Or* (☎05.56.58.96.79; closed Sun & Mon, all July & two weeks at Christmas) in **ARCINS** on the D2 a couple of kilometres south of Lamarque. Not only is the cooking excellent – from omelettes to local lamb or *tripe de porc* – and good value on the 65F/€9.91 lunchtime menu, but you can even take your own wine – local reds only. If they're full or closed, head to Lamarque and the very agreeable *L'Escale* (closed Wed & eves off season), down by the port; in season look out for elvers (*pibales*), shad (*alose*), lamprey (*lamproie*) and other local delicacies on their well-priced regional menus (from 60F/€9.15).

St-Julien to Pauillac

After crossing lower, marshy land given over to poplars and pasture, the D2 wine-route crests a slight rise before being met by the vines of **St-Julien**. Here you're back among the big-name estates – including Talbot, Branaire and Léoville-Barton, the latter graced by a beautiful eighteenth-century *chartreuse* still owned by the Irish Barton family. Here on the undulating higher ground the estuary is more in evidence and **Château Beychevelle** (☎05.56.73.20.70; May–Sept Mon–Sat 10am–noon & 1.30–5pm; Oct–April Mon–Fri 10am–noon & 1.30–5pm, by appointment only; free) in particular takes full advantage, with its long prospect down sloping lawns to the river over a kilometre away. Its name recalls that the Duc d'Épernon, Grand Admiral of France, lived here in the seventeenth century; as ships passed by the command was issued to *baisse-voile* ("strike sail") in salute. The château itself is a classic, long low white-stone Médoc mansion fronted by immaculate lawns and iron railings.

Two kilometres further on you pass through **ST-JULIEN** village, where the **restaurant** *Le St-Julien* (☎05.56.59.63.87; closed Tues eve & Wed Oct–March; menus from 95F/€14.48), known for its excellent local dishes, makes a good lunch stop. Otherwise, there's no reason to linger here. Better instead to press on northwards to the neighbouring **Pauillac** district and the most important of the Bordeaux vineyards: no fewer than three of the five Premiers Crus come from these stony soils. Vineyards here occupy larger single tracts of land than elsewhere in the Médoc, and consequently neighbouring wines can differ markedly: a good vintage Lafite is perfumed and refined, whereas a Mouton-Rothschild is strong and dark and requires long ageing to reach its best.

Though not among the top three, **Château Pichon-Longueville** (☎05.56.73.17.17; daily 9–11.30am & 2–5pm; free), one of the first châteaux you come to from the south, is not only a striking building but its state-of-the-art facilities provide one of the area's most interesting visits. Since acquiring the estate in 1987, the French insurance group AXA has invested enormous sums in restoring the château – installing, among other things, a severely rectangular lake to reflect its Disneyland spires – and in completely rebuilding the vinification plant and *chais* which are now partially underground. Their design allows year-round visits and enables you to see everything from where the grapes are sorted to the bottling plant and a store room containing one million precious bottles.

A visit to **Château Mouton-Rothschild** (by appointment only, ☎05.56.73.21.29; April–Oct daily 9.30–11am & 2–4pm; Nov–March Mon–Fri same times; 30F/€4.57, or 80F/€12.20 with one tasting), 2km northwest of Pauillac, on the other hand, is more about the mystique of the place. Though it is now one of the area's three Premiers Crus – the others being Lafite-Rothschild and Latour, with its distinctive round tower – Mouton-Rothschild was ranked only as a Second Growth until the classification was revised in 1973. That this happened was largely thanks to the efforts of Baron Philippe de Rothschild (1902–88), a great publicist and innovator who built up the estate after 1922 and the first producer to bottle all his wines at the château to ensure quality. The *mouton*, by the way, does not refer to a sheep, but is believed to derive from the little hill (*monton* in local dialect) on which the best vines grow; the two rams on the family crest came along later as a visual pun.

The château itself (not open to the public) is pretty but surprisingly unassuming. The old underground *chais*, however, are suitably atmospheric, the tunnel walls thick with a purple-black deposit accumulated over decades of condensing wine vapour. Two of the tunnels contain the family's private cellar of some 200,000 bottles of the world's top wines and there is also a priceless "archive" of every vintage produced on the estate over more than a century. Since 1955 international artists – Braque, Henry Moore and Warhol amongst others – have been invited to design the labels for each vintage, while even greater art treasures are in store, from Mesopotamian wine jugs to French tapestries, in the next-door museum of "wine in art" created by the baron in 1926, where the tour ends.

As these great estates developed in the eighteenth century, so **PAUILLAC** grew into a bustling port, then faded somewhat after the arrival of steamships, which sailed on up to Bordeaux, before reviving in recent years. It is now easily the largest town in the Médoc but, while its little fishing harbour and riverfront are pretty enough, they can't counteract the looming presence of the nuclear power plant across the Gironde. Nevertheless, it serves as a reasonable base, with transport services, banks, a post office and a few accommodation options in the area. It is also home to an endearing museum, **Le Petit Musée d'Automates** (July & Aug Mon–Sat 10.30am–7pm, Sun 2.30–7pm; May, June & Sept Tues–Sat 10.30am–12.30pm & 2.30–7pm; Oct–April Thurs–Sat or daily in school hols 10.30am–12.30pm & 2.30–7pm; 20F/€3.05); turn up semi-pedestrianized rue Aristide-Briand from the quay near the jetty and it's a few doors along on the right. Behind the Aladdin's cave of a shop the owners have created several anthropomorphic scenes of animals' lives, of which the highlight is a chaotic classroom. Great for kids.

Practicalities

Pauillac is the terminus for **buses** on the #705 route from Bordeaux and from early September to June there is also one daily connection (route #714; Mon–Fri only) on to St-Estèphe; buses stop on the riverfront near the *mairie* and at the **gare SNCF** on the northern edge of town, about five minutes' walk from the centre. The huge and helpful **Maison du Tourisme et du Vin** (July to mid-Sept daily 9am–7pm; June & mid-Sept to Oct daily 9.30am–12.30pm & 2–6.30pm; Nov–May Mon–Sat 9.30am–12.30pm & 2–6pm, Sun 10am–12.30pm & 2.30–6pm; ☎05.56.59.03.08, fax 05.56.59.23.38, *www.pauillac-medoc.com*) lies south along the waterfront. They don't reserve rooms but can provide you with a list of *gîtes* and *chambres d'hôtes*, rent out bikes and make appointments for you to visit the surrounding châteaux (25F/€3.81 per château). In summer (July to mid-Sept) they organize various activities such as introductory tasting courses (90F/€13.72) and their own vineyard tours (45F/€6.86). You can also buy wines here at châteaux prices, or try the area's two private **cellars**: La Cave des Mets d'Oc, at 68 rue du Maréchal-Joffre on the D2 near the *gare SNCF*, and La Pauillacaise, one kilometre further north. Both sell a good range of local wines, from vintage bottles to wine *en vrac* (by the litre), and other regional produce.

Wine also features strongly at **festivals** in Pauillac, one of the most active towns in the Médoc. Events include the Fête du Vin et du Terroir in late July and the Fête de l'Agneau in May (see box on p.70–71 for details).

The best place to **stay** in central Pauillac is the cheerful two-star *Hôtel de France et d'Angleterre*, opposite the little harbour (☎05.56.59.06.43, fax 05.56.59.02.31, *www.hotelfranceangleterre.com*; ④). Rooms are bright and comfortable if not exactly oozing character, but the restaurant is good, with menus from 75F/€11.43 and an excellent choice of Médoc wines (Oct–March closed Sun & Mon). Alternatively, there's an excellent *chambres d'hôte* about 8km northwest near the village of **CISSAC**: *Château Gugès* (☎05.56.59.58.04, fax 05.56.59.56.19; ④), in a large nineteenth-century house attached to a vineyard on the road to Gunes. If money is no object, treat yourself to a night at the plush *Château Cordeillan-Bages* (☎05.56.59.24.24, fax 05.56.59.01.89, *www.cordeillanbages.com;* closed mid-Dec to end Jan; ⑨; restaurant closed Mon & lunchtime Tues & Sat), a seventeenth-century manor house with 25 immaculate rooms surrounded by vines on Pauillac's southern outskirts. Even if you can't afford the room charges, it's worth considering for their reasonable 195F/€29.73 weekday lunch menu. The hotel doubles as a very upmarket school where you can take courses in appreciating local wines and gastronomy. At the other end of the scale, there's a spruce, welcoming riverfront **campsite** (☎05.56.59.10.03; April to mid-Sept) a kilometre south of the tourist office on route de la Rivière.

Apart from the hotels mentioned above, Pauillac is a bit short on decent **restaurants**. There are a number of café-brasseries along the riverfront and along rue Aristide-Briand near the museum. *Tielo*, at no. 28 (closed Sun & Mon), is popular for its mix of pizzas, salads and local dishes; menus from 55F/€8.38.

St-Estèphe and around

North of Pauillac, the wine commune of **St-Estèphe** is Médoc's largest *appellation*, consisting predominantly of Crus Bourgeois vineyards and producers belonging to the local *cave coopérative*, **Marquis de St-Estèphe**, on the D2 (July & Aug daily 9am–noon & 2–7pm; Sept–June Mon–Fri 9am–noon & 2–6pm). One of the *appellation*'s five Crus Classés is the unmistakable **Château Cos d'Estournel**, also on the D2 about 4km north of Pauillac. There's no château as such but its *chais* are housed in an over-the-top nineteenth-century French version of a pagoda, complete with a door from the Sultan of Zanzibar's palace. Except during August and the harvest, the *chais* can be visited, but requests must be made in writing at least two days in advance (☎05.56.73.15.50, fax 05.56.59.72.59, *estournel@estournel.com*). Otherwise, you can walk up to the front from the road.

The village of **ST-ESTÈPHE** itself is a sleepy affair dominated by its landmark, the eighteenth-century **church of St-Étienne**, every inch of its interior painted, gilded and sculpted; the choir is particularly beautiful. The small, active **Maison du Vin** (mid-June to mid-Sept daily 10am–7pm; April to mid-June & mid-Sept to Oct Mon–Fri 10am–noon & 2–6pm, Sat 2–6pm; Nov–March Mon–Fri 10am–noon & 2–5pm; ☎05.56.59.30.59), is hidden in the church square.

St-Estèphe marks the end of the wine-route. Beyond here you enter a more hilly, but also more marshy area which wasn't reclaimed until the nineteenth century. Local vineyards produce high-quality table wines mostly under the Médoc *appellation*, which often need laying down for several years. It's worth making a brief excursion to visit two châteaux with wine-related museums. The first you come to, some 3km north of St-Estèphe on the coast and still just within the Haut-Médoc wine region, is **Château Verdus** (☎05.56.73.17.31; Mon–Fri 9.30–11am & 2–5pm, Sun 2.30–5pm; 20F/€3.05 including tasting). The château has been in the same family since 1200 and boasts a huge, circular pigeon house beside the entrance. It's all a bit crumbling these days, but their collection of family heirlooms is of interest for the number of original documents; the wine, a Cru Bourgeois, is good too. Five kilometres further on, the pretty, rose-coloured **Château Loudenne** (☎05.56.73.17.80; Mon–Fri 9.30am–noon & 2–5.30pm; free) produces another very good Cru Bourgeois under the Médoc AOC as well as white and rosé Bordeaux wines. The museum is very well laid out, following a year in the life of the vineyard, and includes some rare pieces, such as an astonishingly large Spanish terracotta fermenting jar. Afterwards, take the time to wander round the gardens and down to the river.

Practicalities

From early September to June Citram **buses** (☎05.56.43.68.43) make a daily run on weekdays from Pauillac to Jau via St-Estèphe and twice daily to Lesparre where you can pick up **trains** on the Bordeaux–Pointe de Grave line. For an elegant place to **stay**, head south two kilometres to the village of **LEYSSAC**, also home to the nearest *gare SNCF*, where the elegant *Château Pomys* (☎05.56.59.73.44, fax 05.56.59.35.24; ④) offers ten comfortable rooms in a mansion set in its own park; it's also a working vineyard producing a Cru Bourgeois St-Estèphe. There are also several welcoming *chambres d'hôte* in the area, including *Le Clos de Puyzac* 3km west in Pez village (☎ & fax 05.56.59.35.28; ③) and, further west again near **VERTHEUIL-EN-MÉDOC**, the hacienda-style *Cantemerle* (☎ & fax 05.56.41.96.24, *www.bbfrance.com/tardat.html*; ④), both offering *tables d'hôte* on request.

Graves

The **Graves** region, encompassing a band of vineyards hugging the left bank of the Garonne southeast of Bordeaux, is the oldest of the city's wine-producing areas, originally planted during Roman times. Though now largely eclipsed by the Médoc, red Graves wines once provided the bulk of Bordeaux's wine exports, notably from the Pessac-Léognan *appellation* on the city's southern outskirts, where Château Haut-Brion still maintains a toehold amongst the suburban sprawl. The Graves heartland contains a series of wine towns which were once bustling river ports, linked by the main Bordeaux–Toulouse train line and busy N113. Though this isn't an area in which you'll want to linger, it's worth ducking off the main roads to visit fourteenth-century **Château de la Brède**, home to the philosopher Montesquieu, and at least some of the Graves' myriad wine producers. A good starting point is **Portets**, one of the more appealing riverside towns with a clutch of châteaux noted for their gardens or architecture in addition to their wines. For other ideas, call in at **Podensac's** well-run information centre, the Maison des Graves, which showcases a broad selection of local producers.

The region is relatively well served by **public transport**. Both local trains and regional bus services out of Bordeaux (see p.91) track the Garonne river, stopping at Portets and Podensac.

La Brède and around

One of the first villages you come to on leaving Bordeaux is surprisingly free of vines. Instead, sleepy **LA BRÈDE** is famous as the home of the philosopher Baron de Labrède et Montesquieu who was born in nearby **Château de la Brède** (30min guided tour: July–Sept Mon & Wed–Sun 2–6pm; April–June Sat & Sun 2–6pm; Oct to mid-Nov Sat & Sun 2–5.30pm; closed mid-Nov to March; 35F/€5.34) in 1689. The little castle, still occupied by the same family, is encircled by a picturesque moat and a vast English-style park – created by Montesquieu – which help soften the building's grey, rather austere edges.

Though he spent his winters in Paris hobnobbing with fellow philosophers, Montesquieu revelled in the peace and quiet of his country retreat. This is where he wrote some of his best-known essays, among them the highly influential political treatise *L'Esprit des Lois* ("The Spirit of Laws"), and where he amassed a

GRAVES WINES

The name **Graves** derives from *grabas*, the local term for the bed of sand and river pebbles, up to three metres thick in places, deposited over the centuries by the Garonne. Though hostile to most other crops, these harsh, gravelly soils provide the perfect conditions for vines – not only are they well drained but the stones' reflected heat also ensures good, all-round ripening. The region contains three *appellations*: **Graves** and **Pessac-Léognan**, both producing red and dry white wines, and the medium-sweet **Graves Supérieures**. Within this area the Sauternes enclave merits its own *appellation* (see p.104).

Until the eighteenth century Graves was Bordeaux's foremost wine-producing region. The red wines in particular were much in demand, with as much as sixteen million litres being exported annually to London by the late twelfth century, a figure that was not equalled until the 1960s. Graves' **golden age**, however, was the fifteenth to eighteenth centuries when many of today's great vineyards developed. Most notable among these was **Château Haut-Brion** where modern techniques introduced by the Pontac family revolutionized the production process. The Pontacs were also the first to market their wine under its château name, an event recorded by the London diarist Samuel Pepys in 1663: "Drank a sort of French wine, called Ho Bryan, that hath a good and most particular taste that I ever met with".

As the Médoc's star rose in the eighteenth century, so Graves' began to wane. Outbreaks of oïdium and then the deadly **phylloxera** in the late 1800s led many growers to turn their land over to pine trees, the only other crop able to tolerate such stony soils, and by 1935 the area under vines had decreased from 5000ha to a mere 1500ha. In the post war period, however, Graves wines have enjoyed a **renaissance** and previously neglected vineyards are once again producing quality wines. In recognition of this fact a **classification** system was introduced in the 1950s establishing sixteen Crus Classés, all of which fall within the Pessac-Léognan area. (Previously, only Château Haut-Brion was deemed worthy of Premier Cru Classé status when Bordeaux wines were classified in 1855.)

Red wines comprise two-thirds of Graves output. In general they have more body than the Médoc reds and age well over five-to-ten years to yield a fine, aromatic wine. Their distinctive flavour results from the balance of Cabernet Sauvignon, Merlot and Cabernet Franc grape varieties. Dry white Graves – a blend of Sémillon, Sauvignon and Muscadelle grapes – have evolved considerably over recent years to rank among the region's finest. The best, now often aged in oak barrels, peak at three-to-four years of age. Though Graves Crus Classés fetch up to 300F/€45.73 a bottle, the majority of Graves wines go for well under 100F/€15.24.

fabulous library of five thousand books, which was so weighty that in the nineteenth century the ceiling of the entrance hall below had to be strengthened with six stout, oak supports. Sadly, they are no longer required. In 1926 Montesquieu's cash-strapped descendants were forced to sell 1500 volumes, followed in 1939 by his manuscripts; the remaining books were donated to Bordeaux library for safekeeping in 1995.

Otherwise, the rooms you see on the tour have changed little since Montesquieu's time. Two sturdy trunks sit ready in the entrance hall surrounded by souvenirs of his travels, while his writing table occupies pride of place in the wood-panelled bedroom upstairs. Here too is a rare likeness in bas-relief sculpted just before he died in 1755. Towards the end of his life, his sight failing but his mind as sharp as ever, Montesquieu obliged his secretary to sleep in a small, adjoining bedroom, ready to take notes whenever inspiration struck. Records show that few secretaries sustained the onslaught for long.

After exploring the château's park and forest, there's nothing to detain you in La Brède itself beyond a couple of decent **restaurants**. *Maison des Graves*, 4 avenue Charles-de-Gaulle (☎05.56.20.24.45; closed Sun eve and Mon) has the edge, serving a good-value weekday lunch menu (78F/€11.89 including coffee and wine).

Portets to Podensac

PORTETS, set slightly off the N113 east of La Brède, is one of the Graves' more promising riverside towns with its neat church square and a quiet picnic spot down by the *halte nautique*. The main reason for coming here is to visit the delightful **Château de Mongenan** (July–Sept daily 10am–7pm; Easter–June daily 2–6pm; mid-Feb to Easter & Oct–Dec Sat & Sun 2–6pm; closed Jan to mid-Feb; 30F/€4.57) on Portets' western outskirts. This pretty little château contains a museum of eighteenth-century life commemorating one of its former owners, Antoine de Valdec de Lessart, who served as foreign minister under Louis XVI before being executed during the Revolution. Rare original documents, period costumes, faïence and fabrics fill every corner. There's a room devoted to de Lessart's herbarium as well as a *lieu à l'anglaise* – an indoor toilet complete with grape-draped cover, all the rage in the late 1700s – and a somewhat spooky mock-up of a Masonic lodge.

In 1741 de Lessart's predecessor, Baron de Gasq, created a beautiful, walled botanical garden inspired by Jean-Jacques Rousseau. It still exists today in front of the house, heavy with the perfume of old-fashioned roses, herbs, aromatic and medicinal plants alongside almost-forgotten varieties of vegetables. The family also continue traditional methods of wine production and you can end the visit by sampling their red and white Graves (20F/€3.05). Tastings are also available in nearby **Château de Portets** (by appointment only; ☎05.56.67.12.30), a much grander building a few hundred metres away overlooking the river, which also once belonged to the de Gasq family. You can't see inside, but the lovely formal garden is worth a visit – and the wines are good.

For information about other local vineyards, head south another 8km to **PODENSAC** where you'll find the helpful **Maison des Graves** (mid-April to mid-Nov Mon–Fri 9.30am–6.30pm, Sat & Sun 10.30am–6.30pm; mid-Nov to mid-April Mon–Fri 9am–5.30pm; ☎05.56.27.09.25). After watching a short video about the region and the process of wine production, you can browse their cellars, representing 300 wines from 150 properties in the Graves and Pessac-Léognan regions; prices are only marginally above châteaux rates. To help narrow the choice, it's possible to sample a couple of wines for free. Though staff can't arrange châteaux visits for you, they'll provide details of those that accept visitors.

One of the larger vineyards in the area and one of the easier to visit is **Château de Chantegrive** (Mon–Fri 9am–noon & 2–5pm; ☎05.56.27.17.38, *www.chantegrive.com*) on the southern edge of Podensac. It's of interest mainly for its ultra-modern vinification techniques and superb red-wine *chais* of 600 oak barrels. They produce a range of well-rated Graves red wines in addition to a prestigious, oak-aged dry white and a sweet wine under the Cérons *appellation*.

Sauternes and Barsac

The little Ciron river forms the eastern boundary of a region famous for a sweet white wine justly described as "bottled sunlight". Compared with the Graves, the **Sauternes** hills are slightly higher, the landscape more rolling and every inch of space is covered with neat rows of vines presided over by noble châteaux. The foremost of these, **Château d'Yquem**, requires a bit of organizing to visit, but plenty of others are more than happy to offer tastings and tours of their *chais*. **Château de Malle** also provides a rare opportunity to peek inside a lived-in château and stroll round its elegant Italianate garden. The region boasts a number of recommended restaurants, either in Sauternes village itself or across the Ciron in **Barsac**, which has its own sweet white *appellation*, while the main service town here is **Langon**, just outside the Sauternes region to the east, which also provides a convenient jumping-off point for the extravagantly decorated **Château Roquetaillade**, one of several local "Clémentine" fortresses built by relatives of Pope Clément V.

As regards **public transport**, you can reach both Barsac and Langon by local trains on the Bordeaux–Agen line and by regional bus services operating out of

SAUTERNES WINES

The distinctive golden wine of **Sauternes** is certainly sweet, but also round, full-bodied and spicy, with a long aftertaste. It's not necessarily a dessert wine, either: the balance of sugar and acidity marries well with Roquefort and other strong cheeses, delicately flavoured fish and foie gras. Sauternes should be drunk chilled but not icy, somewhere around 8–10°C.

The main grape variety is Sémillon, blended with Sauvignon and usually a tiny amount of Muscadelle for its musky aroma. Gravelly terraces with a limestone subsoil help create the smooth, subtle Sauternes taste, but mostly it's due to a peculiar microclimate of morning autumn mists and hot, sunny afternoons which causes the *Botrytis cinerea* fungus, or **"noble rot"**, to flourish on the grapes. By penetrating the skin, the mould allows water to evaporate, thus concentrating the sugars and pectins and intensifying the flavours.

Harvest time is a nerve-racking period for Sauternes producers. The climate has to be just right for *Botrytis* to work its magic: too much rain and the grapes soak up water again like a sponge; leave it too late and there's a risk of frost damage. As a result, harvests are both unpredictable and time-consuming. Each grape is individually picked only when it's reached the exact point of shrivelled, rotting maturity, a process which can take up to two months with pickers passing over the same vine again and again. Many grapes are rejected, giving an average yield of perhaps only one glass per vine – as opposed to one to three bottles elsewhere in the region. Though they can be drunk young and fruity, Sauternes wines only develop their full body at around ten years and are not truly at their best until at least twenty, even thirty years old. Not surprisingly, they are real luxuries, with bottles of Château d'Yquem, in particular, fetching thousands of francs.

Sauternes wines first came to the fore in the seventeenth century, when they were much prized in Holland. Such was their importance, in fact, that the wines were included in the **classification** at the Paris exhibition in 1855, when Château d'Yquem was awarded Premier Cru Supérieur. At the same time 21 other producers – now 26 as a result of land subdivision – were designated Crus Classés.

Bordeaux (see p.91). If you want to explore slightly further inland though, particularly around Sauternes, you really need your own transport.

Sauternes village

SAUTERNES itself is a trim but sedate village dominated by the **Maison du Sauternes** (Mon–Fri 9am–7pm, Sat & Sun 10am–7pm; ☎05.56.76.69.83) at one end, and a pretty church at the other. The *maison* is a treasure trove of golden bottles with white and gold labels. Although they do offer tastings, staff are unfortunately rather snooty about it unless you obviously intend to buy.

You can pick up information about visiting Sauternes châteaux, among other things, at the helpful **tourist office** (May–Oct daily 10am–noon & 2–5pm; Nov–April Mon–Sat same hours; ☎05.56.76.69.13, fax 05.57.31.00.67, *www.ot-sauternes.com*) halfway down the hill towards the church. They also offer **bike rental** (Tues–Sat only) should you wish to cycle round the vineyards. There's only one place **to stay** in the area, *chambres d'hôte de Broquet* (☎05.56.76.60.17, fax 05.56.76.61.74; ③), with four simple rooms and a swimming pool, about a kilometre southeast of the village.

There are, however, a couple of good **eating** opportunities in Sauternes. *Auberge Les Vignes* (☎05.56.76.60.06; closed Mon eve & Feb) is an atmospheric country restaurant beside the church with regional specialities such as *grillades aux Sarments* (meats grilled over vine clippings), a great wine list and a well-priced 65F/€9.91 menu. Otherwise, there's the more refined *Le Saprien* (☎05.56.76.60.87; closed five weeks Dec–Jan, also Mon & eves on Sun & Wed; menus from 130F/€19.82), opposite the tourist office, with the added bonus of a pleasant summer terrace. They serve lots of fish and modern variations of local dishes such curried sweetbreads and *lamproie au Sauternes* – the latter definitely an acquired taste.

The châteaux

The Sauternes *appellation* covers nearly 250 producers tending two thousand hectares of vines. The landscape is peppered with handsome châteaux, the majority of which offer tastings. Below we recommend a few to aim for.

Right on the southern edge of Sauternes village, **Château Filhot** (by appointment only Mon–Fri 8.30am–6pm; free; ☎05.56.76.61.09, *www.filhot.com*) was one of the Crus Classés designated in 1855. The elegant Neoclassical edifice looks out over its balustrades and terraces to a sheep-grazed English-style park. Its vineyard, which belongs to a branch of the same Lur-Saluces family who own Château d'Yquem, is one of the largest in Sauternes with an annual production of over 100,000 bottles.

Another Cru Classé vineyard is to be found at the more modest **Château Clos Haut-Peyraguey** (daily 9am–noon & 2–6pm; free), on the road north from Sauternes to Preignac, where you're guaranteed a warm welcome and a tour round the *chai*. Unfortunately, the same can't be said for **Château d'Yquem** further east along the same ridge of hills. To visit this world-famous château, the region's sole Premier Cru Supérieur, you have to apply in writing at least three weeks in advance (☎05.57.98.07.07, fax 05.57.98.07.08, *www.chateau-yquem.fr*; visits Mon–Fri 2.30 & 4pm). There's not even a sign at the entrance, but it's easy enough to spot, a honey-coloured sixteenth-century manor house with pepper-pot towers looking down over Château Lafon. The wines of Château d'Yquem were already highly valued in the sixteenth century but really came to prominence in the mid-1800s when the Lur-Saluces family perfected the technique of selecting the overripe grapes.

Continuing northwards, the next hill belongs to **Château de Suduiraut** (no fixed times; by appointment only; ☎05.56.63.61.92; *www.suduiraut.com*) surrounded by a walled park and looking down over the Garonne valley. The long, low château is now used for seminars, but you'll be shown round the *chai* and get a peek at the formal seventeenth-century gardens designed by Le Nôtre before tasting their Premier Cru Classé and AOC Sauternes wines.

Château de Malle (April–Oct daily 10am–noon & 2–6.30pm; 45F/€6.86 including tasting; ☎05.56.62.36.86, *www.chateau-de-malle.fr*), in the lowlands just beyond the motorway, straddles the Graves and Sauternes *appellations*. Alongside a Cru Classé, it produces not only a cheaper AOC Sauternes but also Graves reds and dry whites. This is also one of the few local châteaux you can actually see inside, albeit a mere four rooms, heavy with wood panelling and period furniture under the watchful gaze of ancestral portraits. More engaging is the manicured Italian park complete with fountains, statues, terraces and an open-air theatre. The château was built in the early seventeenth century by Jacques de Malle, a member of the Bordeaux parliament, before passing into the ubiquitous Lur-Saluces family by marriage.

Barsac

BARSAC, immediately west of the River Ciron, is a potentially attractive village ruined by the main road cutting through its centre. Although they fall within the Sauternes region, Barsac's sweet white **wines** are permitted their own *appellation*. In general they are lighter and fruitier than the neighbouring Sauternes, but it's a very subtle difference and the grape varieties, harvesting and production process (see box on p.104) are pretty much identical. To find out more about the area, call in at the **Maison du Vin** (daily 9am–7pm; ☎05.56.27.15.44, fax 05.56.27.03.71) which doubles as a tourist office and showcase for Barsac wines; find it on the main road, opposite the church.

On a back lane a couple of kilometres west of Barsac, **Château de Myrat** (year-round by appointment only; ☎05.56.27.15.06) is a medium-sized vineyard which has been revitalized in recent years. You can only get a glimpse of the château, hiding among trees behind wrought-iron gates, but the old-fashioned *chais* contain some nice antique presses and huge wooden collecting vats. The end product is a velvety-smooth Cru Classé.

Though there are no decent hotels around, there's a very nice place to **eat**, *Restaurant du Cap* (☎05.56.63.27.38; closed three weeks in Nov, also Sun eve & Mon; menus from 120F/€18.29), further east along the Garonne banks just before **PREIGNAC**. It's in a delightful position, with a duck pond and views across the river to Ste-Croix-du-Mont (see p.111).

Langon and Roquetaillade

With its transport connections and hotels, **LANGON**, 8km east of Sauternes village, provides a convenient base for exploring the Sauternes region, as well as further north into Graves, the southern reaches of Entre-Deux-Mers just across the

Garonne (see p.108), and the **Château de Roquetaillade** (see below). Two hundred years ago the town was an important river-port, linked to Bordeaux by passenger-steamer in 1818, but modern Langon has nothing particular in the way of sights beyond **St-Gervais church**, whose Chartres-like steeple dominates the old town centre.

The heart of Langon is place du Général-de-Gaulle. From here cours du Général-Leclerc leads west to the **gare SNCF**, where you'll also find the terminus for regional **buses**. The **tourist office** is located just off the central square at 11 allées Jean-Jaurès (July & Aug Mon–Sat 9am–5pm, Sun 10am–1pm; Sept–June Mon–Sat 9am–12.30pm & 2–6.30pm, Sun 9.30am–12.30pm; ☎05.56.63.68.00, fax 05.56.63.68.09, *office-du-tourisme-langon@wanadoo.fr*). They can help arrange châteaux visits and bike rental is also available, alongside detailed maps of the bicycle tracks and footpaths crisscrossing the area.

Langon boasts a range of **hotels**. The most appealing is the central, three-star *Claude Darroze*, 95 cours du Général-Leclerc (☎05.56.63.00.48, fax 05.56.63.41.15, *darroze@ot-sauternes.com*; closed Sun eve & Mon lunchtime, mid-Oct to mid-Nov & two weeks in Jan; ④). Its clutch of simple but comfortable rooms play second fiddle to one of the region's top restaurants, offering imaginative cuisine in elegant surroundings or, in summer, on a quiet shady terrace (menus from 220F/€33.54). For a mid-range hotel, try the *Horus*, 2 rue des Bruyères (☎05.56.62.36.37, fax 05.56.63.09.99; ③), located near the *autoroute* toll booths about 500m from the centre. Though characterless, the rooms are perfectly adequate, all with bathroom, TV and phone, and there's a decent in-house restaurant (menus from 70F/€10.67). Finally, there's the very basic *Mary-Lou* near the church at 38 cours Sadi-Carnot (☎05.56.63.09.32; restaurant with menus from 57F/€8.69; ①); note that cheaper rooms only merit the use of a communal shower and toilet.

Apart from the hotel **restaurants** mentioned above, there are a couple of good-value brasseries in town, though neither serve evening meals. *Le Maubec* (closed Sun), on place du Général-de-Gaulle, is popular with locals for its 65F/€9.90 *formule* and *plats du jour*. The smarter *Cercle des Amis Réunis*, opposite the tourist office on allées Jean-Jaurès, serves a limited range of salads and main courses for under 50F/€7.62.

Château de Roquetaillade

The **Château de Roquetaillade** (July & Aug daily 10.30am–7pm; Easter–June, Sept & Oct daily 2.30–6pm; Nov–Easter Sun 2.30–6pm; 35F/€5.34, or 45F/€6.86 including farm museum) sits in a twenty-hectare park about 7km south of Langon. With its solid central keep, crenellations and massive walls, it bears a strong resemblance to an English fortress – not so surprising given that it dates from the early 1300s when Aquitaine belonged to the English crown and new ideas of military architecture were being introduced. The castle was built by Cardinal Gaillard de la Mothe, nephew of Pope Clément V, and has been in the same family ever since, which partly explains why it is so well preserved. Another reason is the spunky character of former owner Marie Henriette de Lansac, who reputedly saved Roquetaillade from destruction in the Revolution. When the labourers arrived to demolish the castle she is said to have doubled their pay, asking them in return not to touch anything except the "good wine of Roquetaillade".

Even so, the castle you see today is not entirely genuine – the interiors in particular underwent extensive renovations in the late nineteenth century under the creative hands of **Viollet-le-Duc**, a restorer much in vogue at the time, but who has since been roundly criticized for his fairy-tale conception of medieval architecture. At Roquetaillade one of his colleagues went to work on the twelfth-century chapel with a colourful hotchpotch of Oriental, North African and European motifs. Viollet-le-Duc saved his own energies for the main castle where he added an extra gateway, decorative windows and machicolations around the parapet to create what he considered a medieval look.

Contemporary engravings show that, in fact, Viollet-le-Duc didn't tamper too much with the original facade, but **interiors** are another matter. The work was commissioned in 1886 by the then owner, Mauvesin, who wanted nothing but the best and could afford it thanks to his highly profitable Médoc vineyards. Viollet-le-Duc set to with gusto. He filled the entrance hall with a monumental white-stone staircase, painted every inch of wall – including two charming tricolour-winged angels in the Pink Room which presage the arrival of Art Nouveau – and even designed a complete dining-room suite. So long did all this take, however, that Mauvesin ran out of money in the mid-1870s when the architect was only halfway through the Great Hall. A small watercolour shows what he had in mind, but it's still an impressive room, dominated by a suitably exuberant Renaissance chimney piece. As you leave the castle's inner courtyard, look back at the carvings over the door: the two middle faces depict Mauvesin and his wife; that on the left, with the smile, is said to be Viollet-le-Duc.

Entre-Deux-Mers

The landscape of **Entre-Deux-Mers** (literally "between two seas") – so called because it is sandwiched between the tidal waters of the Dordogne and Garonne – is the prettiest of the Bordeaux wine regions. It's an area of gentle hills and scattered medieval villages, many of them *bastides* (see box on p.310) founded by the English during the Hundred Years' War, the most typical examples of which are **Sauveterre-de-Guyenne** and **Monségur**. Earlier builders and craftsmen left a legacy of Romanesque churches decorated with splendid carvings, which reached their apogee in the ruined abbeys of **La Sauve-Majeure**, **Blasimon** and **St-Ferme**. Moving on a few centuries, the artist Toulouse-Lautrec is commemorated at Château Malromé near **Verdelais**, where he spent much of his life, while **La Réole** is home to a wonderful collection of vintage cars.

Entre-Deux-Mers produces a wide variety of **wines**, but is best known for the dry whites which are regarded as good but inferior to the super-dry Graves (see p.102). The vineyards of Cadillac, Loupiac and Ste-Croix-du-Mont, three *appellations* overlooking the Garonne, also produce a sweet white wine comparable with many Sauternes, but at lower prices. Several Maisons du Vin scattered through the area provide tastings and advice on vineyard visits, as well as the opportunity to buy. For more general **information** about the region, contact the Office du Tourisme de l'Entre-Deux-Mers, 4 rue Issartier, Monségur (☎05.56.61.82.73, fax 05.56.61.89.13, *www.haut-entre-deux-mers.fr*).

While most of the sights of Entre-Deux-Mers are widely scattered, a surprising number are still accessible by **public transport**. Trains on the Bordeaux–Agen line stop at Langon (see p.106) and La Réole. These two towns are also the start of several useful bus routes, notably to Monségur, St-Ferme, Cadillac and Sauveterre-de-Guyenne. From Sauveterre buses also head west to La Sauve-

Majeur, en route to Bordeaux, and northwards via Blasimon to Libourne, where
they connect with trains on the Bordeaux–Paris mainline.

La Sauve-Majeure

The one place you should really try to see is the ruined Benedictine abbey in the
centre of Entre-Deux-Mers, about 23km east of Bordeaux, at **LA SAUVE-
MAJEURE** (June–Sept daily 10am–6.30pm; Oct–May 10am–12.30pm &
2.30–5.30pm; 25F/€3.81). Set in a tranquil valley of small vineyards and cornfields, it was once all forest here, the abbey's name being a corruption of the Latin
silva major ("big wood"). It was founded in 1079 by a hermit later known as St
Gérard and became an important stop for pilgrims en route to Spain's Santiago de
Compostela. Thanks to royal and papal backing, at its height La Sauve boasted
over seventy dependant priories stretching from England to Spain, but then fell
into slow decay until now only the apse and stumps of wall topped by a defiant
octagonal belltower remain.

Despite such neglect, a series of outstanding **sculpted capitals** – big, bold and
unusually low on the walls – has survived from the twelfth century. The finest are
those around the transepts and choir, some illustrating stories from the Old and
New Testaments, others showing fabulous beasts and vegetal motifs. In the little
chapels either side of the apse look out for Adam clutching his throat as Eve
hands him the apple, and a pensive Daniel in the lions' den. But the most remarkable scene occurs on a capital on the southern wall, near the entrance to the
tower, where the story of John the Baptist is depicted in astonishing detail. On
one side Salome dances as Herod twirls his moustache in appreciation; on the
other you see John's head being removed from the prison.

There's a small museum at the abbey entrance, containing keystones from the
fallen roof and fragments of painted wall, and the nearby grange now houses a
welcoming **Maison du Vin** (June–Sept daily 11am–6pm; Oct–May Mon–Fri
11am–noon & 2–5pm; ☎05.57.34.32.12) showcasing the dry white wines of the
Entre-Deux-Mers.

If you have the time, stroll over to the parish church of **St-Pierre**, visible on the
neighbouring hill, where St Gérard is buried (ask at the *mairie* if the church is
locked). Though built around the same time as the abbey, the church has survived intact, including its thirteenth-century frescoes (all bar one retouched in the
nineteenth century) showing St James and pilgrims on their way to Compostela.

La Sauve is on the **bus** route from Bordeaux to Targon, with a daily connection
(Mon–Fri) on to Sauveterre-de-Guyenne (see p.116). There's nowhere to stay in
the village, but you can **eat** well at the *Restaurant de l'Abbaye*, just below the ruins
(closed Sun eve & Mon), where fish features strongly (menus from 55F/€8.38).
Another good option would be the *Auberge du Lion d'Or* (☎05.56.23.90.23; open
daily for lunch, plus Fri & Sat eves) in the centre of **TARGON**, 6km southeast.
They offer traditional, country fare from a big choice of menus starting at
53F/€8.08 for lunch and 105F/€16.01 in the evenings.

Cadillac

Twenty kilometres south of La Sauve-Majeure, on the banks of the Garonne,
CADILLAC is as famous for its name as for the dour Renaissance **château** dom-
inating the town. According to local legend, Antoine Laumet, the founder of

Detroit, Michigan – home city of General Motors – originally came from Cadillac. Sadly, this is just too good to be true. He was born in St-Nicolas-de-la-Grave (see p.331), and on emigrating to Canada simply took the name of Lamothe-Cadillac, a family who had no connections with the town. It's recorded fact, however, that Cadillac was founded by the English in 1280, from which time a surprisingly long stretch of wall still exists, pierced by two gates: porte de l'Horloge to the south and westerly porte de la Mer. Though it lacks any particular charm, Cadillac's range of accommodation and eating options make it a useful base.

In the late sixteenth century the newly named Duc d'Épernon, a favourite of Henri III, was given permission to reconstruct a medieval castle at the confluence of the rivers Œuille and Garonne. His **Château de Cadillac**, on the north side of town (July & Aug daily 10am–8pm; April–June & Sept Tues–Sun 9.30am–12.30pm & 2–6pm; Oct–March Tues–Sun 10am–noon & 2–5.30pm; 25F/€3.81), took nearly thirty years to build and was so luxurious – with sixty bedrooms, twenty fireplaces, tapestries and richly painted woodwork – that it was said to rival the king's own palaces. No doubt it brought rich pickings to the revolutionaries who sacked the place in the 1790s, after which its echoing halls were turned into a notoriously harsh **women's prison**, the Maison Centrale de Force et de Correction. It's this last usage which seems most fitting as you cross the wide, bare courtyard, and which also provides the most interesting exhibits inside. Very little remains of the original decoration, with the notable exception of one or two painted ceilings and some magnificent Renaissance **fireplaces**, several of which are crumbling to pieces under the weight of years and over-exuberant plasterwork. Nevertheless, there's plenty to read about the history of the château and its occupants, including photos and documents relating to the prison, the majority of whose inmates were guilty of infanticide – often committed in the place of abortion. Conditions were extremely strict: absolute silence, a bread-and-water diet and no privacy. The great halls were converted into overcrowded dormitories and even the fireplaces were pressed into service as makeshift latrines. In stark contrast, the basement kitchen hides the most beautiful, slender stone spiral staircase tucked out of sight in its far corner.

While building his château, the Duc d'Épernon was also planning a grand mausoleum for himself in the nearby **church of St-Blaise**. Though his funeral monument was largely destroyed during the Revolution, the celebrated bronze statue of *Renommée* – a winged trumpeter – somehow survived (the original is in the Louvre); contemporary sketches on the chapel walls indicate what it must have looked like. The church's ornate altarpiece also dates from the same period. It features the Duke and Duchess's patron saints, Ste Marguerite and St John, to either side of a crucifixion scene.

Cadillac's sweet white wines – the result of a microclimate similar to that in Sauternes (see box on p.104) – are featured in a smart, new showroom, **La Closière** (May to mid-Sept daily 10am–12.30pm & 1.30–7pm; mid-Sept to April Mon–Fri 10am–12.30pm & 1.30–5pm; *www.cadillacgrainsnobles.com*), just out of town on the D10 to Langon. It also stocks other regional wines, notably under the Premières Côtes de Bordeaux Blancs and Rouges *appellations*, in addition to offering free tastings and vineyard tours.

Practicalities

Cadillac's nearest **gare SNCF** lies across the Garonne at Cerons, from where a taxi will cost around 40F/€6.10E, while **buses** between Bordeaux and Langon stop outside the ramparts on place de Lattre-de-Tassigny. The **tourist office** (July & Aug daily 9am–noon & 1–7pm; Sept–June Tues–Sat 9am–noon & 2–6pm, Sun 9am–noon & 3–6pm; ☎05.56.62.12.92, fax 05.56.76.99.72, *www.cadillac-tourisme.com*) is conveniently located in front of the château on place de la Libération.

The only decent **hotel** in Cadillac is the modern *Château de la Tour* (☎05.56.76.92.00, fax 05.56.62.11.59, *www.chateaudelatour.fr*; ⑤), with a garden, swimming pool and a good restaurant (menus 95–340F/€14.48–51.83; Nov–April closed Fri eve, Sat & Sun), beside the D10 just north of town. There are, however, several excellent **chambres d'hôtes** in the area. Pick of the bunch, *Château du Grand Branet* (☎05.56.72.17.30, fax 05.56.72.17.30; ③), a wine-château 11km north near **CAPIAN** village, offers splendid accommodation in big, en-suite rooms, with *table d'hôte* on request. Other options include *Château Le Vert* (☎ & fax 05.56.23.91.49; ④), 7km northwest on the D11 to Targon, also offering *table d'hôte*, and the more modest *Château du Broustaret* (☎05.56.62.96.97, fax 05.56.76.93.73; Easter–Oct; ③), 5km from Cadillac on the same road. This last overlooks an artificial swimming and fishing lake, the lac de Laromet, where you'll also find a two-star **campsite**, *Camping de Hontanille* (☎05.56.62.12.72; mid-June to mid-Sept).

When it comes to **eating**, there's a clutch of cafés and brasseries around central place de la République – venue for a Saturday morning market. The town's top restaurant lies just north of this square on rue de l'Œuille, where *Entrée Jardin* (☎05.56.76.96.96; closed Mon; menus from 62F/€9.45) serves up imaginative dishes such as duck breast with honey and spices; allow plenty of time, however, since service can be slow. *Les Remparts* (☎05.56.76.90.77; closed Wed), on the main road just outside porte de la Mer, is a popular pizza place which also turns out decent salads and a choice of local dishes; there are no fixed menus, but you can eat well for 100F/€15.24 or less.

Upstream to Verdelais

Either side of Cadillac the Entre-Deux-Mers plateau edges closer to the Garonne. There are good **viewpoints** all along the escarpment, but one of the finest is from the village of **STE-CROIX-DU-MONT** about 6km to the southwest. Aim for the terrace running in front of the church and the medieval Château de Tastes, now the *mairie*, perched on the cliff edge. The **cliff** itself is also of interest. Its top layer, ranging in thickness from three to eight metres and extending back under the village, is composed of fossilized oyster shells deposited some 25 million years ago. The bed has been hollowed out in various places into shallow caves, one of which now forms an unusual showroom for the local wine growers' association, in the cliff below the church (April to mid-Oct Mon, Tues, Thurs & Fri 2.30–6.30pm, Sat & Sun 10am–12.30pm & 2.30–7/8pm). From the grassy terrace you can raise a glass of their sweet white wine (10F/€1.52 per glass), which merits its own *appellation*, to the rival Sauternes vineyards on the far side of the Garonne.

A few kilometres east of here, **VERDELAIS** offers more views and an ornate Baroque **church**, every inch covered with votive plaques dedicated to a miracle-performing statue of the Virgin and Child. Verdelais' first recorded miracle took place in 1185 and pilgrims have been flocking here ever since. Many of them left gifts of paintings, silver hearts and bejewelled cloaks for the statue in thanks, and a fraction of the collection is on display at the nearby **Musée d'Art Religieux** (July & Aug daily 3–7pm; May, June & Sept–Nov Wed–Sun 3–7pm; Dec–April Tues–Fri 2–6pm; 20F/€3.05). The most interesting exhibits are the paintings portraying young children returned to health, and various storm-tossed ships – you'll also find lovely, scale-model boats donated by shipwrecked sailors from the latter.

Verdelais' main claim to fame these days, however, is the **tomb of Toulouse-Lautrec** (see box below) which lies across the road in the church cemetery; go straight ahead from the entrance gate to find it last on the left. From here you can walk on up past the Stations of the Cross, represented here by sculpted tableaux, for views south to Langon and west to Ste-Croix.

Henri Toulouse-Lautrec spent his summers a couple of kilometres northeast of Verdelais in the enchanting **Château Malromé** (30min guided tour: July & Aug daily 10am–noon & 2–6.30pm; April–June & Sept–Nov Thurs–Sat 3–5pm, Sun 2–6pm; closed Dec–March; *www.malrome.com*; 30F/€4.57). His mother, the

---

TOULOUSE-LAUTREC

Known for his provocative portraits of Parisian low-life, **Henri Toulouse-Lautrec** was born in Albi, northeast of Toulouse, in 1864. His father, Count Alphonse de Toulouse-Lautrec, was a highly eccentric man with a passion for hunting, illicit affairs and bizarre outfits, who married his first cousin. This genetic mismatch is blamed for Henri's stunted growth and delicate constitution, exacerbated by two childhood accidents which left him permanently crippled. Nevertheless, encouraged by an uncle and two family friends who spotted his artistic talent, Henri went to study in Paris under Bonnat and Cormon before setting up his own studio in **Montmartre** in 1884.

Henri was in his element. He produced hundreds of paintings and sketches portraying the unglamorous reality of life in the cabarets, theatres, bars and brothels of *fin-de-siécle* Paris. Among his most famous works are those associated with the **Moulin Rouge**, which Henri began to frequent in 1890, recording events offstage as well as the great music-hall artists of the day: Yvette Guilbert, Jane Avril and May Belfort, among many others. The portraits are often grotesque, with a strong element of caricature, but his affection for his subjects shines through. This is particularly true of his works in the *maisons closes*, when the prostitutes – if not their clients – are treated with great sympathy and sensitivity.

The bohemian life and excess of alcohol gradually took its toll. In 1900 Henri returned to southwest France to set up a studio in Bordeaux where the café and theatre world provided ample subject matter. But the following year, as his health began to deteriorate, he was taken back to Malromé, where he died on September 9, aged 37 years. Though originally buried in the nearby cemetery of St-André-du-Bois, in 1908 Henri's body was moved to **Verdelais**, where his mother eventually joined him.

Thanks to the uncompromising nature of much of his work, Toulouse-Lautrec met with little critical success during his lifetime. His portraits were far too shocking for mainstream contemporary tastes and even in the 1920s both the Louvre and Toulouse city refused the family's gift of six hundred paintings, posters and sketches. The magnificent collection went instead to Albi. Since then Toulouse-Lautrec has been recognized as one of the founders of modern advertising, while his dynamic, almost calligraphic lines and bold swathes of colour have won worldwide acclaim.

Countess Adèle de Toulouse-Lautrec, bought the château in 1883 and had it renovated in neo-medieval style according to the then-fashionable ideas of Viollet-le-
Duc (see p.108). Though the mansion is still occupied, the interiors have been
preserved much as they were in Henri's time with dark wall-fabrics and period
furniture. There's even a jaunty self-portrait sketched on one wall, which was discovered during 1950s restoration work, and one or two engaging family photographs, including the eccentric, kimono-clad Henri balancing a carafe of wine
on his head. The paintings and drawings on display – all copies – give a further
glimpse into the artist's extraordinary life, combining the rural gentility of
Malromé with his favourite stomping ground among the bars and brothels of
Montmartre. The tour ends with a *dégustation*; after she acquired the château
the countess rescued its neglected vineyard, which now produces eminently
palatable red and white wines and a Clairet, a light red wine drunk chilled in
summer.

If you're looking for somewhere to stay in the area, head south to St-Macaire (see
below), or continue north on the D19 to St-Germain-de-Graves, where you'll find a
simple country **hotel**, the *Auberge du Pot de Fonte* (☎ & fax 05.56.76.41.12; closed
three weeks Jan–Feb; ②), at the end of a lane among woods and vines. Their restaurant is in the same vein, serving regional dishes such as *trempique*, a chilled summer soup, and local wines (menus from 80F/€12.20; closed Tues & Wed).

St-Macaire

Just across the Garonne from Langon (see p.106), and some 12km southeast of
Cadillac, **ST-MACAIRE** provides a more attractive alternative base, though it's a
bit dead out of season. The town was founded in the first century AD by an itin-
erant Greek monk called Makarios. Later it grew wealthy on the winetrade, so
that by the mid-fourteenth century the population had reached 6000, only to
decline from the early 1600s onwards as the river shifted and the port silted up.
These days St-Macaire musters a mere 1500 souls but still retains several of its
original gates and battlements as well as a beautiful medieval church.

St-Macaire's glory days are also still evident in the number of dignified edifices,
the homes of wealthy merchants, many of which are now being done up. Some of
the most handsome lie just inside **Porte Benauge**, the main north gate, and
around the old market square, **place Mercadiou**, to the east. The **church of St
Sauveur**, on the other hand, occupies an abandoned river cliff on the south side
of town – nothing remains of the original Benedictine priory beyond a fragment
of cloister-wall, but the fourteenth-century murals inside the church are what
everybody comes to see. They were somewhat crudely restored – and embell-
ished – in 1825, but even so present a fine spectacle; it's worth forking out
10F/€1.52 for the lighting. While the scenes behind the altar are based on St
John the Evangelist's Revelation, his miracles and martyrdom in a vat of boiling
oil are depicted over the transept.

St-Macaire might not seem the natural home for tropical fish, but the little
underground **aquarium** (April–Oct daily 9am–7pm; 35F/€5.34) just outside
Porte Benauge is better than one might expect. This is mostly thanks to its passionate owner, Pierre Rodriguez, who has gathered together over 350 of the
world's most colourful and unusual varieties, including piranha, puffer fish, wispy
rascasse volante – a type of scorpion fish – and the glorious emperor angel fish.

Practicalities

A couple of **trains** a day stop at St-Macaire station, less than half a kilometre north of town, or there are more frequent services to Langon (see p.106), from where **buses** headed for Bordeaux or Sauveterre-de-Guyenne will drop you outside Porte Benauge. St-Macaire's well-organized **tourist office** (April–Sept Tues–Sat 10am–12.30pm, Sun 2–7pm; Oct–March Tues–Sat 10am–noon & 2–6pm; ☎05.56.63.32.14, fax 05.56.76.13.24) occupies a handsome, sixteenth-century merchant's house just inside the gate. The office doubles as a Maison du Pays promoting regional produce, which here means honey and wine. Staff can help arrange visits to the *chais* and in season (April–June Sat & Sun; July & Aug daily) they organize tastings hosted by various local wine-makers. Wine also figures prominently during St-Macaire's biggest **festival**, Les Nuits Macariennes, which takes place during July and August, featuring concerts in the church, theatre, folk music and outdoor cinema.

The nicest **hotel** in town is *Les Feuilles d'Acanthe* (☎05.56.62.33.75, fax 05.56.76.12.02; closed Jan; ④) occupying another beautifully restored building opposite the tourist office. The decor is modern but stylish, featuring exposed stone walls and terracotta tiles, in addition to gleaming en-suite bathrooms. Their *Le Pampillet* restaurant serves a choice of *crêpes* and more substantial regional dishes – menus start at 50F/€7.62 for a weekday lunch. Another good option is *Les Tilleuls* (☎05.56.62.28.38, fax 04.79.59.13.44; closed four weeks Jan–Feb; ③; restaurant from 85F/€12.96, closed Wed), which offers bright, spacious rooms with cooking facilities.

As far as **eating** goes, *L'Abricotier* (☎05.56.76.83.63; closed mid-Nov to mid-Dec), west of town on the busy N113, may not look much from the outside but this is one of the region's top restaurants. It's best in summer when tables spread out into the pretty, walled garden, but the food remains excellent all year, featuring shad, lamprey and other local fish as well as game in season (menus from 115F/€17.53, closed Mon & Tues eves). They also have three very comfortable rooms, again with kitchenettes (④); advance booking is essential.

La Réole and around

LA RÉOLE, 20km east of St-Macaire along the same escarpment, hides a wealth of medieval architecture among its narrow, hilly streets, but somehow feels cramped and dowdy as opposed to quaintly aged. That said, France's oldest town hall and the well-preserved Benedictine abbey – with expansive views over the Garonne and the surrounding countryside – reward a stroll through the town, while a couple of nearby museums are also worth a visit. Good transport connections and a choice of restaurants make La Réole a possible overnight stop, but you'll have to go out of town to find any particularly inspiring accommodation.

Starting next to the tourist office on place de la Libération, crossed by the busy N113, semi-pedestrianized **rue Armand-Caduc** leads southwest to the church of St-Pierre and the entrance to the former cloister of the **Benedictine abbey**, founded in the tenth century by the Bishop of Bazas; the town name derives from Regula, meaning Benedictine Rule. The abbey was rebuilt in the early 1700s but by the time it was complete Revolution was in the air and in 1791 the buildings were taken over by the local administration, which is still in residence. The building's main attributes are a grand stone staircase with an elegant iron banister lit by a graceful, elliptical lantern, and some good wrought ironwork by local master-craftsman Blaise Charlut, who was also responsible for the screens in Bordeaux cathedral (see p.82). You can admire the best of his craftsmanship in the gates of the southern door from where a pretty double staircase leads down onto a wide terrace overlooking the Garonne. On a clear winter's day it's even possible to see the Pyrenees from here.

In medieval times La Réole was the region's second largest town after Bordeaux. To ensure their loyalty, Richard the Lionheart granted its townspeople a certain degree of self-government and ordered the building of a town hall. Even today, La Réole is fiercely proud of what is France's oldest surviving **Hôtel de Ville**. Not that there's much to see. The big, open hall downstairs has a few carved capitals, while proclamations were presumably made from the modest balcony on the north side; for now the first-floor meeting hall is closed to the public for safety reasons. To reach the hall, retrace your steps along rue Armand-Caduc and take a left down rue Peysseguin, one of La Réole's most atmospheric streets with one or two handsome town houses and a smattering of half-timbered facades.

There's no shortage of exhibits, on the other hand, at **Les Musées de la Réole** (mid-June to mid-Sept daily 10am–6pm; April to mid-June & mid-Sept to Nov Wed–Sat 2–6pm, Sun 10am–6pm; Dec–March Wed & Sat 2–6pm, Sun 1–6pm; closed two weeks in Dec; *www.les-musees.com*; 60F/€9.15), next to the main N113 on the eastern outskirts of La Réole. The former tobacco factory combines four museums – classic cars, trains, military vehicles and agricultural equipment – of which the undoubted highlight is the stunning collection of over 100 gleaming cars. All the big names from automobile history are here besides a number of extremely rare vehicles – from Auburn and AC Cobra to Rolls Royce and Renault. Look out, too, for a Citroën from the Paris–Peking rally of 1931–32 and a Model T Ford supposedly used in the Laurel and Hardy films. The military section, with its limited array of tanks, radio cars and command vehicles, is also worth a quick look, while railway buffs will appreciate the model train sets and related paraphernalia on the top floor.

The second museum of interest is a couple of kilometres south of La Réole, just the other side of the Canal des Deux-Mers, in the village of **FONTET**. The bizarre **Musée d'Artisanat Monuments en Allumettes** (March–Sept daily 2–6pm; Oct–Feb Sun 2–6pm; 15F/€2.290) is dedicated to scale models made of matchsticks. So far the enthusiastic owner has used over 600,000 – he buys them without sulphur direct from the factory – to create his architectural models of Notre-Dame, complete with swinging bells which took three years to construct, and the abbey of La Réole, among others. Needless to say, sparking up is strictly forbidden. The museum has recently expanded to include works by other local artisans such as model ships, trains and agricultural scenes. Afterwards, walk along the canal to find a pleasant picnic spot beside the *halte nautique*.

Practicalities

La Réole's **gare SNCF** is located a little way east of town, from where it's a steep ten-minute walk to the centre. If you're travelling by **bus** you'll have to come via Sauveterre-de-Guyenne (see overleaf); buses stop on central place de la Libération while some also take in the *gare*. Place de la Libération is also home to the **tourist office** (Mon 3–6pm, Tues–Sat 9am–noon & 3–6pm; Easter–Oct also open Sun 3–6pm; ☎05.56.61.13.55, fax 05.56.71.25.40), where you can buy an English-language leaflet (10F/€1.52) outlining a walking tour of the main sights.

For **accommodation**, the central, two-star *Hôtel de l'Abbaye*, 42 rue Armand-Caduc (☎05.56.61.02.64, fax 05.56.71.24.40; ③), on the road up to the abbey, is a bit chaotic, but the rooms, all with bathroom, TV and phone, are clean and not too bad for the price. La Réole's only other hotel consists of a handful of very basic rooms above the *Auberge Réolaise* (☎ & fax 05.56.61.01.33; closed Fri, also one week in April & three weeks in Nov; ①), on the N113 near the automobile museum (ask for rooms at the back), which is more of interest for its traditional restaurant (menus from 60F/€9.15). Otherwise, it's best to head three kilometres north on the D21 to St-Sève, where you'll find two **chambres d'hôtes**: the stylish and very popular *Domaine de la Charmaie* (☎05.56.61.10.72, fax 05.56.61.27.21; ④; meals on request), and the more rustic *Au Canton* (☎ & fax 05.56.61.04.88; ④). Finally, La Réole's well-run, two-star municipal **campsite**, *Le Rouergue* (☎05.56.61.04.03; Easter–Oct), lies just across the old suspension bridge, with great views back to the abbey.

A good **restaurant** is the light and airy *Les Fontaines* on rue de Verdun (☎05.56.61.15.25; closed Sun eve & Mon; also fifteen days in both Feb & Nov), with a terrace looking across to the old Hôtel de Ville. The food consists of classic French cuisine, albeit with a modern touch, and there's a wide choice of menus 85–240F/€12.96–36.59). You'll also find a warm welcome just off rue Armand-Caduc at *Le Régula*, 31 rue André-Benac (05.56.61.13.52; closed Tues eve & Wed; July & Aug closed Tues eve only), where they continue serving till relatively late. Menus (from 60F/€9.15) feature regional favourites such as *croustillant de canard* and foie gras, or you can try kangaroo fillet. *Le Colvert*, 54 rue Armand-Caduc, dishes up reasonable brasserie fare, and you can get a no-nonsense meal at the *Auberge Réolaise* (see "accommodation" above).

La Réole's main **market** takes place on Saturday mornings on the esplanade des Quais along the Garonne – a good place to stock up on picnic provisions if you're passing. A few stalls also gather on Wednesdays beside the Hôtel de Ville, and on place de la Libération on Sunday mornings.

Sauveterre-de-Guyenne and around

The majority of *bastides* in Entre-Deux-Mers were founded by the English. Of these, perhaps one of the most typical is **Sauveterre-de-Guyenne**, 14km north of La Réole, which was established under Edward I in 1281. The surrounding countryside is peppered with Romanesque churches, some with lovely carved portals, such as at **Castelviel** and **Blasimon**.

Sauveterre-de-Guyenne

With its large, arcaded central square, gate-towers and gridiron street plan, **SAUVETERRE-DE-GUYENNE** is a good example of a *bastide* (see box on p.310). The ramparts themselves were demolished in 1814, replaced by what is now a ring-road, but they must have been a bit battered – Sauveterre changed hands ten times during the Hundred Years' War before finally falling to the French in 1451. The town boasts no real sights of its own, but is big enough to merit a couple of hotels and services grouped round place de la République, the venue for a lively Tuesday-morning **market**. The square is also home to the **Maison du Vin** (Tues–Fri 8am–12.30pm & 3–7pm, Sat 9am–noon & 3–7pm; ☎05.56.71.61.28), where you can buy local wines at the producers' price.

Sauveterre has good bus connections to Langon, Libourne and La Réole; **buses** stop on the ring-road just outside westerly porte Saubotte. You can find out more about these services and get other local information at the well-organized **tourist office** (Feb–Dec Tues–Fri 10am–noon & 2–6pm, Sat & Sun 9am–noon & 3–6pm; ☎05.56.71.53.45, fax 05.56.71.59.39) in the southwest corner of the central square.

There's a choice of two modest **hotels**, both with decent **restaurants**. On the market square, *Le Croix Blanche* (☎05.56.71.50.21; ②) offers four simple rooms, though only two have windows and they suffer a bit from being next to the kitchens. The restaurant, however, is the marginally better of the two, offering an excellent-value 58F/€8.84 menu including wine, plus a good range of salads, omelettes and so forth. The *Hôtel de Guyenne* (☎05.56.71.54.92, fax 05.56.71.62.91, *www.logis-de-france.fr*, ①), on the ring-road outside porte Saubotte, has a choice of rooms with or without en-suite facilities. The former are larger and offer better value for money, but ask for a room at the back to avoid traffic noise. Their two-course *menu express* (48F/€7.32 including wine) is a popular choice. The municipal **campsite** (☎05.56.71.56.95; open all year) is in the throes of moving – check with the tourist office for the latest situation.

Around Sauveterre-de-Guyenne

Seven kilometres southwest of Sauveterre, through a rolling landscape of vines and windmills, lies the tiny, flowery village of **CASTELVIEL**, worth a visit for the carved south portal of its well-buttressed, twelfth-century **church**, lying in the southwest corner. Though they're a bit worn in places, it's still possible to make out a wealth of detail on the portal's five tiers. The outer arch depicts scenes from rural life; on the second the Vices confront the Virtues; the third, which resembles a tug-of-war, represents the faithful united by their common bond. Monsters, biblical characters and layers of interlocking vegetation overspill from the remaining tiers to two small, flanking arches.

The same distance north of Sauveterre, **BLASIMON**, founded by the English in 1322, was one of the very last *bastides* constructed in the region. The town occupies a rocky promontory looking north over the Gamage valley and a ruined **abbey** (see below; 10F/€1.52) established by Benedictine monks in the seventh century. The cloister and abbey buildings, which were obviously fortified at some time, were abandoned in the thirteenth century, but the church itself has survived. Again, it's the twelfth century Romanesque carvings round the **west door** that are most absorbing. The elongated, sinuous figures of the Vices and Virtues in particular are so incredibly delicate it's hard to believe their age. In other places the soft stone has weathered badly, though not so much that you can't identify the angels adoring the Lamb of God on the inner tier, hunting scenes on the outer edge, and at least get the gist of the exuberant motifs in between. The interior is contrastingly unadorned save for the captivating faces on the capitals to either side of the entrance door.

If the church is locked, ask for the key either at the *mairie* on the main village square or at the **tourist office** (June–Sept daily 8–11am & 4–9pm; Oct–May Mon–Fri 10am–noon & 2–7pm; ☎05.56.71.59.62, fax 05.56.71.53.37) located at the *Camping du Lac*, 3km northwest on the Rauzan road. Blasimon lies on the **bus** route between Sauveterre and Libourne; two to three services a day (Mon–Sat) in each direction make it a possible day-trip.

If you're looking for **accommodation** in the area, a good choice would be *Château Lardier* (☎05.57.40.54.11, fax 05.57.40.72.35, *chateau.lardier@free.fr*; closed Nov–Feb; ③) signposted east off the D17 to Castillon-La-Bataille some 7km north of Blasimon. This handsome, ivy-covered wine château offers eight very comfortable, en-suite rooms, swimming pool and lush garden. They don't serve food, but you can picnic or rustle up a barbecue and there are a couple of good **restaurants** not too far away. The nicest is the *Auberge Gasconne* (☎05.57.40.52.08; closed Sun eve & Mon; also one week in both Feb & April, two weeks Aug–Sept) in **ST-PEY-DE-CASTETS**, west of the D17. It's a typical village inn, with an excellent 65F/€9.91 weekday lunch menu including wine, and other menus from 135F/€20.58. At present they're only open for dinner on Friday and Saturday, but may offer additional days in season so it's worth phoning to check. The other option is in **RAUZAN** village, 6km northwest of Blasimon, where the smarter *Le Gentilhommière* (☎05.57.84.13.42; closed Mon) serves well-prepared traditional dishes; menus are 62–98F/€9.45–14.94. Rauzan also boasts an excellent, two-star **campsite**, *Camping du Vieux Château* (☎05.57.84.15.38, fax 05.57.84.18.34; April–Oct), in the valley beneath the ruined castle ramparts. Blasimon's campsite, the three-star *Camping du Lac* (☎05.56.71.55.62; mid-April to Sept), is also recommended. Part of a leisure complex 3km northwest of Blasimon, it comprises a fifty-hectare park with swimming lake (supervised in season), playground, snack bar and so forth.

Monségur and St-Ferme

On the eastern fringes of the Entre-Deux-Mers region, some 20km northeast of La Réole, **Monségur** makes a good base for exploring the fertile Dropt valley and neighbouring Duras (see p.182). It's also within striking distance of the abbey of **St-Ferme**, home to more exquisite carvings.

Monségur

Like Sauveterre-de-Guyenne, **MONSÉGUR** is another good example of a *bastide*, in this case occupying a hill-top site. It was founded a couple of decades earlier, in 1265, also by the English, and though its **market square** is much more confined, there are one or two attractive houses in the narrow streets. Where the **ramparts** once stood a grassy two-kilometre walkway now takes you almost three-quarters of the way round the town; on the north side, look out for the fortified mill down on the River Dropt. That just about exhausts Monségur's sights, but it makes up for it with some reasonable options for eating or even an overnight stay, and if you happen to visit on the first weekend in July you'll hit its biggest annual bash, the *24 Heures du Swing* **jazz festival**, which takes place throughout the town (entry by ticket only).

Monségur is served by **buses** from La Réole and Sauveterre. The **tourist office** is located east of the central square at 33 rue des Victimes (June–Sept Tues–Sat 9am–12.30pm & 2.30–6pm, Sun 9.30am–12.30pm; Oct–May Tues & Fri 8.30am–noon & 2–5pm, Sun 10am–noon; ☎ & fax 05.56.61.89.40). There's a great traditional **market** on Friday mornings under the nineteenth-century *halle*, a smaller farmers' market on Tuesdays and a *foire au gras* on the second Sunday in December and in February, while early May brings a riot of colour with its *foire au fleurs*.

Modest, old-fashioned **accommodation** is available at the *Grand Hotel* (☎05.56.61.06.28, fax 05.56.61.63.89; ②) on the central square; note that cheaper rooms are equipped with a shower and basin, but no toilet. You can eat here, too – unspectacular but perfectly acceptable and plentiful home cooking (menus 53–170F/€8.08–25.92). *Château de la Bûche*, 10 avenue Porte-des-Tours (☎05.56.61.80.22, fax 05.56.61.85.99; closed Nov–March; ③), on Monségur's eastern edge, offers five spacious *chambres d'hôtes* in a nineteenth-century château with a garden running down the valley side. The friendly owners provide evening meals on request (120F/€18.29) – though there's also a well-equipped kitchen – and also offer introductory wine-tasting courses in English. Campers should head for *L'Étoiles du Drot* (☎05.56.61.67.54), a well-tended, two-star municipal **campsite** just below the village on the La Réole road. It's one of the few in the area open all year.

For **eating**, in Monségur itself there's a choice between the *Grand Hotel* (see above) and the more rustic *Les Tilleuls* (menus from 60F/€9.15; lunch only; closed Sat & Sun) with outdoor seating on place des Tilleuls to the west of the main market square. Alternatively, *Café des Sports*, one of several cafés under the market arcades, serves decent sandwiches and other snacks. At *Les Charmilles*, just outside Monségur on the road to St-Ferme (☎05.56.61.68.91; closed Sun eve & Mon), you're guaranteed a wonderful riverside location and good-quality traditional cuisine (menus 95–180F/€14.48–27.44), but not always the warmest welcome.

St-Ferme and around

The last stop in Entre-Deux-Mers is **ST-FERME**, 11km north of Monségur. The village clusters round the solid, grey **abbey** – founded by Benedictine monks sometime before the eleventh century – from which it takes its name. The fortifications added to the abbey buildings during the Hundred Years' War came in handy again during the Wars of Religion when Protestant forces attacked on at least two occasions. Happily, the **church** (daily 8am–7pm) withstood the onslaught. There's no grand portal, but instead the twelfth-century craftsmen went to work on the **capitals** in the three bays around the altar. Best of the lot is the first pillar on the far wall of the north bay, depicting Daniel being saved from lions with two angels above, while on the opposite wall of the same bay, David aims his sling at Goliath. Other recognizable scenes feature Adam, Eve and the serpent, behind the altar, and what appears to be Jonah being regurgitated by the whale on the first pillar on the left of the southernmost bay.

The rest of the abbey, which was rebuilt during the Renaissance, houses the local *mairie* and can only be visited on a **guided tour** (mid-June to mid-Sept Mon & Wed–Sun 10am–noon & 2.30–5.30pm; mid-Sept to mid-June Wed–Sat 9am–noon & 2–5pm; 20F/€3.05); at present tours are only conducted in French, but this may change in future. Not that there's not a great deal of interest inside. Apart from the monks' scriptorium and an eighteenth-century fresco representing Justice, the highlight is a lively stained-glass window by local English artist Jennifer Weller, illustrating abbey-life in the Middle Ages.

A couple of kilometres east of St-Ferme on the D127 to Duras, the welcoming **chambres d'hôtes** *Manoir de James* (☎05.56.61.69.75, fax 05.56.61.89.78; closed mid-Dec to mid-Jan; ④) occupies a quiet spot among fields. The rooms are a touch expensive, but big and airy, with sizeable bathrooms, plus there's a swimming pool and the English-speaking owners can help arrange visits to local wine producers.

The countryside north of St-Ferme is attractive, too. Take the D16 towards St-Foy-la-Grande, then turn left just before Pellegrue on the D126 to find a succession of castles between **AURIOLLES** and **LISTRAC-DE-DURÈZE**. Cutting back southwest, signs indicating *point de vue* lead you to a grassy hillock outside **SOUSSAC** with 360-degree views.

St-Émilion

ST-ÉMILION, roughly 40km east of Bordeaux, or directly north of Sauveterre along the D670, is the oldest wine town in France. It lies at the heart of one of the world's most densely cultivated wine regions, located on the north bank of the River Dordogne shortly before it flows into the Gironde. The **vineyards** alone justify a visit, but there's a lot more to St-Émilion than first meets the eye. The town has hardly grown in size beyond its original twelfth-century ramparts, an appealing collection of old grey houses nestled in a south-facing amphitheatre of low hills, with the green froth of the summer's vines crawling over its walls. Underneath its pretty, cobbled streets, the hillside has been hollowed out to create Europe's largest **underground church** and is riddled with catacombs and quarries that provide ideal conditions for storing the precious wine. Some of St-Émilion's most famous **wine châteaux**, notably Ausone and Belair, sit right on its doorstep, while the limestone plateau to the north is peppered with countless châteaux, country-houses and Romanesque churches hemmed in by the rows of pampered vines.

While the Romans had introduced vines to the area before the third century, the history of St-Émilion really starts some five hundred years later when the monk **Émilion** (or Émilian) arrived here from Brittany and decided to stay. Making his hermitage in an enlarged natural cave he soon gathered a sizeable following, drawn as much by tales of miracle cures as by his piety. After Émilion's death in 767, the religious community continued to grow until the town boasted a population of around 10,000 (as opposed to under 3000 today) when it passed into the hands of the English crown in 1152 as part of the Duchy of Aquitaine. Richard the Lionheart considered the town sufficiently important to grant it the status of a self-governing commune, later ratified in a charter dated 1199 by his successor and brother King John. Thus was born the **Jurade**, an assembly presiding over local justice, taxes, defence, and, of course, the town's economic life blood, the wine. Indeed, so sought-after was St-Émilion wine that when King Edward II of England reconfirmed the Jurade in 1312, following a brief period when the town was under French rule, he did so in exchange for "fifty barrels of clear, pure and good wine, to be delivered by Easter". Despite such strong English affiliations, St-Émilion retained its privileges after the Hundred Years' War and right up until the Revolution. The Jurade resurfaced again in 1948, but limited strictly to promoting and maintaining the quality of the wine.

Half a million visitors descend on St-Émilion each year, the majority during the summer months of July and August, and this will undoubtedly increase even further following the recent addition of St-Émilion and its vineyards to UNESCO's World Heritage list. To avoid the worst of the crowds it's best to come in the early morning or late afternoon, and better still to overnight here, though accommodation tends to be expensive. St-Émilion is a feasible day-trip from Bordeaux, either by yourself, or on one of the vineyard tours organized by the Bordeaux tourist office (see p.76).

Arrival and information

St-Émilion's **gare SNCF** lies down in the valley 2km to the south. Since only three trains a day stop here at best, you could also alight at more-frequently served Libourne, 7km further west on the Bordeaux–Paris line, and take a taxi from

---

THE WINES OF ST-ÉMILION

Louis XIV described **St-Émilion wines** as the "nectar of the gods". The best – notably the wines of Château Ausone and Château Cheval-Blanc – certainly rate on a par with the top Médocs (see p.93). They are the heartiest of the Bordeaux reds, though within the region there is considerable variety due to its complex geology and the fact that many producers are still small, family-run businesses – the average vineyard is a mere 70,000 square metres.

St-Émilion wines were not included in the 1855 **classification** (see pp.74–75), partly for local political reasons (the Bordeaux-based merchants who selected the wines tended to look down on St-Émilion), but won great acclaim in the Paris Exhibition of 1867 and again in 1889, when sixty producers collectively won the Grand Prix. It wasn't until 1954, however, that the wines were fully classified. They were subdivided into two *appellations* – St-Émilion and St-Émilion Grand Cru – and then the latter category organized in three tiers, Grands Crus, Grands Crus Classés and Premiers Grands Crus Classés, of which the top is further subdivided into "A" and "B" wines. The system is unique in that all the wines are tasted and the Grands Crus reviewed each year, while the two top tiers are reclassified every ten years. Following the last major overhaul in 1996, 55 wines are presently entitled to the Grands Crus Classés label and thirteen to Premiers Grands Crus Classés; Ausone and Cheval-Blanc are the only top-ranked "A" wines.

The two St-Émilion *appellations* cover the eight villages of the medieval jurisdiction, the Jurade (see opposite), with a total of 540 square kilometres under vines and an average annual production of over 250,000 hectolitres (more than three million bottles). Nearly half of this is exported. In addition, wines produced in four communes to the north – St-Georges, Montagne, Puisseguin and Lussac – are entitled to the St-Émilion name, but preceded by that of the commune: St-Georges-St-Émilion, for example.

The region's **soils** range from sand-gravel on the Dordogne valley floor to the limestone plateau around the town, in places capped with layers of clay, and the coarse gravel plains of the north and east. Merlot is the predominant **grape variety**, followed by Cabernet Franc (here called Cabernet Bouchet) and with smaller quantities of Cabernet Sauvignon and, occasionally, Malbec. The end result is a smooth, round wine which ages well, though some are ready to drink after only five years. But even a brief tasting session will reveal the tremendous variety among these wines which, combined with the relatively small output from some vineyards, adds to the prestige – and price – of the best ones. A good bottle of Château Ausone, for example, will set you back at least 2000F/€304.90, but among the Grands Crus you should be able to find some very fine wines, good enough for laying down, for around 80F/€12.20 a bottle.

For more information on these wines, call in at St-Émilion's **Maison du Vin** (see overleaf). For general tips on visiting vineyards see p.94.

there at a cost of around 90F/€13.72. The alternative is an only slightly less spo-radic **bus** service (operated by Marchessau; ☎05.56.43.68.43) from Libourne's *gare SNCF*, which drops you on place Maréchal-Leclerc, the roundabout at the north end of rue Gaudet, St-Émilion's main street. If you're driving, note that the town centre is closed to traffic during the day but that there's free **parking** on place Bouqueyre to the south and on avenue de Verdun, which runs along the northwestern ramparts.

The super-efficient **tourist office**, on place des Créneaux beside the belfry (daily: July & Aug 9.30am–8pm; April–June, Sept & Oct 9.30am–12.30pm & 1.45–6.30pm; Nov–March 9.30am–12.30pm & 1.45–6pm; ☎05.57.55.28.28, fax 05.57.55.28.29, *www.saint-emilion-tourisme.com*), produces all manner of useful publications, including suggested walking routes in the area and details of over ninety local vineyards where visitors are welcome. From May to September you can join one of their bilingual vineyard **tours** (Mon–Sat; 51F/€7.77), and they also rent out **bikes** for those who would rather be independent. The town's **Maison du Vin** is round the corner on place Pierre-Meyrat (Aug daily 9.30am–7pm; March–July & Sept–Nov Mon–Sat 9.30am–12.30pm & 2–6.30pm, Sun 10am–12.30pm & 2.30–6.30pm; Dec–Feb Mon–Sat 10am–12.30pm & 2.30–6pm, Sun 10am–12.30pm & 2.30–6.30pm; ☎05.57.55.50.55, fax 05.57.55.53.10). They sell a large selection of wines at producers' prices and can also advise on **vineyard visits**, but don't offer tastings.

As you would expect, the most important of St-Émilion's annual **events** revolve around wine. In June members of the Jurade dust off their finery for the Fête de Printemps, and again in September to announce the harvest (see box on pp.70–71 for more). On the first weekend in May around twenty châteaux throw their doors open to the public, while throughout the year keep an eye out for concerts held in the châteaux – accompanied by a tasting of course.

Accommodation

St-Émilion offers a number of good but expensive **hotels**, while for those on a stricter budget there are some very reasonably priced **chambres d'hôtes** and a **campsite** in the surrounding area. In summer (notably July and August) and dur-ing the two main festivals (see above), everywhere gets booked up weeks in advance. The tourist office won't make reservations for you, but they will be able to advise on where rooms are still available.

In St-Émilion

Auberge de la Commanderie, rue des Cordeliers (☎05.57.24.70.19, fax 05.57.74.44.53). Choose between old-fashioned country-style in the main building and larger, arty rooms in the annexe across the road, the latter with bold stained-glass windows but lacking the vine-yard views. Despite its address, the hotel is located about halfway along rue Gaudet. Closed mid-Jan to mid-Feb. ④.

Hostellerie de Plaisance, pl du Clocher (☎05.57.55.07.55, fax 05.57.74.41.11). This is St-Émilion's top hotel, with a prime location next to the belfry and stunning views from its ter-raced garden. It's small – only thirteen rooms and three suites – but the rooms, some verg-ing on the Baroque, all have the four-star comforts you'd expect. The elegant restaurant offers equally high-class cuisine and a lengthy wine list (menus 150–280F/€22.87–42.69). Closed Jan. ⑥.

Logis de la Cadène, 3 pl du Marché-au-Bois (☎05.57.24.71.40, fax 05.57.74.42.23). With only three rooms, you need to book ahead for this homely *chambres d'hôtes* right in the town centre, on the lane that leads from the belfry down to the Église Monolithe. One room has an en-suite bath, but none has its own toilet. The *Logis* is also a restaurant, with a menu at 110F/€16.77. Closed Sun eve and Mon; also late Dec to late Feb. ③.

Logis des Remparts, 18 rue Gaudet (☎05.57.24.70.43, fax 05.57.74.47.44; *logis-des-remparts @saint-emilion.org*). Though its rooms don't have the same character, this clean, tidy hotel makes a good alternative if the *Auberge de la Commanderie* is full. The plus points are a terrace and pool. ⑤.

Around St-Émilion

Bonsaï Hotel, rte de Castillon (☎05.57.25.25.07, fax 05.57.25.26.59). A few kilometres west of St-Émilion on the main D670, this modern chain hotel is the cheapest option around. The rooms are predictably boxy but comfortable enough, all with en-suite facilities and satellite TV, and there's a pool, garden and restaurant (menus from 85F/€12.96). ③.

Chambres d'hôte France Prat, 3 chemin de Courbestey, Lavagnac (☎ & fax 05.57.47.13.74, *perso.wanadoo.fr/france.prat*). Not the most convenient location, but it's worth going out of your way for this absolutely pristine *chambres d'hôte* 10km south of St-Émilion on the banks of the Dordogne – though the virginal white carpets and glistening parquet might not suit children and muddy walking boots. To find it, take the D670 south towards La Réole and Pau into Lavagnac village, then turn left down a lane just before the river. ③.

Camping Domaine de la Barbanne, rte de Montagne (☎05.57.24.75.80, fax 05.57.24.69.68). Excellent three-star campsite 3km north of St-Émilion signed off the D122 Montagne road. In the midst of vines and next to a large lake, with swimming pool, canoes and tennis courts amongst other facilities. Closed mid-Oct to March.

Château Millaud Montlabert, rte de Pomerol (☎05.57.24.71.82, fax 05.57.24.62.78). A more rustic but nevertheless well-equipped *chambres d'hôte* in a typical Girondin farmhouse 4km northwest of St-Émilion on the D245 to Pomerol. No meals, but there's a kitchenette, and you can sample the owners' Grand Cru wines. ④.

Château de Roques, Puisseguin (☎05.57.74.55.69, fax 05.57.74.58.80). Another vineyard location for this hotel in a rambling château about 10km northeast of St-Émilion on the D17. The rooms are plain – the cheapest not en suite – but represent good value nonetheless. Ancient grain stores beneath the château now serve as the *chais*, which you can visit. From May to October they also run a restaurant (menus from 100–200F/€15.24–30.49; closed Sun eve to Tues lunchtime). ②.

La Gomerie, Château Meylet, rte de Libourne (☎ & fax 05.57.24.68.85). Last but by no means least, an exceptionally welcoming and well-kept *chambres d'hôte* among the vines less than 2km outside St-Émilion on the D243 to Libourne. The rooms are all light and airy with good modern bathrooms. Again, no meals, but there's a kitchenette. Bikes available. ③.

The Town

St-Émilion is built on a steepish south-facing hill, with its belfry providing a convenient landmark in the town centre above the rock-hewn church with its entrance on place du Marché. From beside the belfry rue du Clocher and its extension, rue des Girondins, run east to meet St-Émilion's main street, **rue Gaudet**, which links place Bouqueyre in the south with northerly place Maréchal-Leclerc on the plateau.

A good place to get your bearings is beside the belfry on **place des Créneaux**, from whose terrace edge you get a marvellous view over the huddled roofs. Better still, if you have the energy, to climb the **tower** itself (same hours as the

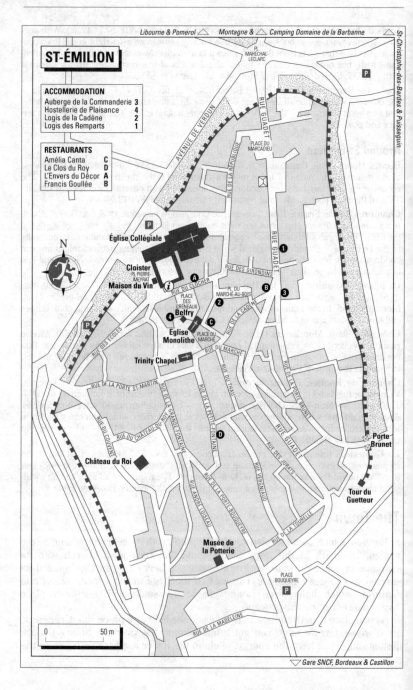

△ Libourne & Pomerol △ Montagne & △ Camping Domaine de la Barbanne ▷ St-Christophe-des-Bardes & Puisseguin

ST-ÉMILION

ACCOMMODATION
Auberge de la Commanderie 3
Hostellerie de Plaisance 4
Logis de la Cadène 2
Logis des Remparts 1

RESTAURANTS
Amélia Canta C
Le Clos du Roy D
L'Envers du Décor A
Francis Goullée B

N

Église Collégiale

Cloister
PL. PIERRE-MEYRAT
Maison du Vin

Belfry

Église
Monolithe

Trinity Chapel

Château du Roi

Musée de
la Potterie

PL. MARECHAL-LECLERC

PLACE DU MARCADIEU

PLACE DES CRENEAUX

PL. DU MARCHÉ-AU-BOIS

PLACE DU MARCHÉ

RUE DU CLOCHER

RUE DES GIRONDINS

RUE DE LA CADÈNE

RUE DU MARCHE

RUE DU TRAIT

RUE DE LA PORTE ST-MARTIN

RUE DU COUVENT

RUE DU CHATEAU DU ROY

RUE DE LA GRANDE-FONTAINE

RUE DE LA PETITE-FONTAINE

RUE ANDRÉ LOISEAU

RUE DE LA PORTE BOUQUEYRE

RUE DES JURATS

RUE GUADET

RUE VERGNAUD

RUE DE LA TOURELLE

RUE DE LA MADELEINE

RUE DE LA PORTE BRUNET

AVENUE DE VERDUN

RUE DE LA RÉPUBLIQUE

RUE GUADET

RUE DES ECOLES

Porte
Brunet

Tour du
Guetteur

PLACE BOUQUEYRE

0   50 m

▽ Gare SNCF, Bordeaux & Castillon

tourist office; 6F/€0.91) for a panorama that sweeps beyond the town walls over the vines' serried ranks. The other point to starting your explorations here is that you can sign up for a tour of the underground church (see below) at the tourist office on place des Créneaux.

While you're waiting for the tour to begin, take a look in the lovely fourteenth-century **cloister** accessed via the tourist office (same hours; free). Though it belongs to the Collégiale church (daily 9.30am–12.30pm & 2–7pm; free), the connecting door is sealed up; instead, to reach the church turn right outside the tourist office and right again to enter via its Romanesque west door. Inside, look out for the twelfth-century frescoes of St Catherine's martyrdom on the south wall of the nave, and a lovely slender Virgin just round the corner, but the main draw is the statue of **St Valéry** on the transept's northeast wall. Carved and painted in the sixteenth century, he bears a staff, sack, gourd, scythe and a natty pair of pointy slippers – the work is not particularly outstanding, but the man is: St Valéry is none other than the patron saint of local wine growers.

The rock on which this upper part of St-Émilion is built is a veritable honeycomb. It's estimated that 120,000 square metres has been excavated from under the town alone, including the vast subterranean **Église Monolithe** (45min guided tours daily 10–11.30am & 2–5pm; 33F/€5.03 from the tourist office). The tour starts in a dark hole in someone's backyard, supposedly the **cave** where St Émilion lived a hermit's life in the eighth century. A rough-hewn ledge served as his bed and a carved seat as his chair, where women trying to conceive reputedly still come to sit in the hope of getting pregnant. Back outside, directly above the "cave" is the simple thirteenth-century **Trinity Chapel**, built in honour of St Émilion and converted into a cooperage during the Revolution; fragments of frescoes are still visible, including the kneeling figure of what is thought to be Émilion. On the other side of the yard, a passage tunnels beneath the belfry to the **catacombs**, where three chambers dug out of the soft limestone were used as a cemetery and then later, through lack of space, as an ossuary from the eighth to the eleventh century. In the innermost chamber – discovered by a neighbour enlarging his cellar 55 years ago – an eleventh-century tombstone bears the inscription "Aulius is buried between saints Valéry, Émilion and Avic"; St Émilion's remains were later moved to the Collegiate Church and then disappeared during the Wars of Religion.

The **church** itself is an incredible place. Simple and huge, the entire structure – barrel-vaulting, great square piers and all – was hacked out of the rock by Benedictine monks between the ninth and twelfth centuries. It is nearly forty metres long, twenty wide and eleven metres at its maximum height. Unfortunately, it's difficult to appreciate the volume because of the massive concrete supports installed as a temporary measure after cracks were discovered in the bell tower above in 1990; so far no better solution has been found. You can still see various bas-relief carvings around the altar: a pair of four-winged angels, two zodiacal signs and an unfinished scene of a man wrestling with a snake-headed monster. The whole interior was also painted at one time, but only faint traces have survived the damp and the Revolution, when saltpetre was collected from the walls to make gunpowder.

In the lower part of town, a couple of minutes' walk from place des Créneaux down rue de la Grande-Fontaine, a stretch of underground gallery makes an unusual home for the well-documented **Musée de la Poterie**, 21 rue André-Loiseau (daily 10am–7pm; 20F/€3.05); ask to borrow their English-language guide. This private collection covering two thousand years of pottery from southwest France contains all sorts of interesting and unusual pieces, from earthen-ware fire-dogs sporting human faces to glazed roof finials (*épi de faîtage*) in the form of birds or humans, including a smartly turned-out gentleman in a top hat.

Some of the rock dug from the museum's galleries undoubtedly went in to building the massive square keep of the **Château du Roi** (daily: June–Sept 10am–12.45pm & 2.45–8.30pm; Oct–May 10am–12.45pm & 2.45–6.45pm; 6F/€0.91) presiding over St-Émilion from the west, and constructed in the thir-teenth century as a forceful reminder of the king's power in this otherwise inde-pendent town. Nowadays it comes into its own in June and September when the members of the Jurade, in their red and white robes, proclaim the judging of the new wines and the start of the grape harvest from its summit.

Eating and drinking

On a sunny day, there's nothing better than to sit at one of the **cafés** on place du Marché beneath the sky-piercing belfry. There are a number of simple **restau-rants** round the square and a couple of more upmarket places in addition to the *Hostellerie de Plaisance* listed on p.122. For picnic fodder, there's a Sunday-morn-ing **market** on place Bouqueyre at the south end of rue Gaudet, and a small supermarket right at the north end of town beyond the roundabout. While you're here you should try the local **macaroons** (*macarons*) – the Blanchez family, 9 rue Gaudet near the post office, still bakes the tiny melt-in-the-mouth biscuits to the original recipe devised by Ursuline sisters in 1620.

Amélia Canta, pl du Marché. The food isn't bad, but this brasserie is recommended mainly for its location, particularly if you can sit outside. The menu includes a wide range of salads and omelettes as well as regional fare. *Plat du jour* 45F/€6.86; menus from 95F/€14.48. Closed Dec & Jan.

Le Clos du Roy, 12 rue de la Petite-Fontaine (☎05.57.74.41.55). Reservations are recom-mended at St-Émilion's most appealing restaurant, where the subtle, inventive cuisine includes a large number of fish and seafood dishes, such as langoustine risotto. It need not break the bank, either, with menus from 100F/€15.24. Closed Wed; also two weeks in early Nov & three weeks in Feb.

L'Envers du Décor, rue du Clocher. Relaxed contemporary-style bistro, just along from the tourist office, with a good range of local wines by the glass (from 20F/€3.05). There are *plats du jour* for 65F/€9.91, a menu at 95F/€14.48 and standard dishes such omelettes and salads. In summer you can sit out in their cosy courtyard. Nov–April closed Sat & Sun.

Francis Goullée, 27 rue Gaudet (☎05.57.24.70.49). St-Émilion's most famous restaurant offers a seasonal variety of traditional dishes and modern creations: spiced pigeon in a pas-try crust, pig's trotters, and foie gras with sea salt. Best value are the 90F/€13.72 lunch menu and that at 190F/€28.97 including two glasses of wine (both daily except Sun). Closed Sun eve & Mon; also two weeks in late Nov.

A tour of the vineyards

The **vineyards** of St-Émilion are the first ever classified by UNESCO as being – in combination with the town – of sufficient cultural, historical and scenic importance to merit inclusion on the World Heritage list. Every spare inch of ground is cov-ered with vines. Their trellised rows march from the valley floor up over the lip of the plateau, accentuating its gentle undulations, and nestle round the pale-grey limestone walls of the myriad **châteaux**. On the whole these are more modest buildings than you'll find in the Médoc or Sauternes wine regions, though St-Émilion does have its share of handsome seventeenth- and eighteenth-century piles. Most are still family homes, and therefore not open to the public, the one exception being the first weekend in May when about twenty châteaux accept visitors under the *portes ouvertes* initiative organized by St-Émilion tourist office; some also host the occasional concert. But the real reason to visit is the wine, and from that point of view owners are more than happy to receive visitors – provided you phone ahead. Below we suggest a representative selection of the region's tremendous variety where English-language tours are usually available on request.

To start your vineyard tour there's no need to do more than stroll round St-Émilion's western ramparts to find the **Château Belair** (☎05.57.24.70.94; Mon–Fri 3–7pm; free) on the hillside just outside the town. They produce one of the region's top wines, a Premier Grand Cru Classé since 1954, using various traditional techniques which are explained during the tour. Belair is also of interest for its underground vinification plant and ageing cellars, the latter spread over three kilometres of tunnels on three levels. The tunnels are the remnants of old stone quarries and, after quarrying was banned in 1872, were first used for cultivating mushrooms, before the owners of Belair and other châteaux along this hillside realized that their constant temperature (around 12–16°C) and high humidity were ideal for ageing and storing wine.

Three kilometres east along the same scarp on the D243, just beyond the village of **ST-CHRISTOPHE-DES-BARDES**, **Château Laroque** (☎05.57.24.77.28; Mon–Fri 9am–noon & 2–6pm; tastings 20F/€3.05) is one of the area's grander edifices. You approach through elaborate wrought-iron gates, then down a long alley of cedars towards the seventeenth-century château overlooking immaculate lawns and Italianate statues in one direction and the Dordogne river to the south. The round tower standing slightly apart is all that remains of the original feudal château while the *chais* occupy the outbuildings across the courtyard. Château Laroque attained Grand Cru Classé status in 1996 following two decades of investment and technical innovation.

In the same commune but just north of St-Christophe on the D130 Parsac road, **Château Toinet-Fombrauge** (☎05.57.24.77.70; daily 9am–noon & 2–7pm; tastings 15F/€2.29) is a good example of a small, family-run vineyard. Not that their wines are anything to sneeze at – in addition to the standard St-Émilion they produce a very reasonable Grand Cru at under 70F/€10.67 a bottle.

The next stop on this brief vineyard tour takes you a kilometre or so northwest of St-Émilion to visit **Château Laniote** (☎05.57.24.70.80; daily 9am–12.30pm & 1.30–7pm; free) signed off the D243 Libourne road. This is another Grand Cru Classé, but produced on much smaller scale than at Château Laroque, and of interest for those wishing to go into the technical intricacies of wine-making in more detail.

To learn about the history of wine and viticulture in the region continue three kilometres further north to the hilltop village of **MONTAGNE** with its pretty Romanesque church and **Ecomusée du Libournais** (mid-Jan to late-Dec daily 10am–noon & 2–6pm; 28F/€4.27). The museum combines replica artisans' workshops with displays concerning the life of the vine and the process of vinification, though none of the documents are translated. Afterwards you can follow a four-kilometre nature trail through the vines – ask at the ticket desk for the map and explanatory leaflet.

travel details

Trains

Bordeaux to: Agen (15–20 daily; 1hr–1hr 35min); Angoulême (at least 1 hourly; 1hr); Barsac (2–5 daily; 35min); Bergerac (4–8 daily; 50min–1hr 30min); Brive (1–2 daily; 2hr 15min); Langon (8–16 daily; 25–45min); La Réole (7–12 daily; 35–50min); Lesparre (2–8 daily; 1hr–1hr 30min); Libourne (15–30 daily; 20–30min); Margaux (2–7 daily; 20–50min); Moulis-Listrac (2–7 daily; 55min); Paris (3–8 daily; 3–4hr); Pauillac (2–8 daily; 50min–1hr); Périgueux (8–15 daily; 1hr–1hr 25min); Podensac (2–5 daily; 15–30min); Portets (2–6 daily; 15–20min); St-Émilion (1–3 daily; 35min); St-Macaire (1–3 daily; 25–40min); Sarlat (3–4 daily; 2hr 30min); Soulac (1–8 daily; 1hr 20min–1hr 45min); Toulouse (10–15 daily; 2hr–2hr 40min).

Buses

Bordeaux to: La Brède (Mon–Sat 1–2 daily; 40min); Barsac (Mon–Sat 2–4 daily; 1hr 10min); Cadillac (2–8 daily; 1hr 20min); Langon (3–12 daily; 1hr 20min); Lesparre (3–6 daily; 1hr 20min); Libourne (4–25 daily; 45min–1hr); Margaux (2–10 daily; 45min–1hr); Pauillac (2–10 daily; 1hr–1hr 20min); Podensac (Mon–Sat 2–4 daily; 1hr); Portets (Mon–Sat 2–4 daily; 45min); St-Julien (2–10 daily; 1hr–1hr 20min); La Sauve-Majeure (1–4 daily; 40min); Sauveterre-de-Guyenne (Mon–Fri 1 daily; 1hr 20min).

Langon to: Barsac (Mon–Sat 1–3 daily; 20–30min); Cadillac (2–8 daily; 30–40min);

Podensac (Mon–Sat 1–3 daily; 30min); Portets (Mon–Sat 1–3 daily; 40min); Sauveterre-de-Guyenne (Mon–Fri daily; 50min).

Lesparre to: Bordeaux (3–6 daily; 1hr 20min); Soulac (3–5 daily; 45min); Pointe de Grave (3–5 daily; 1hr).

Pauillac to: Lesparre (Sept–June only Mon–Fri 2 daily; 50min); St-Estèphe (Sept–June only Mon–Fri 1 daily; 15min).

La Réole to: Monségur (Mon–Sat 2–3 daily; 15min); Sauveterre-de-Guyenne (Mon–Sat 2–3 daily; 15–20min); St-Ferme (Mon–Fri 1–2 daily; 25min).

St-Émilion to: Libourne (3–5 daily; 7min).

Sauveterre-de-Guyenne to: Blasimon (Mon–Sat 2–3 daily; 10min); Bordeaux (Mon–Fri 1 daily; 1hr 20min); Libourne (Mon–Sat 2–3 daily; 1hr 10min); St-Ferme (Mon–Fri 1–2 daily; 30min–1hr); La Sauve-Majeure (Mon–Fri 1 daily; 40min).

Ferries

Lamarque to: Blaye (4–10 daily; 30min).

Planes

Bordeaux to: Lille (1–2 daily; 1hr 20min); Lyon (2–5 daily; 1hr 5min); Marseille (1–3 daily; 1hr 5min); Nice (1 daily; 1hr 15min); Paris CDG (5 daily; 1hr 20min); Paris Orly (1–2 hourly; 1hr 15min); Strasbourg (1–3 daily; 1hr 40min).

CHAPTER TWO

PÉRIGUEUX AND THE NORTH

The north of the Dordogne *département* is its least known and most rural corner, a land with few people and large tracts of pasture and woodland, its intimate green valleys lending it the name of the **Périgord Vert**. It extends north and east to the departmental border and is bounded to the south by the **Périgord Blanc**. This latter region of limestone plateaux and wide, gentle valleys cuts a broad swathe across the heart of the Dordogne, following the course of the River Isle. On its way the river flows through just one major city, the capital of both Périgord Blanc and the whole *département*, **Périgueux**. It is easy to spend a day or two exploring the old city centre with its pineapple-capped cathedral, Roman remains and its archeological museum – a first taste of the wealth of prehistoric art to come – but it is in the countryside around that the region's best attractions lie.

One of the loveliest stretches is the **Dronne valley**, which shadows the Isle to the north. At **Brantôme** the Dronne's still, water-lilied surface mirrors the limes and weeping willows along its banks, before flowing on past the twin fortresses of **Bourdeilles** to **Ribérac**, a market town much-loved by the British, and **Aubeterre** on the Charente border. Like Brantôme, the river-carved cliffs at Aubeterre have been hollowed out into primitive churches by twelfth-century monks. Others built dozens of little Romanesque churches on the sunny hills around, while south of the Dronne their successors helped tame the marshy, insalubrious plateau of the **Double**. In doing so they created the pine and chestnut forests which blanket the area today.

Upstream from Brantôme, two tributaries of the Dronne lead northeast to the tiny village of **St-Jean-de-Côle** and the **Château de Puyguilhem**, a marvellous Renaissance pile whose towers, gun-ports and machicolations were intended for decorative purposes rather than to be used in anger. Further northeast again

---

ACCOMMODATION PRICE CODES

All the hotels and *chambres d'hôtes* listed in this book have been price-coded according to the following scale. The prices quoted are for the **cheapest available double room in high season**, although remember that many of the cheap places will have more expensive rooms with en-suite facilities.

① Under 160F/€24
② 160–220F/€24–34
③ 220–300F/€34–46

④ 300–400F/€46–61
⑤ 400–500F/€61–76
⑥ 500–600F/€76–91

⑦ 600–700F/€91–107
⑧ 700–800F/€107–122
⑨ Over 800F/€122

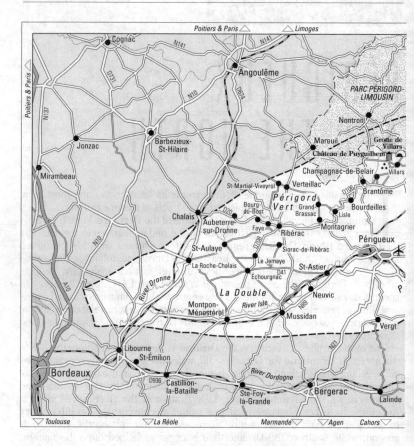

there's no mistaking the warlike nature of **Jumilhac** castle's granite hulk, though its roof towers add a nicely fanciful touch. As a break from the château trail, connoisseurs of foie gras should head south to the little museum in **Thiviers**, while truffle-lovers might like to pop in on **Sorges**, where there is a marked path through truffle country and another small museum to explain it all. These two towns are close to the southeast border of the Périgord Vert, where the scenery becomes softer and more open again towards the lovely Auvézère valley. Here, in a spectacular spot high over the river, the **Château de Hautefort** marks a return to the Périgord Blanc.

East of Hautefort, across the border in the Corrèze *département*, **Brive-la-Gaillarde** lies on an important crossroads and provides an alternative to Périgueux as a gateway to the region. For such a large city, Brive has a surprisingly compact and enjoyable old centre where the historical museum is well worth visiting. The countryside around also holds a few surprises, from the national stud at **Arnac-Pompadour** to the appropriately named **Collonges-la-Rouge**, a village built of a rich, red sandstone.

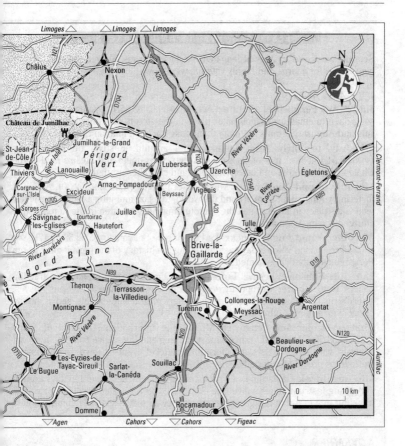

Both Périgueux and Brive are major **transport** hubs. In addition to domestic airports, with daily flights to Paris, they both have reasonable train connections to other towns in the region. Local bus services, however, are very sporadic.

Périgueux

PÉRIGUEUX, capital of the Dordogne, is a small, busy and not particularly attractive market town for a province made rich by tourism and specialized farming. Its name derives from the Petrocorii, the local Gaulish tribe, but it was the Romans who transformed it into an important settlement. Whilst a few **Roman remains** survive, among them an impressive sacred tower, it is the city's **medieval and Renaissance core** that gives Périgueux its particular appeal. Pretty, stone-flagged squares and a maze of narrow alleys harbour richly ornamented merchants' houses. And above it all rises the startlingly white spire of **St-Front Cathedral** flanked by its cluster of pinnacled, Byzantine domes. The cathedral, a nineteenth-century reconstruction, looks best at night – particularly from across the river – when

FESTIVALS, EVENTS AND MARKETS

Second weekend in May St-Jean-de-Côle: Les Floralies. Flower stalls fill the village centre for a large and highly rated flower show.

JULY AND AUGUST

July & Aug Périgueux: La Truffe d'Argent (☎05.53.53.55.17). A festival of French song open to amateurs, which takes place in the streets on Thursday evenings in July and August. Entrants are judged and take part in a final on the last night.

Mid-July to early Aug Hautefort and around: Festival du Pays d'Ans (☎05.53.51.13.63). A mix of classical concerts, jazz, opera and theatre held in the Château de Hautefort and other châteaux and churches around about.

Mid-July to mid-Aug Ribérac: Musiques et Paroles (☎05.53.92.52.30). Aimed at fostering young talent from around the world, this jazz and international music festival takes place in Ribérac and the surrounding villages, often in the Romanesque churches or the open air.

Mid-July to mid-Aug Périgueux: La Légende de St-Front (☎05.53.53.55.17). *Son et lumière* on each Wednesday evening telling the history of the hermit after whom Périgueux's cathedral is named.

Late July Brântome: Festival Européen du Pain. A two-day bread-fest attracting bakers from all over Europe to demonstrate their traditional artisans' loaves. There's also a Mass, displays of antique agricultural implements and a mobile bread-oven amongst other things.

First week in Aug Périgueux: Mimos, the International Festival of Mime (☎05.53.53.55.17). One of France's most exciting and innovative contemporary art festivals, with street artists and more formal ticket events. Clowns, acrobats and workshops provide fun for all the family.

Mid-Aug Brive-la-Gaillarde: Les Orchestrades Universelles. Over ten days around 700 young instrumentalists give free classical concerts in the streets of Brive culminating in a grand open-air concert when they all play a specially commissioned piece.

NOVEMBER

First weekend Brive: La Foire du Livre. A book fair held in Brive's market hall, which attracts some 300 authors and artists presenting their new works, and some 10,000 book-lovers keen to snap up signed editions.

Early Nov Périgueux: Salon International du Livre Gourmand (☎05.53.53.55.17). Another book fair, this time dedicated to wine and cuisine, which takes place every two years. Events take place over four days in the NTP hall (1 avenue d'Aquitaine; 10F/€1.52), including book exhibitions, cooking demonstrations and opportunities to sample the results.

MARKETS

The most important **weekly markets** in this region are: Brântome (Fri); Brive (Tues, Thurs & Sat); Excideuil (Thurs); Périgueux (Wed & Sat); Ribérac (Fri); Thiviers (Sat). In winter many local towns hold **foie gras**, **truffle** and **walnut markets**, generally on the same day as their weekly market. Where we haven't given a specific information number contact the relevant tourist office.

floodlights soften the sharper edges and accentuate its exotic silhouette. For many visitors, however, Périgueux's prime attraction is the **Musée du Périgord** with its important collection of archeological finds from the surrounding region. Unfortunately, some of the Roman art works have been withdrawn in anticipation of a new Gallo-Roman museum, but the Paleolithic exhibits alone justify a visit.

Some history

Périgueux began life sometime after the fourth century BC as a fortified settlement inhabited by the **Petrocorii** ("Four Tribes"), whose craftsmen were noted for their ironwork. After 51 BC, however, the area came under Roman rule and a thriving town known as **Vesunna** (Vésone in French) began to develop, complete with amphitheatre, temples and luxurious villas. By the first century AD its population had reached an estimated 20,000, but the glory was shortlived. Under the *pax romana*, Vesunna, like many other towns, had neglected its defences and was caught unprepared by a succession of **barbarian invasions** in the third century. When Germanic tribes swept through the area in 275 AD, the population used stone from the surrounding civic monuments to construct defensive walls which helped the town survive, but in a much reduced state, and as it faded, it became known as La Cité des Pétrocores, then simply **La Cité**.

In the meantime, **St Front** arrived on the scene sometime in the fourth century to convert the local population to Christianity. After giving La Cité a new breath of life by founding what eventually became St-Étienne Cathedral, St Front was later buried on a neighbouring hilltop, or *puy*, where his tomb became a pilgrimage centre. By the thirteenth century it had spawned a small but prosperous town of merchants and artisans known as **Le Puy-St-Front**, which began to rival La Cité, now the seat of the Counts of Périgord. Though the two communities were joined by an act of union in 1240, they continued to glare at each other over their encircling walls – indeed, at the start of the **Hundred Years' War** La Cité sided with the English and Le Puy with France. For a while following the Treaty of Brétigny in 1360, Périgueux fell under English rule, but the loyal burghers of Le Puy soon rallied to Charles V, and by 1369 Périgueux had been liberated by Bertrand du Guesclin, who then chased the English back towards the coast. Even so, by the early fifteenth century the city was in ruins, its population decimated by war, plague and famine and its buildings crumbling through neglect.

With peace, however, came renewed prosperity and a building boom that left Périgueux its wonderful legacy of **Renaissance** architecture, though much was lost or damaged during the **Wars of Religion**: despite being predominantly Catholic, Périgueux was held by the Protestants for six years after 1575, during which time they vandalized many religious buildings, amongst them St-Étienne. This proved to be the final blow for La Cité, which fell into slow decline, culminating in the transfer of cathedral status to St-Front in 1669.

Up to this time La Cité and Le Puy-St-Front remained firmly inside their respective walls, separated by open space, but in the eighteenth century Périgueux began to expand into today's **modern city**. In the process the medieval walls gave way to wide boulevards, while in the nineteenth century the canal and railway brought further development to what was by then the capital of Périgord. The old city centre was left largely untouched, so that in 1979 some twenty hectares were designated a preservation district. Nevertheless, Périgueux is still the *département*'s most industrialized town: its biggest current claim to fame – a result of

1970s decentralization policies – is the printing works where all French postage stamps, tax discs and the like are produced.

Arrival, information and accommodation

Périgueux boasts a small domestic **airport** at Bassillac, 7km east of the city, with daily flights from Paris. There are no facilities – though rented cars can be picked up here if booked in advance – and no convenient bus links; instead, a taxi into town will take less than twenty minutes (70–80F/€10.67–12.20). On the opposite side of the city, the **gare SNCF** lies roughly ten minutes' walk from the centre, along rue des Mobiles-de-Coulmiers and rue du Président-Wilson, or you can take bus #1 (direction Boulazac) to place Bugeaud or St-Front (€7.50F/1.14). There are several car rental outlets in and around the *gare* (see "Listings", p.143) and although its **left-luggage** lockers are currently out of action, you can leave bags at the ticket office (30F/€4.57 per bag per 24hrs). If you're **driving** you can park for free along the river below St-Front Cathedral, or there's plenty of pay-parking along allées Tourny, in place Montaigne and underneath place Francheville. This last *place* is where long-distance buses terminate at the **gare routière**, and also where you'll find the **tourist office** (July & Aug Mon–Sat 9am–7pm, Sun 10am–6pm; Sept–June Mon–Sat 9am–6pm; ☎05.53.53.10.63, fax 05.53.09.02.50, *tourisme.perigueux@perigord.tm.fr*). Here you can pick up free city **maps**, including one in English with recommended walking routes, and book up for their excellent **city tours** covering medieval and Renaissance Périgueux or the Gallo-Roman city (mid-June to Sept & school holidays Mon–Sat 1–3 tours per day; Sept to mid-June Wed & Sat 2.30pm only; 25F/€3.81). The medieval tour is particularly recommended as it takes you into some of the city's hidden corners. Though the tours are predominantly in French, some guides also speak English.

Surprisingly, central Périgueux doesn't offer a particularly good range of **hotels**. There's only one reasonable option in the old city itself and the other alternatives are located within walking distance of the centre, with the best value for money to be found near the train station. For anything smarter you'll have to head further out. There is, however, a conveniently located **youth hostel** and a choice of **campsites**.

Hotels

All the accommodation listed is marked on the map opposite, apart from *L'Univers*, which is marked on the map on p.137.

Château des Reynats, av des Reynats (☎05.53.03.53.59, fax 05.53.03.44.84, *reynats@ chateau-hotel-perigord.com*). In the village of Chancelade, roughly 5km northwest of central Périgueux, the plush rooms (some in a newer annexe) and excellent restaurant in this little nineteenth-century château make it one of the city's top hotels. Restaurant closed for lunch Mon, Tues & Sat; in winter also for dinner Sun & Mon (menus from 140F/€21.34). Hotel closed Jan & Feb. ⑥.

Etap Hotel, 33 rue du Président-Wilson (☎05.53.05.53.82, fax 05.53.35.93.42). One of the new breed of Etap Hotels, located in the city centre rather than on the outskirts. Otherwise the formula is the same (a large double bed with single bunk above, an en-suite bathroom, phone and satellite TV), though the rooms are more spacious than usual and the bathrooms positively gleam. Off-season rates (Sept–June) fall to 165F/€25.15 for up to three people. ②.

du Midi et Terminus, 18 rue Denis-Papin (☎05.53.53.41.06, fax 05.53.08.19.32). Simple, spruce hotel opposite the station. The cheapest rooms (with a washbasin but no shower or toilet) are rather small for two people. Recommended restaurant offering good-value regional cuisine (menus from 75F/€11.43; Nov–March closed Sat). ①.

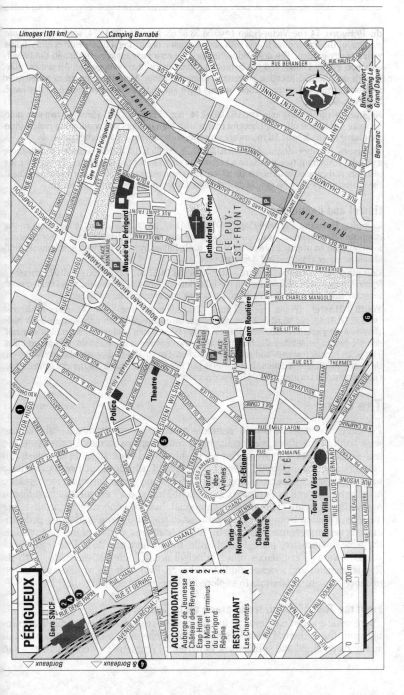

du Périgord, 74 rue Victor-Hugo (☎05.53.53.33.63, fax 05.53.08.19.74, *www.logis-de-france. fr*). One of the few central hotels with any character, occupying a nineteenth-century house with a pretty garden. The downside is its location on a busy main road, though the homely entrance, comfy lounge and old-fashioned rooms more than compensate. All are en suite, though only behind partition screens in cheaper rooms. Meals are served in a well-rated restaurant overlooking the garden (menus from 75F/€11.43; Oct–Feb closed all day Sat & Sun eve). ③.

Régina, 14 rue Denis-Papin (☎05.53.08.40.44, fax 05.53.54.72.44). Pleasant, two-star hotel opposite the station offering cheerful rooms with high ceilings and windows to match (double-glazed on the front). All rooms are en suite, with satellite TV at higher rates. ③.

L'Univers, 18 cours Montaigne (☎05.53.53.34.79, fax 05.53.06.70.76). Fourteen rooms above a popular restaurant (see p.142) on a pedestrian street in the old city centre. Though the furnishings and cabinet bathrooms (in all but the cheapest rooms) are in need of an overhaul, the rooms are clean, with new beds and linen. Closed for three weeks in Jan. ②.

Hostel and campsites

Camping Barnabé, Barnabé-Plage (☎05.53.53.41.45, fax 05.53.54.16.62). Charming two-star campsite fifteen minutes' walk northeast of the city along the Isle. It has a lovely riverside location, with an overspill site on the other bank, linked by boat. Bar with snack meals available in summer (March–Oct). Open all year.

Camping Le Grande Dague, Atur (☎05.53.04.21.01, fax 05.53.04.22.01, *camping. legrandedague@wanadoo.fr*). Lost in the hills 7km southeast of Périgueux, this Dutch-owned, four-star site is less convenient, but it's spacious and immaculate. April–Sept.

Youth Hostel (Foyer des Jeunes Travailleurs), rue des Thermes-Prolongés (☎05.53.06.81.40, fax 05.53.06.81.49, *fjtdordogne@wanadoo.fr*). With only sixteen bunk beds (four to a very small room), reservations at this HI-affiliated hostel are essential in summer, notably July to September. Each room has its own shower and washbasin, though no toilet. The price includes sheets and a buffet breakfast. Lunch and dinner are also available, but there are no kitchen facilities. The hostel is just five minutes' walk from the city centre along rue Lakanal. No curfew; 73F/€11.13 per person.

The City

Périgueux's compact **historic centre** – much of it pedestrianized – sits on the west bank of the River Isle, occupying a rough square formed by the river, the tree-shaded allées Tourny to the north, boulevard Montaigne to the west and cours Fénelon to the south. Though the hill-top **Cathédrale St-Front** provides a natural magnet, the surrounding streets hide some particularly fine Renaissance architecture as well as Périgueux's excellent **Musée du Périgord** and a remnant of **medieval wall**. The main commercial hub is concentrated around rue Taillefer, running from the cathedral west to place Bugeaud, and along pedestrianized rue Limogeanne to the north. At the southwest corner of the old town lies the wide, unattractive place Francheville, from where rue de la Cité leads westwards towards Périgueux's other principal area of interest, **La Cité**, with its Roman remains and a rather mutilated church. Everything is within easy walking distance, making it possible to explore the city comfortably in a day.

From the Tour Mataguerre to place de la Clautre

There's still a slight medieval air to **Le Puy-St-Front**, the district tumbling downhill from the cathedral west to place Francheville and to cours Fénelon in the south. Its confined and cobbled alleys harbour Périgueux's oldest buildings – the former homes of wealthy merchants – as well as the last remaining fragment of the medieval fortifications; Le Puy was originally surrounded by 28 defensive towers, of which only stout, circular **Tour Mataguerre**, protecting the southwest corner, remains. The tower, beside the tourist office, makes a good place from which to start exploring the city. According to legend, it was named after an English captain imprisoned here during the Hundred Years' War, but the present structure dates from the late fifteenth century, when it was rebuilt using leper labourers. The tower is only accessible on guided tours organized by the tourist office (see p.134); there's little to see inside – just the prison and a simple guardroom above – but views from the roof are good.

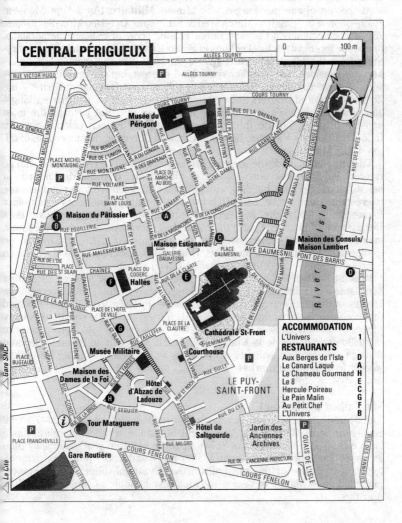

From beside Tour Mataguerre, rue de la Bride runs into rue des Farges, where, at no. 6, you'll find Périgueux's most venerable building, **Maison des Dames de la Foi**, dating from the late twelfth century. The name, "House of the Ladies of Faith", refers to a convent established in the seventeenth century for young Protestant women wishing to convert to Catholicism. Two hundred years earlier, during the Hundred Years' War, it's said that Du Guesclin stayed here while preparing to liberate nearby Chancelade Abbey from the English. The house is now privately owned and very much in need of attention. In fact you'd be forgiven for walking straight past; the only evidence of its more illustrious past is the blocked-in window arches on the second floor.

At the top of rue des Farges, the **Musée Militaire** (April–Sept Mon–Sat 10am–noon & 2–6pm; Jan–March Wed & Sat 2–6pm; Oct–Dec Mon–Sat 2–6pm; 20F/€3.05) contains a vast and rather chaotic array of military memorabilia, one of the foremost such collections in France. The exhibits, which cover everything from the Franco-Prussian War to the Gulf War and today's UN peace-keeping missions, are of rather specialized interest, but the museum contains some noteworthy pieces. There's a fine collection of Oriental uniforms – the Zouaves' natty red trousers and embroidered jackets are particularly striking – and poignant sketches of trench life in World War I. But perhaps the most unusual displays, on the third floor, relate to the French colonial wars in Indochina (today's Vietnam, Laos and Cambodia), among them a couple of tattered Viet Minh flags.

Turning right outside the museum brings you into rue de l'Aubergerie with its two fortified fifteenth-century houses, of which **Hôtel d'Abzac de Ladouze** at no. 16, a typically dour building with an octagonal defensive tower, is the more interesting. The massive, blind arch low on the wall is evidence of much older foundations, while the incongruous ornamental balustrade above is a Renaissance addition. Note also the cockleshell carving on the side of the tower, indicating that the house once received pilgrims en route to Santiago de Compostela. Further down the street, **Hôtel de Saltgourde**, at no. 6, sports an impressive tower, complete with a machicolated parapet.

Rue St-Roch leads east from near Hôtel d'Abzac past several interesting houses, one retaining its wood-timbered upper storey, others their overhanging latrines or decorative arcaded windows, to **rue du Calvaire**. This was the road that criminals in the Middle Ages climbed on their way to the courthouse, identifiable by its studded Renaissance door. The condemned would then continue to the gallows on **place de la Clautre**, which also served as an execution ground during the Revolution. Nowadays it provides a more peaceful setting for a twice-weekly fresh-produce **market** (Wed & Sat) against the backdrop of the cathedral.

The Cathédrale St-Front

The domed and coned **Cathédrale St-Front** (daily: July & Aug 8am–7.30pm; Sept–June 8am–12.30pm & 2.30–6.30pm) began life in the sixth century as a simple chapel over the tomb of St Front. Seven hundred years later – by then an important abbey – it was rebuilt after a fire and in the process the architects created one of the most distinctive Byzantine churches in France, modelled on St Mark's in Venice and on Constantinople's Church of the Holy Apostles.

Unfortunately, the cathedral of today is no beauty, thanks to the zealous attentions of the nineteenth-century restorer **Paul Abadie**, who went on to build
Paris's Sacré-Coeur. The result is too white, too new and too regular, and the roof
is spiked all over with ill-proportioned nipple-like projections; "a supreme example of how not to restore", Freda White tartly observed in her travelogue, *Three
Rivers of France*. Nevertheless, the Byzantine influence is still evident in the interior's Greek-cross plan – unusual in France – and in the massive clean curves of
the domes. The bell tower also survived largely intact and is one of the few vestiges of the twelfth-century reconstruction.

The overriding impression inside the cathedral is of echoing, empty space.
There are few windows to alleviate the gloom, but it's not opprressive: the architects managed to play tricks with the domes' supporting columns, whose hollow
centres belie the weight of stone above. The extravagant copper and glass chandelier over the central altar is another Abadie touch, designed for the wedding of
Napoléon III in Paris's Notre-Dame, but the main attraction is a handsome
Baroque **altarpiece** in the far eastern bay. Carved in oak and walnut, it depicts
the Assumption of the Virgin Mary, with a humorous little detail in the illustrative
scenes from her life of a puppy tugging the sheets off the infant Jesus' bed.
Nearby, a particularly muscle-bound Hercules supports an equally ornate pulpit.

North of the cathedral

North of the cathedral crowd the renovated buildings of the **Renaissance** city.
Though we suggest a few highlights to aim for below, the best approach is simply
to wander, taking any enticing alley that strikes your fancy. Make sure you leave
sufficient time, however, for Périgueux's wide-ranging municipal museum on the
district's northern boundary.

The longest and finest street in this part of town is narrow **rue Limogeanne**,
leading north from place de la Clautre via rue Salinière. Lined with elegant mansions, now turned into swish boutiques and *pâtisseries*, its most notable facade
belongs to **Maison Estignard** at no. 5, whose elaborate architecture – mullions,
dormer windows and ornamental columns – is typical of the Renaissance. It's also
worth popping into the more sober courtyard of no. 3 to see a salamander carved
above the inner door; this was the insignia of Francis I (1515–47), who brought
Italian Renaissance style to France. Opposite, impasse Limogeanne leads into a
series of courtyards and passageways known as **galerie Daumesnil** after the
famous general born at 7 rue de la Clarté in 1776 (see box overleaf). The area,
containing a mix of architectural styles, comprises one of Périgueux's most successful restoration projects.

Though nearby place du Coderc and place de l'Hôtel-de-Ville are both strong
contenders, **Place St-Louis**, to the west of rue Limogeanne, is probably the prettiest of Périgueux's squares. In its southeast corner stands the handsome, turreted **Maison du Pâtissier** – built by a man who made his forutne from *pâté en
croûte* (pâté in a pastry crust) – with a lovely Renaissance door bearing a warn-
ing on its lintel: "remember death awaits us all. Let he who takes pleasure in
speaking ill of those who are no longer with us, know that this house is forbidden to him. The supreme glory is to offend the wicked." There are more fine
houses over to the east of rue Limogeanne on rue de la Constitution; from here
the lanes begin to drop steeply to the river where you'll find the fifteenth-century
Maison des Consuls beside the bridge. It's a grand house with a semi-fortified

DAUMESNIL: THE PEG-LEG GENERAL

A devoted follower of Napoléon Bonaparte, **Baron Pierre Daumesnil** (1777–1832) was fiery, impetuous, loyal, patriotic and, above all, brave. He first distinguished himself during the Italian campaign (1796–97) when he rescued the drowning Napoléon from a river during the Battle of Arcole. Then at Acre in 1799 Daumesnil threw himself in front of his hero when a bomb landed at Napoléon's feet. It failed to explode, but Daumesnil, by now a major, was less lucky at the **Battle of Wagram** in Poland in 1809 when his left leg was so badly mutilated that it had to be amputated. Three years later he was promoted to general and made **Governor of the Château de Vincennes** – the country's largest arsenal – which he twice refused to hand over to the allied European armies fighting Napoléon. The second time, in 1815, he declared: "I will give up Vincennes when you give me back my leg". Nevertheless, Daumesnil was forced to retire a few months later following Napoléon's defeat at Waterloo and eventually died of cholera in 1832, though his wooden leg was preserved and is now on display in Paris's Musée de l'Armée. In Périgueux you'll find a statue of him towards the south end of boulevard Michel-Montaigne proudly pointing at his peg-leg.

third-floor gallery, while **Maison Lambert** next door – added in the sixteenth century – is almost lost behind a double gallery edged with sturdy balustrades.

The last sight in this area is the **Musée du Périgord** (April–Sept Mon & Wed–Fri 11am–6pm, Sat & Sun 1–6pm; Oct–March Mon & Wed–Fri 10am–5pm, Sat & Sun 1–6pm; 20F/€3.05, free mid-Sept to mid-June Mon–Fri noon–2pm) housed in a grand, nineteenth-century building at the top of rue St-Front, overlooking the broad, tree-lined allées Tourny. Given the importance of this museum, notably its prehistoric collection, there's a disappointing lack of information in English – you can get a photocopied sheet from the desk, but it's not always easy to follow.

The museum's most rewarding exhibits are in the east wing (to the left of the entrance hall as you enter), starting upstairs with an outstanding collection of **stone tools** – many from sites around Périgord – from the early and middle Paleolithic eras (100,000–35,000 BC). The local region also yielded the oldest human skeleton yet found in France, believed to be around 70,000 years old, which was discovered at Régourdou near Montignac (see p.222) in 1957; the one here is a replica. The second room, salle Michel-Hardy, traces human development up to 5000 BC. The tools are more precise, delicate and varied, and some show the first evidence of decorative art – look out for the superb "parade of bison" carved on a fragment of bone more than 12,000 years ago. It was found near Chancelade, 6km northwest of Périgueux, along with the nearby skeleton – another replica – known as **Chancelade Man**. Buried in a foetal position and surrounded by tools and more engraved bones, he was discovered in 1888 by Michel Hardy and Maurice Féaux, the then curators of the museum.

The ground floor houses an important ethnographic collection and a small natural history section, including a mammoth tusk found near Bergerac. Though some exhibits will be moved to the museum currently under construction in La Cité (see below), for the moment the highlight is the display of archeological finds from **Gallo-Roman** Vesunna. There are some stunning pieces: frescoes and mosaics in excellent condition, lovely bronze figurines, jewellery and a rare, wooden water pump preserved in Périgueux's marshy ground for nearly two thousand years.

The museum's west wing is devoted to a somewhat motley collection of Fine Arts. A couple of Canalettos stand out, as does the illuminated Rabastens Diptych, painted on leather in 1286, and the exquisite Limoges enamels near the exit.

La Cité

Remnants of the Roman town of Vesunna, now known as **La Cité**, lie southwest along rue de la Cité from place Francheville. Named after a local divinity, Vesunna was an important and prosperous town. By the first century AD it extended over some seventy hectares, complete with a forum, basilica, thermal baths and a seven-kilometre-long aqueduct. Today the most visible vestiges – a ruined amphitheatre, the remains of a temple complex and an excavated villa – lie scattered around the hulk of Périgueux's first cathedral, St-Étienne-de-la-Cité.

Approaching from the east, **St-Étienne**'s domes dominate La Cité. The church was founded by St Front in the fourth century, then rebuilt in its present form, with a Romanesque nave comprised of big square bays, some six hundred years later. The original building comprised four bays but two were destroyed, along with the bell tower, by Huguenots in 1577, leaving the church's west facade roughly truncated. The first bay you enter is the older of the two, dating from the eleventh century: the dome is more massive, the windows smaller and fewer and the stone less regular. The second bay was added a century later, then restored as an exact copy in the 1600s. Apart from being lighter and higher, its main feature is the line of decorative columns along the walls which stand out in the otherwise unornamented church.

The pretty **Jardin des Arènes** (daily: April–Sept 7.30am–9pm; Oct–March 7.30am–6.30pm; free), a circular garden northwest of St-Étienne, conceals a few remnants – comprising an entrance arch and traces of the foundations – of an enormous **amphitheatre** capable of holding 20,000 people or more. Built in the first century AD, it was dismantled two hundred years later to construct defensive walls (see p.133), of which you can see a fragment, the **Porte Normande**, along nearby rue Turenne. In the panic, the walls were cobbled together with whatever came to hand: a column, some capitals, a carved lintel, all pilfered from neighbouring monuments.

Heading southeast from here, past the empty carcass of twelfth-century Château Barrière and across the train lines, you reach Périgueux's most imposing Roman monument, the **Tour de Vésone**, in another public garden (same times as des Arènes; free). This high, circular tower was once the sanctuary of a temple dedicated to Vesunna's eponymous guardian goddess. The gaping breach on the north side is said to have been created when St Front exorcized the pagan gods; more prosaically, the bricks and stones probably went into local building works.

Just behind the tower the foundations of a **Roman villa**, discovered by chance in 1959, will form the basis of a new Gallo-Roman museum to be opened in 2002, alongside other local finds from the era currently on display in the Musée du Périgord (see above). For the moment you have to be content with peering through the chain-link fence. The villa was no humble abode. Spread over 4000 square metres, it had at least sixty rooms, baths and central heating as well as a garden – an indication of just how wealthy Vesunna was in those days.

Eating, drinking and entertainment

Surprisingly for the region, there is no great abundance of good **restaurants** in Périgueux. The most promising area is the old city, notably from rue Taillefer north to place St-Louis. In addition to those recommended below, there are several **cafés** along boulevard Montaigne, where you'll also find a **cinema** (☎08.36.68.14.45) with regular screenings of foreign-language films. The Nouveau Théâtre de Périgueux (NTP) at 1 avenue d'Aquitaine (☎05.53.53.18.71) puts on a varied programme of **theatre**, dance, concerts and variety shows. There's information about **what's on** in the local papers, or look out for *L'araignée du Square*, a twice-monthly free broadsheet covering Périgueux and its surroundings, available in the tourist office and bars around town.

Restaurants

All the following restaurants are marked on the map on p.137, except *Les Charentes* which appears on p.135.

Aux Berges de l'Isle, 2 rue Pierre-Magne. Pretty little restaurant at the east end of Pont des Barris (entrance through the *Hôtel des Barris*), offering unrivalled views of the cathedral and traditional cuisine at reasonable prices. Specialities include lamprey, soufflé of foie gras and Limousin beef. There's a wide choice of menus, starting at 89F/€13.57, except on Sundays, when it's à la carte only. Closed Sun eve.

Le Canard Laqué, 2 rue Lanmary. Authentic Chinese food, including Peking duck and dim sum, served in a stone-walled room. Menus start at 55F/€8.38 (except Sun) for a starter, *plat* and dessert. Closed Sun and last day of the month.

Le Chameau Gourmand, 2 rue des Farges. Another atmospheric restaurant, this time specializing in mountains of couscous with all the trimmings (from 60F/€9.15). Try to save room for one of their mouthwatering, home-made sweetmeats. Closed Mon.

Les Charentes, 16 rue Denis-Papin. It may not look much, but this hotel-restaurant opposite the station is gaining a reputation for its well-priced regional fare. They use locally produced organic and old-fashioned vegetables, to which they hope to add organic meat and wines in future. Weekday menus from 66F/€10.06. Closed one week early Nov.

Hercule Poireau, 2 rue de la Nation (☎05.53.08.90.76). One of Périgueux's best restaurants, in a stone-vaulted room with cheerful red-check fabrics, offering top-quality local cuisine at surprisingly affordable prices. House speciality is the luxurious *rossini de canard* (duck with a slice of foie gras in a truffle sauce). Menus from 99F/€15.09. Closed Sat lunchtime & Sun.

Le 8, 8 rue de la Clarté (☎05.53.35.15.15). Bright, modern colours and floral fabrics add a Mediterranean touch to this well-rated restaurant near St-Front. Dishes including oysters and *foie gras chaud* are matched by an extensive list of regional wines. Menus start at 165F/€25.15 for three courses, and you can order half-portions from 40F/€6.10. Closed Sun and Mon.

Le Pain Malin, 10 rue St-Silain. This tiny, informal restaurant makes a good lunch stop – arrive early to be sure of a table. *Pains malins* (from around 40F/€6.10) are open grilled sandwiches with a choice of toppings served with salad. Alternatively, there's a good range of salad platters, a *plat du jour* (Tues–Fri) or a choice of menus from around 90F/€13.72. Closed Sun & Mon.

Au Petit Chef, 5 pl du Coderc. Non-smoking restaurant that does a great-value lunchtime menu (70F/€10.67), including a self-service hors-d'oeuvres buffet. If that doesn't appeal, there's a whole range of *formules* and more elaborate menus to choose from, as well as a *plat du jour* and the *carte* (around 150F/€22.87 for three courses). Closed Thurs & Sat eve, Sun. July & Aug open daily.

L'Univers, 3 rue Éguillerie. The restaurant of the *L'Univers* hotel (see p.136) is stylishly decked out in plush reds behind frosted windows. There's plenty of fish on offer, including fresh lobsters, and generous portions of vegetables. Vegetarian meals available on request. Menus from 90F/€13.72. Closed Sun eve & Mon.

Bars and cafés

Café de la Place, 7 pl du Marché-au-Bois. Lovely old bar-brasserie on an attractive square, which also does decent food. Free concerts on Friday evenings – predominantly jazz, blues or accordion.

Le Fébus, 11 rue de la Vertu. Best in summer when you can sit outside in the quiet square. Tapas and other snacks available. Closed Sun.

Le St-Louis, 26 rue Éguillerie. A fairly ordinary café-cum-brasserie recommended for its prime position on place St-Louis, especially when you can sit outside.

Star Inn, 17 rue des Drapeaux. Snug Anglo-Irish pub patronized by a mixed crowd of local expats and anglophiles. Happy hour from 8pm, book exchange, board games and – of course – darts and quiz nights. Mon–Sat 8pm–1am.

Listings

Airlines Air France (☎05.53.02.79.71 or 08.02.80.28.02, www.airfrance.com) operates daily flights to Paris Orly.

Airport Bassillac (☎05.53.02.79.71).

Bike rental Try Cycles Cum's, 41 bis cours St-Georges (☎05.53.53.31.56), just across the river, or Cycles Evasion Peugeot, 46 rond point Chanzy (☎05.53.05.21.80), near the *gare SNCF*.

Boat trips From Easter to September boats depart from beneath the cathedral for a fifty-minute excursion along the Isle (40F/€6.10; ☎05.53.24.58.80).

Books and newspapers Maison de la Presse, 11 pl Bugeaud, stocks the widest selection of English-language newspapers and magazines. Librairie Marbot, 21–23 bd Montaigne, has some English-language books and a decent range of local guides and maps.

Bus departures Long-distance buses leave from the *gare routière* on pl Francheville. Most routes are operated by CFTA, which has an information office on site (☎05.53.08.43.13). In July & August Eurolines buses (☎08.36.69.52.52), en route from Toulouse to London, call in at the *gare routière*.

Car rental ADA, 4 bis rue Henri-Barbusse (☎05.53.05.40.28); Avis, *gare SNCF* (☎05.53.53. 39.02); Budget, 20 rue Denis-Papin (☎05.53.35.94.76); Europcar, 7 rue Denis-Papin (☎05.53.08.15.72); Hertz, place de la Gare (☎05.53.53.88.88). All these agents are located near the train station. With Avis, Budget, Europcar and Hertz you can also arrange for cars to be picked up at the airport.

Hospital Central Hospitalier, av Georges-Pompidou (☎05.53.07.70.00), to the north of centre along bd Michel-Montaigne.

Markets Périgueux's largest markets take place on Wednesday and Saturday mornings principally in place de la Clautre, place du Coderc (both fresh foods) and place Francheville (clothes and household goods). There's also a small, daily fresh-food market in place du Coderc's covered hall. In winter (mid-Nov to mid-March), stalls selling foie gras and truffles set up in place St-Louis for the annual *marché de gras* (Wed & Sat morning).

Police Comissariat de Police, rue du 4-Septembre (☎05.53.06.44.44).

Post Office The central post office is at rue du 4-Septembre, 24000 Périgueux.

Shopping The best place to look for regional produce is along rue Taillefer, where Pierre Champion (no. 21) sells local wines and truffles as well as duck and goose in all its guises. Apart from the markets listed above, you can buy picnic food in the Monoprix supermarket on place Francheville. There's also an excellent cheese shop on place du Coderc and other tempting, specialist shops along rue Limogeanne.

Taxis Call Allo Taxi Périgueux on ☎05.53.09.09.09. Alternatively, there's a taxi stand outside the train station and another on place Bugeaud.

Brantôme, the lower Dronne valley and the Double

Thirty kilometres north of Périgueux, the town of **Brantôme** is often described as the "Venice of Périgord". While that's rather overdoing it, the river walks and waterside restaurants are what draw most people here, with the added attraction of a Benedictine abbey's troglodyte vestiges. By contrast, the country along the **River Dronne** remains largely undisturbed. It is tranquil, very beautiful and restoring, best savoured at a gentle pace, perhaps by bike or even by canoe along the river. **Bourdeilles**, the first sizeable town downstream from Brantôme, was the seat of one of Périgord's four Baronies (see p.355), as its great tower testifies, while the Renaissance château next door contains a marvellous collection of furniture. From the foot of the castle, the Dronne meanders through water meadows to one of the Dordogne's most famous market towns, **Ribérac**. Though Ribérac itself holds little else of interest, it makes an agreeable base from which to visit a crop of Romanesque churches scattered in the countryside around. **Aubeterre-sur-Dronne**, with another, better-preserved troglodyte church and a splendid position, represents the final stop along the river. From here, if time allows, plunge south into the empty, enclosed world of the **Double** forest. Among isolated pockets of habitation, the spire of a Cistercian abbey provides a rare landmark and a focus for exploring the area's farms and myriad lakes, before dropping south again to a little-visited Renaissance château at **Neuvic**.

While there is no public transport along the Dronne valley or into the Double, there are **buses** from both Périgueux and Angoulême to Brantôme and Ribérac. From Angoulême, on the Paris–Bordeaux train line, there is also a bus service to Aubeterre.

Brantôme

When local monks dug a mill-stream across a tight meander of the River Dronne about a thousand years ago, they created the island on which **BRANTÔME** now stands. It's a pretty setting, with gardens and parks surrounding much of the town, the mill beside an ancient, dog-leg bridge and a Romanesque belfry silhouetted against the wooded scarp behind. The **abbey** and the **caves** at the base of this hill constitute Brantôme's principal sight, although there's also an engaging **museum** of dolls' houses in the old centre. Another attraction is the range of accommodation in the area, making it worth considering as an alternative base to Périgueux.

The Town

Aerial views show Brantôme's **old centre** packed on to an almost circular island, seemingly tethered to the surrounding bank by its bridges. A modern by-pass takes the worst of the traffic, but in summer it's still a bottleneck along the main road, rue Gambetta, which cuts north across the island to place de Gaulle on the far bank of the Dronne.

The town owes its existence to some rock-shelters – where the first hermits set up home around the fifth century – and a spring now hidden behind the church and convent buildings of the former **Benedictine abbey** standing on the river's far north bank. The first church was built under the cliffs here sometime before 817 – according to local tradition, it was Charlemagne (742–814) who founded the abbey with the endowment of St Sicaire's relic, one of the infants massacred by Herod. It had a rocky start, but by its twelfth-century heyday the abbey supported 24 parishes and had spawned a thriving town. Nevertheless, things started going downhill again with the Hundred Years' War and, after being rebuilt on several occasions, the abbey was finally abandoned after the Revolution. The present buildings, which date from the seventeenth century but were heavily restored two hundred years later, house the **Hôtel de Ville**, whose staring, serried windows still hint at ascetic institutional life. Not that self-denial was a virtue associated with this monastery's most notorious abbot, Pierre de Bourdeilles, the sixteenth-century author of *Les Dames Galantes* and other scurrilous tales of life at the royal court.

The abbey **church** recalls some of this history. The death of St Sicaire is the subject of a stained-glass window behind the altar, while bas-reliefs to either side depict the Massacre of the Innocents and Charlemagne offering Sicaire's relic to the church. After a quick look in the neighbouring chapterhouse, with its palm-frond vaulting, next stop is the **caves** (July & Aug daily 10am–7pm; April–June & Sept Mon & Wed–Sun 10am–12.30pm & 2–6pm; Feb, March & Oct–Dec Mon & Wed–Sun 10am–noon & 2–5pm; closed Jan; 20F/€3.05), accessed through this northeastern corner of the Hôtel de Ville. Despite being used as a quarry over the years, there's still considerable evidence of the monks' earlier troglodytic existence. The most interesting of the caves contains a large, rather crude **sculpture** of The Last Judgement, believed to date from the fifteenth century, in the aftermath of the Hundred Years' War. On a plinth decorated with geometric symbols and eight faces, each in different headgear, two angel trumpeters flank the skeletal image of Death. The figure of God, faintly etched and massive, looms out of the rock above. The cave's right-hand wall bears a much finer Crucifixion scene in front of a very European-looking Jerusalem.

A later, more worldly generation of monks built themselves an Italian-style, walled garden, now a public **park**, to the south of the abbey and across the old stone bridge from the water mill. It's a pleasant picnic spot and a walk along the balustraded **riverbanks** is a must. In summer you can also take a **boat trip** around the island from beside the old bridge (May–Sept; 35F/€5.34).

The more modern bridge directly in front of the abbey leads into rue Puy-Joli, Brantôme's main shopping street, where you'll find the **Musée de Rêve et Miniatures** at no. 8 (July & Aug daily 11am–6pm; April–June Mon–Thurs, Sat & Sun 2–6pm; Sept to mid-Nov Mon–Thurs, Sat & Sun 2–5pm; 38F/€5.79). Though not to everyone's taste, the six dolls' houses and displays of furniture through the ages, including real silver and glassware all shrunk to one-twelfth normal size, show stunning craftsmanship – some pieces of furniture even have real locks and keys.

Practicalities

Buses on the Périgueux–Angoulême route, timed to connect with TGV trains in Angoulême, stop on the Champs de Foire, at the south end of rue Gambetta. The **tourist office** is located in the Hôtel de Ville ticket office (July & Aug daily 10am–7pm; April–June & Sept Mon & Wed–Sun 10am–12.30pm & 2–6pm; Feb, March & Oct–Dec Mon & Wed–Sun 10am–noon & 2–5pm; closed Jan; ☎ & fax

05.53.05.80.52). For 450 years the streets of central Brantôme have been filled with a Friday-morning **market**, its stalls augmented in winter (Nov–Feb) with truffles, foie gras and local walnuts. You can rent **canoes** and **bikes** from Brantôme Canoë, just out of the centre on the road east to Thiviers (☎05.53.05.77.24).

The cheapest **accommodation** in town is the friendly *Hôtel Versaveau*, 8 place de Gaulle (☎05.53.05.71.42; ①; good restaurant from 65F/€9.91; closed three weeks in Nov & Sat Sept–May), with just eight simple rooms. Prettier and more comfortable rooms are available just across the river at the *Hôtel Chabrol* (☎05.53.05.70.15, fax 05.53.05.71.85, *www.logis-de-france.fr*; ③; closed mid-Nov to mid-Dec & Feb), whose restaurant, *Les Frères Charbonnel*, is in the gourmet class but still good value with its cheapest menu at 165F/€25.15 (Oct–June closed Sun eve & Mon). If you're feeling self-indulgent, you could treat yourself to a room at the beautiful *Moulin de l'Abbaye* in the old mill to the west of the abbey (☎05.53.05.80.22, fax 05.53.05.75.27, *moulin@relaischateaux.fr*; ⑧; closed Nov–April; restaurant closed for lunch Mon–Sat, except July & Aug closed Mon lunch only; menus from 240F/€36.59). Alternatively, there's a stylish, English-owned **chambres d'hôtes**, the *Maison Fleurie*, at 54 rue Gambetta (☎05.53.35.17.04, fax 05.53.05.16.58, *holsfrance@aol.com*; ④; closed Feb, school hols and one week in Nov), with a pool and quiet courtyard garden. Or try the *Château de la Borie-Saulnier* (☎05.53.54.22.99, fax 05.53.08.53.78, *chateau-de-la-borie-saulnier@wanadoo.fr*; ④; eve meals on request), also with a pool and extensive grounds, signed off the D82 4km northeast near the village of Champagnac-de-Belair. Those with a tent should head for the well-run **municipal campsite** east of Brantôme on the D78 Thiviers road (☎05.53.05.75.24; May–Sept).

In addition to the hotel **restaurants**, other options in Brantôme include *Les Jardins de Brantôme*, just north of place de Gaulle on the road to Angoulême (menus from 70F/€10.67). It doesn't look much from the outside, but the food is good and there's a nice garden behind for summer dining. Also best in fine weather is *Au Fil de l'Eau*, west of centre on quai Bertin (from 110F/€16.77; closed Jan & Feb, also Mon eve & Tues), with tables down by the river. Under the same management as the *Moulin de l'Abbaye*, it offers lighter meals at more affordable prices. For a real splurge in an idyllic setting, though, head for the *Moulin du Roc*, also a hotel, 6km away at Champagnac-de-Belair (☎05.53.02.86.00; closed Jan & Feb; restaurant closed Tues & lunch on Wed). Except on Sundays, lunch at this one-star Michelin restaurant costs just 165F/€25.15 including apéritifs and two glasses of wine; evening menus start at 240F/€36.59.

Bourdeilles

BOURDEILLES, 16km down the Dronne from Brantôme by a beautiful back road, the D106, is relatively hard to reach – perhaps the most appealing way is by canoe (for rental from Brantôme see above). It's a sleepy backwater, an ancient village clustering round its **château** (July & Aug daily 10am–7pm; May, June & Sept Mon & Wed–Sun 10am–12.30pm & 2–6.30pm; early Feb to April & Oct–Dec Mon & Wed–Sun 10am–12.30pm & 2–5.30pm; closed Jan & early Feb; 30F/€4.57) on a rocky spur above the river. The château consists of two buildings: one a thirteenth-century fortress, the other a subdued Renaissance residence begun by the lady of the house, Jacquette de Montbrun, wife of André de

Bourdeilles, as a piece of unsuccessful favour-currying with Catherine de Medici – unsuccessful because, though she passed through the area, Catherine never came to stay and so the château remained unfinished.

The Renaissance château is now home to an exceptional collection of furniture and religious statuary. Among the more notable pieces are some splendid Spanish dowry chests; the gilded bedroom suite of a former Yugoslav king; and a sixteenth-century Rhenish entombment whose life-sized statues embody the very image of the serious, self-satisfied medieval burgher. The *salon doré*, the room Catherine de Medici was supposed to sleep in, has also been preserved. Its elaborate furnishings and floor-to-ceiling decoration seem almost guaranteed to give a restless night. To clear your head, climb the octagonal keep and look down on the town's clustered roofs, the weir and the boat-shaped mill parting the current, and along the Dronne to the cornfields and the manors hidden among the trees.

There's a small **tourist office** just downhill from the château entrance (mid-June to mid-Sept daily 10.30am–noon & 3–6pm; ☎05.53.03.42.94, fax 05.53.54.56.27). For a simple, old-fashioned **hotel**, *Les Tilleuls* (☎ & fax 05.53.03.76.40; ②; menus from 70F/€10.67), right across the street, makes a cheap and pleasant place to stay, or try the newly renovated *Hôtel du Donjon* opposite (☎05.53.03.73.48, fax 05.53.04.66.69; ②; menus from 90F/€13.72; closed Oct–May). The nicest option, however, is the *Hostellerie des Griffons* (☎05.53.45.45.35, fax 05.53.45.45.20, *www.griffons.fr*; ⑤; closed Oct–Easter) in a sixteenth-century house beside the hump-back bridge, with top-notch regional cuisine (menus from 134F/€20.43).

If you're heading along the Dronne to Ribérac (see below), you could stop for lunch at the *Moulin du Pont* (menus from around 70F/€10.67; closed mid-Nov to Feb), a **restaurant** 8km downstream near the village of **LISLE**. Get there early to sit on the terrace with the weir on one side and the restaurant's trout ponds on the other. You could even arrive by river; **canoe** rental is available in Bourdeilles from Canoës Bourdeilles Loisirs (☎05.53.04.56.94) at the *Hôtel du Donjon*.

Ribérac and around

Surrounded by an intimate, hilly countryside of woods and hay meadows and drowsy hilltop villages, **RIBÉRAC**, 30km downstream from Bourdeilles, is a pleasant if unremarkable town, whose greatest claim to fame is its Friday **market**, bringing in producers and wholesalers from all around. There's nothing really in the way of sights, but the country around is dotted with numerous **Romanesque churches** that provide a focus for leisurely wandering – before setting off, you might want to collect information on these from Ribérac's tourist office (see overleaf). Nowadays many are kept locked, but the route described below takes in a representative sample of those that are more likely to be open. Their most distinctive features are a line of domes over the nave and the lack of decoration, just the occasional carved portal or capitals. Many have also been heavily fortified.

Ribérac's own **Collégiale Notre-Dame** (mid-June to mid-Sept daily 2–7pm; otherwise during exhibitions; free), now an exhibition and concert hall a couple of hundred metres away on the hill to the east of town, makes a good place to start. It's a pleasing building, with its squat tower and semicircular apse designed on a grander scale than its country cousins, but the west end and interior have been extensively altered; if it's open, it's worth popping in to see the recently restored seventeenth- and eighteenth-century frescoes. The **church of St-Pierre** in the village of **FAYE**, 1km west of Ribérac on the D20, on the other hand, has great charm even though it is no architectural beauty. Its diminutive single nave seems barely able to carry the fortress of a tower above. There's more reason to stop at **BOURG-DU-BOST**, 6km further downstream, where the **Notre-Dame** (daily 9am–7pm) harbours some very faded twelfth-century murals: the four Evangelists inside the dome, and the twelve Apostles around the choir.

From here the route cuts north and climbs to an undulating plateau with good views back over the Dronne's river meadows, then meanders through a string of villages. The first one to aim for is **ST-MARTIAL-VIVEYROL**, roughly 15km due north of Ribérac. Its church (daily 9am–6pm) more resembles a castle keep; the windows are reduced to narrow slits, there's just a single, simple door at ground level and the belfry doubles as a watchtower with, behind it, a guardroom big enough to hold the whole village along the length of the nave. Looping southeast around Ribérac, the **church of St-Pierre-et-St-Paul** (daily 9am–7pm) in **GRAND-BRASSAC** is unusual in that sculptures were added over its north door. They show Christ in majesty flanked by St Peter and St Paul above a frieze of the Adoration with traces of earlier paintwork.

The last of the Romanesque churches, **St-Pierre-ès-Liens** (daily 9am–7pm), is also one of the most prettily sited. It lies in wooded country 6km south of Ribérac and is best approached from the west with the roofs of **SIORAC-DE-RIBÉRAC** clustered behind. From the hastily erected rubble walls it's easy to see where, in the fourteenth century, the nave was raised a couple of metres and a guard tower added at the west end. Again, there are almost no windows and the walls are up to three metres thick – which explains why the nave is so surprisingly narrow.

Practicalities

Ribérac lies on the south bank of the Dronne. Its main street starts in the south as rue Jean-Moulin, runs through the central **place Nationale** and then continues northwards as rue du 26-Mars-1944. From place Nationale, rue Gambetta heads east to **place du Gaulle** and the vast market square beyond. **Buses** for Périgueux and Angoulême stop on the other side of this square near the Palais de Justice, which is where you'll also find Ribérac's **tourist office** (July & Aug Mon–Fri 9am–12.30pm & 1.30–7pm, Sat 10am–noon & 2–7pm, Sun 10am–1pm; Sept–June Mon–Sat 9am–noon & 2–6pm; ☎05.53.90.03.10, fax 05.53.91.35.13). In summer (late-June to mid-Sept) they organize tours to the Romanesque churches, guided walks and farm visits. You can rent **bikes** at Cycles Cum's, 35 rue du 26-Mars-1944 (☎05.53.90.33.23), and at the campsite (see below), which also has **canoes**.

There are two good **hotels** in Ribérac. The cheaper is the *Hôtel du Commerce* at 8 rue Gambetta (☎05.53.91.28.59; ①; closed Sun eve & Wed out of season), with a decent restaurant offering Antilles specialities as well as local fare from 55F/€8.38. More attractive and excellent value is the *Hôtel de France*, on the north side of place de Gaulle at 3 rue Marc-Dufraisse (☎05.53.90.00.61, fax 05.53.91.06.05, *www.logis-de-france.fr*; ②), with a terrace garden and a restaurant of some originality and local renown (menus from 85F/€12.96; closed Mon & lunchtime Tues out of season). There's also a municipal **campsite** just across the Dronne on the Angoulême road (☎05.53.90.50.08, fax 05.53.91.35.13; June to mid-Sept). The two hotels are the best places to eat in Ribérac, but for a **drink** you can't beat the old-style *Café des Colonnes* on rue Gambetta.

Aubeterre-sur-Dronne

Rather touristy, but very beautiful with its ancient galleried and turreted houses, **AUBETERRE-SUR-DRONNE** hangs on a steep hillside above the river, some 30km west of Ribérac. Its principal curiosity is the cavernous subterranean **church of St-Jean** (daily: mid-June to mid-Oct 9.30am–12.30pm & 2–7pm; mid-Oct to mid-June 9.30am–12.30pm & 2–6pm; 20F/€3.05), in the lower town, just north of Aubeterre's central square, the lime-shaded and café-lined **place Trarieux**. Carved out of the soft rock by twelfth-century Benedictine monks, it took at least a century to excavate the twenty-metre-high chamber and gallery above. It's from up here that you get the best views over the capacious baptismal font, designed for total immersion, and the two-tiered, hexagonal structure, possibly a reliquary, cut from a single piece of rock – its precise arches seem strangely out of place against the rough walls. The side-chapels are riddled with rock-hewn tombs, while a now-blocked-off tunnel connects the gallery with the château on the bluff overhead.

On the opposite, southern hillside, the upper town consists of a single street of houses culminating in the **church of St-Jacques**, where only the beautiful, sculpted west facade remains of the original twelfth-century church. The great tiered and decorated arch around the main door is lovely, but don't overlook the frieze of zodiacal signs on the smaller arch to the left: Taurus, Aries and Pisces are easy enough to recognize, then come Capricorn, Aquarius and Sagittarius. The other half of the frieze is missing.

Aubeterre's **tourist office** (July & Aug Mon 2.30–6.30pm, Tues–Sun 10am–noon & 2.30–6.30pm; Sept–June daily 2–6pm; ☎05.45.98.57.18, fax 05.45.98.54.13) faces onto the town's main car park to the west of place Trarieux. There are two good **hotels** to choose from: the Dutch-owned *Hôtel de France*, a simple, cheerful place on the central square (☎05.45.98.50.43, *obakker@planete. net*; ②), and the recently renovated *Hostellerie du Périgord* (☎ & fax 05.45.98.50.46; ③; closed Jan & one week in Nov) down by the bridge on the Ribérac road. The latter offers spacious en-suite rooms and a small pool and winter-garden, as well as a recommended **restaurant** (from 110F/€16.77; closed Tues). There's also a three-star municipal **campsite** (☎05.45.98.60.17; mid-June to mid-Sept) just across the bridge, with a small beach nearby and the possibility of **canoe** rental in summer. On weekdays there is a daily **bus** to Angoulême (which departs from near the Gendarmerie on the main road to the south of the bridge), while Chalais, which is on the Angoulême–Bordeaux train line, is only 12km away; call ☎05.45.98.28.11 if you need a taxi.

The Double and beyond

South of the Dronne valley the landscape and atmosphere change dramatically as you enter the region known as the **Double**. This high, undulating plateau is strewn with lakes and brooding **forests** of oak, chestnut and pine, interspersed with pockets of vines and scattered farmhouses. The larger lakes have been developed for tourism and in summer the Double is a popular destination for walkers, cyclists and nature-lovers; the best place to pick up information is from Ribérac tourist office (see opposite). Until the late nineteenth century, however, it was largely uninhabited thanks to its poor soils and malarial marshes. Then Napoléon III decreed that it should be drained and planted with maritime pines in similar fashion to the great Landes forest further south.

This work was partly carried out by Trappist monks who arrived from Port-Salut in 1868. They settled near the only village of any size, **ÉCHOURGNAC**, plum in the middle of the plateau nearly 20km southwest of Ribérac, where they founded the **Abbaye de Notre-Dame de Bonne-Espérance**. Since 1923 the walled abbey has sheltered a small community of Cistercian sisters – these days numbering about thirty, some under a vow of silence – who not only continued in the monks' spiritual footsteps but also in their role as local cheese-makers. But the enterprising and energetic sisters didn't stop there. In their well-stocked **shop** opposite the church entrance (summer daily 10am–noon & 3–6pm; winter 10am–noon & 2.30–5.30pm; but phone for confirmation ☎05.53.80.82.50) you'll find the original Le Trappe Échourgnac, a firm, mild orange-crusted cheese much like Port-Salut, and a new version laced with walnut liqueur, as well as jams, pâté and jellied sweets.

Five kilometres east of the abbey, on the D41 from Échourgnac, the **Ferme du Parcot** (July & Aug daily 2.30–5.30pm; May, June & Sept Sun same times; 15F/€2.29) has been preserved as a more typical example of local architecture. With walls of mud and straw on latticed timber frames, protected by a limestone plaster, these farm buildings are quite unlike the sturdy stone houses found elsewhere in the Dordogne. They date from 1841 and, from the grandeur of the barn, it seems the farmer was relatively affluent. In true rural style, however, the house itself, which was inhabited up to 1990, consists of just two very spartan rooms containing a few bits and pieces of furniture and old implements. The farm also marks the start of a gentle **nature trail** (2.5km; accessible all year) through the fields and forest to a fishing lake.

With a bit of planning, you can then go on to **eat** at the *Ferme Auberge du Perrier*, a working farm dishing up hearty meals made from its own produce – which means lots of duck (menus from 60F/€9.15, including wine; ☎05.53.90.59.04; closed Mon). They're located near one of the biggest lakes in the Double, the **étang de la Jemaye**, signed off the D708 Ribérac road about 8km northeast of Échourgnac.

If you're heading back to Périgueux from here, it's worth dropping down to the Isle valley, which marks the edge of the Double to the south and east, to visit an imposing Renaissance château with a botanical garden on the outskirts of **NEUVIC**, roughly 15km east of Échourgnac. Heading east across the valley floor, a great bank of red-tiled roofs pinpoints the largely sixteenth-century **Château de Neuvic** (daily 1.30–6pm; 35F/€5.34 including the garden; 45F/€6.86 for a guided tour) which now makes an unusually grand school for deprived children. Since the interiors have been extensively modified, there's not a lot to see beyond some badly damaged frescoes and an elegant eighteenth-century salon furbished with pastoral scenes. But it is the scale of the building, and particularly its handsome western facade, that grabs the attention. The best vantage point is from the recently established **botanical garden** to the west of the château (daily: July & Aug 10am–7pm; March–June, Sept & Oct 10am–noon 1.30–6pm; Nov–Feb 1.30–6pm; 22F/€3.35), though you'll find your attention diverted by a wonderful collection of scarecrows made by the pupils. The idea only started in 1998, but looks set to become a regular feature after their truly imaginative designs won an international competition the following year.

The château also houses three **chambres d'hôtes** (☎05.53.80.86.65, fax 05.53.82.22.77; ④) in those rooms that escaped modernization, and a popular **restaurant** offering lunches in the salon for around 100F/€15.24 (by reservation;

closed during school hols). Otherwise, cross back over the Isle and head upstream on the D3 for another 10km, to find two more good eating options in the attractive town of **ST-ASTIER**. The smartest is *La Palombière* (menus from 68F/€10.37; closed Tues eve & Wed, also two weeks both in March & Sept), with its pretty terrace beside the towering abbey church, while the *Auberge du Chapeau Rouge* (menus from 65F/€9.91; closed Mon eve & Sat midday, also the first week of July) is one of those glorious, no-nonsense locals' places where you can have a *plat du jour* for 38F/€5.79. To find it walk west from the church through place Gambetta and fork right in front of the post office along rue Montaigne.

While there is no **public transport** in the Double, both St-Astier and Neuvic are on the train line from Périgueux to Bordeaux and the bus route to Mussidan, though services in both cases are few and far between.

From St-Jean-de-Côle to Hautefort

This sweep across the northern reaches of the Dordogne *département* starts among the lush river valleys of the Périgord Vert, where the enchanting village of **St-Jean-de-Côle** sits on a tributary of the River Dronne. The country around – gentle, rolling and green – is home to the Renaissance **Château de Puyguilhem**, set against oak woods, and the **Grotte de Villars**, a cave system which provides a modest taster of those along the Vézère valley to the south. From Villars the route cuts east and south through the towns of **Thiviers** and **Sorges**, respectively centres of foie gras and truffle production, as described in their small museums. North of Thiviers, the **Château de Jumilhac** merits a detour for its sheer scale and severity, softened by a bristling roof line, if nothing else. A very different castle awaits to the east of Sorges, among the higher, grander landscapes of the Périgord Blanc, where, beyond the attractive town of **Excideuil** with its own impressive castle, the **Château de Hautefort** presents a magnificent sight on its commanding spur, endowed with an elegance quite unlike the normal rough-stone fortresses of the Dordogne.

Those relying on public transport can reach Thiviers by **train** from Périgueux, and there are limited **bus** services from Périgueux and Thiviers to Excideuil. It is even possible to reach Hautefort by bus, but the timings are such that you'll have to stay two nights in the village.

St-Jean-de-Côle and around

Twenty kilometres northeast of Brantôme, **ST-JEAN-DE-CÔLE** ranks as one of the loveliest villages in the Périgord Vert. An ancient church and château constitute its major sights, and, with a hotel and a couple of restaurants it makes a good lunchtime or overnight stop. From here the splendid **Château de Puyguilhem** lies within easy striking distance and, on the return journey, you could loop north via the **Grotte de Villars**, notable for its formations rather than the smattering of prehistoric artwork.

Tiny and very picturesque, without being twee, St-Jean's unusually open, sandy square is dominated by the charmingly ill-proportioned late-eleventh-century **church of St-Jean-Baptiste**. The view as you approach is harmonious enough – layers of tiled roofs from the low, square market-hall to the steeply pitched belfry

– but on entering the single, lofty bay it becomes apparent that the nave was never completed, due to a lack of funds. Beside the church stands the rugged-looking **Château de la Marthonie** (July & Aug daily 10.15am–noon & 2–7pm; 20F/€3.05) which dates from the twelfth century, but has since acquired various additions in a pleasingly organic fashion. Apart from a huddle of houses round the square, the rest of the village consists of a line of pastel-plastered cottages stretching west to a hump-backed bridge over the River Côle and the inevitable watermill. The whole ensemble makes a perfect backdrop for the Floralies **flower festival** held on the second weekend in May.

St-Jean's **tourist office** (daily: June–Sept 10am–1pm & 2–7pm; April, May & Oct 9.30am–12.30pm & 2–5pm; ☎ & fax 05.53.62.14.15, *www.ville-saint-jean-de-cole.fr*) is on the square, as well as two attractive **restaurants**: the *Coq Rouge* (☎05.53.62.32.71; closed Wed & Jan–March), whose excellent regional menus start at around 100F/€15.24; and *Le Templier*, with menus from 78F/€11.89 (closed Mon & Tues, & Dec–Feb). Though it doesn't have the same views, you'll also eat well at the village **hotel**, the wisteria-covered *Hôtel St-Jean* (☎05.53.52.23.20; ②; restaurant from 70F/€10.67, closed Sun eve) on the main road near the entrance to the square. It's a real old-fashioned country hotel, nothing fancy but welcoming and well maintained.

Around St-Jean-de-Côle

About 10km west of St-Jean, the **Château de Puyguilhem** (July & Aug daily 10am–7pm; May, June & Sept daily 10am–12.30pm & 2–6.30pm; April daily 10am–12.30pm & 2–5.30pm; early Feb to March & Oct–Dec Tues–Sun 10am–12.30pm & 2–5.30pm; closed Jan & early Feb; 30F/€4.57) is a perfect example of early French Renaissance architecture. It was erected at the beginning of the sixteenth century by the La Marthonie family of St-Jean-de-Côle on the site of an earlier and more military fortress. The lake that once filled the foreground has long gone, but the château still makes an enchanting prospect, with its steep roofs, stone balustrades, mullion windows, carved chimney stacks and an assortment of round and octagonal towers reminiscent of contemporaneous Loire châteaux.

Though the **interior** suffered more from neglect and pillaging, it too has been beautifully restored and contains some noteworthy pieces of furniture and Aubusson tapestries. Its most remarkable features, however, are two magnificent fireplaces: the first, in the guardroom, depicts three Greek soldiers, while upstairs in the banqueting hall the theme is continued with six of the twelve Labours of Hercules. Both are heavily restored, but no less remarkable for that. The sculptors also went to work on the entrance hall and main staircase, leaving a wealth of oak, vine and acanthus leaves, thistles, fleur-de-lis and a few salamanders for good measure. Right at the top, it was the turn of the master carpenters, whose superb hull-shaped roof timbers have lasted five hundred years.

The ruined Cistercian **abbey of Boschaud**, 3km away in the next valley south, merits a quick visit while you're in the area. Standing in the middle of a field, reached by a lane not much bigger than a farm track, its charm rests as much in the fact that it is – for once – unfenced, unpampered and free, as in the pure, stark lines of its twelfth-century architecture.

Both the château and abbey lie in the commune of **VILLARS**, 8km to the west of St-Jean. The village itself has nothing particularly to recommend it apart from another appealing **hotel**, the *Relais de l'Archerie* (☎05.53.54.88.64, fax 05.53.54.21.92; ②; restaurant from 80F/€12.20; closed Nov & Feb, and weekends Oct–March), in a little nineteenth-century château with terrace and gardens.

In 1953 speleologists discovered an extensive cave system in the hills 3km north of Villars, part of which has been opened to the public. While the **Grotte de Villars** (daily: July & Aug 10am–7pm; May, June & Sept 10am–noon & 2–7pm; April & Oct 2.30–6.30pm; 38F/€5.79) boasts a few prehistoric paintings – notably of horses and a still unexplained scene of a man and bison – the main reason for coming here is the variety of stalagmites and, in particular, stalactites. Some are almost pure white and as fine as needles, others ochre yellow. There are cascades, semi circular basins and hanging curtains of semi-translucent calcium carbonate. The final cave you come to contains the paintings, dating from 17,000 years ago, the same age as those at Lascaux (see p.223). And look out, too, for the bears' claw marks further back from the entrance, where generations of tiny cubs also left their imprints.

Thiviers and Jumilhac

Not far east of St-Jean-de-Côle, the small market town of **THIVIERS** sits on the main road and rail links between Périgueux, 40km to the south, and Limoges. The N21 bypasses the town these days, leaving its old centre – comprising a clutch of pretty, old houses round the church and along pedestrianized rue de la Tour – relatively peaceful. The one exception is during the Saturday **market**, when the streets present a lesson in local agriculture: walnuts, apples, Limousin beef, pork, duck and goose and all manner of associated foodstuffs. From mid-November to mid-March the *foies* come out in force at the *marché au gras*, some of them destined to go into a new local speciality, *L'autre fois de Thiviers*, consisting of duck or goose liver robed in pâté (see the box on p.154 for more on foie gras). Thiviers' accommodation options make it a good base should you wish to make a detour to visit the **Château de Jumilhac** to the north.

Up until the 1920s Thiviers was an important centre for porcelain, a few pieces of which are displayed in a small **museum** (10F/€1.52) accessed via the tourist office (see below). But the pretty blue and white porcelain plays second fiddle to the museum's prime concern – the history and production of foie gras. Thiviers' only other claim to fame is that **Jean-Paul Sartre** spent some of his early childhood and subsequent school holidays here with his grandparents. In this case, though, there is merely an inconspicuous plaque – above an estate agent at the top end of rue Jean-Jaurès near the church – since Sartre recorded his memories of the place in less than complimentary terms.

The **gare SNCF**, with services to Bordeaux, Périgueux and Limoges, is located just north of Thiviers' centre, behind the *Hôtel de France et de Russie* (see below). In school term-time **buses** depart from the station for Excideuil on weekdays only (2–3 daily; 30min). The helpful **tourist office**, on central place Foch (Mon & Tues 10am–noon & 2.30–6pm, Wed–Fri 9am–7pm, Sat 9am–1pm & 2–7pm, Sun 10am–1pm & 2–6pm; ☎ & fax 05.53.55.12.50), can provide information on farm visits and walks in the local area, as well as lists of *chambres d'hôtes* and other **accommodation** options. One of the nicest places to stay is the attractive and well-priced *Hôtel de France et de Russie*, 51 rue du Général-Lamy (☎05.53.55.17.80, fax 05.53.52.59.60; ③), on the road north from the tourist office. Or try the *Auberge de* *la Belle Isle* (☎05.56.62.00.80; ②; menus from 80F/€12.20) run by a friendly English–French couple in the village of **CORGNAC-SUR-L'ISLE**, 5km southeast of Thiviers. They only have a handful of rooms, the cheapest not en suite, and note

---

FOIE GRAS

It is generally agreed that it was the Egyptians who first discovered the delights of eating the **enlarged livers** of migratory geese and ducks gorging themselves in the Nile delta, and that it was the Romans who popularized the practice of force-feeding domesticated birds, generally with figs. Indeed, the first-century cook Apicius wrote a number of recipes for what we now call foie gras, literally "fat liver". For many the name is off-putting enough, let alone the idea of force-feeding the birds, while for others a slice of succulent, pale rose-coloured foie gras is a pleasure not to be missed.

Foie gras is produced throughout southwest France and also in Alsace, Brittany and the Vendée, although the yellowish-hued livers from the Périgord, where the birds are traditionally fed on local yellow – as opposed to white – maize, and where producers jealously guard their methods of preparation, are particularly sought after. Périgord farmers now favour hybrid Mulard or Barbary **ducks** over the more traditional **geese** for a variety of reasons: they fatten more quickly, are easier to raise and force-feed, and the liver is easier to cook with. The softer goose livers, on the other hand, have a more subtle flavour and smoother texture. They are also much larger – 700g to 900g for an average goose liver (*foie gras d'oie*) as opposed to 400g to 500g for duck (*de canard*).

So how do the livers get so big? The young birds are raised outside to the age of four months, after which they are kept in the dark and fed over one kilo per day of partly cooked maize for between two and three weeks. During this time the livers can quadruple in size. This **gavage**, or force-feeding, was traditionally carried out using a funnel to introduce the grain into the bird's throat and then stroking it down the neck by hand. Modern techniques follow the same principle but use a mechanized feeder. It's not nearly as terrible as it might sound and most small producers are very careful not to harm their birds, if for no other reason than that this will ruin the liver.

All round, it's best to **buy** foie gras from small family concerns, either direct from the farm – local tourist offices can advise – or at the region's many *marchés au gras* that take place from November to March. If you're buying fresh liver, choose one which is not too big and is firm but gives slightly to the touch; the average prices are around 250F/€38.11 per kilo for foie gras of duck and 400F/€60.98 for goose. The alternative is the ready-prepared preserved version, of which there is a bewildering variety. The majority is de-veined, seasoned (wherein the secret recipes) and then sterilized by cooking briefly (*mi-cuit*) before being vacuum-packed or sealed in jars, either of which is preferable to the canned varieties; the tin taints the flavour. When choosing, check that it is locally produced and then look for the label *foie gras entier*, consisting of one or more whole lobes, or simply *foie gras* which is composed of smaller pieces but is still top quality liver. Next step down is a *bloc de foie gras* made up of reconstituted liver (sometimes *avec morceaux*, visible pieces of lobe) pressed together. Below that come all sorts of *mousses*, *parfaits*, pâtés and so forth, each of which has to contain a specified minimum percentage of foie gras and to indicate this on the label.

The best way to eat foie gras is with a slice of plain country bread and a glass of Sauternes (see p.104). Use a fine, sharp knife dipped in hot water to cut it into thin slices.

that the restaurant is closed in winter (Nov–March). Finally, there's a well-run, three-star **campsite**, *Le Repaire* (☎ & fax 05.53.52.69.75; May–Sept), beside an artificial lake on the eastern outskirts of Thiviers.

Château de Jumilhac

In its upper reaches the Isle valley narrows down between steep, wooded banks to become a mini-ravine. One of its rocky bluffs, some 20km northeast of Thiviers, is home to the vast **Château de Jumilhac** (45min guided tour: June–Sept daily 10am–7pm; mid-March to May & Oct to mid-Nov Sat & Sun 2–6.30pm; 35F/€5.34). While elements of the original thirteenth-century château, such as the stone-paved ground-floor rooms and the family chapel, remain, the present structure largely owes its existence to an ironmaster, Antoine Chapelle, later Count of Jumilhac, who made his fortune manufacturing arms for the future Henry IV during the Wars of Religion.

The body of the château is suitably uncompromising: the hard, grey stone allowed for little decorative detail and what windows there are mostly consist of only narrow slits. But the roof is another matter. It is adorned with no less than eight different **towers**, from great grey-slate wedges to pinnacled turrets and a jaunty pepper pot, topped off with delicate lead statues depicting the angels of justice or more mundane pigeon-shaped weather-vanes.

Inside, however, austerity reigns once again. This is particularly so in the cramped, ground-floor rooms, which date back to the thirteenth century, but also extends to the medieval rooms above, of which the much-vaunted **spinner's room** provides the focus of the tour. Not so much for its architecture – it's a small vaulted chamber decorated with naive frescoes of animals and flowers – but for the story attached. The spinner in question was Louise de Hautefort, wife of the then Count of Jumilhac, who was imprisoned here for thirty years (1618–48) for her alleged infidelity. Not one to mope, Louise took to painting the walls and spinning to occupy her time. Or so it seemed. The shepherd who regularly called under her window, and from whom she bought her wool, was of course her lover in disguise, and the spindles were used to carry secret messages between them. According to one legend, the story ended in the lover being killed in a duel, while another has him retiring to a monastery. To give you some idea what all the fuss was about, there's a portrait of Louise, supposedly painted at the time of her release but still beautiful, defiantly holding her spindle aloft.

The two wings enclosing the courtyard were added later in the seventeenth century and are gradually being restored by the château's present owners, descendants of Antoine Chapelle, who bought it back from the state in 1927. So far the most interesting room on view is the west wing's grand reception room, with its oak panelling and elaborate chimneypiece carved by Limousin craftsmen.

If you're here around lunchtime, try the *Lou Boueïradour* **restaurant**, named after an implement used for blanching chestnuts, on the wide square in front of the château. Their regional menus start at 70F/€10.67.

Sorges

SORGES, a small town on the Périgueux road about 15km south of Thiviers, is worth visiting simply for its informative **Musée de la Truffe** (July & Aug daily 9.30am–12.30pm & 2.30–6.30pm; Sept–June Tues–Sun 10am–noon & 2–5pm; 20F/€3.05), located just off the main road to the south of the old centre. The dry limestone plateau around Sorges is particularly prolific for truffles – in the early 1900s the commune averaged 6000kg per year, and the largest black truffle discovered so far, a monster weighing well over a kilo, was found near Excideuil (see below) in only 1999. By way of comparison, most truffle-hounds would be happy with a mere couple of hundred grams.

You'll unearth all manner of similar facts and figures in the museum, the brainchild of an enterprising local mayor – a former *trufficulteur* – from how the fungus forms to how to create your own truffle-oak orchard, all helpfully translated into English. The tips on choosing a good truffle and what to do with it afterwards will come in handy if you happen to be in Sorges for the annual **truffle market** (the Sunday nearest January 20) or if you're tempted by one of the preserved specimens on sale in the museum. They also have details of a three-kilometre nature trail that gives an idea of how and where truffles grow (see also the box opposite).

The museum doubles as Sorges' **tourist office** (same hours; ☎05.53.05.90.11, fax 05.53.46.71.43), and the town also boasts a very comfortable, reasonably priced **hotel**, called what else but *Auberge de la Truffe* (☎05.53.05.02.05, fax 05.53.05.39.27, *www.auberge-de-la-truffe.com*; ③). Though it's on the main road, the rooms are all double-glazed and most face onto the garden and pool behind, or there's a quieter annexe (*Hôtel de la Mairie*) by the church. Even if you're not staying, try their excellent **restaurant** – naturally, truffles feature strongly (menus from 80F/€12.20).

Excideuil

The old route between Périgueux and Limoges used to run up the Isle and Loue rivers to **EXCIDEUIL**, 15km east of Sorges, where two huge medieval keeps still dominate the little market town. The **castle** was one of the region's most heavily fortified. For a while the viscounts of Limoges held court here, but after the Hundred Years' War the fortress lay in ruins until relatively recently. Now privately owned, you can only enter the precinct. It is, however, a classic and well worth seeing. From the castle, rue des Cendres leads north into the tight knot of streets concentrated around place Bugeaud and the much-restored church with its Gothic portal. This square and the nearby *halle* are the venue for a lively farmers' **market** on Thursday mornings, augmented in winter (Dec to early March) by an important *foire aux gras*.

Excideuil can be reached by **bus** from Périgueux (Mon–Sat) and Thiviers (see p.153 above). There's a bus stop beneath the castle on place du Château, where you'll also find the **tourist office** booth (mid-April to Sept Mon–Sat 9.30am–1pm & 2.30–5pm; Oct to mid-April Mon–Fri same hours; ☎05.53.62.95.56, fax 05.53.62.04.79, *excideuil@wanadoo.fr*) and a nice old-fashioned **hotel**, the *Hostellerie du Fin Chapon* (☎05.53.62.42.38, fax 05.53.52.39.60; ②), which offers simple but agreeable rooms and a good **restaurant** (Oct–May closed Sun) with menus from 80F/€12.20, or 120F/€18.29 for their popular summer Sunday lunch. There's also a basic but prettily sited **campsite** (☎05.53.62.43.72, fax 05.53.62.95.91, *excideuil@wanadoo.fr*; July & Aug) by the river on the east side of town.

Hautefort

Southeast of Excideuil you cross the pretty Auvézère valley, the route of the GR646 footpath, and enter the limestone plateaux of the Périgord Blanc. The views are magnificent, and nowhere more so than around **HAUTEFORT** and its eponymous **château**, standing on a south-facing promontory some 20km from Excideuil and 40km northeast of Périgueux.

The **Château de Hautefort** (guided tours: mid-July to Aug daily 9.30am–7pm; April to mid-July & Sept daily 10am–noon & 2–6pm; Oct daily 2–6pm; mid-Jan to March daily during school hols 2–6pm; during school term Sun 2–6pm; Nov to mid-Dec Sun 2–6pm; closed mid-Dec to mid-Jan; 35F/€5.34) is a stunning sight from whichever direction you approach, a magnificent example of good living on a grand scale, endowed with an elegance that is out of step with the usual rough stone fortresses of Périgord. Indeed, when the then Marquis de Hautefort rebuilt

---

THE BLACK DIAMONDS OF PÉRIGORD

The **black truffle** of Périgord, *Tuber melanosporum*, is one of those expensive delicacies that many people find overrated. This is mainly because it is usually served in such minute quantities or is combined with such strong flavours that its own subtle, earthy taste and aroma are completely overwhelmed. To really appreciate the truffle, it should be eaten in a salad, omelette or simple pastry crust, or, as the writer Colette advised, "eat it on its own, fragrant and coarse-skinned, eat it like the vegetable that it is, hot, and served in generous quantities".

Part of the truffle's mystique inevitably stems from its supposed **aphrodisiac** virtues. Perhaps the most famous proponent was Napoléon I, who attributed the conception of his son to having eaten a basket of Périgord truffles. Madame de Pompadour (see p.164) was also particularly partial to them. It was thanks to truffles, she said, that she retained Louis XV's favours for so many years.

The truffle is a **fungus** that grows entirely underground, and a fussy one at that. It prefers shallow, free-draining limestone soils rich in organic matter, a sunny position and marked seasonal differences, and requires the presence of certain species of oak, or occasionally lime or hazelnut, around the roots of which it grows. It's greedy, too, absorbing so much of the nutrients and water available that the vegetation overhead often dies. This tell-tale ring of denuded earth is just one of the clues truffle-hunters are on the lookout for. Others include small, yellow truffle-flies hovering just above the soil, and the subtle smell – which is where the pig, or more often these days the more amenable dog – comes in.

Even now the **life cycle** of the Périgord truffle – the most prized out of more than forty different varieties – is not completely understood, and attempts to cultivate them on any scale have so far proved elusive. What is clear is that the spores are released in the spring and mature truffles are ready for harvest between December and early March. When ripe, the skin of a Périgord truffle is a deep purple-brown or black while the lighter-coloured flesh is flecked with fine white veins. It should be firm to the touch and give off a pleasantly earthy aroma; an overripe truffle stinks.

The principal truffle **markets** take place at Périgueux, Sarlat and Brantôme, and at Lalbenqeu near Cahors in the Quercy. Prices these days stand at around 3000F/€457 per kilo, reaching up to 5000F/€762 in poor years. In the past, however, truffles were so common that they were considered a pest by vine growers. Ironically, the fungus proved a life-saver for many local farmers when phylloxera hit, ushering in the truffle's "golden age". Since the 1950s the harvest has declined dramatically for a number of reasons – deforestation and rural depopulation amongst others.

it in the mid-seventeenth century, his ambition was to create a château worthy of the Loire.

The original fortress, which was built sometime around 1000, in the twelfth century belonged jointly to the famous troubadour **Bertran de Born** (see p.355) and his brother Constantin, until Bertran persuaded his overlord, Henry II of England, to grant him sole ownership in 1185. The following year Constantin took his revenge and left the place in ruins – at which point Bertran went off to become a monk. The château's recent history has been no less troubled. After decades of neglect, in 1929 Hautefort was bought and meticulously restored by the Baron Henri de Bastard and his wife. Then in August 1968, just three years after the work was completed, a **fire** gutted everything except the chapel in the southeast tower. A year later the indomitable baroness – her husband having died before the fire – set about the whole task again. Master craftsmen were called in to re-create everything from the staircases to the ornate chimney-pieces. There's no disguising the fact that they are brand new, but the quality of work is superb.

The approach lies across a wide esplanade, flanked by immaculate topiary gardens, and over a drawbridge to enter a stylish Renaissance **courtyard** opening to the south. The two wings end in a pair of round towers whose great bulk is offset by grey-slate domes topped with matching pepperpot lanterns; the southwestern tower, nearest the entrance, is the only part of the medieval château still standing. While the main building is equally symmetrical, the overall impression is one of rhythm and harmony rather than severity.

About the only furnishings saved from the fire were four sixteenth-century tapestries, now on display inside, but the real highlight is the **great hall**. This monumental room, 280 metres square, provides the perfect setting for two huge chimney-pieces. Exact copies of the originals and carved from local walnut, each took five thousand hours' work.

After you've finished in the château and its thirty-hectare park, it's also worth wandering through the village to visit the **Musée de la Médécin** (June–Sept daily 10am–7pm; Oct–May Mon–Fri 10am–noon & 2–6pm; 25F/€3.81) in the midst of an open square. It occupies part of a hospice for the poor founded in 1669 by the same marquis who rebuilt the castle, as its architecture – particularly the domed central chapel – suggests. One of the ground-floor rooms presents an early-nineteenth-century ward under the ministration of the Sisters of Charity. As if this wasn't sobering enough, things get worse upstairs among the displays of medical implements through the ages, culminating in examples of dental surgeries up to 1970 – they even have that awful smell.

The museum entrance lies through the **tourist office** (June–Sept daily 10am–7pm; Oct–May Mon–Fri 10am–noon & 2–6pm; ☎05.53.50.40.27, fax 05.53.51.99.73) located in the hospice's north wing, where you can pick up details of places to visit along the Auvézère valley. For an overnight stay in Hautefort, there's a very pleasant **hotel**, the *Auberge du Parc* (☎05.53.50.88.98, fax 05.53.51.61.72; ②; closed three weeks in Nov & Feb) with a good local restaurant (menus from 90F/€13.72), right under the castle walls, and a lakeside **campsite**, *Le Moulin des Loisirs* (☎ & fax 05.53.50.46.55, *www.moulin-des-loisirs.com*; April–Sept), less than 2km to the south. It is possible to reach Hautefort by public transport, but you'll have to stay two nights: a **bus** leaves Périgueux at 5.25pm (Mon–Fri), with the return service departing Hautefort at 7.30am.

Brive-la-Gaillarde and around

A major road and rail junction **Brive-la-Gaillarde** is the nearest thing to an industrial centre for miles around. Though it has no commanding sights, Brive does
offer a few distractions, foremost of which is the Musée Labenche, focusing on
local history, and a core of carefully restored old streets. It also makes an agreeable base for exploring the beautiful towns and villages around, and it's not that
far to Lascaux and the upper reaches of the Dordogne river.

North of Brive, among the green fields and apple orchards of the southern
Limousin, the hilltop town of **Uzerche** presents a grand array of turrets and towers caught in a loop of the River Vézère, while nearby **Arnac-Pompadour** is a
must for anyone remotely interested in horses. Its château, from where Madame
de Pompadour got her name, provides a stately backdrop to a national stud farm,
and a splendid racecourse. Heading south, first stop is the village of **Turenne**.
Two sky-scraping towers and a number of noblemen's houses are all that remain
of this once-powerful town, which enjoyed almost complete independence up to
the eighteenth century. Nearby **Collonges-la-Rouge** also prospered under
Turenne rule, but it is the unexpected shock of the red sandstone as much as the
time worn buildings that gives the village its special appeal.

All these places can be reached by public **transport**. Uzerche and Arnac-
Pompadour lie on two different train lines between Brive and Limoges, while
Brive is also the departure point for buses to Turenne and Collonges.

Brive-la-Gaillarde

The largely pedestrianized old centre of **BRIVE-LA-GAILLARDE** comes as a
pleasant surprise after its sprawling suburbs. It is enclosed within a circular boulevard shaded by plane trees, from where all roads lead inwards to the much-
restored **church of St-Martin**. Brive's other main sight, the wide-ranging
Musée Labenche, lies on the ring road to the southeast, while across the other
side of town the local Resistance museum, the **Musée Edmond Michelet**, is of
more specialist interest.

It's thought that Brive earned its nickname *la Gaillarde* during the Hundred
Years' War when, for much of the time, it was a lone French stronghold surrounded by English. Opinions are divided, but the name (meaning strong,
sprightly or bawdy) refers either to its fortifications or – the generally preferred
option – the spirited, valiant nature of its people. The ramparts disappeared after
the Revolution to make way for today's gardens and ring road, but the "Brivistes"
themselves haven't changed, as they will happily tell you, citing their prowess on
the rugby field as the prime example; Brive not only won the European Cup in
1997, but were also runners up the following year.

Arrival and information

Brive is large enough to have its own **airport**, 4km to the west, from where there
are daily flights to Paris. There are no shuttle buses, but a taxi only costs about
50F/€7.62. The **gare SNCF**, on the Paris–Toulouse and Bordeaux–Lyon main
lines, is located on the south side of town, from where it's a ten-minute walk along
avenue Jean-Jaurès to the boulevard ringing the old town. The local **bus** service
is unusually comprehensive. Local and regional buses depart from various spots

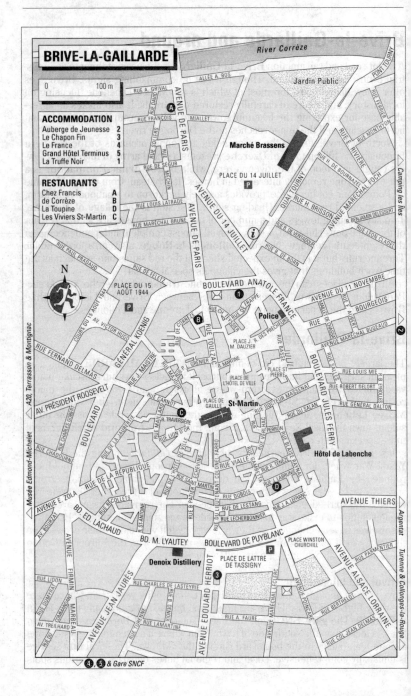

BRIVE-LA-GAILLARDE

0   100 m

ACCOMMODATION

Auberge de Jeunesse	2
Le Chapon Fin	3
Le France	4
Grand Hôtel Terminus	5
La Truffe Noir	1

RESTAURANTS

Chez Francis	A
de Corrèze	B
La Toupine	D
Les Viviers St-Martin	C

round town, including the *gare SNCF* and place du 14-Juillet to the north of the old centre, which is also where you'll find the **tourist office** (July & Aug Mon–Sat 9am–12.30pm & 2–7pm, Sun 10am–1pm; Sept–June Mon–Sat 9am–noon & 2–6pm; ☎05.55.24.08.80, fax 05.55.24.58.24, *tourisme.brive@wanadoo.fr*). It occupies an old pumping station and water tower built in the form of a lighthouse, so you can't miss it. They have a fair amount of information in English, and look out too for the free *Limousin* guide produced annually by *The News* English-language paper.

Accommodation

There are several good cheap **hotels** around Brive station, and a choice of smarter establishments on the ring road. The municipal **campsite**, *Les Îles* (☎ & fax 05.55.24.34.74), is situated across the river nearly half a kilometre east from the old centre.

Le Chapon Fin, 1 pl de Lattre-de-Tassigny (☎05.55.74.23.40, fax 05.55.23.42.52, *www. logis-de-france.fr*). This American-French-owned hotel occupies an attractive bourgeois house on the ring road. The rooms are comfortable enough and all en suite, but they play second fiddle to the restaurant serving regional specialities (menus from 75F/€11.43; Nov–March closed Sun eve). ③.

Le France, 60 av de la Gare (☎05.55.74.08.13, fax 05.55.17.04.32, *www.logis-de-france.fr*). Budget hotel opposite the station offering a choice of clean, functional rooms above a café-style restaurant (three-course menus from 55F/€8.38). ①.

Grand Hôtel Terminus, pl de la Gare (☎05.55.74.21.14). This grand, old railway hotel has hardly changed over the years, from its original cage-lift to the plump beds and old telephones in the huge, high-ceilinged bedrooms. Opt for a room with bath rather than the aged shower cabinets. ①.

La Truffe Noir, 22 bd Anatole-France (☎05.55.92.45.00, fax 05.55.92.45.13, *www.la-truffe-noire.com*). Despite being extensively restored, Brive's best hotel is still full of warm wood panelling and cosy inglenooks. The rooms are equally tasteful, though rather small at the cheaper end, and there's an excellent restaurant – the house specialities of course feature truffles (menus from 135F/€20.58). ⑤.

Youth Hostel, 56 av Maréchal-Bugeaud (☎05.55.24.34.00, fax 05.55.74.82.80, *brive@fuaj.org*). Friendly HI hostel 25 minutes' walk across town from the *gare SNCF*. Rooms come with two to four beds and there's a pleasant garden. There's a members' kitchen and meals are provided. No curfew. 50F/€7.62 per person.

The Town

The compact centre of Brive has been beautifully restored in recent years. As a focus for wandering the old streets, head first to the **church of St-Martin**, plum in the middle. Originally Romanesque in style, now only the transept, apse and a few comically carved capitals survive from that era. St Martin, a Spanish aristocrat, arrived in pagan Brive in 407 AD on the feast of Saturnus, smashed various idols, and was promptly stoned to death by the outraged onlookers; his tomb can be seen in the crypt. The only other point of interest is a large, twelfth-century baptismal font near the west door decorated with the symbols of the four evangelists.

Numerous streets fan out from the surrounding square, **place du Général-de-Gaulle**, with a number of turreted and towered houses, some dating back to the thirteenth century. The most impressive is the sixteenth-century **Hôtel de Labenche**, southeast of the church on boulevard Jules-Ferry, now housing a better-than-usual local history **museum** (Mon & Wed–Sun: April–Oct

10am–6.30pm; Nov–March 1.30–6pm; 27F/€4.12). As you enter, note the busts of the Labenche family leaning forward over each window. The museum's huge collection ranges from archeological finds, including some delightful Gallo-Roman bronzes complete with moulds, to nineteenth-century rural craft industries and a beautiful display of accordions made in Brive by the Dedenis factory prior to 1939. But the museum's highlight is a rare collection of **Mortlake tapestries**. The Mortlake workshop, under the supervision of Dutch weavers, was founded by James I of England in 1620. Though they were only in business until the end of that century, they produced a number of important works which were highly prized at the time. The most interesting of the seven presented here are the three fox-hunting scenes – the colours are still exceptionally vibrant. In the centrepiece a lord and lady dance while another group play *quilles*, a local version of skittles, as dusk falls over the dregs of the hunt dinner.

The tone changes considerably at Brive's other museum, the **Musée Edmond Michelet** at 4 rue Champanatier (Mon–Sat 10am–noon & 2–6pm; free), portraying the Resistance and deportations during World War II through photographs, posters and objects of the time, though little is explained in English. To get there take the main street rue de la République west from St-Martin church as far as the ring road, from where it is signed straight ahead along avenue Émile-Zola. The museum occupies the former home of Edmond Michelet, one of Brive's leading *résistants*, who was arrested here in 1943. He was deported to Dachau but survived to become a minister in de Gaulle's postwar government.

Returning to the centre, turn right along the ring road to find the **Denoix distillery**, founded in 1839, at 9 boulevard Maréchal-Lyautey (Tues–Sat 9am–noon & 2.30–7pm; free; *www.net-creation.fr/denoix*). Their liqueurs are centred around walnuts, notably a very mellow tipple called Suprême Denoix, but they have also resurrected a local mustard. Made with grape must and spices, Moutarde Violette de Brive was first devised in the fourteenth century for Pope Clément VI, a native of Corrèze. Not surprisingly for this area, it goes very well with duck.

Eating and drinking

In summer small **restaurants** and **bars** open in the gardens along the southern stretch of the ring road. Otherwise, avenue de Paris, leading north to the river, is the best place to look for restaurants, while one of Brive's nicest cafés, the old-fashioned *L'Europe*, lies on avenue de 14-Juillet, opposite the tourist office.

Chez Francis, 61 av de Paris (☎05.55.74.41.72). You'll need to book ahead for this friendly, cluttered restaurant down towards the river. The imaginative seasonal menus feature the best of local ingredients, but prices are surprisingly affordable. At lunch you can have a *plat du jour* for just 48F/€7.32, while the fixed menus are priced at 85F/€12.96 and 125F/€19.06. A favourite haunt of writers, actors and artists during Brive's various festivals (see box on p.132), the walls, ceilings and lampshades are covered with messages of appreciation. Closed Sun.

de Corrèze, 3 rue de Corrèze. Another popular, locals' place, this time to the north of St-Martin, with tiled floors and a handful of wooden tables under cheerful, sunflower cloths. The food is equally traditional and comes in hearty portions. Three-course menus start at 55F/€8.38. Closed Sun.

La Toupine, 11 rue Jean-Labrunie (☎05.55.23.71.58). Up-and-coming restaurant in the backstreets of the old town where you need to reserve. They serve lots of fresh fish as well as an assortment of regional dishes. Menus range from 60F/€9.15 to 140F/€21.34. Closed Wed & Sun, two weeks in Feb and two weeks in Aug.

Monument aux Girondins, Bordeaux

Château Margaux, Médoc

MICHAEL BUSSELLE/ROBERT HARDING

Château Latour, Pauillac

ADAM WOOLFITT/ROBERT HARDING

Place de la Myrpe, Bergerac

TONY GERVIS/ROBERT HARDING

Streetside café, Périgord

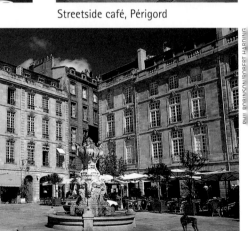

PHIL ROBINSON/ROBERT HARDING

Place du Parlement, Bordeaux

Poppy field, Périgord

St-Front Cathedral, Périgueux

Taking the water at Brântome

River Dordogne at Limeuil

Château de Monbazillac, near Bergerac

Boating on the River Dordogne, near Trémolat

Les Viviers St-Martin, 4 rue Traversière. Its worth seeking out this pretty little restaurant in a backstreet just west of St-Martin church for its simple, good-value cooking. There's a wide range of menus, starting at 59F/€8.99, as well as salads, *moules* and pasta. Service can be slow at times, but this is one of the few places open on Sundays.

Listings

Airlines Air Liberté (☎05.55.86.88.36 or 08.03.80.58.05) operates daily flights to Paris-Orly.

Airport Brive-Laroche (☎05.55.86.88.36).

Bus departures For information on buses around the *département*, call the Conseil Général's transport office on ☎05.55.93.72.17. Eurolines buses en route from Toulouse to London depart from outside the post office on pl Winston-Churchill.

Car rental Avis, 56 av Jean-Jaurès (☎05.55.24.51.00), Europcar, 2 av Jean-Jaurès (☎05.55.74.14.41), and Hertz, 54 av Jean-Jaurès (☎05.55.24.26.75) are all located near the train station, with airport pick-ups available.

Hospital Centre Hospitalier, bd Docteur-Verlhac (☎05.55.92.60.00).

Markets The modern, open hall behind the tourist office is the venue for a famous market on three mornings a week (Tues, Thurs & Sat) and four important *foires grasses* for foie gras, truffles and other local produce held between December and February. During the first weekend in November each year the fruit and veg gives way to a book fair, La Foire du Livre, which attracts a number of well-known authors and artists.

Police Commissariat de Police, 4 bd Anatole-France (☎05.55.17.46.00).

Post office The central post office is at pl Winston-Churchill, 19100 Brive-la-Gaillarde.

Taxis Call ☎05.55.24.24.24.

Around Brive

The country around Brive offers a variety of rewarding day-trips. To the north, **Uzerche** retains evidence of a more noble – and less peaceful – past in its mansions and fortified church perched above the river. Further west comes **Arnac-Pompadour**, home to one of France's best-known stud farms set in the grounds of a striking fifteenth-century château. The viscounts of **Turenne**, to the south of Brive, once ruled over vast tracts of Limousin and Périgord. Now only vestiges of their castle remain, though the aristocratic houses clustered in its lee have fared better, as has the viscounts' administrative centre, **Collonges-la-Rouge**, whose red sandstone lends it a warm, rosy appeal which survives the onslaught of visitors.

Uzerche

Thirty-five kilometres north of Brive, or a half-hour train ride along the course of the bubbling River Vézère, the town of **UZERCHE** is impressively located above a loop in the river's course. It's worth a passing visit as the town has several fine old buildings dating from the sixteenth and seventeenth centuries when it was the capital of the Bas-Limousin, as this region was, and is, known. Despite the cramped site, on a long narrow knuckle of rock oriented north–south, the wealthier citizens managed to erect surprisingly substantial mansions. They also had a passion for towers, which can be best appreciated from across the river when their full height becomes apparent.

All traffic is funnelled along the main road running beside the river on the east side of Uzerche. From here steep steps lead up to the town's highest tower, that of the fortified **abbey church of St-Pierre**. Consecrated in 1097, the church combines Romanesque barrel vaults and carved capitals with a beautifully light and airy Limoges-style ambulatory and radiating chapels. South from the church, the place des Vignerons is a pretty spot with views out across the river, while to the north rue Pierre-Chalaud and rue de la Justice slope gently down past a number of fine Renaissance houses. One of the more ornate is the **Maison Eyssartier**, west of the abbey church at the bottom of the steeply sloping place de la Libération. It was originally owned by several generations of apothecaries – hence the pestle-and-mortar crest on the facade.

Uzerche's **gare SNCF** lies 2km north of the old town along the main road, while **buses** from Brive will drop you beside the river. The **tourist office** (mid-June to Sept daily 10am–12.30pm & 1.30–6.30pm; Oct to mid-June Mon–Fri 10am–noon & 2–5pm; ☎05.55.73.15.71, fax 05.55.73.88.36, *ot.uzerche@wanadoo.fr*) is next door to the Maison Eyssartier; it's worth dropping in for their annotated walking route. If you need a place to **stay**, *Hôtel Teyssier*, by the river (☎05.55.73.10.05, fax 05.55.98.43.31; ③; closed Wed; restaurant from 95F/€14.48), is a good option, or there's *Hôtel Ambroise* round the corner (☎05.55.73.28.60, fax 05.55.98.45.73, *www.logis-de-france.fr*; ②; closed Sun eve & Mon off season and in Nov; restaurant from 80F/€12.20). There's also a three-star municipal **campsite** (☎05.55.73.12.75, fax 05.55.98.44.55; May–Sept) 2km south along the river.

Arnac-Pompadour and around

Roughly 20km west of Uzerche, and also accessible by train from Brive, **ARNAC-POMPADOUR** is dominated by its grey, turreted château overlooking one of the most picturesque racecourses in France. The town is probably most famous for its association with Madame de Pompadour, mistress of Louis XV, but it is also home to the country's second most important stud farm (*haras*), where Anglo-Arabs – the all-round horse used for racing, jumping, cross-country and dressage events – were first bred. As a result it's a very horsey place.

The present château largely dates from the fifteenth century. When the Pompadour line died out in 1745, it was ceded to Louis XV who promptly bestowed the title on his mistress. Though she never bothered to visit, the **Marquise de Pompadour** started breeding horses on her estate before being forced to sell for financial reasons in 1760; she nevertheless kept the title. On regaining possession of the castle the following year, Louis founded the Royal Stud, which became a **National Stud** in 1872. In between, the horses were sold off during the Revolution, but Napoléon I soon re-established the stud to keep his cavalry supplied. He sent four Arab stallions, booty from his Egyptian campaign, which were crossed with English thoroughbred mares to produce the first Anglo-Arabs.

The **château** itself was gutted by fire in 1834 and now houses the stud's headquarters. You can visit its terraces on a half-hour guided tour (daily: April–Sept 10–11.30am & 2–5.30pm; early Feb to March 2–5.30pm; Oct to early Feb 2–4.30pm; 10F/€1.52), but the *dépôt des étalons*, where the stallions are kept, are more interesting (1hr guided tours daily: July–Sept 10–11am & 2–5.30pm; Oct–June 2.30–4.30pm; 25F/€3.81). They lie across the chestnut-shaded esplanade from the château. During the spring breeding season (March–June) there are fewer stallions in the *dépôt*, but this is the best time to visit the mares (*juments*) at the **Jumenterie de la Rivière** (45min guided tours daily: mid-Feb to March 2–4.15pm; April–June 2–5pm; July–Sept 3–5pm; 20F/€3.05), 4km southeast near the village of Beyssac. In late spring (May–June) the fields around are full of mares and foals, the best being kept for breeding, the rest sold worldwide as two-year-olds. At any time of year, however, you will see horses being exercised round the magnificent track in front of the château. In addition, from May to October there are frequent **race meetings**, as well as dressage and driving events, shows and open days; the tourist office can provide a calendar of events.

For those less enamoured of horses, the Romanesque **abbey church** of Arnac (part of the Pompadour domains), 2km to the northwest, is of interest for its carved capitals. Though exceptionally high, enlarged photos beside each pillar help identify the striking images, including Daniel in the lions' den among several depicting lions.

Arnac-Pompadour lies on a minor **train** line between Brive and Limoges. It can also be reached from Brive by **buses**, which stop by the château before terminating at the **gare SNCF**, 500m southeast on the D7 to Vigeois. The **tourist office** (daily: April–Sept 10am–noon & 2–6.30pm; Oct–March 2–6pm; ☎05.55.98.55.47, fax 05.55.98.54.97), in the gatehouse of the *dépôt des étalons*, sells tickets for the château, *dépôt* and Jumenterie, though at the last of these you can also buy tickets on the spot. There's even a reasonable place to **stay**: the *Hôtel du Parc* (☎05.55.73.30.54, fax 05.55.73.39.79, *www.logis-de-france.fr*, ③; closed weekends Nov–March), behind the château. In addition to cheerful rooms and a small pool, the hotel boasts a good regional **restaurant** (menus 85–330F/€12.96–50.31). The other option in the area is the modern *Auberge de la Mandrie* (☎05.55.73.37.14, fax 05.55.73.67.13, *www.logis-de-france.fr*, ③), 4km west on the D7, with chalet rooms around a pool, and more refined cuisine (menus from 72F/€10.98).

Turenne

TURENNE, just 16km south of Brive, is the first of two very picturesque villages in the vicinity. In this case slate-roofed, mellow stone houses crowd under the protective towers of a once-mighty fortress. At their peak during the fifteenth century, the viscounts of Turenne ruled over a vast feudal domain containing some 1200 villages. It was one of the most powerful estates in France, and virtually autonomous. The viscounts retained the right to raise taxes and mint their own coins, amongst other privileges, up until 1738 when Louis XV bought the viscountcy in the aftermath of the Fronde rebellion (see p.358).

Although Louis also ordered that the castle be demolished, two towers still sprout from the summit; to reach them, take the lane running northeast from the main road and keep climbing. One of the towers is occupied by the present owners of the château, but the round **Tour de César** can be visited (July & Aug daily 10am–7pm; April–June, Sept & Oct daily 10am–noon & 2–6pm; Nov–March Sun 2–5pm; 18F/€2.74) and is worth climbing for vertiginous views away over the ridges and valleys to the mountains of Cantal. On the way up to the castle you pass a number of elegant Renaissance houses and the all-important salt store, as well as a **church** hurriedly thrown up in 1662 during the Counter-Reformation to bring the local populace back to Catholicism; take a peek inside at the gilded altar and unusual mosaic ceiling.

Buses from Brive stop on the main road near the **tourist office** (mid-June to mid-Sept daily 10am–12.30pm & 3–6pm; mid-April to mid-June & mid-Sept to mid-Oct Sat & Sun 10am–12.30pm & 3–6pm; closed mid-Oct to mid-April; ☎05.55.85.94.38), where you can get walking maps of the village; or from the souvenir shop opposite. There's a lovely small **hotel**, *La Maison des Chanoines*

(☎05.55.85.93.43; ④; closed Wed & Nov–March), on the old village square just up from the tourist office. The rooms are decorated with the same flair and imagination that's apparent in their **restaurant**, where you'll eat extremely well for around 160F/€24.39 (closed Wed and lunchtime on Tues & Thurs; reservations essential). Across the square, *La Vicomté* (closed Mon & Nov–Feb, also closed for dinner Sept–June) offers wonderful views of the château from its terrace and a traditional regional menu for 110F/€16.77.

Collonges-la-Rouge

There's a great view back to Turenne as you head southeast on the D20 before cutting eastwards on pretty back lanes through meadows and walnut orchards to reach **COLLONGES-LA-ROUGE** some 10km later; alternatively, you can walk between the two on the GR446. The village is the epitome of bucolic charm with its rust-red sandstone houses, pepperpot towers and pink-candled chestnut trees, although you need to time your visit carefully, as it is very much on the tourist route. Though small-scale, there is a grandeur about the place. This is where the nobles who governed Turenne on behalf of the viscounts built their mini-châteaux, each boasting at least one tower – there's a wonderful view of the bristling roofs as you approach from the west.

On the main square the twelfth-century **church** is unusual in having two naves, of which the shorter, north nave – the one used today – was a later addition. They came in handy during the sixteenth century when Turenne supported the Huguenot cause; here at least, Protestants and Catholics conducted their services peacefully side by side. Outside, the covered **market hall** still retains its old-fashioned baker's oven, while rather different local traditions are on show at the **Musée Vivant de l'Oie** (April–Oct daily 10am–noon & 2–7pm; free) on the southeastern outskirts of the village. You can learn all about the history and mythology of geese and the various different species and, if you've got the stomach for it, watch the *gavage* – the method of force-feeding with maize to produce foie gras (see box on p.154 for more).

Buses from Turenne and Brive pass Collonges on their way to the terminus at Meyssac (see below). They stop on the main road at the northern entrance to the village, beside the **tourist office** (July & Aug daily 10.30am–12.30pm & 2.30–7pm; April–June & Sept Mon–Sat 2–5pm; closed Oct–March; ☎ & fax 05.55.25.47.57). There's an attractive but slightly expensive **hotel** in the village, the *Relais de St-Jacques de Compostelle* (☎05.55.25.41.02, fax 05.55.84.08.51, *www.multimania.com/relaistjacques/index.htm*; ②–④; closed mid-Nov to mid-March; restaurant 70–250F/€10.67–38.11). The cheaper rooms, with communal toilet and showers, are in a less interesting annexe, but those in the main building have lovely views. If you want somewhere quieter, head east 2km to **MEYSSAC**, a smaller town built in the same red sandstone, to the very pleasant *Relais du Quercy* (☎05.55.25.40.31, fax 05.55.25.36.22, *www.logis-de-france.fr*; ③; closed three weeks in Nov), with a pool and pretty restaurant (menus start at 70F/€10.67). Alternatively, there's a two-star **campsite**, *Moulin de Valane* (☎05.55.25.41.59; May–Sept), halfway between Collonges and Meyssac.

Collonges has a number of *créperies* and snack bars, but if you're looking for a proper **restaurant**, try the *Auberge Le Cantou* (closed last week of June & mid-Dec to mid-Jan, also Sun eve & Mon off season) with its flower-filled terrace on the main street. They serve good old-fashioned country cooking, with menus from 78F/€11.89.

travel details

Trains

Brive-la-Gaillarde to: Arnac-Pompadour (2–3 daily; 35–50min); Bordeaux (1–2 daily; 2hr 15min); Cahors (4–8 daily; 1hr 10min); Paris Austerlitz (7–10 daily; 4hr–4hr 30min); Périgueux (3–5 daily; 1hr); Souillac (3–6 daily; 25min); Toulouse (4–7 daily; 2hr 30min); Uzerche (3–5 daily; 25–30min).

Périgueux to: Bordeaux (8–15 daily; 1hr–1hr 25min); Brive (3–5 daily; 1hr); Neuvic (1–2 daily; 20–30min); Paris Austerlitz (1–2 daily; 5hr); St-Astier (6–9 daily; 10–20min); Terrasson (5–6 daily; 40–50min); Thiviers (10–12 daily; 20–30min).

Buses

Aubeterre-sur-Dronne to: Angoulême (Mon–Fri 1–2 daily; 1hr 15min–2hr).

Brantôme to: Angoulême (1–3 daily; 1hr–1hr 15min); Périgueux (1–4 daily; 45min).

Brive to: Argentat (Mon–Sat 2 daily; 1hr 15min–1hr 40min); Arnac-Pompadour (Mon–Sat 1 daily; 2hr–2hr 20min); Beaulieu-sur-Dordogne (school term Mon–Sat 1–3 daily, school hols Tues, Thurs & Sat 1–2 daily; July & Aug Mon, Tues & Thurs–Sat 1–2 daily; 1hr–1hr 30min); Collonges-la-Rouge (Mon–Sat 1–4 daily; 25min–1hr); Meyssac (Mon–Sat 1–4 daily; 30min–1hr); Montignac (Mon–Sat 1 daily; 1hr 30min); Sarlat (school term Mon–Sat 1 daily, rest of year Tues, Thurs & Sat 1 daily; 2hr); Turenne (Mon–Sat 1–4 daily; 25–40min); Uzerche (2 daily; 1hr 10min–1hr 30min).

Périgueux to: Angoulême (1–3 daily; 1hr 40min–2hrs); Bergerac (Mon–Sat 2–4 daily; 1hr–1hr 20min); Brantôme (1–4 daily; 45min); Excideuil (Mon–Sat 3–5 daily; 1hr); Hautefort (Mon–Fri 1 daily; 40min); Montignac (Mon–Sat 1–2 daily; 1hr); Neuvic (school term Mon–Fri 1 daily; school hols 1 weekly; 40min); Ribérac (Mon–Sat 1–4 daily; 1hr); Sarlat (Mon–Sat 1–2 daily; 1hr 30min); St-Astier (school term Mon–Fri 1 daily; school hols 1 weekly; 30min); Thiviers (1 weekly during school term; 40min); Villars (school term-time 1 weekly; 1hr).

Ribérac to: Angoulême, via Mareuil (Mon–Sat 1–2 daily; 1hr 30min–1hr 45min); Périgueux (Mon–Sat 1–4 daily; 1hr).

Turenne to: Brive (Mon–Sat 1–4 daily; 20–35min); Collonges-la-Rouge (school term Mon–Fri 1–2 daily, July & Aug Tues & Thurs 1 daily; 15min); Meyssac (school term Mon–Fri 1–2 daily, July & Aug Tues & Thurs 1 daily; 20min).

Planes

Brive-la-Gaillarde to: Paris Orly (1–3 daily; 1hr 15min–1hr 30min).

Périgueux to: Paris Orly (1–3 daily; 1hr 10min).

CHAPTER THREE

BERGERAC AND AROUND

In its lower reaches the Dordogne slides wide and slow through a landscape of vine-planted hills. This is the heart of the **Périgord Pourpre**, a major wine-growing area that blends seamlessly into the Bordelais vineyards to the west. For centuries the region's most important market town, port and commercial centre has been **Bergerac**, the second largest city in Dordogne *département*, but still a pleasantly provincial place with a clutch of worthwhile sights amongst its twisting lanes. As to the wine region itself, its foremost sight is the Renaissance **Château de Monbazillac**, clearly visible on the ridge to the south, surrounded by its prestigious vineyards, originally planted by monks in the Middle Ages, which produce a very palatable sweet white wine. The high country further south of Bergerac, where the gentle River Dropt marks the border of Dordogne and Lot-et-Garonne *départements*, wasn't always such a bucolic scene, as a glance at the remaining fortifications of **Issigeac** and particularly **Eymet** – the ramparts built in the run-up to the Hundred Years' War – goes to show. The prevailing sense of unease following more than a century of war, plague and famine is caught in the fifteenth-century frescoes of the Last Judgement in the little church of **Allemans-du-Dropt**, while further downstream at **Duras** another semi-ruined château dominates the valley.

To the west of Bergerac the Dordogne valley becomes wider, busier and less attractive. Nevertheless, there are one or two appealing sights, notably the Gallo-Roman remains at **Montcaret** and the nearby **Château de Montaigne** were the eponymous philosopher wrote his original, wide-ranging *Essais*, before the river slips between St-Émilion's trellised vines (see p.120). North of here, the **Forêt du Landais** stretches north across the top of the Périgord Pourpre. It's a pretty region of wooded hills, meandering streams and sparse habitation, good for wandering, though without any particularly compelling sights.

ACCOMMODATION PRICE CODES

All the hotels and *chambres d'hôtes* listed in this book have been price-coded according to the following scale. The prices quoted are for the **cheapest available double room in high season**, although remember that many of the cheap places will have more expensive rooms with en-suite facilities.

① Under 160F/€24
② 160–220F/€24–34
③ 220–300F/€34–46
④ 300–400F/€46–61
⑤ 400–500F/€61–76
⑥ 500–600F/€76–91
⑦ 600–700F/€91–107
⑧ 700–800F/€107–122
⑨ Over 800F/€122

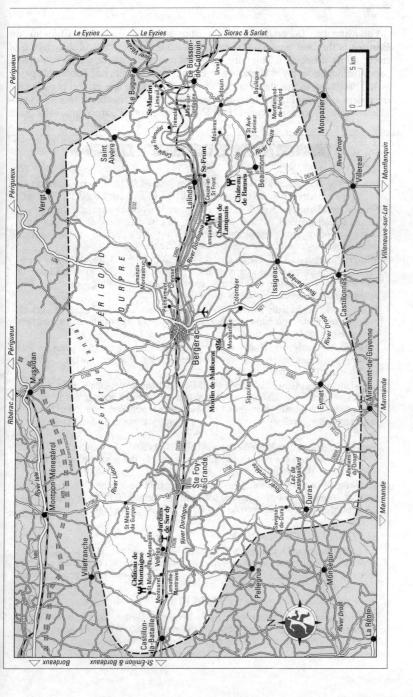

Following the Dordogne upstream from Bergerac the noble **Château de Bannes** is the best preserved of many châteaux built to control this stretch of river and its tributaries. The pure waters of one such tributary later spawned a paper-making industry at **Couze-et-St-Front**, where traditional, handmade paper is still produced to this day. Further east the Dordogne has carved two gigantic meanders at **Trémolat** and **Limeuil**; the views from the northern river-cliffs provide a classic Dordogne scene. Here also the Périgord Pourpre gradually gives

---

FESTIVALS, EVENTS AND MARKETS

JULY AND AUGUST

July & Aug Bergerac: Les Mercredis du Jazz (☎05.53.57.71.51). Free concerts by French jazz artists on Wednesday evenings in the Clôitre des Récollets.

Second weekend in July Issigeac: Foire aux Paniers. Unique and hugely successful basket-weavers' fair held on the place du Château. Some fifty artisans from all regions of France demonstrate their different techniques and styles, including the local spiral-shaped baskets. Entry fee 10F/€1.52.

Mid-July Bergerac: La Table de Cyrano (☎05.53.74.66.66). The old town is transformed into a gigantic outdoor restaurant for this magnificent food festival held over four days. Everyone eats at large, convivial tables, sampling local dishes and wines, and there are free concerts every night.

Third weekend in July Duras: Fête de la Madeleine. A combination of agricultural fair, town fête with music and feasting, and market stalls, culminating in a fireworks display on the final night.

Late July or early Aug Duras: Le Parvis. A highly rated local circus troupe puts on three night-time spectacles over a weekend in the château courtyard. Tickets available from the tourist office.

Late-July to mid-Aug Castillon-la-Bataille: La Bataille de Castillon (☎05.57.40. 14.53, *www.batailledecastillon.com*). Local citizenry stage a spectacular floodlit re-enactment of the battle that ended the Hundred Years' War. Some five hundred actors and fifty cavaliers take part, giving roughly a dozen performances over a month.

Mid-Aug Bergerac: La Table de Roxane (☎05.53.74.66.66). A repeat of the Table de Cyrano (see above) but held in odd-numbered years – the next one will be in 2003 – on the place de la République.

Mid-Aug Duras: Fête du Vin. One-day wine-fest held beside the château with free tastings (you have to buy a glass at the entrance for 10F/€1.52). In addition, seventeen hot-air balloons offer free rides from the foot of the château.

SEPTEMBER AND OCTOBER

Late Sept to early Oct Bergerac: Fêtes des Vendanges (☎05.53.63.57.55). Various festivities take place in Bergerac – starting with a procession of *gabares* – and its surrounding wine-villages over one week to celebrate the end of the grape harvest.

MARKETS

The main **markets** in this region are at Bergerac (Wed & Sat); Eymet (Thurs); Issigeac (Sun); Lalinde (Thurs); Ste-Foy-la-Grande (Sat). Where we haven't given a specific information number contact the relevant tourist office.

way to wooded hills on the western edge of the Périgord Noir. The change is perhaps most obvious in the landscapes south of the river, where the *bastide* town of **Beaumont** and the nearby abbey of **St-Avit-Sénieur** stand isolated on the edge of a high, open plateau. Just a few kilometres to the east, however, **Cadouin**'s abbey-church sits in a hidden valley deep among the chestnut forests.

Overall, exploring this region by **public transport** is not easy. Although the Sarlat–Bordeaux train line runs along the Dordogne valley and through Bergerac, services to smaller intermediary stations are infrequent. Heading inland, away from the river, there are a couple of useful bus routes, but again services are few and far between.

Bergerac

For much of the year **BERGERAC**, lying mostly on the Dordogne's north bank overlooking its wide flood plain, is a rather sleepy place, which then bursts into life for the summer tourist season when cafés and restaurants spill out into the cobbled squares and alleyways. It suffered particularly badly during the Wars of Religion, but in recent years the old streets fanning out from the former port have been carefully restored to bring out the best in the rows of half-timbered cottages and more bourgeois, stone-built residences. Among several interesting and attractive reminders of the past, the main sights are a surprisingly rewarding **museum** devoted to tobacco and a former **monastery** which in summer opens as an information centre on the local wines. In the immediate vicinity of Bergerac the vineyards of **Pécharment** and **Monbazillac** (see p.179) provide rewarding excursions, the latter easily combined with more extensive forays south, while there's another interesting museum, this time dedicated to river life, in the village of **Creysse** to the east.

Some history

The largest town in the Dordogne valley, Bergerac owes its existence and prosperity to the river. By the twelfth century it was already an important bridging point and port, controlling the trade between its Périgord hinterland and Bordeaux, particularly the burgeoning **wine trade**. Things began to take off after Henry III of England sought to keep the townspeople sweet by giving them certain privileges in 1254: they were exempted from local taxes, given the right of assembly and allowed to export their wines to Bordeaux unhindered. Local burghers took advantage of the new dispensations to ship their own wines first, while the less privileged were forced to sell later, at disadvantageous prices, and were also charged a tax of five *sous* per barrel. Bergerac's wine aristocracy were thus able to corner the lucrative foreign market until the seventeenth century, when the technique of ageing wines was discovered.

The town's heyday came in the decades preceding the Wars of Religion (1561–98) when Bergerac was among the foremost centres of **Protestantism** in southwest France. One of many truces between the warring factions was even signed here in 1577, but in 1620 the Catholic Louis XIII seized the town and ordered that the ramparts and fortress be demolished. Worse was to come when Catholic priests arrived to bring Bergerac back into the fold. They met with mixed success – the majority of the Protestant population fled, principally to Holland, where they soon established a long and mutually profitable business importing Bergerac wines.

Since then wine has continued to be the staple of the local economy. Up until the railway arrived in the 1870s, the bulk of it was transported by river, leading to a thriving **boat-building** industry all along the Dordogne. Though most have long disappeared, a few sturdy *gabares* are still being built to cater to the tourist trade.

Arrival, information and accommodation

There are daily flights from Paris to Bergerac's **airport**, 4km southeast of the city on the Agen road; from here it's a 10–15min taxi-ride (60–90F/€9.15–13.72). The **gare SNCF**, on the other hand, is located at the north end of cours Alsace-Lorraine, ten minutes' walk from the old town. You can leave bags at the station's ticket desk (30F/€4.57 per day) – note that they close at 7.30pm – and various car rental firms (see p.178) have offices near the *gare*. Most **bus** services also terminate at the station, though some stop on either place du Foirail or place de la République (see "Listings", p.177 for details). Driving in, you'll find free **parking** in the cobbled area beside the old port and on place du Foirail near the tourist office.

Bergerac's main **tourist office** is at 97 rue Neuve-d'Argenson (July & Aug daily 9.30am–7.30pm; Sept–June Mon–Sat 9.30am–12.30pm & 2–7pm; ☎05.53.57.03.11, fax 05.53.61.11.04, *www.bergerac-tourisme.com*), while in summer they also open an annexe in the Clôitre des Récollets (mid-June to mid-Sept daily 10am–1pm & 2.30–7pm). **Guided tours** of the old town, organized by the tourist office, take place daily in high season (mid-July to late-Aug) and less frequently at other times (1hr 30min; 25F/€3.81); most guides are bilingual.

Accommodation

Bergerac offers a choice of mid-level and budget **hotels** scattered around the town centre, in addition to one upmarket option on the northeastern outskirts. There's also a small, simple **campsite**, *La Pelouse* (☎ & fax 05.53.57.06.67; open all year), in a pleasant spot on the south bank of the river.

de Bordeaux, 38 pl Gambetta (☎05.53.57.12.83, fax 05.53.57.72.14, *www.logis-de-france.fr*). With its gastronomic restaurant, swimming pool and small but pleasant garden, central Bergerac's top hotel lurks behind a rather austere 1930s facade. The larger, more expensive rooms have recently been renovated and upgraded with modern, ochre-coloured furnishings. There's a good buffet breakfast (50F/€7.62) and the restaurant (Nov–March closed Sat lunch & Sun) serves menus from 110F/€16.77. Closed mid-Dec to end Jan. ④.

Family, 3 rue du Dragon (☎05.53.57.80.90, fax 05.53.57.08.00). Family-run budget hotel with just eight en-suite rooms tucked in a corner of the central pl du Marché-Couvert – booking is advisable at any time of year. Though on the small side, the rooms are clean and comfortable, equipped with TV and phone, new shower units and good, firm beds. The restaurant, *Le Jardin d'Epicure* (closed Sun), also offers hearty, family cooking at reasonable prices: *plat du jour* for 42F/€6.40 and menus from 82F/€12.50. ②.

La Flambée, 153 av Pasteur (☎05.53.57.52.33, fax 05.53.61.07.57, *www.laflambee.com*). The entrance of this upmarket hotel beside a Renault garage, about 1.5km out of the centre on the road to Périgueux, isn't too promising, but inside the rooms are tastefully decorated in a range of styles from antique pine to North African. There's also a sizeable garden, tennis court and pool, and an excellent restaurant serving local delicacies (menus from 98F/€14.94). ④.

de France, 18 pl Gambetta (☎05.53.57.11.61, fax 05.53.61.25.70). Slightly cheaper option than the nearby *Bordeaux* (see above), with a swimming pool squeezed into the back yard.

THE WINES OF BERGERAC

The **Bergerac wine region** extends along the north bank of the Dordogne from Lamothe-Montravel in the west to Lalinde in the east, and south as far as Eymet and Issigeac. It comprises no less than twelve different *appellations*, of which just over half the total output – 680,000 hectolitres (around 90 million bottles) in 1999 – is red wine, although the region's most famous wine is the sweet white Monbazillac.

There is evidence of wine production around Bergerac since Roman times, but the vineyards really began to develop in the thirteenth century to supply the English market. Demand from Holland, for sweet white wines in particular, led to a second spurt in the sixteenth century and then again after the Wars of Religion when Protestant émigré merchants virtually monopolized the market in Monbazillac wines. By the nineteenth century vines covered 100,000 hectares around Bergerac, only to be decimated by phylloxera in the 1870s; the area under AOC wines today covers a mere 12,000 hectares.

Pre-eminent among the Bergerac wines is **Monbazillac**. This pale golden, sweet white wine is blended from Semillon, Sauvignon and Muscadelle vines grown on the chalky clay soils of the valley's north-facing slopes. As with Sauternes, a key element is the cold, autumn-morning mists which lead to the development of *Botrytis cinerea*, or "noble rot", on the grapes (see p.104). The result is an intensely perfumed, concentrated wine best consumed chilled with foie gras, desserts or as an apéritif. Though they can't compare to the finesse of Sauternes, even top-quality Monbazillacs are eminently affordable at around 100F/€15.24 or less a bottle.

Pécharment, the best of the local reds, is often compared unfavourably to Bordeaux wines (see pp.74–75), though some are now beginning to rival a number of less prestigious St-Emilions. Pécharment wines are produced from Cabernet Sauvignon, Cabernet Franc and small quantities of Malbec or Merlot grapes, grown on the most favourable pockets of sand and gravel soils found to the north and east of Bergerac. They are thus far more complex and full-bodied than other Bergerac reds and some will age well up to seven years.

In summer you can sample the range of local AOC wines at Bergerac's Maison des Vins (see p.175). Alternatively, many producers offer **tastings and visits** to their *chais* – for a full list see the brochure *Route des Vins de Bergerac* available at the Maison du Vin or Bergerac tourist office. For general tips on visiting the vineyards see box on p.94.

The concrete-box exterior is a bit off-putting, but the rooms are comfortable enough and are gradually being upgraded and the bathrooms modernized. ③.

Le Moderne, av du 108e Régiment-d'Infantrie (☎05.53.57.19.62, fax 05.53.61.80.50). Simple, cheerful rooms at a good price right opposite the station. Phone and TV are standard, though cheaper rooms share spruce communal toilets and showers, and those on the front are a little noisy. There's a decent bar-brasserie downstairs, with menus from 63F/€9.60 (closed Fri). Closed two weeks in early Oct. ②.

The Town

Although Bergerac sits astride the Dordogne, nearly everything of interest is located on the north bank. The best place to start is beside the old port, a short hop from the entertaining **Musée du Tabac**, just inland. From here the compact *vielle ville* spreads gently uphill, a calm and pleasant area to wander, with drinking fountains on the street corners and numerous late-medieval houses. Its main artery is the Grand'Rue, which runs north from the central church of St-Jacques to join rue de la Résistance, the old town's northern perimeter; these two form Bergerac's principal shopping streets. Just beyond their junction, across the wide place de Lattre-de-Tassigny, stands another useful landmark, the **Notre-Dame** church.

The Musée du Tabac

Rue de l'Ancien-Pont leads northwards from portside rue Hippolyte Taine to the splendid seventeenth-century Maison Peyrarède, which houses the informative **Musée du Tabac** (Tues–Fri 10am–noon & 2–6pm, Sat 10am–noon & 2–5pm, Sun 2.30–6.30pm; 17.50F/€2.67), detailing the history of tobacco, though rather glossing over its more dire medical effects. Nevertheless, this is a stunning collection of pipes, snuffboxes, cigar holders, tobacco jars, graters and various tools of the trade.

The museum occupies three floors, starting with the first discovery of tobacco in pre-Columbian America and its introduction to Europe in the mid-seventeenth century. Somewhat conveniently, the displays only go as far as the early twentieth century, before the question of health risks came to the fore. Though the plant takes its botanical name, Nicotiana, from the Frenchman Jean Nicot, who sent some leaves from Portugal to Catherine de Medici in 1561 to help cure her migraines, his compatriot André Thevet had already planted several seeds in his Angoulême garden five years earlier. With Catherine de Medici's endorsement, however, the "divine weed" took off. So popular did it become, among both men and women, that tobacco smoking soon had to be banned from churches as the smoke overpowered the incense. It was also widely consumed for medicinal reasons as a powder and in drinks, oils, pills and unguents. Such usage continued into the early nineteenth century, when tobacco came to be viewed with greater alarm, but mainly for moral rather than health reasons: tobacco-consumption was blamed for laziness, brutality, criminality, madness and sexual perversion.

The tale is told in great detail and accompanied by some marvellous illustrations and superb examples of the connoisseur's accoutrements. There are wooden graters etched with religious scenes, snuffboxes engraved with the busts of Napoléon and Marie Antoinette, blushing young beauties adorn porcelain pipe-bowls and hunting scenes are fashioned out of meerschaum. Among many rare and beautiful pieces, the museum's prize possessions are an incredibly ornate Viennese meerschaum-and-amber cigar holder depicting a Sicilian wedding and an intriguing machine, invented in the 1860s, for carving fourteen brier pipes at once. Look out, too, for the clay pipe in the ominous form of a skull with glittering glass eyes.

The rest of the old town

North of the museum, you cross the attractive place du Feu, one of many such well-restored squares in central Bergerac, to enter the **Clôitre des Récollets**. This simple, galleried cloister dates from the seventeenth century when, in the aftermath of the Wars of Religion, Louis XIII dispatched five monks of the Franciscan Récollets order to bring Protestant Bergerac back to the faith. They were not warmly welcomed – it took a visit by Louis himself, in 1621, to assure their authority – but by the end of the decade the Récollets had succeeded in founding a new chapel and monastery. Not that they had the last word. After the Revolution, Bergerac's remaining Protestant congregation bought the chapel and re-established a temple on the site which is still used for regular, Sunday-morning worship.

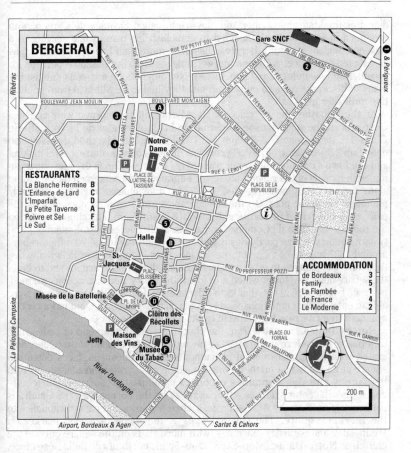

The monks' vaulted grain and wine cellars, on the cloister's south side, are used nowadays for meetings of the Consulat de la Vinée, which decides those wines meriting the AOC label, while in summer the **Maison des Vins** occupies the monks' former reception rooms above (June–Sept daily 10am–7pm; free; ☎05.53.63.57.55, *vin.civrb@wanadoo.fr*). In addition to free tastings, they offer weekly wine-tasting lessons (10F/€1.52; reservations required) and produce the very detailed *Route des Vins de Bergerac* as a guide to visiting the vineyards around the town.

On its north side the Clôitre des Récollets opens onto one of Bergerac's most picturesque squares, the cobbled **place de la Myrpe** (also spelt Mirpe) lined with stone and half-timbered labourers' cottages. All very pretty now, but until not so long ago this frequently flooded area within spitting distance of the port would have lived up to its name, meaning malodorous. Which perhaps explains the presence of a statue, erected in 1977, honouring Edmond Rostand's fictional hero **Cyrano de Bergerac** in typically haughty pose, and with his formidable nose very much in evidence. The character was inspired by a seventeenth-century soldier, free-thinking philosopher and playwright called Savinien de Cyrano, who was born in Paris and only decided to embellish his name while serving in a Gascon company – though Bergerac has been more than happy to claim him as an adopted son. It seems Cyrano was well able to match the Gascon reputation for swaggering boastfulness and impetuosity. Not only was he a famous duellist but many of his works were so outspoken that they had to be withheld from publication until after his death.

At the opposite end of place de la Myrpe, on the corner with rue des Conférences, the small **Musée Régional de la Batellerie et de la Tonnellerie** (Tues–Fri 10am–noon & 2–5.30pm, Sat 10am–noon; mid-March to mid-Nov also open Sun 2.30–6.30pm; 6F/€0.91) contains displays on viticulture, barrel-making and the town's once bustling river trade. This latter section is the most interesting, with models of the *gabares* alongside engravings showing men hauling them along the river – a practice banned in 1837 for humanitarian reasons – and early photos of Bergerac port. On the hillside above, up rue St-Jacques, stands the patchwork **church of St-Jacques** (Mon–Sat 8.30am–5pm). The church, a stop on the route to Santiago de Compostela, has had a chequered past. Founded in the twelfth century, it was partly destroyed in the Hundred Years' War, then rebuilt around 1537 only to be ruined three decades later in the Wars of Religion, when the stone was pillaged to erect ramparts against the Catholic armies and to build the square defensive tower which now forms the belfry. Reconstruction on a modest scale began in 1639 but, thanks to a donation by Louis XIV, the architects were able to enlarge their ambitions. Today's church is fairly modest, but has a certain grandeur in its narrow, high nave lit by stained-glass windows.

Rue St-James runs east from the church across the top end of pedestrianized **place Pélissière** in the heart of the old town. An elegant town house, decorated with traditional musical instruments and cockleshells, faces down the square at no. 26, while further along are some rustic *colombage* facades. From here pretty **rue des Fontaines** continues uphill past prosperous, fourteenth- and sixteenth-century houses – that at no. 29 on the corner with rue Gaudra is particularly noteworthy with its large, arched windows and carved capitals – to the **market square**. The covered *halle* is the focus of a vast market on Wednesday and Saturday mornings, with more stalls on the square outside the church of **Notre-Dame** (Mon–Sat 8.30am–5pm), north of rue de la Résistance. While there, it's worth strolling into the nineteenth-century Gothic church to see two large oil paintings in the east chapel: *The Adoration of the Shepherds*, attributed to a pupil of Leonardo de Vinci, and *The Adoration of the Magi* from the Venetian School.

Eating and drinking

When it comes to **places to eat**, the streets of old Bergerac present the most promising hunting ground. Here you'll find cosy restaurants serving top-notch Périgord cuisine alongside more modest brasseries and an excellent Moroccan specialist. Don't forget, also, the hotel-restaurants mentioned above on p.172. The vine-shaded terrace of *La Treille*, overlooking the old port at 12 quai Salvette, is a popular spot for a **drink**, while the best place to look for a **café** is on place Pélissière, with a few more workmanlike places around the market hall and on place Gambetta to the west of Notre-Dame.

La Blanche Hermine, pl du Marché-Couvert. Cheerful crêperie offering an imaginative range of buckwheat *crêpes* as well as copious salads, steak and chips and a more extensive evening menu – including such novelties as tuna-filled grapefruit or "gothic pork chop", with an apricot and mustard sauce. Most dishes are under 40F/€6.10. Closed Sun & Mon.

L'Enfance de Lard, pl Pélissière (☎05.53.57.52.88). Reservations are recommended at this intimate, first-floor restaurant run by a delightful French-English team. From an innovative menu, try pan-fried foie gras – served in summer with fried peaches – followed by meat grilled in front of you over a wood fire, and home-made desserts. There's a well-priced, three-course menu at 150F/€22.87, and in winter they also stage the occasional dinner-concert (250F/€38.11 including wine). Open daily except Tues for dinner and all day Sunday (lunch by reservation only). Closed for ten days in late Sept.

L'Imparfait, 8 rue des Fontaines (☎05.53.57.47.92). Another highly-rated restaurant which has the added benefit of a spacious summer terrace (reservations recommended for dinner in season). Fish features strongly, from salt-baked herbed sea bass to langoustine cooked with prawns, foie gras, fresh truffles and a sauce laced with Madiran and brandy. Menus – which change daily – start at around 100F/€15.24 for a weekday lunch. Dec–Easter closed Sun & Mon; also closed for three weeks from mid-Nov.

La Petite Taverne, 13 bd Montaigne (☎05.53.63.25.65). If you fancy a change from foie gras and *confit*, join the locals round steaming piles of *choucroute garnie* – pickled cabbage with various toppings – in five different varieties (from 50F/€7.62). They also do oysters and seafood platters as well as more standard dishes. Menus start at around 100F/€15.24. Closed Tues.

Poivre et Sel, 11 rue de l'Ancien-Pont. A forest of pot plants opposite the entrance to the Musée du Tabac announces this relaxed restaurant in an attractive, stone-walled room, with the option of outdoor tables in summer. The food is above-average local fare, such as *confit de canard* and *magret*, though they also serve a range of fish dishes. Menus start at around 80F/€12.20. Late Oct to April closed Mon.

Le Sud, 19 rue de l'Ancien-Pont (☎05.53.27.26.81). Feast on *couscous Royale*, exotic salads and, if you still have room, home-made desserts or eye-boggling ice creams at this good-value, welcoming Moroccan restaurant. A three-course meal will only set you back about 125F/€19.06, while in summer they also offer a light 60F/€9.15 menu on the terrace, weather permitting. There's a good choice of North African wines and one or two well-priced Bergeracs. Reservations advisable on Sat eve. Closed Sun & Mon, also two weeks in June and two weeks at Christmas.

Listings

Airlines Air France (☎05.53.22.25.25 or 08.02.80.28.02, *www.airfrance.com*) operates daily flights to Paris Orly.

Airport Roumanière (☎05.53.22.25.25).

Bike rental Périgord Cycles, 11 pl Gambetta (☎05.53.57.07.19), offers bike rental in summer, or by reservation at other times of year.

Boat trips From Easter to the end of October you can take an hour-long trip (40F/€6.10) by *gabare* from the old port along the Dordogne to a nature reserve, home to herons, cormorants and kingfishers, amongst other wildlife. Departures at least once daily, up to once an hour in July & Aug. Bilingual commentary. For further information call ☎05.53.24.58.80.

Books and newspapers The best place to try for local guides and English-language papers is the Maison de la Presse, 33 rue de la Résistance, opposite the post office.

Bus departures Most buses around the region depart from outside the *gare SNCF*, with the exception of those for Lalinde (Les Car Boulet; ☎05.53.61.00.46) which leave from place du Foirail, a five-minute walk east of the old town. The tourist office has timetables for this and other routes out of Bergerac: to Villeneuve-sur-Lot (SAB; ☎05.53.40.23.30), Périgueux (CFTA; ☎05.53.08.43.13) and Marmande via Issigeac and Eymet (Cars Bleus;

☎05.53.23.81.92). In July and August, Eurolines buses (☎08.36.69.52.52, *www.eurolines.fr*) stop beside pl de la République on bd de Varsovie.

Car rental The following are all located near the *gare SNCF*: Avis, 26 cours Alsace-Lorraine (☎05.53.57.69.83); Budget, 32 av du 108e Régiment-d'Infantrie (☎05.53.74.20.00); Europcar, 3 av du 108e Régiment-d'Infantrie (☎05.53.58.97.97); and Hertz, 15 av du 108e Régiment-d'Infantrie (☎05.53.57.19.27). Airport pick-ups available on demand.

Hospital Central Hospitalier Samuel Pozzi, 9 bd du Professeur-Calmette, the eastern extension of rue du Professeur-Pozzi (☎05.53.63.88.88).

Markets There's a fresh-food market in the central *halle* daily except Sunday, while Bergerac's main market takes place on Wednesday and Saturday mornings in the *halle*, on pl Gambetta and in front of Notre-Dame church. Pl de la Myrpe is the venue for a flea market on the first Sunday of the month.

Police Commissariat de Police, 37 bd Chanzy (☎05.53.57.61.02).

Post Office The main post office is at 36 rue de la Résistance, 24000 Bergerac.

Taxis There's a taxi stand outside the station. Otherwise, call Cyrano Taxi (☎05.53.63.39.39), Allo Radio Taxi Bergerac (☎05.53.57.20.70) or Taxi Bergeracois (☎05.53.23.77.64).

Tourist train From early July to late August there's also a tourist train, the *Autorail Espérance*, which runs along the Dordogne valley from Bergerac to Sarlat, via Lalinde and Le Buisson; en route they serve various local products, including a glass of wine. The train departs Bergerac's *gare SNCF* around midday on the hour's journey (Mon–Sat) and you then return on a regular SNCF service. Tickets cost 72F/€10.98 return (there are no one-way fares) and reservations are required: phone the Association l'Autorail Espérance on ☎05.53.31.53.46, or the *gare SNCF* at Sarlat on ☎05.53.59.00.21.

Near Bergerac: Pécharmant and Creysse

The vineyards to the north of Bergerac produces wines – notably the reds of Pécharment and whites of Rosette – which are a cut above the surrounding Côtes de Bergerac and Bergerac *appellations*. Just beyond the town's northeastern outskirts, near the village of **PÉCHARMANT**, the family-run **Domaine du Haut-Pécharment** (Mon–Sat 9am–noon & 3–6pm; ☎05.53.57.29.50) is a good place to aim for. It stands in the thick of the vines with views across to Monbazillac (see opposite) and produces a typically full-bodied, aromatic wine which ages well. The Domaine is signed left off the D32 Ste-Alvère road 6km northeast of Bergerac. Opposite the turning, at the end of a long alley, the much grander **Château de Tiregand** (April–Oct Mon–Fri 9–11.30am & 2–5pm, Sat 9–11.30am; ☎05.53.23.21.08) also offers tastings and, if you phone ahead, visits to its extensive park and seventeenth-century *chais*.

Dropping down to the valley from here you hit the busy D660 to Sarlat and, strung out along it 8km east of Bergerac, the village of **CREYSSE**. The only reason to stop here is the **Musée de la Pêche** (daily: June–Sept 10am–noon & 2–7pm; Oct–May 10am–noon & 2–6pm; 35F/€5.34) located under the riverside terrace in the village centre. The museum covers the history of fishing along the Dordogne, with examples of the different boats, nets and traps employed, but of greater interest is the surprising variety of river life displayed in the tanks around. Indigenous species such as salmon, trout, eel and bream were joined in the nineteenth century by zander, black bass and catfish. The river is also home to a number of unique species: shad (*alose*) and sea lamprey (*lamproie*) – both popular local dishes – which migrate upstream to breed, in addition to the increasingly rare river lamprey and a local type of sturgeon.

South of Bergerac

In the wine-producing hills to the south of Bergerac, **Monbazillac**, with its imposing château now housing a local history museum, marks an engaging start to a
southerly route following the **Dropt valley** southwest towards the Garonne. First
stop on the itinerary is **Issigeac** with its picturesque medieval centre, situated on a
tributary of the Dropt. From there you can follow quieter backroads all along the
valley to **Eymet**, a *bastide* of passing interest, and on to **Allemans-du-Dropt** where
the focus of interest is a remarkable series of frescoes in its otherwise unassuming
church. Last but not least comes **Duras**, the town from which the twentieth-century novelist Margaret Duras took her pen-name after spending part of her childhood
in the region. Duras's semi-ruined but still forbidding castle holds a commanding
position on Périgord's southwestern border; if you continue down the Dropt from
here you'll soon reach Monségur in the Entre-Deux-Mers region (see p.108), or,
you can head north to Ste-Foy-la-Grande back in the Dordogne valley (see p.184).

As far as public transport is concerned, there is just one **bus** service from
Bergerac to Marmande via Issigeac, Eymet and Allemans. Even using this, however, it will take careful planning and at least one overnight stop in Eymet to
explore the area, since there are only one or two buses a day in each direction,
not always at convenient times.

Monbazillac and around

Half-a-dozen kilometres south of Bergerac, **MONBAZILLAC** is the name not
only of a village but also, more famously, of a château and a sweet white wine similar to those of the Sauternes (see p.173 for more on Monbazillac wines). Visible
from across the valley floor, the handsome sixteenth-century **Château de
Monbazillac** (July & Aug daily 10am–7.30pm; June & Sept daily 10am–noon &
2–7.30pm; May & Oct daily 10am–noon & 2–7pm; April daily 10am–noon &
2–6pm; mid-Feb to March & Nov to mid-Jan Tues–Sun 10am–noon & 2–5pm;
closed mid-Jan to mid-Feb; 36F/€5.49; *www.chateau-monbazillac.com*) looks
down over the gentle slopes of its long-favoured vineyards. An eye-catching blend
of Renaissance residence and mock-medieval fortress, its corners reinforced by
four sturdy towers, the château was a Protestant stronghold during the Wars of
Religion. Surprisingly, it has survived virtually intact and now contains a moderately interesting **museum**. Best are the wine-related displays in the cellar, including antique bottles specially labelled for the Dutch market (see p.173), and the
ground-floor grand salon with its richly decorated ceiling and a parquet floor of
oak, pine and cherry wood. Upstairs again two local personalities are remembered in the Baroque furniture of the equally exuberant Bergerac-born actor Jean
Mounet-Sully (1841–1916), and a good collection of caricatures by SEM (aka
Georges Goursat) born in Périgueux in 1863; SEM's most famous drawing of an
animated scene in Paris's *Maxim's* restaurant still adorns their menus.

The Château de Monbazillac now belongs to the local wine producers' co-
operative, the **Cave de Monbazillac** (Tues–Sat: July & Aug 8.30am–7pm;
Sept–June 10am–12.30pm & 1.30–7pm), whose showroom lies 2km west on the
D933 Bergerac–Marmande road. They offer free tastings of the velvety sweet
white wine and, of course, the opportunity to buy. Monbazillac village boasts a

very grand **chambres d'hôtes**, *Domaine de la Rouquette* (☎05.53.58.30.60, fax 05.53.73.20.36; ④), in an eighteenth-century mansion a few hundred metres west along the ridge from the Château de Monbazillac, while you'll find a well-rated **restaurant** (☎05.53.58.38.93; closed Sun eve, Mon & Jan to mid-Feb; menus from 95F/€14.48) attached to the château itself, and another 3km further west again at the *Tour des Vents* (☎05.53.58.30.10; closed Jan, Sun eve & Mon) near the **Moulin de Malfourat**, a ruined windmill perched on the highest point for miles around. Though it's not an attractive building, the views from the restaurant's picture windows and terrace are superb – and the food is excellent value; menus start at 98F/€14.94.

After whetting your appetite at the Cave de Monbazillac, it's worth investigating some of the area's private vineyards. There are two good options to the east of Monbazillac near the village of **COLOMBIER**. The first you come to on the D14E, after about 4km, is the sixteenth-century **Château de la Jaubertie** (☎05.53.58.32.11, *jaubertie@wanadoo.fr*; July & Aug Mon–Fri 10am–6pm, Sat & Sun 3–6pm; Sept–June Mon, Tues, Thurs & Fri 10am–noon & 1.30–5.30pm; free), which was supposedly built by Henry IV for his mistress, Gabrielle d'Estrée, and later belonged to a doctor of Marie Antoinette. Now owned by the English Ryman family, the estate produces a variety of very reasonable wines under the Bergerac *appellation*. In Colombier itself, the **Domaine de l'Ancienne Cure** (☎05.53.58.27.90) has won any number of awards for its high-quality Monbazillac, Bergerac and Pécharment wines – their Cuvée Abbaye and the highly concentrated L'Extase are particularly recommended. You can visit the *chais* by appointment, but tastings are available at any time at their shop just below the village on the main N21 Bergerac–Agen road (April–Oct Mon–Sat 9am–7pm; Nov–March Mon–Sat 9am–6pm).

Issigeac

An almost perfectly circular huddle of houses in the midst of pastureland and orchards 8km southeast of Colombier along the D14, **ISSIGEAC** owes its prosperity to the bishops of Sarlat who established a residence here in 1317. Only fragments of the outer walls remain, and in recent years the village has been considerably tarted up, but otherwise its core of half-timbered medieval buildings is largely unspoiled and the narrow streets mercifully traffic-free.

The seventeenth-century **bishop's palace**, now containing various administrative offices, and the **Maison des Dîmes**, the former tax office, with its immense roof, command the village's north entrance. Behind the palace, and not much larger, the Gothic **church of St-Félicien** contains little of interest beyond some polychrome statues. Better instead to wander the old streets, starting with the **Grand'Rue** leading south to Issigeac's most famous building, known as the **Maison des Têtes** for its roughly carved, almost grotesque crowned and grimacing heads. It stands on the corner with rue Cardénal, at the east end of which a house with a half-timbered upper storey on a narrow stone pedestal – allowing carts to pass on either side – resembles nothing so much as a toadstool. From here, take rue Sauveterre circling southwest past more medieval houses and then cross over the southern end of the Grand'Rue to find the rue de l'Ancienne-Poste, which meanders generally back northwards to the Maison des Dîmes.

Issigeac receives sufficient visitors to have its own **tourist office**, located in a vaulted cellar beneath the bishop's palace (May–Sept Tues–Sun 9.30am–12.30pm & 2.30–6.30pm; Jan–April Mon–Fri 2–6pm, Sun 9.30am–1pm, closed Sat; Oct–Dec Tues 2–5pm, Wed–Sat 10am–noon & 2–5pm, Sun 9.30am–1pm; ☎ & fax 05.53.58.79.62). The busiest time is on Sunday mornings when the village fills with **market** stalls. If you are here on a Sunday, make sure you book ahead at *Chez Alain* (☎05.53.58.77.88; closed mid-Jan to early Feb, Sept–April closed Sun eve & Mon), a classy **restaurant** just across the ring road from the bishop's palace. They serve an excellent buffet lunch daily in season (Aug–Sept; 89F/€13.57); dinner and weekend menus from 119F/€18.14. **Buses** from Bergerac stop on place du Foirail on the southwest side of Issigeac.

Eymet

In contrast to Issigeac's meandering medieval streets, **EYMET**, 15km to the southwest, is laid out on a typical *bastide* chequerboard plan around a well-preserved arcaded central square, **place Gambetta**. Founded in 1270 by Alphonse de Poitiers (see p.356), Eymet changed hands on several occasions – not always by force – during the Hundred Years' War and later joined Bergerac as a bastion of Protestantism. Indeed, locals are still proud of the fact that in 1588 Henry of Navarre, the then leader of the Protestant armies and future King Henry IV, wrote a letter from Eymet to his mistress, Diane d'Andouins. With its corner tower and trefoil windows, the house in which he supposedly set pen to paper is the grandest on place Gambetta; it is naturally called the **Maison d'Amour**.

Apart from the square and a missable **museum** of local history in the semi-ruined thirteenth-century tower to the north (July–Sept Mon–Wed, Fri & Sat 3–6.30pm, Thurs 10am–noon, closed Sun; 10F/€1.52), there's not much else to see in Eymet. The town does, however, make a possible overnight stop, particularly if you're travelling by **bus**; buses stop on the main D933 which skirts Eymet to the east. There's a **tourist office** under the arcades (July & Aug Mon–Sat 10am–12.30pm & 2–6.30pm, Sun 10–12.30pm; Sept–June Tues–Fri 10am–12.30pm & 2–5.30pm; ☎ & fax 05.53.23.74.95, *OT.eymet@perigord.tm.fr*) and a comfortable **hotel**, *Les Vieilles Pierres* (☎05.53.23.75.99, fax 05.53.27.87.14; ③; closed one week in Nov & ten days in Feb; restaurant 60–220F/€9.15–33.54, closed Sun eve), with a pool and garden just off the D933 to the south. Alternatively, there's a well-run two-star municipal **campsite** between the museum tower and the river (☎05.53.23.80.28, fax 05.53.22.22.19; May–Sept).

The nicest place to **eat** is the *Maison d'Amour*, a *crêperie* and *salon du thé* on place Gambetta (closed Nov to mid-Feb; ☎05.53.22.34.64), which does a special breakfast menu on market day (Thurs). Otherwise, expect to pay 30–50F/€4.57–7.62 for a well-stuffed *galette* or a salad platter. They also rent out **canoes** and **bikes** for some gentle exploration of the Dropt valley.

Allemans-du-Dropt

A good place to head – by whatever means of transport – is downstream 10km from Eymet to **ALLEMANS-DU-DROPT**. The village is so tiny there's not much more than a homely little central square and its **church of St-Eutrope** (Mon–Sat

9am–6pm, Sun 10am–noon; free). The church's top-heavy lantern-tower and grand west door – both nineteenth-century additions to the much-altered tenth-century building – are rather misleading because inside the walls are covered with recently restored fifteenth-century **frescoes** depicting the Crucifixion and Last Judgement. A number of scenes have been lost or damaged over the years, but on the whole the paintings, which were only rediscovered in 1935, are unusually complete. They read from left to right as you enter, starting with the Last Supper and ending with a particularly graphic view of Hell. Despite the best efforts of St Michael, clad in medieval armour, a mere two souls seem bound for heaven while the damned are being carried off by the basket-load, or skewered on a spit, to be thrust into a boiling cauldron.

Once you've had enough of that, take a stroll to Allemans' western outskirts to see a splendid **pigeonnier** standing in a farmyard beside the D211 Pont de Duras road. Such pigeon-houses, which only noblemen had the right to build, are fairly common throughout southwest France, but this elegant hexagonal brick and oak-framed structure, raised up on seven pillars, each capped to prevent rats climbing up, is a particularly fine example.

Though Allemans is easy enough to find your way around, it's still worth picking up an English-language walking guide from the **tourist office** (July & Aug Mon–Sat 10am–12.15pm & 2–6.30pm; Sept–June Tues–Sat 3–5pm; ☎ & fax 05.53.20.25.59) beside the church; outside these hours ask at the nearby newsagent. **Buses** stop on place de la Mairie, southwest of the church, which is where you'll also find an old-fashioned country **hotel**, *L'Étape Gasconne* (☎05.53.20.23.55, fax 05.53.93.51.42; ③). It's a quiet spot with a pool and a decent restaurant serving traditional fare; menus from 65F/€9.91 (Oct–April closed for dinner Fri–Sun, rest of year closed Sat lunch). There's also a low-key municipal **campsite** (☎05.53.20.23.37, fax 05.53.83.65.45; May–Oct) beside the river, north across the old stone bridge from the village. In July and August they rent out **canoes** (☎06.89.60.68.31).

Duras

From Allemans the Dropt winds its way northwest for 10km to where the castle-town of **DURAS** lords it over the valley from its rocky outcrop. The château towers were truncated during the Revolution, but they still afford fine views beyond the Dropt to the country around, an enchanting region of rolling hills topped with windmills, of pasture, orchards, woods and, particularly to the north, of vines. It was the wine trade which ushered in Duras's eighteenth-century golden era and which has, since 1937, played a part in its economic revival through the Côtes de Duras *appellation*, one of the first created.

The chequered history of Duras is evident in the mix-and-match architecture of the **Château des Ducs de Duras** which dominates the town (daily: June–Sept 10am–7pm; April & May 10am–noon & 2–7pm; Oct 10am–noon & 2–6pm; Nov–March 2–6pm; 28F/€4.27). The château was founded in 1137, but then rebuilt after 1308 by Bertrand de Goth, nephew of Pope Clément V; it is said he used money confiscated from the Templars. Rebuilt again after the Hundred Years' War, it was then extensively remodelled during the more peaceful and prosperous late-sixteenth and seventeenth centuries. The finishing touches were added in 1741, just in time to be thoroughly ransacked during the Revolution, after which the château was left to crumble until the commune bought it in 1969. They are still in the midst of a massive restoration project, but a fair number of rooms are open to the public, containing displays on archeology, rural crafts and agriculture amongst others. On your way round, look out for wells cut straight through the bedrock and freshwater tanks in case of siege, and a monstrous kitchen fireplace big enough to roast a whole ox. The dukes obviously liked to build on a grand scale – across a wide, open courtyard the entrance hall is impressive enough, but the ceremonial hall above is heated by no less than eleven chimneys.

Miniaturization is the order of the day, however, at the **Musée Vivant du Parchemin** (daily: July & Aug 10am–noon & 3–7pm; April–June & Sept 3–7pm; closed Oct–March; 40F/€6.10), a couple of minutes' walk northeast following the ramparts along boulevard Jean-Brisseau. Established by two artisans, the museum-workshop provides a fascinating introduction to medieval parchment and the art of illumination. After a video presentation (English version available on request) and a short guided tour explaining, among other things, how parchment is made from hides and the different coloured inks from minerals, plant dies, oak galls and the like, you get to try your hand at a little fancy lettering with a goose-quill pen.

Practicalities

The nearby **tourist office**, at 14 boulevard Jean-Brisseau (mid-June to mid-Sept Mon–Sat 9am–noon & 1.30–6pm; mid-Sept to mid-June Mon–Fri same hours; ☎ & fax 05.53.83.63.06, *www.pays-de-duras.com*), has plentiful English-language information on the Duras region and also doubles as a **Maison du Vin**, offering free tastings and advice on vineyard visits.

Also on boulevard Jean-Brisseau, near the museum and tourist office, the *Hostellerie des Ducs* (☎05.53.83.74.58, fax 05.53.83.75.03, *www.logis-de-france.fr*; ③) makes a very comfortable place **to stay**. In addition to a pool and flowery terrace, there's also an excellent **restaurant** serving upmarket regional cuisine with menus from 90F/€13.72 (July–Sept closed for lunch Sat & Mon; Oct–June closed Sat lunch, Sun eve & Mon). Otherwise, try the *Auberge du Château*, on place Jean-Bousquet (closed Wed & Jan), the square opposite the castle entrance, for its good-value, no-nonsense meals (from 70F/€10.67). Duras has a decent choice of **campsites** too, starting with a basic municipal site right under the château's north wall (☎05.53.83.70.18, fax 05.53.83.65.20; July & Aug only). Continue on this road, the D203 to Savignac, another 600m and you'll come to *Le Cabri*, a well-equipped *camping à la ferme* (☎05.53.83.81.03, fax 05.53.83.08.91; June–Sept). Finally, there's a three-star site beside the Castelgaillard leisure lake (☎ & fax 05.53.94.78.74; May–Sept), signed off the main D708 8km northeast of Duras, with a wide variety of **activities** in season; if you're not camping, there's an entry fee of 12F/€1.83 at weekends in May and daily from June to August.

West to Castillon-la-Bataille

Downstream from Bergerac the steep, north slopes of the Dordogne valley are once again clothed in vines all the way along to the more illustrious vineyards of St-Émilion (see Chapter 1). The valley here is flat and uninteresting, dominated by a major road and rail line, but there are a few diversions en route. First is **Ste-Foy-la-Grande**, a pleasant enough town whose strict grid plan and arcaded central square reveal its origin as a *bastide*, though its prime interest lies in its transport links, hotels and other facilities. More immediately engrossing are the Gallo-Roman remains further west at **Montcaret**. The partially excavated villa with its well-preserved mosaics is one of the region's best. From Montcaret you can strike up into the hills to pay homage to the influential Renaissance thinker and confirmed sceptic, Michel de Montaigne, who wrote most of his famous *Essais* at the **Château de Montaigne**. Last stop is **Castillon-de-Bataille**, a busy market town famous for the nearby battleground where the Hundred Years' War came to a spectacularly bloody end. Its other attraction is a number of good-value red wines produced on the very border with St-Émilion.

Public transport along this stretch of the Dordogne is limited to **trains** on the Sarlat–Bordeaux line. With just a couple of trains per day between some of these towns, it requires careful planning and a fair bit of walking to reach the area's more interesting sites.

Ste-Foy-la-Grande

Heading west from Bergerac along the River Dordogne, the first place you come to of any size is the *bastide* town of **STE-FOY-LA-GRANDE**, whose die-straight streets retain a sprinkling of half-timbered houses. One of the finest is now occupied by the tourist office (see below) on the main street, **rue de la République**, running parallel to the river. Follow this road west and you reach the central place Gambetta, partially filled by the more modern *mairie* but still one of the town's most appealing corners. Also worth a wander is the riverside esplanade a short walk to the north, from where you can cross the river via the pont Michel-Montaigne to visit Ste-Foy's modest museum, the **Maison du Fleuve** (July & Aug daily 2–6pm; May, June, Sept & Oct Tues–Sun same hours; 15F/€2.29), covering riverlife – its boats, fish and fishing – and its role in local history; if you've already seen the museum at Creysse (see p.178 above), however, you won't need to bother. But it's definitely worth timing your visit to Ste-Foy to catch the Saturday morning **market**, one of the region's biggest and most important, when the whole town centre is closed to traffic.

Practicalities

Though Ste-Foy boasts few sights, it is worth considering as a base, particularly if you are travelling on to Montcaret (see below) by public transport. The **gare SNCF** lies five minutes' walk south of town; from the station, walk north along avenue Paul-Broca and then rue Victor-Hugo, Ste-Foy's other major shopping street. Where Victor-Hugo crosses rue de la République, turn right to find the **tourist office** at no. 102 (mid-June to mid-Sept Mon–Sat 9.30am–12.30pm & 2.30–5.30pm, Sun 10.30am–12.30pm; mid-Sept to mid-June Mon 2.30–5.30pm & Tues–Sat 9.30am–12.30pm & 2.30–5.30pm; ☎05.57.46.03.00, fax ☎05.57.46.16.62, *ot.sainte-foy-la-grande@wanadoo.fr*) in a grandiose, sixteenth-century residence.

For **accommodation** in central Ste-Foy, you can't do better than the *Grand Hôtel*, with its magnolia-shaded back terrace and airy, old-fashioned rooms, a little further east at 117 rue de la République (☎05.57.46.00.08, fax 05.57.46.50.70, *www.grandhotel-mce.com*; ③; restaurant from 65F/€9.91, closed Sat lunch & Wed). With your own transport, however, there's also the option of the *Escapade* (☎05.53.24.22.79, fax 05.53.57.45.05, *www.logis-de-france.fr*; ③; closed mid-Nov to late Jan, Oct–April closed Sun & Fri). Despite being only just south of the main

D936 less than 4km west of Ste-Foy, this hotel has more of a country feel than one would expect. There are twelve unfussy rooms in a converted tobacco-drying barn as well as a pool, sauna, squash courts and gym in which to work off the chef's generous Périgord cooking (menus from 95F/€14.48; eves and Sun lunch only reservations recommended). Another good-value **restaurant** where you'll need a reservation is *Au Fil de l'Eau* (☎05.53.24.72.60; closed Mon) back in Ste-Foy at 3 rue de la Rouquette on the north side of pont Michel-Montaigne; menus start at 85F/€12.96.

Anyone with a tent should head east about 500m along the river's south bank on avenue Georges-Clémenceau – the extension of rue de la République – to the three-star municipal **campsite** (☎05.57.46.13.84, fax 05.57.46.53.77; mid-March to Oct). In season you can rent **canoes** from the *base nautique* (☎05.53.24.86.12; June–Sept) on the north side of the river opposite the campsite. Alternatively, **bike rental** is available from either Ets. J. David, right opposite the tourist office at 29 rue Jean-Jacques-Rousseau (☎05.57.46.19.49), or J. Vircoulon at 41 rue Victor-Hugo (☎05.57.46.02.67).

Downstream to St-Michel-de-Montaigne

Travelling west on the D936 from Ste-Foy, garden-lovers might like to make a brief detour after about ten kilometres up into the hills north of the river to visit the **Jardins de Sardy** (April–Oct daily 10am–6pm; 30F/€4.57). Though not huge, the gardens – a combination of English and Italian style – occupy a pretty, sheltered spot overlooking the Dordogne. The centrepiece is an informal pond-garden set against the wisteria-covered farmhouse, where it's tempting to linger on the terrace over a cold drink or a light lunch (75F/€11.43; June–Sept only) surrounded by the heady scents of aromatic plants.

Three kilometres further along the main road, another right turn brings you to the village of **MONTCARET** and the remains of a fourth-century **Gallo-Roman villa** (daily: July & Aug 9am–1pm & 2–7pm; April–June & Sept 9am–noon & 2–6pm; Oct–March 10am–noon & 2–4pm; 25F/€3.81) with superb mosaics and an adjoining museum displaying some of the many objects found on the site. While only about one-tenth of the villa has been fully excavated, that is more than enough to demonstrate the occupants' affluent lifestyle, from underfloor heating and a variety of hot and cold baths to a grand reception room measuring 350 square metres. The floors, baths and covered walkways were laid with elaborate mosaics, of which large areas have survived relatively intact, notably in the cold bath decorated with shellfish, dolphins and octopuses, and the more abstract pattern of shields and fish scales in the "dining room". This latter is the villa's best-preserved room and has been incorporated into the museum building; note, however, that from mid-November to mid-April those mosaics outdoors are covered to protect them from frosts and are therefore not on view.

Back lanes lead another three kilometres northwest to the sleepy village of **ST-MICHEL-DE-MONTAIGNE**, where Michel Eyquem, Lord of Montaigne (1533–92), wrote many of his chatty, digressive and influential essays on the nature of life and humankind. Even if you haven't read any of his works, it's worth making the pilgrimage to the **Château de Montaigne** (July & Aug daily 10am–6.30pm; Feb–June & Sept–Dec Wed–Sun 10am–noon & 2–5.30pm; closed Jan; 20F/€3.05), just beyond the village to the north, to learn more about this engaging, if somewhat quirky and complex, character.

Montaigne was the third son of a Catholic father and a mother from a wealthy Spanish-Portuguese Jewish family. His unusual education involved everyone, including the servants, speaking to him in Latin, and being woken by a musician to ensure "his brain not be damaged". It certainly seems to have caused no harm, since Montaigne went on to become a councillor and later mayor of Bordeaux and was highly respected for his tolerance, wisdom and diplomacy. There is evidence that he also possessed a mischievous sense of humour – throughout the bitter Religious Wars, the Catholic Montaigne apparently took pleasure in ringing his chapel bell as loudly and as often as possible to annoy his Protestant neighbours. On the other hand, it must also be said that Montaigne, who held the Protestant leader Henry of Navarre in great esteem, played an important role in resolving the conflict, though he didn't live to see peace restored in 1598.

Though he attended Mass regularly before his death, and received the last sacrament, Montaigne's writings are renowned for their scepticism; in a typical outburst he declares "Man is insane. He wouldn't know how to create a maggot, and he creates Gods by the dozen." His philosophical standpoint was essentially an argument for introspection – "if man does not know himself, then what can he know?". While it is criticized as being inconclusive, his legacy is rather his great originality of thought and his essays' wide-ranging questioning of generally accepted truths. His chapel occupies the ground floor of a fourteenth-century **tower** where Montaigne closeted himself away after 1571 to work on his three volumes of essays. Unfortunately his priceless library of more than a thousand books, all carefully annotated, were dispersed immediately after his death, but some trace of the philosopher can still be found in the Greek and Latin maxims he inscribed on the beams – note where he replaced some with later favourites. Indeed, it is something of a miracle that the tower exists at all, since the rest of the château was completely destroyed by fire in 1885; the subsequent reconstruction is not open to the public, though you are welcome to wander the extensive park.

Afterwards, you can refuel at the excellent-value *routiers'* **restaurant**, the *Auberge du Péricou* (lunch menus from 63F/€9.60; closed Mon), down on the main road in **LAMOTHE-MONTRAVEL**. If you're travelling by public transport, both Montcaret and Lamothe are served by infrequent **trains** from Bergerac via Ste-Foy to Castillon and St-Émilion, leaving you with an eight-kilometre walk and a long wait for the evening train. A better option would be to rent bikes in Ste-Foy (see p.185) and then follow the quieter side roads running parallel to the D936.

Castillon-la-Bataille

As you travel the final five kilometres west from Lamothe-Montravel to **CASTILLON-LA-BATAILLE** you'd be forgiven for not noticing as you cross the Lidoire valley. In 1453 this is where the French routed the English in the last major **battle** of the Hundred Years' War (see box opposite). There's nothing to mark the site, save an uninspiring monument to the English General Talbot on the spot where he supposedly died close to the River Dordogne, two kilometres east of Castillon, but every summer the local citizenry stage a spectacular floodlit re-enactment with some five hundred actors and fifty cavaliers (late-July to mid-Aug; ☎05.57.40.14.53; *www.batailledecastillon.com*).

The town makes the most of its history, and has one or two pretty corners, notably along the river and its one remaining medieval gate, but the only real

THE BATTLE OF CASTILLON

What is now known as the **Hundred Years' War** had been rumbling back and forth through southwest France from 1337, but in the 1440s the French, led by the great military commander Bertrand du Guesclin, began to push the English armies back. In reply, the English despatched the equally renowned **Sir John Talbot**, Earl of Shrewsbury, with orders to regain the lost territory. He took Bordeaux in 1452 and had swept through to Castillon by July 1453.

Here a large French force was waiting for him camped beyond the town, but when the Castillon garrison withdrew without much of a fight, Talbot believed it would be an easy battle. Instead he was walking straight into a trap. The French had gathered 300 pieces of artillery – a relatively new development – and ranged them in the hills either side of the valley. On **July 17**, after Talbot had heard Mass, a messenger reported mistakenly that the French were breaking camp and retreating when all they were doing was moving the baggage to the rear. Talbot hastily rallied his men and led them in pursuit straight into the mouth of the valley and a murderous crossfire. Talbot and four thousand of his men were killed – if not immediately, then by the pursuing archers or simply drowning as they attempted to flee across the Dordogne. As news of the carnage spread, other English-held towns quickly capitulated until more than a century of warfare finally came to an end.

reason to stop here is the helpful **Maison du Vin** facing the church across the central place de Gaulle (☎05.57.40.00.88, *www.vins-bordeaux.fr/cotes-de-castillon*). You're getting close to St-Émilion here and, while the Côtes de Castillon are no match for the big St-Émilion wines, since the early 1990s some have been making their mark – particularly when you consider that even the best only cost around 70F/€10.67 a bottle. Two names to look out for, both of which offer tastings by appointment, are Château Cap de Faugères (☎05.57.40.34.99, *www. chateau-faugeres.com*), a couple of kilometres northwest from Castillon outside the village of Ste-Colombe, and Vieux Château Champ de Mars (☎05.57.40.63.49), some 7km north along the D123 and then right towards Les-Salles-de-Castillon. Alternatively, the Maison du Vin stocks a representative sample and can advise on other vineyards in the area.

Castillon's **gare SNCF** is located on the northeast side of town about five minutes' walk along rue Gambetta, while its **tourist office** is on place Marcel-Paul (July & Aug Mon–Sat 9.15am–noon & 2–6pm, Sun 10am–noon; Sept–June Mon, Tues & Thurs–Sat 9.15am–noon & 2–6pm; ☎05.57.40.27.58, fax 05.57.40.49.76); to find it take rue Victor-Hugo heading west from the north end of place de Gaulle. There's really nothing much in the way of **hotels**, just the overpriced *Bonne Auberge* at 12 rue du 8-Mai (☎05.57.40.11.56, fax 05.57.40.21.66; ③; closed two weeks in Nov; restaurant from 75F/€11.43), at the south end of rue Gambetta. Better instead to head to one of the **chambres d'hôtes** around, such as the friendly *Chambres d'hôte Robin* (☎05.57.40.20.55; ③), in a small vineyard two kilometres north of Castillon on the D119 to Belvès; the tourist office can provide lists of others in the area. There's also a small two-star municipal **campsite**, *La Pelouse* (☎05.57.40.04.22; May to early Sept), along the river to the east of Castillon, with the possibility of **canoe** rental in July and August.

When it comes to **eating**, head straight for the *Gourmandine* at 4 rue Waldeck-Rousseau (☎05.57.40.24.48; closed Sun eve & Tues), one block west of the tourist office, for their traditional dishes washed down with local wines (menus from around 80F/€12.20). The other good option is the pizzeria-grill *Le Mounan* just outside Castillon on the Bergerac road (menus from 57F/€8.69; closed Mon).

East to Le Buisson

The Dordogne river begins to get more interesting upstream from Bergerac, largely thanks to the two great meanders it makes near **Trémolat** and **Limeuil** before the hills begin to close in. The castles, abbeys and villages south of the river are also worth exploring, giving the option of two routes: along the Dordogne itself or looping inland to the little-visited **Château de Bannes**, guarding an ancient road up the heavily wooded Couze valley, and the village of **Cadouin** with its austere abbey-church and elaborately carved cloister.

Transport along the Dordogne valley is provided by **trains** on the Bergerac–Sarlat line. These call at most of the towns and even some villages, though note that in certain cases the services are fairly infrequent. The inland route is even more problematic: there are **buses** from Bergerac along the river's north bank to Lalinde, but only twice-weekly services on to Cadouin (Wed & Sat).

Along the Dordogne

Following the Dordogne east from Bergerac the first sight of any interest is the half-completed **Château de Lanquais**, as much for the story behind its architecture as for its somewhat dilapidated interiors. The working paper mills at **Couze-et-St-Front** also merit a quick stop, while **Lalinde** provides hotels, transport and other tourist facilities, before you meet the first of the Dordogne's great loops, the **Cingle de Trémolat**. At the top of the second meander the feudal village of **Limeuil** marks where the River Vézère flows into the Dordogne and where you pass into the Périgord Noir, while the final destination, **Le Buisson-de-Cadouin**, sits on an important rail junction on the Bergerac–Sarlat and Agen–Périgueux lines.

Lanquais and Couze-et-St-Front

The **Château de Lanquais** (July & Aug daily 10am–7pm; May, June & Sept Mon & Wed–Sun 10.30am–noon & 2.30–6.30pm; April, Oct & Nov Mon & Wed–Sun 2.30–6pm; closed Dec–March; 35F/€5.34), 15km east of Bergerac on the south side of the river, is described in tourist literature as "Périgord's unfinished Louvre". The story goes that in the mid-sixteenth century, when Bergerac and much of the surrounding country was under Protestant sway, Lanquais was owned by a Catholic, Isabeau de Limeuil, cousin to Catherine de Medici. In a brave – or foolhardy – move Isabeau commissioned the architects of the Louvre in Catholic Paris to add a wing in similar style to her castle. Before the work could be completed, the Protestant armies besieged the château in 1577 and left the facade pitted by cannonballs.

They didn't destroy it, however, and you can still discern the change in styles where the Renaissance wing, with its dormer windows and ornamentation, was grafted on to the medieval fortress. It is an imposing rather than an attractive building and some of the interiors are in need of restoration, but there are one or two rooms worth a peep. As in many Périgord châteaux, it's the fireplaces that steal the show, notably that occupying one whole wall of the "blue salon" with its two enigmatic bulls'-skull carvings.

The present owners of the château have set aside two immense rooms with period furniture and en-suite bathrooms as **chambres d'hôtes** (☎05.53.61.24.24, fax 05.53.73.20.72; closed Dec–March; ⑥). Alternatively, there's cheaper but still very pretty *chambres d'hôtes* accommodation half a kilometre south of the château at the welcoming *Domaine de la Marmette* (☎05.53.24.99.13, fax 05.53.24.11.48, *www.france-publicite.com/24/marmette.html*; ④). They offer evening meals on request (130F/€19.82 including wine) or otherwise there's a typical country **restaurant** in **LANQUAIS** village, just north of the château, the *Auberge des Marronniers* (☎05.53.24.93.78; closed Wed, also two weeks both in early March & late Oct) with good-value weekday lunches at 65F/€9.91 and other menus from 80F/€12.20.

Two kilometres from Lanquais you drop down to the Dordogne again at what was once an important paper-making centre, **COUZE-ET-ST-FRONT**. Of thirteen mills along the banks of the River Couze, only two still churn out handmade paper in time-honoured fashion. In the first, the fifteenth-century **Moulin de la Rouzique** under a cliff in the town's northwest corner (daily: June–Aug 10am–noon & 2–6.30pm; April, May, Sept to mid-Oct 2–6.30pm; closed mid-Oct to March; 30F/€4.57), you can see paper being made and examine its collection of antique watermark paper in the drying rooms upstairs. Then at the equally venerable **Moulin de Larroque**, on the main road through the town centre, they make traditional cotton- and linen-rag paper (Mon–Fri 9am–noon & 2–5pm; free); there's also an array of paper products on sale (Mon–Sat 9am–noon & 2–6.30pm).

Departing from Couze-et-St-Front you have the choice either to continue east along the river to Lalinde or delve inland along the Couze valley to Beaumont (see p.192).

Lalinde

The only town of any size along this stretch of the Dordogne, **LALINDE** guards an important river-crossing 3km upstream from Couze and 23km from Bergerac. In 1267 Henry III of England chose the little settlement on the river's north bank to become the first English *bastide*. The central market square, grid plan and fragments of wall remain, but Lalinde's most attractive aspects are its riverside position and a large canal basin immediately to the north; in July and August you can take various trips along the canal by *gabare* (☎05.56.68.33.14). The canal was built in the nineteenth century to bypass a dangerous set of rapids, made more hazardous in legendary times by the presence of a dragon, La Coloubre, which lurked in a cave on the opposite bank. According to legend, St Front (see p.133) got rid of the monster in the fourth century by burning it on an enormous bonfire on the hill above the dragon's lair– grateful citizens later erected the tiny cliff-top **Chapelle de St-Front** in his honour.

Nowadays Lalinde is a bustling market town (Thursday is market day) and prosperous commercial centre. Its **gare SNCF** lies three minutes' walk across the canal, while **buses** stop on the central place de la Halle. The **tourist office** (July & Aug Mon–Sat 9am–7pm & Sun 9am–noon; May, June & Sept Mon–Sat 9am–12.30pm & 2–4.30pm; Oct–April Mon, Tues & Thurs–Sat 9am–1pm & 2–4pm; ☎05.53.61.08.55, fax 05.53.61.00.64, *www.lalinde-perigord.com*) is on the riverbank near the old bridge. You can rent **bikes** from the Centre VTT Lalinde, Maison de l'Écluse (☎ & fax 05.53.24.12.31, *centre-vtt-lalinde@libertysurf.fr*), beside the canal bridge.

The town also has two good **hotel-restaurants**. Smarter of the two is *Le Château*, 1 rue de Verdun (☎05.53.61.01.82, fax 05.53.24.74.60, *www.logis-de-france.fr*; Nov–March closed Sun, also late Dec to mid-Feb & third week in Sept; ④)), overlooking the river to the west of the tourist office, where the larger, more expensive rooms offer better value for their balconies and river views. The restaurant lives up to its reputation with dishes such as snails stuffed with foie gras and walnut butter, and trout with *rillettes* (menus start at 125F/€19.06; July & Aug closed Mon lunch; rest of year closed Sun eve & Mon). You'll also eat extremely well at the *Hôtel du Périgord*, 1 place du 14-Juillet (☎05.53.61.19.86, fax 05.53.61.27.49, *www.logis-de-france.fr*; ③; Sept–June closed Sun eve & Mon, also two weeks in Dec & one in March), on the main boulevard de la Résistance to the north of central Lalinde. Despite its unpromising exterior, the rooms are well equipped and enlivened by the owner's bold abstract canvases – an artistic flair he also brings to his award-winning cooking, such as pigeon stuffed with foie gras, or soup with truffles *en croute* (lunch menus from 90F/€13.72; evenings 100–450F/€15.24–68.60).

Trémolat to Le Buisson-de-Cadouin

Some 8km upstream from Lalinde the Dordogne snakes its way through two huge meanders, of which the first you come to, the **Cingle de Trémolat**, is the tighter and therefore more impressive. The best views are from the limestone cliffs to the north – follow signs to the Panorama de Trémolat, or on upwards to the Belvedere de Rocamadou – from where the whole meander is visible. Over to the east, a heavily fortified church tower pinpoints the picturesque village of **TRÉMOLAT**, where the *Bistrot d'en Face* makes a good pit stop (menus from 65F/€9.91; closed Thurs & Jan). The **restaurant** belongs to the nearby *Vieux Logis* (☎05.53.22.80.06, fax 05.53.22.84.89, *vieuxlogis@relaischateaux.fr*; ⑨), a beautiful luxury **hotel** in a former priory with a large pool, formal gardens – with a lovely terrace for summer dining (menus from 210F/€32.01; closed for lunch except weekends and holidays) – and all sorts of cosy nooks and crannies. Last but not least, there's an excellent three-star **campsite** (☎05.53.35.50.39, fax 05.53.06.03.94, *semitour@perigord.tm.fr*) beside the river less than a kilometre northwest of Trémolat on the road to the viewpoint. The **gare SNCF** is located just over a kilometre to the south of the village.

Take the D31 east from Trémolat and it will lead you over the ridge for a bird's-eye view of the second meander. The road then drops down to the honey-stoned village of **LIMEUIL** on the confluence of the Vézère and Dordogne rivers. It's an attractive sight straggling down the hillside from the church. At the bottom is a grassy area beside the first of two bridges perpendicular to each other where, in summer, there are outdoor cafés and people canoeing and swimming in the river. Limeuil reached its first peak in the Middle Ages, thanks to its strategic location, and then another in the nineteenth century when local craftsmen built boats for the booming river trade.

The village has changed little since then, as you'll soon discover by wandering under the old gate and up narrow, central rue du Port to the hilltop **park** (July–Sept daily 11am–7pm; Oct–June weekends only same hours; 15F/€2.29) where the château once stood. Afterwards, it's worth heading 1km northeast on the Le Bugue road to the **Chapelle St-Martin** (May–Sept daily 9am–7pm; free); out of season, the house opposite holds the key. A Latin inscription inside this dumpy little Romanesque chapel records that it was dedicated to St Thomas à Becket, the Archbishop of Canterbury murdered by Henry II's courtiers in 1170 after the king famously asked who would rid him of "this turbulent priest". The inscription goes on to relate that the chapel was founded in 1194 by Henry's son and successor, Richard the Lionheart, together with Philippe II (Philippe Auguste) of France on their return from the Third Crusade, "to beseech the pardon of God". There are also the remnants of fifteenth-century frescoes in the choir: to the right a Crucifixion scene and the Descent from the Cross; to the left the Flight from Egypt. Note also the *pisé* floor – giving the appearance of pebbles, but actually made of long, narrow stones placed upright – and the roof of stone slates, *lauzes*, over the choir. You'll meet these architectural features again and again as you penetrate deeper into the Périgord Noir.

The nearest **gare SNCF** to Limeuil is at Alles-sur-Dordogne, a couple of kilometres to the southeast, but there are more frequent services to Le Buisson (see below) and Le Bugue (see p.191), 5km north on the Agen–Périgueux line. There's a small **tourist office** at the bottom of rue du Port (April–Oct Tues–Sun 10am–noon & 2–6pm; Nov–March Mon–Fri 2–6pm; ☎05.53.63.38.90, *si.limeuil@perigord.tm.fr*) and, at the top of the same road, you'll find the appropriately named **hotel**, *Le Bon Acceuil* (☎05.53.63.30.97, fax 05.53.73.33.85; ①; closed Fri & Nov–March). Rooms are spotlessly clean but basic – none have their own toilets and the cheapest rooms use communal showers – but this is more than made up for by the vine-covered terrace, views along the valley and good, homely cooking (menus from 85F/€12.96). You can rent **canoes** and **bikes** from Canoës Jean-Rivière Loisirs (☎ & fax 05.53.63.38.73) and there's also an excellent **riding centre**, La Haute Yerle in Alles-sur-Dordogne (☎ & fax 05.53.63.35.85), which offers treks from half a day up to a week's circuit of the Périgord Noir.

LE BUISSON-DE-CADOUIN, 5km south of Limeuil, is the last stop on this stretch of river. While it has nothing in the way of sights, Le Buisson is a junction on the Bordeaux–Sarlat and Agen–Périgueux train lines and its **gare SNCF**, to the north of the town centre, is also the closest station to Cadouin (see p.193); for a **taxi** call Denis Valadié on ☎05.53.22.04.77. There's a **tourist office** on place du Général-de-Gaulle (mid-June to mid-Sept Mon–Sat 10am–noon & 2–6pm, Sun 10am–noon; mid-Sept to mid-June Tues–Sat 10am–noon; ☎ & fax 05.53.22.06.09, *www.perigord.com/ot.buisson-de-cadouin*), a couple of minutes' walk south from the station, and a rather lovely **hotel** less than two kilometres east on the road to Siorac. The *Manoir de Bellerive* (☎05.53.22.16.16, fax 05.53.22.09.05, *www.manoir-bellerive.com*; ⑥; closed Jan & Feb), an elegant little nineteenth-century château in an English-style park on the banks of the Dordogne, offers far more than you'd expect for the price. The rooms have been completely modernized, with gleaming en-suite bathrooms, and decorated with great flair: period furniture in the château itself and more modern touches in the *orangerie* annexe. Their **restaurant**, *Les Délices d'Hortense*, won its first Michelin star in 2000 for delicacies such as scallops with a truffle vinaigrette or duck *façon Rossini* (menus 160–450F/€24.39–68.60; closed Mon & midday on Tues and Wed). There's also a tennis court, pool and a perfect breakfast spot on the terrace overlooking the Dordogne.

Inland via Beaumont and Cadouin

Where the River Couze joins the Dordogne at the paper-making town of Couze-et-St-Front (see p.189), this inland route strikes southeast to follow the quiet, green tributary valley. It was once a far more important routeway, as the **Château de Bannes**, snug behind stout walls, drawbridge and well-defended gate-tower, clearly demonstrates. The same need for defence created and shaped the nearby *bastide* of **Beaumont** and its colossal Gothic church, though the latter at least has survived in surprisingly good shape. Better than the neighbouring abbey-church of **St-Avit-Sénieur**, one of the biggest in the region, which was never completed due to a succession of fires, wars and lack of funds. Further upstream the little chapel above the village of **Montferrand-du-Périgord** has also seen more prosperous times, but in this case its frescoes are still there – battered but largely visible. Another abbey-church at **Cadouin**, further to the northeast, suffered a rather different fate when its holy relic, supposedly the shroud that covered Christ's head in the tomb, was found to be too recent by a thousand years and the pilgrims stopped coming. Nevertheless, its late-Gothic cloister is worth a look and the town's location in a bowl of chestnut-forested hills makes it the sort of place that's difficult to leave.

The Couze valley

Since Gallo-Roman times there's been a fortress on the nobble of rock six kilometres up the **Couze valley** now occupied by the **Château de Bannes** (July & Aug Wed–Sun 3–6.30pm; June & Sept Sat & Sun same times; 30F/€4.57). The castle was captured by the English in 1409, then retaken thirty years later by the French, who promptly tore it down to prevent it falling into enemy hands again. Towards the end of the century the then Bishop of Sarlat, Armand de Gontaud-Biron, bought the ruin and rebuilt it largely in the prevailing medieval style before adding a few Renaissance flourishes in the early 1500s. Since then the exterior has hardly changed. The château is still lived in, so only a handful of rooms are open to the public, best of which is the grand drawing room where the Renaissance fireplace sports a life-size – and lifelike – sculpture of an Indian chief's head complete with feather-plume; a reminder that Columbus had discovered the Americas only a few decades previously.

Four kilometres further on, on another spur overlooking the valley, **BEAUMONT** was founded as a *bastide* by Edward I in 1272. Like many such towns, its church, **St-Front**, was built for military as well as religious reasons – a final outpost of defence in times of attack – hence the bulky tower at each of the four corners and the well inside. Its only decorative touch comprises a frieze over the west door depicting the four animals symbolizing the Evangelists in the midst of mermaids, monsters and a man pulling a cheeky face. The nearby central square retains some of its arcades and off to the west you'll find Porte de Luzier, one of the original sixteen town gates, but otherwise there's little to detain you. Beaumont does, however, boast a **tourist office** on the central square (July–Sept daily 10am–noon & 2.30–6.30pm; Oct–June Mon–Sat 10am–noon & 2–5pm; ☎05.53.22.39.12, fax 05.53.22.05.35, *ot.beaumont@perigord.tm.fr*) and a good two-star **campsite**, *Les Remparts* (☎ & fax 05.53.22.40.86; May–Sept), in a pine wood just southwest off the D676 to Villeréal.

On the other side of the valley, roughly 4km by road, the semi-ruined abbey of **ST-AVIT-SÉNIEUR** stares across at Beaumont from another rocky knoll. It grew up around the burial place of a fifth-century hermit, Avitus, who was born at Lanquais and later served in the Visigoth army until taken prisoner in 507 by the Frankish King Clovis, a recent convert to Christianity. At some point during his fourteen years' captivity in Paris Avitus followed suit and was then instructed in a vision to return to Périgord, where he lived as a hermit until his death in 570. Tales of his miracles soon attracted pilgrims and the simple chapel grew into a monastery, then the present **church** (Tues–Sun 10am–noon & 3–6pm; free) was founded in the early twelfth century; an inscription records that the saint's bones were brought here in 1117. Like Beaumont's St-Front, it's another huge building, over fifty metres long and twenty wide, heavily fortified and plain save for the remnants of fifteenth-century geometric patterns painted on the walls and ceiling. In this case, however, the ravages of war and time have left deeper scars.

The D26 continues southeast up the narrowing valley for another 8km to the seemingly forgotten village of **MONTFERRAND-DU-PÉRIGORD**, where a clutch of typical Périgord houses shelters beneath the semi-ruined château. A single street leads up past a sixteenth-century market hall – bigger than some of the surrounding houses – to where a path takes off west through the woods. Roughly a kilometre later it comes out near the hilltop **church of St-Christophe**, standing on its own in a cemetery. It used to be the parish church but has gradually been diminished over the years to little more than a stocky bell tower – it's surprising to find that the twelfth- and fifteenth-century frescoes have survived. The moon's face smiles down as you enter, while to either side are scenes of the Last Supper and a monstrous mouth gobbling up souls. The oldest painting is that on the north wall of the choir portraying St Leonard releasing prisoners. According to legend, Leonard was the godson of Clovis and refused a bishopric to become a hermit; his connection with prisoners dates from after his death when a crusader prince, released by his Arabic captors in 1103, went to pay homage at St Leonard's grave.

For **accommodation** or somewhere to eat in the area, you couldn't do better than the little creeper-covered country hotel back down on the main road. Owned by a young, friendly English–French couple, the *Lou Peyrol* (☎ & fax 05.53.63.24.45, *www.logis-de-france.fr*; ②; closed Oct–Easter) boasts a handful of rustic rooms, all but one en suite, and a restaurant with well-priced menus from 85F/€12.96 (April–June & Sept closed Wed lunchtime). There's another good option 3km further up the valley, where Jacqueline Belgarric runs a welcoming *chambres d'hôtes* (☎ & fax 05.53.63.26.42; ③; closed mid-Dec to early Jan) in **BOULÈGUE** hamlet; evening meals available on request (90F/€13.72).

Cadouin

At the same time that Augustinian monks were busy building their church in honour of St Avit (see opposite), the Cistercians founded a typically austere **abbey** in what is now the village of **CADOUIN**, 8km to the northeast up the D25. Their efforts were given a boost when in 1117 they were given a piece of cloth believed to have been part of Christ's shroud by Crusaders returning from the Holy Land. For 800 years it drew flocks of pilgrims – including Eleanor of Aquitaine, Richard the Lionheart and King Louis IX – until in 1935 the two bands of embroidery at either end were shown to contain an Arabic text from the early eleventh century. The cloth is now on display in the flamboyant Gothic **cloister** accessed via a separate entrance to the north of the church door (July & Aug daily 10am–7pm; May, June & Sept Mon & Wed–Sun 10am–12.30pm & 2–6.30pm; early Feb to April &

Oct–Dec Mon & Wed–Sun 10am–12.30pm & 2–5.30pm; 30F/€4.57) where it plays second fiddle to the finely sculpted but badly damaged capitals: look out for two merchants squabbling over a goose and the parable of Lazarus. There are some more good carvings on the cloister's north wall, either side of the abbots' seat, showing Jesus carrying the Cross while two soldiers dice for his tunic, and a procession of monks alongside a prostrate Mary Magdalene – the remains of a Crucifixion scene.

Adjacent to the cloister stands the contrastingly austere Romanesque **church** with a stark, monumental west wall and unusual, double-tier belfry roofed with chestnut shingles. Inside, the triple nave is equally spartan and so high that the pillars appear to bulge outwards. You can still see the chains above the altar where the shroud was suspended in its casket, but the main point of interest is the stained-glass windows, installed around a century ago, retelling the story of the shroud's journey from Jerusalem.

If you've had enough of all these churches the **Musée du Vélocipède** (daily 10am–7pm; 30F/€4.57), just up the hill from the church, provides an engaging diversion. This unique collection of vintage bikes covers 150 years of cycling history, from the aptly named bone shaker of 1817 up to the end of World War II. The owners have tracked down bicycles ridden by Victor Hugo and Jules Verne, a rare American penny-farthing and a bike from the first Tour de France in 1903, amongst many other weird and wonderful contraptions.

Cadouin is the terminus for **buses** from Bergerac via Lalinde (Wed & Sat only), but the most convenient way to get here by public transport is to take the **train** to Le Buisson (see p.191) and then a taxi for the final 6km; if you need a **taxi** in Cadouin, call Taxi de l'Abbaye (☎05.53.63.44.75). The village offers an unexpected range of **accommodation**. Adjacent to the cloister, the monks' dormitories have been turned into an excellent HI *Auberge de Jeunesse* (☎05.53.73.28.78, fax 05.53.73.28.79; dorms 73F/€11.13; private rooms ②; rates include breakfast) with a well-equipped kitchen and bikes on loan. Then, on the opposite side of the church, there are five en-suite rooms above the *Restaurant de l'Abbaye* (☎05.53.63.40.93, fax 05.53.61.72.08; ②; closed Mon) – which also does very good-value meals (menus from 68F/€10.37; closed Mon; mid-Oct to mid-April closed eves except Sat). For more comfortable accommodation and elaborate cooking, take the D54 a couple of kilometres southeast to find the delightful *Auberge de la Salvetat* (☎05.53.63.42.79, fax 05.53.61.72.05, *www.logis-de-france.fr*; ④; closed Nov & Dec; menus from 140F/€21.34; restaurant closed Wed lunchtime) with its pool, garden and pretty, rustic rooms in the middle of nowhere.

Those looking for **campsites** are equally well provided for. Closest is a small one-star municipal site (☎05.53.63.46.43, fax 05.53.73.36.72; mid-June to mid-Sept) just above the village on the Montferrand road. With your own transport, however, you can reach the extremely welcoming and well-equipped three-star *La Grande Veyière* (☎05.53.63.25.84, fax 05.53.63.18.25; April–Sept) 3km southwest on the road to Molières.

Leaving Cadouin, most people drop straight down to the Dordogne at Le Buisson, from where the caves around Les Eyzies (see p.209) are within easy striking distance. But if time allows, take a short detour east through the woods to **URVAL** where you'll find a mere handful of houses and a fortified Romanesque church which is really no more than a tower containing a diminutive nave.

travel details

Trains

Bergerac to: Alles-sur-Dordogne (1–2 daily; 35min); Bordeaux (4–8 daily; 50min–1hr 30min); Castillon-la-Bataille (5–8 daily; 30–50min); Couze (1–2 daily; 20min); Lalinde (2–6 daily; 16–20min); Lamothe-Montravel (2–4 daily; 35–45min); Le Buisson (2–6 daily; 35min–1hr); Libourne (4–10 daily; 45min–1hr 10min); Montcaret (1–3 daily; 30–40min); Sarlat (2–6 daily; 1hr–1hr 30min); St-Émilion (1–3 daily; 55min); Ste-Foy-La-Grande (5–10 daily; 20min); Siorac-en-Périgord (1–2 daily; 1hr); Trémolat (2–5 daily; 25–30min).

Castillon-la-Bataille to: Bergerac (5–8 daily; 30–50min); Bordeaux (4–8 daily; 30–40min); Lamothe-Montravel (2–4 daily; 5–10min); Montcaret (1–3 daily; 10min); St-Émilion (1–3 daily; 8min); Ste-Foy-La-Grande (5–10 daily; 15–25min).

Le Buisson to: Agen (2–5 daily; 1hr 15min–2hr); Bergerac (2–6 daily; 35min–1hr); Couze (Sun–Fri 1–2 daily; 25min); Lalinde (4–6 daily; 20min); Le Bugue (2–6 daily; 8min); Les Eyzies (2–6 daily; 15min); Paris Austerlitz (1–2 daily; 6hr); Périgueux (2–6 daily; 45–50min); Sarlat (3–6 daily; 30min); Trémolat (4–6 daily; 10min).

Ste-Foy-La-Grande to: Bergerac (5–10 daily; 20min); Bordeaux (4–8 daily; 45min–1hr); Castillon-la-Bataille (5–10 daily; 15–25min); Lamothe-Montravel (2–4 daily; 15–20min); Montcaret (1–3 daily; 14min); St-Émilion (1–3 daily; 35min).

Buses

Bergerac to: Cadouin (Wed & Sat 1 daily; 45min); Eymet (1–2 daily; 1hr–1hr 20min); Issigeac (1–2 daily; 30–40min); Lalinde (Mon–Sat 2–3 daily; 30min); Marmande (1 daily; 2hr); Périgueux (Mon–Sat 2–3 daily; 1hr–1hr 25min); Port de Couze (Mon–Sat 2–3 daily; 25min); Port de Lanquais (Mon–Sat 2–3 daily; 20min); Villeneuve-sur-Lot (Mon–Fri 1–2 daily; 1hr 15min).

Cadouin to: Bergerac (Wed & Sat 1 daily; 1hr 20min); Lalinde (Wed & Sat 1 daily; 40min); Port de Couze (Wed & Sat 1 daily; 50min); Port de Lanquais (Wed & Sat 1 daily; 50min).

Eymet to: Allemans-du-Dropt (2–3 daily; 15min); Bergerac (1–2 daily; 1hr); Issigeac (1–2 daily; 20min); Marmande (3–4 daily; 45min–1hr).

Lalinde to: Bergerac (school term Mon–Sat 1–3 daily, school hols 1–2 daily except Mon & Fri; 45min); Cadouin (Wed & Sat 1 daily; 15min); Port de Couze (as for Bergerac; 5–7min); Port de Lanquais (as for Bergerac; 6–10min).

Planes

Bergerac to: Paris (1–4 daily; 1hr 20min).

CHAPTER FOUR

SARLAT AND THE PÉRIGORD NOIR

The central part of the Dordogne valley and its tributary, the valley of the Vézère, comprise the heart of the **Périgord Noir**. This is distinctive Dordogne country: deep-cut valleys enclosed within limestone cliffs, with fields of maize in the alluvial bottoms and dense, dark oak woods on the heights. Orchards of walnut trees (cultivated for their oil), flocks of ducks and low-slung grey geese, and primitive-looking stone huts called *bories* are other hall-marks of the region. You'll also find mottled-grey roofs made of limestone slabs (*lauzes*), although the cost of maintaining these – the stones weigh on average 500kg per square metre – means that they are gradually being replaced with ter-racotta tiles. A floor made out of *lauzes* is called *pisé*, and is commonly found in châteaux and chapels, the stones inserted upright into a bed of clay and lime. None of these features is unique to the Périgord Noir, of course, but their preva-lence here adds a defining stamp to the region.

No more so than in the well-preserved medieval town of **Sarlat**, the capital of the Périgord Noir. Though it boasts no great monuments, the warren of old lanes, hidden courtyards and fine architecture, the background for many a period drama, not to mention its excellent weekly market, are not to be missed. And there's no shortage of sights in the country around, of which the **Manoir d'Eyrignac** stands out for its evergreen gardens. Sarlat is also within spitting dis-tance of the highlight of the Périgord Noir, the **Vézère valley**, which cuts diago-nally across the region from the northeast. The valley's slightly overhanging cliffs have been worn away by frost action over the millennia to create natural rock-shelters where humans have sought refuge for thousands of years, leaving an incredible wealth of archeological and artistic evidence from the late Paleolithic era. There are more **prehistoric caves**, shelters and related sites around **Les**

ACCOMMODATION PRICE CODES

All the hotels and *chambres d'hôtes* listed in this book have been price-coded accord-ing to the following scale. The prices quoted are for the **cheapest available dou-ble room in high season**, although remember that many of the cheap places will have more expensive rooms with en-suite facilities.

① Under 160F/€24
② 160–220F/€24–34
③ 220–300F/€34–46
④ 300–400F/€46–61
⑤ 400–500F/€61–76
⑥ 500–600F/€76–91
⑦ 600–700F/€91–107
⑧ 700–800F/€107–122
⑨ Over 800F/€122

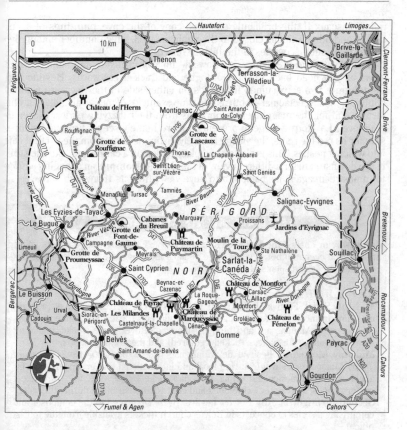

Eyzies, the Vézère's main town, to keep the real enthusiast happy for days. For most visitors, however, a selection will suffice, starting with the most beautiful of the caves still open to the public, the **Grotte de Font-de-Gaume**, where the quality of the paintings is quite outstanding; also nearby is the **Abri du Cap Blanc**, famous for its frieze of horses exquisitely depicted in bas-relief, while in the **Grotte des Combarelles** prehistoric artists went to town with hundreds of animal engravings.

Nature has also gone to work in the limestone caves along the Vézère, with dazzling displays of multicoloured stalactites and stalagmites, columns, fistules, draperies, eccentrics, triangles and pearls – the weird and wonderful shapes of crystallized calcite. The big daddy of crystal caves around here, despite all its commercialization, is the **Gouffre de Proumeyssac** near the southerly town of **Le Bugue**. Following the Vézère upstream, the valley's most eye-catching sight is the kilometre-long cliff of **La Roque St-Christophe**, where people lived for at least 50,000 years, first in simple shelters and then building increasingly sophisticated dwellings against the rock face until, in medieval times, it constituted a self-sufficient town. But the prime reason everyone treks up here is **Lascaux**, or rather Lascaux II, the brilliantly executed copy of the **cave paintings** of oxen, horses and other animals closed to the public in 1963, which number among the most significant discoveries in the history of art.

Having sated on prehistory, it's now the turn of châteaux and sublime river views as you head back to the Dordogne and track it eastwards. **Beynac** and **Castelnaud**, two semi-ruined fortresses on either side of the river, are without doubt the most spectacular – both as supreme examples of medieval military architecture and for the magnificent panoramas from their dizzying eyries. Closer to river-level, **La Roque-Gageac** presents a more homely scene. From a distance, save for its red-tile roofs, the village is barely distinguishable from the vertical cliff into which it nestles. This is also a good place to hop on a **canoe** and take a leisurely trip downstream for a different view of the river. At **Domme**, an engaging *bastide* town upstream again, it's back to bird's-eye views from its 160m-high belvedere.

FESTIVALS, EVENTS AND MARKETS

Late May or early June Sarlat: La Ringueta (☎05.53.31.53.31). At Pentecôte (Whit Sunday) in even-numbered years place de la Grande-Rigaudie is the venue for traditional games and sports of the Périgord.

JULY & AUGUST
Mid-July Sarlat: Festival des Jeux du Théâtre (☎05.53.31.10.83). One of France's most important theatre fests, ranging from children's theatre and mime to classical pieces by Maupassant and Molière. It's staged over three weeks, including many open-air performances (tickets required) and theatre workshops.
Mid-July Montignac: Festival de Montignac (☎05.53.50.14.00, *alm24@perigord .tm.fr*) Major arts festival featuring local and international folk groups from as far afield as South America and China. As well as ticket-only events, there are street performances, food stalls, exhibitions and crafts demonstrations during the week.
Second fortnight in July Belvès: Festival Bach. Dedicated to the composer and comprising a series of concerts in Belvès church (tickets available from the tourist office).
Late July to late Aug St-Léon-sur-Vézère and around: Festival du Périgord Noir (☎05.53.51.95.17). Baroque and classical music concerts in the churches of St-Léon, St-Amand de Coly and others throughout the region.
Early Aug Sarlat: Fête de la Bierre (☎05.53.31.02.95 or 05.53.31.08.21). Organized by the rugby club, the entertainments revolve around a giant *choucroute* (pickled cabbage garnished with sausages and other meats) washed down with Alsace beer, to the accompaniment of a Bavarian orchestra.

NOVEMBER
Early Nov Sarlat: Festival du Film (☎05.53.29.18.13). One-week festival previewing some 30 films a day from around the world, including special screenings of student productions. Discount tickets available.

MARKETS
The main **markets** in this region are at Belvès (Sat); Le Bugue (Tues & Sat); Domme (Thurs); Montignac (Wed & Sat); St-Cyprien (Sun); Sarlat (Wed & Sat); Terrasson (Thurs). Where we haven't given a specific information number contact the relevant tourist office.

With so many first-class sights in such a compact area, it's not surprising that this is one of most heavily touristed inland areas of France, and as a result has all the concomitant problems of crowds, high prices and tack. It is really worth coming out of season, but if you can't, seek accommodation away from the main centres, try to visit places first thing in the morning and always drive along the back roads – the smaller the better – even when there is a more direct route available.

Though you will be reliant on your own transport for exploring much of the area, two **train** lines cut through the Périgord Noir. Sarlat is the terminus of a line from Bordeaux via Bergerac, while trains between Agen and Périgueux stop at Le Bugue and Les Eyzies. You can change between the two lines at Siorac-en-Périgord and Le Buisson (see p.191). In addition, the northern Vézère valley can be accessed from Terrasson, on the Brive–Bordeaux main line. There is also a smattering of **bus** routes, though as usual services are not always very frequent nor at particularly convenient times.

Sarlat-la-Canéda and around

Very picturesque and very touristy, **SARLAT-LA-CANÉDA** is held in a green hollow between hills 7km or so north of the River Dordogne. You hardly notice the modern suburbs, as it is the mainly fifteenth- and sixteenth-century houses of the old town in mellow, pale ochre-coloured stone that draw the attention. Sarlat has one of the best-preserved centres you could wish for, an excellent example of organic, medieval growth where cobbled lanes open onto delightful little squares and where you'll find steep roofs stacked with characteristic *lauze* tiles. Of the many fine bourgeois houses scattered about the district, the most notable are the **Maison de la Boétie** and **Hôtel Plamon**. Since none are open to the public, however, unless you are in Sarlat for the Saturday market, it won't take more than half a day to explore. Sarlat's range of accommodation options, both in and just outside the town, also make it the most natural base for exploring the Périgord Noir.

The hills above Sarlat contain a good range of sights, from the **Moulin de la Tour**, a water mill making walnut oil by traditional methods, to the topiary gardens of the **Manoir d'Eyrignac**, with perhaps a detour to the picturesque village of **St-Geniès**. Heading westwards, the still-occupied **Château de Puymartin** tends to be overshadowed by the more famous castles along the Dordogne, but contains some unusual interior decorations, while the nearby **Cabanes de Breuil**, a harmonious group of what were probably shepherds' huts, represent a completely different architectural tradition.

Though it started life as a **Gallo-Roman** settlement, Sarlat really came to prominence in the late eighth century when Benedictine monks established an abbey here, later dedicated to a former bishop of Limoges, St Sacerdos. In 1147 **Bernard of Clairvaux** also left his mark when he preached to the second Crusade – according to legend he miraculously cured the sick by offering them bread he had blessed. In spite of this, the townspeople were keen to gain independence from church rule and in 1298 were eventually granted the right to elect their own consuls by Louis VIII. In return, they remained loyal to the French crown during the Hundred Years' War and staunchly Catholic in the Wars of Religion, when the town suffered considerably at the hands of the Protestants. Prosperity returned, however, in the mid-fifteenth century, which led to a building boom whose legacy is the

Renaissance facades you see to this day. That they are so well preserved is large-ly due to the fact that Sarlat went into slow decline after the late 1700s and thus for the most part escaped the ravages of modernization. Indeed, by the early twenti-eth century the centre was in a pretty poor state but was saved from further decay by the Malraux Act of 1962 which helped fund a huge restoration project and brought life back to the town. As a result it is now one of the most popular tourist destinations in the whole Dordogne valley, packed to the gunnels in summer, though still relatively undisturbed during the winter months.

Arrival, information and accommodation

Sarlat's **gare SNCF** is just over 1km south of the old town on the road to Souillac. **Buses** from Périgueux pull in to place de la Petite-Rigaudie at the north end of Sarlat's main street, rue de la République. Those from Brive and Souillac call at the station before terminating on place Pasteur at the southern extremity of the same street. If you're driving you can **park** for free around the ring road (except boulevard Eugène-Le-Roy on the west side). Otherwise the most convenient pay-parking is on place de la Grande-Rigaudie immediately south of centre. The **tourist office** (July & Aug daily 9am–7.30pm; May, June & Sept–Nov daily 9am–7pm; Dec–April Mon–Sat 9am–noon & 2–6pm; ☎05.53.31.45.45, fax 05.53.59.19.44, *ot24.sarlat@perigord.tm.fr*) lodges in the sixteenth-century Hôtel de Maleville on place de la Liberté in the centre of the old town. Amongst all sorts of useful leaflets, they produce a free English-language walking guide to the medieval city, while from June to September you can join one of their **guided tours** (2–3 daily 1hr 30min; 15F/€2.29). They also sell booklets detailing hiking and bike trails around the Périgord Noir.

For most of the year finding **accommodation** is not a problem and you'll have a good choice of hotels, *chambres d'hôtes* and campsites in and around Sarlat. Note, however, that during the peak holiday season (June–Sept) you'd be advised to book several weeks, if not months, ahead. If you arrive without a reservation, the tourist office will do what they can to assist, but they can't guarantee to find anything; note that they charge a nominal fee of 10F/€1.52 during these months.

Accommodation in Sarlat

Auberge de Jeunesse, 77 av de Selves (☎05.53.59.47.59). Relaxed, old-fashioned municipal youth hostel five minutes' walk north from the old centre, with just fifteen beds in three dorms. There's a small kitchen area and space for five two-person tents in the garden. In the-ory the hostel is only open for individuals from April to October, catering to groups for the rest of the year, but it's always worth ringing in the off-season to see if there are places to spare. HI membership not required. Closed Jan. 55F/€8.38 for the first night; 50F/€7.62 thereafter.

Camping Les Périères, route de Ste-Nathalène (☎05.53.59.05.84, fax 05.53.28.57.51). Sarlat's closest campsite lies in a little valley 1km northeast of centre up rue Jean-Jaurès. It's spacious and extremely well equipped – facilities include heated indoor pool, outdoor pool, Jacuzzi, sauna, washing machines, tennis courts and grocery shop – but it costs almost as much as a cheap hotel. Daily rates for two people start at around 110F/€16.77, rising to 140F/€21.34 in July and August, when there's a one-week minimum stay. Closed Oct–Easter.

La Couleuvrine, 1 pl de la Bouquerie (☎05.53.59.27.80, fax 05.53.31.26.83, *www.hotels-restau-dordogne.org/couleuvrine*). Built into the northern ramparts, *Le Couleuvrine* has a medieval feel in its exposed stone walls and big fireplaces downstairs, while the smallish rooms are decked out with country-style furniture – best is the tower room with views across town. Restaurant menus from 98F/€14.94 (closed three weeks in Jan & two weeks in Nov). April to late Sept half-board preferred. ③.

de la Madeleine, 1 pl de la Petite-Rigaudie (☎05.53.59.10.41, fax 05.53.31.03.62, *hotel.madeleine@wanadoo.fr*). Sarlat's best hotel occupies a smart town house just outside the old core. The rooms are all modernized, with light woods and floral fabrics, though the cheapest are on the small side. The restaurant serves suitably classic cuisine; menus from 130F/€19.82 (closed Mon lunchtime). Closed Jan to early Feb. ⑤.

des Récollets, 4 rue Jean-Jacques-Rousseau (☎05.53.31.36.00, fax 05.53.30.32.62, *otelrecol@aol.com*). The nicest and most reasonable place to stay in Sarlat is this small hotel in the former Récollets' cloister on a quiet street to the west of rue de la République. They offer a range of comfortable rooms in bright modern colours with immaculate en-suite bathrooms, and a warm welcome. ③.

St-Albert, pl Pasteur (☎05.53.31.55.55, fax 05.53.59.19.99, *www.logis-de-france.fr*). A choice of rather characterless but perfectly decent rooms in the main hotel or the slightly more spacious annexe (the *Montaigne*) across the road. The main plus is their restaurant serving highly traditional Périgord cuisine (Mon–Fri bistro menu at 65F/€9.91; other menus start at 115F/€17.53). Located on the main road immediately south of town, so ask for a room at the back. Nov–March closed Sun eve and Mon. ③.

Accommodation around Sarlat

L'Arche, Les Chanets, Proissans (☎05.53.29.08.48). Well-priced *chambres d'hôtes* in a lovely Périgord farmhouse beside a country lane to the southwest of Proissans village, about 5km northeast of Sarlat. The immaculate en-suite rooms are pretty in a frilly sort of way with lots of nick-nacks. Closed mid-Nov to Feb. ③.

Aux Trois Sources, Pech-Lafaille (☎05.53.59.08.19, fax 05.53.28.83.30). Another *chambres d'hôtes* in a handsome old manor house, in this case 3km east of Sarlat on the road to Ste-Nathalène. The rooms, rather squeezed into a converted barn, are well equipped and all en suite, but for attractiveness don't quite live up to the surrounding park, with its chestnut trees and pond. ③.

Camping La Palombière, Ste-Nathalène (☎05.53.59.42.34, fax 05.53.28.45.40). A four-star job, this is one of the region's best campsites, roughly 10km east of Sarlat on the D47. It's in a lovely, peaceful location in eight hectares of woodland, very well equipped – including restaurant, bar, grocery store, bikes, pool and tennis courts – and puts on all sorts of kids' events in summer. Closed Oct–April.

Camping Les Terraces du Périgord, Pech d'Orance (☎05.53.59.02.25, fax 05.53.59.16.48). Another welcoming, well-tended campsite, this time in a superb hilltop position 2.5km north of Sarlat on the Proissans road. Plenty of flowers and spacious plots make this one of the nicest sites around. Closed Oct–April.

La Hoirie, rue Marcel-Cerdan, La Girange (☎05.53.59.05.62, fax 05.53.31.13.90, *lahoirie@club-internet.fr*). This vine-covered thirteenth-century hunting lodge with a pool and small park lies 2km south of Sarlat, signed off the Souillac road. Though a touch on the expensive side, the rooms are a decent size and range from rustic beams to huge fireplaces and period furniture. There's also a good restaurant (closed for lunch on weekdays) with menus from 95F/€14.48. Closed mid-Nov to mid-March. ⑤.

La Mas de Castel, Le Sudalissant (☎05.53.59.02.59, fax 05.53.28.52.62). It's best to reserve well in advance for this friendly hotel in a quiet spot 2.5km south of Sarlat, also signed off the road to Souillac. The rooms are freshly decorated in pastel tones, the larger ones overlooking the garden. There's a pool but no restaurant. Closed Nov–March. ③.

Le Relais de Moussidière, Moussidière-Basse (☎05.53.28.28.74, fax 05.53.28.25.11, *www.chateauxhotels.com/moussidiere*). Turn left off the busy D57 Bergerac road beside the Citroën garage to find this luxury hotel nestled among trees in a seven-hectare park. The hotel occupies a new wing attached to a very attractive Périgordin manor house and incorporates open-plan communal areas full of palms and comfortable nooks and crannies. Most of the 35 rooms have their own balcony or terrace and a slightly Middle Eastern air in the hessian wall-coverings, tiles and chunky wooden furniture. There's a pool and restaurant serving evening meals only (from 170F/€25.92). July & Aug half-board obligatory. Closed Nov–March. ⑦.

The Town

The ramparts surrounding old Sarlat were torn down in the late 1800s, at about the same time that the north–south **rue de la République** was cut through the centre to create its main thoroughfare. The streets to the west remain relatively quiet; the east side is where you'll find the majority of sights. During the July and August peak much of central Sarlat is closed to cars, including rue de la République and its eastern shadow: rue Tourny, rue de la Liberté and rue des Consuls.

Sarlat's labyrinthine lanes fan out from **place de la Liberté**, the central square where the big Saturday **market** spreads its stands of geese, flowers, foie gras, truffles, walnuts and mushrooms according to the season. The square's finest building is the **Hôtel de Maleville**, now home to the tourist office, tucked into its southwest corner. On this side, overlooking the square, it consists of a tall, narrow building in French Renaissance style with ornate window surrounds; turn down the lane beside it to see its more classical Italianate facade, with a balustraded terrace and two medallions above the door representing Henry IV and, according to popular belief, his mistress Gabrielle d'Estrée. The lane continues through a series of passages and geranium-filled courtyards to emerge beneath Sarlat's most famous house, the **Maison de La Boétie**. Though its tiers of mullion windows, each within a sculpted frame, and prominent gables are certainly eye-catching, much of the building's fame derives from the fact that the poet and humanist Étienne de La Boétie, a close friend of Michel de Montaigne (see p.185), was born here in 1530. He went on to study law in Orléans, where he wrote his most famous work, *Discourse on Voluntary Servitude*, though it wasn't published until after his premature death at the age of 33. A treatise on the tyranny of power, and thus a very early expression of anarchism, the *Discourse* later struck a cord with Rousseau and other radical thinkers in the run up to the Revolution.

Opposite the Maison de la Boétie, the former bishop's palace also sports a Renaissance gallery and windows, while the large and unexciting **Cathédrale St-Sacerdos** to which it is attached mostly dates from a seventeenth-century renovation. More interesting are the two pretty courtyards to the south of the cathedral – **cour des Fontaines**, filled with the sound of playing water, and **cour des Chanoines** surrounded by a pleasing assembly of buildings – and the passage around the chevet where Sarlat's nobles were laid to rest in arched niches, *enfeux*, let into the wall. Less-illustrious mortals were buried in the cemetery above, presided over by a curious bullet-shaped tower, the **Lanterne des Morts**, built in the twelfth century. Its exact purpose is unknown. Although it's called a "Lantern of the Dead" – after similar such monuments found further north in the Limousin – in this case there's no access to the upper chamber where the fire would normally be lit. Local tradition maintains that it commemorates St Bernard's visit in 1147 (see p.199).

Further north along the same slope you come to the **Présidial**, the former seat of royal justice, now a restaurant (see p.204). It is distinguished by its great stone staircase and interior court lit by a lantern under a peculiar, bell-shaped roof several sizes too large. From here drop back down to place de la Liberté and pass behind the back of the badly mutilated church of Ste-Marie to find the place du Marché-aux-Oies – a delightful corner decorated by three bronze geese – and the **rue des Consuls**. Of several handsome houses along here the most remarkable is the **Hôtel Plamon**. Built by wealthy drapers in the fourteenth century, it was

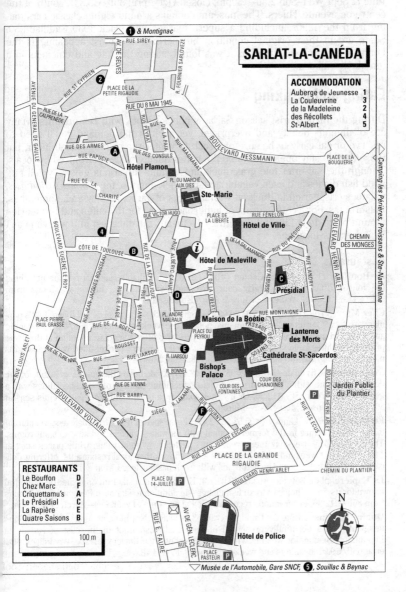

SARLAT-LA-CANÉDA

ACCOMMODATION

Auberge de Jeunesse	1
La Couleuvrine	3
de la Madeleine	2
des Récollets	4
St-Albert	5

RESTAURANTS

Le Bouffon	D
Chez Marc	F
Criquettamu's	A
Le Présidial	C
La Rapière	E
Quatre Saisons	B

0   100 m

then added to over the next three hundred years, starting with a lovely row of flamboyant Gothic windows on the first floor.

It's worth crossing over rue de la République to wander the western sector, particularly **rue Jean-Jacques-Rousseau**, but Sarlat's only other sight as such is the **Musée de l'Automobile** (July & Aug daily 10am–noon & 2–6pm; May, June & Sept Wed–Sun 2.30–6.30pm; closed Oct–April; 35F/€5.34), south of the centre on avenue Thiers. The museum contains around eighty classic cars dating from the 1890s, including a superb maroon and black 1930 Cadillac 330. Some are in their original condition but perhaps the most appealing is the Lorraine Dietrich displayed as it was found among the hay and chickens in a tumble-down barn.

Eating and drinking

During the main tourist season Sarlat is chock-a-block with **restaurants**. Many are of dubious quality and overpriced, yet such is the demand you'll need to reserve or eat early to be sure of a seat. In winter the pickings are thinner, but those that do stay open tend to be the better quality places patronized by locals. Though they all offer foie gras, duck and walnuts in various guises, you'll find good fish dishes and even vegetarian fare. Look out, too, for *pommes sarladaises*, potatoes crispy-fried in duck fat with lashings of garlic, parsley and, sometimes, mushrooms. For a coffee, drink or light snack, head for the **cafés** and **brasseries** around place de la Liberté; though by no means the cheapest in town, you can't beat them for location.

Restaurants

Le Bouffon, 11 rue Alberic-Cahuet (☎05.53.31.03.36). Reliable regional restaurant behind the tourist office with a pretty courtyard and exposed-stone interiors. Menus from 78F/€11.89. Closed Wed except July & Aug, also closed Dec.

Chez Marc, 4 rue Tourny (☎05.53.59.02.71). Small place south of pl de la Liberté that's popular with locals for its well-priced menus, notably the weekday lunch at 55F/€8.38. Evening and weekend menus start at 85F/€12.96 and they also offer a vegetarian option at the same price. Specialities include *feuilleté Périgourdin* – a flaky-pastry pocket filled with a foie gras mousse and *morilles* mushroom sauce. Closed Sun & Mon.

Criquettamu's, 5 rue des Armes (☎05.53.59.48.10). A safe bet on the quieter west side of rue de la République with a good variety of dishes, including platters of local specialities with a glass of wine from 85F/€12.96. Or try their *tourtier*, a potato and *cêpes* pie. Menus start at 80F/€12.20. Closed Mon & Nov–March.

Le Présidial, 6 rue Landry (☎05.53.28.92.47). For a special treat, try this classy restaurant to the east of centre in the former tribunal with its walled garden and airy, elegant rooms. The 115F/€17.53 weekday menu represents particularly good value, while prices start at 145F/€22.11 at weekends. The cuisine is a cut above other local restaurants, offering delicacies such as kidneys and sweetbreads with fresh pasta. Closed Mon & Dec–Jan.

La Rapière, pl du Peyrou (☎05.53.59.03.13). Highly rated restaurant opposite the cathedral known for its good choice of fresh fish dishes – in addition to standard Périgord fare. Menus from 85F/€12.96. Reservations recommended at any time of year. Oct–March closed Sun.

Quatre Saisons, 2 Côte de Toulouse (☎05.53.29.48.59). Not huge portions, but the food is imaginative and beautifully presented in this small restaurant to the east of rue de la République. Best in fine weather when you can eat on their flowery terrace. Weekday lunches at 65F/€9.91; evenings and weekends from 95F/€14.48.

Listings

Bike rental Bikes are available from Cycles Sarladais, 36 av Thiers (☎05.53.28.51.87, *cycles.sarladais@wanadoo.fr*), and Christian Chapoulie, 4 av de Selves (☎05.53.59.06.11). The latter also rents scooters.

Books and newspapers For local guides and foreign-language newspapers and magazines, try the Maison de la Presse, 34 rue de la République, or Librairie Majuscule, 43 rue de la République.

Bus departures Regional buses for Périgueux (CFTA; ☎05.53.59.01.48) leave from pl de la Petite-Rigaudie on the north side of town; those for Brive (also CFTA) and Souillac (SNCF; ☎05.53.59.00.21) from southerly pl Pasteur and the *gare SNCF*.

Car rental The following are all on pl de Lattre-de-Tassigny on the road to the train station: Budget (☎05.53.28.10.21); Europcar (☎05.53.30.30.40); Hertz (☎05.53.59.05.94).

Centre Hospitalier Jean-Leclaire, rue Jean-Leclaire (☎05.53.31.75.75) to the northeast of the centre.

Markets Sarlat's main market takes place on Saturdays in and around pl de la Liberté, with mostly foodstuffs in the morning and general goods after lunch; in winter (Dec–Feb) stalls selling foie gras and truffles swell the morning crowds. There's also a smaller fresh-foods market on Wednesday mornings.

Police Commissariat de Police, 1 bvd Henri-Arlet (☎05.53.59.05.17).

Post office The main post office is at pl du 14-Juillet, 24200 Sarlat.

Shopping While the markets are the best place to buy foie gras, walnuts, walnut oil, prunes and other local foods straight from the farmer, pl de la Liberté, rue de la Liberté and rue des Consuls are full of speciality shops. The Distillerie du Périgord (*www.perigord.com/distillerie_perigord*), on pl de la Liberté, makes delectable liqueurs from walnut and plum, amongst other things, and fruits in alcohol – try their Guinettes, containing local Morello cherries.

Taxis Allo Philippe Taxi ☎05.53.59.39.65; Brajot ☎05.53.59.41.13.

Tourist train In addition to regular services, from early July to late August the tourist train *Autorail Espérance* runs along the Dordogne valley from Sarlat to Bergerac, via Lalinde and Le Buisson; en route they serve various local products, including a glass of wine. The train departs from Sarlat mid-morning on the hour's journey (Mon–Sat), after which you return on a regular SNCF service. Tickets cost 72F/€10.98 return (there are no one-way fares) and reservations are required: phone Sarlat's *gare SNCF* (☎05.53.59.00.21) or the Association l'Autorail Espérance in Bergerac (☎05.53.31.53.46).

Around Sarlat

While the major sights are the castles and towns of the Dordogne valley (see pp.225–234), there are a number of worthwhile destinations in the hilly country above Sarlat. Heading eastwards first of all, you can see what happens to at least some of the local walnut crop at the **Moulin de la Tour**, where they produce various nut oils using creaking antique mills and presses, all driven by water power. Five kilometres further up into the hills, an abundance of water also helped create the surprisingly lush and very beautiful **Jardins du Manoir d'Eyrignac**, famous for their topiary. From there you can head further north again to admire the classic Périgord village of **St-Geniès**, or drop down to the west of Sarlat to the **Château de Puymartin**. Its fairytale towers, machicolations and crenellations make a stirring sight, while inside you'll find an interesting collection of tapestries and murals. The **Cabanes de Breuil**, northeast of Puymartin, consist of a more lowly clutch of traditional stone-built huts which are nonetheless preserved as a historic monument. You'll need your own **transport** to reach any of these places, with the exception of St-Geniès which lies on the Sarlat–Périgueux bus route.

East and north of Sarlat

On the banks of the River Enéa, 9km east of Sarlat and 2km north of **STE-NATHALÈNE** on the Proissans road, a sixteenth-century water mill still grinds out walnut oil in time-honoured fashion. The pressing room of the **Moulin de la Tour** (July & Aug Mon, Wed, Fri 9am–noon & 2–7pm, Sat 2–7pm; April–June & Sept Wed & Fri 9am–noon & 2–7pm; Oct–March Fri same hours; 25F/€3.81), where creaking cog-wheels drive a cylindrical grinding stone set at right angles to the flat base, is dark, cosy and full of the most delicious aromas. Here the nuts – ready-shelled by local pensioners – are ground to a paste, heated gently over a wood fire and then pressed to extract the oil; an average pressing gives roughly fifteen litres of oil from thirty kilos of nuts. It's best to time your visit for a grinding day (see times above), but otherwise you can buy their walnut, hazelnut and almond oils at the mill shop (Mon–Sat 9am–noon & 2–7pm).

The River Enéa rises among oak woods on a plateau to the north of Ste-Nathalène. Though the hills appear scrubby and dry, one of the Enéa's tributaries is fed by seven springs, the same springs that prompted a seventeenth-century noble, Antoine de Costes de la Calprenède, to build a manor house here, the **Manoir d'Eyrignac**, and which now sustain his descendants' glorious **gardens**, signed to the northeast along backroads from Ste-Nathalène (1hr guided tours daily: June–Sept 9.30am–7pm; April & May 10am–12.30pm & 2–7pm; Oct–March 10.30am–12.30pm & 2.30pm–dusk; 40F/€6.10; house not open to the public). The garden isn't huge, but, consisting of lush evergreens – mainly hornbeam, box, cypress and yew – clipped and arranged in formal patterns of alleys and borders, achieves remarkable effects with almost no colour. The regimented lines are softened by the occasional pavilion or fountain and informal stands of trees framing the countryside around. The original formal garden was laid out by an eighteenth-century Italian landscaper, and later converted to an English romantic garden according to the fashion of the times. What you see today is the work of the last forty years, the creation of the present owner's father in a combination of Italian and French styles. The most striking features are the "**hornbeam avenue**", a hundred-metre-long alley lined with cylindrical yews between spiralling hornbeam ramps, and the parterre in front of the manor house with its trompe l'oeil effect. To retain their immaculate lines, the hedges are cut – by hand – four times a year; it takes ten gardeners a full seven days to cut the hornbeam avenue alone.

The complex also contains a small exhibition hall, next to the ticket office, where you can watch a video about the garden and its history, and a snack bar offering drinks, sandwiches and simple meals (*plat du jour* around 55F/€8.38). Alternatively, bring your own food and take advantage of their picnic tables.

With time to spare, cut across country northwestwards to the cluster of buildings some 14km north of Sarlat known as **ST-GENIÈS**. It's a typical Périgord Noir village with its partly ruined château and fortress-like church, all constructed from the same warm-yellow stone under heavy *lauze* roofs. It won't take long to explore. Once you've done a quick circuit of the village, the only sight is the **Chapelle de Cheylard** standing on its own on a small knoll to the east. The fourteenth-century frescoes inside have suffered over the years – at one time the chapel served as a dance hall – but a number remain visible: St Michael weighing souls in a balance, the martyrdom of St Catherine, St George slaying his dragon and, over the door, a particularly manic bunch pelting St Stephen with stones.

West of Sarlat

Eight kilometres northwest of Sarlat on the D47, the **Château de Puymartin** (45min guided tours: April to early Nov daily 10am–noon & 2–6pm; 32F/€4.88) stands guard over the headwaters of the Petite Beune river which flows down to join the Vézère at Les Eyzies (see p.209). The castle, which underwent extensive remodelling in the seventeenth and nineteenth centuries, has been in the same family since 1450 and is remarkably well preserved. Among a large collection of family heirlooms, most noteworthy are the **tapestries**, particularly those in the grand hall, depicting the Siege of Troy. The Classical theme continues in the seventeenth-century trompe-l'oeil paintings on the chimneypiece here and again in the guest bedroom, where Zeus visits Danaë in a shower of gold – presumably he would have been surprised to find her clothed and holding a cross, a liberty taken in the more puritanical 1800s. The same sensibilities demanded that a number of naked figures in the "**mythological room**" also be dressed. It is an extraordinary room, not large, but completely covered in monochrome scenes from mythology: snake-haired Medusa, Argus with his hundred eyes and Althaea murdering her son Maleagra by means of a burning brand. The general consensus is that the room was a place of meditation, though surprisingly it also served as a children's room for some time. Like all good castles, Puymartin also has its ghost, in this case La Dame Blanche, who supposedly haunts the north tower. In real life she was Thérèse de St-Clar, the lady of the household during the sixteenth century, who, on being surprised in the arms of a lover, was walled up in the tower until she died fifteen years later. More prosaically, it's worth climbing up into the roof here to admire the elaborate timber framework supporting the *lauzes*. If tales of ghosts don't put you off, the château also offers very comfortable **chambres d'hôtes** accommodation (☎05.53.59.29.97, fax 05.53.29.87.52, *ch.puymartin@ lemel.fr*; closed Nov–March; ⑧).

At the opposite end of the architectural scale are the **Cabanes du Breuil** (June–Sept daily 10am–7pm; April, May & Oct daily 10am–noon & 2–6pm; Nov–March Sat & Sun 10am–noon & 2–6pm; 20F/€3.05; *www.cabanes-du-breuil.com*), a couple of kilometres up in the hills to the northwest of Puymartin. You'll find these dry-stone circular huts under conical *lauze* roofs scattered throughout the region, but none so picturesque as this group belonging to a small, working farm. Known locally as *bories*, the huts were originally used for human habitation, then for animals or storage. These particular examples are so in keeping with their location, that they appear to grow out of the ground – especially the row of three under one undulating roof. In season (June–Sept) there's a video presentation explaining how the huts are made, but really these beautiful structures speak for themselves.

The Vézère valley and around

Billed as the "Vallée de l'Homme", the **Vézère valley** is home to the greatest concentration of **prehistoric sites** in Europe. They are by no means the oldest, but it is the sheer wealth and variety that is quite stunning. It was here also that many important discoveries were made in the nineteenth and early twentieth centuries

THE CRO-MAGNON AND THEIR CAVES

The first signs of human habitation (in the form of flint tools) in the Vézère valley area date from around 400,000 years ago, but things don't really start to get interesting until the appearance of **Cro-Magnon** people – named after a rock-shelter in the middle Vézère valley where the first skeleton was found in 1868, but more broadly known as *Homo sapiens sapiens*, in other words, us – who swept across Europe a mere 30,000 to 40,000 years ago. The Cro-Magnon were nomadic people, tracking herds of reindeer across what was then steppe, only occasionally settling in riverside rock-shelters. Following on from their Neanderthal cousins, who were dying out around this time, they developed increasingly sophisticated tools using bone, ivory and antlers as well as stone, and then used fire to mould and strengthen them. They crafted ornaments such as necklaces and also started to decorate their tools and stone blocks with crude engravings and to sculpt small figurines.

By around 20,000 years ago the Cro-Magnons were depicting supremely realistic animals on their rock-shelter walls by means of engraving and sculpting with flints, or painting with dyes made from charcoal, manganese dioxide and red ochre. But the real explosion of prehistoric **cave art** was heralded by the widespread use of the tallow lamp, using reindeer fat, about 3000 years later at the start of the **Magdalenian** era (17,000–10,000 years ago); the era was named after the rock shelter at La Madeleine (see p.219) but its apogee is to be found in Lascaux's painted caves (see p.223). The lamps allowed Magdalenian artists to penetrate deep into the limestone caves, where they covered the walls with drawings, paintings and engravings, the vast majority being animals, but also occasional human figures and various abstract signs – dots, rectangles and parallel lines being the most common – whose meanings are the subject of endless debate: they were perhaps forms of communication or ritualistic symbols. There is also much speculation as to why such inaccessible spots were chosen, but it seems likely that the caves were sanctuaries and, if not actually places of worship, they at least had spiritual significance. However, we will never know for certain, which in many respects adds to the attraction.

which not only helped prove that early man did indeed possess artistic capabilities but also added greatly to our knowledge of our ancestors' way of life.

The valley, now listed by UNESCO as a World Heritage site, draws some 1.5 million visitors a year. The epicentre of all this activity is **Les Eyzies** where the National Museum of Prehistory contains many important finds and gives a good overview of what's on offer. The choice is bewildering, but at the very least you should visit the **Grotte de Font-de-Gaume** and the **Abri du Cap Blanc**, both in the Beune valley to the east of Les Eyzies. They harbour the best cave paintings and bas-relief sculptures still open to the public. With a bit of extra time, the nearby **Grotte des Combarelles** also stands out for its wealth of engravings, while the **Grotte du Grand Roc** combines a classic rock-shelter with a limestone cave decorated with spectacular displays of stalactites and stalagmites. Further afield, directly to the north of Les Eyzies, the **Grotte de Rouffignac** is one of the area's largest caves, where the superb drawings of more than two hundred mammoths, horses and bison, amongst others, seem so fresh they could have been done yesterday.

Towards the south end of the Vézère valley, near **Le Bugue**, there are more colourful concretions in the **Gouffre de Proumeyssac**, with its very touristy but nonetheless dramatic *son et lumière*. Then north of Les Eyzies the sights begin to get more diversified. The semi-troglodytic settlements at **La Madeleine** and **La Roque St-Christophe** – where a whole town was built into a cliff-face – continue from where prehistoric man left off, and one of the most appealing châteaux along the Vézère, the **Château de Losse**, stands further upstream near the picturesque village of **St-Léon**. There are now several prehistoric parks in the area, of which **Le Thot**, also north of St-Léon, is of most general interest for its collection of live animals frequently depicted in cave art, and as an introduction to cave art, particularly the legendary paintings of **Lascaux**. Located near **Montignac**, towards the northern end of the Vézère valley, Lascaux cave itself is no longer open to the public, but the paintings and engravings – with all their exceptional detail, colour and realism – have been faithfully reproduced in **Lascaux II**.

Most of the Vézère sites can only be visited on **guided tours**. Some are offered in English while others provide a translated text, but they are tiring – and the talks get repetitive – so it's best to select just a few of those covered below. At several caves, notably Font-de-Gaume, Combarelles and Lascaux II, visitor numbers are limited so you need to buy **tickets** in advance. And note that in high season it pays to visit the more famous places in the early morning or at lunchtime, when they are quieter, or to concentrate on the less well-known ones, some of which are every bit as enjoyable.

Finally, it's difficult, but not impossible, to explore the valley by a mixture of public **transport**, taxis and walking – good planning is required to cover more than one site per day. Les Eyzies, Le Bugue and Terrasson, the northern gateway to the valley, are all on major train lines, while with a few early starts, Montignac, Le Bugue and Rouffignac can all be reached by bus.

Les Eyzies-de-Tayac

The principal base for visiting the Vézère valley is **LES EYZIES-DE-TAYAC**, 20km northwest of Sarlat. Despite a promising position between the river and a towering cliff, it's a small, unattractive one-street town which nevertheless merits a visit for its museum of Paleolithic art, the largest collection in France. While out of season it offers a good choice of hotels and restaurants, Les Eyzies gets completely overrun in summer.

Arrival and information

A stop on the Périgueux–Agen train line, Les Eyzies' **gare SNCF** lies about half a kilometre northwest of centre along the main road, on which you'll also find the **tourist office** right in the town centre (July & Aug Mon–Sat 9am–8pm, Sun 10am–noon & 2–6pm; June & Sept Mon–Sat 9am–7pm, Sun 10am–noon & 2–6pm; Oct–May Mon–Sat 9am–noon & 2–6pm; ☎05.53.06.97.05, fax 05.53.06.90.79). In addition to plentiful information on local sights, *chambres d'hôtes* and hiking trails, they also provide **bike rental**. You can rent **canoes** from Canoës Vallée Vézère (☎05.53.05.10.11; April to mid-Oct) and Les 3 Drapeaux (☎05.53.06.91.89; April–Sept), located either side of the bridge upstream from Les Eyzies on the Périgueux road. If you need a **taxi**, call Taxi Tardieu (☎05.53.06.93.06).

Accommodation

Most **hotels** in Les Eyzies are pricey and may require *demi-pension* in high season, when it's better anyway to stay in one of the villages around. Note that many

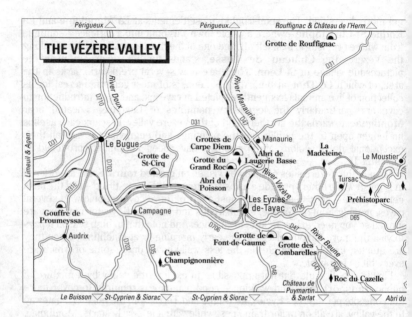

THE VÉZÈRE VALLEY

Périgueux △   Périgueux △   Rouffignac & Château de l'Herm △

River Doux

River Manaurie

Grotte de Rouffignac

D31

D710

D31

D47

Limeuil & Agen ◁

D31

D703

Le Bugue ●

Grotte de St-Cirq

D31E

Grottes de Carpe Diem

Grotte du Grand Roc

Abri du Poisson

● Manaurie

Abri de Laugerie Basse

River Vézère

La Madeleine

Le Moustier ●

Tursac

Préhistoparc

Gouffre de Proumeyssac

● Campagne

Les Eyzies-de-Tayac

D706

D47

D65

D706

River Beune

D703

D35

● Audrix

Cave Champignonnière

Grotte de Font-de-Gaume

Grotte des Combarelles

D48

D47

D48

Château de Puymartin

♦ Roc du Cazelle

Le Buisson ▽   St-Cyprien & Siorac ▽   St-Cyprien & Siorac ▽   & Sarlat ▽   ▽ Abri du

also close in winter. The closest **campsite** is the well-tended, three-star *La Rivière* (April–Oct) under the same management as the hotel of the same name listed below.

Le Centenaire (☎05.53.06.68.68, fax 05.53.06.92.41, *www.hotelducentenaire.fr*). Les Eyzies' most luxurious hotel sits on a busy junction at the southeast end of town, though you soon forget the traffic once you're inside. While not huge the rooms are certainly plush – in a clean, modern style – and the service excellent. There's also a pretty garden and pool with views of the surrounding cliffs, and a top-class restaurant which offers best value with its lunch menu at 180F/€27.44 (Thurs & Fri only); at other times the starting price is nearly double that (closed lunchtime Mon–Wed). Closed Nov–April. ⑦.

du Centre (☎05.53.06.97.13, fax 05.53.06.91.63, *www.logis-de-france.fr*). The ivy-covered *Hôtel du Centre* is in a prime spot right in the centre beside the tourist office but set back from the road with a riverside terrace. The smart, airy rooms have recently been refurbished and there's a decent restaurant serving dishes such as rabbit *confit* with truffles and ceps (menus 100–195F/€15.24–29.73; closed Tues lunchtime). Closed Nov–Jan. ③.

Les Falaises (☎05.53.06.97.35). The cheapest hotel in Les Eyzies is one of the few open all year with fourteen simple rooms above a café opposite the Abri Pataud. It's worth paying a little extra for the balcony rooms with proper en-suite bathrooms; cheaper rooms contain just a cubicle shower and partitioned-off toilet. ②.

Le Moulin de la Beune (☎05.53.06.93.39, fax 05.53.06.94.33). This converted mill in a lovely spot across the road from the *Centenaire* is undoubtedly the finest place to stay in Les Eyzies. The rooms offer extremely good value, not opulent but fresh with white walls and big windows all overlooking the mill-race gardens. The restaurant, *Le Vieux Moulin*, is also excellent, both for the setting and its well-priced regional menus (125–400F/€19.06–60.98; closed lunch Tues & Wed). Closed early-Nov to April. ④.

La Rivière (☎05.53.06.97.14, fax 05.53.35.20.85). A good choice at the lower end of the market about 1km from Les Eyzies on the Périgueux road. There are just six unfussy rooms, all

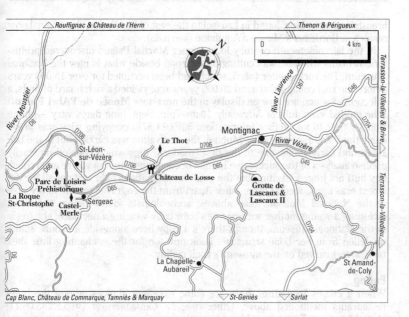

en suite, in a typical Périgord farmhouse with access to the same facilities as the campsite: pool, bike and canoe rental, river beach, and a restaurant with simple meals from 68F/€10.37. Closed Oct–April. ②.

des Roches (☎05.53.06.96.59, fax 05.53.06.95.54, *www.roches-les-eyzies.com*). With forty-odd rooms, this is a good bet if everywhere else is full, even if it is a touch overpriced. It's set back from the road – the D47 to Sarlat – behind a garden and pool, but even so it's still worth upgrading to one of the slightly more expensive rooms in the newer annexe at the back. Closed Oct–April. ④–⑤.

The Town

Les Eyzies' single, unnamed street runs parallel to the jutting limestone cliff which dominates the town. Beneath its overhang, Paul Dardé's 1930 statue of Neanderthal man, portrayed as an ape-like hunk, stands staring out over the Vézère, while beside him the **Musée National de Préhistoire** (Mon & Wed–Sun: July & Aug 9.30am–7pm; mid-March to June & Sept to mid-Nov 9.30am–noon & 2–6pm; mid-Nov to mid-March 9.30am–noon & 2–5pm; 22F/€3.35) occupies the remains of a castle built into the rock. As such only a tiny proportion of its collection is displayed in less than perfect conditions, but this is all set to change with the opening of a new building in 2002. For the present the museum starts with a vast array of increasingly sophisticated stone tools of the Paleolithic era (2 million to 10,000 years ago), the tools which enabled man to create the engravings and sculptures that follow. Some are copies, but many are originals, such as the large limestone block with two aurochs (primitive wild cattle) beautifully superimposed to provide perspective, and the tiny female figure from the nearby Abri Pataud (see below). Look out, too, for the still small but much more exaggerated bas-relief known as the Vénus à la Corne ("Venus with the Horn") with her pendulous breasts and stout hips; found in Laussel to the east of Les Eyzies, the original now resides in Bordeaux's Musée d'Aquitaine (see p.83).

In the late nineteenth century local farmer Martial Pataud discovered prehistoric remains when he was cutting a new road beside what is now the National Museum. The rock-shelter (*abri*), which had been occupied for over 15,000 years before the roof collapsed around 20,000 years ago, yielded a rich hoard of finds, a selection of which are now on display in the next-door **Musée de l'Abri Pataud** (1hr guided visit: July & Aug daily 10am–7pm; Sept–June dates vary – phone ☎05.53.06.92.46 for further information; 30F/€4.57) occupying what was previously the Pataud's wine cellar. Much of the excavation was carried out in the late 1950s and early 1960s, one of the first "modern" digs which enabled unusually precise analysis of the successive human occupations – unless you're an archeology buff not hugely exciting but the guide's explanations help sort out all the different eras mentioned at other sites. Apart from the engraved female figure now in the National Museum (see above), archeologists found eleven skeletons, including a young mother with her newborn baby wearing a necklace; she too is in the National Museum, though there's a copy here alongside a bronze statue modelled from her bone structure. Look out, too for the enchanting little ibex (*bouquetin*) carved on the museum's rock ceiling.

Eating

When it comes to **eating**, there are some excellent choices among the hotel restaurants mentioned above. Otherwise, *Le Chateaubriant* (☎05.53.35.06.11; closed Jan & for dinner Dec–March), north along the main street from the tourist office, is your best bet. They're strong on grills and fresh fish, with good-value menus starting at 70F/€10.67; reservations are recommended in season, especially for the terrace. Or, for something cheaper, *La Grignotière*, east of the tourist office, serves no-nonsense brasserie-style food: sandwiches, omelettes and salads, as well as full menus from 58F/€8.84.

East of Les Eyzies

Les Eyzies sits on the confluence of the River Vézère and the Beune flowing in from the east. Like the Vézère, the Beune valley hides a wealth of prehistoric rock-shelters and caves, but here it is the great variety of cave art on offer that makes it so attractive. Closest to Les Eyzies, and arguably the best single sight in the whole area, the **Grotte de Font-de-Gaume** is one of the few places where you can still see original cave paintings on such a scale. Numbers are restricted so **advance booking** is highly recommended. The same applies to the **Grotte des Combarelles**, further east, the walls of which are covered with engravings. They're not always easy to make out but the sense of mystery as you proceed deep into the dimly lit tunnel is compelling. To put it all in context the mock-up scenes at nearby **Roc du Cazelle** give an enjoyable view of what prehistoric life might have been like. You're back to the real thing, though, at the **Abri du Cap Blanc** where early man sculpted an unusually large frieze of horses way up in the hills.

Grotte de Font-de-Gaume

Since they were first discovered in 1901, over two hundred Magdalenian-era (18,000–10,000 years old) polychrome paintings and engravings have been found in the narrow tunnel of the **Grotte de Font-de-Gaume** (40min guided tours: Mon, Tues & Thurs–Sun: April–Sept 9am–noon & 2–6pm; March & Oct 9.30am–noon & 2–5.30pm; Nov–Feb 10am–noon & 2–5pm; 35F/€5.34; ☎05.53.06.86.00, fax 05.53.35.26.18; maximum 20 people per tour), just over a kilometre from Les Eyzies along the D47 to Sarlat. In order to preserve them, only two hundred people are allowed to enter the cave each day. During the peak season (July & Aug) it is essential to book several days, even a week, ahead. At other times a couple of days will be sufficient, or you may be lucky and get them on spec first thing in the morning. Phone reservations are accepted, though during the peak season they may ask you to confirm by fax.

The cave mouth is no more than a fissure concealed by rocks and trees above a small lush valley. Inside is a narrow twisting passage of irregular height over 100m long, where you quickly lose your bearings in the dark. The majority of the paintings depict bison, but also horses, mammoths, reindeer and wild cats, and many unexplained signs such as the so-called "tectiforms", comprising a very gently inclined, upside down "V" with vertical lines beneath. The first you come to is a frieze of bison at about eye level: reddish-brown in colour, massive, full of movement and an almost palpable force. Further on a horse stands with one hoof slightly raised, resting, and another appears to be galloping or jumping. But the most miraculous of all is a frieze of five bison discovered in 1966. The colour, remarkably sharp and vivid, is preserved by a protective layer of calcite. Shading under the belly and down the thighs is used to add volume with a sophistication that seems utterly modern. Another panel consists of superimposed drawings, a fairly common phenomenon in cave-painting, sometimes the result of work by successive generations, but here an obviously deliberate technique: a reindeer in the foreground shares legs with a large bison to indicate perspective.

Grotte des Combarelles and Roc du Cazelle

The myriad engravings of the **Grotte des Combarelles** (40min guided tours: same hours as Font-de-Gaume; 35F/€5.34; maximum six people per tour), a short distance further along the D47, were discovered a few days before Font-de-Gaume in 1901. Up to this date only five decorated caves were known so, with the jury still out on primitive man's artistic abilities, they were an incredibly significant find. As with Font-de-Gaume, numbers are restricted and prebooking is recommended, especially in peak season; apply to the Font-de-Gaume booking office (see above).

Again, you make your way down a long, claustrophobic tunnel, stopping every now and then while the guide picks out a tiny selection of the six-hundred-plus **engravings** identified so far. It is a veritable Magdalenian menagerie: mostly horses, but also bison, reindeer, mammoths, rhinos, bears, ibex, aurochs and wild cats. Stylized human figures and geometric symbols also feature. A good deal of imagination is required to recognize some of the fainter outlines, often superimposed one upon another, while others are astounding in their simplicity and realistic treatment – among the finest are the heads of a horse and a lioness where the dips and projections in the rock provide eyes, nostrils and even bone structure.

Continue along the D47 for another couple of kilometres and you'll be greeted by mammoths roaring and the sound of people chipping flints at **Roc du Cazelle** (daily: July & Aug 10am–8pm; June & Sept 10am–7pm; March–May, Oct & Nov 10am–6pm; Dec–Feb 11am–5pm; 31F/€4.73), a theme park which reconstructs life 12,000 years ago. It's really best for children, but the imaginative design helps bring the surrounding caves to life. Various scenes – from hunting and gathering to painting and sculpting – are scattered around a wooded valley once occupied by prehistoric man, culminating in a real troglodyte fortress and a troglodyte farm that was inhabited up to the 1960s.

Abri du Cap Blanc and beyond

Not a cave but a natural rock-shelter, the **Abri du Cap Blanc** (45min guided tours daily: July & Aug 9.30am–7pm; April–June, Sept & Oct 10am–noon & 2–6pm; closed Nov–March; 31F/€4.73) lies on a steep wooded hillside above the River Beune about 7km east of Les Eyzies; it's signed left off the D47 shortly after Les Combarelles. The shelter contains a superb **sculpted frieze** of horses and bison dating from the middle Magdalenian period (16,000–13,000 years ago), discovered in 1909 behind thick layers of sediment. Unfortunately, the excavation was carried out in such a hurry that the frieze had been badly damaged before anyone realized it was there. Even so, it is quite remarkable, mainly for its scale – the middle horse, which closely resembles the wild Przewalski horse of Central Asia, is virtually life-size – but also the depth of some of the sculptures. The bodies were obviously polished to set them off against the rough background, while traces of ochre and manganese pigments indicate that they were also painted at one time.

Continuing up the Beune valley from Cap Blanc you come to the elegant sixteenth-century Château de Laussel (closed to the public). On the opposite side of the valley stand the romantic ruins of the **Château de Commarque**, now undergoing extensive restoration. The easiest way to reach it is by a footpath starting below Cap Blanc.

The next right turn, the D6, brings you to the little hilltop hamlet of **MARQUAY** about 4km from Cap Blanc, where the *Hôtel des Bories* (☎05.53.29.67.02, fax 05.53.29.64.15, *www.logis-de-france.fr*; ②; closed Nov–March) makes a pleasant alternative to staying in Les Eyzies. It's in a lovely spot, with marvellous views, a swimming pool and nicely rustic rooms; you need to book several months in advance for July and August. They also run the excellent *L'Estérel* restaurant, just round the corner, offering unusual dishes such as buffalo steaks and African tilapia fish – a welcome change from duck (menus from 85F/€12.96; closed Wed lunch & Nov–March).

There's another good, slightly more upmarket hotel back across the Beune valley at **TAMNIÈS**, perched even higher, some 13km northeast of Les Eyzies. The geranium-decked *Hôtel Laborderie* (☎05.53.29.68.59, fax 05.53.29.65.31, *www.logis-de-france.fr*; ③; closed Nov–March; good restaurant with regional menus from 85F/€12.96) occupies four separate buildings, with larger rooms in the newer blocks overlooking the extensive garden and pool; again, early booking is advisable in summer.

Northwest of Les Eyzies

As well as prehistoric cave art, you can see some truly spectacular stalactites and stalagmites around the Vézère valley. The closest of these to Les Eyzies is the **Grotte du Grand Roc**, just a few kilometres upstream. It can be combined with **Abri de Laugerie Basse** – another treasure-trove of Magdalenian art and artefacts – located under the same dramatic overhang. The Laugerie Basse finds are now scattered around various museums, including Les Eyzies' National Museum (see p.211), but one splendid piece of art in the area is still *in situ*. Up a little side-valley known as the Gorge d'Enfer, the **Abri de Poisson** is named after the life-size salmon carved in the roof; visits are by appointment only and well worth the trouble. Further upstream again the Vézère is joined by the River Manaurie, whose valley boasts its own small crystalline cave, the **Grottes de Carpe Diem**. Then, way up in the hills to the north, the **Grotte de Rouffignac** is one of the largest decorated caves in Europe, so large that you enter by electric train to find caverns splattered with beautifully observed mammoths, horses, bison and other beasts deep in the bowls of the earth. If time allows, continue north to the **Château de l'Herm** whose overgrown ruins provide an antidote to all these caves.

Grotte du Grand Roc and around

Two kilometres north of Les Eyzies on the D47 to Périgueux, the entrance to the **Grotte du Grand Roc** (30min guided tours: July & Aug daily 9.30am–7pm; April–June, Sept & Oct daily 9.30am–6pm; Feb, March, Nov & Dec Mon & Wed–Sun 10am–5pm; 38F/€5.79, or 48F/€7.32 including Laugerie Basse; *www.grandroc.com*) lies under the cliffs that line much of the Vézère valley. There's a great view from the mouth of the cave and, inside, along some 80m of tunnel, a fantastic array of rock formations. Most unusual are the still-unexplained *excentriques* growing in all directions and triangles formed by calcite crystallizing in still, shallow pools.

The cave was discovered in 1924 in the continuing search for prehistoric art. Sixty years earlier Edouard Lartet and Henry Christy had discovered a rock-shelter further along the same cliff. The **Abri de Laugerie Basse** (same hours as Grotte du Grand Roc; 28F/€4.27) was inhabited almost constantly over the last 15,000 years – most recently in the form of farmhouses built against the rock – and yielded hundreds of engravings and sculptures, not on the rockface but on pieces of bone or fashioned out of individual stones. The majority date from the late Magdalenian period (13,000–10,000 years ago) when prehistoric art reached its peak. They include a mysterious engraving of a very pregnant woman lying under a reindeer, and a sculpted female torso, the first so-called "Venus figure" – obviously symbols of fertility, though it's not known whether they relate to fertility rites – discovered in France. These and other important finds are presented in a slide-show before visiting the shelter; there's little to see otherwise, though during the visit you learn a lot about the history of the excavations and what conditions were like during the Magdalenian era.

More interesting, though, is the **Abri de Poisson** (1hr guided tours: Mon, Tues & Thurs–Sun: July & Aug 10am–6pm; April–June & Sept 9am–noon & 2–6pm; March & Oct 9.30am–noon & 2–5.30pm; Nov–Feb 10am–noon & 2–5pm; 15F/€2.29) which lies on the road from Les Eyzies just before the Grotte du Grand Roc. The rock-shelter – one of many along a side-valley – contains one of the very few sculpted fish in prehistoric art. It's a real beauty too, a metre-long male salmon complete with gills and beak probably carved about 25,000 years ago. The deep-cut rectangular outline is not a prehistoric picture-frame, however, but the remains of an abortive attempt by a Berlin museum to acquire the salmon soon after it was discovered in 1912. Since then the shelter has been kept sealed up and can now be visited by appointment only by a maximum of forty people per day; for reservations and tickets apply to the office at Font-de-Gaume (see p.212).

Onward to Rouffignac and the Château de l'Herm

Soon after Grand Roc the D47 turns northwest to follow the Manaurie valley. Another left turn in **MANAURIE** village takes you up a lane to the **Grottes de Carpe Diem** (30min guided tours: July & Aug daily 9.30am–7pm; April–June, Sept & Oct daily 10am–6pm; Nov–March Sat, Sun & school hols 2–5pm; 30F/€4.57), roughly 5km from Les Eyzies; Carpe Diem, meaning "seize the day", is simply the name chosen by the man who discovered the caves in 1927. They comprise a 200m-long tunnel the ceiling of which is covered with tiny stalactites in brilliant white. It's nowhere near as exciting as Grand Roc, but on the other hand it's less crowded and more natural, without all the wire mesh necessary to keep souvenir hunters at bay in the more popular caves.

If you continue up the D47 from Manaurie for 7km, you'll find a right turn signed to the **Grotte de Rouffignac** (1hr guided tours daily: July & Aug 9–11.30am & 2–6pm; April–June, Sept & Oct 10–11.30am & 2–5pm; closed Nov–March; 36F/€5.49) another 7km uphill among dense woods; unfortunately the tour is in French only and there's no English-language leaflet. You take a little electric train a kilometre along the bed of an underground river which dried up about three million years ago. On the way the guide points out where hibernating bears scratched their nests and human visitors left their mark in the form of graffiti – including a priest, Abbé de la Tour, in 1808. In fact records show that the cave was known about in the sixteenth century, but it took until 1956 before the 13,000-year-old monochromatic drawings and engravings were recognized. Around 270 animal figures have been identified so far. The vast majority are mammoths, including a superb patriarch, his great tusks arcing under a piercing eye, in the final chamber. The chamber's ceiling is covered with mammoths, woolly rhino, horses, bison and ibex depicted with an astonishing economy of line.

The cave is located about 5km south of **ROUFFIGNAC** town, which was destroyed by German troops in 1944 and subsequently rebuilt. They drove everyone out before torching it; the only buildings to survive were the church, with its carved portal and unusual, twisted columns inside, and the adjacent house. Four kilometres further north, the **Château de l'Herm** (April, May & July to mid-Sept daily 10am–7pm; June Sun 10am–7pm; mid-Sept to mid-Nov daily 11am–6pm; mid-Nov to March by appointment only, ☎05.53.05.46.61; 24F/€3.66) also has an unhappy history, in this case a complicated tale of murders, forced marriages and disputed inheritance rights. In the end the castle was abandoned and has been crumbling away for more than three centuries to leave an atmospheric ruin engulfed by trees. Two big round towers and some decorative touches from the fifteenth and sixteenth centuries remain: a late-Gothic doorway opens on to a spiral stone staircase at the top of which is a beautifully worked palm-tree vault, while three sculpted fireplaces cling one above the other to the wall of an otherwise empty shell. Much is made of the fact that the château featured in local novelist Eugène le Roy's famous work *Jacquou le Croquant* (see p.222) based a sixteenth-century peasant revolt (see p.358).

Le Bugue and around

LE BUGUE lies on the north bank of a meander in the Vézère 11km downstream from Les Eyzies, for which it provides an alternative base. It's not only marginally less crowded in season but also a more attractive town, with its riverfront setting and scattering of old houses along the River Doux, which flows into the

Vézère from the north, and the lane generously called Grand Rue running east of and parallel to the Doux. Between the two, rue de Paris represents Le Bugue's main shopping street, while the **place de Mairie**, on the river bank at the south end of rue de Paris, is what passes for the town centre. From this square avenue de la Libération heads south over the Vézère, and the main D703 to Les Eyzies, here called rue de la République, scoots southeast. On its way it takes you past Le Bugue's two rather second-tier sights located side by side roughly 1km from the centre.

The more interesting, particularly for younger kids, is the **Village du Bournat** (daily: May–Sept 10am–7pm; Feb–April & Oct–Dec 10am–5pm; closed Jan; last entry 1hr before closing; 50F/€7.62), a fair re-creation of a Périgord village in the early 1900s complete with *lauze*-roofed cottages, chapel, schoolhouse, baker, café and so forth – but no real animals. The entry price seems expensive, but there's a lot to see, including demonstrations of local crafts, such as clog- and barrel-making, potting and basketry, and you can come and go as you please within a day. Next door, the **Aquarium du Périgord Noir** (daily: June–Aug 9am–7pm; April, May & Sept 10am–6pm; mid-Feb to March & Oct to mid-Nov 10am–noon & 2–5pm; closed mid-Nov to mid-Feb; July & Aug open till midnight on Sat; 48F/€7.32) will also appeal mostly to children. The aquarium concentrates on European freshwater fish – though they've recently added more colourful tropical species as well – kept for the most part in open tanks, some of which you can walk under.

Practicalities

Trains on the Périgueux–Agen line pull into Le Bugue's gare SNCF roughly 2km southeast on the D703; call Archambeau (☎05.53.07.10.70) if you need a taxi. You can also reach Le Bugue from Périgueux by bus (operated by Voyages Rey; %05.53.07.27.22); buses stop on place de la Mairie. Walk west from this square and along rue du Jardin-Public to find the tourist office (July & Aug daily 9am–1pm & 3–7pm; April–June, Sept & Oct Mon–Sat 9.30am–12.30pm & 2.30–6.30pm, Sun 10am–1pm; Nov–March Tues–Sat 9.30am–12.30pm & 2.30–6.30pm; %05.53.07.20.48, fax 05.53.54.92.30, www.perigord.com/bugue) just across the River Doux. In addition to the normal services, they also operate an exchange bureau and double as an SNCF ticket office; note that you can't buy tickets at the station. Canoe rental is available from Les 3 Drapeaux (%05.53.03.51.99; June–Sept) beside the Village du Bournat.

The cheapest place to **stay** is the welcoming, old-fashioned *Hôtel de Paris*, 14 rue Paris (☎05.53.07.28.16, fax 05.53.04.20.89, *hotel.de.paris.le.bugue@wanadoo.fr*, ②), a short walk north of the central square. *Le Cygne*, Le Placage (☎05.53.07.17.77, fax 05.53.03.93.74, *www.logis-de-france.fr*; ③; closed late Dec to Jan & two weeks in Oct) is a more stately place just west of the tourist office. It offers well-priced rooms – overlooking the road at the cheaper end – and a popular traditional restaurant with menus from 88F/€13.42 (closed Sun eve & Mon out of season). If you'd rather be more in the country, try the friendly *Les Fontenilles* (☎05.53.07.24.97, fax 05.53.07.24.70; ③; Feb, March & Oct–Dec closed Fri, also Jan) set back from the D703 a few kilometres southeast of Le Bugue with simple rooms, a pool and a decent restaurant (menus 65–150F/€9.91–22.87).

For somewhere simple to **eat**, there's the grill and pizza joint, *La Pergola*, 16 avenue de la Libération, just across the Vézère. They also offer salads, pasta, fondues and two regional menus at 85F/€12.96 and 120F/€18.29. At the other end of the scale *Les Trois As* is well known for its original and varied cuisine. It's best in summer (April–Sept) when they occupy a riverside terrace in the *Royal Vézère* hotel on place de la Mairie; when the hotel closes they decamp to 78 rue de Paris (menus from 110F/€16.77; closed for lunch Tues & Wed).

Le Bugue's main **market** takes place on Tuesday mornings on rue de Paris and place de la Mairie, with a smaller market on Saturdays. There's also an excellent **wine shop**, Julien de Savignac, on avenue de la Libération, selling their own Bergerac wines in addition to a good selection from around the southwest.

Around Le Bugue

High-tech has hit the Vézère in a big way at the **Gouffre de Proumeyssac** (45min guided tours daily: July & Aug 9am–7pm; May & June 9.30am–6.30pm; March, April, Sept & Oct 9.30am–noon & 2–5.30pm; Feb, Nov & Dec 2–5pm; closed Jan; 44F/€6.71), a vast and spectacular limestone cavern 5km south of Le Bugue on the D31E. Its forty-metre-high vault dripping with multicoloured stalactites ranging from fine needles to massive petrified waterfalls is dubbed the "crystal cathedral". To heighten the sense of atmosphere you enter in the dark, then the music builds as lights pick out various formations before revealing the whole chamber in a grand finale. It's cleverly done, though some will find it too commercialized, even down to stacks of calcite-coated pottery souvenirs, and a far cry from when the cave was discovered in 1907. At that time the only way in was via a basket lowered through a hole in the roof under flickering torchlight – you can still make the descent by two-person basket for 85F/€12.96 per person including the entry fee.

By contrast, the **Grotte de St-Cirq** (daily except Sat: mid-June to mid-Sept 10am–6pm; mid-Sept to mid-June noon–4pm; 20F/€3.05), is a very low-key affair which receives refreshingly few visitors. The small, blackened cave contains a rare and explicitly male figure, popularly known as the sorcerer, engraved on the ceiling alongside a human head, ibex, horses and bison. They're all small and rather difficult to make out but a big part of the attraction is the location. The cave lies in the hamlet of **ST-CIRQ** on the north bank of the Vézère more or less midway between Le Bugue and Les Eyzies, on a back road leading right off the D31. Go to the top of the village, then left past a row of houses set into the cliffs where bamboo and banana trees flourish. Knock at the last *lauze*-roofed cottage and the elderly Mr Palluzzano who will proudly show you his little museum of prehistoric bits and pieces before taking you to the cave.

On the opposite side of the Vézère there's one last cave to visit, but rather than carvings and concretions this ancient stone quarry contains a mushroom farm, the **Cave Champignonnière** (30min guided tours daily: July & Aug 10–11am & 1–6pm; April–June & Sept 10–11am & 2–5pm; early Oct 11am, 3pm & 4pm; closed mid-Oct to March; 30F/€4.57). In addition to ordinary button mushrooms, they grow shiitake, oyster mushrooms and grass, or straw, mushrooms. After the whole process has been explained (in French only) you can buy fresh or dried mushrooms – all organically grown – on the spot.

The cave lies on the D35 St-Cyprien road just outside **CAMPAGNE**, a pretty village gathered round a château and diminutive church 4km upstream from Le Bugue. There's also an excellent **hotel** where you'll find big, bright rooms and a good regional restaurant: the *Hôtel du Château* (☎05.53.07.23.50, fax 05.53.03.93.69; ③; closed mid-Oct to Easter; restaurant 100–235F/€15.24–35.82).

Northeast along the Vézère: La Madeleine to Le Thot

The D706 tracks the Vézère as it meanders northeastwards from Les Eyzies. Here again the valley sides are peppered with cliff-dwellings, from prehistoric rock-shelters to the remnants of a full-blown town. One of the first you come to is the relatively recently abandoned village of **La Madeleine** where a little chapel still survives, straddling the path, alongside the shells of several houses built into the rock cavity. Further on, the **Préhistoparc** with its life-size replicas of prehistoric animals and people will amuse the kids, while **La Roque St-Christophe** provides the most dramatic sight along this stretch of the valley. Until the sixteenth century this great wall of cliff provided accommodation for hundreds of people on five levels – a forerunner of the multistorey – accessed by ladders and just one heavily defended ledge-path. Beyond lies the exquisite riverside village of **St-Léon-sur-Vézère**, near which there's another imaginative prehistoric theme-park and a cluster of rock-shelters, and the **Château de Losse**. A handsome sight with its towers and turrets reflected in the Vézère, the château contains a particularly good collection of furniture and tapestries. Afterwards, head up over the lip of the valley to learn about caveart at **Le Thot**.

La Madeleine and the Préhistoparc

First stop along the Vézère is a semi-troglodytic medieval settlement near the village of **TURSAC**, 5km upstream from Les Eyzies. **La Madeleine** (daily: July & Aug 9.30am–7pm; Sept–June 10am–6pm; 30F/€4.57) lies on the river's north bank near the neck of a huge meander where the river takes a three-kilometre loop to cover less than 100m as the crow flies. The cliffs here have been inhabited on and off for the last 15,000 years. Indeed, the prehistoric rock-shelter down by the water's edge yielded such a wealth of late-Paleolithic tools and engravings that archeologists named the era Magdalenian; one of the more intriguing finds was a carving of a man with a bestial head, believed to be a mask, now on display at Les Eyzies' museum (see p.211). Further up the cliff subsequent settlers constructed a whole village complete with fortress, drawbridge, village square and chapel dating back to the tenth century. Le Madeleine was inhabited until 1920 and the Maquis used it as a hide-out, but now the chapel is the only building completely intact. Nevertheless, enough remains to give a good sense of what such cliff-dwellings were like.

Plastic Neanderthals hunting mock mammoths to an accompanying soundtrack won't be everyone's cup of tea, but the **Préhistoparc** (daily: July & Aug 9.30am–7.30pm; March–June & Sept–Nov 10am–6pm; closed Dec–Feb; 31F/€4.73), a little further along the D706, is another attempt to re-create the daily life of prehistoric man. If you've already visited the more varied Roc du Cazelle (see p.213), you can give this a miss, but otherwise it's fun to take in one of these parks, especially if you've got children in tow. Again, a woodland walk takes you past tableaux of encampments, people making flints, painting, sculpting and generally being busy in a prehistoric sort of way.

Tursac is also home to two good **campsites**. First is the simple but spectacularly located *La Ferme du Pelou* (☎05.53.06.98.17; mid-March to mid-Nov), a two-star site perched on the hilltop overlooking La Madeleine and its meander from the east; it's signed off the D706 to the south of Tursac. North of the village, *Le Vézère Périgord* (☎05.53.06.96.31, fax 05.53.50.78.96; April–Sept) is a well-run, spacious and friendly three-star site set back from the main road among trees.

La Roque St-Christophe

The enormous natural refuge of **La Roque St-Christophe** (45min guided tours daily: July & Aug 10am–7pm; May, June & Sept 10am–6.30pm; March, April & Oct 10am–6pm; Jan, Feb, Nov & Dec 11am–5pm; 35F/€5.34; *www. roque-st-christophe.com*), 3km upriver from Tursac, is made up of about one hundred rock-shelters on five levels hollowed out of the limestone cliffs. The whole complex is nearly a kilometre long and up to 80m above ground-level, where the River Vézère once flowed. The earliest traces of occupation go back over 50,000 years, although permanent settlement dates from around the ninth century when the site's natural defences really came into their own. At its peak during the Middle Ages it had grown into a veritable town clinging to the rock-face – with its own marketplace, church, prison, abattoir, baker and artisans' workshops – and able to shelter over one thousand people in times of trouble. And there was no shortage of those, culminating in the Wars of Religion when Protestant sympathizers took refuge here. After they were kicked out in 1588, Henri III ordered the town and fortress demolished. Which means you need a good imagination to re-create the scene from the various nooks and crannies hacked into the rock. The guides are instructive but during the summer peak the tour gets rather tedious – better if possible to come at lunchtime (noon–2pm) when you can wander at your own pace with the aid of their well-written English-language leaflet.

St-Léon-sur-Vézère and around

ST-LÉON-SUR-VÉZÈRE, 6km above Tursac, is by far the most attractive village along the whole Vézère valley. It sits in a quiet bend of the river guarded by two châteaux – one topped by a fairy-tale array of turrets – and boasts one of the region's most harmonious Romanesque churches. In summer the church serves as one of the principal venues, along with St-Amand-de-Coly (see p.224), for classical music concerts during the summertime **Festival du Périgord Noir** (see box on p.198). For the best views of the whole ensemble, walk over the iron-girder bridge and turn left along a footpath on the opposite bank.

The path continues to a series of rock-shelters and the remains of a semi-troglodytic settlement known as Le Conquil, now part of the **Parc de Loisirs Préhistorique** (daily: May–Sept 10am–7pm; April & Oct 10am–6pm; closed Nov–March; 50F/€7.62). The advertising is a bit twee, but the activities – fashioning flint tools and needles from bones, making fire and throwing spears, among others – are well organized and should appeal to all ages. On the whole the caves themselves aren't particularly interesting, with the exception of one pitted with square niches in rows along the back and side walls (one theory attributes them to a Neolithic burial site), but it's fun scrambling among the cliff dwellings, particularly the little fort right at the top before you walk back through the woods.

St-Léon's *Auberge du Pont* (closed Tues & Nov–March) is a lovely wisteria-covered **restaurant** beside the bridge, which offers well-presented regional menus from 68F/€10.37 and a wicked array of home-made ice creams. The owners also run a pleasant **hotel**, *Le Relais de la Côte de Jor* (☎05.53.50.74.47, fax 05.53.51.16.22; ③; closed Nov–March), located in the pine-forested hills 2.5km north of St-Léon with views down the valley to La Roque St-Christophe. As for **campsites**, there's a choice between St-Léon's small *Camping Municipal*, beside the bridge (☎05.53.50.73.16, fax 05.53.50.20.32; May–Sept), and the luxurious *Le Paradis* (☎05.53.50.72.64, fax 05.53.50.75.90, *www.camping-le-paradis.com*; closed Nov–March) complete with heated pools, 3km down the road to Les Eyzies. You can rent **canoes** at *Le Paradis* and also through Canoës-Loisirs (☎05.53.51.02.19) who set up by the bridge in St-Léon from April to October depending on the weather.

South across the Vézère from St-Léon, the rock-shelters of **Castel-Merle** (July & Aug daily 10am–7pm; April–June & Sept Mon–Fri 10am–noon & 2–6pm, Sat 10am–noon; 25F/€3.81) are of fairly specialist interest, but have the advantages that the site is rarely crowded and that you can borrow an unusually thorough English-language booklet outlining the history and importance of the four shelters. Only one still contains any cave art, including three rather poorly preserved bison sculptures from the same era as Cap Blanc (see p.214). However, the site has yielded a terrific number of flints, bones and beads. A good number of these are on show in a small private **museum** (no fixed hours; if the owner's not there, call ☎05.53.50.77.54; free) in the village of **SERGEAC** 500m below Castel-Merle. The owner takes great delight in explaining the objects, many of them unearthed by his archeologist father, of which the highlight is a collection of six necklaces strung together about 30,000 years ago. One is made up of shells from the Atlantic, presumably obtained by trade, and another of various animal teeth including wolf's.

The same family also own a **hotel**, the *Auberge de Castel-Merle* (☎05.53.50.70.08, fax 05.53.50.76.25; ③; closed Nov–Feb) on the hill above the prehistoric shelters. It's a handsome Périgord building and the rooms are cheerful, but the main attribute is its cliff-top terrace where on fine days you can eat lunch overlooking the Vézère (menus from 69F/€10.52; closed Mon).

Château de Losse and Le Thot

Of several castles along the Vézère valley, the Renaissance **Château de Losse** (45min guided tours daily: June–Aug 10am–7pm; April, May & Sept 10am–12.30pm & 1.30–6pm; closed Oct–March; 35F/€5.34) stands out as the most striking. It occupies a rocky bluff 4km upstream from St-Léon on the main D706, though the best views are from the opposite bank, where the D65 provides a quiet and picturesque back road from St-Léon to Montignac (see below). The present castle was constructed in the 1570s by Jean II de Losse, royal tutor and the Governor of Guyenne, on medieval foundations. It has changed little since then, a well-proportioned L-shaped building surrounded by dry moats and watch-towers. Inside, the château's present owners have established an impressive collection of sixteenth- and seventeenth-century furniture and tapestries. Among the latter, the Florentine "Return of the Courtesan" is particularly successful in its use of perspective, while the colours of this and the Flemish rendition of knights preparing for a tournament remain exceptionally vibrant. There's also a rare, tulip-decorated tapestry dating from around the time of the Dutch Tulipomania in 1634 when tulips cost more than gold. On your way out, note the inscription over the unusually imposing gatehouse which quotes one of Jean II's favourite maxims: "When I thought the end was in sight, I was only beginning". His perhaps jaundiced view is forgivable – of his five sons, four were killed in war and the fifth had no heirs to inherit the family estates.

It's back to prehistory at the next stop, **Le Thot** (April–Sept daily 10am–7pm; Oct to early Nov daily 10am–12.30pm & 2–6pm; early Feb to March & early Nov to Dec Tues–Sun 10am–12.30pm & 2–5.30pm; closed Jan to early Feb; 30F/€4.57), 1km into the hills west of the château. Described as an "Espace Cro-Magnon", the combined museum and animal park focuses on prehistoric art, not only the technical aspects but also some of the wildlife that provided inspiration: reindeer, Przewalski horses with their erect manes, ibex, deer and European bison are all resident here. You'll also see aurochs, though these primitive wild cattle really died out in the 1600s – the beasts here are a close approximation achieved through selective breeding in the early twentieth century. In the museum the different techniques and styles of cave art are explained, but the most interesting part is a video showing the painstaking re-creation of the Lascaux caves (see opposite). For once, it's subtitled in English and the majority of displays here have English-language explanations.

Montignac and around

Some 26km upstream from Les Eyzies, **MONTIGNAC** is a more attractive town, with several wooden-balconied houses leaning appealingly over the river, and a lively annual **arts festival** in mid-July, featuring international folk groups (see box on p.198). It serves as the main base for exploring the Vézère valley's northern sights, foremost of which is **Lascaux**'s painted cave, though the Romanesque abbey-church of **St-Amand-de-Coly** is also worth a visit.

Apart from wandering the riverbanks, Montignac's only sight is the **Musée Eugène-Le-Roy** (July to mid-Sept daily 9am–6.15pm; mid-Sept to July Mon–Sat 9–11.15am & 2–5.15pm; 10F/€1.52), occupying the second floor of a sixteenth-century hospital on place Bertran-de-Born in the town centre. The museum commemorates the novelist Eugène le Roy, who died in Montignac in 1907, with a reconstruction of his bureau and scenes of village life based on his works – the most famous being *Jacquou le Croquant* – which deal with the harshness of the peasants' lot and the depredations of the local squirearchy.

Practicalities

Montignac straddles the Vézère, with its church and central square, place Carnot, on the west bank and the majority of tourist facilities across the river along rue de 4-Septembre. **Buses** from Périgueux, Brive and Sarlat stop on place Carnot and place Tourny, the latter being at the east end of rue de 4-Septembre. Also on this road the **tourist office** occupies the same building as the museum on place Bertran-de-Born (July to mid-Sept daily 9am–7pm; mid-Sept to June Mon–Sat 9am–noon & 2–6pm; ☎05.53.51.82.60, fax 05.53.50.49.72). In summer note that in principal **tickets for Lascaux II** (see opposite) must be bought from the office on the ground floor (April–Oct daily 9am–6pm). There are two **canoe rental** outlets: Les 7 Rives (☎05.53.50.19.26; July & Aug) beside the more northerly Pont de la Paix; and Kanoak (☎05.53.04.36.92; April–Sept) below the old bridge. The main **market** takes place on place Carnot and the streets around on Wednesday mornings, with a smaller one on Saturdays.

Accommodation, as everywhere around here, can be a problem in high season. The *Hôtel de la Grotte*, 63 rue du 4-Septembre (☎05.53.51.80.48, fax 05.53.51.05.96; ②; restaurant from 65F/€9.91), is the cheapest in town, with basic rooms and a small streamside garden. Then it's a big leap up to the very comfortable *Relais du Soleil d'Or*, 16 rue du 4-Septembre (☎05.53.51.80.22, fax 05.53.50.27.54, *www.soleil-dor.com*; ④; closed mid-Jan to mid-Feb), whose restaurant menus start at 110F/€16.77. They've got a lovely big garden, with pool, but for not much more you can stay in the more homely ivy- and wisteria-clad *Hostellerie de la Roseraie*, across the river in quiet place d'Armes (☎05.53.50.53.92, fax 05.53.51.02.23; ③; closed Nov–March; restaurant from 175F/€26.68). The rooms are prettily decorated with period furniture, and they boast an even bigger garden, landscaped pool and a riverside terrace. Finally, there's a well-tended, two-star **campsite**, *Le Moulin du Bleufond* (☎ & fax 05.53.51.83.95; closed mid-Oct to March), on the riverbank 500m downstream.

The other option is to stay in one of the surrounding villages. St-Amand-de-Coly (see p.224) is within striking distance, and there are a couple of attractive places near **LA CHAPELLE-AUBAREIL**, about 6km beyond Lascaux. The first you reach is *La Table du Terroir* (☎05.53.50.72.14, fax 05.53.51.16.23, *www.logis-de-france.fr*, ③; closed late Nov to March), occupying several converted farm buildings in the middle of nowhere but well signposted all around, with a swimming pool and an excellent restaurant (menus from 70F/€10.67) – though note that in summer it gets swamped; everything derived from duck is home-produced. In the village itself, *La Cavatine* (☎05.53.50.79.99, fax 05.53.50.80.22; ③; closed Jan & Feb) is a simple place run by a very welcoming Argentinian-Dutch couple who rustle up all sorts of international fare – from Creole to Javanese – and will serve late on request (menus from around 80F/€12.20; closed mid-Oct to mid-March to nonresidents).

Grotte de Lascaux and Lascaux II

The **Grotte de Lascaux** was discovered in 1940 by four teenagers in search of their dog, which had fallen into a deep cavern near Montignac. The cave was found to be decorated with marvellously preserved animal paintings, executed by Cro-Magnon people some 17,000 years ago, which are among the finest examples of prehistoric art in existence. Lascaux was opened to the public in 1948 and over the next fifteen years the humidity created by more than a million visitors caused algae and then an opaque layer of calcite to form over the paintings. The algae can be cured by disinfection, but the "white disease" is a more serious problem and in 1963 the authorities decided to close the cave and build a replica.

Opened in 1983, some 200m from the original cave, **Lascaux II**, signed 2km south from central Montignac (40min guided tours: July & Aug daily 9am–8pm; April–June & Sept daily 9.30am–6.30pm; early Feb to March Tues–Sun 10am–12.30pm & 2–6pm; Oct to early Nov daily 10am–12.30pm & 2–6pm; early Nov to Dec Tues–Sun 10am–noon & 2–5.30pm; closed Jan to early Feb; 50F/€7.62; combined ticket with Le Thot – see p.221 – 57F/€8.69; *www.culture.fr/culture/arcnat/lascaux/en*), was the result of ten years' painstaking work by twenty artists and sculptors led by Monique Peytral, using the same methods and materials as the original cave painters. The almost perfect facsimile comprises ninety percent of the Lascaux paintings concentrated in the Hall of Bulls and the Axial (or Painted) Gallery, a distance of less than 100m. While it can't offer the excitement of the real thing, the reproduction is still breathtaking. In the Hall of Bulls five huge aurochs – one 5.5 metres long with an astonishingly expressive head and face – dominate the ceiling, while the Axial Gallery is covered with more cattle surrounded by deer, bison and horses rendered in distinctive Lascaux style with pot-bellies and narrow heads. Some are shaded or spotted with different coloured pigments, others, like the bulls, drawn in black outline. You don't have to be an expert to appreciate the incredible skill employed by the prehistoric artists, who would have painted these animals from memory by the light of flickering oil lamps, nor to appreciate their sense of perspective and movement, the sheer energy they manage to convey.

Even so, if you want to appreciate the paintings at their best, it's important to avoid July and August, when groups of forty are herded through conveyor-belt style. Two thousand **tickets** are on sale each day, but these go fast during the peak holiday periods, when it's best to buy your tickets in advance either by going to the ticket office in person or making a credit-card booking over the phone (July & Aug ☎05.53.51.96.23; Sept–June ☎05.53.51.95.03); bookings can be made up to seven days in advance. Note also that in winter (Nov–March) tickets are on sale at the site, while in summer (April–Oct) they are only available from an office beneath Montignac tourist office – the system varies from year to year, however, so check in Montignac before heading up to the cave. Tours are conducted in either French or English.

St-Amand-de-Coly

Nine kilometres east of Montignac, the village of **ST-AMAND-DE-COLY** boasts a superb fortified Romanesque church. Despite its size and bristling military architecture, the twelfth-century abbey-church manages to combine great delicacy and spirituality. It is supposedly built over the burial place of the sixth-century St Amand, who gave up soldiering to become a hermit. Despite a promising start, however, the abbey never really prospered and had largely been abandoned by the late 1400s. In 1575 a Protestant garrison withstood a heavy siege here for six days, after which the buildings continued to crumble until 1868 when it was classified as a historic monument. Since then it has been entirely restored.

With its purity of line and simple decoration, the church is at its most evocative in the low sun of late afternoon or early evening. Its defences, added in the fourteenth century, left nothing to chance: it is encircled by ramparts, its walls are 4m thick, and a passage once skirted the eaves, with numerous positions for archers to rain down arrows, and blind stairways to mislead attackers.

Near the church, unsophisticated **accommodation** offered by the small *Hôtel Gardette* (☎05.53.51.68.50; ②; restaurant from 70F/€10.67, closed Oct–Easter) makes it possible to stay overnight in this tiny, idyllic place. If you're lucky enough to be here in July or August you might catch a classical music concert in the church during the **Festival du Périgord Noir** (late-July to late-Aug).

Terrasson-la-Villedieu

Beyond Montignac the prehistoric sites die out and the Vézère valley becomes busier and more industrialized as it opens out towards **TERRASSON-LA-VILLEDIEU**, 15km upstream, and Brive (see p.159). The old part of Terrasson, a knot of lanes on the river's south bank leading up from the arched stone bridge to the church, merits a quick wander, but the main reason for coming here is to visit its resolutely contemporary garden, **Les Jardins de l'Imaginaire** (1hr 15min guided tours only: July & Aug daily 10am–6.10pm; April–June & Sept to mid-Oct Mon & Wed–Sun 10–11.20am & 2–5.20pm; 30F/€4.57) on a terraced hillside to the west of the church.

Opened in 1996, the **gardens** were designed by American landscaper Kathryn Gustafson. In them she explores common themes found in gardens throughout history and among different cultures, from the Romans' sacred groves and the Hanging Gardens of Babylon to moss, water and rose gardens, the last a magnificent display of nearly two thousand roses. In this respect it is much more than "just" a garden, which is why they insist you go with a guide to explain the complicated symbolism; English-language texts are available. Afterwards, however, you can wander at leisure to enjoy the garden on its own terms. It is full of imaginative touches: a forest of wind chimes, a stark line of weather-vanes and, above all, the use of water to splendid effect.

If you're travelling by public transport, you might find yourself passing through Terrasson since it lies on the Brive–Bordeaux train line and has bus links to Montignac and Brive. The **gare SNCF** lies on the north side of town at the far end of avenue Jean-Jaurès. **Buses** stop at the station and place de la Libération, on the main west–east Brive road, near the old bridge. Place de la Libération is also where you'll find the **tourist office** (July & Aug daily 9.30am–noon & 2–7pm; Sept–June Mon–Fri 9.30am–noon & 2–6pm, Sat 9.30am–noon & 2–5pm; ☎05.53.50.37.56, fax 05.53.51.01.22). If you need a **hotel**, your best bet is the very basic but friendly *Terrasson* (☎05.53.50.06.93, fax 05.53.50.44.72; ①; Oct–April closed Sun; menus from 60F/€9.15) at the south end of avenue Jean-Jaurès. There's also a good and rather classy **restaurant**, *L'Imaginaire*, just below the gardens on place du Foirail (☎05.53.51.37.27; closed Sun eve, Mon & second & fourth Tues of the month), in two elegant stone-vaulted rooms. Menus start at 160F/€24.39.

The middle Dordogne: St-Cyprien towards Souillac

The stretch of river to the south of Sarlat sees the Dordogne at its most appealing, forming great loops between rich fields, wooded hills and craggy outcrops. This is also castle country, where great medieval fortresses eyeball each other across the valley. Most date from the Hundred Years' War, when the river marked a frontier of sorts between French-held land to the north and English territory to the south.

For the visitor today things start slowly in the west with the service town of **St-Cyprien** and nearby **Belvès**, now a sleepy little place where people once lived in troglodyte houses beneath its streets, but châteaux come thick and fast thereafter. The first you reach on the river's north bank is **Beynac**. Clamped to the rock out of which it appears to grow, Beynac and its village of russet-hued, stone-roofed cottages cascading to the river, presents one of the valley's most dramatic sights – and, from the castle keep, one of its best panoramas. A short distance further upstream the **Château de Marqueyssac** provides respite among its Italian-style terraced gardens and woodland promenades with views of both Beynac and its arch rival over on the south bank, the **Château de Castelnaud**. Castelnaud is all that a medieval castle should be: barbicans, curtain walls, inner courtyards, fluttering pennants and watchtowers surrounding a seemingly indomitable keep. It also contains an excellent museum of medieval warfare and, as at Beynac, the views are superb. Then a brief diversion westwards brings you to the far-from-militaristic castle of **Les Milandes**, once owned by the cabaret artist Josephine Baker and now set up as a museum in her honour.

Heading back upstream, the next stop is **La Roque-Gageac**. This lovely village caught between the river and the rock-face is up there with Beynac and Castelnaud as one of the Dordogne's most photographed – and visited – sights. Across on the south bank, **Domme**, a fortified *bastide* town perched on the cliff edge, is no pushover on either the tourist stakes or as regards its views. Both take in a ten-kilometre sweep of the river, giving you a foretaste of the **Cingle de Montfort**, a particularly picturesque meander set off by yet another glorious château to the east. Which leaves just one more castle to go, the **Château de Fénelon** with its attractive blend of medieval and Renaissance architecture, and good collections of furniture and weaponry to match, before you cross from Dordogne *département* into Lot.

As far as public transport is concerned, although **trains** run along the valley from Le Buisson (see p.191) to Sarlat, the only intermediary station still functioning is Siorac-en-Périgord, between St-Cyprien and Belvès. Like Le Buisson, Siorac sits on the junction of the Sarlat–Bordeaux and Agen–Périgueux lines, with connections for Les Eyzies and the Vézère valley (see p.209). The only place accessible by **bus** is Carsac-Aillac, a village with a pretty church just east of Montfort which is a stop on the Sarlat–Souillac bus route.

St-Cyprien and around

Despite its location, just 20km west of Sarlat and 10km south from Les Eyzies, **ST-CYPRIEN** remains a refreshingly workaday place set back from the busy D703. Admittedly, it hasn't got much in the way of sights, but the whole place really comes to life on Sunday mornings for one of the area's best **markets** after Sarlat. The hillside setting is also attractive and, with a number of decent hotels around, it's worth considering St-Cyprien as a base.

The old centre's narrow lanes of medieval houses and labourers' cottages, a good number still unprettified, hold the greatest interest. They zigzag up towards the austere **abbey-church** founded by twelfth-century Augustinian monks. You certainly can't accuse the church of being pretty either, though there's a certain robust grandeur about its Romanesque tower and the echoing nave. The altar containing a thorn from Christ's crown was stolen in 1997, leaving pole position to a rather more grizzly relic, the heart of a former archbishop of Paris, Monseigneur Christophe-de-Beaumont, bricked up in the second pillar on the right.

The helpful **tourist office**, on place Charles-de-Gaulle in the centre of the lower town (Mon–Sat 9.30am–12.30pm & 3–6.30pm, Sun 10am–12.30pm; ☎05.53.30.36.09, fax 05.53.59.54.75), produces a good walking map of St-Cyprien and will point you to local **accommodation**. In the town itself, the nicest is the *Hôtel de L'Abbaye* (☎05.53.29.20.48, fax 05.53.29.15.85, *www.abbaye-dordogne.com*; ⑤; closed mid-Oct to mid-April) round a beautiful courtyard on rue de l'Abbaye leading up to the church from the east, with good views from the terraced gardens and pool. The antique furniture, comfy sofas and inglenooks give the place a country-house feel, and you'll be made to feel equally welcome in the restaurant where they serve lighter versions of local dishes, as well as plenty of fish, vegetables and home-grown herbs (menus from 155F/€23.63; restaurant open to nonresidents eves only). Further down the same road, *La Terrasse* (☎05.53.29.21.69, fax 05.53.29.60.88, *www.logis-de-france.fr*; ③; Oct to mid-April closed Sun eve & Mon, also closed Jan & Feb) offers functional but decent-size rooms and good traditional meals (menus from 65F/€9.91).

There are a couple more good places to stay and eat in the hills 5km to the north of St-Cyprien near the typical Périgord village of **MEYRALS**. You'll need to book up early to get one of the twelve stylish rooms at *La Ferme Lamy* (☎05.53.29.62.46, fax 05.53.59.61.41; *ferme_lamy@wanadoo.fr*; ⑤) on the C3 north of the village. The whole place is immaculate, from the en-suite bathrooms to the big, landscaped pool and flower-filled garden, not to mention the breakfast-spread of home-made jams and breads. They don't offer main meals, but you only have to pop up the road to *Fort de la Rhonie* (☎05.53.29.24.83, fax 05.53.29.62.58, *coustaty2@wanadoo.fr*; ③; closed early Dec to end Feb), where the Coustaty family run an excellent *ferme auberge* (meals 90–130F/€13.72–19.82; July & Aug closed Sat, rest of year Tues eve & Wed). For those that want to stay in this idyllic spot, they also offer good-value *chambres d'hôtes* accommodation and a campsite (June–Sept) with space for just eight tents.

Belvès

Before setting off up the Dordogne from St-Cyprien, it's worth taking a detour south about 12km, via **SIORAC-EN-PÉRIGORD** – a junction on the Sarlat–Bordeaux and Agen–Périgueux train lines but otherwise missable – to **BELVÈS**. There's no mistaking the town's strategic importance, encircled by ramparts on a promontory above the Nauze valley and bristling with seven towers – even the central square is called place d'Armes. These days, however, the only battles likely to take place here involve haggling over prices at the Saturday-morning **market** under the old *halle*, or a hotly disputed game of *boules*.

In 1907 the wheel of a cart crossing place d'Armes broke through the roof of a warren of **troglodyte houses** (45min guided tours: mid-June to mid-Sept daily 10.30am–12.30pm & 3–7pm; mid-Sept to mid-June Mon–Sat at 11.30am, 3.30pm & 5.30pm, though it's best to confirm with the tourist office – see below – in advance; 20F/€3.05; tickets from the tourist office. Hollowed into the rampart wall, these damp, dark insalubrious dwellings were inhabited from the twelfth century up to the mid-1700s, after which they were blocked up and forgotten. So far eight "houses" have been opened. They consist of single rooms averaging a mere twenty square metres apiece for a family plus animals. It's hard to imagine what they must have been like to live in, even if the more sophisticated dwellings boast chimneys, raised sleeping areas and shelves cut into the soft rock. Afterwards, walk down rue Jacques-Manchotte, leading west from the market square and, if it's open, pop into the **Organistrum** at no. 14 (no fixed hours; ☎05.53.29.10.93), a combined museum and workshop producing medieval instruments. Music-lovers might also be interested in Belvès' principal annual event, the **Festival Bach**, dedicated to the composer, which takes place in the church during the second fortnight of July (see box on p.198).

Like Siorac, Belvès lies on the main Agen–Périgueux train line, with the **gare SNCF** down on the main road below the town. Its **tourist office**, 1 rue des Filhols (July & Aug daily 10am–1pm & 3–7pm; Sept–June Mon, Tues & Thurs–Sat 10am–12.30pm & 3–6.30pm, though the closing days may vary; ☎ & fax 05.53.29.10.20, *www.perigord.com/belves*), occupies the ground floor of the fifteenth-century Maison des Consuls, just off the market square, while the town's two **hotels** stand next to each other on place de la Croix-des-Frères, at the far west end of rue Jacques-Manchotte. First choice should be *Le Home* (☎05.53.29.01.65, fax 05.53.59.46.99; ①; Oct–May closed Sun) for its excellent-value rooms, friendly service and hearty country cooking (menus from 60F/€9.15). The *Belvédère* (☎05.53.31.51.41, fax 05.53.31.51.42, *www.logis-de-france.fr*; ③; closed Jan & Oct–May closed Mon) is a fancier place with another good restaurant (menus from 78F/€11.89), but the rooms are overpriced for what you get. The nearest **campsite** is the three-star *Les Nauves* (☎ & fax

05.53.29.07.87; mid-May to mid-Sept) in a quiet spot 4km southwest off the Monpazier road. Alternatively, *Le Bon Accueil* (☎05.53.29.08.49; open all year) offers basic *camping à la ferme* a couple of kilometres east across the Nauze in the hamlet of Gratecap near St-Amand-de-Belvès.

Beynac-et-Cazenac and around

The stretch of river east of St-Cyprien sees the Dordogne at its most dramatic. The river still takes its time, but here the valley sides begin to close in as you approach the two great fortresses of **Beynac** and **Castelnaud**. They glare across at each other from their eyries, instantly recognizable from countless promotional posters, postcards and films. The area's second-tier sights inevitably pale by comparison. Close to Beynac the ridge-top gardens of the **Château de Marqueyssac** offer pleasant walks and expansive views, while **Les Milandes**, a Renaissance pile west of Castlenaud, serves as a sort of shrine to cabaret star Josephine Baker – much loved in France – who once owned it.

Beynac-et-Cazenac

Clearly visible on an impregnable cliff edge on the Dordogne's north bank, the eye-catching village and castle of **BEYNAC-ET-CAZENAC** was built in the days when the river was the only route open to traders and invaders. Now the busy main road squeezes between the cliffs and the water, creating a horrible bottleneck from July to mid-September. At this time you're best advised to arrive first thing in the morning to escape the worst of the crowds.

It is three kilometres by road from the waterfront to the **Château de Beynac** (1hr guided tours daily: June–Sept 10am–6.30pm; March–May 10am–6pm; Oct & Nov 10am–dusk; Dec–Feb 11am–dusk; 40F/€6.10) or, alternatively, it takes fifteen minutes to walk up the steep lane among the *lauze*-roofed cottages. The lichenous-grey castle is protected on the landward side by double walls and ditches; elsewhere the sheer drop of almost 150m does the job. The redoutable Richard the Lionheart nevertheless took and held Beynac for a decade, until a gangrenous wound ended his term of blood-letting in 1189; apparently the heart-shaped keys and keyholes were fashioned in his memory. Though the English regained the castle briefly – thanks to the Treaty of Brétigny rather than any military prowess – in essence Beynac remained loyal to the French crown during the Hundred Years' War.

The buildings are in surprisingly good condition thanks to a mammoth restoration project over the last forty years which is scheduled to continue until at least 2030. You enter into a guardroom lit by flickering oil lamps, one of the castle's more atmospheric rooms along with the great hall where the nobles of Beynac, Biron, Mareuil and Bourdeilles – the four Baronies of Périgord (see p.355) – met; note the unusual ox-skull motif over the fireplace, previously found at the Château de Lanquais (see p.188). Also good are the twelfth-century kitchens, complete with a cobbled ramp allowing horses access to the central courtyard, and kitted out with no-nonsense tables, vats, meat-hooks and great pulleys. If it looks familiar, that's because it featured in Luc Besson's recent epic, *Jeanne d'Arc*. For most people, however, it's the views that steal the show, notably from the top of the keep, where you get a stupendous – and vertiginous – sweep over the surrounding châteaux: Marqueyssac, Feyrac and Castelnaud (see below).

To get a very different perspective of all these castles, it's worth taking a **river-trip** with Gabarres de Beynac (April–Oct 10am–6pm; 40F/€6.10; ☎05.53.28.51.15), if possible on one of their replica *gabares*, the traditional wooden river-craft. Boats leave from a jetty beside the **tourist office** booth (May–Sept Mon–Sat 9.30am–12.30pm & 2–6pm, Sun 10am–12.30pm & 2–6pm; Oct–April Mon–Sat 9.30am–12.30pm & 2–5.30pm; ☎ & fax 05.53.29.43.08, *ot.beynac@ perigord.tm.fr*). You'll also find a small pay **car park** here, but there are bigger, free car parks on the road to the château opposite. The nearest **canoe rental** outlet is Couleurs Périgord (☎05.53.30.37.61, *perso.wanadoo.fr/couleurs.perigord*; open all year) about a kilometre east of Beynac where the railway crosses the river.

Beynac's best **hotel** is the *Hostellerie Maleville* (☎05.53.29.50.06, fax 05.53.28.28.52, *www.logis-de-france.fr*; ③; closed Jan), as long as you ensure you get a room in its annexe, the *Hôtel Pontet*, on the road up to the castle; their recommended riverside restaurant (menus from 80F/€12.20) overlooks a pint-size beach. The more atmospheric of the other two options – both on the main drag, so ask for rooms at the back – is the old-fashioned *Hôtel Bonnet* (☎05.53.29.50.01, fax 05.53.29.83.74; ④; closed Nov–March), right under the castle as you come into Beynac from the east, with a decent restaurant serving menus from 85F/€12.96. You'll find smarter rooms and better value, however, at the *Hôtel du Château* (☎05.53.29.50.13, fax 05.53.28.53.05, *www.perigord.com/spih*; ③; restaurant from 82F/€12.50), opposite the tourist office. Finally, there's a riverside **campsite**, *Le Capeyrou* (☎05.53.29.54.95, fax 05.53.28.36.27; mid-May to mid-Sept), immediately east of the town.

Château de Marqueyssac

Three kilometres east of Beynac the Dordogne loops south round a long and narrow wooded promontory. At its tip the **Château de Marqueyssac** (daily: July & Aug 9am–8pm; May, June & Sept 10am–7pm; mid-Feb to April & Oct to mid-Nov 10am–6pm; mid-Nov to mid-Feb 2–5pm; 30F/€4.57, or 58F/€8.84 with Château de Castelnaud) presides over its terraced **gardens**. The château itself, a typically mellow Périgord mansion of the late eighteenth century, is rarely open to the public, but the view, encompassing the châteaux of Beynac, Feyrac and Castelnaud, is magnificent. The gardens were first laid out in the 1600s by the then owner, Bertrand Vernet de Marqueyssac, under the inspiration of Le Nôtre, the landscaper responsible for Versailles. However, most of the features you see today were added two centuries later when the half-kilometre long Grand Allée was established, thousands of box trees clipped into plump cushions, and six kilometres of woodland walks opened up along the ridge to the east. All paths lead to a 130m-high belvedere from where you can see La Roque-Gageac nestling under its cliff (see p.231).

Castelnaud-la-Chapelle

Rivals for centuries, the feudal fortresses of Beynac and **CASTELNAUD-LA-CHAPELLE**, on the Dordogne's south bank, now vie over visitor numbers. There's no question that Beynac has the edge with its more dramatic location, and arguably the better views, but the **Château de Castelnaud** (July & Aug daily 9am–8pm; May, June & Sept daily 10am–7pm; March, April & Oct to mid-Nov daily 10am–6pm; mid-Nov to Feb Mon–Fri & Sun 2–5pm; 38F/€5.79, or 58F/€8.84 with Château de Marqueyssac; *www.castelnaud.com*) provides the more entertaining visit.

JOSEPHINE BAKER AND THE RAINBOW TRIBE

Born on June 3, 1906, in the black ghetto of East St Louis, Illinois, **Josephine Baker** was one of the most remarkable women of the twentieth century. Her mother washed clothes for a living and her father was a drummer who soon deserted his family, yet by the late 1920s Josephine was the most celebrated cabaret star in France, primarily due to her role in the legendary Folies Bergère show in Paris. On her first night, de Gaulle, Hemingway, Piaf and Stravinsky were among the audience, and her notoriety was further enhanced by her long line of illustrious husbands and lovers, which included the Crown Prince of Sweden and the crime novelist Georges Simenon. She also mixed with the likes of Le Corbusier and Adolf Loos, and kept a pet cheetah, with whom she used to walk around Paris. During the war, she was active in the Resistance, for which she was awarded the Croix de Guerre. Later on, she became involved in the civil rights movement in North America, where she insisted on playing to non-segregated audiences, a stance which got her arrested in Canada and tailed by the FBI in the US.

By far her most bizarre and expensive project was the château of **Les Milandes**, which she rented from 1938 and then bought in 1947, including 300 hectares of land, after her marriage to the French orchestra leader Jo Bouillon. Having equipped the place with two hotels, three restaurants, a minigolf course, tennis court and an autobiographical wax museum, she opened the château to the general public as a model multicultural community, popularly dubbed the "village du monde". Unable to have children of her own, in the course of the 1950s she adopted babies (mostly orphans) of different ethnic and religious backgrounds from around the world. By the end of the decade, she had brought twelve children to Les Milandes, including a black Catholic Colombian and a Buddhist Korean, along with her own mother, brother and sister from East St Louis.

Over 300,000 people a year visited the château in the 1950s, but her more conservative neighbours were never very happy about Les Milandes and the "Rainbow Tribe". In the 1960s, Baker's financial problems, divorce and two heart attacks spelled the end for the project, and despite a sit-in protest by Baker herself (by then in her sixties), the château and its contents were auctioned off in 1968. Still performing and as glamorous as ever, Josephine died of a stroke in 1975 and was given a grand state funeral at La Madeleine in Paris, mourned by thousands of her adopted countryfolk.

Like Beynac, Castelnaud was founded in the twelfth century and bitterly fought over on many occasions, starting with the bellicose Simon de Montfort who seized it as early as 1214 during his Cathar Crusades (see p.356). Then during the Hundred Years' War the lords of Castelnaud sided with the English. They slugged it out for nearly four decades with the French at Beynac until Charles VII besieged Castelnaud in 1442. After holding out for three weeks a treacherous English captain handed over the keys in return for his life and the princely sum of 400 crowns.

Heavily restored in the last decades, the château now houses a highly informative **museum of medieval warfare**. Its core is an extensive collection of original weaponry, including all sorts of bizarre contraptions, such as an "organ" which sprayed lead balls from its multiple barrels, and a fine assortment of armour. The displays are interspersed with interesting video presentations (in French only) on the history of warfare. In summer (July & Aug) they give demonstrations of the various siege engines dotted around the ramparts, and also hold evening visits led by guides in period costume (July 9–Aug 31 daily at 7.30pm; 40F/€6.10; in French only).

On the road down from the village, where it joins the D57, it's worth stopping off briefly at the **Eco-musée de la Noix du Périgord** (April–Oct 10am–7pm; 25F/€3.81) for everything you ever wanted to know about nuts – walnuts, specifically. Not only pressing them for oil, but also their history, including such gems as that Louis XI's beard was trimmed using heated walnut shells, and that they are used in the insulation of American spaceships. They also point out the nuts' many health benefits, before shepherding you through the well-stocked shop. If you're lucky the mill itself will be working, but otherwise there's a self-explanatory video featuring St-Nathalène's more authentic Moulin de la Tour (see p.206). The adjacent orchard spattered with giant cement walnuts and picnic tables is particularly good for children; you can buy salads and sandwiches on site.

While there are no hotels in Castelnaud, you'll find a quiet and well-managed **campsite**, *Lou Castel* (☎05.53.29.89.24, fax 05.53.54.56.54; May–Oct), among oak woods on the plateau a couple of kilometres to the south.

Les Milandes

From Castelnaud it's a scenic drive 5km west along the river past **Château de Fayrac** (not open to the public) with its slated pepperpot towers – an English forward position in the Hundred Years' War, built to watch over Beynac – to **Les Milandes** (1hr guided tours daily: June–Aug 9am–7pm; April, May & Sept 10am–6pm; mid- to end March & Oct 10am–noon & 2–5pm; closed Nov to mid-March; 48F/€7.32; *www.milandes.com*). Built in the late 1400s, the ivy-clad château was the property of the Caumont family (the lords of Castelnaud) until the Revolution, but its most famous owner is the Folies Bergère star, **Josephine Baker** (see box opposite), who fell in love with it while visiting friends in the area in 1937.

It's easy to see why. The Renaissance château sitting high above the Dordogne has all the necessary romantic ingredients: towers, machicolations, balustrades, gargoyles, ornate dormer windows and terraced gardens shaded by great, glossy-leafed magnolias. After she bought Les Milandes in 1947, Josephine set about modernizing it, adding creature comforts such as the en-suite bathrooms, whose decor was inspired by her favourite perfumes – Arpège-style black tiles with gold taps and ceiling in one, Dioresque pink marble with silver-leaf in another. But it's really the stories surrounding Josephine and Les Milandes that are more intriguing than the château itself. Her roller-coaster life story is enough to fill a book, but you get a basic outline as the guide takes you round the collection of photos, posters and those of her costumes which escaped the auctioneer's hammer in 1968, though these are somewhat moth-eaten after mouldering in the cellar for 25 years.

From the terrace in front of the château, where they hold **falconry demonstrations** (May–Oct), you can look down on the J-shaped swimming pool belonging to one of the many fun-parks Josephine established in the area.

La Roque-Gageac

The village of **LA ROQUE-GAGEAC**, on the river's north bank 5km east from Beynac, is almost too perfect, its ochre-coloured houses sheltering under dramatically overhanging cliffs. Regular winner of France's prettiest village contest, it inevitably pulls in the tourist buses, and since here again the main road separates the village from the river, the noise and fumes of the traffic can become oppressive. The best way to escape is to slip away through the lanes and alleyways that wind up through the terraced houses. The other option is to rent a canoe and paddle over to the opposite bank, where you can picnic and enjoy a much better view of La Roque than from among the crowds milling around beneath the village, at its best in the burnt-orange glow of the evening sun.

Look carefully at the cliff above the village and you'll see guard-posts, ramparts and other remnants of a **troglodyte fort** (Mon–Fri & Sun: May–Sept 10am–7pm; Oct–April 10am–6pm; 25F/€3.81). At one time belonging to the bishops of Sarlat, who built themselves a château within the ramparts, the fort provided the villagers with a virtually impregnable refuge from the Vikings' ninth-century invasions right up until the early 1800s when it was largely dismantled; only the Protestant armies were able to take it by force. The remaining defence-works are of only moderate interest, but it's worth tackling the vertigo-inducing ladder for the views.

A less athletic option, and highly recommended, is to take a **boat ride** down to Castelnaud. From April to October two companies offer these one-hour round-trips (with commentary in English) in a *gabare*: Gabares Norbert (☎05.53.29.40.44; *www.perigord.com/gabares-norbert*; 45F/€6.86), the main operator, and Les Caminades (☎05.53.29.40.95; same price). If you'd rather go under your own steam, you can rent **canoes** from Canoë Dordogne (☎05.53.29.58.50, *contact@canoe-dordogne.fr*; open all year) just east of La Roque on the Sarlat road.

Practicalities

For more information about activities in the area contact La Roque's **tourist office** (April–Oct Mon–Thurs 10am–noon & 3–7pm, Fri–Sun 10am–noon & 2–7pm; Nov–March telephone enquiries only Mon–Fri 9am–noon & 2–6pm; ☎05.53.29.17.01, fax 05.53.31.24.48, *si.la.roque.gageac@freesbee.fr*) in a hut by the main car park, also on the Sarlat side of town. Since most people just come here for a day-trip, outside the summer peaks there's usually space if you want to **stay** the night. The most pleasant and best-value option is *La Belle Étoile* (☎05.53.29.51.44, fax 05.53.29.45.63; ④; closed Nov–March), on the main road below the fort, whose restaurant serves good traditional cuisine (from 125F/€19.06; closed Mon except in July & Aug). You can also **eat** well further along the riverfront at *La Plume d'Oie* (☎05.53.29.57.05; closed Dec to early Feb; menus from 195F/€29.73), though you'll need to book ahead. Of the many **campsites** in the vicinity, *Le Lauzier* (☎05.53.29.51.56, fax 05.53.59.69.54; mid-June to Sept) is one of the closest, while *Le Beau Rivage* (☎05.53.28.32.05, fax 05.53.29.63.56, *www.camping-beau-rivage.com*; March to mid-Oct) offers three-star luxury and lots of activities in season; they're both east of La Roque on the D703 Sarlat road.

Domme and around

High on the scarp on the south bank of the river 5km southeast from La Roque-Gageac and 10km due south of Sarlat (see p.199), **DOMME** is an exceptionally well-preserved, terribly pretty *bastide*, now wholly given over to tourism. Its foremost attraction, however, is its position. From the chestnut-shaded **Esplanade**

du Belvédère at the town's northern edge you look out over a wide sweep of river country encompassing everything from Beynac to the Cingle de Montfort (see overleaf). The drop here is so precipitous that when the *bastide* was founded in 1281 fortifications were deemed unnecessary. They lived to regret it: in 1588 a small band of Protestants scaled the cliffs at dawn to take the town completely by surprise. The intruders stayed four years, during which time they destroyed the church amongst other buildings, before they were forced to abandon the town again to Catholic control.

Much of Domme's thirteenth-century walls and three of the gateways they skirted remain. Of the latter, the best-preserved and most interesting is easterly **Porte des Tours**, flanked by two round bastions. In 1307 a group of Templar knights was imprisoned here for eleven years; if you peer through the openings you can just make out the graffiti – Crucifixion scenes, the Virgin Mary, angels and various secret signs – they carved on the walls. Alternatively, you can visit by appointment with the tourist office, or there are photos of the carvings in the **Musée d'Art et de Traditions Populaire** (July & Aug Mon–Fri & Sun 10.30am–7pm, Sat 10.30am–12.30pm & 3–7pm; April–June & Sept daily 10.30am–12.30pm & 2.30–6pm; closed Oct–March; 18F/€2.74, or 35F/€5.34 including caves) on central place de la Halle. Its displays of local life are nicely done, though not wildly interesting. Whereas the **caves** (Feb to mid-Nov & Christmas hols daily 10.30am–noon & 2.15–5.15pm; 35F/€5.34 including museum; tickets from the tourist office), which extend hundreds of metres under the village from beneath the timbered market hall, can definitely be given a miss. The concretions are badly discoloured with algae and can't compare with any of the area's other limestone caverns; the only good point is the exit onto the cliff face with a panoramic lift up to the top and a pleasant stroll back along the promenade de la Falaise.

On the way to – or from – Domme, it's worth making a brief stop in **CÉNAC**, down by the river, to admire its Romanesque **church**, located a short distance along the D50 to St-Cybranet. Apart from a lovely *lauze* roof, its main draw is the remarkably distinct carving on the capitals, featuring various animals and demons, including Daniel taming the lions.

Practicalities

Domme's **tourist office** (July & Aug daily 10am–7pm; Feb–June & Sept to mid-Nov daily 10am–noon & 2–6pm; mid-Nov to Jan Mon–Fri 10am–noon & 2–6pm; ☎05.53.31.71.00, fax 05.53.31.71.09) is located on place de la Halle. On **market** days (Thursday mornings) stalls spill out of the square south down the main commercial street lined with souvenir shops, the Grand-Rue. At the top of this road, *Le Nouvel Hôtel* (☎05.53.28.38.67, fax 05.53.28.27.13; ③; closed Sun eve & Mon except in July & Aug) offers several simple, reasonably priced **rooms** above a restaurant serving regional fare to match (menus from 70F/€10.67). For those on a more generous budget, the smartest place to stay is *L'Esplanade*, right on the cliff edge (☎05.53.28.31.41, fax 05.53.28.49.92; ④; closed early Nov to mid-Feb; recommended restaurant from 180F/€27.44); note that rooms with a view are premium-rated.

The nearest **campsite** is Cénac's one-star municipal site (☎05.53.28.31.91, fax 05.53.31.41.32; closed mid-Sept to mid-June) beside the bridge. In summer at least three separate **canoe rental** places set up here; Randonnée Dordogne

(☎05.53.28.22.01, *randordogne@wanadoo.fr*) offers good prices, while Cénac Périgord Loisirs (CPL; ☎05.53.29.99.69) also has **bikes** for rent.

Upstream towards Souillac

Taking the prettier north bank of the Dordogne from Domme, a white-walled castle bristling with turrets soon hoves into view atop its well-defended promontory. So coveted was the superb strategic position that the **Château de Montfort**'s history is a long tale of destruction and reconstruction, most recently in the nineteenth century – hence the Disneyesque skyline (the château is not open to the public). To complete the picture it overlooks the almost perfect curve of the **Cingle de Montfort**, not the biggest but certainly the tightest of the Dordogne's many meanders, almost encircling a tongue of land covered in walnut orchards.

Two kilometres further on another inviting little Romanesque **church** below the village of **CARSAC-AILLAC** makes a good place to pause. Again it's the carvings that are most of interest, in this case Arabic-influenced capitals around the choir and some later keystones, though the meadow setting is also delightful. Note, too, the Stations of the Cross made by Russian abstract artist Léon Zack, who was a refugee here during World War II. Carsac also has a couple of good **hotels**, which could be used as a base for Sarlat, only 10km to the northwest and accessible by bus. In the village itself the family-run *Hôtel Delpeyrat* (☎05.53.28.10.43, fax 05.53.29.35.13, *www.logis-de-france.fr*; ②; closed Oct & Nov) is a charmingly old-fashioned place offering well-priced rooms, most of them set back from the road overlooking a small garden, and equally homely cooking (menus from 80F/€12.20; restaurant closed Sun eve & Dec–April Sat lunchtime). The more upmarket option is *Le Relais du Touron* (☎05.53.28.16.70, fax 05.53.28.52.51; ④; closed Nov–March; eve meals provided on request) set in extensive grounds a short distance along the Sarlat road. Its twelve bright and cheery rooms occupy a modern block, with pool, behind the owners' lovely old manor house.

From Carsac you need to cross back over the Dordogne and continue along its south bank for some 5km to find the **Château de Fénelon** (45min guide tours daily: June–Sept 9.30am–7pm; Oct–May 10am–noon & 2–6pm; 35F/€5.34) clamped to its own rocky outcrop. With its triple walls and great round towers topped with *lauzes*, the castle exudes all the might of the original medieval fortress. As you get closer, however, the Renaissance-era additions and other, later embellishments, become more apparent – the large mullion windows and the gallery closing the interior courtyard, for example. The then lords of Fénelon swore allegiance to the English in 1360, but after it was taken by the French fifteen years later the castle came into the hands of the Salvignac de Lamothe-Fénelon family, very big cheeses in the Périgord, who owned it for the next four centuries. Their most illustrious member was Francois Salvignac de Lamothe-Fénelon, who was born here in 1651. Private tutor to the heir to the throne and later Archbishop of Cambrai, he fell from grace when King Louis XIV interpreted his work *Télémaque* – which recounts the adventures of Ulysses' son – as a thinly veiled attack on the crown. His intention had been to teach the young prince the finer points of kinghood, but for his pains Fénelon was banished to Cambrai where he died in 1715. He is remembered with much pride at Fénelon today.

There's a mock-up of his study and numerous portraits, but the present owners have also amassed a worthwhile collection of period furniture, tapestries and medieval weaponry. The ornate walnut chimneypieces are also eye-catching.

From the Château de Fénelon the route continues east along the Dordogne, past one of its main rivals, the Château de Rouffillac (not open to the public), on the opposite bank, before finally reaching Souillac 17km later.

travel details

Trains

Belvès to: Agen (2–6 daily; 1hr–1hr 40min); Le Bugue (2–5 daily; 20–45min); Le Buisson (4–5 daily; 20–35min); Les Eyzies (2–5 daily; 30–40min); Périgueux (4–6 daily; 1hr–1hr 15min); Siorac-en-Périgord (3–4 daily; 6min).

Le Bugue to: Agen (2–5 daily; 1hr 40min); Belvès (2–5 daily; 20–45min); Le Buisson (2–5 daily; 8–20min); Les Eyzies (4–6 daily; 7min); Limoges (1 daily; 2hr 10min); Périgueux (4–6 daily; 35–40min); Siorac-en-Périgord (2–5 daily; 5–10min).

Les Eyzies to: Agen (2–5 daily; 1hr 45min); Belvès (2–5 daily; 30–40min); Le Bugue (2–5 daily; 7min); Le Buisson (2–5 daily; 15–20min); Limoges (1 daily; 2hr); Périgueux (4–6 daily; 30–35min); Siorac-en-Périgord (2–5 daily; 25–40min).

Sarlat to: Alles-sur-Dordogne (1–2 daily; 40–45min); Bergerac (4–6 daily; 1hr–1hr 30min); Bordeaux (3–4 daily; 2hr 15min–2hr 40min); Le Buisson (4–6 daily; 25–40min); Castillon-la-Bataille (4–6 daily; 1hr 35min–2hr); Lalinde (4–6 daily; 45min–1hr); Ste-Foy-la-Grande (4–6 daily; 1hr 20min–1hr 45min); Siorac-en-Périgord (1–3 daily; 20–40min); Trémolat (4–6 daily; 35–50min).

Siorac-en-Périgord to: Agen (3–4 daily; 1hr 10min–1hr 50min); Belvès (3–4 daily; 6min); Bergerac (1–3 daily; 45min–1hr 10min); Bordeaux (1–2 daily; 2hr–2hr 20min); Le Buisson (2–5 daily; 7–20min); Le Bugue (2–5 daily; 5–10min); Les Eyzies (2–5 daily; 25–40min); Périgueux (2–5 daily; 45min–1hr 15min); Sarlat (1–3 daily; 20–40min).

Terrasson-la-Villedieu to: Brive (5–7 daily; 15min); Périgueux (4–5 daily; 35–50min); Bordeaux (1–3 daily; 2hr–2hr 20min).

Buses

Le Bugue to: Périgueux (school term Mon–Fri 1–2 daily, school hols Wed only; 1hr).

Carsac-Aillac to: Sarlat (3–5 daily; 20min); Souillac (4 daily; 30min).

Montignac to: Brive (Mon–Sat 1 daily; 1hr 15min); Périgueux (July & Aug Wed 2 daily, Sat 1 daily; Sept–June Mon–Sat 1–2 daily; 1hr); St-Geniès (school term Mon, Wed, Fri, Sat 1–2 daily; school hols Mon–Sat 1–2 daily; July & Aug Wed 2 daily, Sat 1 daily; 15min); Sarlat (as for St-Geniès; 30min); Terrasson (Mon–Sat 1 daily; 25min).

Sarlat to: Brive-la-Gaillarde (school term Mon–Fri 1 daily; rest of year Tues, Thurs & Sat 1 daily; 1hr 40min); Carsac-Aillac (4 daily; 20min); Montignac (July & Aug Wed 2 daily, Sat 1 daily; rest of year Mon–Sat 1–2 daily; 30min); Périgueux (July & Aug Wed 2 daily, Sat 1 daily; rest of year Mon–Sat 1–2 daily; 1hr 40min); St-Geniès (July & Aug Wed 2 daily, Sat 1 daily; rest of year Mon–Sat 1–2 daily; 15min); Souillac (3–4 daily; 1hr).

CHAPTER FIVE

THE UPPER DORDOGNE VALLEY AND ROCAMADOUR

I n its upper reaches the River Dordogne cuts a green swathe through the rocky limestone plateau of **Haut-Quercy**, as the northern sector of Lot *département* is traditionally known. Though the cliffs rise to considerable heights in places, the valley here lacks the drama of the perched castles and towns immediately downstream. Instead, away from the main towns, it offers quieter lanes, more modest castles and a succession of unspoilt riverside villages where it's pleasant to kick back for a couple of days.

The main gateway to the upper Dordogne valley is **Souillac**, a busy little town whose major attraction is its domed abbey-church, containing the finest of several examples of Romanesque carving scattered along the valley. A short distance upstream of Souillac an attractive back road strikes off along the River Ouysse, a minor tributary of the Dordogne, heading southeast to the spectacular pilgrimage town of **Rocamadour**, whose seven religious sanctuaries are built almost vertically into a rocky backdrop. The town has been an important pilgrimage centre since the ninth century, though nowadays pilgrims are outnumbered by tourists, to the tune of over one million a year, who come here simply to wonder at the sheer audacity of its location.

Due north of Rocamadour, but on the other side of the Dordogne, the market town of **Martel** sees surprisingly few tourists, given its medieval centre full of turreted mansions, while further east **Carennac** merits a stop for its picturesque

---

ACCOMMODATION PRICE CODES

All the hotels and *chambres d'hôtes* listed in this book have been price-coded according to the following scale. The prices quoted are for the **cheapest available double room in high season**, although remember that many of the cheap places will have more expensive rooms with en-suite facilities.

① Under 160F/€24   ④ 300–400F/€46–61   ⑦ 600–700F/€91–107
② 160–220F/€24–34   ⑤ 400–500F/€61–76   ⑧ 700–800F/€107–122
③ 220–300F/€34–46   ⑥ 500–600F/€76–91   ⑨ Over 800F/€122

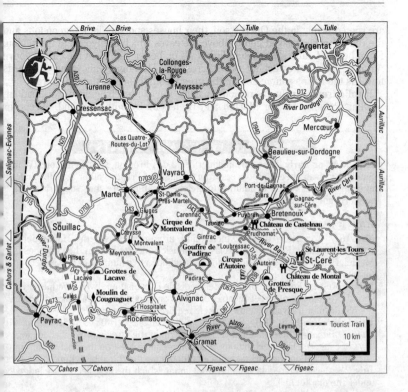

lanes and the twelfth-century carved portal adorning its church. Carennac also lies within striking distance of the **Gouffre de Padirac**, several kilometres to the south, where a collapsed cavern has left a gaping hole in the limestone plateau. Down below, a river leads deep underground through passages festooned with giant stalactites. East of Carennac the Dordogne valley begins to open out to form a broad plain around its confluence with the Cère. **Bretenoux**, the main town guarding the Cère valley, isn't in itself a particularly engaging place, but it's more than compensated for by the nearby **Château de Castelnau**, an impregnable fortress standing on the frontier between the old provinces of Quercy and the Limousin, which still dominates the country for miles around. To the north of Bretenoux, **Beaulieu-sur-Dordogne** is a more pleasing town, featuring an abbey-church with another magnificent tympanum carved in the same style as those at Souillac and Carennac.

To the south of Bretenoux, **St-Céré**, like Beaulieu, provides another good base for exploring the region, and, beneath the brooding towers of its ruined château, a scattering of stone and half-timbered town houses attest to the town's fifteenth- and sixteenth-century heyday. There's more Renaissance architecture on show on the facades and in the superb stone staircase of the **Château de Montal**, a few kilometres to the west. The nearby villages of **Autoire** and **Loubressac**, meanwhile, are rooted firmly in the Quercy soil, their houses sporting little pigeon-lofts and the red-tile roofs splayed gently above the eaves which are typical of the region. From beside Loubressac's encircling walls or, better still, from the cirque above Autoire, there are sweeping views across the Dordogne valley and eastwards towards the river's source among the green foothills of the Massif Central.

Public transport in this region is patchy. You can reach Souillac, Rocamadour, St-Denis-Près-Martel (for Martel) and Bretenoux by both train and, except for

---

FESTIVALS, EVENTS AND MARKETS

Late May or early June Rocamadour: Fête des Fromages. At Pentecôte (Whit Sunday) artisan cheese producers from throughout France gather at L'Hospitalet to show off their wares. In addition to the cheeses, there are sheep-dog trials, folk concerts and other events.

JULY & AUGUST

Mid-July to mid-August Martel and around: Festival du Haut-Quercy (☎05.65.37.43.13). Religious and classical music concerts held in the churches of Martel, Beaulieu, Carennac and Souillac, in addition to a number of free street performances.

July & August Rocamadour: Les Mercredis de Rocamadour. Every Wednesday, a varied programme of street theatre, concerts and open-air cinema takes place in the old town or the valley below. Tickets required for some events.

Third weekend in July Souillac: Souillac en Jazz (☎05.65.37.81.56; *info@ souillacenjazz.net*). International jazz acts let rip in the streets of Souillac for four days of concerts, films, exhibitions, a jazz Mass and a feast on the final night. The big-name, ticket-only events take place outdoors next to the abbey-church.

July 23 Martel: Foire à la Laine. A wool fair, in which the best fleeces are judged under the market hall.

Late July to mid-August St-Céré: Festival de Musique (☎05.65.38.28.08, *festival. saint-cere@wanadoo.fr*). Two-to-three weeks of opera, recitals, orchestral works and workshops in St-Céré and the Château de Castelnau. Tickets required.

Second weekend in August Souillac: Festival du Mime d'Automate (☎05.65.37.07.07). About fifteen groups of mime artists give free performances in the streets of Souillac on the Friday and Saturday.

SEPTEMBER

Sept 2–9 Rocamadour: Semaine Mariale. The week dedicated to the Virgin Mary is celebrated with pilgrimages, prayers and Masses, including torchlight processions to the Chapelle Notre-Dame.

Last weekend in September Rocamadour: Rassemblement Européen de Montgolfières. More than twenty hot-air balloons take off from the valley below Rocamadour; for the best views, take up position early on the Belvédère in L'Hospitalet.

MARKETS

The main **markets** in this region are at: Beaulieu-sur-Dordogne (Wed & Sat); Bretenoux (Tues & Sat); Martel (Wed & Sat); St-Céré (Sat & first and third Wed of month); and Souillac (Fri). In addition to the weekly market, two-to-three truffle markets are held in Martel between mid-December and the end of January.

Rocamadour, by bus. There are buses also to Martel, Carennac, Beaulieu and St-Céré, but services are fairly infrequent and the connections between the smaller towns not particularly good. If you plan to do a lot of bus journeys, it would be worth getting hold of the comprehensive timetable, *Les Bus du Lot*; tourist offices in larger towns such as Souillac and Bretenoux should hold copies, or you can phone the Conseil Général's central information desk (☎05.65.53.27.50).

Souillac and southeast towards Rocamadour

Traffic-ridden **SOUILLAC** suffers from being the major gateway to both Sarlat and the Périgord Noir to the west (see Chapter four) and to the upper reaches of the Dordogne valley to the east, and though it should quieten down considerably once the stretch of the A20 *autoroute* around the town is completed towards the end of 2001, it will never be a terribly pretty place. The town's main attraction is the **Église Ste-Marie**, with its exquisite carvings, but it also holds a small area of old streets, which are worth a quick wander, and a couple of decent museums, the more engaging of which holds a large collection of automated dolls.

Immediately upstream from Souillac, the valley has been ruined by the new A20 road-bridge, but a few meanders of the river later and you're back among quiet lanes and unspoilt scenery. One place to head for is **Lacave**, a village on the south bank with some passably interesting limestone caves. From Lacave you can take an attractive detour south along a tributary river, the Ouysse, as it cuts its way through a mini-gorge in the limestone plateau, to visit a six-hundred-year-old working flour mill. Continue on this route and you will eventually find yourself in Rocamadour (see p.243).

Arrival and information

Getting to Souillac by public transport is not a problem since it lies on the main Paris–Toulouse **train** line. The *gare SNCF* lies just over a kilometre northwest of town; from the station take avenue Jean-Jaurès and then avenue Martin-Malvy, which will bring you out at the west end of avenue Gambetta, the old quarter's main east–west artery. **Buses** from Sarlat, Brive and Gourdon – all operated by Voyages Belmont (☎05.65.37.81.15) – and from St-Denis-Près-Martel (on the Brive–Figeac train line; SNCF ☎05.65.32.78.21) terminate at the *gare*, while Eurolines buses (tickets from Voyages Belmont, rte de Sarlat; ☎05.65.37.81.15, *www.eurolines.fr*), en route between Toulouse and London, Brussels and Amsterdam, stop in central Souillac on the place du Foirail, a large square to the east of the main N20, here called boulevard Louis-Jean Malvy. This square also provides the most convenient **car parking** for the centre.

Note that there are no **car rental** outlets in Souillac, but you can rent **bicycles** from Carrefour du Cycle, 23 avenue de Gaulle (☎05.65.37.07.52), the northern extension of boulevard Louis-Jean Malvy. Bikes and **canoes** are also available from Quercyland (☎05.65.32.72.61, *canoe@mail.netsource.fr*), next to the campsite (see below), and canoes only from Safaraid (☎05.65.32.72.00, *www.canoe-dordogne.com*), beside the pont du Lanzac, a couple of kilometres south of Souillac on the N20.

The **tourist office** (July & Aug daily 9.30am–12.30pm & 2–7pm; rest of year Mon–Sat 10am–noon & 2–6pm; ☎05.65.37.81.56, fax 05.65.27.11.45, *souillac@ wanadoo.fr*) is located in the town centre on boulevard Louis-Jean Malvy, just across the road from place du Foirail. Souillac's main **market** takes place on Friday mornings: stalls selling fresh foods set up around the abbey-church, while clothes and so forth can be found on place du Foirail.

Accommodation

Among Souillac's **hotels**, the best-value budget option is the homely *Auberge du Puits*, 5 place du Puits (☎05.65.37.80.32, fax 05.65.37.07.16, *www.souillac. net/aubpuits*; ①; closed Sun evening, Mon & Dec–Jan), on a pretty square opening onto avenue Gambetta, which also serves copious country menus starting at 80F/€12.20. Moving up a notch, there's the appealingly old-fashioned *Grand Hôtel*, next to the tourist office at 1 allée de Verninac (☎05.62.32.78.30, fax 05.65.32.66.34, *www.logis-de-france.fr*; ②; closed Nov–March), with a wide range of comfortable if somewhat bland rooms, and an excellent restaurant (closed Wed; menus from 75F/€11.43); ask for a room at the back to avoid road noise. Souillac's most upmarket hotel is *La Vieille Auberge*, 1 rue de la Recège (☎05.65.32.79.43, fax 05.65.32.65.19, *www.la-vieille-auberge.com*; ④; closed 5 weeks Nov–Dec), across the old quarter at the west end of avenue Gambetta. The rooms in the main building are well equipped but disappointingly functional, while the annexe rooms, near the Musée de l'Automate, are larger, brighter and nicely furnished. Facilities include a pool (free to residents), sauna and jacuzzi (50F/€7.62 for 30 min) and a fine restaurant with menus from 120F/€18.29 (Jan–March closed Sun eve & Mon). Finally, you could try the welcoming *Puy d'Alan*, a couple of minutes' walk south of the station down avenue Jean-Jaurès at 1 rue de Présignac (☎05.65.37.89.79, fax 05.65.32.69.10; ②), offering clean, simple rooms, a pool and a small garden.

Souillac's nearest **campsite** is *Les Ondines* (☎05.65.37.86.44; closed Oct–April), a large, three-star municipal site down by the river to the south of town. Alternatively, with your own transport, you could head for the more luxurious four-star *Domaine de la Paille Basse* (☎05.65.37.85.48, fax 05.65.37.09.58, *paille.basse@wanadoo.fr*), in a lovely, high spot 9km northwest of Souillac, signed off the D15 to Salvignac.

The Town

Souillac's sights are all concentrated in the compact old quarter to the west of boulevard Louis-Jean Malvy. A handy landmark to aim for is the semi-ruined **belfry** of St-Martin church, partially destroyed in the Wars of Religion, on the southeast corner of the old centre.

Walk one block west of the belfry and you come to a wide open space dominated by the beautiful Romanesque **abbey-church of Ste-Marie**. Its byzantine domes are reminiscent of the cathedrals of Périgueux and Cahors, though on a smaller scale, while its largely unadorned interior conveys a far greater sense of antiquity. The first church on this site belonged to a priory founded in the tenth century which became an abbey five hundred years later. Badly damaged both in the Hundred Years' War and Wars of Religion, the church was restored during the seventeenth century before being abandoned at the Revolution. Sadly, only fragments of the **Romanesque sculptures** that once graced the main, west portal have survived, but those that do remain – now reassembled inside the west door – are superb. Those on the tympanum tell the story of a local monk, Théophile, who was dismissed from the treasury for corruption. Desperate to regain his position, he is said to have made a pact with the Devil, but then fell seriously ill and, full of remorse, beseeched the Virgin Mary for forgiveness. His luck was in – the final scene depicts Théophile's dream of the Virgin accompanied by St Michael driving the Devil away. Other carvings portray sin as an entangled couple, chaos as a seething mass of beasts devouring each other, and redemption as God staying Abraham's hand as he prepares to sacrifice his son Isaac. The greatest piece of craftsmanship, however, is the bas-relief of the prophet Isaiah to the right of the door. Fluid and supple, it appears that the elongated, bearded figure clutching his parchment and with one leg extended is dancing for joy as he proclaims news of the coming of the Messiah.

Behind the church to the west, the **Musée de l'Automate** (Jan–March, Nov & Dec Wed–Sun 2–5pm; April, May & Oct Tues–Sun 10am–noon & 3–6pm; June & Sept daily 10am–noon & 3–6pm; July & Aug daily 10am–7pm; 30F/€4.57, or 45F/€6.86 with the Musée des Attelages – see below) contains an impressive collection of nineteenth- and twentieth-century mechanical dolls and animals which dance, juggle and perform magical tricks. Most come from the once-famous Roullet-Decamps workshops in Paris and include such pieces as a life-sized 1920s jazz band, Charlie Chaplin and a woman doing the twist. Look out, too, for the irresistible laughing man.

Afterwards, if you've got half an hour to spare, it's worth taking a peek in the **Musée des Attelages de la Belle Époque**, to the south of St-Martin's belfry on rue Paul-Chambert (April, May & Oct Tues–Sun 10.30am–noon & 2.30–5pm; June & Sept daily 10.30am–noon & 2.30–5pm; July & Aug daily 10.30am–1pm & 2–6.30pm; closed Nov–March; 25F/€3.81, or 45F/€6.86 with the Musée de l'Automate above), which comprises a varied collection of mostly nineteenth-century horse-drawn carriages, all in excellent condition, though lacking in English-language information. There are some elegant wickerwork carriages, a fire engine, a Russian troika and a sporty-looking American buggy, while pride of place goes to a carriage in which Tsar Nicolas II of Russia once rode.

Eating and drinking

The hotel **restaurants** mentioned above are all worth trying, but the best place to eat in Souillac – despite its inconvenient location about 1km south of centre along boulevard Louis-Jean Malvy – is quiet and elegant *Le Redouillé*, 28 avenue de Toulouse (☎05.65.37.87.25; closed Sun eve & Mon, also mid-Feb to mid-March; menus from 95F/€14.48), which makes innovative use of local produce to create such mouthwatering dishes as smoked duck breast doused in a cep and cream sauce. For simpler meals and snacks, try *Le Beffroi*, 6 place St-Martin (closed Mon; *plats du jour* at 38F/€5.79, menus from 59F/€8.99), beneath the old bell tower, particularly if it's warm enough to eat out on the terrace under the wisteria. Alternatively, if you fancy a more novel eating experience, head for the Lycée Hôtelier, avenue Roger-Couderc (☎05.65.27.03.00; closed Mon, Wed eve and during school hols; menus from around 100F/€15.24), on a hill to the west of the old quarter, where you act as guinea-pigs for trainee chefs and waiting staff. Don't be put off, though – the food is generally excellent and you'll need to book up several days in advance.

Amongst an uninspiring array of cafés along the main road, the best place for a **drink** is the terrace of the *Grand Hôtel*. Better still, head for the relaxed *L'Atelier* wine bar at 32 rue de la Halle (daily June to mid-Sept; rest of year closed weekends and eves), a lane striking north off avenue Gambetta. They offer a fair selection of regional wines from 15F/€2.29 a glass, or even less for the *vin du jour*, and from Easter to October you can also eat here – usually lunchtimes only (menus from 80F/€12.20), though at other times they'll rustle up a sandwich. The bar occasionally holds wine-tastings and concerts, notably during the **festival** Souillac en Jazz (see box on p.238).

Lacave and south towards Rocamadour

Following the Dordogne upstream along the D43 you soon leave the *autoroute* behind as you crest the hill and drop down to **LACAVE**, on the river's south bank 14km southeast of Souillac. A cavernous hole in the limestone cliffs overshadowing the village marks the entrance to a series of underground lakes, together making up the **Grottes de Lacave**, which can be visited on 1hr 15min guided **tours** (daily: March & Oct to mid-Nov 10am–noon & 2–5pm; April–June 9.30am–noon & 2–6pm; July 9.30am–12.30pm & 1.30–6pm; Aug 1–25 9.30am–6.30pm; Aug 26–Sept 9.30am–noon & 2–5.30pm; 43F/€6.56). You travel the first few hundred metres by electric train, after which there's a lift up to the kilometre-long gallery resplendent with all manner of stalactites and stalagmites, from petrified "waterfalls" to great organ pipes. But the highlight here is the magical reflections in the lakes' mirrored surfaces – at one point they also use ultraviolet light to reveal the glittering fluorescence of the "living" water-filled formations while the older, dry deposits remain lost in the darkness.

There's a **hotel-restaurant** right opposite the cave entrance, but it's overpriced and very basic. If you can afford it, treat yourself instead to a meal at the Michelin-starred *Le Pont de l'Ouysse* (☎05.65.37.87.04, fax 05.65.32.77.41; ⑨; closed mid-Nov to March), which also has eleven immaculate rooms. It's in an idyllic spot beside the tumbling River Ouysse about a kilometre west of Lacave on the Souillac road, and you can enjoy a four-course feast there for a very reasonable 180F/€27.44 (restaurant closed for lunch on Mon & Tues; menus 180–600F/€27.44–91.47). Heading 2km out of Lacave in the opposite direction, on the D23 northeast to Meyronne, more rustic fare is available at the friendly *Ferme-Auberge Clavel* (☎05.65.37.87.20; reservations required; July to mid-Sept daily except Thurs; rest of year weekends only; menus at 85F/€12.96 & 95F/€14.48 including wine), which also offers a basic *camping à la ferme* with space for a few tents (closed mid-Sept to March).

From where the River Ouysse empties into the Dordogne just west of Lacave, a minor road heads south along the Ouysse, winding its way up the valley side with grand views as you climb up onto the plateau near the village of **CALÈS** 5km later. The village is a neat and tidy place with little more than a couple of decent **hotels** in its centre. The more appealing of the two is *Le Petit Relais* (☎05.65.37.96.09, fax 05.65.37.95.93, *www.le-petit-relais.fr*; ③; closed Christmas & New Year hols; restaurant closed Sat lunch; good regional menus from 78F/€11.89), with a rustic atmosphere, spick-and-span rooms and pretty, flowery terrace.

Cingle de Montfort, River Dordogne

Ste-Marie, Souillac

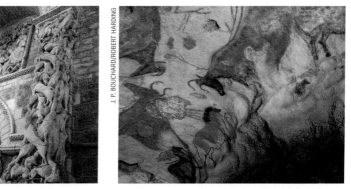

The Axiel Gallery, Lascaux II

Topiary gardens at the Manoir d'Eyrignac

River Dordogne at Beynac

Cliffside dwellings, La Roque-Gageac

River Dordogne at Carennac

St Cirq-Lapopie

Riverfront houses, Beaulieu-sur-Dordogne

Pont Valentré, Cahors

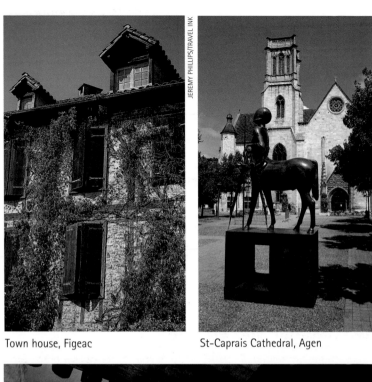

JEREMY PHILLIPS/TRAVEL INK

DAVID MARTYN HUGHES/ROBERT HARDING

Town house, Figeac

St-Caprais Cathedral, Agen

ROBERT HARDING

Place des Cornières, Monpazier

At Calès the road from Lacave joins the D673 and turns east before dropping back down to the Ouysse, which has here carved out a mini-gorge. For an interesting diversion, turn left just after crossing the river and about a kilometre later you'll reach the **Moulin de Cougnaguet**, a fourteenth-century fortified mill, which only ceased working commercially in 1959. During thirty-minute guided tours (daily: April to mid-Sept 10am–noon & 2–6pm; 17F/€2.59), the enthusiastic owner points out its many defensive features – including arrow slits and sluice gates which, when opened from inside the mill, unleashed a torrent of water to sweep away anyone attempting to ford the millrace – and also puts the mill through its paces. Standing close to 1.5 tonnes of stone spinning at 80 revolutions per minute you get a real feel for the pent-up power of the water waiting calmly upstream.

From the mill it's only another 12km to Rocamadour. The D673 takes you back up onto the plateau and into Rocamadour from the north, but for a more dramatic approach follow the footpath (the GR6) along the valley. It runs alongside the River Ouysse past another mill – this was once big wheat country and even in high summer the Ouysse, part of which flows underground, never dries up – before turning eastwards along the River Alzou. Gradually the valley closes in until you round a bend and see the pilgrimage town of Rocamadour clinging to the cliff like some lost city.

Rocamadour and around

Halfway up the northern cliff face of the deep and abrupt canyon of the River Alzou, the spectacular setting of **ROCAMADOUR** is hard to beat, with the turrets and spires of the **Cité Religieuse** at its heart, sandwiched between the jumbled roofs of the medieval town and the château's crenellated walls above. However, as you draw closer the spell is broken by the constant stream of pilgrims and more secular-minded visitors, particularly in summer, who fill lanes lined with shops peddling incongruous souvenirs. The main reason for Rocamadour's popularity – going back centuries – is the supposed miraculous properties of the statue of the **Black Madonna**, enshrined in the *cité*'s smoke-blackened Chapelle Notre-Dame. Modern tourists are also courted with a number of secondary attractions, including two wildlife parks, scattered on the plateau to the north and east of town. Even if those don't appeal, it's worth venturing up to the hamlet of **L'Hospitalet**, on the cliff to the east of Rocamadour, for the finest views of the town.

The first mention of Rocamadour's Chapelle Notre-Dame dates from 1105, although evidence suggests pilgrims started coming here as early as the ninth century. However, things really got going when a perfectly preserved body was discovered in a rock-hewn tomb beside the chapel in 1166. It was promptly declared to be that of Zacchaeus, later **St Amadour**; according to one legend, Zacchaeus – a tax-collector in Jericho at the time of Christ – was advised by the Virgin Mary to come to France and lived out his years in Rocamadour as a hermit. As tales of the saint and associated miracles spread, the faithful began to arrive in droves from all over Europe. St Bernard, numerous kings – including Henry II of England and Louis IX of France (St Louis) – and thousands of ordinary mortals crawled up the grand staircase on their knees to pay their respects and to seek forgiveness or cures. Others came simply to plunder the shrine –

among them Henry Short-Coat (see box on p.251) – but they were easily out-classed by the Huguenots, who, in 1562, tried in vain to burn St Amadour's corpse and finally resigned themselves to hacking it to bits. In the meantime, centuries of warfare and plague led to a decline in the number of pilgrims. The buildings gradually fell into ruin until the bishops of Cahors – hoping to revive the flagging pilgrimage – financed a massive reconstruction in the early nineteenth century and so gave us the Rocamadour we see today.

Arrival and information

Getting to Rocamadour by public transport is awkward. There are no buses, and Rocamadour-Padirac **gare SNCF**, on the Brive–Figeac line, lies 4km away to the northeast; if you don't want to walk, you can call a taxi (☎05.65.33.72.27) or rent a bike – though you'll need to book in advance since the station only has a handful (daily 11.30am–7pm; ☎05.65.33.63.05). Rocamadour is pedestrianized, so if you arrive **by car** you'll have to park in L'Hospitalet or else in the valley several hundred metres below the town. A **lift** (daily: mid-Feb to April 9am–6pm; May & June 8am–8pm; July & Aug 8am–10pm; Sept to mid-Nov 8am–6pm; closed mid-Nov to mid-Feb; every 3min; 11F/€1.68 one-way, 15F/€2.29 return) links the town's main street, rue de la Couronnerie, with the sanctuaries above, while **cable cars** (daily: April & Oct 9am–12.30pm & 1.30–6pm; May, June & Sept 8am–8pm; July & Aug 8am–8pm; closed Nov–March; every 3min; 15F/€2.29 one-way, 23F/€3.51 return) depart from just east of the *cité* to emerge on the cliff-top near the château.

Rocamadour boasts two **tourist offices**: the main one is located on the western outskirts of L'Hospitalet (April & May daily 10am–noon & 2–6pm; June & Sept daily 10am–noon & 2–7pm; July & Aug daily 10am–8pm; Oct–March Mon–Fri 10am–noon & 2–5.30pm, Sat & Sun 2–5.30pm; ☎05.65.33.22.00, fax 05.65.33.22.01, *www.rocamadour.com*), and you'll find a second on rue de la Couronnerie next to the Hôtel de Ville (daily: April to mid-July & Sept 10am–12.30pm & 1.30–6pm; mid-July to Aug 9.30am–7.30pm; Oct to mid-Nov 10am–noon & 2–5.30pm; mid-Nov to March 2.30–5.30pm; ☎05.65.33.63.26). Both can help book hotels and change money (25F/€3.81 flat-rate commission on traveller's cheques or cash). They also sell a number of useful publications, including a town map, either on its own (5F/€0.76) or in a pack along with a brief guidebook, lists of hotels and other facilities, and details of four walks in the area (10F/€1.52).

Accommodation

One of the benefits of staying over in Rocamadour is that you can enjoy the town at its quietest in the early morning and late evening, and the **hotels** here are not too expensive. The downside is that everywhere is completely booked out in summer for miles around, and most places close during the winter months. Outside these periods, there are some good options, with a choice between central Rocamadour, the modern places in L'Hospitalet or somewhere in the countryside around.

The nearest **campsite** to Rocamadour is the two-star *Relais du Campeur* (☎05.65.33.63.28, fax 05.65.33.69.60; closed mid-Oct to March), situated next to the *Comp'Hostel* (see below) and under the same management – facilities are limited, but there's a mini-market close by and plenty of restaurants in the vicinity.

Hotels in the old town

Beau Site, rue de la Couronnerie (☎05.65.33.63.08, fax 05.65.33.65.23, *www.bw-beausite. com*). Rocamadour's top hotel occupies a lovely old mansion – its entrance all flagstone floors and oak beams – right in the centre, with more modern rooms in an annexe across the road. It has an excellent restaurant, the *Jehan de Valon* (see p.248), and a pool 2km away. Closed mid-Nov to early Feb. ④.

Lion d'Or, Porte Figuier (☎05.65.33.62.04, fax 05.65.33.72.54, *www.liondor-rocamadour.com*). Just inside the old city gate at the east end of rue de la Couronnerie, this old-fashioned, family-run hotel is the cheapest option in the old quarter, offering small but adequate en-suite rooms. Their restaurant is right across the street with good but equally no-nonsense menus from 68F/€10.37. Closed Nov–March. ②.

Sainte-Marie, place des Senhals (☎05.65.33.63.07, fax 05.65.33.69.08, *saintemarie@ rocamadour.com*). If the *Lion d'Or* is closed, try this friendly place halfway up the pilgrims' staircase. The rooms are simple and some quite small, but the location and restaurant with superb views down into the valley make up for it (*plat du jour* at around 50F/€7.62 and menus from 65F/€9.91). Closed mid-Oct to March. ③.

Le Terminus des Pèlerins, place de la Carreta (☎05.65.33.62.14, fax 05.65.33.72.10, *www.logis-de-france.fr*). Another good option on rue de la Couronnerie at the bottom of the grand staircase. Some rooms have terraces overlooking the valley, while all are decked out in fresh, modern colours with spacious bathrooms. They also offer traditional and regional cuisine with a *plat du jour* at around 50F/€7.62 and menus from 70F/€10.67. Closed Nov–March. ③.

Hotels in L'Hospitalet and around

Le Belvédère (☎05.65.33.63.25, fax 05.65.33.69.25, *www.logis-de-france.fr*). This is not the most beautiful hotel, and rooms are functional, though comfortable enough, but the main thing here is the location, on the cliff edge as you come into L'Hospitalet from Rocamadour – make sure you ask for a room overlooking the *cité*. You can also enjoy the views from the restaurant's big picture windows (menus from 69F/€10.52). Closed Nov–March. ③.

Le Comp'Hostel, place de l'Europe (☎05.65.33.73.50, fax 05.65.33.69.60). No views from this modern hotel a hundred metres north of the *Belvédere*, but squeaky clean rooms – some with a small terrace – a swimming pool and a warm welcome. Closed mid-Oct to March. ③.

Le Troubadour, Belveyre (☎05.65.33.70.27, fax 05.65.33.71.99, *troubadour@racamadour. com*). A small, spruce hotel, 1km north of L'Hospitalet on the D673, with flowery, en-suite rooms, where you can truly get away from the crowds. There's a pool and bikes, and a residents-only restaurant, open for dinner only (from about 100F/€15.24). Closed mid-Nov to mid-Feb. ②.

Les Vieilles Tours, Lafage (☎05.65.33.68.01, fax 05.65.33.68.59, *roger.zozolli@wanadoo.fr*). A surprisingly affordable country-house hotel offering a spot of luxury 3km west of L'Hospitalet just off the D673. The buildings have been beautifully restored – one room incorporates a mini-tower – and there are splendid views all around, as well as a pool and an excellent restaurant (menus from 125F/€19.06; Mon–Sat closed midday). Closed mid-Nov to March. ④.

des Voyageurs, place de la Gare (☎05.65.33.63.19). Opposite Rocamadour-Padirac station, this hotel is not only the cheapest in the area, but also one of very few that stays open all year. The nine rooms are bright and well kept, though only one boasts an en-suite toilet, while locals patronize the restaurant for its hearty *menu du jour* (65F/€9.91). Oct–Easter closed Sun. ①.

The Town

Rocamadour is divided into two parts: the medieval town containing the **Cité Religieuse**, where you'll find all the most important sights, and the cliff-top hamlet of **L'Hospitalet**, one and a half kilometres by road to the east. The old town is easy enough to find your way around since there's just one street, pedestrianized rue de la Couronnerie, which runs west from porte du Figuier – one of Rocamadour's four medieval gateways – to the wide stone staircase leading up to the sanctuaries roughly 300m later. Follow the main road east from porte du Figuier, on the other hand, and it will take you winding up the valley side to L'Hospitalet; pedestrians can use the quieter Voie Sainte, a narrow lane which branches off left after a couple of hundred metres.

La Cité Religieuse

The steep hillside above rue de la Couronnerie supports no fewer than seven chapels, known collectively as "Les Sanctuaires", or the **Cité Religieuse**. There's a lift dug into the rock-face (see above), but it's far better to climb the 216 worn and pitted steps of the **Grand Escalier**, up which the devout once dragged themselves on their knees to the doors of the *cité*. Inside lies a small square, the *parvis*, completely hemmed in by the various chapels. The largest of these, lying straight ahead of you, is the **Basilique St-Sauveur** (daily 8.30am–6pm), which up until 1900 provided lodgings for pilgrims who couldn't afford anything better. There's nothing much to see inside, however, so turn left for the little **Chapelle Notre-Dame** (daily 8.30am–6pm), nestled against the rock and the basilica wall, where the miracle-working twelfth-century Black Madonna resides. The crudely carved statue, less than 70cm tall, still wears a faint smile despite her mutilated state, though the adult-featured Jesus balanced on her knee looks decidedly out of sorts. The rest of the chapel is unremarkable, but note the empty recess in the rock outside, where St Amadour's body was found, and a rusty sword protruding from the cliff above. According to local tradition this is Durandal, the trusty blade of the legendary Roland whose heroic exploits are recorded in the twelfth-century *Chanson de Roland* (The Song of Roland), though it's not revealed exactly how it got here from northern Spain, where Roland supposedly died in battle against the Moors in 778. Beside the chapel's ornately carved door there are also some faded fifteenth-century frescoes depicting a macabre fight between the Living and the Dead.

Opposite the Chapelle Notre-Dame two incredibly well-preserved twelfth-century polychrome paintings of the Annunciation and the Visitation adorn the **Chapelle St-Michel**, which, along with the other four chapels, is only accessible on guided tours of the *cité* (1hr: April–June, Sept & Oct Mon–Fri 10.30am, 2.30pm & 4.30pm according to demand; July & Aug at least four visits daily; rest of the year for groups by appointment only ☎05.65.33.23.23; 20F/€3.05); tickets are available from the guide on the *parvis*. However, don't worry if you miss it, since most of the chapels' remaining carvings, reliquaries and other treasures have been removed for safe-keeping to the **Musée d'Art Sacré** (Feb–June, Sept & Oct daily 10am–noon & 2–5pm; July & Aug daily 10am–7pm; Nov–Jan Mon–Fri 10am–noon & 2–5pm; 28F/€4.27), located immediately inside the *cité* gate on the left as you enter. The museum is dedicated to the French composer Francis Poulenc (1899–1963), who wrote his *Litanies à la Vierge Noire* after visiting the shrine in 1936, and contains a wide-ranging and well-presented collection of religious art from the twelfth to the twentieth centuries. Best are the earlier exhibits from Rocamadour's golden age (the twelfth and thirteenth centuries), such as the pilgrims' insignia, *sportelles*, which were made nearby on the place des Senhals, a fragment of stained glass from St-Sauveur and reliquaries covered in beautiful Limoges enamel.

East of the Cité there's a sandy esplanade and the cable car (see above) which will take you to the top of the cliff. Alternatively, you can walk up the shady zig-zag path, *La Calvarie*, past tableaux depicting the Stations of the Cross, or take a more direct and steeper path to come out near the château, a full 150m above the river below. While the château itself, a mostly nineteenth-century reconstruction, is private, you can walk round the **ramparts** (daily 8am–dusk; 15F/€2.29) for vertiginous views.

East to L'Hospitalet

The road leading east from the château brings you almost immediately to the first of Rocamadour's two wildlife parks, the **Rocher des Aigles** (April–June & Sept Mon–Fri 10am–noon & 2–5pm, Sun & school hols 10am–noon & 2–6pm; July & Aug daily 10am–6pm; Oct & Nov Mon–Fri 2–4pm, Sun & school hols 2–5pm; closed Dec–March; 40F/€6.10), a breeding centre for birds of prey. The cages seem uncomfortably small, but with a production rate of nearly a hundred chicks a year the birds can't be overly stressed about it. There's a film explaining the breeding programme, which aims to reintroduce a number of rare species to the wild, and you can also see the hatching room where scrawny chicks warm themselves under sun lamps. Best, though, are the thirty-minute flying demonstrations (April–June & Sept Mon–Fri 11am, 3pm & 4pm, Sun & school hols also at 5pm; July & Aug 11am–5.30pm roughly every hour; Oct & Nov Mon–Fri 3pm, Sun & school hols 3pm & 4pm), in which a dozen or so condors, fish eagles and other such majestic birds are allowed to soar free over the valley.

Continuing east about 700m along the cliff edge you join the main road, the D673 from Calès (see p.242), and then after another 150m reach the modern, plate-glass tourist office which marks the western extent of **L'Hospitalet**. The name refers to a pilgrims' hospital founded on the cliff-top here in the thirteenth century, of which only a few ruined walls and a chapel containing a copy of the Black Madonna remain. A crossroads lying immediately to the northeast of the chapel represents the centre of modern L'Hospitalet, which consists of a scattering of hotels, cafés and shops.

A hundred metres east of this crossroads, along the D36 to Gramat and Figeac, is **La Féerie du Rail**, essentially a landscaped model railway, albeit it an amazingly detailed one, which took more than fifteen years to build. Forty-five-minute mini-*son et lumière* shows (daily: April to mid-June & Sept at 11.15pm, 2.45pm & 4.30pm; mid-June to mid-July 11.15am, 2.40pm & 3.30pm; mid-July to Aug 10.45am–5.50pm roughly every hour; Oct 2.45pm & 4.15pm; closed Nov–March; 38F/€5.76) highlight different scenes: not only do trains scuttle about, but there are also automated cars, boats, fairs and fire engines, and even skiers and hot-air balloonists. It may not be everyone's cup of tea, but the whole thing is extremely well done and full of imaginative touches, and it's a must for kids.

Another couple of hundred metres east along this same road is the second of the wildlife parks, the **Forêt des Singes** (April–June & Sept daily 10am–noon & 1–6pm; July & Aug daily 10am–7pm; Oct to mid-Nov Mon–Sat 1–5pm, Sun & school hols 10am–noon & 1–5pm; 40F/€6.10); it's one of the better such parks, with some 120 Barbary apes roaming 20 hectares of oak and scrubland in relative freedom. Again, the aim is conservation – so far around 600 young monkeys have been reintroduced to north Africa. The monkeys continue feeding, grooming and playing regardless of human intruders, but the best time to visit is during the cool of the early morning or evening and in early summer when the youngsters are frisking about.

Even if none of the above sights appeal, it's still worth coming up to L'Hospitalet for the tremendous views of the medieval *cité* from the cliff-edge **Belvédère**, beside the eponymous hotel, just south of the central crossroads. It's stunning at any time, but particularly magical at night when the buildings are illuminated (March–Nov & Christmas hols). To return to Rocamadour from here, take the Voie Sainte, the old pilgrims' route running down beside the *Belvédère* hotel to arrive beside the porte du Figuier around eight minutes later.

Eating

In general, the best of Rocamadour's **restaurants** are those attached to the hotels (see p.245), notably the superb *Jehan de Valon*, listed below along with a few more everyday recommendations; note that most places are closed in winter. The local speciality, which you'll find on every menu, is *Rocamadour*, a round disc of goats' cheese, often served on toast or with a walnut salad, or occasionally flambéed in brandy or drizzled with honey. Elsewhere in the region it is known as *cabécou*, but cheeses produced around Rocamadour warrant their own special *appellation* – and even their own festival (see box on p.238). You can buy it at shops selling the inevitable foie gras and other regional produce, but for other **picnic fare** the only proper food shop hereabouts is the mini-market near the *Comp'Hostel* in L'Hospitalet.

Chez Anne-Marie, rue de la Couronnerie (☎05.65.33.65.81). A jolly little place just west of the *Hôtel Beau Site* that's popular for its cheap-and-cheerful mix of grills, omelettes and salads in addition to regional dishes. They also serve a vegetarian menu. *Plat du jour* at 50F/€7.62 and menus from 70F/€10.67 with lots of choice. Closed Jan.

Le Globe, rue de la Couronnerie. A few doors west from *Chez Anne-Marie* along the main street, this welcoming hotel-restaurant offers salads, pizzas and pasta. Their most expensive dish costs less than 70F/€10.67, or there's a choice of *plats du jour* for under 60F/€9.15. Closed mid-Nov to late Dec & Jan, and Mon eve & Tues.

Jehan de Valon, *Hôtel Beau Site*, rue de la Couronnerie (☎05.65.33.63.08). You need to book ahead for a table in this elegant restaurant, with panoramic views over the Alzou valley. Their seasonal menus include a good variety of fresh fish as well as local specialities, with prices starting at 115F/€17.53; count on at least 250F/€38.11 à la carte. Simpler fare is on offer in their adjoining brasserie where a *plat du jour* will set you back 52F/€7.93 and a three-course menu 78F/€11.89. Closed mid-Nov to early Feb.

Au Panorama, L'Hospitalet. If you're looking for somewhere to eat in L'Hospitalet, try this unpretentious café-restaurant across from the *Belvédère* hotel. They serve an eclectic mix of regional dishes, pizzas, salads and snacks, and breakfasts from 8am to cater for the nearby campsite. Pizzas cost 35–65F/€5.34–9.91, while full-blown menus start at 100F/€15.24. Closed mid-Nov to March.

Upstream from Lacave to Beaulieu-sur-Dordogne

Upstream from Lacave (see p.242), the Dordogne meanders in a northeasterly direction through walnut orchards and dozing villages. Its valley sides occasionally rise up to form rocky crags, the most dramatic of which are those around **Gluges** where the river has carved the **Cirque de Montvalent** out of the plateau. On the dry uplands to the north of Gluges, the market town of **Martel** somehow escapes the worst of the crowds, despite the attractions of its well-preserved medieval centre, while further east the river glides past the typical Quercy village of **Carennac**. The carved portal on its abbey-church is, like Souillac's, a superb example of Romanesque craftsmanship, and its cloister harbours a beautifully expressive entombment scene from the Renaissance era. With a couple of good hotels, Carennac also makes a good base for exploring this stretch of river, or for a foray south to the enormous limestone sinkhole known as the **Gouffre de Padirac**. From the bottom of the cavity you follow an underground river by boat and on foot through equally oversized caverns hung with gigantic stalactites.

At **Bretenoux**, some 10km to the east of Carennac, the River Dordogne turns northwards. Though the town has little to recommend it beyond a pretty medieval square and reasonable transport connections, the nearby **Château de Castelnau** makes a worthwhile excursion, if only to admire the fortress's impregnable defences or to take in the views from its ramparts. A short hop north of Bretenoux, **Beaulieu-sur-Dordogne** is a more attractive spot with its riverside walks and lanes of ancient houses, and is also home to another finely carved Romanesque portal ornamenting its abbey-church.

Public transport along this stretch of the river is relatively good. St-Denis-Près-Martel, 7km from Martel, lies on both the Brive–Figeac and Brive–Aurillac train lines, while services on this latter line also call at Bretenoux-Biars, the nearest station for both Bretenoux and Beaulieu. Bus services are more comprehensive, covering Martel, St-Denis, Carennac, Bretenoux, Beaulieu and St-Céré, though it involves a bit of toing and froing, and there's a gap in the network between St-Denis and Carennac.

From Lacave to Creysse and Gluges

From Lacave, the D23 takes a leisurely route northeastwards as it tracks the twists and turns of the Dordogne. Seven kilometres upstream you come to the sleepy hilltop village of **MEYRONNE**, where the road crosses from the south bank to the north. In the eleventh century the bishops of Tulle, northeast of Brive, built a château here to defend what was then an important bridging point. Their residence is now a splendid **hotel**, *La Terrasse* (☎05.65.32.21.60, fax 05.65.32.26.93; ④; closed Nov–Feb), complete with spiral stairs, old chimneys and an excellent restaurant (menus from 100F/€15.24).

On the north side of the bridge turn right onto the tiny D114, which hugs the river for the next 4km east to **CREYSSE**. This idyllic hamlet, with its dinky market hall and fast-running stream, sits in the lee of a knuckle of rock where a fortified gate and scraps of wall are all that remain of a château once owned by the viscounts of Turenne (see p.165). Their twelfth-century **chapel**, standing immediately above the village (Mon, Thurs & Fri 3–5pm, Sun 10.30am–noon, or ask for the key at the Mairie next door), has fared rather better, and is worth a look for its *pisé* floor and unique arrangement of two absidial chapels. There's a simple but very appealing **hotel**, the *Auberge de L'Île* (☎05.65.32.22.01, fax 05.65.32.21.43, *www.logis-de-france.com*; ③; closed Nov–March), straddling the stream in the village centre, whose plane-tree-shaded terrace is hard to resist; they offer a brasserie menu of salads, omelettes, sandwiches and so forth in addition to full meals (menus from 100F/€15.24). Campers, meanwhile, should head for the excellent two-star **campsite**, the *Camping du Port* (☎05.65.32.27.59, fax 05.65.32.20.40; closed Oct–April), down beside the Dordogne a hundred metres east of the village – **bikes** and **canoes** are available for rent on site from Port-Loisirs (☎05.65.32.20.82).

The cliffs lining the Dordogne valley get more dramatic upstream from Creysse. For the most impressive scenery, follow the D23 northeast for a good two kilometres and then branch off right along the D43. The road quickly narrows down to a single track – with passing spaces – cut into the rock. You emerge two kilometres later at another huddle of houses, **GLUGES**, whose prime attraction is its location under the cliffs and its views south to the **Cirque de Montvalent**, where the meandering river has carved a great semicircle out of the cliffs; for a sweeping panorama, climb up to the hilltop Belvédère de Copeyre, signed off the main road one kilometre above Gluges to the east. Otherwise, apart from a quick wander round Gluges' medieval lanes, the only thing to do is relax on the terrace of the welcoming and recently renovated **hotel** *Les Falaises* (☎05.65.27.18.44, fax 05.65.27.18.45; ③; closed Nov–March; restaurant from 120F/€18.29, evenings only) at the western entrance to the village. There's a three-star riverside **campsite** opposite, also called *Les Falaises* (☎05.65.37.37.78, fax 05.65.32.20.40; closed Oct–April), though it's not under the same management. You can rent **canoes** and **bikes** from Copeyre Canoë (☎05.65.37.33.51, fax 05.65.37.31.71) down by the water.

Martel

Five kilometres north of Gluges, and fifteen east of Souillac, **MARTEL**'s medieval centre is built in a pale, almost white, stone, offset by warm reddish-brown roofs. Another Turenne-administered town (see p.165), its heyday came during the thirteenth and fourteenth centuries when the viscounts granted certain freedoms, including the right to mint money, and established a royal court of appeal here. Martel was occupied briefly by English forces during the Hundred Years' War and suffered again at the hands of the Huguenots in the sixteenth century, but on the whole the compact old centre has survived remarkably intact.

The exception to this is the ramparts, which have been dismantled to make way for the wide boulevard which now rings Martel's pedestrianized centre. Take any of the lanes leading inwards and you will soon find yourself in the cobbled main square, **place des Consuls**. It is mostly taken up by the eighteenth-century *halle*, scene of a busy market on Wednesdays and Saturdays, but on every side there are reminders of the town's illustrious past, most notably the grand Gothic **Palais de la Raymondie** on the square's east side, now occupied by the Mairie. Begun in 1280, it served as both the Turenne law courts and fortress, hence the large square tower – one of seven which gave the town its epithet, *la ville aux sept tours*. On the square's south side is another of the towers – a circular five-storeyed turret belonging to the **Maison Fabri**. According to tradition, this striking building is where Henry Short-Coat died in 1183 (see box opposite).

One block south of here, rue Droite leads east to the town's main church, **St-Maur**, built in a fiercely defensive, mostly Gothic style, with a finely carved Romanesque tympanum depicting the Last Judgement above the west door.

Practicalities

Without your own transport, the best way to get to Martel is via one of two SNCF **bus services** (☎05.65.37.81.15), both of which stop on the ring road to the

THE TALE OF HENRY SHORT-COAT

At the end of the twelfth century, Martel provided the stage for one of the tragic events in the internecine conflicts of the Plantagenet family. When Henry Plantagenet (King Henry II of England) imprisoned his estranged wife Eleanor of Aquitaine, his sons took up arms against their father. The eldest, **Henry Short-Coat** (Henri Court-Mantel), even went so far as to plunder the viscountcy of Turenne, at which point his father immediately handed over Henry's lands to his next son, Richard the Lionheart. With no income but a considerable army to maintain, Henry Short-Coat began looting the treasures of every abbey and shrine in the region, including Rocamadour (see p.243). This last act was to be his downfall. Ill with a fever, Henry fled to Martel, where, guilt-ridden and fearing for his life, he confessed his crimes and asked his father for forgiveness. It duly came but Henry Short-Coat died soon after, leaving Richard the Lionheart heir to the English throne.

southwest of the centre. One route comes from Brive and the second from Souillac, passing through Martel on its way to the **gare SNCF** at **ST-DENIS-PRÈS-MARTEL**, 7km to the east, on the Brive–Figeac and Brive-Aurillac train lines; if there's no convenient bus heading back from St-Denis to Martel, call Daubet (☎05.65.37.34.87) for a taxi. In season, a **tourist train** runs along a splendid stretch of decommissioned line from Martel towards St-Denis and back – but not as far as St-Denis station – along cliffs 80m above the Dordogne (departures by diesel train: April, May, June & Sept Thurs 4.30pm; July & Aug Tues–Sun 2.30pm & 4pm; 35F/€5.34; departures by steam train: April–Sept Sun 2.30pm & 4pm, also mid-July to mid-Aug Wed same times; 50F/€7.62; ☎05.65.37.35.81). It departs from the otherwise disused station two hundred metres south of town; reservations are recommended.

The small **tourist office** in the Palais de la Raymondie on place des Consuls (July & Aug daily 9am–8pm; rest of year Mon–Sat 9am–noon & 3–6pm; ☎05.65.37.43.44, fax 05.65.37.37.27) can provide further information about the train and about Martel's **festivals**, of which the most important is the Festival du Haut-Quercy, with concerts in St-Maur and other churches around the region (see box on p.238 for more).

For an overnight **stay**, try the basic, old-fashioned *Hôtel Le Turenne* on avenue Jean-Lavayssière (☎05.65.37.30.30; ②; closed Dec–Feb; menus from 75F/€11.43), the ring road to the west of town, or, if you have money to spare, the expensive but absolutely gorgeous *Relais Ste-Anne* (☎05.65.37.40.56, fax 05.65.37.42.82; ⑥; closed mid-Nov to late March), south across the ring road from the old centre down rue du Pourtanel. It occupies a former girls' boarding school set in gardens with its own chapel, pool and beautifully appointed rooms. For campers, there's a decidedly spartan municipal **campsite**, *La Callopie* (05.65.37.30.03, fax 05.65.37.37.27; closed Oct–April), on Martel's northern outskirts on the road to Les Quatres-Routes.

If you're looking for somewhere to **eat**, you could try the bars and brasseries around place des Consuls but, better still, follow the signs west across the ring road to *La Mère Michèle* on rue de la Remise (☎05.65.37.35.66; closed Sun eve), a tiny little place serving well-presented dishes such as lamb with honey and thyme, and confit of pigeon with raisons soaked in armagnac (*plat du jour* 38F/€5.79;

menus from 65F/€9.91). Another good choice, where you definitely need to ring ahead, is the *Ferme Auberge Moulin à Huile de Noix* (☎05.65.37.40.69; closed Nov–March), attached to a working walnut-oil mill 3km east off the D703 to St-Denis and Bretenoux. Don't be put off by the modern concrete exterior; the dining rooms upstairs have a bit of character and the food – all regional dishes with a strong preference for duck and walnuts – is both excellent and plentiful (menus 78–132F/€11.89–20.12).

Carennac and around

CARENNAC is without doubt one of the most beautiful villages along this part of the Dordogne valley. It sits on a terrace above the river's south bank 16km or so east of Martel – backtrack to Gluges and then head upstream on the D43 for the prettiest route – and is best known for its typical Quercy architecture and the richly carved tympanum of its Romanesque priory-church. Founded in the eleventh century by Benedictine monks, the priory grew rich from pilgrims en route to Santiago de Compostela. Sacked during the Hundred Years' War, it then enjoyed a second golden age in the late fifteenth and sixteenth centuries, when the church was restored and a château built alongside. But by the 1700s the rot had set in as the monks became lazy and corrupt, and the priory was finally closed after the Revolution.

You get one of the best views of the village's towers and higgledy-piggledy russet-tiled roofs as you approach from the west. The houses cluster so tightly round the priory buildings that it's hard to tell them apart, but if you follow the road along the riverbank, you'll soon find a gateway leading to a cobbled courtyard and the **Église St-Pierre**. Straight ahead of you the church's twelfth-century tympanum – in the style of Moissac and Cahors – dominates its recessed west door. The carvings are in exceptionally good condition: Christ sits in majesty with the Book of Judgement in his left hand, surrounded by the four symbols of the Evangelists and animated portraits of the Apostles – the twelfth is missing – ranged on either side. There's not a lot to see inside, but in July and August the church makes an atmospheric venue for concerts during the Festival du Haut-Quercy (see p.238 for more).

South of the church, still inside the courtyard, you gain access to the **cloister and chapter house** via the tourist office (see below for hours; 10F/€1.52). The cloister's Romanesque and flamboyant Gothic galleries were somewhat mutilated during the Revolution, but they are in any case overshadowed by the late-fifteenth-century, life-size *Mise au Tombeau* (Entombment of Christ) on display in the chapterhouse. So supremely detailed is the sculpture that you can even see the veins in Christ's hands and legs. Joseph of Arimathea and Nicodemus, holding either end of the shroud, are richly attired as a fifteenth-century nobleman and pilgrim respectively, while behind them Mary Magdalene, her hair a mass of ringlets, ostentatiously wipes away a tear.

In the sixteenth century the *doyens* (deans) in charge of the priory and its dependant churches built themselves a grand residence, referred to nowadays as the **château**, abutting the church's north wall. Its most famous occupant was François de Savignac de La Mothe-Fénelon (see p.234) who served as *doyen* of Carennac for fifteen years from 1681; according to local tradition he penned his infamous book *Télémaque* here. A few stone chimneypieces and the great hall's painted ceiling remain from this era, but little else, since the building has been partially modernized to house the **Maison de la Dordogne Quercynoise**

(April–Oct daily 10am–1pm & 2–7pm; 30F/€4.57). This museum covers the geography, history, fauna and flora of the Dordogne valley from Bretenoux downstream to Lacave; it's not hugely exciting but the displays are well done and provide a good overview of what the region has to offer.

Practicalities

Buses from Brive, Gramat and St-Céré (all operated by Cars Quercy Corrèze; ☎05.65.38.71.90) will drop you near the Mairie on the south side of Carennac. The nearest **gare SNCF** is Vayrac, 8km northwest on the other side of the river, on the Brive–Aurillac line; call ☎05.65.10.92.92 if you need a taxi. However, services are more frequent to St-Denis-Près-Martel, 10km to the west (see p.251), on the Brive–Figeac line. Carennac's helpful **tourist office** is located in the priory courtyard (March–June Mon–Fri 10am–noon & 1.30–6.30pm, Sat & Sun 2–6.30pm; July to mid-Sept daily 10am–7pm; mid-Sept to Oct daily 10am–noon & 1.30–6.30pm; Nov–Feb Mon–Fri 10am–noon & 1.30–5.30pm, Sat & Sun 2–5.30pm; ☎ & fax 05.65.10.97.01).

The village also boasts two comfortable and reasonably priced **hotels**, both with pools and good restaurants specializing in traditional regional cuisine. Marginally better of the two is the *Auberge du Vieux Quercy*, on the D20 immediately south of the village (☎05.65.10.96.59, fax 05.65.10.94.05, *www. logis-de-france.fr*, ③; closed mid-Nov to March), whose restaurant offers well-priced menus from 98F/€14.94 (April, Oct & Nov closed Mon). The alternative is the more rustic *Hôtel Fénelon* on the main street to the east of the château (☎05.65.10.96.46, fax 05.65.10.94.86, *www.logis-de-france.fr*, ③; closed Jan to mid-March, also Fri & Sat lunch except in July & Aug; restaurant from 100F/€15.24). There's also a good municipal **campsite**, *L'Eau Vive*, beside the river 1km east of Carennac (☎05.65.10.97.39, fax 05.55.28.12.12; closed Oct–April).

Though you can eat very well in either of the above hotels, there are also a couple of **restaurants** worth seeking out in the countryside around Carennac. For something special, try the *Côté Jardin* (☎05.36.38.49.51; reservations required; menu at 130F/€19.82), just north of Tauriac, a pretty village roughly 3km east of Carennac on the other side of the river. The exquisitely prepared dishes using ultra-fresh ingredients taste their best on summer evenings under the fairy lights. The *Relais de Gintrac* (Oct–April closed Mon eve, also closed second fortnight in Sept; menus from 60F/€9.15), in the hamlet of Gintrac, about 3km from Carennac southeast along the D30, lies at the opposite end of the spectrum, offering copious country cooking washed down with well-priced wines.

The Gouffre de Padirac

Not surprisingly, local legend holds the Devil responsible for opening the gaping mouth of the **Gouffre de Padirac** (1hr 30min guided tours daily: April–July 9 & Sept 9am–noon & 2–6pm; July 10–31 9am–6.30pm; Aug 8.30am–6.30pm; Oct 9am–noon & 2–5pm; *www.gouffre-de-padirac.com*; 49F/€7.47) in the middle of the limestone plateau 10km south of Carennac. The hole is over 30m wide and 75m deep, its sides festooned with dripping ferns and creepers, though the sense of mystery is somewhat diminished these days by the presence of a lift-cage built against the side. Rather than the Devil, the chasm was probably formed by a cave roof collapsing centuries ago; locals took refuge here during the Hundred Years' War and probably long before. The cave system was not properly explored, however, until 1889 when spectacular stalactites – the biggest a staggering 75m tall – and lakes were discovered.

The visit starts with a half-kilometre-long **boat trip** along an underground river, after which you walk on past barrages and massive cascades formed by calcite deposits over the millennia. The lakes are pretty, but the most notable feature here is the sheer scale of the formations and the height of the passages carved out of the rock, reaching nearly 100m at their highest. Be warned, though: it is very, very touristy and best avoided at weekends and other peak periods, when you'll wait an age for tickets. And in wet weather you'll need a waterproof jacket.

The nearest **gare SNCF** is Rocamadour-Padirac, more than 10km to the west; from the station you could take a taxi (☎05.65.33.72.27) or rent a bike (see p.244). The best **accommodation** in the vicinity is the ivy-covered *Auberge de Mathieu* (☎05.65.33.64.68, fax 05.65.33.69.29; ②; closed Sat & mid-Nov to Feb; menus from 78F/€11.89), 300m south of the Gouffre on the D90, with plain rooms but a nice terrace and garden. Alternatively, try *Les Chênes* (☎05.65.33.65.54, fax 05.65.33.71.55; closed mid-Sept to April), a very well-organized four-star **campsite** just south of the *Auberge*, with a bar, restaurant and pool.

Bretenoux and around

Some 10km east of Carennac, the *bastide* town of **BRETENOUX**, founded in 1277 by the barons of Castelnau, sits on the south bank of the River Cère just upstream from where it joins the Dordogne. It was obviously a pretty little place at one time – the cobbled and arcaded **place des Consuls** behind the tourist office is a delight, especially on **market** days (Tues & Sat am) – but these days the town suffers from a busy main road and too much modern development. With its transport connections, however, Bretenoux is a useful staging post for the nearby towns of St-Céré and Beaulieu-sur-Dordogne (see p.257 & opposite).

It also lies within striking distance of the **Château de Castelnau** (30min guided tours: April–June & Sept daily 9.30am–12.15pm & 2–6.15pm; July & Aug daily 9.30am–6.45pm; Oct–March Tues–Sun 10am–12.15pm & 2–5.15pm; 32F/€4.88), 2.5km to the southwest, which is one of this region's most outstanding examples of medieval military architecture. The great fortress dominates an abrupt knoll to the east of the village, its sturdy towers and machicolated red-brown walls visible for miles around. It dates from the mid-tenth century, but took on its present form – a triangular fort with a massive square keep and three round towers, the whole lot surrounded by ramparts and dry moats – during the Hundred Years' War under the ownership of the powerful barons of Castelnau. By the early eighteenth century, however, the Castelnau family had died out. Their abandoned château was sacked during the Revolution, sustained even greater damage in a fire in 1851 and was left to rot until it was salvaged, somewhat bizarrely, in 1896 by a celebrated tenor of the Parisian Comic Opera, Jean Mouliérat. He threw his fortune into its restoration and amassing the valuable but rather dry collection of religious art and furniture from the fifteenth to eighteenth centuries which populate the handful of rooms you see on the guided tour. The views from the ramparts, though, are extremely impressive; on a clear day you can just make out the towers of Turenne, nearly 30km to the north (see p.165).

As you exit the castle's inner enclosure, turn left along the walls to take a quick look in the **Collégiale St-Louis**. Built of the same red stone and with powerful buttresses, this little Gothic church contains a fine fifteenth-century polychrome statue of the baptism of Christ – note the startled expression of the angel holding his clothes – and a macabre treasure in the form of a bone from the arm of St Louis (alias King Louis IX of France). In 1970 the relic was taken to St Louis in America to commemorate the founding of the city.

Practicalities

Bretenoux's **gare SNCF**, on the Brive–Aurillac line, is officially known as Bretenoux-Biars since it is located some 2km north of the River Cère in the town of Biars. Taxis wait outside (or call ☎05.65.10.90.90), and **buses** operated by Chauvac (☎05.65.38.08.28) shuttle between the station, Bretenoux and St-Céré three times a day at 11.50am, 2.50pm and 3.50pm; in Bretenoux the bus stop is on the main road, rue de la Libération, near the post office a couple of hundred metres south of the river.

There's a well-organized **tourist office** (July & Aug Mon–Sat 9am–12.30pm & 2.30–7pm, Sun 10am–1pm; rest of year Mon–Sat 9am–noon & 2–6pm; ☎05.65.38.59.53, fax 05.65.39.72.14, *ot.bretenoux@wanadoo.fr*) on rue de la Libération just south of the bridge. Carry on a bit further south along this road and you'll find Cycles Bladier (☎05.65.38.19.32), where you can rent **bikes** for a trip out to the Château de Castelnau.

Bretenoux has nothing to recommend in the way of **hotels**, but there are a couple of possibilities 6km northeast on the D14 in the village of **PORT-DE-GAGNAC**, on the north bank of the Cère. The nicer of the two is the homely *Auberge du Vieux Port* (☎05.65.38.50.05, fax 05.65.38.52.73, *www.logis-de-france.fr*; ②; closed Dec 15–31), serving excellent-value regional cuisine (menus from 78F/€11.89; Nov–Feb closed Sun eve). If they're full, try the *Hostellerie Belle Rive* (☎05.65.38.50.04, fax 05.65.38.47.72; ②; closed 1 week at Christmas; restaurant closed Fri eve, Sat lunch and Sun eve except in July & Aug; menus from 85F/€12.96) right next door. The other alternative is to stay in St-Céré, 9km to the south, or Beaulieu-sur-Dordogne, 8km to the north (see p.257 & below respectively), or at one of the local **campsites**. The three-star *Camping de la Bourgnatelle* (☎05.65.38.44.07; closed Oct–April), located on an island just across the bridge from Bretenoux, is not only the best option but also the most convenient. Otherwise, there's a quiet *camping à la ferme* (☎05.65.38.52.31; closed Oct–May) on the riverbank a couple of kilometres west along the D14 towards Prudhomat. **Canoe** rental is available in July and August at the *Bourgnatelle* campsite (☎05.65.35.91.59).

Again, Bretenoux has nothing much to offer in the way of **places to eat**, beyond a few cafés along the main road. The *Auberge* in Port-de-Gagnac represents your best option, or you could head south to St-Céré (see p.257).

Beaulieu-sur-Dordogne and beyond

At Bretenoux the River Dordogne turns northwards as it leaves the Lot *département* for neighbouring Corrèze. The valley here is wide and industrial – with factories such as Andros churning out enough jam to make this the "jam capital" of Europe – but things get better as you recross the river 8km north of Bretenoux to find **BEAULIEU-SUR-DORDOGNE** beautifully situated on a wide bend in the river. It's a perfectly proportioned town, with an abbey-church that boasts another of the great masterpieces of Romanesque sculpture, and yet is refreshingly untouristy. It even appears to be in gentle decline.

Arriving from Bretenoux, the main road skirts south of Beaulieu's compact and semi-pedestrianized core of old streets. On its way it passes through a large square, **place Marbot**, which represents the town's modern centre, off which rue de la République leads north to **place du Marché** (markets take place on Wednesday and Saturday mornings). Here, you'll find some nicely jaded stone and half-timbered buildings, along with the twelfth-century **abbey-church of St-Pierre**, a surprisingly large building, whose architecture reflects its position on the border between Limousin and Languedoc. The pairs of rounded arches piercing the belfry, for example, are typical Limousin styling, while the subject matter and style of carving on the magnificent **south portal** belongs firmly to the south. This doorway is unusually deep-set but even a quick glance reveals similarities between the sculptures here and those at Souillac, Carennac and Moissac, both in the design and the wonderfully fluid lines; it is likely that they were all fashioned by craftsmen from Toulouse. In this case, the tympanum is presided over by an Oriental-looking Christ with one arm extended to welcome the chosen on the Judgement Day. Around him a mass of angels and Apostles, even the dead rising from their graves below, seem bursting with vitality. The church interior is contrastingly sober, but it's worth venturing inside to see the little twelfth-century silver statue of the Virgin and Child kept in the north transept – it's only 60cm high but crafted in beautiful detail.

It won't take long to cover the rest of Beaulieu, and it's worth devoting half an hour or so to wandering its maze of lanes. In particular, there are a number of jaunty half-timbered houses along **rue Ste-Catherine**, running east from place du Marché, while if you continue northwest along **rue de la Résistance** and **rue Chapelle** you'll pass some handsome sculpted facades before emerging in an attractive spot on the riverbank.

Upstream from Beaulieu the Dordogne valley becomes wilder as you enter the first forest-covered foothills of the Massif Central. It makes for a lovely drive along the D12 as far as **ARGENTAT**, the last town of any size on the river, where it's easy to while away an hour or so sitting at one of the waterside cafés. Beyond Argentat, however, the Dordogne changes character entirely, due to a series of hydroelectric dams that turn the river into a succession of huge reservoirs.

Practicalities

It's just over 6km from Beaulieu to the Bretenoux-Biars **gare SNCF** (see p.255). Unfortunately there are no connecting **buses**, although you can get to Beaulieu by bus from Brive (☎05.55.93.72.17); services terminate on place du Champs-de-Mars, a large shady square just west of place Marbot. If you need a **taxi** in Beaulieu, call ☎05.55.91.00.76. The **tourist office** is located on the south side of place Marbot (April, June & Sept daily 9.30am–12.30pm & 2.30–6pm; July & Aug daily 9am–1pm & 2–7pm; Oct–March Mon–Sat 9.30am–12.30pm & 2.30–6pm; ☎05.55.91.09.94, fax 05.55.91.10.97).

The town has a decent range of **hotels**. Most appealing is the riverside *Charmilles*, 20 bd St-Rodolphe-de-Turenne (☎05.55.91.29.29, fax 05.55.91.29.30, *charme@dubinternet.fr*; ④; closed Nov), on the northeast side of town, a bright, clean, cheerful place with just eight rooms and a flowery terrace – you'll eat well here, too; menus start at 105F/€16.01 (restaurant closed Tues & Wed except in

July & Aug). A good alternative is the *Hôtel Le Turenne*, in a former abbey on place Marbot (☎05.55.91.10.16, fax 05.55.91.22.42; ③; closed mid-Nov to mid-March), with spacious rooms and a fine restaurant (closed Sun eve & Mon except in July & Aug; menus from 75F/€11.73). For cheaper rooms head further north to the *Hôtel Fournié*, on place du Champ-de-Mars (☎05.55.91.01.34; fax 05.55.91.23.57; ②; closed Tues & mid-Nov to April; menus from 100F/€15.24), or, better still, the welcoming **HI hostel** (☎05.55.91.13.82, fax 05.55.91.26.06, *beaulieu@fuaj.org*; dorm bed 48F/€7.32; closed Oct–March) at the far end of rue de la Chapelle in a magnificent half-timbered and turreted building; it has comfortable modern dorms, a well-equipped kitchen, and meals are available on request.

Beaulieu's two **campsites** are located on an island either side of the main road bridge. The three-star *Camping des Isles* (☎05.55.91.02.65, fax 05.55.91.05.19; closed Oct–April), to the north of the bridge, is the better value and more attractive of the pair. The two-star municipal site, *Camping du Pont* (05.55.91.00.57, fax 05.55.91.24.73, *mairie.beaulieu@wanadoo.fr*; closed mid-Sept to mid-June), lies immediately to the south. *Camping du Pont* offers **canoe** rental in July and August (Saga Team; ☎05.55.28.84.84) as do Safaraid (☎05.55.91.21.83, *www.canoe-dordogne.com*) at the *base nautique* on the other side of the river; you can drive round or get there via a footbridge to the north of the town centre.

Once again, the hotel **restaurants** are the best places to eat, but there's also a nice little *crêperie, Au Beau-Lieu Breton*, on rue du Presbytère, behind the church, where you can get *crêpes* and salads for around 40–50F/€6.10–7.62 (closed Tues & Wed except in July & Aug).

St-Céré and around

About nine kilometres south of Bretenoux on the River Bave, a minor tributary of the Dordogne, you come to the medieval town of **ST-CÉRÉ**, dominated by the brooding ruins of the Château de St-Laurent-les-Tours. The château is now home to an engaging museum dedicated to tapestry designer Jean Lurçat, who revitalized contemporary French tapestry, but the town's prime attraction is its old centre peppered with picturesque half-timbered houses.

St-Céré also makes a useful base for exploring the surrounding area. The town lies on the border between the empty but glorious wooded hills of the Ségala to the east and south, and the dry limestone *causse* to the west. However, the region's most impressive sight, and one not to be missed, is the Renaissance **Château de Montal**, 2km west of St-Céré, with its sculpted facade and grand staircase. From there you can loop south via the **Grottes de Presque** – a limestone cave with a tremendous variety of unusually colourful concretions – to arrive at the lip of the Cirque d'Autoire for dramatic views over the russet-red roofs of **Autoire** village, which provide a splash of colour in the valley far below. On the way back to St-Céré the route passes through another captivating little village, **Loubressac**, which can hardly have changed for centuries.

It's possible to reach St-Céré by bus from Bretenoux, Cahors and Figeac, but you'll need your own **transport** to explore the rest of the area. If you've got the energy to tackle some of these hills, you can always rent a bike in St-Céré (see p.259).

The Town

Arriving in St-Céré from the north the first things you see are the two powerful keeps of the Château de St-Laurent-les-Tours, once part of a fortress belonging to the viscounts of Turenne (see p.165). The town itself sits in the valley to the south-west where the old houses cluster round place du Mercadial and place de l'Église. These two squares lie north and south respectively of rue de la République, the main shopping street cutting through the old centre which, at its southeast end, comes out into **place de la République**. This big, open square is where you'll find car parks, cafés and the town's main tourist facilities.

St-Céré owes its existence to the martyrdom of **Ste Spérie** in 780. Born the daughter of the then lord of St-Laurent, Sérenus, Spérie pledged her life to God at an early age, and when later she refused to marry a local nobleman, she was beheaded by her brother and buried on the riverbank. Later a chapel was erected on the spot around which the town began to develop in the tenth century. It lay initially under the jurisdiction of the counts of Auvergne, but was transferred to the Turenne viscounts in 1178. They beefed up the fortress and, as usual, granted the town a certain degree of autonomy. Its heyday didn't arrive, however, until after the fifteenth century when St-Céré's wealthy merchants began investing in the noble houses which can still be seen today.

The best of these lie in the streets to the north of rue de la République, notably around **place du Mercadial**, which, with its fountain and cobbles, is particularly appealing; to find it, walk one block north from rue de la République and turn left along rue du Mazel. You come out opposite the town's most eye-catching building, the **Maison des Consuls**, where the administrative council used to meet – it now hosts various free art exhibitions in summer. Beneath a steeply pitched tile roof, the building's most striking feature is the slightly overhanging upper storey of neatly layered brick in a timber frame. The same design is echoed in the **Maison Arnoud**, on the north side of the square, whose ground floor is a mere three metres wide. Rue St-Cyr, the lane to the right of this house, takes you east and then south past several elegant Renaissance buildings and into a recently ren-ovated area of courtyards and alleys. Where rue St-Cyr eventually joins rue du Mazel, look out on the right for a particularly fine fifteenth-century residence with two round towers and a pair of escutcheons above the doorway.

There's less of interest on the south side of rue de la République, though the **church of Ste-Spérie**, largely rebuilt after the Wars of Religion, is worth a quick peek for its eighteenth-century altarpiece with a statue of Ste Spérie standing on the left. It was carved by a local monk who received 240 *livres* and, for some rea-son, four handkerchiefs for his pains.

St-Céré is rather prouder of another, more recent local artist, **Jean Lurçat** (1892–1966), who first came to the Lot to join the Resistance in 1941, then decid-ed to settle in Château St-Laurent after the war. His wide-ranging talents took in sketching, painting, engraving and pottery, but he is best known for his big, bold tapestries, of which the most famous is the eighty-metre-long *Le Chant du Monde* (The Song of the World), which portrays the vagaries of human existence and our inherent power for both good and evil. The tapestry is now on display in Angers, but you can get an idea of Lurçat's distinctive style – typically incorporating ani-mals and birds, both real and fantastic, against dark blue or black backgrounds – by visiting the **Galerie d'Art Casino**, avenue Jean-Mouliérat (July–Sept daily

9.30am–noon & 2–6.30pm; rest of year Mon, Tues & Wed–Sat same hours; free), a hundred metres northeast of the old town; from place de la République walk north on boulevard Lurçat a short distance before turning right down avenue Jean-Mouliérat. Built as a casino in 1938 but never used, the gallery keeps at least thirteen Lurçat tapestries on permanent display.

You can see more of his work in his former studio in the **Château de St-Laurent-les-Tours** a kilometre or so above St-Céré – take avenue du Docteur-Roux heading northeast past the hospital and then follow the signs winding uphill. Of the Turenne fortress only the ramparts and two square towers remain, the smaller one dating from the late twelfth century and the taller, eastern tower from the 1300s. The rest of the castle was destroyed during the Wars of Religion, but around 1895 the then owner built himself a neo-Gothic mansion between the two towers. It is this building in which Jean Lurçat set up his studio in 1945 and which is now the **Atelier-Musée Jean Lurçat** (mid-July to Sept daily 9.30am–noon & 2.30–6.30pm; also two weeks at Easter same hours; ☎05.65.38.28.21; 15F/€2.29). Alongside his sketches and illustrations, a slide show of *Le Chant du Monde* and a short biographical film, the museum's most interesting feature is the artist's unmistakable paintings covering the ceilings and doors.

Practicalities

The nearest **gare SNCF** to St-Céré is Bretenoux-Biars (see p.255), a good 10km to the north, from where there are three **buses** a day (Mon–Sat; Chauvac; ☎05.65.38.08.28) on to St-Céré. You can also reach St-Céré by bus from Cahors via Gramat (also operated by Chauvac), and from Figeac (Cars Delbos; ☎05.65.38.24.19). All these services terminate on place de la République, on the north side of which you'll find the **tourist office** (June & Sept Mon–Sat 9am–noon & 2–7pm; July & Aug Mon–Sat 9am–noon & 2.30–7pm, Sun 10am–12.30pm; Oct–May Mon–Sat 10am–noon & 2–6pm; ☎05.65.38.11.85, fax 05.65.38.38.71, *www.quercy.net/quercy/saint-cere*). The office stocks English-language leaflets outlining a walking tour of the old centre and details of events in the area, of which the most important is the summer music festival (see p.238). For exploring the countryside around St-Céré, you can rent **bikes** from Peugeot Cycles, 45 rue Faidherbe (☎05.65.38.03.23), to the west of place de la République.

There are a couple of decent **hotels**, as well. You'll get a warm welcome at the Irish/French-run *Hôtel Victor Hugo*, 7 av des Maquis (☎05.65.38.16.15, fax 05.65.38.39.91, *www.hotel-victor-hugo.fr*; ③; closed 2 weeks in March & 3 weeks in Oct), beside the old bridge in the southeast corner of place de la République. Although most rooms lack windows, they are all en suite and have been decorated with flair by the chef, who also puts his artistic talents to good use in the restaurant (closed Mon & Oct–March also Sun eve; menus 60–200F/€9.15–30.49). The other option is the modern, more upmarket *Hôtel de France*, 181 av François-de-Maynard (☎05.65.38.02.16, fax 05.65.38.02.98; ④; closed Nov–Easter), east off place de la République, with well-priced en-suite rooms, a pool and a flowery garden where you can eat out under a huge chestnut tree (closed lunch; menu at 130F/€19.82). For campers, there's the three-star *Le Soulhol* **campsite** (☎05.65.38.12.37, fax 05.65.10.61.75; closed Nov–March) beside the river a short walk east of the *Hôtel Victor-Hugo*.

The *Victor-Hugo* is by far the best place to **eat** in St-Céré. Otherwise, there are cafés and brasseries around place de la République, or you could treat yourself to a meal at the Michelin-starred *Les Trois Soleils*, near the Château de Montal (see below). For picnic fodder, there's a small **market** on Saturday mornings on place du Mercadial and a much larger affair spreading throughout the old town on the first and third Wednesdays of the month.

Château de Montal

Two kilometres west of St-Céré, the **Château de Montal** (30min guided tours: April–Sept daily except Sat 9.30am–noon & 2.30–6pm; 30F/€4.57) is a superb example of French Renaissance architecture. Its interesting history started in 1523 when Jeanne Balzac d'Entraygues, the widow of Amaury de Montal, started transforming the medieval fortress into a Renaissance palace, as was currently all the rage. But then came news that her eldest son, Robert, had been killed in Italy and poor Jeanne lost the heart to continue. Nevertheless the de Montal family continued to own the château up to the Revolution, after which it was bought by a certain Monsieur Macaire who gradually sold off the chimney pieces, sculptures and even the carved window surrounds. Rescue was at hand, however, in the form of Maurice Fenaille, a rich industrialist and patron of the arts, who bought the château in 1908 and began to restore it to its former glory. In just five years he managed to track down nearly everything that had been sold, including some of the original wall-coverings, and also filled the rooms with a fine collection of Renaissance and Louis XIII furnishings, before giving the whole caboodle to the State in 1913. Later, during World War II Montal was chosen as a hiding place for thousands of paintings from the Louvre, including the *Mona Lisa*, which were moved from Paris for safekeeping.

As you approach, the rear of the château still exudes a thoroughly medieval air with its small windows, steep *lauze* roof and pepper-pot towers, but turn the corner into the **inner courtyard** and you're immediately transported to sunny Italy. The lovely pale stone of the two facades is worked into delicate carvings, including a frieze of mermaid-like sibyls and, above, busts representing three generations of the de Montal family: Jeanne is flanked by her husband and son Robert on the west wing, while her parents take pride of place over the front door.

The craftsmen went to work inside, too, on a magnificent **staircase** made from the same local limestone. As you climb up, notice the carving on the panels above, each bearing a different design, which gets finer and more elaborate towards the top. The rest of the interior can't quite compare, but there are some massive old oak tables, a good, homely kitchen and an excellent collection of tapestries, including a rare example featuring a pastoral scene with descriptive boxes of text, like an early cartoon.

As long as you make sure to book, you can combine a visit to Montal with a meal at *Les Trois Soleils* (☎05.65.10.16.16; closed Nov & Jan; Oct–March closed Sun eve to Tues midday inclusive), a one-star Michelin **restaurant** immediately west of the château surrounded by immaculate gardens. Their 150F/€22.87 menu is a bargain for such a perfect setting, and for dishes which see the best of the region's cuisine given a creative twist. Alternatively, you can eat in their grill, *Les Près de Montal* (same phone number), where menus start at 115F/€17.53 (closed mid-Oct to mid-March).

Grottes de Presque

About three kilometres southwest along the D673 from the Château de Montal the road cuts through a hillside as it climbs up on to the *causse*. When they were digging this road in 1825, engineers discovered the entrance to the **Grottes de Presque** (40min guided tours daily: mid-Feb to June & Sept 9am–noon & 2–6pm; July & Aug 9am–7pm; Oct to mid-Nov 10am–noon & 2–5pm; *www.grottesdepresque.com*; 33F/€5.03). The cave system is not only unusually accessible, with few stairs, but it also contains a marvellous variety of stalactites and stalagmites, some up to 10m high, as well as columns, semi-translucent curtains and glistening crystalline cascades. The other notable feature is the amount of colour, from pure white to grey, yellow and deep orange. This is the result of rainwater picking up iron, manganese and other minerals as it percolates through the 90m of rock above, minerals which are then deposited along with the calcite drip by drip inside the cave.

Autoire and Loubressac

Further west along the same line of hills, the River Autoire has carved an impressive canyon, the **Cirque d'Autoire**, into the limestone plateau; to get here from the Grottes de Presque, follow the D673 southwest for another 4km and then turn right on the D38. This brings you in above the cirque – for the best views, walk west from the car park for about five minutes, following the footpath across a bridge and up onto the opposite hillside. In the valley bottom, some two kilometres below you, lies the hugely pretty little village of **AUTOIRE** where the ochre-hued houses, including several rather grand piles built by nobles from St-Céré in the fifteenth and sixteenth centuries, snuggle round a very plain, solid Romanesque church.

The village also boasts a good **hotel** and pit stop in the form of the *Auberge de la Fontaine* (☎05.65.10.85.40, fax 05.65.10.12.70, *www.logis-de-france.fr*; ③; closed Jan, also Sun eve & Mon except in July & Aug) on the main street opposite the church, a simple country inn offering basic but well-kept rooms and family cooking washed down with local Côtes de Glanes wines (menus from 65F/€9.91). In season there's also *La Cascade* across the road, serving *crêpes*, salads and regional dishes in a cheerful stone-walled room or on a terrace with views up to the cirque (closed Oct–March, also Tues except in July & Aug; menus from around 70F/€10.67).

It's only 8km back to St-Céré from Autoire, but it's worth taking a short diversion 6km northwest along the D135, little more than a country lane, to **LOUBRESSAC**. The narrow lanes of this fortified hilltop village are full of flowers and typical Quercy houses. You can't visit the château standing on the cliff edge, but there are grand views to be had from the look-out point immediately to the east of the village, taking in the whole sweep of the Dordogne, Bave and Cère valleys across to St-Céré and the châteaux of Castelnau and Montal.

In season a helpful **tourist office** (April, May, Sept & Oct Tues–Sat 2–6pm; June Mon–Sat daily 10am–12.30pm & 2.30–6.30pm; July & Aug Mon–Sat 9.30am–12.30pm & 2.30–6.30pm; ☎05.65.10.82.18) opens up just outside Loubressac's southern gateway. There are also a couple of decent **hotels**. The simpler of the two is the *Lou Cantou* (☎05.65.38.20.58, fax 05.65.38.25.37, *www.logis-de-france.fr*; ③; closed late Oct for 3 weeks, Christmas hols, also Mon & Sun eve Oct–March) on the southwest side of the village, with good views from its front rooms and the picture windows of its restaurant (menus from 70F/€10.67). Moving up a few notches, the modern *Relais de Castelnau* (☎05.65.10.80.90, fax 05.65.38.22.02; ④; closed Nov–March, also Sun eve & Mon Oct–April) sits just outside the village on the main road west to Padirac. Apart from more splendid views, it also boasts a pool and a highly rated restaurant (menus from 90F/€13.72). There's also a very pleasant little three-star **campsite**, *La Garrigue* (☎ & fax 05.65.38.34.88; closed Oct–March), with a pool and restaurant among fields a couple of hundred metres south of the village.

travel details

By bus

Carennac to: Brive (school term Mon & Sat 1 daily; 1hr); Gramat (Wed & Fri 1 daily; 25min); St-Céré (school term Mon–Fri 1–2 daily, rest of year Mon & Wed 1 daily; 20min).

Beaulieu-sur-Dordogne to: Argentat (July & Aug Mon–Sat 3 daily; 40min); Brive (school term Mon–Sat 1–3 daily, July & Aug Mon–Sat 1–2 daily, rest of year Tues, Thurs & Sat 1 daily; 1hr).

Bretenoux-Biars to: Bretenoux (Mon–Sat 3 daily; 5min); St-Céré (Mon–Sat 3 daily; 15min).

Martel to: Brive (1 weekly; 55min); St-Denis-Près-Martel (Mon–Sat 2–3 daily; 15min); Souillac (Mon–Sat 2 daily; 45min).

St-Céré to: Bretenoux (Mon–Sat 3 daily; 10min); Bretenoux-Biars (Mon–Sat 3 daily; 15min); Cahors (Mon, Fri & Sat 1 daily; 1hr 45min); Carennac (school term Mon–Fri 1 daily, rest of year Wed & Fri 1 daily; 20min); Figeac (school term 1 weekly; 1hr 30min); Gramat (school term Mon–Sat 1–2 daily, rest of year Mon, Fri & Sat 1 daily; 30–55min).

Souillac to: Amsterdam (2–4 weekly; 18hr 30min); Brive (school term Mon–Sat 1–2 daily, rest of year Tues–Sat 1–2 daily; 50min–1hr 15min); Brussels (2–4 weekly; 15hr); London (2–3 weekly; 15hr); Martel (Mon–Sat 2–3 daily; 20–25min); St-Denis-Près-Martel (Mon–Sat 2–3 daily; 35–40min); Sarlat (3–6 daily; 50min–1hr).

By train

Bretenoux-Biars to: Brive (4–5 daily; 40–50min); St-Denis-Près-Martel (4–5 daily; 20min); Vayrac (1–2 daily; 15min).

St-Denis-Près-Martel to: Brive (4–6 daily; 20–30min); Figeac (5–6 daily; 1hr); Gramat (5–6 daily; 20–35min); Rocamadour-Padirac (5–6 daily; 15–20min); Paris (1–2 daily; 5hr); Vayrac (2 daily; 5min).

Souillac to: Brive (7–9 daily; 25min); Cahors (7–9 daily; 40–45min); Gourdon (7–9 daily; 15min); Montauban (6–8 daily; 1hr 20min); Paris (4–5 daily; 4hr 40min); Toulouse (6–8 daily; 1hr 50min).

CHAPTER SIX

THE LOT VALLEY AND AROUND

L ike the Dordogne, the **River Lot** rises in the foothills of the Massif Central and is dammed in its upper reaches to form huge reservoirs. It begins to get more interesting, however, where it enters the Lot *département*, the boundaries of which roughly coincide with the old province of **Quercy**. Here the river has carved a wide gorge as it meanders back and forth in great lazy loops. In the east the land on either side is high and dry, part of the limestone plateau that extends north to the Dordogne and south almost to the Aveyron. Following the river westwards, the surrounding country suddenly becomes wooded and then gradually opens out into rolling farmland before the hills die out altogether where the Lot draws near to the Garonne.

The largest town in the Lot valley, and the capital of the *département*, is **Cahors**. It may lack the higgledy-piggledy charm of Sarlat or Bergerac, but compensates for this with a pleasingly workaday atmosphere and a wonderful location in the middle of a meander. It also boasts the best example of a fortified medieval bridge left in France, the **Pont Valentré**, while the country round about produces an extremely distinctive dark, almost peppery red **wine**.

The Lot valley is at its most picturesque upstream from Cahors. The scenery may not be as dramatic as the middle reaches of the Dordogne, but the cliffs here rise to considerable heights and host their fair share of perched fortresses and feudal villages. Foremost among these is **St-Cirq-Lapopie**, one of the most spectacular sights along the valley, while the nearby **Grotte de Pech-Merle** draws almost as many visitors with its glittering rock formations and prehistoric cave art. Pech-Merle lies in the hills above the wild and pretty **Célé valley**, which leads northeast to **Figeac**, the Lot's second largest town. Figeac is a captivating place, just big enough to swallow the tourists who come to admire its web of medieval lanes, but not so big as to lose its intimacy. The town is also home to a rewarding

---

ACCOMMODATION PRICE CODES

All the hotels and *chambres d'hôtes* listed in this book have been price-coded according to the following scale. The prices quoted are for the **cheapest available double room in high season**, although remember that many of the cheap places will have more expensive rooms with en-suite facilities.

① Under 160F/€24
② 160–220F/€24–34
③ 220–300F/€34–46
④ 300–400F/€46–61
⑤ 400–500F/€61–76
⑥ 500–600F/€76–91
⑦ 600–700F/€91–107
⑧ 700–800F/€107–122
⑨ Over 800F/€122

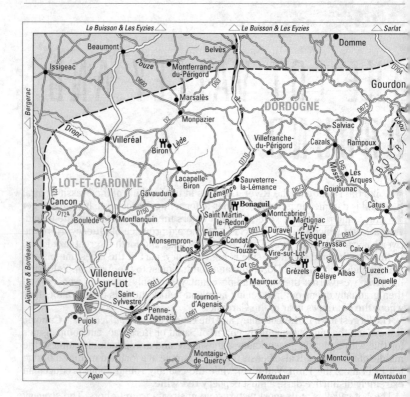

museum devoted to Jean-François Champollion, the man who cracked the hiero-glyphic code in the early nineteenth century.

North and west of Figeac stretches the **Causse de Gramat**, the biggest and wildest of the region's limestone *causses*. With its huge vistas, it makes a welcome change from the confining valleys and a great place for walking or cycling, though it has few notable sights beyond the village of **Assier**, in the far southeast, with its extraordinary church. On its western edge the Causse de Gramat suddenly gives way to a lovely area of gentle wooded hills known as the **Bouriane**. Again, there are no must-see sights, though its capital, **Gourdon**, a once-prosperous town built of butter-coloured stone, makes an engaging place to stay, and the nearby **Grottes de Cougnac**, with a smattering of prehistoric cave paintings and some exceptionally delicate limestone concretions, repay a visit.

Returning to the Lot valley, the river south of Cahors wriggles its way west-wards through vineyards and past ancient towns and villages. By far the most striking of these is **Puy-l'Évêque**. An outpost of the bishops of Cahors, the town's medieval and Renaissance houses jostle for space on a steep incline, reaching upwards like trees for light, though none is equal to the bishop's thirteen-cen-tury keep towering above. An even more dramatic sight lies in store in the country northwest of Puy-l'Évêque where the **Château de Bonaguil** is an

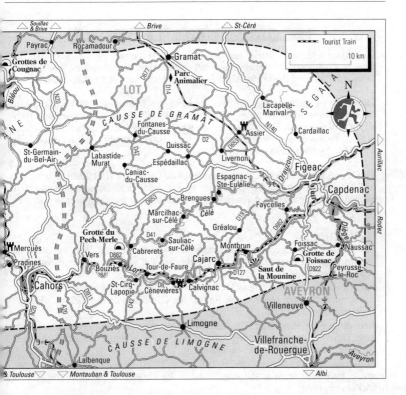

outstanding example of late-fifteenth-century military architecture, its great bulk silhouetted against the wooded hillside.

Further downstream things begin to quieten down again as the valley flattens out towards **Villeneuve-sur-Lot**. Despite unattractive modern suburbs, Villeneuve holds a certain allure thanks to the river sliding through its old centre built of stone and warm, red brick, and to its decent supply of hotels and restaurants. Villeneuve – as its name indicates – was also one of the many "new towns", or *bastides*, founded in this area in the thirteenth and fourteenth centuries. The best examples of *bastide* architecture are to be found in the hills to the north, where the villages of **Monflanquin** and **Monpazier** seem hardly to have changed since the Middle Ages. The same can't be said for the much-altered **Château de Biron**, lying between the two, but its superb hilltop location makes it hard to resist.

Travelling by **public transport** is made relatively easy by two **bus services** running along the Lot valley from Cahors east to Figeac and west to Fumel, from where there's a connecting service downstream to Villeneuve. Other buses head north from Cahors and Figeac to Gourdon and Gramat, though these towns are also served by trains on the Toulouse–Brive and Figeac–Brive main lines. If you're planning to use the buses a lot, you'll need the departmental timetables for the Lot and Lot-et-Garonne, available at larger tourist offices; otherwise contact

FESTIVALS, EVENTS AND MARKETS

Late March to early April Cahors: Le Chaînon Manquant (☎05.65.22.62.62). Six days of contemporary performance art introducing up-and-coming talent from France and around the world. Mix of street performances and ticket events.

Late May or early June Puy-l'Évêque: Les Fêtes Médiévales (☎05.65.30.81.45). Over the weekend of Pentecôte (Whit Sunday) Puy-l'Évêque lets its hair down with all sorts of merry medieval japes: music, dance, games and a full-on medieval banquet (tickets required) on the Sunday night. Most events take place on place de la Truffière, by the tourist office.

Late June to early July Cahors: Printemps de Cahors (☎01.41.12.80.50 or 05.65. 53.94.75, *www.printempsdecahors.com*). Wide-ranging and highly recommended festival of photography and visual arts held throughout the town over two weeks; no entry charge.

JULY & AUGUST
Early July Cazals: Encontre Chorégraphique (☎05.65.22.86.41). Well-regarded festival of contemporary dance over three days in the streets (free) and Salle des Fêtes (tickets required).
July Gourdon: Les Rencontres Estivales (☎05.65.41.20.06). A handful of classical music concerts take place in the Église des Cordeliers or the Église St-Pierre. Tickets required.
July & August Monpazier. Throughout the summer season Monpazier stages a huge variety of events, including outdoor theatre and cinema, books and antiques fairs, concerts and crafts demonstrations.
Mid-July Cahors: Blues Festival (☎05.65.35.22.29). French and international artists bare their souls in the streets and in the Théâtre de Verdure, rue Wilson (tickets required).

the transport information desk of the relevant Conseil Général (Lot ☎05.65.53.27.50; Lot-et-Garonne ☎05.53.69.42.03).

You'll need your own transport, however, for exploring the Célé valley, the Bouriane and other places off the beaten track. Look out for the Promenades et Randonnées **walking guides** detailing footpaths throughout the Lot *département*, on sale in bookshops and tourist offices (37F/€5.64). Another, more leisurely possibility is to rent a **houseboat** and pootle along the Lot (see box on p.268).

Cahors

CAHORS, a sunny southern backwater built in a tight meander of the River Lot, was the chief town of the old province of Quercy and is now the modern capital of the Lot *département*. Its somewhat troubled history has left a warren of dark medieval lanes, a rather knocked about cathedral and impressive fortifications, among them Cahors' famous landmark, the turreted **Pont Valentré**. Another reason to come here is to sample the local **wines**, heady and black but dry to the taste, which have undergone a revival in recent years (see box on p.270).

Second two weeks in July Monflanquin: Musique en Guyenne (☎01.48.73.27.90 or 05.53.36.31.12). Varied programme of classical, jazz and contemporary concerts held in the places des Arcades (free) and the church (tickets required), as well as other towns in the region.

First weekend in August Gourdon: Grande Fête Médiévale. Gourdon lets rip with two days of junketing complete with jugglers, fire-eaters, musicians and the works. Entry 20F/€3.05.

First weekend in August Assier: Jardins dans tous ses États. Jazz and theatre festival with events taking place in local gardens, the church and the château courtyard. Some free events.

Early August Puy-l'Évêque: Fête Votive. One of the area's most important local fêtes, lasting five days with a free dance every night, a funfair and a fireworks spectacular with music on the Sunday.

Early to mid-August Lot *département*: L'Été Musical dans la Vallée du Lot (☎05.65.35.35.21, *www.atlantis-cf.fr/musica-lot/accueil*). Classical concerts (some free) at various locations including Cahors, Gourdon and Gramat.

Early to mid-August Château de Bonaguil: Festival du Théâtre (☎05.53.71.17.17). The inner court and moats make a spectacular venue for this festival of French theatre held over nine days. There's a play or other musical event every night (tickets required), as well as workshops, street theatre and lectures.

Mid-August Monflanquin: Journées Médiévales. Three days of mead, minstrels and merry japes as Monflanquin goes medieval. Jousting, banquets, siege engines, fireworks – you name it. You can even rent costumes.

MARKETS

The region's main **markets** take place at Cahors (Wed & Sat); Cajarc (Sat); Figeac (Sat); Duravel (Sat); Fumel (Tues, Fri & Sun); Gourdon (Tues & Sat); Gramat (Tues & Fri); Luzech (Wed); Monflanquin (Thurs); Monpazier (Thurs); Monsempron-Libos (Thurs); Puy L'Évêque (Tues); and Villeneuve-sur-Lot (Tues, Wed & Sat).

Some history

Both the names Quercy and Cahors derive from the area's first-known inhabitants, the local Gaulish tribe known as the **Cadurci**. During the first century BC they founded a settlement near a sacred spring, immediately across the river to the southwest of modern Cahors, which the Romans later called **Divona Cadurcorum**. Following successive Vandal and Frankish invasions after the fifth century, only a few fragments of Roman stonework remain, as well as the spring, which continues to supply Cahors' drinking water. It wasn't until the seventh century that the then Bishop, later Saint, Didier finally erected a wall to protect the nascent town and his rapidly growing cathedral.

The bishops of Cahors gradually spread their net until they not only ruled over a vast area extending down the Lot as far as Puy-l'Évêque but also controlled the all-important river trade. By the early thirteenth century Cahors was entering its **golden age** as powerful local merchants, known as Caorsins, together with Lombard bankers fleeing the Cathar Crusades, turned the town into Europe's chief banking centre. The more enthusiastic of these moneylenders earned such a reputation for usury that in his *Divine Comedy* (1321) Dante compared the town to Gomorrah when describing the structure of Hell. Nevertheless, the merchants

---

BOATING ON THE LOT

The **River Lot** is navigable to **houseboats** between St-Cirq-Lapopie and Luzech, a distance of some 65km. The boating season lasts from April 1 to November 15, at the latest, after which the current is too swift and the river too high to be safe. Four **companies** offer houseboat rental: Lot Navigation Nicols (Bouziès; ☎05.65.30. 24.41, fax 05.65.31.72.25, *www.nicols.com*); Babou Marine (Port St Mary, Cahors; ☎05.65.30.08.99, fax 05.65.23.92.59, *www.baboulene-jean.fr*); Locaboat Plaisance (Luzech; ☎05.65.30.71.11, fax 05.65.30.53.17, *www.locaboat.com*); and Crown Blue Line (Douelle; ☎05.65.20.08.79, fax 05.65.30.97.96, *www.crown-blueline.com*). Rates range from 5000F/€762 to 10,000F/€1525 per week for a four- to six-person boat depending on the season and level of comfort. The Lot can be a capricious river, and you are strongly advised to purchase a copy of *Carte Guide de Navigation Fluvial* (87.80F/€13.39), outlining the potential hazards, before setting off; it is available in local bookstores, from major tourist offices, or from the departmental tourist office (see p.27).

---

helped finance any number of noble town houses, two new bridges, various embellishments to the cathedral and further fortifications enclosing the peninsula to the north. When the local Bishop Jacques Duèze was named **Pope John XXII** in 1316, Cahors had reached its apogee. His greatest legacy was a university which remained one of the most important in France for the next four centuries.

By now, however, the English and French armies were at loggerheads. Cahors was never attacked during the Hundred Years' War, but the end result was the same: under the Treaty of Brétigny (1360) it succumbed reluctantly to **English occupation**. When French rule was eventually restored around 1440, the Cadurciens set about rebuilding their ravaged town, adding a few Italianate flourishes and developing a distinctive decorative style comprising carved or moulded rose blossoms, flaming suns and the so-called "*bâtons écotés*" (pruned branches), which is still in evidence today.

Unlike several of its neighbours, Cahors remained staunchly Catholic during the **Wars of Religion**. As a consequence it was sacked by the Protestant Henry of Navarre, the future King Henri IV of France, when he seized it after a brief battle in 1580. Later the same year, however, one of many peace treaties saw the town returned to the Catholic fold. By way of recompense, Henry later donated 6000 *livres*, half of which went towards restoring the cathedral.

Over the years Cahors gradually expanded to fill the entire peninsula, though it was not until the nineteenth century that Bishop Didier's ramparts were finally razed. They were replaced by a tree-lined boulevard which was later named after Cahors' most famous son, the politician **Léon Gambetta** (see box on p.274). Adorned with municipal buildings – the town hall, library, law courts and theatre – in Neoclassical style, it remains modern Cahors' principal thoroughfare.

Arrival, information and accommodation

The heart of present-day Cahors is place François-Mitterrand, a wide, open square towards the middle of the main boulevard Gambetta. East of here medieval houses cluster round the cathedral, while the post-seventeenth-century town spreads west towards the **gare SNCF**, 500m away along rue Joachim-Murat.

The station is also the terminus for some regional **buses**, while others – including Eurolines coaches from London, Brussels and Amsterdam – stop on place de Charles-de-Gaulle at the north end of the main boulevard.

Cahors' **tourist office** (July & Aug Mon–Fri 9am–12.30pm & 1.30–6.30pm, Sat to 6pm, Sun 10am–noon; rest of year closed Sun; ☎05.65.53.20.65, fax 05.65.53.20.74, *www.quercy-tourisme.com/cahors*) occupies a handsome building on the north side of place François-Mitterrand. It provides detailed walking maps of the town, with an English-language insert, and also organizes **guided tours** (July & Aug Mon–Sat;

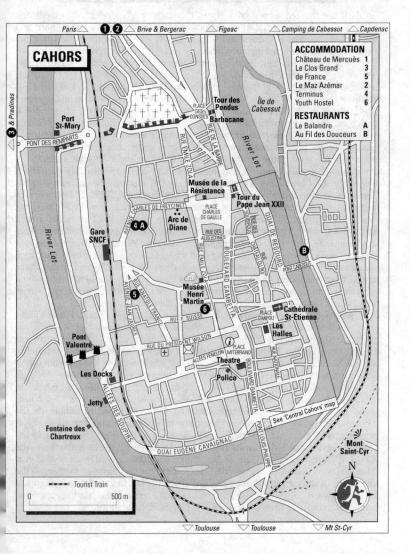

less frequent at other times; 35F/€5.34) covering either the cathedral or the medieval streets. The tours are generally conducted by bilingual guides.

Cahors boasts a broad range of **hotels**, though the choice, particularly in the middle price categories, is not particularly inspiring. Instead, there's better value for money to be had in the surrounding region, though you'll need your own transport to take advantage of it.

THE WINES AND VINEYARDS OF CAHORS

So dark are the red **wines of Cahors** that they're often referred to as "black wines". They are by far the most distinctive of the southwestern wines, hard and full-bodied with lots of tannin, and they generally need long ageing to bring out their best. The dominant **grape variety** is Auxerrois (also known as Malbec or Cot), which gives the wine its rich tannin content, its colour and its ability to age. The other thirty percent is made up of Merlot and Tanat – Merlot for roundness and aroma, Tanat to help the ageing process. They are planted on the clay-limestone terraces beside the Lot, on the south-facing slopes and even up on the *causse* itself, where the harsh conditions produce a correspondingly hard wine, but one which can improve dramatically with age. The distinctive bite of a young Cahors wine goes well with *charcuterie* and stews, while the more aromatic older wines usually accompany red meats, game and the local goats' cheese, *cabécou*.

As through most of the southwest it was the Romans who brought vines to the area, though it wasn't until the Middle Ages that Cahors wines really caught on. Pope John XXII (see p.268) kicked things off by introducing "Vieux Cahors" as his communion wine and table wine of choice. Then François I (1494–1547) ordered a vineyard of Auxerrois grapes to be planted at Fontainebleau, and Peter the Great (1672–1725) imported the wine to Russia, where it was adopted by the Greek Orthodox Church. However, the good times came to an abrupt end when phylloxera hit in 1877. The vines weren't replanted until after World War II, and then over a much smaller area. After struggling for a while, Cahors wines earned their *appellation* in 1971, and over the last decade have come back into fashion again. There are now approximately 42 square kilometres under vines in the *appellation*, which stretches from Cahors west along the Lot for 30km to Soturac, producing on average 240,000 hectolitres (roughly 32 million bottles) per annum.

Before **visiting the vineyards**, pick up a copy of the free *Livret du Vin de Cahors* giving details of the two hundred or so producers in the *appellation*; it's available from the tourist office and wine merchants in Cahors (see p.269 & p.278 respectively), or from the Maison du Vin de Cahors, 430 av Jean-Jaurès (Mon–Fri; ☎05.65.23.22.24), opposite the station; note that the Maison du Vin does not otherwise cater to individuals. (For general tips on vineyard visits see p.94.)

As an introduction to what's on offer, head for the imposing **Château Lagrézette** (daily: July & Aug 10am–7pm; rest of year 9am–12.30pm & 2–6.30pm; ☎05.65.20.07.42, *www.chateau-lagrezette.tm.fr*), 7km northwest of Cahors on the D12 midway between Douelle and Mercués. In addition to sampling their award-winning wines you get a tour of the magnificent, state-of-the-art *chais* dug into the hillside. Also worth a visit for its reliably good wines if not for its ambience is the **Côtes d'Olt** co-operative (July & Aug daily 9am–noon & 2–6.30pm; rest of year Mon–Fri 9am–noon & 2–6pm; ☎05.65.30.71.86) in the commune of Parnac, on the river's south bank about 17km west of Cahors on the D8. In general you can expect to pay between 50F/€7.62 and 100F/€15.24 for a very decent Cahors, although some of the region's prestige wines fetch 150F/€22.87 or more.

Hotels in town

A l'Escargot, 5 bd Gambetta (☎05.65.35.07.66, fax 05.65.53.92.38). This small hotel-restaurant at the north end of boulevard Gambetta offers the best value for money in Cahors; make sure you book well ahead in season. The rooms are small and simple but absolutely spotless, all with sparkling en-suite bathrooms. The restaurant offers simple menus from 62F/€9.45. Closed Sun eve & Mon except in July & Aug. ③.

de France, 252 av Jean-Jaurès (☎05.65.35.16.76, fax 05.65.22.01.08). A large hotel in a modern block near the train station offering en-suite facilities, satellite TV and phone as standard. Cheaper rooms are boxy and the furnishings bland, though the newly renovated bathrooms are a welcome improvement. Closed 15 days over Christmas and New Year. ③.

de la Paix, place de la Halle (☎05.65.35.03.40, fax 05.65.35.40.88). Apart from the hostel (see below) this is by far the cheapest option in town. Facilities are old and very basic – with a shared shower at lower rates – but clean enough, and you couldn't be more central, right on the market square. They serve simple food, with a three-course menu at 68F/€10.37 (restaurant closed Sun). Closed 15 days over Christmas and New Year. ②.

Terminus, 5 av Charles-de-Freycinet (☎05.65.53.32.00, fax 05.65.53.32.26). Cahors' most opulent hotel occupies a nineteenth-century bourgeois residence near the station. Though extensively renovated, a few original features remain, such as big, tiled bathrooms with luxurious tubs in some rooms, while all boast the modern comforts of double-glazing, air-conditioning and satellite TV. The hotel is equally well known for its superb restaurant, *Le Balandre* (see p.276). ⑥.

Hotels outside town

Château de Mercuès, Mercuès (☎05.65.20.00.01, fax 05.65.20.05.72, *mercues@ relaischateaux.fr*). High on its promontory 6km to the northwest of Cahors, for centuries this was the humble residence of the bishops of Cahors. It is now a luxury hotel with pool, tennis courts, excellent wine cellars (tastings available July & Aug; free) and a 1-star Michelin restaurant (closed Tues lunch & Mon except in July & Aug; menus from 200F/€30.49). Closed Oct–Easter. ⑨.

Le Clos Grand, 12 rue des Claux Grands, Labéraudie, Pradines (☎05.65.35.04.39, fax 05.65.22.56.69, *www.logis-de-france.fr*). In Pradines, a suburb 5km northwest of Cahors, this welcoming hotel looks out over fields and has a pleasant, shady garden. Most rooms occupy a purpose-built annexe beside the pool, each with a little terrace or balcony and en-suite bathroom. Locals come here for the good-value cooking (menus 66–170F/€10.06–25.92). ③.

Le Maz Azémar, rue du Mas de Vinssou, Mercuès (☎05.65.30.96.85, fax 05.65.30.53.82). A welcoming and characterful *chambres d'hôtes* on the western outskirts of Mercuès village; follow signs down the D145 Luzech road. All rooms are different, but with plenty of exposed beams and stone walls and views over the flowery garden, complete with heated pool, and vineyards beyond. Evening meals available on request (from 150F/€22.87 including wine). ④.

Hostel and campsite

Camping Rivière de Cabessut, rue de la Rivière (☎05.65.30.06.30, fax 05.65.23.99.46). Three-star campsite in a quiet spot beside the river just over 1km from Cahors across Pont de Cabessut. Facilities include a shop, snack bar, small pool and canoe rental. Closed Nov–March.

Youth hostel, 20 rue Frédéric-Suisse (☎05.65.35.64.71, fax 05.65.35.95.92). One of the more centrally placed youth hostels, occupying part of a former convent, with rows of bunk beds in large, spartan dormitories. Breakfast (20F/€3.05) and other meals available, or there's a small self-catering kitchen, as well as a laundry and TV room. No curfew. HI membership required. 55F/€8.38 per person per night.

The Town

Compact and easily walkable, Cahors is surrounded on three sides by the River Lot and protected to the north by a series of fourteenth-century fortifications. Most of interest lies within the cramped confines of the medieval streets on the peninsula's eastern edge, focused around the twin domes of the **Cathédrale St-Étienne**. From here, **rue Nationale** leads south past the former homes of wealthy merchants to the flood-prone artisans' quarter, while north of the cathedral the land continues to slope gently upwards along **rue du Château-du-Roi**, where bankers and aristocrats once lived, towards the old town gate with its guardhouse and tower. Of medieval Cahors' three fortified bridges, only westerly **Pont Valentré** remains – one of the finest surviving bridges of its time. More recent history is commemorated in a couple of passably interesting **museums** and, on a fine day, there are good views to be had from the summit of **Mont St-Cyr**, which overlooks the town from the southeast.

The cathedral and around

The oldest and simplest in plan of the Périgord-style Romanesque churches, the **Cathédrale St-Étienne** dates largely from the early twelfth century, when Bishop Didier's original cathedral was rebuilt in part to house the relic of the Holy Coif. According to local legend, this cloth, said to have covered Christ's head in the tomb, was brought back from the Holy Land around this time by Bishop Géraud de Cardaillac. From the thirteenth century on, various modifications took place. First the choir was rebuilt in Gothic style and the massive west facade added to form the church's main entrance in place of the original, north door. Then the cloister was reconstructed in the late 1400s, after which there was a pause until the nineteenth century when extensive restoration work on the whole edifice was carried out by Paul Abadie among others (see p.139).

As a result of so many accretions, the cathedral's exterior is not exciting, with the notable exception of the elaborately decorated portal above the **north door**. Carved around 1140, it depicts Christ's Ascension. He dominates the tympanum, surrounded by the Apostles and angels falling back in ecstasy, while cherubim fly out of the clouds to relieve him of his halo. Side panels show scenes from the life of St Stephen (St Étienne), the first Christian martyr who was stoned to death around 35AD, while the outer arch portrays people being stabbed and hacked with axes.

Inside, the cathedral is much like Périgueux's St-Étienne (see p.141), with a nave lacking aisles and transepts, roofed with two monumental domes. The extensive murals round the apse – depicting, for example, St Stephen's martyrdom and the Adoration of the Magi – suffered from rather heavy-handed, nineteenth-century restoration work. The fourteenth-century frescoes high in the west dome are, however, original – they again depict the stoning of St Stephen, encircled by eight giant prophets. In 1988 further paintings from the same era were discovered behind layers of plaster just inside and above the west door. They consist of faded but beautiful Creation scenes including Adam and Eve in the Garden of Eden and many finely observed birds and animals.

To the right of the choir, the aptly named Deep Chapel bears earlier scars from the Wars of Religion when Protestant armies hacked away at its carvings. They also caused irreparable damage to the **cloister**, accessed by a door next to the Deep Chapel, though the Flamboyant Gothic colonnades still retain some intricate craftsmanship. The best example occupies a niche on the northwest corner pillar where the Virgin is portrayed as a graceful girl with broad brow and ringlets to her waist. The door surrounds are also beautifully carved, if rather battered; that on the northeast wall leads into **St-Gausbert's Chapel** (July & Aug Mon–Sat 10am–12.30pm & 3–6pm; variable opening hours out of season – contact the tourist office for the current schedule; 15F/€2.29), which holds the Holy Coif – a decidedly unimpressive, rather grubby looking piece of padded cloth – among chalices, gilded statues and other treasures. The unusually complicated vaulted ceiling and the mural adorning the chapel's west wall are of far greater interest. The latter portrays the Last Judgement, with the dead rising from their tombs as a dashing St Michael weighs their souls – despite the best efforts of a little devil trying to tip the balance in his favour.

The square on which the cathedral stands, **place Jean-Jacques-Chapou**, commemorates a local Resistance leader killed in a German ambush in July 1944. On its west side, look for a sign above what is now a

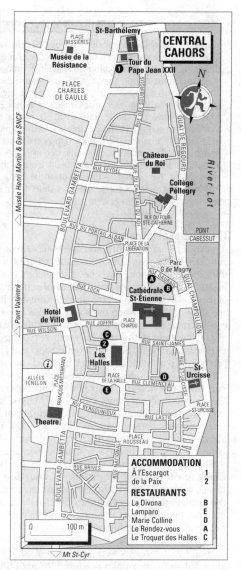

bank announcing *Bazar Gênois: Gambetta Jeune et Cie.* This is where **Léon Gambetta**, the son of an Italian grocer, spent his childhood (see box overleaf). At its southern end the square extends into place Galdemar, popularly known as place de la Halle. The covered **market hall** at its centre, built as a corn exchange in 1865, provides the focus for Cahors' lively markets (see p.277).

LÉON GAMBETTA

Heralded as the "father of the Republic", **Léon Gambetta** was born in Cahors in 1838. After graduating as a lawyer, he specialized in defending republican sympathizers accused of political crimes against Emperor Napoléon III. A charismatic man and great orator, the republicans soon rallied around Gambetta and, when Napoléon was forced to surrender to an invading Prussian army in 1870, he was among those who quickly proclaimed the **Third Republic**, the regime which continued to govern France until 1940. It had a rocky start, however. With the Prussians besieging Paris, Gambetta fled the capital by balloon to organize the war effort in the provinces. While he opposed the armistice signed in 1871, Gambetta and his band of moderate republicans, or "Opportunists", were able to keep the Republic afloat despite constant attacks from both the monarchist majority and the radical Left. He served as President of the National Assembly from 1879 to 1882, but later that year his career was cut short when he accidentally shot himself with a revolver and died soon after.

The medieval streets

A warren of narrow lanes and alleys fills the area between boulevard Gambetta and the eastern riverbank, where the majority of houses, turreted and built of flat, thin, southern brick, have been handsomely restored during recent decades. From the market square, **rue Nationale** cuts almost due south through the heart of medieval Cahors to where the old Roman bridge once stood – the foundations are still just visible when the water level is low. On the way it passes a number of eye-catching merchants' houses and some pleasing half-timbered frontages on place Rousseau. Other roads worth exploring in the area are canyon-like rue Bergougnioux and its easterly extension rue Lastié, which comes out among a pretty group of brick and timber buildings around place St-Urcisse.

One of Cahors' most attractive corners lies just north of the cathedral along **rue Daurade** where a lovely row of buildings overlooks a little park named after the sixteenth-century poet Olivier de Magny, who lived at no. 12. His house is overshadowed, though, by the thirteenth-century **Maison du Bourreau**, the "executioner's house", with its big arched openings and line of double windows above. The name dates from the Revolution, when the public executioner lived here; naturally, the house is said to be haunted.

Continuing north along rue Daurade you reach the southern end of **rue Château-du-Roi** and its extension, **rue des Soubirous**. This is the "upper town", where the houses become distinctly grander. One of the most imposing is the fourteenth-century **Château du Roi** itself, built by cousins of Pope John XXII but later taken over by the king's emissary when the bishops lost their stranglehold on Cahors in the fifteenth century. Its massive, featureless walls now contain the local prison.

Wealthy Cadurciens were very fond of adding turrets to their homes and there are a number of examples scattered through the Soubirous quarter. To see them properly it's best to head down to the river – rue du Four-Ste-Catherine provides the most interesting route – to a vantage point across Pont de Cabessut. Cahors' skyline stretches in front of you from the cathedral domes in the south via Collège Pélegry, with its crenellated hexagonal turret, and the square, solid tower of the Château du Roi. In the far distance the **Tour du Pape Jean XXII** and the **Tour**

des Pendus pinpoint Cahors' northern ramparts, which still stretch partway across the peninsula.

The museums

Back in the centre, Cahors' two museums deserve a brief stop. The first, in a small building on the north side of place Charles-de-Gaulle, is the **Musée de la Résistance** (daily 2–6pm; free), which documents very thoroughly the history of the local Resistance movement against the broader context of German occupation, deportations and finally, Liberation in 1945. The most interesting section, on the ground floor, deals with local history, where you can read about Jean-Jacques Chapou, after whom the cathedral square is named (see p.273), and about the *Mona Lisa*'s sojourn in the area (see p.333).

Continuing south down rue Émile-Zola, you come to the **Musée Henri Martin** at no. 792 (March–Nov daily except Tues 10am–1pm & 2–6pm; times vary during temporary exhibitions; ☎05.65.30.15.13; 20F/€3.05), in the seventeenth-century former Episcopal palace. Exhibits range from Gallo-Roman pots to works by nineteenth- and twentieth-century artists such as Dufy, Vlaminck and Utrillo. However, pride of place goes to seventeen oil paintings by local artist Henri Martin (1860–1943), whose mix of Impressionism and Pointillism evokes perfectly the lazy sun-filled landscapes of this part of France, and an important collection dedicated to Léon Gambetta. With over 2000 documents, photographs, sculptures and paintings, only a fraction is on show at any one time. The displays are predictably worthy, although the caricatures help liven things up a bit.

Pont Valentré

The reason most people venture to Cahors is to see the dramatic **Pont Valentré**, which guards the western river crossing. Its three powerful towers, originally closed by portcullises and gates, made it an independent fortress, which was so imposing, in fact, that the bridge was never attacked. Building it was a problem, however. Work started in 1308, but the bridge was not completed for another seventy years. According to legend, the Devil was to blame – at least in part. The story goes that the architect, exasperated at the slow progress, sold his soul in exchange for the Devil's assistance. As the bridge was nearing completion, he tried to wriggle out of the deal by giving the Devil a sieve with which to carry water for the masons. The Devil took revenge by creeping up the central tower every night to remove the last stone, thus ensuring that the bridge would never be finished. If you look carefully at the top of the tower's east face, you'll see a little devil which was added when Pont Valentré was renovated in 1879.

Mont St-Cyr

All around Cahors rise the dry, scrubby uplands of the *causse*. From Roman times until the nineteenth century, when phylloxera hit, these valley sides were carpeted with vines. For a while after the land was used for grazing sheep but now only the lines of tumbled-down stone walls and abandoned farmhouses remain. One of the few landmarks around is the red-and-white TV mast on the summit of **Mont St-Cyr**, overlooking Cahors to the southeast. At 264m, this is the place to head for bird's-eye views of the town: the division between medieval and seventeenth-century Cahors becomes very apparent from the summit, particularly in summer when tree-lined boulevard Gambetta picks out the former course of the ramparts.

Pont Valentré is just visible in the distance, while on clear days you can see the Château de Mercuès way to the north.

It's a stiff but easy climb to the summit of Mont St-Cyr. From the southern end of boulevard Gambetta, cross Pont Louis-Philippe, then take the steps to the right of the Virgin's statue and keep going up for about twenty to thirty minutes. Though you can drive, it takes almost as long, as the road winds for about 5km among stunted oaks and pines across the plateau. Apart from the views, there are picnic tables at the top and a little log-cabin **restaurant**, *Agripaume*, serving snacks and basic meals (closed Mon & Tues Oct–May; menus from 85F/€12.96).

Eating, drinking and entertainment

Cahors has no shortage of good **places to eat**, from the classy *Balandre* – the place to go for a splurge – to very much more modest establishments. Most are concentrated in the streets of the medieval town, though you'll also find brasseries, pizzerias and cafés along boulevard Gambetta.

There's little in the way of **nightlife**, especially out of season, but one of the livelier spots is the *Irish Pub* (Mon–Sat 6pm–2am), to the northwest of place des Consuls, which hosts various live bands three nights a week (Wed, Thurs & Sat; 20F/€3.05). For other **events**, ask at the tourist office, which publishes lists of the many festivals (see box on p.266 for more), exhibitions, concerts and plays taking place in Cahors. For plays, the principal venue is the newly renovated Neoclassical Municipal Theatre on place François-Mitterrand (☎05.65.23.82.60, *www.mairie-cahors.fr/theatre*), which puts on a varied programme of theatre, dance, concerts and opera. Classical concerts are also held in the cathedral, while pop concerts take place in Les Docks, 430 allées des Soupirs (☎05.65.22.36.38, *www.mairie-cahors.fr/docks*), a new complex beside Pont-Valentré.

Restaurants

Le Balandre, *Hôtel Terminus*, 5 av Charles-de-Freycinet (☎05.65.53.32.00). Cahors' top restaurant serves refined takes on Quercy cuisine, with plenty of local lamb, duck, truffles and foie gras, in a dining room to match: all chandeliers, plasterwork and pretty, Art Nouveau stained glass. They also offer a very impressive wine list, including over 70 Cahors wines. There are three menus at 180–450F/€27.44–68.60, or you can eat for around 250–300F/€38.11–45.73 from the *carte*. Mid-Sept to June closed Sun & Mon.

La Divona, 46 rue Daurade. This little bistro in the lovely rue Daurade is a safe bet for traditional regional dishes, mostly simple country fare such as magret, tripe, trout or various types of mushroom. Menus from 70F/€10.67. Oct–June closed Mon.

Au Fil des Douceurs, 90 quai de la Verrerie (☎05.65.22.13.04). A floating restaurant moored on the far side of Pont Cabessut, with splendid views of the Cahors skyline. The food is refined – *crêpes* with morsels of duck, lamb brochette and plenty of fish – but not outrageously expensive. Menus start at 75F/€11.43 for three courses. Reservations recommended Sat eve and Sun lunch. Closed Sun eve & Mon.

Lamparo, place de la Halle. Large, bustling first-floor restaurant, decked out in sunny blues and yellows and lots of greenery, that's justifiably popular for its generous portions and very reasonable prices. Though the speciality is pizza, there's something for everyone, including salads and local dishes plus enticing desserts to follow. *Plats du jour* 48F/€7.32; menus from 65F/€9.91.

Marie Colline, 173 rue Georges-Clemenceau (☎05.65.35.59.96). You need to reserve or wait till around 1pm to find space at this bright, airy vegetarian restaurant run by two sisters. The choice is limited – two entrées and two main dishes which change daily – but it's all freshly made, using locally produced vegetables. Save room for one of their scrumptious desserts. *Plats du jour* 42F/€6.40, or three courses for under 90F/€13.72. Open Tues–Fri lunchtime only. Closed Aug.

Le Rendez-vous, 49 rue Clément-Marot (☎05.65.22.65.10). Top-notch cuisine at affordable prices means that you need to book ahead at this elegant little restaurant in the heart of the old town. Seasonal dishes include Quercy lamb with herbs and garlic, foie gras raviolis and smoked duck breast with *cabécou*, accompanied by a good selection of local wines. Menus from 99F/€15.09 including wine, or around 150F/€22.87 per person à la carte. Closed Sun & Mon; also for two weeks in Nov and two weeks in late April to early May.

Le Troquet des Halles, 55 rue St-Maurice. An unpretentious locals' restaurant tucked into a corner of the marketplace behind old-fashioned lace curtains. No-nonsense home cooking is the order of the day, such as roast pork with prunes or *faux filet*. Prices start at 40F/€6.10 for a *plat du jour* and soup, going up to 60F/€9.15 for three courses including wine. Open lunchtime only. Closed Sat.

Listings

Bike rental Cycles 7, at 417 quai de Regourd near the town centre (☎05.65.22.66.60), rents out bikes from April to October. Cycl'Espace 46 at 1049 av Anatole-de-Monzie (☎05.65.35.75.63), in the southern outskirts, has more bikes but is open in July and August only.

Boat trips From April to November Safaraid (☎05.65.35.98.88) organizes river tours, with commentary in English on request, from beside Pont Valentré (1hr 30min; 50F/€7.62). In July and August they also offer combined boat and train trips up the Lot river in association with Quercyrail (see p.278). If you'd rather captain your own boat, contact Babou Marine (☎05.65.30.08.99, *www.baboulene-jean.fr*) at Port St-Mary, beside the Pont des Remparts. In addition to small boats you can rent by the hour or day, they also have houseboats for weekly rental (see p.268 for more about boating on the Lot).

Books and newspapers The Maison de la Presse, 73 bd Gambetta, stocks the biggest range of English-language papers and magazines as well as local guides, while Librairie Calligramme, 75 rue du Maréchal-Joffre, is a more serious bookshop carrying a few English-language titles.

Bus information The tourist office stocks bus timetables, or phone the Conseil Général's central information desk (☎05.65.53.27.50). Tickets for Eurolines buses are available from Voyages Belmon, 2 bd Gambetta (☎05.65.35.59.30), at the north end of the boulevard.

Car parks Free parking is available on allées Fénelon and place Charles-de-Gaulle.

Car rental Both Avis, 512 av Jean-Jaurès (☎05.65.30.13.10), and Hertz, 385 rue Anatole-France (☎05.65.35.34.69), are located near the train station.

Cinema Of Cahors' two cinemas, the three-screen ABC, 24 rue des Augustins (☎05.65.35.03.11), is the more likely to show English-language films, usually in the original version (*v.o.*). The other cinema is Le Quercy, 871 rue Émile-Zola (☎05.65.22.20.05), near the Musée Henri-Martin.

Hospital Centre Hospitalier Jean Rougier, 449–335 rue du Président-Wilson (☎05.65.20.50.50).

Internet access You can log on at the new Les Docks complex, 430 allées des Soupirs (daily 2–6pm; ☎05.65.22.36.38, *www.mairie-cahors.fr/docks*; 10F/€1.52 per hour), and at the Bureau Information Jeunesse du Lot, 20 rue Frédéric-Suisse, in the same building as the youth hostel (closed Sun; 20F/€3.05 per hour).

Markets There's a fresh food market in the *halle* on place Galdemar (daily except Sun pm & Mon) and a more extensive market on Wednesday and Saturday mornings spreading north into the cathedral square. Place François-Mitterrand, near the tourist office, hosts an antiques fair-cum-flea market on the first and third Saturdays of the month, while in winter (Nov to mid-March) there's a *marché au gras*, selling all manner of duck and goose products, every Saturday morning in the *halle*.

Police Commissariat de Police, 1 rue de l'Ancienne-Gendarmerie (☎05.65.35.27.00).

Post office The main post office is at 257 rue du Président-Wilson, 46000 Cahors.

Shopping Apart from buying directly from the producers (see box on p.270), the best place to shop for Cahors wine is the big L'Atrium showroom on the N20 as you come into town from the south. It's under the same ownership as the châteaux de Mercuès and de Haute-Serre, but features other wines as well, at close to château prices. They provide tastings and can also advise on vineyard visits, as can the smaller La Cèdre Valentré, 32 av André-Breton, at the east end of Pont Valentré (closed mid-Jan to mid-Feb; *www.quercy.net/com/cedre*).

Taxis There's a taxi stand outside the train station (☎05.65.35.20.31) and another on bd Gambetta (☎05.65.35.20.49).

East along the Lot

Upstream from Cahors the Lot valley becomes narrower and the cliffs higher. The river is confined to ever tighter meanders and castles sprout from all the most inaccessible knuckles of rock, often with red-tiled villages clinging to their flanks. One such provides the most dramatic sight in the whole valley: **St-Cirq-Lapopie**, 30km or so east of Cahors, perched precariously on the edge of a 100m drop. Its castle is now a ruin, but the village itself is a delightful – if very touristy – place where noble mansions stand testimony to a more illustrious past. Further along the river's south bank on the D8, the Renaissance **Château de Cénevières** also boasts an interesting history, as well as some unusual frescoes and a good collection of period furniture. The only major settlement along this stretch of river is **Cajarc**, an important market town and a stop on the pilgrims' road to Santiago de Compostela. Cajarc's only sight is an incongruous modern art gallery, featuring some world-class names, but it has sufficient accommodation and other facilities to provide a useful base. Upstream, the scenery takes over once again as the Lot winds its way past more medieval villages and castles, and beneath a 300m-high belvedere, the **Saut de la Mounine**, on the valley's southern lip. There's nothing particular to stop for along the last stretch of river heading northeast to **Capdenac**, near Figeac (see p.287). Instead, you could

---

THE QUERCYRAIL TOURIST TRAIN

A leisurely way to enjoy the Lot valley is to take the **Quercyrail tourist train**, which runs vintage diesel locomotives along an otherwise redundant line between Cahors and Capdenac. Various round trips of a day or half-day are available, including a walk along the towpath at Bouziès, or a visit to the Château de Cénevières. Prices are 100–160F/€15.24–24.39 return, with departures from Cahors station (May–Oct) or, in July and August only, from Capdenac. You can make reservations – highly recommended – and buy tickets in Cahors from the tourist office (see p.269) or the Quercyrail office beside the *gare SNCF* (☎05.65.23.94.72), and from Capdenac station (☎05.65.64.74.87). In July and August you can also combine the train ride from Cahors with a **boat trip**; tickets are available from Safaraid (☎05.65.35.98.88) or Quercyrail and cost 150F/€22.87 (plus 75F/€11.43 for a restaurant lunch), with departures on Tuesdays and Fridays at 9am.

take a diversion south across the *causse* to where the **Grotte de Foissac** harbours some prehistoric remains alongside a varied and colourful array of stalactites and stalagmites, and then continue on across country to the atmospheric ruins of **Peyrerusse-le-Roc**.

The Lot valley is unusually well served by **public transport**, with an SNCF **bus** running along the river's north bank from Cahors via Figeac to Capdenac. It stops at almost every village en route, though you'll have to walk across to those south of the river, and will need your own transport to explore the high country on either side.

From Cahors towards St-Cirq-Lapopie

Immediately east of Cahors, the Lot valley is taken up with a busy main road, train tracks and scattered modern developments, in addition to engineering works for the new A20 *autoroute*. However, things improve dramatically after the village of **VERS**, some 15km upstream, where the main D653 to Figeac strikes off northeastwards. Vers itself doesn't merit a stop, unless you are in search of overnight **accommodation**. The most attractive option – as long as you get a room in the main hotel rather than the old and noisy annexe across the road – is *La Truite Dorée* (☎05.65.31.41.51, fax 05.65.31.47.43, *www.logis-de-france.fr*; ③; closed mid-Dec to mid-Feb, also Sun eve & Mon from Oct to April), at the entrance to the village overlooking the River Vers where it flows into the Lot from the north; it has a good-value restaurant with menus from 65F/€9.91. You can rent **bikes** at La Roue Libre, place du Communal (☎05.65.31.45.57), in the centre of the village near the church, which is also where you'll find the **bus stop**.

East of Vers, the D662 hugs the north bank of the Lot as it meanders back and forth beneath cliffs that loom ever higher as you near **BOUZIÈS**, located on the south bank across a narrow suspension bridge. The main reason for coming here is to walk along the **chemin de halage**, a towpath cut into the cliff just above water level on the river's south bank. In pre-railway days it was used by men hauling *gabares* (traditional wooden river craft) laden with produce upstream. It now forms part of the GR36 long-distance footpath, indicated by red and white markers, which you can join at the car park on the east side of Bouziès. The rock-hewn section starts after about 500m and extends for some 300m; if you're feeling energetic, you can then continue on to St-Cirq-Lapopie (see below).

Another way of exploring the riverbank is to take to the water. Bouziès is a **boating** and **canoeing** centre, with several companies setting up shop on the south side of the bridge in the summer. You can rent canoes from the hotel (see below) and Safaraid (July & Aug; ☎05.65.30.74.47, *www.canoe-dordogne.com*). Safaraid also has 12-person "picnic boats" for rental by the day (mid-June to mid-Sept; reservations recommended at least one week in advance; ☎05.65.35.98.88; 900F/€137.20 per day), while Lot Navigation Nicols rents out houseboats for longer excursions (see box on p.268 for more). Finally, you can take a one-and-a-half-hour river trip, with running commentary (in English on request), from Bouziès to St-Cirq-Lapopie and back with Safaraid (April–Nov 3–4 trips daily; ☎05.65.35.98.88; 50F/€7.62), with the option of an evening voyage on Fridays (mid-June to mid-Sept 10pm) to admire the floodlit cliffs.

SNCF **buses** stop on the main road near the bridge. There's no tourist office, but Bouziès' welcoming **hotel**, *Les Falaises* (☎05.65.31.26.83, fax 05.65.30.23.87, *www.crdi.fr/falaises*; ④; closed late Nov to early March; restaurant from

82F/€12.50), in the village centre, is a mine of information – and a hive of activity. They offer everything from accompanied walks and canoe trips to trekking, rock climbing and potholing. Note that the rooms in the main building overlooking the pool and gardens are preferable to the older block behind.

St-Cirq-Lapopie

Next stop up the valley is the cliff-edge village of **ST-CIRQ-LAPOPIE**, 5km east of Bouziès, perched high above the south bank of the Lot. With its cobbled lanes, half-timbered houses and gardens, virtually unspoilt by modern intrusions, the village is an irresistible draw for the tour buses, but it's still worth the trouble, especially if you visit early or late in the day.

There has been a fortress on this rocky protuberance, known as La Popie, since Gallo-Roman times if not before. So important was the site strategically that in the Middle Ages it was shared by the Viscount of St-Cirq with the other three viscounts of Quercy (Gourdon, Cardaillac and Castelnau) and a feudal town grew up within the protection of its walls. It wasn't a particularly safe haven: St-Cirq took a battering from the English during the Hundred Years' War, then in the Wars of Religion it was seized by the Protestant Henry of Navarre who ordered the castle destroyed in 1580 to keep it from the Catholics. Undaunted however, local craftsmen built up a reputation for their skill in wood turning, specifically boxwood which they fashioned into goblets, furniture and taps for casks. They continued to ply their craft into the nineteenth century, but then along came industrialization and St-Cirq went into steep decline until it was rediscovered in the early twentieth century by the artistic fraternity, most famously Henri Martin (see p.275) and the surrealist poet André Breton, who came to live here in the 1950s.

St-Cirq today consists of one main street running steeply downhill for 500m from porte de la Payrolerie in the west to easterly porte de Pélissaria; in between it is variously known as rue de la Payrolerie, **rue Droite** – between the central market square, place du Sombral, and the church – and rue de la Pélissaria. All along are stone and half-timbered houses, under steeply pitched and gabled Quercy roofs.

Starting from porte de la Payrolerie, the first place to head for is the ruined **château** to the north of place du Sombral. Precious little remains of the castle, but the site is fantastic, plunging down to the river 100m below. Further east along the cliff edge, the fortified **church of St-Cirq** is now the village's dominant building. It's in a pretty sorry state itself, though you can still make out faint traces of thirteenth-century murals where the original Romanesque chapel was incorporated into a larger church three hundred years later.

Below the church to the east, the **Musée Rignault** (April–Oct daily except Tues 10am–12.30pm & 2.30–6pm; 10F/€1.52) occupies a lovely fortified mansion with a romantic little rock garden and various other embellishments added by an art dealer who came to live here in 1922. A few pieces of his wide-ranging art collection are on display, while the rest of the space is given over to temporary exhibitions. On the way back up the hill, St-Cirq's local history museum, the **Musée de la Memoire** (daily: March to mid-June & mid-Sept to mid-Nov 10.30am–12.30pm & 2–7pm; mid-June to mid-Sept 10am–8pm; 10F/€1.52), in a Renaissance mansion one block south of rue Droite, is worth a peek for its small exhibition on wood turning.

Practicalities

Buses on the Cahors–Figeac run drop you across the river in the hamlet of Tour-de-Faure; from there you can call a **taxi** (Lonjou; ☎05.65.31.26.15) or leg it up the steep hill for the last 2km. If you're driving, the most convenient **car park** is that outside porte de la Payrolerie at the top of the village (Easter to mid-Nov 12F/€1.83 per day, including one free entry to the Musée de la Mémoire; rest of the year free). The **tourist office**, on place du Sombral (daily: May to mid-June, Sept & Oct 10am–1pm & 2–7pm; mid-June to Aug 10am–1pm & 2–8pm; Nov–April 10am–1pm & 2–6pm; ☎ & fax 05.65.31.29.06, *saint-cirque.lapopie@wanadoo.fr*), can furnish you with a handy English-language walking guide to the village.

There are various **accommodation** options, all of which get booked up weeks ahead in summer. Of the two hotels, *La Pélissaria* (☎05.65.31.25.14, fax 05.65.30.25.52; ⑤; closed Nov–March), in a sixteenth-century house perched on the cliff just inside St-Cirq's eastern gateway, provides the most atmospheric sur-roundings – all polished wood floors and exposed stonework, and a pretty ter-raced garden. The alternative is the *Auberge du Sombral* (☎05.65.31.26.08, fax 05.65.30.26.37; ④; closed mid-Nov to March) on place du Sombral, which offers plain but perfectly adequate rooms in addition to an excellent restaurant (Oct–June closed Tues eve & Wed; menus from 100F/€15.24). Cheaper accom-modation is available in a very comfortable and well-equipped **gîte d'étape** in the same building as the Musée de la Mémoire (☎ & fax 05.65.31.21.51; 60F/€9.15 per person; open all year), and at two well-run three-star **campsites**: *Camping de la Plage* (☎05.65.30.29.51, fax 05.65.30.23.33, *www.les-campings.com/plage*; open all year), down by the bridge, and the spacious *La Truffière* (☎05.65.30.20.22, fax 05.65.30.20.22; closed Oct–April), on the plateau 3km southeast of St-Cirq via the D42. You can rent **canoes** and **bikes** from Kalapca (☎05.65.30.29.51, *perso.wanadoo.fr/bureau-sports-nature*), next door to – and under the same man-agement as – the *Camping de la Plage*; they also organize trekking, caving, rock climbing and other activities.

As for **restaurants**, in addition to the *Auberge de Sombral*, you can eat very well at *L'Oustal* (☎05.65.31.20.17; closed Nov–Easter; menus from 75F/€11.43), a tiny little place tucked into a corner at the top end of rue de la Pélissaria just south of the church. For unbeatable views, however, head for the terrace of *Lou Bolat* (closed mid-Nov to Feb, also Tues except in July & Aug), at the top of the village just inside porte de la Payrolerie, which serves a varied menu of *crêpes*, salads and regional dishes, with menus starting at 60F/€9.15. In July and August there's a small **market** in place du Sombral on Wednesday mornings, but note that the nearest **food shop** is a small grocer down in Tour-de-Faure.

The Château de Cénevières and around

Travelling on eastwards from St-Cirq, rather than carry on along the main D662 it's preferable to take the smaller and quieter D8 along the river's south bank. Seven kilometres later you reach the **Château de Cénevières** (1hr guided tours daily: April–Sept 10am–noon & 2–6pm; 27F/€4.12), perched on another rocky spur just beyond Cénevières village; the nearest **bus stop** is in St-Martin-Labouval, a good kilometre downstream and across on the north bank. The château belonged to the de Gourdon family for 900 years until the line petered out in 1616, though the present building largely dates from the sixteenth century. The last in line, Antoine de Gourdon, was a fervent supporter of the Reformation, so much so that the Protestant leader Henry of Navarre stayed here before attacking Cahors in 1580. Antoine brought back a rich haul which included the cathedral's principal altar – the boat carrying it, however, capsized and the altar is now somewhere at the bottom of the Lot. The château was saved from being torched during the Revolution by a quick-thinking overseer who opened the wine cellars to the mob, though he couldn't save the library, nor the coat of arms and other carvings on the façade. Cénevières was sold only once during its long history, to the ancestors of the present owners in 1793. Over the years they have uncovered several unusual Renaissance-era **frescoes**: notably, a frieze of the Istanbul skyline in the grand salon, and scenes from Greek mythology alongside what is believed to be a representation of an alchemist's fire and the philosopher's stone adorning a little vaulted chamber.

The valley's next rocky eyrie is occupied by the village of **CALVIGNAC**, 5km east from Cénevières on the D8, where a handful of ancient houses cluster round the remnants of another medieval stronghold. Apart from the views, the main point of coming here is to take a pit stop at *La Terrasse Romantique* (☎05.65.30.24.37; closed mid-Sept to mid-May; menus from 62F/€9.45), under the tower on the village's east side: the **restaurant** lives up to its name, serving salads, *crêpes* and more substantial regional dishes on a tiny terrace nestled into the rock face.

Cajarc

CAJARC, which lies on the river's north bank, 9km upstream from Calvignac, is the biggest town on the Lot between Cahors and Capdenac. It consists of a small core of old lanes encircled by the boulevard du Tour-du-Ville, where you'll find facilities such as banks, food shops and a post office as well as cafés and brasseries. The town's only sight as such is the **Maison des Arts Georges-Pompidou** (hours vary for each exhibition; ☎05.65.40.63.97; 20F/€3.05) on the northeastern outskirts on the D19 Figeac road. The gallery is named in honour of the former French prime minister, who bought a holiday home near here in 1963, and hosts four major contemporary art exhibitions a year, including artists such as Jean-Pierre Bertrand and Vicente Pimentel; phone ahead to see if there's anything of interest.

SNCF **buses** stop on the north side of town on place du Foirail, a big open square where you'll also find the **tourist office** (late May to June & Sept Mon–Sat 3.30–6.30pm, Sun 10am–12.30pm; July & Aug daily 10am–1pm & 3.30–7.30pm; ☎05.65.40.72.89, fax 05.65.40.39.05); the *gare*, now only used by Quercyrail tourist trains (see box on p.278), lies across town to the southeast. A **market** takes place on Saturday afternoons on place du Foirail, with larger *foires* (country fairs) on the 10th and 25th of each month. **Bike rental** is available at Garage Couybes, also on place du Foirail (☎05.65.40.66.48).

Cajarc has two **hotels**, the smarter of which is *La Ségalière* (☎05.65.40.65.35, fax 05.65.40.74.92, *perso.wanadoo.fr/hotelsegaliere*; ④; closed mid-Nov to March; good restaurant from 80F/€12.20), around 400m east on the D662 to Capdenac. It's a modern, concrete building – not beautiful, but airy and with nicely decorated rooms, some with a small balcony overlooking the pool and spacious gardens. In season you can arrive here on the little Quercyrail tourist train which stops at the bottom of the garden (see above). Cajarc's other hotel is *La Promenade*, place du Foirail (☎05.65.40.61.21, fax 05.65.40.79.12; ②; closed Feb and last fortnight of June, also Sun eve & Mon mid-Sept to June), with a handful of simple rooms above a high-quality restaurant; try their roast lamb or snails with saffron sauce, among other local specialities (menus from 70F/€10.67). There's also a two-star municipal **campsite**, *Le Terriol* (☎05.65.40.72.74, fax 05.65.40.39.05; closed Oct–April), beside the river roughly 200m southwest of the centre.

In addition to the above hotel **restaurants**, *Cajarc Gourmand* (☎05.65.40.69.50; April–June & Sept closed Thurs, Nov–March open Fri eve to Sun lunch only) on a quiet square beside the church is worth trying. They serve traditional regional fare, with various *formules* starting at 58F/€8.84 and full menus at 85F/€12.96.

On to Capdenac

Upstream from Cajarc the Lot twists through one more giant meander and then straightens out until you reach the next big loop at Capdenac. Buses follow the northerly route past a succession of picturesque villages and castles, but if you've got your own transport, the less-travelled roads along the river's south bank provide the more interesting route. They take you through walnut orchards and past weathered farm buildings snuggled into the landscape's folds, then up on to the *causse* where the scene changes to flat, empty country with little sign of habitation, past the occasional dolmen or *cabane*, the traditional, stone-built shepherds' huts.

Where the D127 first climbs up from the river, 7km from Cajarc, it skirts along the edge of a 300m-high cliff formed by the meander. The spot is known as the **Saut de la Mounine** (Monkey's Leap) after a legend concerning a local lord who ordered his daughter thrown off the cliff when she fell in love with a boy he disapproved of. A hermit took pity on the girl and secretly dressed a monkey in her clothes instead. When the poor beast was chucked over the edge, the lord repented, of course, and was only too relieved to discover he'd been outwitted. He apparently forgave his daughter, but history doesn't relate whom she married. Whatever the outcome, it's a marvellous view from up here, taking in the meander filled with patchwork fields and the ruined Château de Montbrun on the far hillside – where the lord and his daughter once lived.

A few kilometres further on you drop back down to the river along tiny lanes that wend their way northeastwards for about 15km before hitting the main D922. Turn left here and you'll be in Figeac (see p.287) in about ten minutes. Alternatively, if you cross over and follow the D86 along the river, another 7km will bring you to **CAPDENAC**, a major railway town on the south bank of the River Lot. There's a majestic view from the high ridge above the town and river to the north, but otherwise Capdenac is of little interest unless you plan to take a Quercyrail excursion (see box on p.278).

The Grotte de Foissac and Peyrerusse-le-Roc

On reaching the D922, instead of heading immediately north to Figeac or carrying on to Capdenac, it's worth taking a detour south towards Villefranche, to visit one of the less-frequented caves, the **Grotte de Foissac** (1hr guided tours: April, May & Oct daily except Sat 2–6pm; June & Sept daily 10–11.30am & 2–6pm; July & Aug daily 10am–6pm; 40F/€6.10); it is signposted about 6km down the D922 and lies another 3km west across the *causse* through Foissac village. The cave was discovered in 1959 by a local potholing club, who found not only a huge cavern of colourful and varied concretions, including delicate needles, some bulging out into onion shapes, but also evidence of human activity going back at least 4000 years. From the number of skeletons and their positions it seems that, unusually, the cave was used as a cemetery. It was also a source of clay – you can still see where people dug it out with their hands, and they also left large and beautifully fashioned pots, probably for storing grain. But the most moving evidence is the lone footprint left by a child deep inside the cave.

Twenty kilometres to the east of Foissac, via beautiful back lanes through Naussac and along the Roselle, the ruined towers of **PEYRERUSSE-LE-ROC** are also well worth a look. The "modern" village, a tiny weatherworn huddle of half-timbered houses gathered round a seventeenth-century church, sits above a narrow valley. On the valley sides, hidden in the steep woods, lie the scattered remains of a fortified medieval town which once sheltered some 4500 people – a sizeable population in those days – come to seek their fortunes in the local silver mines. But their luck ran out in the early sixteenth century, when silver from the recently discovered Americas began to flood the market, and the town was eventually abandoned around 1700. There are moves afoot to clear the undergrowth and tidy up the site, but for the moment at least, it remains a moving and atmospheric place.

A path leads from the northwest corner of the church square to a pinnacle of rock crowned by **twin towers**, all that's left of the medieval fortress which protected the town. If you've got a head for heights, you can scramble up the iron ladders for a vertiginous view of the gorge. From here a cobbled mule trail leads steeply down through the woods, where the stones of a Gothic church, synagogue and hospital stand roofless, to the river and a little thirteenth-century chapel, complete but not open to the public. To return to the modern village, follow the river downstream and pick up another path which takes you past the old market hall to the village gate.

The Célé Valley

Instead of following the River Lot east from Cahors, you can take an alternative route to Figeac along the wilder and narrower **Célé valley**, which joins the Lot a kilometre or so upstream from Bouziès (see p.279). A single road winds through the luxuriant canyon-like valley, frequented mainly by canoeists and walkers on the GR651, which runs sometimes close to the river, sometimes on the edge of the *causse* on the north bank. The major settlement along here is **Cabrerets**, a village not far upstream from the Célé's confluence with the Lot, which serves as a base for the nearby **Grotte de Pech-Merle**. Well hidden on the scrubby hillsides to the west of the river, this enormous cave system combines superb examples of prehistoric art with an array of calcite deposits in all shapes and sizes. Continuing northeast, the valley is punctuated by a succession of villages and hamlets built against the cliff face. Of these, two in particular stand out: **Marcilhac-sur-Célé**, about halfway along the valley, for the atmospheric ruins of its abbey; and the tiny hamlet of **Espagnac-Ste-Eulalie** in the north, where another, more substantial church sports a delightfully whimsical belfry.

There's no **public transport** along the Célé, but you can rent bicycles in St-Cirq-Lapopie (see p.281), which lies on the bus route from Cahors to Figeac.

Another good option is to descend the Célé by canoe; rental outlets in St-Cirq, Figeac and near Cabrerets will organize the necessary transport.

Cabrerets

CABRERETS lies 4km up the Célé from its confluence with the Lot, the approach guarded by the sturdy **Château de Gontaut-Biron** (not open to the public), on a small flood plain where the River Sagne joins the Célé. It's a pretty enough spot, but the only real reason to linger here is to take advantage of its tourist amenities.

Firstly, there's a small **tourist office** in the village centre on the road to Pech-Merle (April & first two weeks Oct Tues–Sun 10am–12.30pm & 2–5.30pm; May, June & Sept Wed–Sun 10am–12.30pm & 2–6.30pm; July & Aug daily 10am–12.30pm & 2–7.30pm; ☎05.65.31.27.12, fax 05.65.24.38.11), which sells handy guides detailing walks in the area. There's also a pair of two-star **hotels**. In the village itself, overlooking the Célé, *Les Grottes* (☎05.65.31.27.02, fax 05.65.31.20.15, *hotel.grottes@wanadoo.fr*; ③; closed Nov–March) is a welcoming place with functional rooms – the cheapest without en-suite facilities – and a decent restaurant (menus from 89F/€13.57). The alternative is the slightly smarter and absolutely spotless *Auberge de la Sagne* (☎05.65.31.26.62, fax 05.65.30.27.43, *www.logis-de-france.fr*; ④; closed mid-Sept to mid-May), 1km west of the village on the road to the caves; there's a pool, well-tended garden and a restaurant offering good quality home cooking (evenings only; menus at 90F/€13.72 & 130F/€19.82; reservations recommended). In addition, there's simple **chambres d'hôtes** accommodation available at *Chez Bessac* (☎05.65.31.27.04; ③; closed Nov–Easter) near Cabreret's tourist office; they also run a **gîte d'étape** (50F/€7.62 per night; open all year) with its own kitchen and a modern dormitory. The last option is a small two-star **campsite**, *Le Cantal* (☎05.65.31.26.61; closed Nov–March), immediately north of Cabrerets on the other side of the Célé.

Apart from the hotel **restaurants**, you can also eat well in the *O'Louise* (☎05.65.30.25.56; closed at Christmas and 2 weeks in Feb, also Sun eve except in July & Aug), a rustic little place halfway between the church and the Célé, popular among locals for its well-priced menus (from 65F/€9.91) and – from mid-June to mid-September only – its pizzas.

Grotte de Pech-Merle

Up in the hills 3km west of Cabrerets by road, or 1km via the footpath from beside the Mairie, the **Grotte de Pech-Merle** (1hr guided visits: mid-Jan to March and Nov to mid-Dec group reservation only; April–Oct daily 9.30am–noon & 1.30–5pm; ☎05.65.31.27.05; mid-June to mid-Sept 44F/€6.71, rest of year 38F/€5.79) takes some beating. Discovered in 1922 by two local boys, the galleries are not only full of the most spectacular limestone formations – structures tiered like wedding cakes, hanging like curtains, or shaped like discs or "cave pearls" – but also contain an equally dazzling display of more than 500 **prehistoric drawings**. To protect the drawings tickets are restricted to 700 per day (it's advisable to book at least a day ahead in July and August) and the guides make sure you're processed through in the allotted time. It's worth arriving in plenty of time to visit the **museum**, located beside the ticket office (same hours; same ticket), before your scheduled tour. A twenty-minute film, subtitled in English, provides an excellent overview of Pech-Merle and its prehistoric art.

The drawings date mostly from the early Magdalenian era (around 16,000–17,000 years ago), contemporaneous with much of the cave art in the Vézère valley (see p.207), with which they share many similarities. The first drawings you come to are in the so-called **Chapelle des Mammouths**, executed on a white calcite panel that looks as if it's been specially prepared for the purpose; note how the artists used the contour and relief of the rock to do the work, producing utterly convincing mammoths with just two lines. In addition to the mammoths, there are horses, oxen and bison charging head down with tiny rumps and arched tails; the guide will point out where St-Cirq's André Breton (see p.280) added his own mammoth – he was fined but the damage was done. Next comes a vast chamber containing the glorious **horse frieze**, the oldest of the drawings (at around 25,000 years). Two large horses stand back to back, the head of one formed by a natural protuberance of rock, and their hindquarters superimposed to provide perspective. The surface is spattered with black dots of some unknown symbolic significance and silhouettes of hands, while the ceiling is covered with finger marks preserved in the soft clay. On the way you pass the skeletons of cave-hyena and bears that have been lying there for thousands of years, and, finally, the footprints of an adolescent preserved in a muddy pool some 8000 years ago.

Upstream to Marcilhac-sur-Célé

Back down on the D41 heading up the Célé from Cabrerets, after 3km you emerge from a tunnel to find old bikes, mannequins, even the shells of cars hanging from the rock face. They belong to the gloriously eccentric **Petit Musée de l'Insolite**, the "little museum of the extraordinary" (April–Oct 9am–1pm & 2–8pm; rest of year by appointment; ☎05.65.30.21.01; free), run by a wood sculptor with an engaging sense of humour. Both his garden and gallery are full of bizarre montages fashioned out of tree stumps, old machines and other bits of scrap.

Along the river here you'll also find two **canoe rental** outlets: Les Amis du Célé (open all year; ☎05.65.31.26.73) and Nature et Loisirs (April–Oct; ☎05.65.30.25.69). Both organize descents of the Célé and have **bikes** for rent, while the former also offers rock-climbing and potholing outings.

The next village of interest is **MARCILHAC**, 16km upstream from Cabrerets, whose partly ruined Benedictine **abbey** (April–June & Sept Wed–Sat 10am–noon & 2–5pm, Sun 2–5pm; July & Aug daily 10am–noon & 2–7pm; 15F/€2.29; tickets from the tourist office – see below), with its gaping walls and broken columns, conjures a strongly romantic atmosphere. Founded sometime prior to the ninth century, the abbey had the good fortune to be in charge of the modest sanctuary at Rocamadour (see p.243) in which St Amadour's body was discovered in 1186. The subsequent revenue from pilgrims and benefactors led to a brief golden age, which came to a grinding halt when English troops laid waste to the abbey in the Hundred Years' War. It never really recovered and was abandoned after the Reformation.

Entering the abbey from the south, a rather primitive and badly damaged ninth-century Christ in majesty decorates the tympanum over the ruined door. In the damp interior of the church itself are late-fifteenth-century frescoes of the Apostles and another Christ in majesty, with the coats of arms of the local nobility below. The few religious treasures that survived – such as a seventeenth-century polychrome pietà and a nicely rendered statue of a pilgrim – are now on display in the small **Musée d'Art Sacré** in a handsome half-timbered house immediately west of the abbey church, which also doubles as a **tourist office** (April–June & Sept Wed–Sat 10am–noon & 2–5pm, Sun 2–5pm; July & Aug daily 10am–noon & 2–7pm; ☎05.65.40.68.44).

It's worth timing your visit to **eat** at the attractive *Café des Touristes* on the main street, to the northwest of the abbey (☎05.65.40.65.61; Easter–Oct lunch & dinner, rest of year lunch only), where you'll feast on hearty home cooking for around 100F/€15.24. There's a **gîte d'étape** in the abbey (☎05.65.40.61.43; 32F/€4.88; closed Nov–Easter), as well as a municipal **campsite** (☎05.65. 40.77.88, fax 05.65.40.61.43; closed Oct–April) just north of the village.

Espagnac-Ste-Eulalie

The tiny and beautiful hamlet of **ESPAGNAC-STE-EULALIE** lies about 12km upriver from Marcilhac and is reached across an old stone bridge. Immediately across the bridge, an eye-catching octagonal lantern crowns the belfry of the priory **church of Notre-Dame-du-Val-Paradis** (1hr guided tours: daily 10.30am, 4.30pm & 5pm by appointment; Mme Bonzani ☎05.65.40.06.17; donation expected). The building itself is strangely ill-proportioned, a result of the nave being truncated in the Hundred Years' War, which somehow adds to its charm. Inside, apart from a typically over-the-top altarpiece of the Counter Reformation, the most interesting features are the ornate tombs of the church's thirteenth-century benefactor, Aymeric d'Hébrard de St-Sulpice, a local man who became Bishop of Coimbra in Portugal, and those of the Duke of Cardaillac and his wife, who financed the rebuilding of the choir in the fourteenth century.

An ancient fortified gateway south of the church now houses a **gîte d'étape** (☎05.65.40.08.34; 60F/€9.15 per night; open all year). Simple but good-quality **meals** are available at *Les Jardins du Célé* (daily except Sun eve; by reservation only; same number as *gîte*; 80F/€12.20), under the same management as the *gîte*, in the row of houses next to the church. The only other accommodation around comprises two good riverside **campsites** in **BRENGUES**, a hamlet 3km back downstream from Espagnac: the three-star *Le Moulin Vieux* (☎05.65.40.00.41, fax 05.65.40.05.65; closed Oct–April), with a restaurant, pool and **canoe** rental, and the smaller municipal site (☎05.65.40.06.82; closed Oct–May).

Figeac

Situated on the River Célé some 70km east of Cahors, **FIGEAC** is a most appealing town with an unspoilt medieval centre which is, surprisingly, not too encumbered by tourism. Its principal church, the **Église St-Sauveur**, contains a sumptuous rendition of the Passion of Christ in a side-chapel, and there's an excellent **museum** devoted to locally born Jean-François Champollion, who solved the mystery of hieroglyphics. But best of all is simply to wander its narrow lanes, lined with a delightful array of houses, both stone and half-timbered, adorned with carvings, ornate colonnaded windows and elaborate ironwork.

Like many other provincial towns hereabouts, Figeac owes its beginnings to the foundation of an **abbey** in the early days of Christianity, one which quickly became wealthy thanks to its position on the pilgrim roads to both Rocamadour (see p.243) and Compostela. In the Middle Ages the town flourished as a trading centre exporting wine and woollen fabrics throughout Europe, so much so that the wealthy merchants began to challenge the abbey's authority. In 1302 King Philip IV (the Fair) resolved the issue by sending his representative, the Viguier, to bring Figeac directly under royal control. At the same time he granted the town the all-important right to mint money. Figeac's fortunes declined during the Hundred Years' War, then revived in the Renaissance era, but it was the Wars of Religion that pushed it into eclipse. The town threw in its lot with the Protestants in 1576, providing them with an important safe-haven, until it was brought forcefully back into line in 1622. Figeac later became an important centre for tanning hides, and received a further boost with the arrival of the railway in 1862.

During **World War II** the Germans converted the Ratier metal workshop into a factory churning out propellers for Luftwaffe bombers. When the Maquis destroyed the plant in 1944, more than 500 local men were carted off to labour and concentration camps, from which at least 120 failed to return at the end of the war. By the 1960s Figeac's old quarter had declined to such an extent that the majority of buildings were declared uninhabitable. It was designated a preservation zone in 1986, since when the authorities have put a tremendous effort into restoring the medieval and Renaissance buildings.

Arrival, information and accommodation

Figeac's **gare SNCF** – on the Toulouse–Brive and Toulouse–Clermont-Ferrand main lines – lies about 600m south of the town centre. SNCF **buses** from Cahors, Gramat and Villeneuve-de-Rouergue terminate at the train station, while most other services drop you at the *gare routière* on avenue Maréchal-Joffre, a couple of minutes' walk west of centre. If you're arriving **by car**, note that the old quarter is largely pedestrianized. The most convenient parking is along the riverbank or on place Vival, where you'll also find the **tourist office** (May & June Mon–Sat 10am–noon & 2.30–6pm, Sun 10am–1pm; July to mid-Sept daily 10am–1pm & 2–7pm; mid-Sept to April Mon–Sat 10am–noon & 2.30–6pm; ☎05.65.34.06.25, fax 05.65.50.04.58, *www.quercy-tourisme.com/figeac*) in the very striking Hôtel de la Monnaie. They supply a useful do-it-yourself guide to Figeac and sell booklets outlining walks in the surrounding area, while in summer you can sign up for one of their excellent **guided tours** (in French only), of which "À la découverte de Figeac" provides the best general introduction (April, May & Sept Sat 4.30pm; July & Aug daily 5pm; 1hr 30min; 25F/€3.81).

Figeac has a mixed bag of **accommodation**. There are a couple of possibilities in the old quarter at completely opposite ends of the spectrum, and then a scattering over on the south bank of the river and towards the *gare SNCF*. The tourist office can supply lists of *chambres d'hôtes* in the area.

The nearest **campsite** is the well-equipped three-star *Camping Les Rives du Célé*, by the river 2km east of town in the Domaine de Surgié leisure complex (☎05.65.34.59.00, fax 05.65.34.83.83; closed Oct–March); it contains a restaurant, shop, several pools and **canoes** for rent.

Hotels

des Bains, 1 rue du Griffoul (☎05.65.34.10.89, fax 05.65.14.00.45). For those on a modest budget, this attractive hotel just across from the old town is by far the nicest place to stay in

Figeac, particularly if you fork out a few francs more for a balcony room. Cheaper rooms have access to spotlessly clean communal toilets and showers. Closed mid-Dec to mid-Jan. ②–③.

Le Champollion, 3 pl Champollion (☎05.65.34.04.37). This welcoming place offers ten functional but clean en-suite rooms above a popular café right in the centre. Try and get one of the two rooms overlooking the square. ③.

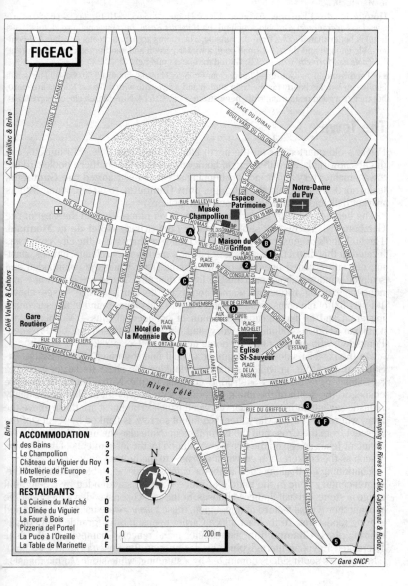

FIGEAC

ACCOMMODATION

des Bains	3
Le Champollion	2
Château du Viguier du Roy	1
Hôtellerie de l'Europe	4
Le Terminus	5

RESTAURANTS

La Cuisine du Marché	D
La Dînée du Viguier	B
La Four à Bois	C
Pizzeria del Portel	E
La Puce à l'Oreille	A
La Table de Marinette	F

0 200 m

Château du Viguier du Roy, rue Émile-Zola (☎05.65.50.05.05, fax 05.65.50.06.06, *www.chateau-viguier-figeac.com*). Figeac's one and only luxury hotel occupies a magnificent medieval residence, formerly the seat of the king's representative, the Viguier. Each room is individually designed, for example in Renaissance or Venetian style. There's a pool, pretty cloister garden and a top-notch restaurant, *La Dinée du Viguier* (see p.292). Closed late Oct to March. ⑧.

Hôtellerie de l'Europe, 51 allée Victor-Hugo (☎05.65.34.10.16, fax 05.65.50.04.57, *www.logis-de-france.fr*). One block behind the *Hôtel des Bains*, on a busy main road, this 1930s hotel is better than it looks from the outside. The rooms are by no means exciting, but comfortable enough and there's a small pool, a winter garden and another excellent restaurant, *La Table de Marinette* (see p.292). Closed mid-Jan to mid-Feb. ②.

Le Terminus, 27 av Georges-Clemenceau (☎05.65.34.00.43, fax 05.65.50.00.94). This small family-run hotel is handy for the train station and a favourite with walkers. Rooms are basic, but there's a good restaurant, with menus from 100F/€15.24. Nov–March closed Sun eve. ③.

The Town

Figeac's old quarter sits on the north bank of the River Célé, its ramparts and ditches now replaced with a ring of boulevards. From the southern boulevard the town's main artery and principal shopping street, pedestrianized **rue Gambetta**, leads north from the old stone bridge, **pont Gambetta**, to place Carnot, with its market hall, and neighbouring place Champollion.

The best place to start your explorations is on **place Vival** to the west of rue Gambetta, where the tourist office occupies the striking **Hôtel de la Monnaie**. The building's origins go back to the thirteenth century when the city's mint was located in this district. It is typical of Figeac's medieval merchants' houses, starting off with arcaded openings on the ground floor, while the colonnaded and sculpted windows above indicate the living quarters. These are now home to a none-too-exciting **museum** (same hours as the tourist office – see above; 10F/€1.52) of old coins and archeological bits and pieces found in the surrounding area, and an incongruous selection of presidential gifts – Moroccan and Tunisian saddles, Indonesian ivory and the like – passed on by President Pompidou, who owned a holiday home near Cajarc (see p.282).

On the eastern side of rue Gambetta you'll find the much-altered **Église St-Sauveur** on a big, gravelled square overlooking the river. Its large, grey and restrained nave provides a striking contrast to the **Notre-Dame-de-la-Pitié** chapel, to the south of the choir, decorated with heavily gilded but dramatically realistic seventeenth-century carved wood panels. The finest are those above the altar, where the Virgin Mary, her face full of sorrow, is flanked by scenes of the Descent from the Cross and the Entombment. Note also the unusual depiction of an infant Jesus asleep on the Cross surrounded by the instruments of the Passion – such as the cockerel and crown of thorns – to the bottom right.

Continuing north along rue Gambetta, cafés spread their tables under the nineteenth-century *halle* in the middle of **place Carnot**, surrounded by a delightful range of stone and half-timbered houses. Some sport open wooden galleries at the top; another typical feature of this region, these *solelhos* were used for drying and storing foodstuffs. To the east, place Carnot opens into the grander but equally alluring **place Champollion**, named after Jean-François Champollion, who finally cracked Egyptian hieroglyphics by deciphering the Rosetta Stone (see box). The square's south side is dominated by a stunning, white-stone Gothic mansion

CHAMPOLLION AND THE ROSETTA STONE

Jean-François Champollion was born in Figeac in 1790, the son of a bookseller who opened a shop on place Carnot, in what is now *Le Sphynx* café. His interest in Egypt was first sparked by news coming back from Napoléon Bonaparte's 1798 Egyptian adventures, and when an acquaintance showed him the so-far indecipherable script two years later, he became hooked. Declaring that he would solve the puzzle, Champollion set about studying ancient and Middle Eastern languages – he eventually mastered a mind-boggling total of twenty – and pouring over hieroglyphs. One of the most important resources available was the **Rosetta Stone**. A slab of black basalt measuring around 120cm in height and 80cm wide, the stone was discovered in 1799 by French soldiers building fortifications around the town of Rosetta in the Nile delta; three years later it fell into British hands when they seized Egypt from the French, and now resides in London's British Museum.

The crucial significance of the Rosetta Stone is that the same text – a decree issued in 196 BC recording the honours to be accorded to the young Pharaoh Ptolemy – is repeated in three different scripts: **hieroglyphics**, demotic (an abbreviated, cursive form of hieroglyphics used for everyday affairs), and Greek. By being able to translate the Greek, scholars now had fresh clues, but it took until 1822 before Champollion made the final breakthrough when he realized that hieroglyphs were, broadly, not pictograms but phonetic characters. Within two years he had identified the majority of symbols. And all this without having set foot in Egypt. He made his one and only voyage to the country in 1828, but died of a stroke four years later at the age of forty-one.

with a row of handsome ornamental windows, filled with lacy trefoil stonework. Opposite, the **Maison du Griffon** on the corner with rue de Colomb is far less ostentatious, but this is Figeac's oldest house, built in the twelfth century and named after a barely visible griffon carved on one of the pillars on the third floor.

Champollion was born nearby in a house at 4 impasse Champollion, to the northwest of the square, which now contains the fascinating **Musée Champollion** (March–June, Sept & Oct Tues–Sun 10am–noon & 2.30–6.30pm; July & Aug daily 10am–noon & 2.30–6.30pm; Nov–Feb Tues–Sun 2–6pm; 20F/€3.05), dedicated to his life and work. In addition to many beautiful examples of hieroglyphic script, it houses an excellent collection of funerary objects from the sixth and seventh centuries BC – sarcophagi, amulets and statues of the gods and goddesses, such as Bastet, a superb bronze cat, and an exquisitely crafted head of the god-king Osiris.

At the west end of this alley, a gigantic reproduction of the Rosetta Stone – the work of American artist Joseph Kossuth – forms the floor of the tiny **place des Écritures**, above which is a little garden with tufts of papyrus in pots and medicinal herbs. If it's open, you can cut through the **Espace Patrimoine** (April–June & Oct Tues–Sun 2–6pm; July–Sept daily 10am–12.30pm & 3–7pm; free), a one-room exhibition illustrating Figeac's history and architecture, to rue de Colomb.

On the east side of place Champollion, it's worth walking along rue Émile-Zola past the front of the **Hôtel du Viguier**, now a luxury hotel (see opposite). As you go by, look out for three small sculptures on the façade: to the left a very fine portrait of the building's fifteenth-century owner; to the right an architect clutching his callipers; and in the middle the present owner, added during recent renovations. Round the corner on rue Delzhens the large square tower looming over the street is the last vestige of the Viguier's fourteenth-century residence. You'll get a better view of it if you continue on up the hill to the **church of Notre-Dame du Puy**. Transformed into a veritable fortress by the Protestants in the late 1500s, then partially destroyed by Catholic reprisals, it now contains little of interest, but its cedar-shaded terrace is a peaceful spot from which to look down on the roofs of Figeac. When you've done, take cobbled rue St-Jacques twisting and turning down the hillside back to rue de Colomb and place Champollion.

Eating and drinking

Figeac's old centre is well provided with **restaurants**, offering everything from pizza to *haute cuisine*. When it comes to **cafés** or **bars**, your best bets are *Le Champollion* on place Champollion and *Le Sphynx* on neighbouring place Carnot, where tables are set out under the *halle* in warm weather.

La Cuisine du Marché, 15 rue Clermont (☎05.65.50.18.55). A warm welcome, well-spaced tables and varied cuisine, including lots of fish, mean it's best to reserve ahead for this restaurant just east of rue Gambetta. Specialities include such delicacies as terrine of foie gras with artichokes and duck with peach sauce. Menus start at 85F/€12.96, or you can eat *à la carte* for 150–200F/€22.87–30.49. Closed Sun.

La Dînée du Viguier, 4 rue Boutaric (☎05.65.50.08.08). The restaurant of the *Château du Viguier du Roy* hotel (see p.290) isn't as expensive as one might expect for such rarefied cuisine: 150F/€22.87 for two dishes, 220F/€33.54 for a full menu and around 300F/€45.73 à la carte. There are only a handful of tables in its elegant stone-walled room, so reservations are essential. Oct–April closed Sat lunch, Sun eve & Mon; May–Sept closed Mon midday; also closed 3 weeks from mid-Jan.

La Four à Bois, 26 rue Caviale. Join the locals in this rustic little restaurant offering something for everyone: salad, pasta, pizzas and regional dishes. There's a *plat du jour* at 42F/€6.40 and a regional menu at 95F/€14.48, or you can eat from the *carte* for around 150F/€22.87. Closed Sun & Mon lunch.

Pizzeria del Portel, 9 rue Orthabadial. Another good-value place serving tasty pizzas and pasta dishes, big plates of *moules frites*, and the usual local fare. It's not so cosy as *La Four à Bois*, but has the benefit of an outside terrace. Menus at 65F/€9.91 and 105F/€16.01 or expect to pay 150F/€22.87 or so à la carte. Closed Sun lunch & Mon.

La Puce à l'Oreille, 5 rue St-Thomas (05.65.34.33.08). Located north of place Carnot in a handsome fifteenth-century residence with an interior court for fine weather, this place serves rich Quercy fare – make sure you leave room for one of their scrumptious desserts. Menus range from 75F/€11.43 to 190F/€28.97 and there's a fulsome regional wine list. Closed Sun eve & Mon except in July & Aug; also closed 1 week early Nov.

La Table de Marinette, *Hôstellerie de l'Europe*, 51 allées Victor-Hugo. It's worth venturing south across the river for the well-priced menus in this hotel restaurant with its stylish 1930s decor. Specialities include *cassoulet*, Quercy lamb and *pastis*, the local dessert of apple tart topped with a mountain of ultra-fine crinkly pastry. They offer a wide range of menus starting at 78F/€11.89, while eating à la carte will set you back at least 250F/€38.11. Closed mid-Oct to May Sat & Sun eve.

Listings

Bike rental You can rent bikes at Ets Larroque, 10 quai Albert-Bessières (☎05.65.34.10.28), down beside the river.

Books and newspapers Your best bet for local guides and English newspapers is the Maison de la Presse, 2 rue Gambetta, down by the river.

Bus information For details of all bus routes, call the central information desk on ☎05.65.53.27.50.

Car rental The only option in central Figeac is Avis, 10 quai Albert-Bessières (☎05.65.34.10.28), with station pick-ups available on request.

Hospital Centre Hospitalier, rue des Maquisards (☎05.65.50.65.50), to the west of the old quarter.

Markets The main weekly market takes place on Saturday mornings, with fresh food under the *halle* on place Carnot, and dry goods on place Vival.

Police Commissariat de Police, Cité Administrative, pl des Carmes (☎05.65.50.73.73).

Post office The central post office is at 6 av Fernand-Pezet, 46100 Figeac.

Taxis Call Jean-Michel Luc on ☎05.65.50.00.20.

The Causse de Gramat

After the intimate beauty of the Lot and Célé valleys, the wide horizons of the **Causse de Gramat** to the north make a refreshing change. It's an empty land with few people and few villages, filled only with the sound of sheep bells and the cicadas' persistent clamour during the tinder-box-dry summers. Across the gently undulating landscape of scrubby pines and oaks and close-cropped grass spattered with orchids and aromatic plants, you'll come across dolmens, shepherds' dry-stone huts and strange *lacs de St-Namphaise* – water-holes hacked out of the rock – but little else to make you want to stop. The exceptions are mostly along the *causse*'s southern boundary, starting off in the far southeast with **Assier**, a small village put on the map by a vainglorious military man who built a château and church here. From Assier the route tracks westward through a series of picturesque villages to the even more diminutive **Caniac-du-Causse**, last resting place of St Namphaise of *lacs* fame. At Caniac the route turns northwards into the wildest part of the *causse* towards the busy market town of **Gramat**, home to a wildlife park, with an above-average collection of animals.

The main towns in this area are well served by **public transport**. Assier and Gramat both lie on main **train** lines and are also accessible by **bus**. However, to do the *causse* justice you really do need your own means of getting about. With few roads and only a sprinkling of villages, this is a great area for **walking** or mountain-biking; look out in local tourist offices and bookstores for the excellent booklet *Le Causse de Gramat*, in the Promenades et Randonnées series (37F/€5.64), which details eighteen circuits of varying lengths.

Assier

If it weren't for the immoderate – and immodest – nature of Galiot de Genouillac, **ASSIER**, some 17km northwest of Figeac, would probably have remained an insignificant village. Chief of artillery under François I and an inspired tactician, de Genouillac really earned his stripes during the decisive French victory at Marignano in 1515 in the Italian Wars, after which he returned to his native village bathed in glory to erect a **château** befitting his status (April–June & Sept daily except Tues 9.30am–12.15pm & 2–6.15pm; July & Aug daily 9.30am–12.30pm & 2–6.45pm; Oct–March daily except Tues 10am–12.15pm & 2–5.15pm; 20F/€3.05). Built in the latest Renaissance style, it was said to rival the châteaux of the Loire, with its vast interior courtyard flanked by four round towers, its galleries, loggias and carved friezes – and liberal repetition of de Genouillac's motto: *J'aime fortune* (In love with chance/success). After 1768, however, the château and its contents were sold off lock, stock and barrel to raise money, leaving only part of the west wing – and even that is in a pretty poor state.

You can get a better idea of de Genouillac's decorative tastes from the **church** he also had built in the village square. It's an extraordinary edifice, not just because of its size and the feeling that it was built to the glory of de Genouillac rather than God, but mainly due to a frieze running round the exterior depicting Roman centurions, guns being hauled across the Alps, flame-spewing cannon and cities under siege – all beautifully realized but hardly normal church ornamentation. Less surprisingly, the most interesting feature inside is the great man's tomb in an intricately vaulted chapel near the west door. He appears twice: as a bearded man lying with his feet on powder sacks and as a soldier leaning nonchalantly against a cannon.

Assier is a stop on the main Figeac–Brive train line, with a daily service direct to Paris. The **gare SNCF** lies nearly 1km west of the village. All **buses** running between Figeac and Gramat stop at the *gare*, and some also stop on the church square. There's a very helpful **tourist office** (June 15–30 Mon–Fri 2.30–5.30pm; July to mid-Sept daily 9am–noon & 3–6pm; mid-Sept to mid-June Mon & Thurs 2.30–5.30pm; ☎05.65.40.50.60, fax 05.65.40.41.99) on the square's northeast corner, and an equally accommodating **restaurant**, *Chez Noelle*, opposite the church, offering traditional family cuisine (closed 3 weeks in Sept; *plat du jour* at 45F/€6.86, menus from 65F/€9.91).

The southern causse

With your own transport, you can take a circuitous route from Assier through **the southern causse** before cutting northeast to Gramat. There are a few scattered sights to aim for, but on the whole it's the scenery that takes precedence in this high, open country with its grand vistas.

Five kilometres southwest of Assier on the D653 **LIVERNON** is the first of a string of attractive villages, in this case distinguished by a particularly appealing Romanesque belfry, with its rhythmically spaced arches. The route then meanders further south via **ESPÉDAILLAC** – a cluster of crumbling towers and pigeon-lofts – to **QUISSAC**, roughly 10km from Livernon. The main claim to fame of this tiny village is that the ninth-century soldier-turned-hermit **St Namphaise** lived in a nearby grotto. He's a terribly important person on the *causse*, since it was he who, according to legend, dug the shallow ponds in the rock which are characteristic of this region, thus providing water for the flocks of sheep; ironically, he is said to have been killed by an irate bull. There's a statue of Namphaise dressed as a soldier in Quissac church, and you can see one of his famous *lacs* about 1km south of the village beside the Coursac road.

The dying Namphaise supposedly threw away his hammer – with which he presumably created the ponds – and declared that he would be buried wherever it came to rest. It landed 8km away in what is now the village of **CANIAC-DU-CAUSSE**. It's a sleepy, flowery place undisturbed by the trickle of visitors come to view Namphaise's small, unadorned sarcophagus lying in a diminutive twelfth-century crypt beneath the village church.

From Caniac cut north across country on the D42, keeping a look out on the right for signs to the Site de Planagrèze a couple of kilometres later. At the end of a dirt track various footpaths and biking trails strike out across the *causse*, while one of the more accessible dolmen stands a short walk south. On the way you pass a fenced-off area in the middle of which is another typical feature of the *causse*, a limestone sinkhole, the **Igue de Planagrèze**; in this particular case potholers have so far explored 800m of tunnels.

From here the D42 continues north to Fontanes-du-Causse, where there's a choice of routes to Gramat: you can either stick to the back lanes, or cut west to the faster D677.

Gramat

The biggest town on the *causse*, and its capital, **GRAMAT** developed at the junction of two major Roman roads. Its fortunes increased further when pilgrims started passing through en route to Rocamadour (see p.243), and received another boost when the railway came here in 1863. Even today it is an important market town, with two weekly **markets** (Tues & Fri mornings) and bigger *foires* on the second and fourth Thursdays of each month. Though a few vestiges of the medieval town remain, Gramat is most of interest as somewhere to base yourself for a day or so; as well as being an ideal starting point for exploring the *causse*, it's also within easy striking distance of Rocamadour, only 9km away to the northwest, and sights in the upper Dordogne valley (see Chapter Five).

Gramat would be more appealing if it weren't for the busy N140 and D677 funnelling through **place de la République**, a big square on the east side of town. If you walk west from here along the **Grande Rue**, though, you'll suddenly find yourself among the narrow lanes of the old quarter. There's not a lot to see here but both the place de l'Hôtel de Ville, at the top of the Grande Rue, and the market square, south of the Grande Rue down rue Notre-Dame, are attractive corners.

Once you've explored the old town, however, the only thing to do is head 3km south on the D14 for a romp round an unusually good wildlife park, the **Parc Animalier de Gramat** (daily: April–Sept 9am–7pm; Oct–March 2–5pm; 43F/€6.56). Encompassing half a square kilometre of the *causse*, the park is home to 150 mostly European species, including wolves, otters, bears, ibex, with their magnificent curved horns, and *mouflon*, a type of goat crowned with no less than four horns. If possible it's best to visit first thing in the morning, during feeding time, and to avoid the summer's midday heat when nothing stirs save the cicadas. Allow at least two hours if you want to cover the whole park.

Practicalities

Arriving in Gramat by train, you'll pitch up at the **gare SNCF** 1km south of the centre; if no **taxis** are waiting, call Adgie on ☎05.65.38.70.54. Some **buses** call at the station but most drop you on place de la République, which is also where you'll find the **tourist office** (May, June & Sept Mon–Sat 9.30am–12.30pm & 2–7pm; July & Aug Mon–Sat 9.30am–12.30pm & 2–7pm, Sun 9.30am–12.30pm; Oct–April Mon–Sat 9.30am–12.30pm & 2–6.30pm; ☎05.65.38.73.60, fax 05.65.33.46.38, *www.quercy.net/quercy/gramat*) on the east side of the square.

The most appealing place to **stay** in Gramat is the English/French-owned *Relais des Gourmands*, opposite the train station (☎05.65.38.83.92, fax 05.65.38.70.99, *www.logis-de-france.fr*, ④; closed 2 weeks in Feb, also Sun eve to Mon midday inclusive except July & Aug), a delightful flowery spot, with airy rooms, a pool and excellent restaurant serving all the classics as well as lighter versions of regional cuisine (menus from 90F/€13.72). If it's full, try one of the two hotels on place de la République. The more refined *Lion d'Or* (☎05.65.38.73.18, fax 05.65.38.84.50; ④; closed mid-Dec to mid-Jan, also Mon midday Nov–March) occupies a handsome stone building on the north side of the square; its rooms are not particularly stylish, but comfortable enough, while the restaurant offers top-quality cooking (menus from 125F/€19.06). On the square's east side, you can't miss the electric-green shades of *Le Centre* (☎05.65.38.73.37, fax 05.65.38.73.66, *www.lecentre.fr*; ③; Oct–April closed Sat; menus from 80F/€12.20), which is equally cheerful inside, too, with good-value en-suite rooms.

If you'd rather be out in the countryside, you'll find a warm welcome at *Le Cloucau*, a very comfortable **chambres d'hôtes** signed off the D677 roughly 4km west of Gramat (☎ & fax 05.65.33.76.18, *lecloucau@caramail.com*; evening meals available on request at 115F/€17.53 including wine). Alternatively, there's a well-organized three-star **campsite**, *Les Ségalières* (☎05.65.38.76.92, fax 05.65.33.16.48; closed Oct–May), opposite the entrance to the Parc Animalier.

Gourdon and the Bouriane

Thirty-five kilometres west of Gramat, **GOURDON** is an attractive town, its medieval centre of butter-coloured stone houses attached like a swarm of bees to a prominent hilltop, neatly ringed by shady modern boulevards, known collectively as the **Tour-de-Ville**. While it has no outstanding sights, Gourdon makes a quiet, pleasant base, not only for the nearby **Grottes de Cougnac**, with their prehistoric paintings, but also for the **Bouriane** to the south, a hugely pretty area of luxuriant woods and valleys merging into neighbouring Périgord. The Bouriane is primarily a place to wander with no particular destination in mind, but anyone interested in twentieth-century art should visit **Les Arques**, in the south of the region, where a number of Russian exile Ossip Zadkine's powerful, sometimes disturbing, sculptures are on display.

Gourdon lies on the main Toulouse–Brive **train** line and is also accessible by **bus** from Souillac and Cahors. However, to explore the Bouriane you'll need your own means of getting about.

Arrival, information and accommodation

Gourdon's **gare SNCF** is located roughly 1km northeast of the old centre; from the station, walk south on avenue de la Gare, then turn right onto avenue Gambetta to come out on the south side of the Tour-de-Ville. **Taxis** come to meet the trains, or you could try calling one of the two local companies: Pasteur (☎05.65.41.08.63) or Gélis (☎05.65.41.36.31). Arriving by **bus**, services terminate on place de la Libération on the southwest side of the Tour-de-Ville. There are no **car rental** outlets in Gourdon, but you can arrange to pick up cars at the station through Avis in Cahors (see p.277).

The **tourist office**, at 24 rue du Majou in the old centre (March–May & Oct Mon–Sat 10am–noon & 2–6pm; June & Sept Mon–Sat 10am–noon & 2–6pm, Sun 10am–noon; July & Aug Mon–Sat 10am–7pm, Sun 10am–noon; Nov–Feb Mon–Sat 10am–noon & 2–5pm; ☎05.65.27.52.50, fax 05.65.27.52.52, *www.*

quercy.net/quercy/gourdon), dispenses town maps and details of Gourdon's festivities (see box on p.266). You can rent **bikes** from MJC, place Noël-Poujade (☎05.65.41.11.65), immediately behind the tourist office.

For an overnight **stay**, head for the cheerful and very reasonably priced *Hôtel de la Promenade*, on the northwest side of the Tour-de-Ville at 48 bd Galiot-de-Genouillac (☎05.65.41.41.44, fax 05.65.41.41.22; ③), with immaculate rooms and a decent restaurant (closed Sun lunch; menus from 71F/€10.82). Less in the thick of things, though not such good value, there's the *Hostellerie de la Bouriane*, place du Foirail (☎05.65.41.16.37, fax 05.65.41.04.92; ⑤; menus from 85F/€12.96; restaurant closed April–Oct Sat & Mon lunch, rest of year closed Sat lunch, Sun eve & Mon), set in pleasant gardens outside the Tour-de-Ville to the southeast, two minutes' walk down avenue Jean-Admirat. Alternatively, *Le Terminus*, 7 av de la Gare (☎05.65.41.03.29, fax 05.65.41.29.49; ③; menus from 70F/€10.67), near the train station, offers jolly, well-priced rooms and a little pool with views over fields. Finally, there's a good, three-star municipal **campsite**, *Écoute s'il Pleut* (☎ & fax 05.65.41.06.19; closed Oct–May), 1km north on the Sarlat road beside a leisure lake; the name, meaning "listen if it rains", comes from a mill which only functioned when there was sufficient rain to swell the river.

The Town

Where the ramparts once stood, Gourdon's medieval centre is now entirely surrounded by the **Tour-de-Ville**. The best-preserved gateway into the centre is southwesterly port du Majou, which stands guard over the old town's canyon-like main street, **rue du Majou**. The street is lined with mellow stone-built houses, some, like the **Maison d'Anglars**, at no. 17, with its ogive arches and mullion windows, as old as the thirteenth century; look out on the right, as you go up, for the delightfully – and accurately – named rue Zig-Zag.

At its upper end, rue du Majou opens onto a lovely cobbled square beneath the twin towers of the massive fourteenth-century **church of St-Pierre**. Note the traces of fortifications, in the form of machicolations, over the west door, but you'll find nothing of particular interest inside, beyond some seventeenth-century gilded bas-reliefs by a local sculptor depicting the life of the Virgin Mary. The **Hôtel de Ville** – a handsome if unpretentious building whose arcaded ground floor once served as the market hall – stands on the west side of the square, while east of the church in place des Marronniers an ornately carved door marks the home of the Cavaignac family, who supplied the nation with numerous prominent public figures in the eighteenth and nineteenth centuries, including the notoriously brutal general who put down the Paris workers' attempts to defend the Second Republic in June 1848.

From the north side of the church, a path leads to the top of the hill where Gourdon's castle stood until it was razed in the early seventeenth century in the wake of the Wars of Religion. At 264m in height it affords superb views over the wooded country stretching north to the Dordogne valley.

Eating and drinking

The best place to **eat** in Gourdon is *La Bonne Auberge*, the restaurant of the *Hôtel Bissonnier*, 51 bd des Martyrs, on the eastern boulevard, which serves traditional dishes such as pigeon, rabbit and roast lamb from the *causse* (☎05.65.41.02.48; Oct–April closed Sun evening & Mon lunch; menus from 86F/€13.11). Otherwise, *Croque-Note*, with a tiny outdoor terrace at 12 rue Jean-Jaurès on the southeast side of the old town, is a safe bet for its copious salads and regional dishes (mid-April to June & Sept closed Mon, Oct to mid-April closed Mon–Wed & Thurs lunch; menus from 70F/€10.67). A third option is *Le P'tit Bouchon*, just round the corner at 31 bd Cabanès (closed Sun & Mon except in July & Aug), which serves *plats du jours* at 45F/€6.86 and full menus starting at 69F/€10.52; the place also doubles as a **wine bar**, and you can sample local wines from 14F/€2.13 a glass.

For picnic fare, there are fresh-food **markets** on Tuesdays beside the church in place St-Pierre and on Saturdays beside the post office. In July and August an important farmers' market takes place on Thursday mornings in place St-Pierre, while the Tour-de-Ville is closed off on the first and third Tuesdays of the month for a traditional country fair.

The Grottes de Cougnac

Signed off the Sarlat road a couple of kilometres north of Gourdon, the **Grottes de Cougnac** (1hr guided tours daily: April–June, Sept & Oct 9.30–11am & 2–5pm; July & Aug 9.30am–6pm; 34F/€5.18) were discovered in 1949 by a local water-diviner. To begin with all the subsequent explorers found were rock formations – notably ceilings festooned with ice-white needles like some glitzy ballroom decoration – but three years later they hit gold when they came across **prehistoric paintings**. These date from between 25,000 and 19,000 years ago, when Cro-Magnon people (see p.208) ventured deep inside the caves to paint panels of ibex, reindeer and mammoths in elegant outline, using the rock's undulating surface to provide a sense of form and movement. They also left hundreds of mysterious signs – mostly dots and pairs of short lines – in addition to two human figures seemingly pierced by spears, a motif also found in Pech-Merle (see p.285).

Southwest through the Bouriane

The country southwest of Gourdon is a delight. Lanes tunnel through chestnut and pine woods, twisting up the valley sides past the occasional patch of vines and then popping out obligingly on high ground for the views. The **Céou valley** to the south of Gourdon provides one particularly beguiling route, although what sights there are in the Bouriane lie further west and are most easily accessed via the D673.

The first place of any size you come to along this road is the fortified village of **SALVIAC**, 14km from Gourdon, whose Gothic church was built in the late thirteenth century by Jean Duèze of Cahors, the future Pope John XXII (see p.268), and still contains fine stained-glass windows from that era. Seven kilometres further on, the *bastide* town of **CAZALS** has seen better days: its feudal château and ramparts were largely destroyed during the Hundred Years' War, though its big central square remains, and the whole place bursts into life in early July for a major contemporary dance festival (see box on p.266). From here, you can work your way 9km eastwards through enticing back lanes to **RAMPOUX**. This unusually scattered hamlet is home to a Romanesque priory-church in which one of the original frescoes can still be seen – a very faded Christ in majesty in the apse. Better preserved are those from the fifteenth century in the south chapel portraying the life of Jesus.

The next port of call, **LES ARQUES**, is equally buried in the countryside, 10km southwest of Rampoux and 6km south of Cazals. It's a nicely higgledy-piggledy village on a hillock above the River Masse, but its main draw is the Romanesque **church** and the neighbouring **Musée Zadkine** (June–Sept & school hols daily 10am–1pm & 2–7pm; rest of year Mon–Fri 10am–1pm & 2–7pm, Sat & Sun 2–5pm; 15F/€2.29). A Russian émigré and well-known sculptor, Ossip Zadkine set up a studio in Les Arques in 1934 and worked on and off in the village until his death in 1967, producing big, powerful statues full of restless energy. Many are on a mythological or musical theme, such as those of Orpheus and Diana, the latter metamorphosing from tree to woman, and there's a strong Cubist influence, although his works grew more abstract towards the end of his life. Some of his most compelling pieces are displayed inside the church, whose cool stone interior provides the perfect foil for a passionate rendering of Christ on the Cross and, in the crypt, the *Pietà*. Mary sits without hope, her tortured face gazing off into the distance while the broken body of her son lies slumped across her knees, as if forgotten.

In season, it's worth timing your visit to have lunch in the old schoolhouse at the entrance to the village, now home to an attractive **restaurant**, *La Récréation* (☎05.65.22.88.08; closed Dec–Feb, also March–April, Oct & Nov closed Mon–Thurs & Sun eve, May–Sept closed Wed & Thurs lunch). In July and August they serve a two-course lunch menu for 90F/€13.72 (daily except Sun), including coffee and wine, while for the rest of the year there's a single *menu carte* at 150F/€22.87 for five courses. Reservations are required at any time of year, but in summer you'll need to book at least two or three days in advance.

Another possibility for eating, or for an overnight stay, would be to continue southwest for 5km to **GOUJOUNAC**, whose **church** has rather worn Romanesque carvings of Christ in majesty and the four Evangelists over the south door. Opposite the church the pretty *Hostellerie de Goujounac* (☎05.65.36.68.67, fax 05.65.36.60.54; ②; closed 1 week at Christmas, also Sun eve & Mon except in July & Aug; menus from 75F/€11.43) offers honest country cooking in addition to five very simple **rooms**; if you want to stay here, you'll need to book well ahead in the summer season. Otherwise, there's a three-star **campsite**, *Camping La Pinède* (☎05.65.36.61.84; closed mid-Sept to mid-June), immediately west of Goujounac on the D660 Villefranche road.

West along the Lot from Cahors

The Bouriane's southern boundary is marked by the River Lot, which follows a particularly convoluted course downstream of Cahors as it doubles back on itself again and again between cliffs which gradually diminish towards the west. Standing guard over one of the larger meanders is **Luzech**, whose main claim to fame is the scant remains of a Roman encampment on the hill above the town, one of several possible contenders for the site of the Gaulish fort of Uxellodunum, celebrated as being the last to fall to the Roman legions after a heroic battle. Continuing downstream, the route winds through a series of villages perched above the river, culminating in one of the most beautiful along the entire Lot valley, **Puy-l'Évêque**. A castle-town built on a terraced cliff, it dominates the last of the river's meanders, and its wandering lanes, tunnels, staircases and fountains together compensate for the lack of any first-rate sights. The area around **Duravel** and **Touzac**, further west again, with its fine selection of hotels and restaurants, provides a good base for visiting the impressive **Château de Bonaguil** in the hills to the north of the Lot. The last of the medieval castles to be constructed in France, and now partially in ruins, it still bristles with sophisticated defensive devices. Back on the Lot, **Fumel** is a major transport hub and service centre, though otherwise contains nothing to make you dally – better to hurry on downriver to where **Penne-d'Agenais**, with its striking basilica, lords it over the valley.

Public transport along this stretch of the river consists of an SNCF **bus** that threads along the valley from Cahors via Luzech, Puy-l'Évêque and Fumel to Monsempron-Libos, on the Agen–Périgueux train line. On the way it also passes through or close by most of the smaller villages cited below. From Fumel you can continue on by bus to Penne-d'Agenais and Villeneuve-sur-Lot (see p.306), but you'll need your own transport to reach the Château de Bonaguil and the villages north of the valley.

Luzech

Twenty kilometres downriver from Cahors you come to **LUZECH**, sited on the narrow neck of a particularly large meander and overlooked by a twelfth-century **keep**. There's a small area of picturesque alleys to the north of **place du Canal**, the central square spanning the isthmus, where you'll find the **Maison des Consuls** on rue de la Ville. Built in 1270, its most distinguished feature is the sturdy Gothic arch on the ground floor offset by a pair of airy, double-arched windows worked in brick above. The building is now home to the tourist office and an interesting one-room **museum** of archeological finds from around Luzech (July & Aug Mon–Sat 9.30am–12.30pm & 2.30–6pm, Sun 10am–noon & 2–4pm; rest of year Mon–Fri 9.30am–12.30pm & 3–6pm; free). Though there are some delicate Gaulish safety pins and needles, the exhibits demonstrate the huge leap in craftsmanship ushered in by the Romans in the first century BC: look out for the unusual folding spoon and the very fine red-clay pottery from the Tarn, not to mention the Roman coins chopped in half for small change.

The majority of items come from a fortress on a hill above the town occupied since the early Iron Age, later reinforced by the Romans, who also erected a temple on the site. Little remains of their **Oppidum d'Impernal** beyond a few foundation stones, but it's worth trekking up for a splendid view over the Luzech meander. It's 1.5km by road, or you can walk up in about ten minutes: from the north end of rue de la Ville, follow signs for the GR36 footpath, past the castle keep and then just keep climbing. For a less strenuous jaunt, head south for about 2km to visit a tiny chapel, **Notre-Dame de l'Oesle**, surrounded by vines and walnut trees on the very tip of the meander.

Practicalities
Buses from Cahors pull in beside a roundabout at the east end of place du Canal, where you'll find the **tourist office** in the Maison des Consuls (July & Aug Mon–Sat 9.30am–12.30pm & 2.30–6pm, Sun 10am–noon & 2–4pm; rest of year

Mon–Fri 9.30am–12.30pm & 3–6pm; ☎ & fax 05.65.20.17.27, *www.ville-luzech.fr*).
Accommodation is limited to the aged *Hôtel Le Barry*, rue du Barry
(☎05.65.30.33.50, fax 05.65.30.33.59; ②; menus from 85F/€12.96), to the south of
place du Canal, and a more welcoming two-star municipal **campsite**, *Camping de
l'Alcade* (☎05.65.30.72.32, fax 05.65.30.76.80, *maire.luzech@wanadoo.fr*; closed
Oct–April), beside the river immediately west of town on the Albas road.

Luzech marks the end of the navigable river descending from St-Cirq-Lapopie.
Houseboats are available through Locaboat Plaisance (see p.268) 2km north on
the D9. Pleasure **boats** can also be rented by the day or half-day from Navilot
(☎05.65.20.18.19) at the Base Nautique in **CAIX**, 1km further north; they also
offer **canoes** and **bikes**, and you can pitch a tent in their no-frills **campsite**
(closed Oct–June).

On towards Puy-l'Évêque

The prettiest route downstream from Luzech – and that followed by the bus – is
the D8 along the river's south bank. It's especially beguiling in summer when the
intense green of the vines and walnut trees in the valley bottom is offset against
the dark grey cliffs. The river loops back and forth across the flood plain, with a
village at the bottom of each meander. The first you come to, and the most attractive, is **ALBAS**, 5km from Luzech, instantly recognizable by its tall church spire.
The church is nineteenth century and otherwise uninteresting, but the steep
lanes below retain a few noble fourteenth- and fifteenth-century facades, a
reminder of when the bishops of Cahors maintained a residence here.

There are a couple of good pit stops in Albas and its vicinity. In the town itself
the *Restaurant du Port* (closed Tues), which occupies a small vaulted room on the
road from the central square down to the river, serves good old-fashioned menus
from 60F/€9.15, in addition to salads, omelettes and the like. Two kilometres
east, the *Auberge Imhotep* (☎05.65.30.70.91; closed Sun eve & Mon) is a friendly
little **restaurant** named after the ancient Egyptian who supposedly discovered
the art of *gavage* – the process of force-feeding ducks for foie gras – in 2600 BC.
Naturally, duck features strongly on the menu, including innovative dishes such
as duck kebabs with curry sauce, and they also offer an excellent Cahors wine-
list (menus at 78–250F/€11.89–38.11).

Two meanders and 18km west of Albas, **GRÉZELS** was another episcopal seat,
though in this case its **château** – a very sober affair – has survived thanks to a
seventeenth-century rebuild. But the prime attraction here is another **restaurant**,
the rustic *La Terrasse* (☎05.65.21.34.03; July & Aug daily except Sun eve & Mon,
rest of year Tues–Sat open for lunch only, closed first 2 weeks in Sept), on the
main road through the village, renowned for its jovial host and no-nonsense cuisine. There's only one menu which changes daily (85F/€12.96 on weekdays;
135F/€20.58 at weekends). Make sure you've got a healthy appetite, and note
that reservations are strongly recommended.

Puy-l'Évêque and around

Five kilometres from Grézels and 30km from Cahors by the main D911, **PUY-
L'ÉVÊQUE** contends with St-Cirq-Lapopie (see p.280) as the Lot valley's prettiest
village. After 1227 it marked the western extremity of the Cahors bishops'
domains and it is the remains of their thirteenth-century **château**, a big square

keep like that at Luzech, which provides the town's focal point. Puy-l'Évêque changed hands any number of times during the Hundred Years' War, but then withstood a prolonged Protestant siege in 1580 during the Wars of Religion. Ardent anti-clerics tried to change the name to Puy-Libre during the Revolution, then Puy-sur-Lot, but the locals weren't convinced and it soon reverted to Puy-l'Évêque.

There are no great sights to speak of, just lanes of medieval and Renaissance houses built in honey-coloured stone. From the main **place de la Truffière**, beside the castle keep at the top of the town, **rue du Fort** leads steeply down then flattens out beneath an imposing fourteenth-century building distinguished by its Gothic windows, which served as the bishops' audience chamber. As it curves round the hill, rue du Fort becomes rue Bovila and then peters out beside a staircase descending to rue des Capucins. This road heads back east along the hillside to **place Guillaume-de-Cardaillac** and then **place de la Halle**, the town's two most picturesque corners. Downhill from place de la Halle again, you come to rue de la Cale, with the dark alleys of the artisans' quarter off to the left, and the old **port**. For the best **view** of the whole ensemble walk out onto the modern bridge which crosses the Lot here. Alternatively, head for the belvedere in front of the **church of St-Sauveur** which guards Puy-l'Évêque's northeast quarter – literally, since it once formed an integral part of the fortifications; look carefully and you can still see where cannonballs found their target during the siege of 1580.

Practicalities

SNCF **buses** from Cahors stop in front of the church on place du Rampeau and down on rue des Platanes to the southeast of the old centre. The **tourist office** is behind the castle keep on place de la Truffière (July & Aug Mon–Sat 9am–12.30pm & 2.30–6pm, Sun 10am–noon; rest of year Mon–Sat 8.30am–12.30pm & 2–5.30pm; ☎ & fax 05.65.21.37.63, *office.du.tourisme.puy.l.eveque@wanadoo.fr*). This square is also the venue for the main weekly **market** (Tues am), with a small farmers' market taking place on Saturdays in the lower town on place George-Henry, at the west end of rue des Platanes.

For an overnight **stay**, the refurbished *Hôtel Bellevue*, perched on the cliff edge on place de la Truffière (☎05.65.36.06.60, fax 05.65.36.06.61; ⑤; closed Jan), has very stylish rooms, all with ultra-contemporary decor and fine views, and with a restaurant to match (menus from 170F/€25.92, or 75F/€11.43 in the brasserie). Opposite, *La Truffière* (☎05.65.21.34.54, fax 05.65.30.84.47, *www.epicuria.fr/truffier;* ③; closed 2 weeks in March & 2 weeks in Oct) offers a more rustic atmosphere, with aged but well-kept and spacious en-suite rooms, while their restaurant draws the locals with its excellent-value menus (July & Aug closed Sun eve, rest of year closed for dinner Fri–Sun; from 75F/€11.43). Alternatively you could try the very reasonably priced English-owned **chambres d'hôtes** at *Maison Rouma*, 2 rue du Docteur-Rouma (☎ & fax 05.65.36.59.39; ③), at the east end of the bridge. Its three rooms are immaculate and oozing with character, but the highlight is the glorious view of Puy-l'Évêque from the garden. There's also a two-star, Dutch-owned **campsite**, *Camping Les Vignes* (☎ & fax 05.65.30.81.72; closed Oct–March), 3km south along the river on the D28.

As for **eating**, in winter time *Le Fournil de l'Opéra Bouffe*, 24 Grand Rue (☎05.65.36.45.15; closed Tues except in July & Aug; menus from 75F/€11.43, or you can eat à la carte for around 150F/€22.87), on the main road leading from the lower to the upper town, is a nice cosy place offering grills cooked on a wood fire. In summer, on the other hand, the nicest option for a drink or a meal is the riverside *Le Pigeonnier* (☎05.65.21.37.77; April–Sept daily except Mon midday, Oct to early Nov & mid-Jan to March open Sat & Sun), on the far side of the bridge. Apart from splendid views, they also offer good-value salads and *crêpes* (a meal will set you back 50–100F/€7.62–15.24); reservations are recommended from June to September. You can also rent **canoes** here (July & Aug), while **bikes** are available from Loca-Lot (☎05.65.36.59.22), 5km downstream in **VIRE-SUR-LOT**.

Martignac

One of the best excursions in the vicinity is to the hamlet of **MARTIGNAC**, 2.5km north, where the much-altered Romanesque **church of St-Pierre-ès-Liens** contains some remarkable late-fifteenth- and early-sixteenth-century frescoes – hidden under plaster until 1938, they are reasonably well preserved. Characters on the north wall represent the Seven Deadly Sins being escorted to the mouth of hell, each mounted on a different animal: Lust on a billy goat, Gluttony scoffing ham and wine and riding a pig, and scruffy Sloth on a donkey bringing up the tail. The Seven Virtues surround the apse, their grey robes tumbling about them, with Courage and Temperance being the easiest to recognize – the former holds a serpent, while Temperance carefully waters down her wine.

Duravel and around

Downstream of Puy-l'Évêque, the Lot valley begins to open out as the hills along the southern bank fade away. Those to the north continue a while longer, providing a green backdrop for the pretty eleventh-century **church** of **DURAVEL**, 6km from Puy-l'Évêque. Its crypt contains the remains of no less than three saints – Poémon, Agathon and Hilarion, their bodies having been brought back from the Holy Land in the eleventh century – but the village is unfortunately spoilt by the busy main road passing through its centre.

There are, however, a number of excellent **chambres d'hôtes** and **eating** options round about. If money is no object, the *Domaine de Haut-Barran* (☎05.65.24.63.24, fax 05.65.36.59.05, *www.hautbaran.com*; ⑥), in an old Quercy farmhouse in a bowl of hills 3.5km northeast of Duravel, signed off the D911, is the most romantic spot. They offer five immaculate *chambres d'hôtes*, not huge, but all designed with great flair, as well as a pool and glorious views over a willow-fringed lake and walnut orchard to the Lot valley beyond. Meals are available on request (from 120F/€18.29), or you can walk 500m downhill to feast on good old-fashioned home cooking at *Aux Dodus d'Audhuy* (☎05.65.36.44.12; April–June & Sept–Dec open Fri, Sat & Sun lunch, July & Aug open daily for dinner, closed Jan–March; menu at 120F/€18.29), where it's wise to reserve; the name, meaning the roly-poly people of Audhuy, says it all. One kilometre to the south of Duravel, you'll also get a warm welcome and good food at *La Roseraie* (☎05.65.24.63.82, fax 05.65.30.89.79), a busy working farm offering simple *chambres d'hôtes* (③; closed Nov–March), *ferme-auberge* meals (menus from 110F/€16.77; by reservation only; daily in July & Aug; rest of year Sat & Sun only) and dinner-dances on Fridays in July & Aug (125F/€19.06 including wine; reservation required), as well as a farm shop selling everything from duck to ostrich meat; they even produce their own wine.

Five kilometres southwest across the Lot, you'll find an idyllic **hotel**, the *Hostellerie de la Source Bleue* (☎05.65.36.52.01, fax 05.65.24.65.69, *www. sourcebleue.com*; ④; closed Jan–March), just south of the village of **TOUZAC**, in an ancient, spring-fed water mill swamped by luxuriant vegetation. It's worth paying extra for rooms in the old mill; those in the newer building next door are huge but in need of renovation. They don't offer meals, but you can **eat** at *La Source Enchantée* (☎05.65.30.63.18; closed Jan & Feb, also Mon lunch & Wed; menus from 100F/€15.24), conveniently located at the entrance. There's also a shady three-star **campsite**, *Le Clos Bouyssac* (☎05.65.36.52.21, fax 05.65.24.68.51, *camping.leclosbouyssac@wanadoo.fr*; closed Oct–April), a short distance south along the riverbank.

North to the Château de Bonaguil

With your own transport, you can cut northwest across country from Duravel to visit the magnificent ruined castle of Bonaguil. On the way it's worth taking a short detour to **MONTCABRIER**, just over 5km north of Duravel, if for no other reason than because this tiny *bastide* seems to have been forgotten by the renovators and tourist authorities. There is a clutch of once-noble residences around the chestnut-shaded main square, but the village is best known for a diminutive statue lodged in the north nave of its quietly crumbling **church of St-Louis**. It is one of the first stone representations of the saint, formerly King Louis IX, showing him as a bearded figure wearing a painted crown. It is also slightly macabre: when Louis died on a crusade in 1270, his body was immediately chopped into pieces and dispatched around Europe to meet the demand for relics. Apparently, one unspecified piece of the king now resides inside this little statue.

From Montcabrier take the D673 from below the village heading southwest, then turn west through the delightful hamlet of St-Martin-Le-Redon and start climbing. As the road crests the ridge you get a stunning view of the **Château de Bonaguil** (daily: Feb–May & Sept–Nov 10.30am–noon & 2.30–5pm; June 10am–noon & 2–5pm; July & Aug 10am–5.45pm; closed Dec & Jan; 30F/€4.57), 7km from Montcabrier, perched at the end of a wooded spur. The castle dates largely from the fifteenth and sixteenth centuries when Bérenger de Roquefeuil, from a powerful Languedoc family and by all accounts a nasty piece of work, inherited the partially ruined castle. Fearing revolts by his vassals, he decided to transform it into an impregnable fortress, just as his contemporaries were abandoning such elaborate fortifications. It took him around forty years to do so, constructing a double ring of walls, six huge towers, a highly unusual, narrow boat-shaped keep, and sophisticated loopholes with overlapping lines of fire. Perhaps because of such elaborate precautions, Bonaguil was never attacked, and although some demolition occurred during the Revolution, the castle still stands, bloodied but unbowed.

As a result, the site attracts up to 2000 tourists per day in July and August. It's best to arrive first thing in the morning to avoid the worst of the crush, and rather than joining the **guided tours** (1hr; English tours available in July & Aug), which get tedious when it's very busy, it's preferable to buy one of the very comprehensive guide books (25F/€3.81) from the bookstore in the chapel near the ticket gate and do it yourself.

There are a couple of **eating** places below the castle, including the *Auberge les Bons Enfants* (closed mid-Oct to mid-March), which serves drinks and snacks all day as well as more substantial meals from 60F/€9.15. However, you're better off heading north 7km through the back lanes to **SAUVETERRE-LA-LÉMANCE**, where the friendly *Hôtel du Centre*, near the church (☎05.53.40.65.45, fax 05.53.40.68.59; ②; closed mid-Dec to Feb; menus from 75F/€11.43), offers excellent-value regional cuisine in addition to a handful of basic rooms (no en-suite facilities).

Fumel and around

Eight kilometres southwest of Bonaguil and 12km west of Duravel, **FUMEL** – an important stronghold in medieval times – is now a busy industrial town which holds little of interest beyond its transport facilities and a decent hotel. It lies on the north bank of the Lot, spilling along the main road from its old centre – focused around **place du Postel** – in the east, past a huge factory making car parts, and then merges 4km later with the western suburb of **MONSEMPRON-LIBOS**.

It's in Monsempron-Libos that you'll find the **gare SNCF**, set back from the river near the new road bridge at the end of avenue de la Gare. This is where SNCF **buses** from Cahors terminate, having first called in Fumel at place du Postel. Buses from Villeneuve-sur-Lot (operated by Cars Evasion; ☎05.53.40.88.20), on the other hand, drop you on place Voltaire, a short walk north of the old town.

You'll find Fumel's **tourist office** on place Geroges-Escandes, immediately east of place du Postel (mid-July to mid-Aug Mon–Fri 9am–6.30pm, Sat 9am–6pm, Sun 10am–12.30pm; rest of year Mon–Fri 9am–noon & 2.30–6pm, Sat 9am–noon & 3–5pm, Sun 10am–noon; ☎05.53.71.13.70, fax 05.53.71.40.91). **Bike rental** is available from AJF Cycles, 8 place du Postel (☎05.53.71.14.57), and for a **taxi**, call Taxi Fumélois (☎05.53.71.39.50) in Fumel, or Ets Fantin (☎05.53.40.86.77) in Monsempron-Libos.

The best bet for an overnight **stay** is the modern and welcoming, Dutch-run *Hôtel Kyriad*, place de l'Église (☎05.53.40.93.93, fax 05.53.71.27.94; ③), perched on the cliff to the south of place du Postel. Most rooms have valley views, and there's also a pool and a decent **restaurant**, *La Soupière*, offering a choice of a self-service buffet (65F/€9.91), menus from 75F/€11.43 and à la carte around 130F/€19.82. If you're looking for a **campsite**, head 3.5km east through the village of Condat to the two-star *Camping de Condat* (☎05.53.71.45.72, fax 05.53.71.36.69; open all year), a relaxed but well-cared-for place beside the river; SNCF buses stop 1.5km up the road in Condat.

With your own transport, a better option than staying in Fumel would be to head 9km southeast to the *Hostellerie Le Vert* (☎05.65.36.51.36, fax 05.65.36.56.84, *www.logis-de-france.fr*; ③–⑤; closed mid-Nov to mid-Feb), a lovely old farm set in fields just east of Mauroux on the D5 Puy-l'Évêque road, offering a handful of comfortable rooms – the two more expensive rooms in the annexe have more character – and a good **restaurant** serving regional cuisine (closed all day Thurs & Fri lunch; menus from 120F/€18.29).

Penne-d'Agenais

The last stop along the valley before Villeneuve-sur-Lot is the beautiful but touristy old fortress-town of **PENNE-D'AGENAIS**, 15km downstream from

Fumel on the river's south bank, where a silver-domed **basilica** teeters on the cliff edge. **Notre-Dame-de-Peyragude** dates back to 1000, but had the misfortune to be built on a particularly strategic pinnacle of rock. After Richard the Lionheart erected a castle right next door in 1182, the chapel found itself in the crossfire on any number of occasions; in 1412 Penne changed hands no less than four times. The most recent construction was only completed in 1949; there's nothing particular to see inside, and the neighbouring castle was razed during the Wars of Religion, but the climb is rewarded with panoramic views.

From **place Gambetta**, the main square immediately south of the old town, **rue du 14-Juillet** ducks under a medieval gate. From there just follow your fancy uphill along narrow lanes lined with an alluring mix of brick and stone houses – all incredibly spick and span. A few twists and turns later you emerge beside the basilica.

Penne lies on the Agen–Paris main line, its **gare SNCF** a couple of kilometres southeast down the D103 to Agen. **Buses** between Fumel and Villeneuve-sur-Lot drop you 2km north across the river in St-Sylvestre. If you need a **taxi**, call Pallard on ☎05.53.41.22.66. There's a **tourist office**, just inside the gate on rue du 14-Juillet (June to mid-Sept Mon–Fri 9.30am–12.30pm & 2–7pm, Sat Mon–Fri 9.30am–12.30pm & 3–7pm, Sun 3–7pm; rest of year Mon–Sat 9am–12.30pm & 2–6pm, Sun 2–6pm; ☎05.53.41.37.80, fax 05.53.49.38.37, *www.ville-pennedagenais. fr*), and a comfortable if characterless **hotel**, *Le Compostelle*, rue Jean-Moulin (☎05.53.41.12.41, fax 05.53.41.00.20; ③; closed Jan & Feb; restaurant from 65F/€9.91), at the bottom of the hill; it's well signed off the road to the station. As for **campsites**, there's a choice between the small, two-star riverside *Camping Municipal de St-Sylvestre* (☎05.53.41.22.23; closed Oct to mid-May), beside the bridge over the Lot, and the three-star *Camping Municipal de Férrié* (☎05.53.41.30.97; open mid-June to Aug) beside a leisure lake just north of Penne's *gare SNCF*.

Villeneuve-sur-Lot and around

VILLENEUVE-SUR-LOT, straddling the river 10km west of Penne-d'Agenais, is a pleasant, workaday sort of town. It has no terribly compelling sights, but the handful of attractive timbered houses in the old centre go some way to compensate, while the nearby hilltop village of **Pujols** makes for an enjoyable excursion. Founded in 1251 by Alphonse de Poitiers, Villeneuve was one of the region's earliest *bastide* towns (see p.310), and in no time it developed into an important commercial centre, which it remains to this day. As elsewhere, its ramparts have given way to encircling boulevards, but the distinctive chequerboard street plan survives, along with two medieval gates and the old, arched bridge.

Arrival, information and accommodation

While there is no longer a train station in Villeneuve itself, SNCF runs regular **bus services** from Agen, which is on the Bordeaux–Toulouse and Agen–Périgueux lines. These buses call at Villeneuve's former *gare SNCF* (where there's an SNCF ticket office), a good five minutes' walk south of the centre, before terminating near the theatre on the opposite side of town. Other buses

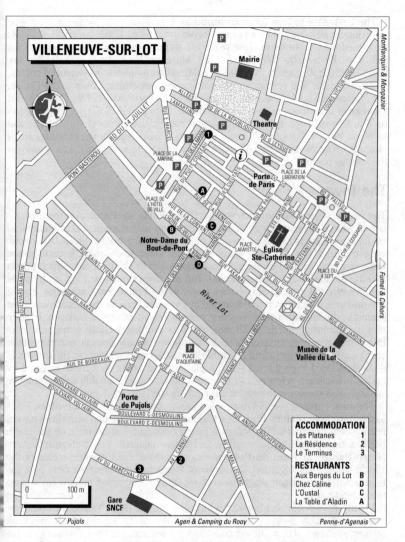

from Fumel, Bergerac, Marmande and Monflanquin stop by the theatre, at the old *gare* or near the post office, but the situation is not static: for further details call the central information desk (☎05.53.69.42.03) or ask at the **tourist office** opposite the theatre at 1 bd de la République (June–Aug Mon–Sat 9am–7pm, Sun 10am–1pm; rest of year Mon–Sat 9am–noon & 2–6pm; ☎05.53.36.17.30, fax 05.53.49.42.98). The tourist office also rents out **bikes** in summer (July–Sept). At other times of year, try Cycles Lamiche, at 11 allées Lamartine (☎05.53.70.42.65), west along the boulevard.

The best place to look for **accommodation** is around the former *gare*, where the friendly *Résidence*, 17 av Lazare-Carnot (☎05.53.40.17.03, fax 05.53.01.57.34; ①; closed for Christmas & New Year), offers unbeatable value for money. If it's full, try the nearby *Terminus*, 2 av Maréchal-Foch (☎05.53.70.94.36, fax 05.53.70.45.13; ③; menus from 58F/€8.84), with completely modernized rooms, a retro-style bar and restaurant downstairs. For something closer to the centre, *Les Platanes*, 40 bd de la Marine (☎05.53.40.11.40, fax 05.53.70.71.95; ①–③; closed 2 weeks at Christmas; restaurant closed Sun, from 70F/€10.67), on the old quarter's northwest corner, has old-fashioned rooms, the cheapest without en-suite facilities, but it's all spotlessly clean. Campers should head for the two-star **campsite**, *Camping du Rooy* (☎05.53.70.24.18; closed Oct to mid-April), 1.5km away in the southern suburbs, signed off the Agen road.

The Town

The *bastide*'s principal entrance was northerly **Porte de Paris**, also the prison – one of whose occupants was an unfortunate, and incompetent, baker incarcerated for the heinous crime of turning out substandard bread. From here semi-pedestrianized rue de Paris leads south to Villeneuve's main square, **place Lafayette**, surrounded by arcaded town houses in brick and stone, which bursts into life on market days (Tues & Sat). But the town's most striking landmark is the 55-metre-tall, octagonal red-brick tower of the **Église Ste-Catherine**, east of rue de Paris. The church was founded at the same time as the *bastide*, but then rebuilt in the late nineteenth century when it was in danger of collapse. In addition to an unusual north–south axis, the new architects chose a dramatic neo-Byzantine style, with a line of three domes above the nave, mosaic portraits of the six St Catherines – including St Catherine of Alexandria, to whom the church is dedicated, third from the left – and a multitude of saints on a frieze inspired by early Christian art. A few relics of the old church remain, notably some attractive stained-glass windows, the oldest dating from the fourteenth century.

The road running parallel to rue de Paris to the west, **rue de Cieutats**, leads to the thirteenth-century **Pont des Cieutats**, originally topped with three towers reminiscent of Cahors' Pont Valentré (see p.275), and, just beside it on the north bank, a tiny chapel full of candles and votive plaques. The sixteenth-century **Notre-Dame du Bout-du-Pont** commemorates a small wooden statue of the Virgin holding Jesus gingerly in her arms. It was found in the river here by a sixteenth-century boatman when his craft mysteriously stopped midstream – or so the legend goes.

Finally, it's worth checking what's on at the **Musée de la Vallée du Lot**, 2 rue des Jardins (daily 2–6pm; ☎05.53.40.48.00; 15F/€2.29), on the north riverbank further upstream. Their fine art collection is missable, but the temporary exhibitions devoted to the history of the Lot, the river trade, its craft, boat-builders and so forth, are generally of interest.

Eating

Villeneuve has a good choice of **restaurants**. The prettiest is *Chez Câline*, 2 rue Notre-Dame (☎05.53.70.42.08; menus from 75F/€11.43), near the old bridge, serving fresh, inventive dishes in a tiny brick-vaulted room. Nearby *L'Oustal*, 24 rue de la Convention (closed Tues eve), is a safe bet, relaxed and friendly, where you can ring the changes with Basque specialities such as *aoxa* (minced veal), *cipirons* (squid) and dishes cooked *à la plancha* (grilled); menus start at 65F/€9.91. Or try the Moroccan *La Table d'Aladin*, 42 rue de Casseneuil (closed Mon; menus from 62F/€9.45), two blocks back from the river, for generous helpings of couscous, tajine and suchlike. For classic cuisine in more luxurious surroundings head back to the river and *Aux Berges du Lot*, 3 rue de l'Hôtel-de-Ville (☎05.53.70.84.41; closed Sun evening & Mon), with its shady terrace, picture-windows and good-value 85F/€12.96 weekday lunch menus. There are also several recommended restaurants in Pujols (see below).

For picnic fare, the main **markets** take place on Tuesday and Saturday mornings on place Lafayette, with an organic market on Wednesdays on place d'Aquitaine, south of the river. Bigger fairs are held on the first and third Tuesdays of the month, while in July and August there are also farmers' night markets on Fridays near the tourist office on boulevard Georges-Leygues.

Pujols

Three kilometres south of Villeneuve the two-street village of **PUJOLS** stands high above the plain behind its thirteenth-century ramparts. It makes a popular excursion, partly because it's a beguiling little place with its flowery nooks and crannies, and partly for views over the surrounding country, although the main reason that locals flock to Pujols is its restaurants.

Immediately inside Pujols' main north gate, it's hard to tell where the fortifications end and the tiny Gothic **church of St-Nicolas** begins. It contains nothing of particular note, whereas the **Église Ste-Foy** (open during temporary exhibitions; free), on the far side of the market square, is decorated with fifteenth and sixteenth-century frescoes. Though faded, many are still visible, such as St George poised over the dragon and St Catherine with her wheel of torture, both around the apse. And look out, too, for a painting in the baptismal chapel (first on the left as you enter) depicting the old bridge at Villeneuve-sur-Lot sporting its three towers.

Top of the list for **restaurants** is the excellent but expensive *La Toque Blanche* (☎05.53.49.00.30; closed Sun eve, Mon & Tues lunch; weekday lunchtime menus from 120F/€18.29, or 215F/€32.78 at weekends and hols), just south of Pujols with views back to the village, whose dishes include classics such as poached eggs in a Périgord sauce, and foie gras wrapped in millefeuille pastry. The panorama is even better from their less formal outlet in Pujols itself, *Lou Calel* (☎05.53.70.46.14; menus from 85F/€12.96; closed Tues evening & Wed), which serves beautifully cooked traditional but light menus. Also worth trying is the up-and-coming *Le Figuier* (☎05.53.36.72.12; closed Mon; menus from 85F/€12.96, or under 150F/€22.87 à la carte), on the market square, offering a small but extremely well-priced selection of dishes.

The bastide country

Although *bastides*, or medieval new towns (see box overleaf), are by no means unique to this stretch of country to the north of the Lot, it's here that you'll find the two finest examples. The more southerly of the pair is **Monflanquin**, which makes a good place to start because of its museum outlining the history, architecture and daily life of the *bastides*. The route then heads northeast, skirting

---

BASTIDES

Bastides, from the Occitan *bastida*, meaning a group of buildings, were the new towns of the thirteenth and fourteenth centuries. Although they are found all over southwest France, from the Dordogne to the foothills of the Pyrenees, there is a particularly high concentration in the area between the Dordogne and Lot rivers, which at that time formed the disputed "frontier" region between English-held Aquitaine and Capetian France.

That said, the earliest *bastides* were founded largely for **economic and political** reasons. They were a means of bringing new land into production – this was a period of rapid population growth and technological innovation – and thus extending the power of the local lord. But as tensions between the French and English forces intensified during the late thirteenth century, so the motive became increasingly **military**. The *bastides* now provided a handy way of securing the land along the frontier, and it was generally at this point that they were fortified.

As an incentive, anyone who was prepared to build, inhabit and defend the *bastide* was granted various perks and concessions in a founding **charter**. All new residents were allocated a building plot, garden and cultivable land outside the town. The charter might also offer asylum to certain types of criminal or grant exemption from military service, or might allow the election of **consuls** charged with day-to-day administration – a measure of self-government remarkable in feudal times. Taxes and judicial affairs, meanwhile, remained the preserve of the representative of the king or local lord under whose ultimate authority the *bastide* lay.

The other defining feature of a *bastide* is its **layout**. They are nearly always square or rectangular in shape, depending on the nature of the terrain, and are divided by streets at right angles to each other to produce a chequerboard pattern. The focal point is the market square, often missing its covered *halle* nowadays, but generally still surrounded by arcades, while the church is relegated to one side, or may even form part of the town walls.

The busiest *bastide* founders were **Alphonse de Poitiers** (1249–1271), on behalf of the French crown, after he became Count of Toulouse in 1249, and **King Edward I of England**, Edward Plantagenet (1272–1307), who wished to consolidate his hold on the northern borders of his Duchy of Aquitaine. The former chalked up a total of 57 *bastides*, including Villeneuve-sur-Lot (1251), Monflanquin (1252), Ste-Foy-la-Grande (1255) and Eymet (1270), while Edward was responsible for Beaumont (1272), Monpazier and Molières (both 1284) amongst others.

---

round the flanks of the imposing **Château de Biron**, seat of one of the four Baronies of Périgord, before reaching **Monpazier**. This is the most typical of the *bastides*, with virtually no modern development around – where the rectangle of streets end the fields begin. There's a small museum here, too, but Monpazier's prime attraction is its atmosphere, "like a drowsy yellow cat, slumbering in the sun" as Freda White so aptly describes it in the *Three Rivers of France* (see p.363).

Nevertheless, some effort is required to reach it. Neither the Château de Biron nor Monpazier are accessible by **public transport**. The best on offer is the early-evening **bus** from Villeneuve to Monflanquin, but even that doesn't run every day.

Monflanquin

Some 17km north of Villeneuve-sur-Lot, pretty **MONFLANQUIN**, founded in 1252 by Alphonse de Poitiers, is nearly as perfectly preserved as Monpazier, less touristy and impressively positioned on top of a hill that rises sharply from the surrounding country and is visible for miles. Despite being constructed on a steep slope, it conforms to the regular pattern of right-angled streets leading from a central square to the four town gates. The ramparts themselves were demolished on Richelieu's orders in 1630, but otherwise Monflanquin has experienced few radical changes since the thirteenth century.

The main square, tree-shaded **place des Arcades** – where the market still takes place on Thursdays as decreed in the *bastide*'s founding charter – derives a special charm from being on a slope. Its grandest building is the Gothic **Maison du Prince Noir** in the northeast corner, where the Black Prince is said to have stayed. On this north side you'll also find the high-tech **Musée des Bastides**, above the tourist office (same hours – see below; 20F/€3.05), which is full of information about the life and history of *bastides*; most of the text is translated into English, but unfortunately not the audio-tapes. Then after a quick wander through Monflanquin's old centre, it's worth heading north past the **church**, which took on its pseudo-medieval look in the early twentieth century, to end up on a terrace with expansive views northeast to the next stop, Château de Biron (see overleaf).

Practicalities

Buses from Villeneuve-sur-Lot stop on the main road below the *bastide* in modern Monflanquin; simply walk uphill until you hit rue St-Pierre heading north to place des Arcades, where you'll find the **tourist office** (July & Aug Mon–Fri 10am–12.30pm & 2.30–7pm, Sat & Sun 10am–12.30pm & 3–7pm; rest of year Mon–Sat 10am–noon & 2–5pm, Sun 2–5pm; ☎05.53.36.40.19, fax 05.53.36.42.91, *office.de.tourisme.monflanquin@wanadoo.fr*); they can furnish you with details of the many **events** taking place here in summer (see box on pp.266–267).

The nearest **hotel** worth recommending is the *Moulin de Boulède* (☎05.53.36.40.27, fax 05.53.36.59.26; *www.logis-de-france.fr*; ③; mid-Sept to April closed Sun eve & Mon), 2km west of Monflanquin on the D124 to Cancon. The rooms aren't brilliant, but it's a nice quiet spot beside the river and the restaurant is reasonable (menus from 70F/€10.67).

For pure atmosphere, however, it's better to eat in one of the **cafés** and **restaurants** on place des Arcades. Pick of the bunch is the welcoming *Le Bistrot du Prince Noir* (closed Jan & Feb, also Oct–May Tues & Wed) in the southwest corner of the square. It's both a wine-bar – with an excellent choice of local wines (from 12F/€1.83 for a glass) – and restaurant, running the gamut from pan-fried foie gras or duck breast with a spicy redcurrant sauce to a selection of Asian dishes; there's also a vegetarian menu and plenty of fresh fish (menus from 60F/€9.15, or around 150F/€22.87 from the *carte*). Another good option, 5km north on the D676 to Villeréal, is the *Ferme Auberge de Tabel* (☎05.53.36.30.57; reservation required), in a flowery corner at the end of a lane, where you'll feast on hearty regional dishes; there's a good range of menus between 65F/€9.91 and 166F/€25.31.

The best place for picnic fodder is the Thursday-morning **market** on place des Arcades, though you can also buy provisions at the **supermarket** on the main road immediately south of town. The neighbouring **wine co-operative**, the Cave des 7 Monts, represents some 200 local vineyards, producing some very palatable and reasonably priced wines; tastings are available free of charge.

Château de Biron

Twenty-two kilometres northeast of Monflanquin, via a picturesque route along the River Lède, the vast **Château de Biron** dominates the countryside for miles around (early Feb to March & Oct–Dec Tues–Sun 10am–12.30pm & 2–5.30pm; April daily 10am–12.30pm & 2–5.30pm; May, June & Sept daily 10am–12.30pm & 2–6.30pm; July & Aug daily 10am–7pm; 30F/€4.57). It was begun in the eleventh century and added to piecemeal over the years by the Gontaut-Biron family, who occupied the castle right up to the early twentieth century. The biggest alterations were made in the fifteenth and early sixteenth centuries, when Pons de Gontaut-Biron started reconstructing the eastern wing. The result is an architectural primer, from the medieval keep through Flamboyant Gothic and Renaissance to an eighteenth-century loggia in the style of Versailles.

Rather than the guided tour (in French only; 45min), at busy times it's better to borrow the English-language text from the ticket desk and wander at will. The most striking building in the grassy **lower court** is the Renaissance chapel where the sarcophagi of Pons and his brother Armand, Bishop of Sarlat, lie. Though their statues were hacked about during the Revolution, the Italianate biblical scenes and three Virtues carved on the sides still show fine craftsmanship. On entering the cobbled and confined **inner courtyard** around its twelfth-century keep, the route takes you to a dungeon and through the lord's apartments, with their Renaissance chimney and wood-panelled hall, to a vast reception room and an equally capacious stone-vaulted refectory. If the rooms decked out as a tannery, torture chamber and weavers' workshop make you feel as though you're walking through a film set, you are – Biron is a favourite for period dramas, the latest being *Le Pacte des Loups* in 2000.

If you're looking for somewhere to **eat**, you could try the *Auberge du Château*, beside the path up to the castle, which serves a decent lunchtime menu at 60–70F/€9.15–10.67 (☎05.53.63.13.33; closed mid-Dec to mid-Feb & Sat Oct–April). Or, better still, head back southeast 5km – by road or on the GR36 footpath – to **LACAPELLE-BIRON**, where *Le Palissy* (closed 3 weeks in Feb, closed Tues eve except June–Aug), on the main road, is a friendly, locals' place offering excellent-value menus from 60F/€9.15. The village also boasts one of the region's best **campsites**, *Le Moulinal* (☎05.53.40.84.60, fax 05.53.40.81.49, *www.lemoulinal.com*; closed mid-Sept to late April), with four-star facilities, including a shop, restaurant and bar, even a cybercafé, beside a leisure lake.

Monpazier

From the Château de Biron it's only another 8km north to **MONPAZIER**, the finest and most complete of the surviving *bastides*, built of a lovely warm-coloured stone on a hill above the River Dropt. It was founded in 1284 by King Edward I of England on land granted by Pierre de Gontaud-Biron, and picturesque and placid though it is today, Monpazier has a hard and bitter history, being twice – in 1594 and 1637 – the centre of **peasant rebellions** provoked by the misery that followed the Wars of Religion (see p.358). Both uprisings were brutally suppressed: the 1637 peasants' leader was broken on the wheel in the square and his head paraded around the countryside. In an earlier episode, Sully, the Protestant general, describes a rare moment of light relief in the terrible **Wars of Religion**, when the men of Catholic Villefranche-de-Périgord planned to capture Monpazier on the same night as the men of Monpazier were headed for Villefranche. By chance, both sides took different routes, met no resistance, looted to their hearts' content and returned home congratulating themselves on their luck and skill, only to find that things were rather different. The peace terms were that everything should be returned to its proper place.

It therefore comes as something of a surprise to find Monpazier has survived so well. Three of its six **medieval gates** are still intact and its central square, **place des Cornières**, couldn't be more perfect with its oak-pillared *halle* and time-worn, stone-built houses, no two the same. Deep, shady arcades pass beneath all the houses, which are separated from each other by a small gap to reduce fire risk; at the corners the buttresses are cut away to allow the passage of laden pack animals.

Monpazier's main north–south axis is **rue Notre-Dame**, which brings you in to the northeast corner of place des Cornières, past the much-altered **church**. The thirteenth-century building opposite is a bit battered but this is Monpazier's oldest house, where the tax collector received his share of the harvest. Of more interest is the local museum, the **Ateliers des Bastides** (May, June & Oct Sat & Sun 2–5pm; July & Aug daily 10am–12.30pm & 3–7pm; free), west of the square along rue Jean-Galmot. It boasts a few prehistoric remains and other historical bits and pieces, but is largely devoted to local adventurer Jean Galmot, who was born here in 1879 and was assassinated in 1928 in French Guiana, then a penal colony, where he was aiding its fledgling independence movement.

During the summer months the museum also hosts a number of temporary art exhibitions, and the town puts on all sorts of other events to draw the tourists, from book fairs to medieval jamborees (see box on p.266). Outside these occasions, however, there's not much else to do in Monpazier beyond soak up the sun at a café on the market square.

Practicalities

Monpazier's very organized and helpful **tourist office** (mid-March to June & Sept to mid-Nov Mon–Fri 9am–12.30pm & 2.30–7pm, Sat & Sun 10am–12.30pm & 2.30–7pm; July & Aug daily 10am–7pm; mid-Nov to mid-March daily 9am–12.30pm & 2.30–5.30pm; ☎05.53.22.68.59, fax 05.53.74.30.08, *www.finest.tm.fr/fr/dordogne/office_monpazier*) is located on the east side of place des Cornières. Amongst all sorts of useful information, they produce a free leaflet of six walks in the area, including a 17km round trip via the Château de Biron (see opposite). You can also rent **bikes** at Jean-Pierre Mouret, at 17 rue St-Jacques (☎05.53.22.63.46), the road forming the west side of the market square, or go **trekking** with the excellent Centre Équestre de Marsalès (☎05.53.22.63.14), 3km northwest in Marsalès village.

The smartest place to **stay** is the *Hôtel de France*, 21 rue St-Jacques (☎05.53.22.60.06, fax 05.53.22.07.27; ③; closed mid-Nov to mid-Dec, also closed April to mid-May Tues & Oct–March Tues–Thurs), in a lovely medieval building on the southwest corner of place des Cornières. It has a fine regional restaurant (menus from 90F/€13.72) while in summer it also offers lighter brasserie-style fare. Another good option is the exceptionally welcoming *Hôtel de Londres*, Foirail Nord (☎05.53.22.60.64, fax 05.53.22.61.98, *corupsis@wanadoo.fr*; ②), just outside the north gate, also with a good restaurant (menus from 60F/€9.15). There are two **campsites** in the vicinity: the two-star *Camping de Véronne* (☎05.53.22.62.22, fax 05.53.22.65.23; closed mid-Sept to mid-June), beside a lake 3km northwest in

Marsalès, and the more luxurious, four-star *Le Moulin de David* (☎05.53.22.65.25, fax 05.53.23.99.76, *www.moulin.de.david.com*; closed early Sept to mid-May) in the Dropt valley roughly the same distance to the south. Make sure you reserve well in advance for the latter.

You'll eat very well in the two hotel **restaurants** cited above. Otherwise, browse around place des Cornières, where *Le Ménestrel* (closed Jan & Feb, and Wed except in July & Aug; menus from 68F/€10.37) in the southeast corner is a safe bet. Or head north along rue St-Jacques to find *La Bastide* at no. 52 (☎05.53.22.60.59; closed Mon & Feb), a good old-fashioned restaurant with a well-deserved reputation for its beautifully presented dishes – try a plate of kidneys and sweetbreads with truffles, roast herbed lamb or zander with a red-wine sauce, as long as you leave room for some of their luscious home-made ice cream and sorbet.

On Thursday mornings place des Cornières comes to life for the weekly **market**, which expands on the third Thursday of each month into a fair. In mushroom season (roughly May–Oct) people also come here on Thursday afternoons to sell their pickings.

travel details

Trains

Cahors to: Brive (7–10 daily; 1hr–1hr 10min); Gourdon (6–9 daily; 25min); Montauban (7–10 daily; 40min); Paris-Austerlitz (8 daily; 5hr 30min–6hr 20min); Souillac (6–9 daily; 40min); Toulouse (7–10 daily; 1hr 10min–1hr 20min).

Figeac to: Assier (5–6 daily; 7–10min); Brive (5–6 daily; 1hr 10min–1hr 20min); Cordes (6–7 daily; 1hr 20min–1hr 45min); Gramat (5–6 daily; 30min); Laguépie (6–7 daily; 1hr–1hr 25min); Najac (6–7 daily; 50min–1hr 15min); Paris-Austerlitz (1–2 daily; 4hr 45min–7hr); Rocamadour (5–6 daily; 40–50min); St-Denis-Près-Martel (5–6 daily; 45–55min); Toulouse (5–6 daily; 2hr 15min–3hr); Villefranche-de-Rouergue (5–6 daily; 40min–1hr).

Gourdon to: Brive (6–9 daily; 40min); Cahors (7–9 daily; 30min); Montauban (7–9 daily; 1hr); Paris-Austerlitz (4–5 daily; 5hr); Souillac (6–9 daily; 15min); Toulouse (7–9 daily; 1hr 30min).

Gramat to: Assier (5–7 daily; 15min); Brive (5–6 daily; 45min–1hr 10min); Figeac (5–7 daily; 30min); Najac (2 daily; 1hr 30min); Paris-Austerlitz (1–2 daily; 5hr–6hr 30min); Rocamadour (5–6 daily; 8min); St-Denis-Près-Martel (5–6 daily; 25min); Toulouse (1 daily; 3hr).

Monsempron-Libos to: Agen (5–7 daily; 35–55min); Le Bugue (4–5 daily; 50min–1hr); Les Eyzies (4–5 daily; 1hr 20min); Paris-Austerlitz (1–2 daily; 6hr 30min–8hr); Penne-d'Agenais (5–7 daily; 15–20min); Périgueux (4–5 daily; 1hr 20min–1hr 40min).

Buses

Cahors to: Albas (4–8 daily; 30min); Amsterdam (2–4 weekly; 20hr); Les Arques (1 weekly; 1hr 05min); Bouziès (3–9 daily; 30min); Brussels (2–4 weekly; 16hr); Cajarc (3–7 daily; 1hr); Calvignac (3–7 daily; 50min); Figeac (3–9 daily; 1hr 45min); Fumel (4–6 daily; 1hr 10min); Gourdon (1st and 3rd Fri of month by reservation ☎05.65.41.10.94; 2hr); Gramat (Mon, Fri & Sat 1–2 daily; 1hr 10min); London (2–3 weekly; 18hr 30min); Luzech (4–8 daily; 20min); Monsempron-Libos (4–6 daily; 1hr 15min); Puy-l'Évêque (4–8 daily; 45min); St-Céré (Mon, Fri & Sat 1–2 daily; 1hr 45min); St-Martin-Labouval (3–7 daily; 40min); Tour-de-Faure (3–7 daily; 35min); Vers (3–9 daily; 15–20min); Villefranche-de-Rouergue (school term only Mon 1 daily; 1hr 30min).

Figeac to: Assiers (Mon–Fri 1 daily; 30min); Cahors (4–6 daily; 1hr 40min–2hr); Cajarc (4–6 daily; 30–35min); Gramat (Mon–Fri 1 daily; 1hr); St-Céré (school term 4 weekly, school hols Tues & Thurs 1 daily; 1hr); Tour-de-Faure (4–6 daily; 1hr); Villefranche-de-Rouergue (1–2 daily; 40min).

Fumel to: Cahors (4–6 daily; 1hr 10min); Condat (4–6 daily; 7min); Duravel (4–6 daily; 15min); Luzech (4–6 daily; 45min); Puy-l'Evêque (4–6 daily; 25min); St-Sylvestre (Sept–July Mon–Sat 1–2 daily; 30min); Touzac (4–6 daily; 12min); Villeneuve-sur-Lot (Sept–July Mon–Sat 1–2 daily; 40min).

Gourdon to: Cahors (1st and 3rd Fri of month by reservation ☎05.65.41.10.94; 2hr); Souillac (school term 1–2 daily, school hols Tues 1 daily; 1hr).

Gramat to: Brive (school term Mon & Sat 1 daily; 1hr 30min); Assier (Mon–Sat 1 daily; 30min); Brive (school term Mon & Sat 1 daily; 1hr 30min); Cahors (Mon, Fri & Sat 1 daily; 1hr–1hr 15min); Carennac (school term Mon & Sat 1 daily; 25min); Figeac (Mon–Sat 1 daily; 1hr); St-Céré (school term Mon–Sat 1–3 daily, school hols Mon, Fri & Sat 1 daily; 35–40min).

Luzech to: Albas (4–8 daily; 10min); Cahors (4–8 daily; 25min); Monsempron-Libos (4–6 daily; 1hr); Puy-l'Evêque (4–8 daily; 30min).

Monsempron-Libos to: Cahors (4–6 daily; 1hr 15min); Condat (4–6 daily; 10min); Duravel (4–6 daily; 20min); Fumel (4–6 daily; 2min); Luzech (4–6 daily; 50min); Puy-l'Évêque (4–6 daily; 30min); Touzac (4–6 daily; 15min).

Puy-l'Évêque to: Albas (4–7 daily; 15–20min); Condat (4–6 daily; 15–20min); Cahors (4–8 daily; 1hr); Duravel (4–6 daily; 5–10min); Fumel (4–6 daily; 15–20min); Luzech (4–8 daily; 20–25min); Monsempron-Libos (4–6 daily; 20–25min); Touzac (4–6 daily; 10–15min).

Villeneuve-sur-Lot to: Agen (8–10 daily; 45–50min); Bergerac (Mon–Fri 1–2 daily; 1hr 15min); Fumel (Sept–July Mon–Sat 1–2 daily; 30–40min); Marmande (Mon–Fri 1–3 daily; 1hr 15min–1hr 30min); Monflanquin (school term Mon–Fri 1 daily, school hols Thurs 1 daily; 20–25min).

CHAPTER SEVEN

SOUTH OF THE RIVER LOT

The southern border of the Dordogne and Lot region is defined by the River Garonne in the west and by the Tarn and Aveyron in the east. On the whole this area to the south of the Lot offers more gentle and less dramatic scenery than further north, but by the same token it sees fewer tourists, and even in midsummer there are still quiet corners to be found. It is a fertile land, full of sunflowers and fruit orchards, particularly along the Garonne and spreading over the hills to the north: plums, pears, peaches, cherries, apples and nectarines all grow here, as well as melons, strawberries and the succulent chasselas grapes. In contrast with such agricultural bounty, the region has few

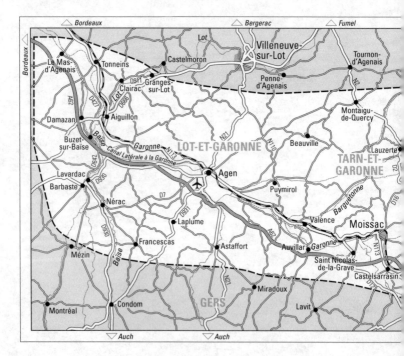

ACCOMMODATION PRICE CODES

All the hotels and *chambres d'hôtes* listed in this book have been price-coded according to the following scale. The prices quoted are for the **cheapest available double room in high season**, although remember that many of the cheap places will have more expensive rooms with en-suite facilities.

① Under 160F/€24
② 160–220F/€24–34
③ 220–300F/€34–46
④ 300–400F/€46–61
⑤ 400–500F/€61–76
⑥ 500–600F/€76–91
⑦ 600–700F/€91–107
⑧ 700–800F/€107–122
⑨ Over 800F/€122

outstanding sights, but, instead, endless opportunities to wander the country lanes between timeworn hilltop villages where life moves at a pace dictated by the slowly turning seasons, and where the local market is the high point of the week.

The first of the region's two gateways is **Agen**, the only major town on the Garonne between Bordeaux and Toulouse, and pleasanter than it first appears, with an old centre built of pink-mottled brick and a fine local museum. Southwest of Agen, what's left of **Nérac**'s castle and its riverside pleasure gardens – where King Henri IV misspent his youth – still exude a slightly decadent air. The river here is the Baïse, which flows north to join the Garonne near **Buzet-sur-Baïse** in the centre of a small wine region, from where it's worth

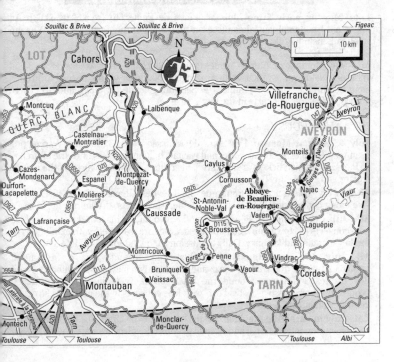

continuing west again to see a tiny painting by Rembrandt in the church of **Le Mas-d'Agenais**.

Heading upstream from Agen, the one sight in this region not to be missed is the abbey-church at **Moissac**. The carvings on its south porch and in its cloister are among the finest examples of Romanesque art to be found in France. The Garonne valley here is at its flattest and most featureless, but north of Moissac things improve as you climb up onto the low, rolling plateau of the **Quercy Blanc** which stretches north almost to Cahors. It's a region of white-stone farmhouses, windmills and *pigeonniers* – pigeon houses often raised on stilts – by the hundred and of sun-drenched hilltop villages. Of these the prettiest is **Lauzerte**, but **Montpezat-de-Quercy** also merits a visit for its display of religious art, including a series of superb tapestries.

Near Montpezat the N20 and new A20 *autoroute* mark the eastern extent of Quercy Blanc and funnel traffic south to **Montauban**. This brick-red city, not far north of Toulouse and on the Paris main line, is the region's second gateway, and justifies a few hours' exploration thanks to its art museum and central square surrounded by elegant town houses. It sits on the banks of the Tarn in the midst of an alluvial plain which, in the east, gives way abruptly to hills. Running through them, the **Gorges de l'Aveyron** are punctuated with ancient villages.

FESTIVALS, EVENTS AND MARKETS

Late May or early June Moissac: Fêtes de Pentecôte (☎05.63.04.63.63). An important traditional fair takes place on the banks of the Tarn over the Whitsun weekend, including fireworks on the final night.

Mid-May Montauban: Alors, Chante! (☎05.63.63.02.36). Over Ascension weekend various well-known, and lesser-known, artists take part in this festival of French song held in the Salle Eurythmie, rue Salvador-Allende (tickets required). There are also a few free concerts in the city centre.

JULY AND AUGUST

July & August Moissac: Les Soirs de Moissac (☎05.63.04.32.69). Varied programme of concerts, choral works and recitals held in the cloister or the church of St-Pierre, for which tickets are required, in addition to free concerts on the church square and beside the Tarn.

Early July Villefranche-en-Rouergue: La Clé des Chants (☎05.65.45.41.12). A week-long competition of French song held in the streets of Villefranche. Free.

Mid-July Cordes-sur-Ciel: Fêtes du Grand Fauconnier. This four-day medieval festival converts the town into a costumed extravaganza, complete with exhibitions on medieval crafts and falconry. Daily admission to the old town is 25F/€3.81.

Mid-July to mid-August Montauban and around: Jazz à Montauban (☎05.63.20.46.72). International jazz and blues artists play in Montauban's Jardin des Plantes and towns around the *département*, including Moissac (tickets required). There's also a "festival off" with free concerts in the cafés and streets of central Montauban.

Late July to early Aug Aiguillon: Festival de Jazz (☎05.53.88.20.20). Open-air concerts featuring international and French groups take place over a weekend in front perched high above the river, while **St-Antonin-de-Noble-Val**, with its core of medieval lanes, lies in the valley bottom caught between soaring limestone crags. Beyond St-Antonin, it's worth making a short detour south across the plateau to the aptly named **Cordes-sur-Ciel**, where noble facades line the steeply cobbled lanes, before rejoining the Aveyron beneath **Najac**'s much-contested fortress. The gorge opens out to the north of Najac, but it's worth continuing the last few kilometres to **Villefranche-de-Rouergue**, at whose centre, in the monstrous shadow of its church tower, lies the most perfectly preserved arcaded market square.

Three major **train** lines fan out across this region from Toulouse: along the Garonne valley to Montauban, Moissac and Agen; north via Montpezat to Cahors; and northeast through Cordes, Najac and Villefranche en route to Figeac. The **bus services** are also fairly comprehensive. Among the more useful routes are those to Nérac, Lauzerte and along the Aveyron to St-Antonin and Laguépie. Another way to get about is by **boat** on the Canal latéral à la Garonne, which shadows the Garonne for nearly 200km from near Langon in the east (see p.106), passing through Buzet, Agen and Moissac, among other places, to Toulouse, where it joins the Canal du Midi.

---

of the Château des Ducs (tickets required). A small "festival off" includes free concerts, workshops and masterclasses.

Late July to mid-August Lauzerte and around: Festival du Quercy Blanc (☎05.65.31.83.12). Concerts of classical and chamber music held mostly in churches around the region, including Montcuq, Montpezat-du-Quercy, Castelnau-Montratier and Cahors. Tickets available from local tourist offices.

Early August Villefranche-en-Rouergue: La Festival en Bastide. Five days of contemporary theatre and performance art animate the streets of the old town. Free.

August 15 Lauzerte: Foire brocante. Secondhand stalls fill the old village on the same day as the concert in the church as part of the Festival du Quercy Blanc (see above).

SEPTEMBER AND OCTOBER

Third weekend in September Moissac: Fête du Chasselas and Fête des Fruits et des Légumes (☎05.63.04.63.63). Every year the Fête du Chasselas celebrates the local grape, with tastings on offer and a competition to find the pick of the bunch; the event takes place in the market hall. In odd years all local fruits and vegetables are on display throughout the town.

Second weekend in Oct Auvillar: Marché Potier. Some 50 exhibitors take part in this important pottery fair held on the place de la Halle.

MARKETS

The main **markets** in the region are at Aiguillon (Tues & Fri); Agen (Wed, Sat & Sun); Cordes (Sat); Laguépie (Wed & Sun); Lauzerte (Wed & Sat); Moissac (Sat & Sun); Montauban (Sat); Montcuq (Sun); Nérac (Sat); St-Antonin-de-Noble-Val (Sun); St-Nicolas-de-la-Grave (Mon); and Villefranche-de-Rouergue (Thurs).

Agen and around

AGEN, capital of Lot-et-Garonne *département*, lies on the broad, powerful River Garonne halfway between Bordeaux and Toulouse. Close to the A62 *autoroute* and connected to both cities by fast and frequent train services, and to Paris by train and plane, it provides a useful gateway to the southern reaches of the Dordogne and Lot region. However, Agen is more than just a transport hub. Inside the ring of hypermarkets and industrial estates lies a core of old lanes lined with handsome brick houses, several churches worth a look and a surprisingly good fine arts museum. Add to that a number of excellent restaurants and a good choice of hotels, and Agen makes for a pleasant half-day's exploration or a base from which to cover the surrounding country. The most interesting jaunts take you southwest to **Nérac**, where kings and queens disported themselves on the Baïse's wooded banks, and west to the wine-town of **Buzet-sur-Baïse**. Further down the Garonne, **Aiguillon** provides more good hotel options as well as a clutch of picturesque medieval lanes, while **Le Mas-d'Agenais** hides a few surprises inside its church.

Of these places, only Nérac and Aiguillon are accessible by **public transport**: the former by bus from Agen, and the latter by train. However, since they all lie on navigable and interconnected waterways – the Baïse, Garonne and the Canal latéral – renting a **boat** would provide a leisurely way of exploring the area.

Arrival, information and accommodation

Flights from Paris arrive at Agen's La Garenne **airport**, around 3km southwest of town; a taxi into the centre costs roughly 50F/€7.62. The **gare SNCF** and **gare routière** are located next to each other on the north side of town. From in front of the station boulevard du Président-Carnot leads south to place Goya, where it crosses the town's other main thoroughfare, the east–west rue de la République. You'll find the **tourist office** south of this crossroads at 107 bd Carnot (July & Aug Mon–Sat 9am–7pm, Sun 10am–noon; rest of year Mon–Sat 9am–12.30pm & 2–6.30pm; ☎05.53.47.36.09, fax 05.53.47.29.98, *otsi.agen@ wanadoo.fr*).

Agen has some good **hotel** options scattered around its centre, especially at the budget end, though you'll also find four-star luxury at a reasonable price. There's also a clutch of chain hotels (such as *Formule 1* and *Campanile*) at the exit from the *autoroute*; see Basics p.37 for more on these chains.

Hotels

des Ambans, 59 rue des Ambans (☎05.53.66.28.60, fax 05.53.87.94.01). The best value of the budget hotels, at the very bottom of this price category, with nine small, tidy rooms; note that the cheapest have to share a toilet. It's clean, friendly and central, which means you need to book well ahead for the summer season. Oct–March closed Sun. ②.

Ibis, 16 rue Camille-Desmoulins (☎05.53.47.43.43, fax 05.53.47.68.54, *www.ibis.fr*). A modern mid-range hotel on a quiet sidestreet near the tourist office. The rooms are comfortable enough, if lacking in character. ④.

Les Îles, 25 rue Baudin (☎05.53.47.11.33, fax 05.53.66.19.25). One of Agen's more attractive hotels, in a lovely brick-built house full of plants and family furniture, about 10 minutes' walk southwest of the station. Its rooms are simple but light and airy, while the cheapest share a toilet on the corridor. Again, with only nine rooms, it fills up quickly at peak periods. ②.

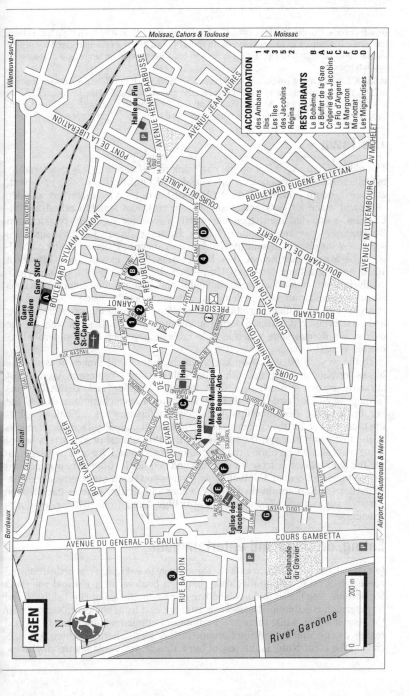

des Jacobins, 1 pl des Jacobins (☎05.53.47.03.31, fax 05.53.47.02.80). Agen's top hotel oozes character. It occupies an elegant nineteenth-century town house swathed in greenery beside the Jacobins church, and its rooms are decked out with antique furniture, gilt mirrors and plush fabrics. ④.

Régina, 139 bd Carnot (☎05.53.47.07.97, fax 05.53.95.69.51). If the *Hôtel des Ambans* above is full, try this welcoming, rambling old hotel on the main road south of the station; it's best to ask for a quieter room at the back. Rooms are on the small side but with good-sized bathrooms and modern, light-wood furnishings. Note that there's an 11pm curfew. ②.

The Town

The old centre of Agen lies on the east bank of the Garonne. It is quartered by two nineteenth-century boulevards – **rue de la République**, running east–west, and north–south **boulevard du Président-Carnot** – which intersect at place Goya and make for easy navigation. To the northeast stands **Cathédrale St-Caprais**, somewhat misshapen but worth a look for its finely proportioned Romanesque apse and radiating chapels. However, Agen's foremost sight lies southwest on place Dr-Esquirol: beside the exuberant, Italianate municipal theatre, the **Musée Municipal des Beaux-Arts** (daily except Tues: May–Sept 10am–noon & 2–6pm; Oct–April 10am–noon & 2–5pm; 20F/€3.05) is magnificently housed in four adjacent sixteenth- and seventeenth-century mansions adorned with stair turrets and Renaissance window details. Inside is a rich variety of archeological exhibits, furniture and paintings – among the latter, five Goyas and a Tintoretto rediscovered during an inventory in 1997. Best, though, are the basement's Roman finds which include intricate jewellery and a superb white-marble Venus.

To the west of place Dr-Esquirol, a clutch of brick and timber houses – the bricks forming neat zigzags within the timber frame – represent Agen's most attractive corner. From here a short and narrow alley, **rue Beauville**, cuts through to rue Richard-Cœur-de-Lion, with more eye-catching facades, and the big, brick **Église des Jacobins** (open during temporary art exhibitions; ask at the tourist office for the current schedule). It was founded by Dominican monks in the thirteenth century, then served as the Protestants' headquarters before being used as a prison during the Revolution. If it's open, it's worth popping in to see the unusual Gothic frescoes of leaves and geometric patterns in trompe l'oeil on the walls and ceiling. Continuing westwards you reach the river and the public gardens of **Esplanade du Gravier**, where a footbridge crosses the Garonne – from it you can see a 550m-long **canal bridge** dating from 1843 further downstream.

Eating, drinking and entertainment

In general, the best place to look for somewhere to **eat** in Agen is pedestrianized rue Émile-Sentini, cutting diagonally between boulevard Carnot and rue de la République. You'll also find a mixed bag of restaurants along rue Lafayette and its extension rue Camille-Desmoulins running east from boulevard Carnot near the tourist office, while there are a number of ethnic restaurants and fast-food outlets on rue Voltaire and rue Garonne further west. There's nothing very special, on the other hand, in the way of **bars**, though you could try the *St Patrick*,

---

PRUNEAUX D'AGEN

Agen grew rich at first on the trade of manufactured goods, such as cloth and leather, flowing through its river port, but the industrial revolution put paid to all that and since then the town's prosperity has been based on agriculture – in particular, its famous **prunes** and **plums**. Plums (*prunes* in French) were introduced to France by Crusaders returning from Syria in the eleventh century. It is believed that Benedictine monks at Clairac, near the confluence of the Lot and Garonne, were the first to cultivate the fruit, a variety known as *prune d'Ente*, which thrives on sun, high humidity and chalky soils and is also excellent for drying thanks to its size and high sugar content. Though plums now grow throughout the region, the dried fruit (*pruneaux*) were originally exported via the port at Agen – and are thus known as **pruneaux d'Agen**.

Nowadays **prunes** are one of this region's principal money-earners and in late August the orchards are a hive of activity as the ripe fruit are shaken from the trees. They are dried slowly in hot-air ovens to retain the flavour – during which process they loose three-quarters of their weight. Even so, the biggest prunes weigh in at 20g.

You can learn more facts and figures about prune production in the specialist *confiseries* of Agen (see overleaf) and also at an enjoyable **farm-museum**, Au Pruneau Gourmand (Jan & Feb Mon–Sat 9am–noon & 2–6pm, Sun 3–7pm; March–Dec Mon–Sat 9am–noon & 2–7pm, Sun 3–7pm; 20F/€3.05), near the village of Granges-sur-Lot, 10km northeast of Aiguillon (see p.327).

---

6 rue Garonne, and there are a couple of decent cafés nearby on rue de la République.

With no less than three **theatres** and its own highly rated troupe, Les Baladins en Agenais, Agen has a reputation for its thespian activities. The main Théâtre Municipal, place Dr-Esquirol (☎05.53.69.47.47), puts on a varied programme of theatre, dance, concerts and opera by local and national artists, while the Théâtre du Jour, 21 rue Paulin-Régnier (☎05.53.47.82.08), stages amateur dramatics and even the occasional English-language play. Last but not least, the Théâtre du Petit Jour, 13 rue Raspail (☎05.53.48.03.72), puts on a variety of children's entertainment.

Restaurants

La Bohème, 14 rue Emile-Sentini (☎05.53.68.31.00). Chunky wooden furniture and raffia screens set the tone in this small restaurant serving a wide-ranging menu; their speciality is *La Marmite*, a platter of Creole delicacies at 120F/€18.29. Fixed menus start at a very reasonable 69F/€10.52, or count on 150F/€22.87 upwards from the *carte*. Closed Sun & Wed eve except in July & Aug.

Le Buffet de la Gare, 1 pl Rabelais. Join the locals in one of three cheap eateries in the *gare SNCF*. There's a self-service snack bar (11am–midnight), a brasserie (*plat du jour* at 49F/€7.47) and a more formal restaurant with menus from around 70F/€10.67. *Nul points* for decor or ambience, but the food isn't bad for the price.

Crêperie des Jacobins, 3 pl des Jacobins. This pretty little brick-walled *crêperie* opposite the Église des Jacobins serves well-stuffed savoury *galettes* and salads for around 40–50F/€6.10–7.62, or you can get a full meal for a touch over 100F/€15.24. Closed Sun & Mon.

Le Flo d'Argent, 24 pl Jean-Baptiste-Durand. Sunny Provençal decor and extremely well-priced menus with something for everyone – grills, pasta, salads, meat and fish dishes in generous portions – make this a good choice. Menus start at 63F/€9.60 including wine, rising to 122F/€18.60.

Le Margoton, 52 rue Richard-Cœur-de-Lion (☎05.53.48.11.55). Stylish little place near the Jacobins church, serving a good range of seafood in addition to local dishes. Menus from 90F/€13.72, or around 200F/€30.49 from the *carte*. Closed Mon.

Mariottat, 25 rue Louis-Vivent (☎05.53.77.99.77). Agen's most elegant restaurant occupies a lovely town house to the south of the Jacobins church. They concentrate on mostly local produce, including duck in all its guises, with menus starting at a very reasonable 105F/€16.01, while eating *à la carte* will set you back about 350F/€53.36. Closed Sun eve & Mon, also Sat lunch except in July & Aug. Also closed 1 week in Feb.

Les Mignardises, 40 rue Camille-Desmoulins (☎05.53.47.18.62). The decor's nothing to shout about, but locals flock here for the excellent-value home cooking. Even in the evening menus start at just 56F/€8.54 for four courses. Closed Sun & Mon, also 2 weeks from late Feb and 3 weeks in August.

Listings

Airport Air France (☎05.53.77.00.88 or 08.02.80.28.02, *www.airfrance.com*) operates daily flights to Paris from Agen's La Garenne airport, 3km southwest of centre.

Boat rental You can rent houseboats from Locaboat Plaisance, quai Dunkerque (☎05.53.66.00.74, *www.locaboat.com*), for pootling along the Canal latéral east to Moissac or west to Buzet, Le Mas-d'Agenais and Aiguillon, from where you can enter the River Lot. For a 3–5 person boat prices are around 5000–11,000F/€760–1680 per week, depending on the season and level of comfort.

Bike rental Bicycles are available from Méca Plus, 18–20 av du Général-de-Gaulle (☎05.53.47.76.76).

Bus information For up-to-date bus schedules ask at the tourist office or phone the transport desk of the Conseil Général on ☎05.53.69.42.03.

Car parks There is free parking along the riverbank and on cours Gambetta.

Car rental Avis, 12 bd Sylvain-Dumon (☎05.53.47.76.47), and Europcar, 120 bd du Président-Carnot (☎05.53.47.37.40), have outlets near the *gare SNCF*. Airport pick-ups are available on request.

Hospital Centre Hospitalier, rte de Villeneuve (☎05.53.69.70.71), located 1.5km northeast of central Agen on the N21 to Villeneuve-sur-Lot.

Markets A fresh produce market takes place every morning in the *halle* on pl Jean-Baptiste-Durand. There are two large farmers' markets on Wednesday and Sunday mornings in the Halle du Pin beside place du 14-Juillet, a smaller one on Saturday mornings on the Esplanade du Gravier, and an organic market, also on Saturdays, on place des Laitiers, bd de la République. The most interesting of several agricultural fairs are the *foire de la prune* (1st or 2nd Mon after Sept 15), devoted to plums and prunes, and the *foire aux oies et canards gras* (2nd Sun in Dec) for foie gras and all manner of products made from duck and goose.

Police Commissariat de Police, 10 rue Palissy (☎05.53.68.17.00), to the south of the old quarter.

Post office The central post office is at 72 bd du Président-Carnot, 47000 Agen.

Shopping The main shopping streets are rue de la République and bd du Président-Carnot, while pedestrianized rue Molinier, south of the cathedral, has a few smarter boutiques. *The* thing to buy in Agen is prunes. You'll find them in the markets and at a number of specialist shops, including Confiserie P. Boisson, 20 rue Grande-Horloge (closed Sun), southwest of the cathedral, which was opened in 1835 and still uses traditional methods to produce chocolate prunes, truffle prunes, prunes in armagnac and stuffed prunes, amongst other delicacies. You can also ask to see a short explanatory film in English.

Taxis There is a taxi stand at the *gare* or call Agen Taxi on ☎05.53.66.39.14.

Nérac

Thirty kilometres across high, rolling hills to the southwest of Agen, you come to the castle town of **NÉRAC** on the banks of the River Baïse. It's hard to believe that this drowsy backwater, seat of the **d'Albret** family, once matched the Parisian court in its splendour and extravagance, and that here the bitter rivalries between Protestant and Catholic were played out. Nowadays, it's an attractive and prosperous little place, where you can happily spend a few hours wandering the riverbanks and what's left of the d'Albrets' castle.

The d'Albrets first came to Nérac around 1150 and over the next three centuries grew to become one of Aquitaine's most powerful dynasties – largely through a talent for marrying well. First they gained the Pyrenean kingdom of Navarre by marriage and then in 1527 Henri II d'Albret wed **Marguerite d'Angoulême**, sister to King François I of France. Intelligent and cultured, Marguerite surrounded her Nérac court with scholars and proponents of the new Protestant faith, including Jean Chauvin (John Calvin) who stayed here briefly in 1534. Neither Henri nor Marguerite converted, but their determined and ambitious daughter, **Jeanne d'Albret**, did so in 1560, thus making Nérac an important Protestant stronghold. Jeanne's son, also Henri, for his part married the young and beautiful **Marguerite de Valois**, sister of the King of France and Catherine de Médici, in 1572 and so ushered in Nérac's golden era. Their court glittered with eminent writers, diplomats and nobles, poets and musicians, while Henri indulged in the innumerable amorous conquests that earned him the nickname, *Le Vert Galant*; Queen Margot, as she was called, was no retiring violet, either, and the marriage was eventually annulled in 1599, by which time Henri had become **Henri IV** of France and removed his court to Paris.

All this while the d'Albrets had been adding to their **château** (April–June Mon 2–6pm, Wed–Sun 10am–noon & 2–6pm; July–Sept daily except Tues 10am–noon & 3–7pm; Oct–March Wed–Sun 10am–noon & 2–5pm; 20F/€3.05) on the river's west bank – at the far end of the bridge coming into Nérac from Agen. By the sixteenth century they had made it into a comfortable palace, of which only the north wing with its Renaissance gallery still exists, the other three having been partially destroyed in 1621 and finished off during the Revolution. It now houses a local history museum, of which the most interesting displays relate to Henri, Queen Margot and their larger-than-life relatives.

To the north of the château stands the Neoclassical **Église St-Nicolas** which was built in the mid-eighteenth century and contains some good nineteenth-century stained glass depicting scenes from the Old and New Testaments. From the terrace here you get good views of the triple-arched **Pont-Vieux** and the ancient roofs of the area known as **Petit-Nérac** on the opposite side of the river. It's worth wandering over the bridge and turning right along rue Sederie, where the wooden balconies of old tanneries overhang the river, to come out beside Nérac port, now bustling in summer with cruise-boats, below the Pont-Neuf.

Continuing south from the port across the main road, avenue Georges-Clemenceau, a shady woodland path leads 1.5km along the riverbank. **La Garenne**, as the area is known, was laid out as a royal pleasure park in the sixteenth century. The aviaries of exotic birds, the arbours and minstrels have long gone, but it's still a pleasant place to stroll or picnic. Not far from the entrance, look out for the **Fontaine de Fleurette**, marked by a statue of a prostrate and scantily clad young woman. According to legend, Fleurette was a gardener's daughter who had the misfortune to be seduced by *Le Vert Galant* and, when his attentions drifted elsewhere, drowned herself in the river. The inscription reads "She gave him all her life. He gave her but one day."

Practicalities

Buses from Agen (Citram; ☎05.56.43.68.43) stop on the central place d'Horloge, immediately west of the château, while the **tourist office** is located across the river in an intrusive new glass building above the port (May–Sept daily 9am–noon & 1–7pm; Oct–April Tues–Sat 9am–noon & 2–6pm; ☎05.53.65.27.75, fax 05.53.65.97.48). In summer you can rent pleasure **boats** at the port through Aquitaine Navigation (☎05.53.65.66.66; from 500F/€76.22 per day), or take a cruise with commentary on a traditional *gabare* a short distance up the Baïse to the first lock and back (1hr; April–Oct; 40F/€6.10).

The most comfortable **accommodation** in Nérac is the centrally located *Hôtel du Chateau*, 7 av Mondenard (☎05.53.65.09.05, fax 05.53.65.89.78, *www.logis-de-france.fr*; ③; closed Jan 1–15; good restaurant from 68F/€10.37, Oct–June closed Fri, Sat lunch & Sun eve), on the main road west of the Pont-Neuf; rooms at the back are quieter. Alternatively, try the welcoming, family-run *Hôtel d'Albret*, 40 allées d'Albret (☎05.53.97.41.10, fax 05.53.65.20.26, *www.logis-de-france.fr*; ③), on the wide boulevard a couple of minutes' walk southwest of the centre, with simple rooms and a cheerful restaurant serving well-priced regional menus from 68F/€10.37 (closed Sun eve & Mon).

Apart from the above hotel **restaurants**, you can get *crêpes*, salads and the like at *L'Escadron Volant* in a nice spot facing the château entrance. But by far the best place to eat in the area is *Le Relais de la Hire* (☎05.53.65.41.59; closed Sun eve & Mon), 10km southeast of Nérac in the village of Francescas, where you can feast on such dishes as artichoke and foie gras soufflé in their elegant eighteenth-century house or its flower-filled garden; menus start at 140F/€21.34, or you can eat à la carte for around 300F/€45.73.

Downstream from Agen

East of Agen the Garonne is sandwiched between the *autoroute*, two busy main roads, and the Bordeaux train line, which doesn't make for a particularly scenic journey. If you're headed this way, however, there are a clutch of interesting places to stop en route. Near the confluence of the Baïse and the Garonne lies the wine town of **Buzet-sur-Baïse**, where the local wine co-operative merits a visit, while over on the Garonne's east bank, **Aiguillon**'s eighteenth-century château presides over the junction of the Garonne and Lot rivers. From Aguillon it's worth continuing downstream as far as **Le Mas-d'Agenais**. This village, which overlooks both the Canal latéral and the Garonne from the west, has an attractive old centre, but it's prime draw is the wealth of carvings and a little oil painting inside its church.

Buzet-sur-Baïse

BUZET-SUR-BAÏSE lies roughly 30km from Agen, in the shadow of the Château de Buzet (not open to the public), which stands high on the green hillside, now separated from its village by the *autoroute*. Buzet itself is rather dull but as the vines on this south bank of the Garonne indicate, you're back in wine country and you shouldn't miss the chance to visit the local **wine co-operative**, Les Vignerons de Buzet (Mon–Sat 9am–noon & 2–6pm; ☎05.53.84.74.30, *www.vignerons-buzet.fr*), east of the village on the D642. Founded in 1955, this is France's largest wine co-operative, with around 300 growers producing 14 million bottles on average per year. The majority are strong red wines which benefit from ageing – Grande Réserve, Baron D'Ardeuil and Château de Gueyze stand out among the many award-winning wines produced by the co-operative (free tastings available). It's also well worth arranging for one of their exceptionally informative **guided tours** of the vinification plant and *chais* (by appointment only; visits in English on request). The tour covers everything, from the place where the grapes are delivered and sorted, via the in-house cooperage, the vast *chais* containing more than 4000 barrels and the bottling plant, to the warehouse where you'll find yourself among some 8 million glistening green bottles.

The other reason to visit Buzet is to rent a **boat** for a trip along the Canal latéral, the Baïse or the Lot. Aquitaine Navigation (☎05.53.84.72.50, *www.aquitaine-navigation.com*), based at the *halte nautique* on the canal below Buzet village, has both small pleasure boats (2–12 person) for rent by the half-day or day, as well as houseboats for longer excursions. They also offer one-way rental for a jaunt up the Baïse to Nérac (see above), from where they will come and collect you.

Aiguillon

Six kilometres north of Buzet on the opposite bank, the hilltop town of **AIGUILLON** stands guard over the confluence of the Lot and Garonne rivers as it has done at least since Roman times. Nowadays Aiguillon's most imposing building is the eighteenth-century, Neoclassical **Château des Ducs** – now a school – which dominates the town centre. It was built by the Duc d'Aiguillon who, having served as an army chief and Governor of Brittany under Louis XV, returned to transform his medieval château into a mini-Versailles, though the grand balls and other festivities were soon cut short by the Revolution. The small area of medieval lanes with their half-timbered houses to the north of the château are worth a wander, but otherwise Aiguillon is more of interest for its hotels and transport connections.

Aiguillon's **gare SNCF**, on the Agen–Bordeaux train line, lies a couple of minutes' walk below the château to the southwest along avenue de la Gare, while **buses** from Agen (Europe Evasion; ☎05.53.79.18.38) stop on the east side of town on rue de Visé. You'll find the **tourist office** beside the château on the central place du 14-Juillet (June–Sept Mon–Sat 9am–12.30pm & 2.30–6.30pm; Oct–May Mon 2.30–6.30pm, Tues–Sat 9am–noon & 2.30–6.30pm; ☎05.53.79.62.58, fax 05.53.84.41.17, *tourisme.aiguillon@wanadoo.fr*). The most appealing place to **stay** is *La Terrasse de l'Étoile*, 8 cours Alsace-Lorraine (☎05.53.79.64.64, fax 05.53.79.46.48, *www.logis-de-france.fr*, ③), in a handsome stone and brick building at the east end of place du 14-Juillet; the rooms are full of character, and there's also a small pool and a good traditional restaurant (menus from 78F/€11.89). The only other hotel is *Le Jardin des Cygnes*, route de Villeneuve (☎05.53.79.60.02, fax 05.53.88.10.22, *www.jardin-des-cygnes.com*; ③; closed Dec 15–Jan 10), offering functional but perfectly comfortable rooms in an unmissable puce-coloured building – also with a garden, pool and decent restaurant (menus from 75F/€11.43) – on Aiguillon's northeastern outskirts.

Le Mas-d'Agenais

From Aiguillon, rather than taking the dreary N113, cross to the Garonne's west bank and follow the D427 northwest for 15km through orchards and poplar plantations to find another ancient village perched above the Garonne, **LE MAS-D'A-GENAIS**. Traces of its ramparts still remain, but Le Mas' pride and joy is its cobbled central square with its old wooden *halle* and Romanesque **Église St-Vincent**. At first glance the church's muddle of brick and stone, and its truncated tower don't look much, but there's a surprising amount to see inside. Firstly, the exceptionally expressive carved capitals all around the choir and the triple-vaulted nave, depicting scenes such as Daniel in the lions' den, Abraham's sacrifice and David and Goliath. Then, in the southwest corner of the nave, there's a white-marble sarcophagus covered with geometric designs, which is said to have held the remains of St Vincent, the third-century evangelizer to whom the church is dedicated. But what most people come to see is a tiny painting in the north absidial chapel: the *Crucifixion* by **Rembrandt**. Dated 1631, the painting was donated to the church by a former parishioner in 1804; it belongs to a series of seven Stations of the Cross, the other six of which are in Munich. Christ is caught in a ray of light against an almost black background, his upturned face revealing the full agony of his question "My God, why have you forsaken me?"

The Canal latéral runs immediately below Le Mas to the east, between the river cliffs and the Garonne. Here, beside the lock just north of the bridge over the Garonne, you'll find another **boating** centre, where Crown Blue Line (☎05.53.89.50.80, *www.crown-blueline.com*) has houseboats for rent. The canal itself makes a pretty route westwards, but otherwise there's little reason to stop beyond Le Mas until you reach La Réole, 30km downstream (see p.114).

Moissac and around

There is nothing very memorable about the modern town of **MOISSAC**, some 40km southeast of Agen, largely because of the terrible damage done by the flood of 1930, when the Tarn, swollen by a sudden thaw in the Massif Central, burst its banks, destroying 617 houses and killing more than 100 people. Luckily, the one thing that makes Moissac a household name in the history of art survived, and that is the cloister and porch of the Benedictine **abbey-church of St-Pierre**, a masterpiece of Romanesque sculpture and model for dozens of churches throughout the region. The flat plains to the south and west of Moissac are less exciting, not least because of the looming presence of a nuclear power plant, but there are, nevertheless, a couple of places worth visiting along the banks of the Garonne: **St-Nicolas-de-la-Grave**, for its little museum devoted to the founder of Detroit, after whom Cadillac cars were named, and **Auvillar** for its exquisite market square.

Moissac is well served by **public transport**, with train and bus connections to Toulouse, Montauban and Agen. You can also reach St-Nicolas and Auvillar by bus from Moissac and Agen.

The Town

Moissac sits with its back to the old river cliffs on the north bank of the Tarn just before its confluence with the Garonne. The town's compact centre is bordered to the south by the Canal latéral, to the east by boulevard Camille-Delthil and to the west by boulevard Lakanal, at the south end of which Pont-Napoléon carries road traffic over the Tarn. Moissac's main east–west thoroughfare, named rue Gambetta in the west, rue St-Catherine and then rue Malaveille, brings you into the central market square, **place des Récollets**, where you'll find the most convenient car park.

From this square rue de la République leads north towards the red-brick belfry of the **Église Abbatiale St-Pierre**. Legend has it that Clovis first founded a church here in 506, though it seems more probable that its origins belong to the seventh century, which saw the foundation of so many monasteries throughout Aquitaine. The first Romanesque church on the site was consecrated in 1063 and enlarged in the following century when Moissac became a stop on the Santiago de Compostela pilgrim route. Since then the church has survived countless wars, including siege and sack by Simon de Montfort in 1212 during the Crusade against the Cathars. Indeed, the fact that it is still standing at all is something of a miracle. During the Revolution the cloister was used as a gunpowder factory and billet for soldiers, who damaged many of the carvings, while in the 1850s it only escaped demolition to make way for the Bordeaux–Toulouse train line by a whisker.

Apart from the dumpy, red-brick belfry, the first thing you see approaching from the south is the great stone arc of the **south porch**, with its magnificent tympanum, completed in 1130. It depicts Christ in majesty, right hand raised in benediction, the Book resting on his knee, surrounded by the Evangelists and the 24 elders of the Apocalypse – every one different – as described by St John in the Book of Revelation. Below, the central pillar bears the figures of St Paul and St Jeremiah, the latter with the most beautifully doleful face imaginable, in the same elongated style as at Souillac (see p.241). In fact, the influence of this craftsmanship, assimilated with varying degrees of success, can be seen in the work of artists who decorated the porches of countless churches across southwest France.

There is more fine carving on the capitals inside the porch, and the **interior** of the church, which was remodelled in the fifteenth century and is painted with intricate patterns, is interesting too, especially for some of the wood and stone statuary it contains. The most outstanding are those in the second chapel on the right as you enter: a lovely stone pietà in which Mary, enveloped in pastel blue, holds her son gently in her arms, and an equally compelling statue of Mary Magdalene with one arm outstretched and a thick tress of hair falling round her knees.

The adjoining **cloister** (same hours as tourist office – see below; 30F/€4.57) is accessed through the tourist office, behind the church to the west, where you can see a ten-minute video (in English on request) describing its main features. The cloister surrounds a garden shaded by a majestic cedar, and its pantile roof is supported by 76 alternating single and double marble columns. Each column supports a single inverted wedge-shaped block of stone, on which are carved with extraordinary delicacy all manner of animals and plant motifs, as well as 46 scenes from the Bible and the lives of the saints, among them Daniel in the lions' den, the Evangelists, fishermen on Lake Galilee, St Peter being crucified upside down and the decapitation of John the Baptist. Despite the damage done during the Revolution, they are in amazingly good shape. An inscription on the middle pillar on the west side explains that the cloister was constructed in the time of the Abbot Ansquitil in the year of Our Lord 1100.

The same ticket gains you entry to the rather less interesting **Musée d'Arts et Traditions Populaires** (Tues–Sat 10am–1pm & 2–6pm, Sun 2–6pm; closed Dec 24–Jan 15), housed in the former abbots' palace on rue de l'Abbaye immediately northeast of the church. Apart from a good collection of local ceramics, including faïence from Auvillar (see opposite), it contains a hotch-potch of furniture, ecclesiastical robes and religious treasures, and a mock-up of a Quercy farmhouse interior.

Practicalities

Moissac's **gare SNCF** lies about 500m west of the centre along avenue Pierre-Chabrié; from the station follow this road east and, where it curves northwards, you'll see steps leading down to the church square. **Buses** from Agen, Montauban and Toulouse, on the other hand, stop on the east side of town beside a roundabout known as the Tribunal on boulevard Camille-Delthil. The **tourist office**, 6 place Durand-de-Bredon (daily: mid-March to June & Sept to mid-Oct 9am–noon & 2–6pm; July & Aug 9am–7pm; mid-Oct to mid-March 9am–noon & 2–5pm; ☎05.63.04.01.85, fax 05.63.04.27.10, *www.frenchcom.com/moissac*), at the west end of the church, has details of Moissac's festivals (see box on p.318 & 319) and of concerts taking place in the church and cloister in the summer months. You can rent **bicycles** from Moissac Loisir, 29 rue Malaveille (☎05.63.04.03.48), on the north side of the market square.

The most pleasant **hotel** in town is *Le Chapon Fin*, 3 place des Récollets (☎05.63.04.04.22, fax 05.63.04.58.44, *www.logis-de-france.fr*, ②), on the south side of the market square. The older and cheaper rooms are a little small, and some have to share a toilet, but it's quiet, comfortable and has a decent restaurant (closed Sun Jan–March; menus from 105F/€16.01). Alternatively, try the nicely old-fashioned *Le Luxembourg*, 2 av Pierre-Chabrié (☎05.63.04.00.27, fax 05.63.04.19.73; ②), halfway along the road to the station, though it suffers slightly from road noise and the train tracks running behind, despite double-glazing. Even if you're not staying here, the restaurant is worth a visit for its good-value traditional meals (menus 62–157F/€9.45–23.93). Lastly, there's the *Le Pont Napoléon*, beside the eponymous bridge at 2 allées Montebello (☎05.63.04.01.55, fax 05.63.04.34.44; ③), with a few very classy rooms above its excellent restaurant (closed Wed; menus from 139F/€21.19, or around 300F/€45.73 à la carte); again, the hotel overlooks a busy road, but inside all is calm. For **campers**, there's a shady two-star site, the *Île du Bidounet* (☎05.63.32.52.52, fax 05.63.04.27.10; closed Oct–March), on a little island 2km from central Moissac across the Pont-Napoléon.

In fine weather, the nicest place to **eat** in Moissac is the magnolia-shaded *Bistrot du Cloître*, on place Durand-de-Bredon beside the tourist office (closed Mon eve & Tues), serving regional menus from 89F/€13.57. Otherwise there are the hotel restaurants mentioned above, as well as the cafés and brasseries on rue de la République and around the market square: the cheap and cheerful *Bar de Paris*, 1 place des Récollets (closed Mon; menu at 72F/€10.98), is popular for its pizzas, salads and simple regional dishes. In July and August, depending on the weather, you can also eat outside at the riverside *Le Kiosque de l'Uvarium*, avenue de l'Uvarium (☎05.63.04.53.16; closed Sun midday & Mon; menus from 85F/€12.96), about five minutes' walk southeast of centre. The food – a limited range of salads, grills and local fare – is fairly average and the service slow, but it's a lovely spot where you can watch the river glide by and old men playing *boules* under the plane trees.

For picnic fodder, there's a small fresh produce **market** in the covered hall on place des Récollets daily except Monday, while on Saturday and Sunday mornings farmers' stalls fill the whole square, a marvel of colour and temptation.

St-Nicolas-de-la-Grave

Eight kilometres southwest of Moissac, the small *bastide* of **ST-NICOLAS-DE-LA-GRAVE** is dominated by a four-square château atop a low rise on the far side of the Garonne. Its oldest tower – the fatter of the four, on the northeast corner – is attributed to Richard the Lionheart, who passed through here on his return from the Third Crusade in the late 1100s. Nowadays, however, it houses the Mairie, and there's nothing to see inside.

St-Nicolas is prouder of its second claim to fame as the home town of **Antoine Laumet**, founder of Detroit in America, who was born here in 1658. His birthplace, just southwest of the central square, now contains the **Musée Lamothe-Cadillac** (July & Aug Mon 9am–noon & 2–6pm, Tues–Sun 10am–noon & 2–6pm; rest of year apply to tourist office – see below; free), worth a quick look in passing as much for the story of Laumet's life as for any of the exhibits, which comprise mock-ups of a period bedroom and kitchen, and masses of documentation, some of it in English. Laumet was an adventurer who, on leaving for Canada in 1683 adopted the upper-crust name of de Lamothe-Cadillac. He later turned up in America in the service of King Louis XIV, where he founded a number of forts, among them a cavalry outpost called *le détroit* between lakes Erie and Huron in 1701. Two hundred years later, a Detroit car company was looking for a name at the same time as the city was celebrating its anniversary. They decided to honour Detroit's founding father, and thus were Cadillacs born.

Buses on the Toulouse–Agen route (Courriers de la Garonne; ☎05.62.72.37.23) stop on place du Platane in front of the château, which is also where you'll find the **tourist office** (July & Aug Mon 9am–noon & 2–6pm, Tues–Sun 10am–noon & 2–6pm; rest of year Mon & Wed 9am–noon, Tues 2–5pm, Thurs 2–4pm; ☎ & fax 05.63.94.82.81). St-Nicolas has no hotels, but the tourist office has details of *chambres d'hôtes* and there's a decent two-star **campsite** (☎05.63.95.50.00, fax 05.63.95.50.01; closed mid-Sept to mid-June) 2km north of the village where the Garonne and Tarn rivers form a large lake; the campsite is part of a leisure complex with **canoe** and **bike rental** amongst other facilities. If you need somewhere to **eat**, try *Le Cadillac*, on the village's northwest corner; it's a simple place serving pizzas, grills, salads and a good hors-d'oeuvre buffet (closed Mon; menus from 65F/€9.91).

Auvillar

AUVILLAR, 14km west of St-Nicolas, is perched on a cliff on the Garonne's south bank. Its feudal château and ramparts were demolished in the eighteenth and nineteenth centuries, but thankfully the wonderful old village centre remains. From the main road skirting south of the village, you duck under the seventeenth-century **Tour de l'Horloge** to find yourself in the gently sloping triangular-shaped **place de la Halle** surrounded by a harmonious ensemble of brick and timber buildings with arcades running all around. At the square's cobbled centre stands a particularly pleasing circular stone-pillared market hall, built in the early nineteenth century. While you're here it's worth poking your nose in the **Musée du Vieil Auvillar** (mid-June to mid-Oct daily except Tues 2–6pm; mid-Oct to mid-June Sat & Sun 2–6pm; 10F/€1.52), on the square's north side, for its collection of local pottery. Auvillar was already known for its pottery production in the sixteenth century, but in the following century they began making *faïence* of sufficiently high quality to rival that imported from Holland and Italy. Local potters still have a good reputation, as witnessed by the big pottery fair held every October (see box on p.319 for details).

The Toulouse-Agen **bus** stops on the main road about 30m east of the Tour de l'Horloge, while you'll find the **tourist office** on place de la Halle next to the museum (daily: June to mid-Oct 9am–noon & 2–7pm; mid-Oct to May 2–5.30pm; ☎ & fax 05.63.39.89.82, *www.auvillar.com*). For somewhere to **stay** or **eat**, head for the *Hôtel de l'Horloge* (☎05.63.39.91.61, fax 05.63.39.75.20; ③; mid-Oct to mid-April closed Fri & lunch on Sat) beside the gate-tower: in addition to a clutch of recently modernized and spacious en-suite rooms, they run a bar-brasserie, where you can eat well for around 100F/€15.24, and a more formal restaurant with menus from 155F/€23.63.

Quercy Blanc

As you head north from Moissac, the land rises gradually to gently undulating, green and woody country, cut obliquely by parallel valleys running down to meet the Garonne and planted with vines, sunflowers and maize, and apple and cherry orchards. It's a very soft landscape, the villages are small and widely scattered and the pace of life seems about equal with that of a turning sunflower. This is the **Quercy Blanc**, named after the area's grey-white soils and building stone, a region with few sights, but one which lives up to the image of deepest rural France. The single most interesting place to head for is **Lauzerte**, atop a river bluff 25km north of Moissac, though it won't take long to explore its spruce central square and endearingly stocky little church, nor the clutch of once-noble houses in the lanes around. Further north again, **Montcuq** distinguishes itself with its solid square keep, the remnants of a twelfth-century fortress, standing guard over the medieval village, while way over to the southeast, **Montpezat-de-Quercy** is home to a Gothic church with a surprising collection of art treasures, including a beautiful and complete set of Flemish tapestries.

Public transport around Quercy Blanc consists of three separate bus services. You can reach Lauzerte from Moissac, and Montcuq from Cahors, while Montpezat is a stop on the route between Cahors and Montauban.

Lauzerte and around

The first of the sleepy hilltop villages that you reach travelling north from Moissac is **LAUZERTE**. It stands on a promontory between two rivers, a press of white-walled houses contained within its medieval ramparts, while the "new" town spills down the south and eastern slopes. The site's strategic importance was not lost on the counts of Toulouse, who took control of Lauzerte in the late twelfth century and granted it the status of a *bastide*, with all the rights and privileges attached, in 1241. The other notable event in its history took place fifty years later when the townspeople threw out the English occupiers. In reward the French king, Philippe IV, elevated Lauzerte to capital of the Bas Quercy (Lower Quercy) region and seat of the royal Seneschal. However, its golden age came to an end in the late sixteenth century when Lauzerte was demoted to a mere district capital in the aftermath of the Wars of Religion.

Nevertheless, a few vestiges of its glory days remain in the old town, which lies clustered around the pretty, arcaded central square, **place des Cornières**, and the church of **St-Barthélémy**. The church's origins go back to the thirteenth century, but it was largely rebuilt after the Protestants wreaked their havoc, and its main point of interest nowadays is the gilded Baroque altarpiece, dedicated to the Virgin Mary and depicting scenes from her life, filling the north chapel. Behind the church, there are good views to be had of the patchwork landscape all around from the **place du Château**, where the castle once stood on the promontory's northern tip. From here **rue de la Garrigue**, and its extension **rue de la Gendarmerie**, double back south of the church, running along the ridge past a number of thirteenth- and fourteenth-century merchants' houses with their big ground-floor arches and colonnaded windows above.

Once you've explored Lauzerte's compact centre, it's worth venturing southeast to visit an interesting museum near **CAZES-MONDENARD**, a village with a pretty Gothic church and a pleasant hotel (see below) 8km from Lauzerte. The core of the **Musée Yvan Quercy** (1hr guided tours; by appointment only; ☎05.63.95.84.02; free), at the end of a long lane signed off the D16 Molières road 2km east of the village, is its collection of hearses, which was started by chance when the owner – Monsieur Quercy – was given an old hearse thirty years ago. Since then he has amassed ninety different models, some horse-drawn, others pulled by hand, from the seventeenth century up to the first motorized model manufactured by Peugeot in 1949. The collection also comprises some fifty regular carriages, all in excellent condition, and a number of early caterpillar tractors. After the tour, you are offered free tastings of wine, pâtés and other local produce, and in season they also run a restaurant (May–Sept daily; menus at 80F/€12.20 & 120F/€18.29; reservations required); the dining room is a bit soulless but the food – all regional dishes – more than compensates.

Practicalities

Lauzerte is served by twice-weekly **buses** from Moissac (Wed & Sat 11.30am; ☎05.63.94.64.44), which drop you at the northern entrance to the lower village. It's then a steep walk along faubourg d'Auriac, or straight uphill via a series of steps and twisting paths, to reach the **tourist office** on place des Cornières (July & Aug daily 9am–1pm & 2–7pm; rest of year Mon–Sat 9am–noon & 2–6pm, Sun 9am–noon & 2–7pm; ☎05.63.94.61.94, fax 05.63.94.61.93, *perso.wanadoo.fr/lauzerte.tourisme*).

The **hotel** on faubourg d'Auriac, the *Hôtel du Quercy* (☎05.63.94.66.36; ②; closed 3 weeks in Oct, also Sun evening & Mon), has a handful of old-fashioned but perfectly comfortable rooms, and a well-deserved reputation for its excellent **restaurant**. In addition to traditional local dishes, such as *cassoulet*, stuffed cabbage and *confit de canard*, the latter also stuffed with foie gras, they serve a good range of fish and seafood dishes and game in season; menus start at 60F/€9.15 at lunch and 195F/€29.73 in the evening; reservations are recommended. The next closest hotel is *Le Luzerta*, north of the village beside the Cahors road (☎05.63.94.64.43, fax 05.63.94.66.67; ②), which consists of several bungalows – functional but clean and en suite – around a pool. They also run a decent restaurant in a converted mill just up the road (closed Sun evening & Tues; menus from 90F/€13.72).

In addition, there are two more good options in the countryside around Lauzerte. The smarter and more comfortable of the two is the Belgian-run *Aube Nouvelle* (☎05.63.04.50.33, fax 05.63.04.57.55; ②; good restaurant from 60F/€9.15), in a handsome brick-built manor house 9km south of Lauzerte on the D2, just before the village of Durfort-Lacapalette. Otherwise, try *l'Atre* (☎05.63.95.81.61, fax 05.63.95.87.22, *www.logis-de-france.fr*; ②; closed Mon), a pleasant, country hotel, offering unfussy en-suite rooms and good home cooking (menus 67–210F/€10.21–32.01) in the centre of Cazes-Mondenard.

Montcuq and around

Thirteen kilometres northeast of Lauzerte along the Petite-Barguelonne valley, **MONTCUQ** – pronounce the q if you don't want to be saying "my arse" – is built around the flanks of a conical hill, on top of which stands a huge square keep. Like Lauzerte, Montcuq guarded the ancient road to Cahors and lies on the Santiago de Compostela pilgrims' route, but it seems to have had the knack of picking the wrong cause: it sided with the Cathars, was condemned for collaborating with the English and later became a Protestant stronghold. As a result, there's not much in the way of sights, though it's an attractive little place and less touristy than Lauzerte.

To get the lie of the land the best thing to do is climb up to the **tower** (mid-June to mid-Sept daily 3–7pm; 7F/€1.07); any of the lanes leading uphill from rue de la Promenade, the wide boulevard to the south of the old town, will take you up there. It was built at the turn of the eleventh century as part of a larger fortress, and although Louis IX ordered the ramparts destroyed, the ditches filled in and the tower's top knocked off in the aftermath of the Cathar Crusades, at 24m it's still a fair climb. The effort is rewarded with all-round views; even when it's closed the pinnacle of rock it stands on is high enough to give a good panorama. Wandering back down the slope through the maze of stone and half-timbered houses, the church of **St-Hilaire** stands out with its octagonal, brick tower, though there's nothing of particular interest inside.

Practicalities

Buses run to Montcuq from Cahors (Raynal Voyages; ☎05.65.23.28.28), stopping on rue de la Promenade near the **tourist office** (July & Aug Mon–Sat 10am–12.30pm & 3–7pm, Sun 10.30am–1pm; rest of year Tues–Fri 10am–noon & 3–5pm; ☎ & fax 05.65.22.94.04, *montcuq@wanadoo.fr*). For a place to **stay**, try the welcoming *Hôtel du Parc* (☎05.65.31.18.82, fax 05.65.22.99.77, *www.logis-de-france.fr*; ③; closed Nov–March), 500m west of Montcuq on the Belmont road, with old-fashioned but comfortable rooms, a big, quiet garden and a decent restaurant (menus from 65F/€9.91). Another good place to **eat** is the *Café du Centre* on place de la République, a little further east along the boulevard from the tourist office. They serve brasserie food – salads, steaks, sandwiches and the like – and a *menu du jour* at 69F/€10.52; note that meals are not served on Sundays. Finally, should you need a new supply of reading matter, Montcuq is also home to Chiméra, an English-owned **bookshop** selling mostly secondhand French and English titles; it's just off place de la République along rue du Faubourg-St-Privat – the road to Castelnau-Montratier.

Southwest to Montpezat-de-Quercy

The route southeast of Montcuq takes you on a roller-coaster ride across the valleys and intervening hills, on one of which stands **CASTELNAU-MONTRATIER**, 20km from Montcuq, with its incongruous neo-Byzantine church and spacious market square. Twelve kilometres further on through more country lanes you come to another, rather more interesting hilltop village, **MONTPEZAT-DE-QUERCY**. Traces of its medieval heyday remain in the arcaded central square and lanes of half-timbered houses, but the main reason to stop here is the **Collégiale St-Martin**, with its unusually rich hoard of treasures, standing at the southeast end of the promontory on which the village is built.

The church was founded in the early fourteenth century by Cardinal Pierre des Prés (1281–1361), a native of Montpezat, who grew wealthy in the service of the Avignon popes. With its high and severe single nave, the interior is unexciting, at least in comparison with the artworks of the fourteenth to sixteenth centuries arrayed in the side-chapels. Best are the battered but still lovely *Vierge aux Colombes*, her face framed by golden ringlets, in the second chapel on the left, a polychrome pietà in the first on the right, and, next door, an English alabaster triptych depicting the Birth, Resurrection and Ascension of Christ – in the last only his feet are visible as he's whisked heavenwards. The church's finest treasures, though, are the five Flemish **tapestries** grouped around the choir. They were made specially for the church in the early sixteenth century, a gift from Jean IV des Prés, Bishop of Montauban, and portray events from the life of St Martin de Tours, to whom the church is consecrated. The most famous scene is that in the first panel, where the future saint – at the time in the service of the Roman army – shares his cloak with a crippled beggar. The workmanship throughout is of superb quality, while the colours remain amazingly vibrant. Also in remarkably good condition is the white marble sarcophagus and statue of Pierre des Prés, to the right of the choir, with his feet resting on a lion while his well-fed face is bathed in a contented grin.

Practicalities

Buses between Montauban and Cahors (Chauderon; ☎05.63.22.55.00) stop on the west side of the village on the boulevard des Fossés, near the helpful **tourist office** (April, May & Oct Tues–Fri 10.30am–12.30pm & 1.30–5.30pm; June & Sept Tues–Sun 10am–1pm & 2–7pm; July & Aug Mon 2–6pm, Tues–Sun 10am–1pm & 2–7pm; Nov–March Tues, Thurs & Sun 11am–5pm; ☎05.63.02.05.55). The office doubles as a Maison du Vin where you can buy the local Coteaux du Quercy wines and get advice on vineyards to visit, though they don't offer tastings.

While there are no hotels in Montpezat, you can stay in a very comfortable German/English-owned **chambres d'hôte**, *Le Barry*, faubourg St-Roch (☎05.63.02.05.50, fax 05.63.02.03.07; ④), built into the southern ramparts with a romantic garden, pool and views, and good-value meals available on request (eves only; 125F/€19.06). You'll also **eat** well at the *Ferme Auberge de Coutié* (☎05.63.67.73.51; menus from 95F/€14.48), on the D20 9km southwest of Montpezat, signed to the east of Espanel hamlet, in a Quercy farm surrounded by ducks and orchards. There's also a well-tended two-star municipal **campsite** (☎ & fax 05.63.02.07.08, *montpezat-accueil@wanadoo.fr*; open all year) in a leisure park on Montpezat's northern outskirts.

Montauban

Lying 20km east of Moissac and 50km north of Toulouse, **MONTAUBAN** is a prosperous middle-sized provincial city, the capital of the largely agricultural *département* of Tarn-et-Garonne. Its beautiful old centre sits on the north bank of the River Tarn, a harmonious ensemble of warm, pink brick which shows its best at sunset, or at night when the steeples, massive old bridge and riverside facades are illuminated. The layout follows the typical *bastide* pattern: a regular grid of streets around an arcaded market square, the glorious **place Nationale**, but between the main streets lie enticing alleys, covered passages and interior court-yards. The greatest delight is simply to wander – the centre is only a ten-minute stroll from end to end – taking in the scattered sights as you go, of which the high-light is the **Musée Ingres**, dedicated to Montauban's most famous son.

The city's origins go back to 1144 when Alphonse Jourdain, Count of Toulouse, decided to create a *bastide* here as a bulwark against English and French royal power. Indeed, it is generally regarded as the first *bastide*, the model for the medieval new towns found throughout this region (see p.310). Montauban has enjoyed various periods of great prosperity, as one can guess from the prolifera-tion of fine houses, mainly based on trade in silk and other textiles. The first fol-lowed the suppression of the Cathar heresy and the final submission of the counts of Toulouse in 1229 and was greatly enhanced by the building of the Pont-Vieux in 1335, making it the best crossing point on the Tarn for miles. The Hundred Years' War did its share of damage, as did Montauban's opting for the Protestant cause in the Wars of Religion, but by the time of the Revolution it had become once more one of the richest cities in the southwest.

Arrival, information and accommodation

Montauban's **gare SNCF** lies roughly 1km west of centre across the Pont-Vieux at the far end of avenue de Mayenne. Most regional **buses** terminate either at the *gare* or nearby on place Lalaque, though buses from Laguépie drop you by the hideous market hall on place Prax-Paris on the northeast side of town. Eurolines buses stop at the top end of rue de Chateauvieux, about 600m north of the old centre, while the *navette* from Toulouse airport brings you into the riverside park-ing lot below the Pont-Vieux. While central Montauban is eminently walkable, you might want to hop on a **city bus** from the train station to the centre (line #3; roughly every 15–20min), stopping on boulevard Midi-Pyrénées near place Prax-Paris; tickets, costing 5.50F/€0.84 for a single journey, can be bought on the bus.

The **tourist office** is located on the south side of place Prax-Paris (July & Aug Mon–Sat 9am–7pm, Sun 2–4pm; rest of year Mon–Sat 9am–noon & 2–7pm; ☎05.63.63.60.60, fax 05.63.63.65.12); you can pick up an English-language do-it-yourself walking map of the old centre here, as well as lists of local events (see box on p.318). They charge 10F/€1.52 for finding accommodation, but this is money well spent in high summer when rooms are hard to come by.

Montauban has a surprisingly poor choice of **hotels**, none of them particularly good value for money. The cheapest in the centre is the homely but rather worn *Hôtel du Commerce*, 9 place Roosevelt (☎05.63.66.31.32, fax 05.63.03.18.46; ①–④), beside the cathedral; it's worth paying a bit more here for en-suite facilities. At the other extreme, the *Hôtel Mercure*, opposite at 12 rue Notre-Dame

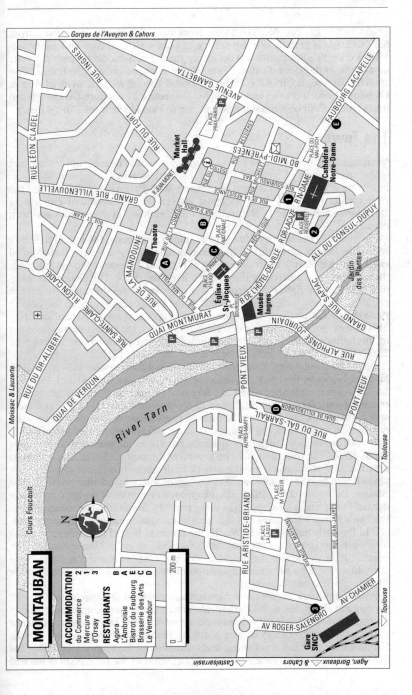

MONTAUBAN

ACCOMMODATION
du Commerce   2
Mercure   1
d'Orsay   3

RESTAURANTS
Agora   B
L'Ambroisie   A
Bistrot du Faubourg   E
Brasserie des Arts   C
Le Ventadour   D

(☎05.63.63.17.23, fax 05.63.66.43.66, *www.mercure.com*; ⑥; restaurant from 85F/€12.96), is getting into the luxury bracket – all mod-cons and nicely furnished, though some rooms are decidedly small. For a middle-range hotel, your best option is the *Hôtel d'Orsay*, 31 rue Roger-Salengro, outside the train station (☎05.63.66.06.66, fax 05.63.66.19.39; ③; closed second & third week of Aug & Christmas hols); it doesn't look much, but the rooms are comfortable enough and it has an excellent restaurant (closed all Sun & Mon lunch; from 130F/€19.82).

The Town

Montauban couldn't be easier to find your way around. The most interesting part is the small kernel of streets based on the original *bastide*, enclosed within an inner ring of boulevards between **boulevard Midi-Pyrénées** to the east and the river on the west. The main shopping streets are pedestrianized **rue de la Résistance** and **rue de la République** which intersect in the *bastide's* southern corner.

In the centre lies the city's finest point, **place Nationale**, the hub of the city's social life. Rebuilt after a fire in the seventeenth century, it is surrounded on all sides by a double row of arcades beneath two- and three-storeyed town houses, their uniformity tempered by the square's irregular shape. The distinctive octagonal belfry of the **Église St-Jacques** shows above the southwestern rooftops, a couple of minutes' walk away. First built in the thirteenth century on the pilgrim route to Santiago de Compostela, the church bears the scars of Montauban's troubled history, not only in its mix of architectural styles, but in the holes gouged out of the belfry's fortified base by cannonballs during an unsuccessful siege by 20,000 Catholic troops – held off by just 6000 locals – in 1621.

On the banks of the river south of the church stands a massive half-palace, half-fortress, begun by the counts of Toulouse, then continued by the Black Prince in 1363. He left it unfinished when the English lost control of the town, and so it remained until 1664 when the Bishop of Montauban chose this very prominent spot for his residence. It is now the **Musée Ingres** (July & Aug daily 10am–noon & 2–6pm; rest of year closed Mon; 20F/€3.05), which houses paintings and more than 4000 drawings left to the city by locally born Jean-Auguste-Dominique Ingres (1780–1867). The collection includes several of the supremely realistic, luminous portraits of women which are the artist's trademark, though not to everyone's taste. It also contains a substantial collection of works by another native, Émile-Antoine Bourdelle (1861–1929), the ubiquitous monumental sculptor and a student of Rodin, and a hotch-potch of other exhibits, from Gallo-Roman mosaics in the Black Prince's basement hall to fifteenth- and sixteenth-century European fine art. In the early days of World War II, the museum hosted more illustrious visitors when the Louvre dispatched over 3000 works of art to Montauban for safekeeping prior to the German invasion. When southern France was occupied in 1942, however, they were moved again to more remote locations, including the Château de Montal (see p.260).

Providing a stark exception to Montauban's red-brick homogeneity is a cold, sore-thumb of a building, the **Cathédrale Notre-Dame**, ten minutes' walk southeast up rue de l'Hôtel-de-Ville. It was erected on the city's highest spot at the turn of the seventeenth century as part of the triumphalist campaign to reassert the Catholic faith after the cruel defeat and repression of the Protestants. Inside the dazzling white classical facade lies an echoing nave, whose main point of interest is another Ingres painting, *Le Vœu de Louis XIII*, hanging in the north aisle. Specially commissioned for the cathedral, the vast canvas depicts Louis offering France, symbolized by his crown and sword, to a Virgin and Child strongly influenced by Raphael's romantic style.

Eating, drinking and entertainment

The simplest way of finding a place to **eat** is to browse round the place Nationale, where you'll find the cheap and cheerful *Agora* under the arcades at no. 9 (closed Sun evening & Mon), serving salads and *plats* at around 40–45F/€6.10–6.86, and the slightly smarter *Brasserie des Arts* at no. 4 (Oct–April lunch only; *plat du jour* at 45F/€6.86, menus from 82F/€12.50), offering a wider choice of salads, fish dishes and regional fare. For traditional cooking, however, you can't beat the *Bistrot du Faubourg*, east of the cathedral at 111 faubourg Lacapelle (☎05.63.63.49.89; closed Sat eve & Sun), a popular locals' place offering excellent value for money: at lunchtime you can eat for 66F/€10.06 including wine. Also good is *L'Ambroisie*, 41 rue de la Comédie, with a summer terrace outside the theatre, which serves well-priced *plats du jours* (45F/€6.86 including a glass of wine) and regional menus from 75F/€11.43. Last but not least, there's Montauban's top restaurant, *Le Ventadour*, 23 quai Villebourbon (☎05.63.63.34.58; closed Sun & Mon; menus 100–220F/€15.24–33.54), magnificently sited in an old house on the west bank near the Pont-Vieux: *the* place for a splurge.

The best place for a **picnic**, on the other hand, is the Jardin des Plantes, a pleasant green space south of the cathedral along the banks of a small tributary to the Tarn. You can buy provisions at the sandwich shops, patisseries and delicatessens on rue de la République and rue de la Résistance. While you're at it, keep an eye open for the **local speciality**, *Montauriols*, a chocolate-coated cherry preserved in armagnac; you'll find them at the *Salon de Thé Marty*, 10 rue de la Résistance, amongst other places.

When it comes to a **drink**, the most atmospheric spot is *Le Flamand* at 8 rue de la République (Oct–April closed Sun), with a wide range of bottled and draft beers, including La Oc' Ale from a local microbrewery; they also do bar food till midnight. Or you could try *Le Maracana*, 3 place National, the liveliest option on the central square, which hosts free **live music** – usually blues, rock and country – most Saturday nights. Another good option is *Le Santa Maria*, north of the Musée Ingres on quai Montmurat (Oct–April closed Sun), with a terrace overlooking the Tarn; they also serve tapas and more substantial Tex-Mex meals.

Listings

Airport The nearest airport is Toulouse-Blagnac (☎05.61.42.44.00).

Bike rental Try Denayrolles, 878 av Jean-Moulin (☎05.63.03.62.02), northeast of town along rue du Fort.

Boat rental On summer afternoons you can rent electric-powered boats (4–5 person) from the *embarcadère* below the Musée Ingres (June–Sept; 70F/€10.67 per hr).

Bus information For tickets and information about Eurolines buses for Amsterdam, Brussels and London, contact Barrière-Voyages, 16 bd Midi-Pyrénées (☎05.63.66.41.03). The *navette* for Toulouse airport leaves hourly from the riverside parking lot below the Musée Ingres (45min–1hr; 170F/€25.92; reservations required at least one day before from Interligne ☎05.63.63.16.00).

Car rental Both Avis, 72 av Aristide-Briand (☎05.63.20.45.73), and Europcar, 21 av Roger-Salengro (☎05.63.20.29.00), are located near the *gare SNCF*.

Car parks The most convenient is the pay parking on pl Prax-Paris or pl Roosevelt. Free parking is available along the riverbanks beneath the Pont-Vieux.

Hospital Centre Hospitalier, rue Léon-Cladel (☎05.63.92.82.82), to the north of the old quarter.

Markets A few stalls sell fresh produce every day on pl Nationale, but the main farmers' market takes place on Saturday mornings on pl Prax-Paris. In winter (Nov–March) there's a special *marché au gras* on pl Nationale & pl Lalaque on Wednesday and Saturday mornings.

Police Commissariat de Police, 50 bd Alsace-Lorraine (☎05.63.21.54.00), northeast of centre, off av Gambetta.

Post office The central post office is on the bd Midi-Pyrénées, 82000 Montauban.

Taxis There are taxi stands at the *gare* and the north end of bd Midi-Pyrénées, or call Radio Taxi Montalbanais ☎05.63.66.99.99.

The Gorges de l'Aveyron and around

In its lower course the Aveyron glides across the dull flood plain surrounding Montauban, offering little reason to stop other than the village of **Montricoux**, with its museum dedicated to a forgotten artist. The scenery begins to get more interesting, however, about 30km east of Montauban where the river has sliced a narrow defile through the hills. The entrance of the **Gorges de l'Aveyron** is guarded by the fortress village of **Bruniquel**, its ancient houses smothered with summer roses, while further east **Penne** is perched beneath a crumbling castle. From here on the gorge gets increasingly dramatic as you work your way upriver to **St-Antonin-Noble-Val**, which, with its compact medieval centre and choice of hotels, makes an excellent base for exploring the gorge and surrounding sights. The most compelling of these is the partially ruined **Abbaye de Beaulieu-en-Rouergue**, located 14km northwest, where the Gothic church has been converted into a contemporary art gallery. Beyond St-Antonin, **Laguépie** is less interesting but provides another possible base, from where you can hop south to the beguiling – if very touristy – hilltop town of **Cordes-sur-Ciel**. At Laguépie the Aveyron valley turns abruptly north, and its sides close in again to form a second increasingly deep, thickly wooded gorge, dominated by the ruins of **Najac**'s mighty fortress. It stands guard over the frontier of the former province of Rouergue, now the Aveyron *département*, and the southern approach to the *bastide* of **Villefranche-de-Rouergue**. A refreshingly unprettified town lying on a bend in the river, Villefranche is centred around a perfectly preserved, arcaded market square above which soars a colossal fortified church tower.

    Buses run along the Aveyron between Montauban and Laguépie (GAU Autocar; ☎05.63.30.44.45) during school term time, with onward services all year from Laguépie to Villefranche (SNCF; ☎05.65.45.03.16) and from Najac to Villefranche (Gauchy; ☎05.65.81.12.92). Note that these buses cater mostly to schoolchildren, which means they don't necessarily run every day and tend to be at inconvenient times. An alternative – and preferable – way of travelling between Laguépie, Najac and Villefranche is the Toulouse–Brive **train** line, which tunnels and weaves along the valleyside; these trains also stop at Cordes on their way south.

Montricoux

Just before you leave the flat alluvial plains, 25km west of Montauban, **MONTRI-COUX** would hardly be worth the stop if it weren't for its intriguing art museum, the **Musée Marcel-Lenoir** (daily: April–June & Sept to mid-Oct 10am–12.30pm & 2.30–6pm; July & Aug 10am–12.30pm & 2.30–7pm; 25F/€3.81), on the west side of the village. Like Ingres (see p.338), Marcel Lenoir was another prolific local artist, who was born in Montauban in 1872 and died in Montricoux in 1931. He was much fêted during his early years, when he was at the forefront of Pointillism and Cubism, and he even presaged Art Deco as he searched for new means of expression. But Lenoir was also an irascible character and managed to offend so many critics, dealers and galleries that he was eventually cast into oblivion. And there he stays, despite the best efforts of the owner of this collection of 140 works spanning Lenoir's whole career. One of the most revealing is the *Kiss of Judas*, in which you see Picasso profiled in blue and Van Gogh cutting off Gauguin's ear, while Judas is portrayed as a well-known art critic of the time.

Buses from Montauban stop on the main road across from the village on the river's south bank, where you'll also find an old-fashioned **hotel**, *Le Relais du Postillon* (☎05.63.67.23.58, fax 05.63.67.27.68; ①; closed Fri eve & Sat lunch except July & Aug), offering basic rooms (none with its own toilet) but excellent regional cooking (menus from 95F/€14.48). There's also a very swish riverside **restaurant**, *Les Gorges de l'Aveyron* (☎05.63.24.50.50; closed Feb, also Sun eve & Mon except in July & Aug; menus from 148F/€22.56), along a lane beside the bridge. For more comfortable accommodation, head 8km southwest to *Chez Terrassier* (☎05.63.30.94.60, fax 05.63.30.87.40, *www.logis-de-france.com*; ③; closed Sun eve, mid-Sept to April closed Fri eve, also 2 weeks in Nov & 1 week in Jan; menus from 70F/€10.67), a pretty, modern place with a pool in the middle of **VAISSAC**.

Bruniquel

East of Montricoux the hills rise suddenly and 5km later the **Gorges de l'Aveyron** really get into their stride as you sight the first of several fortified villages along these rocky crags. Once a Protestant stronghold, **BRUNIQUEL** shelters in the lee of its **castle** (April, June & Sept Mon–Sat 2–6pm, Sun 10am–12.30pm & 2–6pm; May & Oct Sun only same hours; July & Aug daily 10am–12.30pm & 2–7pm; 15F/€2.29), teetering on the edge of a 100m cliff. In fact there are two adjacent castles, since the original twelfth-century fortress had to be divided between rival cousins in 1484, but both are much knocked about and not of tremendous interest, save for the views they afford along the valley. More engaging is the **Maison des Comtes de Payrol** (April–Sept daily 10am–6pm; rest of year Sat & Sun 10am–6pm; 15F/€2.29) to the west of the castle entrance. The thirteenth-century home of a wealthy merchant family, its vaulted cellars and panelled and frescoed rooms now house an unusually good local history museum, including an interesting collection of oil lamps and candle holders.

Buses stop about 250m below Bruniquel to the south, beside a road leading up to the church and the **tourist office** (April–Sept daily 10.30am–noon & 2–6pm; rest of year same hours but variable closing days; ☎ & fax 05.63.67.29.84) at the entrance to the village. For an overnight **stay**, Marc de Baudouin runs a very

good *chambres d'hôtes*, to the right of the church (☎ & fax 05.63.67.26.16; ③;
closed Dec & Jan; evening meals from 95F/€14.48 by request); he's also a keen
mountain-biker and is happy to advise on local trails and footpaths. Right opposite,
the **restaurant** *L'Étape du Château* (closed mid-Nov to Feb, also eves except mid-
May to mid-Sept) serves traditional menus from 85F/€12.96. There's also a
small, two-star **campsite**, *Le Payssel* (☎05.63.67.25.95; closed Oct–April), about
700m south on the D964 to Albi.

Penne and on towards St-Antonin

Six kilometres upriver from Bruniquel you come to the even more beautiful ridge-
top village of **PENNE**, once a Cathar stronghold, with its ruined **castle** perched
on an impregnable pinnacle. Everything is old and leaning and bulging, but holding together nonetheless, with a harmony that would be impossible to create pur-
posely. There's just one cobbled street leading from an arch under the church belfry and through a second gate – where ancient grain measures are cut into the
wall – to a footpath scrambling among the castle ruins. There's not much left, but
it's an atmospheric spot, the piles of stones overrun with dog-roses, clematis and
honeysuckle, with a panorama taking in the village roofs and the wooded country
beyond. If that's worked up an appetite or a thirst, head for the **bar-restaurant** *La
Terrasse* (July & Aug daily, rest of year open for lunch daily except Wed & open
Sat eve; menus from 99F/€15.09), at the north end of the village, from the back
terrace of which you get a first-class view of the castle's airy crag.

Beyond Penne the gorge becomes deeper and more dramatic. To appreciate it
at its best, turn off the main road just after Cazals, 6km from Penne, following
signs for the **Corniche**, a lane which climbs steeply for a kilometre or so on to the
cliffs' edge. You'll be rewarded with tremendous views and, a little further on, a
superbly sited **restaurant**, *La Corniche* (☎05.63.68.26.95; closed Nov–March, also
April–June, Sept & Oct closed Sun eve & Wed, July & Aug closed lunch
Mon–Wed; menus from 90F/€13.72; reservation recommended), offering generous country dishes, in the hamlet of **BROUSSES**. Six kilometres later you drop
down to the river again to the west of St-Antonin-Noble-Val.

St-Antonin-Noble-Val and around

The finest and most substantial town in this lower stretch of the Aveyron valley is
ST-ANTONIN-NOBLE-VAL, 16km northeast of Penne. It sits on the river's north
bank beneath the beetling white cliffs of the **Roc d'Anglars**, where it developed in
the ninth century around an abbey said to house the remains of the evangelizing **St
Antonin**. According to legend, his body was carried here in a boat guided by two
white eagles from Pamiers, in the Ariège, where the saint met his death. Since then
the town has endured all the vicissitudes of this region's history: it sided with the
Cathars, then the Protestants and each time was walloped by the alien power of the
kings from the north, until it eventually sank into oblivion after the seventeenth century. Yet, in spite of all, a marvellous heritage of houses endowed by wealthy merchants remains from its medieval glory days, when St-Antonin was an important
commercial centre, manufacturing linen and leather goods.

The easiest landmark to head for is the spire of the large but uninteresting neo-
Gothic **church**, towards the town's southeast corner. Along the church's west

wall rue du Pont-de-l'Aveyron leads south to the bridge, while rue Guilhelm-Peyre curves northeast to **place de la Halle**. This square is St-Antonin at its most picturesque, with its cafés and pint-sized *halle*, the focus of an important Sunday-morning market, and the town's finest building, the **Maison des Consuls**, whose origins go back to 1125. The facade is pierced with arcades, pairs of colonnaded openings and a contrastingly severe oblong window on the first floor, on one pillar of which Adam and Eve hide their modesty; the old man on the pillar to the left, holding some books and a staff, is Emperor Justinian (483–565), who codified Roman law. The building's most striking feature, however, is the tower with its top-heavy loggia and too-perfect machicolations added by the controversial nineteenth-century architect Viollet-le-Duc (see p.108) – though he did save the building from collapse. It now houses the **Musée du Vieux St-Antonin** (May, June & Sept Mon & Wed–Fri 3–6pm, Sat & Sun 2–6pm; July & Aug daily except Tues 10am–1pm & 3–6pm; 15F/€2.29), with a missable collection of objects to do with the former life of the place, including various prehistoric finds.

Practicalities

Buses on the Montauban–Laguépie route stop near the Crédit Agricole bank on avenue Paul-Benet, the boulevard to the north of the old centre. The **tourist office** is in the Mairie next to the church (April–June, Sept & Oct Mon–Fri 2–5.30pm, Sat & Sun 10am–noon & 2–6.30pm; July & Aug daily 9.30am–12.30pm & 2–6.30pm; Nov–March Tues–Sat 2–5.30pm; ☎05.63.30.63.47, fax 05.63.30.66.33). St-Antonin is also the starting point for canoeing down this lower stretch of the Aveyron: you can rent **canoes** from Variation (☎05.63.68.25.25), on the town's eastern outskirts, and Découverte, 22 bd des Thermes (☎05.63.68.22.46), to the west of the bridge. Découverte also rents out **bicycles**, while both companies organize **caving** and **rock-climbing** expeditions in the area.

St-Antonin has two very good places in which to **stay**. Beside the bridge on boulevard des Thermes there's the simple *Hôtel Les Thermes* (☎05.63.30.61.08, fax 05.63.68.26.23; ②–③; restaurant from 59F/€8.99, closed Wed except in July & Aug) – so called because there was once a spa next door – with a terrace overlooking the water and cheerful, en-suite rooms; it's worth paying an extra 30F/€4.57 to be on the riverfront. The smarter option is *La Résidence*, 37 rue Droite (☎ & fax 05.63.68.21.60, *laresidence@compuserve.com*; ④), a welcoming, English-run *chambres d'hôte* on the road leading northwest out of place de la Halle. The rooms are all en suite, large and light, with tiles or wooden floorboards and high ceilings, and there's a small back garden. The two-star *Camping d'Anglars* is the closest **campsite**, located beside the river 1km upstream on the D115 (☎05.63.30.69.76, fax 05.63.30.67.61; closed mid-Oct to mid-April). With your own transport, however, follow the signs 6km north up onto the *causse* to the spacious and well-organized *Les 3 Cantons* (☎05.63.31.98.57, fax 05.63.31.25.93; closed Oct to mid-April), with three-star facilities including a heated pool, shop and snackbar.

As for eating in St-Antonin, the **restaurant** at *Hôtel Les Thermes* (see above) is a good bet. Or, for simpler fare, along the lines of *steak-frites*, pizzas and salads in addition to basic regional dishes, try *Le Gaspacho*, 25 av Paul-Benet (closed Mon eve except in July & Aug; *plat du jour* 40F/€6.10, menus from 67F/€10.21), on the north side of the old town.

Abbaye de Beaulieu-en-Rouergue

Apart from exploring the gorge itself, the best excursion from St-Antonin takes you 14km northwest to the beautiful Cistercian **Abbaye de Beaulieu-en-Rouergue** (April–June, Sept & Oct daily except Tues 10am–noon & 2–6.30pm; July & Aug daily 10am–noon & 2–6pm; 32F/€4.88), which lies deep among wooded hills. The abbey was founded in 1144, though the present buildings date from the turn of the thirteenth century, and are remarkably unscathed considering it was sacked and burnt during the Wars of Religion, looted again during the Revolution and then used as a barn until the late 1950s; in 1844 Viollet-le-Duc even wanted to rebuild the whole caboodle in St-Antonin but had to give up through lack of funds. The present owners have now restored the church to create a superb exhibition space for their collection of **contemporary art**; displays change several times a year, in combination with temporary exhibitions. The high, light nave with its clean lines and lack of ornamentation, save for the delicate rose windows and a few sculpted capitals, provides the perfect foil for works by Jean Dubuffet, Simon Hantaï and Henri Michaux, amongst others. There's not much else to see – a low, vaulted chapterhouse with a few unidentified frescoes which predates the church, and a vast wine storehouse – but the peaceful setting will make you want to linger.

If you happen to be here around lunchtime, continue a couple of kilometres north to the hamlet of **CORNUSSON**, which comprises little more than a church and the **restaurant** *de la Vallée* opposite (closed Dec, also Sat & evenings; menus 65–130F/€19.82). It's a popular and friendly locals' place serving no-nonsense meals, kicking off with a 65F/€9.91 *menu du jour* of five courses including wine.

Upstream to Laguépie

Upstream of St-Antonin the Aveyron valley widens out for a while and is spoilt by stone quarries. The only reason to stop is the village of **VAREN**, 16km from St-Antonin on the river's north bank. Its Romanesque **church** and tiny area of old streets repay a quick wander, but the prime attraction is another excellent-value though more upmarket **restaurant**, this time a converted mill on the riverbank just east of the village. The *Moulin de Varen* (☎05.63.65.45.10; closed Mon & Tues except in July & Aug) serves a *menu à choix*, from which you select the number of courses you want; the choice is good and the food beautifully presented. Prices start at 80F/€12.20 for a soup, main course, cheese and dessert.

LAGUÉPIE, 9km east of Varen, where the cliffs begin to close in again, guards the confluence of the Viaur with the Aveyron, which here turns north. The village has nothing in the way of sights, but is pretty enough and provides a useful base, served both by buses from Montauban and by trains on the Toulouse–Brive line. The **church** pinpoints the village centre lying in a spit of land between the two rivers. The **gare SNCF** lies 500m northwest on the north bank of the Aveyron, while **buses** terminate beside the church. There's a small **tourist office** (Wed 10am–noon & Sat 2–5pm; ☎ & fax 05.63.30.20.34) on place du Foirail, a big open space with a café and a grocery to the southwest of the church.

Laguépie's one and only **hotel** is the delightfully old-fashioned, welcoming and well-priced *Les Deux Rivières* (☎05.63.31.41.41, fax 05.63.30.20.91, *www.logis-de-france.fr*, ②; closed 2 weeks in Feb), on the north side of the bridge across the Aveyron. It is also a good place to **eat**, offering a choice between a brasserie and a formal restaurant with menus from 95F/€14.48 (mid-Sept to April restaurant closed Sat lunch & for dinner on Mon, Fri & Sun). Another option for food is the rustic *L'Oustal* (Oct–April closed Thurs; menus from 55F/€8.38), one block south of the church, offering chicken with Roquefort sauce, kidneys à la crème and other lip-smacking fare. Finally, you'll find a one-star municipal **campsite**, *Les Tilleuls* (☎05.63.30.22.32; closed Nov–April), in a good shady spot beside the Viaur roughly 1km to the east of Laguépie.

Cordes-sur-Ciel

While you're in this part of the world it would be a shame to miss out on the spectacularly sited fortified town of **CORDES-SUR-CIEL**, 15km south of Laguépie on the D922 across high, rolling farmland, and also accessible by train. The origins of the suffix *sur-ciel* ("in the sky") become obvious as you approach the foot of the sudden hill on which the town is built, girded by several concentric walls and endowed with a score of medieval houses. It is something of an open-air museum and artisanal centre, best avoided during July and August, but otherwise an atmospheric place to spend a few hours.

Founded in 1222 by Count Raymond VII of Toulouse, Cordes grew rich on **leatherworking**: in the following century the walls had to be enlarged no less than seven times to contain the expanding population. Things took a downturn, however, with the arrival of the plague in the fifteenth century, but Cordes later recovered, and developed a notable lace industry in the nineteenth century. However, its real renaissance came in the 1970s, when hippies, including the **craftsmen** and **artisans** whose studios now cram the upper town, arrived to put Cordes back on the map, attracted by its beauty and abandon.

The Town

The layout of the town is simple: Cordes' old citadel – the **upper town** or *cité* – occupies the long and narrow ridge jutting up from the plain, while the modern **lower town** consists of a clump of streets at its eastern foot. The best route uphill is the knee-cracking Grand Rue Basse ascending from the lower tourist office (see below) through a series of medieval gateways, although at busy times it is more pleasant to take one of the less crowded side-streets.

Entering the last of the gates, you reach the **Musée Charles-Portal** (July & Aug daily 11am–noon & 3–6pm; Sept–June Mon–Sat same times, Sun 3–6pm; 15F/€2.29), housing a display about the many medieval wells which were used in time of siege for water supply or to store grain. Further along Grande Rue, the elegant arcaded face of the fourteenth-century **Maison du Grand Fauconnier** conceals the **Musée Yves-Brayer** (same times and price as the Musée Charles-Portal), with one room devoted to the eponymous local figurative painter, and another with a French-only audio presentation about the town's lace-making tradition – hardly worth the stop. Across the street squats the ancient covered market, where you can peer down one of the famously deep wells. Continuing along Grand Rue, the otherwise plain stone facade of the **Maison de Grand Veneur** ("House of the Great Hunter") is festooned with amusingly sculpted and extremely well preserved medieval caricatures of beasts and hunters. A few doors down stands the similarly impressively carved frontage of Raymond of Toulouse's old palace, now home to the *Grand Ecuyer* hotel (named after the finely sculpted horse figure), while, just beyond, the contemporary **Porte des Ormeaux** ("Gate of the Birds") takes you out of the old town.

Practicalities

Trains stop 5km to the west of Cordes at **Vindrac**, where you can also rent **bikes**; otherwise it's a pleasant hour-long walk into town. **Buses** from Albi, 25km to the southwest on the Toulouse–Rodez train line, stop near the lower-town summer-only **tourist office** (July & Aug Mon–Sat 9am–noon & 2–6.30pm, Sun 3–5pm); the main tourist office (year-round same hours; ☎05.63.56.00.52, fax 05.63.56.19.52, *www.cordes-sur-ciel.org*) is in the heart of the *cité*. If you're driving, **parking** can be a challenge – in the summer months space in the lower town soon fills up and cars line the roads all around.

Cordes' top **hotel** is the *Grand Ecuyer* (☎05.63.53.79.50, fax 05.63.53.79.51, *grand.ecuyer@thuries.fr*; ⑤; closed Oct–Easter), housed in Raymond's former palace, with a fine restaurant known for its lamb and truffle dishes (menus 170–470F/€25.93–71.68). Opposite the Charles-Portal museum, *Hôtel de la Cité* is a lower-priced alternative offering the same medieval trappings (☎05.63.56.03.53, fax 05.63.56.02.47; ③; closed Nov to mid-April), while the *Hôtel de la Bride*, on the *place* of the same name (☎05.63.56.04.02; ③; closed Jan; menus from 75F/€11.44), is the cheapest option – rather basic, but well kept. There's also a **campsite** (☎ & fax 05.63.56.11.10; closed Oct–March) 1km southeast on the Gaillac road. The best **restaurants** are in the town's hotels, but other options include the *crêperie La Factorie*, 53 Grand Rue (closed Jan & Dec), and, next door, *Le Grand Veneur* (closed Dec), which serves sixty brands of Belgian **beer** and decent **pizzas** (from 68F/€10.37) in its hokey "salle médiévale".

Najac

Back at Laguépie, the Aveyron valley turns northwards and the river flows through a wooded defile. The most picturesque route along the valley bottom is either the train or the GR36 footpath, while road users should take the D106 and D594 along the western line of hills. Either way, you eventually arrive at a bridge – 15km by road and slightly less on foot – beneath the brooding towers of **NAJAC**'s semi-ruined **castle**.

The castle occupies an extraordinary site on the peak of a conical hill isolated in the river's wide meander – a site chosen in the mid-1200s by **Alphonse de Poitiers** who wanted to bring the area's Cathar sympathizers to heel. He enlarged the original fortress and laid out a new town to the east in an elongated version of a *bastide* with its arcades and central market square. For a short while Najac prospered as the region's capital, but the site proved too restricted and by the end of the thirteenth century it had lost out to Villefranche-de-Rouergue (see below), leaving the castle to be fought over endlessly in the conflicts that ensued. The Protestants pillaged it in 1572 and the revolutionaries had their turn in 1793, but, in spite of all, Najac survived. It's all very attractive and consequently touristy nowadays, with the inevitable resident knick-knack shops and craftspeople, but don't be put off – the setting is quite stunning.

The Town

The heart of modern Najac consists of a big, open square lying to the east of the medieval village, whose grey-tiled houses tail out westwards in a single street along the narrow spur connecting the valley side to the castle hill. Entering from the east you come first to the **faubourg**, the elongated market square bordered by houses raised on pillars. It slopes gently downhill towards a cobbled street, overlooked by more ancient houses, which leads past a fountain to the **château** (April, May & Sept daily 10am–12.30pm & 3–5.30pm; June daily 10am–12.30pm & 3–6.30pm; July & Aug daily 10am–1pm & 3–7pm; Oct Sun 3–5.30pm; last entry 30min before closing; 21F/€3.20). The castle is a model of medieval defensive architecture: its curtain walls reach to over twenty metres in places, within which five round towers supplement the square twelfth-century turret, and the castle is equipped with unusual multistorey loopholes for archers. However, the main reason to visit is for the magnificent all-round view from the top of the keep a full 200m above the river.

Just below the castle, in what was the original medieval village, stands the huge, very solid-looking and austere church of **St-Jean** (April–Sept 10am–noon & 2–6pm, Sun 11am–noon & 2–7pm; free), which the villagers were forced to build at their own expense in 1258 as a punishment for their conversion to Catharism. In addition to a lovely silver reliquary and an extraordinary iron cage for holding candles – both dating from the thirteenth century – the church has one architectural oddity: its windows are solid panels of stone from which the lights have been cut out in trefoil form. Below the church, by a derelict farm, a stretch of Roman road survives and, at the bottom of the hill, a thirteenth-century bridge spans the Aveyron.

Practicalities

Najac's **gare SNCF** lies on the north side of the old bridge, 2km by road below the village; **taxis** can be called on ☎05.65.29.72.48. The daily **bus** from Villefranche terminates on the square to the east of the village, while the **tourist office** is on the south side of the *faubourg* (April–June & Sept Mon–Sat 9am–noon & 2.30–5.30pm; July & Aug Mon–Sat 9am–noon & 2.30–5.30pm, Sun 10am–noon; Oct–March Mon–Sat 9am–noon; ☎05.65.29.72.05, fax 05.65.29.72.29, *otsi.najac@wanadoo.fr*).

There's a good choice of **accommodation** in and around Najac, of which the nicest and most central is the *Maison Authesserre* (☎05.65.29.73.47; ③; closed occasionally in winter), with just three *chambres d'hôtes* in a lovely, blue-shuttered town house at the west end of the *faubourg*. Owned by an artist, the rooms are all en suite, spacious and packed with character; there's also a peaceful courtyard garden at the back. At the *faubourg*'s east entrance you'll find a very comfortable hotel, *L'Oustal del Barry* (☎05.65.29.74.32, fax 05.65.29.75.32, *www.oustal-del-barry.com*; ④; closed Nov–March, also Mon from mid-April to June & mid-Sept to Oct), whose restaurant is renowned for its subtle and inventive cuisine (closed Mon & Tues lunch out of season; menus from 140F/€21.34). Najac's other hotel is the welcoming, old-fashioned *La Belle Rive* (☎05.65.29.73.90, fax 05.65.29.76.88, *hotel.bellerive.najac@wanadoo.fr*; ③; closed Nov–March), in a lovely riverside position near the *gare SNCF*, from whose garden you get an ants'-eye view of the château towering above. They also run an excellent restaurant serving good-value regional cooking with menus from 88F/€13.42. If money is no object, you could treat yourself to a night at *Longcol* (☎05.65.29.63.36, fax 05.65.29.64.28, *longcol@relaischateaux.fr*, ⑧; closed mid-Nov to mid-March; restaurant from 225F/€35.82, closed midday Mon & Wed & all day Tues from mid-Sept to mid-June), perched on the Aveyron's east bank 8km upstream from Najac on the D638. Occupying a cluster of ancient buildings around an intrusive but stunningly designed pool, the rooms – decked out with Asian antiques – are immaculate and the service is impeccable.

Back in Najac, the four-star riverside **campsite**, *Le Païsserou* (☎05.65.29.72.05, fax 05.65.29.72.29; closed Oct–April), to the southwest of the old bridge, is not quite so luxurious, but spacious and very well equipped. You can also rent **canoes** and **bikes** at the neighbouring sports centre (☎05.65.29.73.94).

In addition to Najac's two hotel **restaurants**, *La Salamandre*, at the bottom of the *faubourg*, is a good bet; they serve simple, well-priced meals, with a *plat du jour* at 38F/€5.79 and a menu at 90F/€13.72.

Villefranche-de-Rouergue

The second stretch of the Aveyron gorge peters out about 10km north of Najac, but it's worth continuing upstream the same distance again to the laid-back market town of **VILLEFRANCHE-DE-ROUERGUE**, which boasts one of the most atmospheric central squares in the whole region. As its regular form and the die-straight streets indicate, this is a *bastide*, founded in 1252 by the ubiquitous **Alphonse de Poitiers** as part of the royal policy of extending control over the recalcitrant lands of the south. Villefranche became rich on trade and on copper from the surrounding mines. In 1369 it was also made the seat of the Seneschal, the king's representative, with the right to mint money. While its wealthy merchants built the ornate houses that grace the cobbled streets to this day, conditions in the surrounding countryside were so desperate that in 1643 more than 10,000 peasants, known as **Croquants** (see p.358), besieged the town for a week. As elsewhere, the rebellion was harshly put down and the leaders strung up in the market square.

The Town
Villefranche's medieval quarter lies on the north bank of the Aveyron, accessed by a modern road bridge beside its decommissioned fourteenth-century counterpart. From the old bridge, the town's main commercial street, pedestrianized **rue de la République**, runs northwards up a gentle incline into the heart of the *bastide*. It is attractive enough, but no preparation for the central square you come out into, **place Notre-Dame**. The square, too, is built on a slope and is surrounded by unusually tall houses, arcaded at ground-floor level, some of which bear elaborate window surrounds. If possible, try and visit on a Thursday morning when local merchants and farmers spread out their produce at the weekly **market**, presided over by the colossal porch and bell tower – nearly 60m high and fortified – of the **Collégiale Notre-Dame**, which dominates the square's east side. The church was started in 1260 but wars and fires intervened and it was not finally completed until 1519. Behind the altar are two fine mid-fifteenth-century stained-glass windows: the one on the left depicts the creation; that on the right portrays sixteen characters from the Old and New Testaments. Also worth noting are the oak choir stalls alive with a superb array of beasts and demons as well a

scenes from daily life – they took the craftsman, André Sulpice, fifteen years to complete in the late fifteenth century.

On boulevard Haute-Guyenne, which forms the northern limit of the old town, the seventeenth-century **Chapelle des Pénitents-Noirs** (30min guided tours: July–Sept daily 10am–noon & 2–6pm; 20F/€3.05) boasts a splendidly Baroque painted ceiling and an enormous gilded retable – resplendent after its recent renovation. Another ecclesiastical building worth the slight detour is the **Chartreuse St-Sauveur** (30min guided tours: same hours; 20F/€3.05), in the grounds of a hospital about 1km south of town on the main D922 to Najac and Laguépie. It was completed in the space of ten years from 1450, giving it a singular architectural harmony. The highlight is the second of the two cloisters, a minuscule quadrangle of white, sculpted stone, while the church itself contains more examples of André Sulpice's craftsmanship on the screen and choir stalls.

Practicalities

The **gare SNCF** and **gare routière** are located together a couple of minutes' walk south across the Aveyron from the old centre, while **car rental** is available from Avis, on riverside place St-Jean (☎05.65.45.08.16), in the town's southeast corner. The **tourist office** sits on the river's north bank, on promenade du Giraudet (May–Sept Mon–Fri 9am–noon & 2–7pm, Sat 9am–noon; Oct–April Mon–Fri 9am–noon & 2–6pm; ☎05.65.45.13.18, fax 05.65.45.55.58, *www.villefranche.com*), beside the new bridge.

For an overnight stay, there are two pleasant **hotels**: *L'Univers*, 2 place de la République (☎05.65.45.15.63, fax 05.65.45.02.21; ②), immediately across the river from the tourist office with a good traditional restaurant (closed 3 weeks in Jan, also Fri eve & Sat except July to Sept; menus from 89F/€13.57); and the more modest but cheerful and friendly *Bellevue*, 3 av du Ségala (☎05.65.45.23.17, fax 05.65.45.11.19; ②; closed school hols in Feb & Nov, also Sun & Mon lunch except in July & Aug), which also boasts a decent restaurant (menus 80–280F/€12.20–42.69), a little further out of town on the Rodez road. Even cheaper accommodation is on offer at the excellent new HI-affiliated *Foyer des Jeunes Travailleurs* (☎05.65.45.09.68, fax 05.65.45.62.26; 68F/€10.37 for the first night, 51F/€7.77 thereafter), in a wood-faced building next to the *gare SNCF*, offering individual en-suite rooms, kitchen facilities and canteen meals. There is also a big three-star municipal **campsite** (☎05.65.45.16.24, fax 05.65.45.55.58; closed Oct–March), 1.5km to the south, signed off the D47 to Monteil.

As far as **restaurants** are concerned, you're assured of a warm welcome at the convivial *Café des Halles*, a workers' diner beside the covered market hall immediately east of the church, where you can eat substantial meals for 55F/€8.38 at communal tables. Another simple but good option is *La Gabelle*, 10 rue Belle-Isle (closed Sun lunch & Mon), on the road one block south of the church. It's another locals' place, offering pizzas, grills, salads and the like; you can eat three courses for around 100F/€15.24. Finally, for more upmarket regional cuisine, try *L'Assiette Gourmande*, one block north of the church on place André-Lescure (closed Sun; ☎05.65.45.25.95; menus from 90F/€13.72); meals are served in a pleasant stone-vaulted room or out on the square in fine weather.

travel details

By plane

Agen to: Paris Orly (1–3 daily; 1hr 30min–2hr).

By train

Agen to: Aiguillon (5–8 daily; 15–20min); Bordeaux (15–20 daily; 1hr 10min–1hr 30min); Moissac (2–3 daily; 25–30min); Montauban (12–14 daily; 40–50min); Monsempron-Libos (6–8 daily; 30–40min); Paris-Austerlitz (1–2 daily; 7hr–8hr 30min); Périgueux (4–5 daily; 2hr–2hr 30min); La Réole (7 daily; 40min–1hr); Toulouse (12–14 daily; 1hr–1hr 10min).

Cordes-sur-Ciel (Cordes-Vindrac) to: Brive (1 daily; 2hr 25min); Figeac (4–6 daily; 1hr 30min); Laguépie (4–5 daily; 20min); Najac (4–6 daily; 30min); Paris-Austerlitz (1 daily; 8hr 40min); Toulouse (5–6 daily; 1hr); Villefranche-de-Rouergue (4–6 daily; 45min).

Laguépie to: Brive (1 daily; 3hr); Cordes-sur-Ciel (6–7 daily; 30min); Figeac (4–6 daily; 1hr–1hr 25min); Najac (4–6 daily; 10min); Paris-Austerlitz (1 daily; 8hr 20min); Toulouse (5–6 daily; 1hr 25min); Villefranche-de-Rouergue (4–6 daily; 25min).

Moissac to: Agen (3–4 daily; 30min); Bordeaux (3–4 daily; 40–50min); Montauban (2–3 daily; 20min); Toulouse (2–3 daily; 45min).

Montauban to: Agen (10–15 daily; 35–50min); Brive (8–10 daily; 2hr); Cahors (8–10 daily; 40–45min); Moissac (3–4 daily; 20min); Toulouse (20–30 daily; 30–40min).

Najac to: Brive (1–2 daily; 2hr 20min–3hr); Cordes-sur-Ciel (6–7 daily; 30min); Laguépie (6–7 daily; 10min); Figeac (4–6 daily; 50min–1hr 15min); Paris-Austerlitz (1 daily; 8hr); Toulouse (5–6 daily; 1hr 30min); Villefranche-de-Rouergue (4–6 daily; 15min).

Villefranche-de-Rouergue to: Brive (1–2 daily; 2hr–2hr 45min); Cordes-sur-Ciel (6–7 daily; 45min); Laguépie (6–7 daily; 25min); Figeac (4–6 daily; 35min–1hr); Najac (4–6 daily; 15min); Paris-Austerlitz (1 daily; 7hr 45min); Toulouse (5–6 daily; 1hr 45min).

By bus

Agen to: Aiguillon (Mon–Fri 2 daily; 35–45min); Auvillar (Mon–Fri 1 daily; 55min); Moissac (Mon–Sat 2–4 daily; 1hr 10min–1hr 30min); Nérac (1–8 daily; 35–40min); St-Nicolas-le-Grave (Mon–Fri 1 daily; 1hr 15min); Montauban (Mon–Sat 2 daily; 2hr); Toulouse (Mon–Sat 1 daily; 2hr 40min); Villeneuve-sur-Lot (4–12 daily; 45min).

Cordes-sur-Ciel to: Albi (school term, plus July & Aug Mon–Sat 1–2 daily; 35–50min).

Laguépie to: Bruniquel (1 daily; 1hr); Montauban (1 daily; 1hr 40min); Penne (1 daily; 50min); St-Antonin-Noble-Val (1 daily; 40min); Villefranche-de-Rouergue (school term Mon–Fri 1 daily; 45min).

Moissac to: Agen (Mon–Sat 1–4 daily; 1hr–1hr 20min); Auvillar (Mon–Fri 1 daily; 30min); Lauzerte (Wed & Sat 1 daily; 30min); Montauban (Mon–Sat 3–4 daily; 45min–1hr 05min); St-Nicolas-de-la-Grave (Mon–Sat 2–4 daily; 10–15min); Toulouse (1–4 daily; 1hr 30min).

Montauban to: Agen (Mon–Sat 2 daily; 2hr–2hr 30min); Amsterdam (2–4 weekly; 21hr); Bruniquel (school term Mon–Sat 2–4 daily, school hols Mon–Fri 2 daily; 40min–1hr 10min); Brussels (2–4 weekly; 17hr 30min); Cahors (Mon–Fri 1 daily; 1hr 15min); Laguépie (school term Mon–Sat 1 daily, school hols Mon–Fri 1 daily; 1hr 20min–1hr 45min); London (2–3 weekly; 19hr 30min); Moissac (Mon–Sat 3–6 daily; 40min–1hr); Montpezat-de-Quercy (Mon–Fri 1 daily; 45min); Montricoux (as for Bruniquel; 35–40min); St-Antonin-Noble-Val (as for Laguépie; 45min–1hr); St-Nicolas-de-la-Grave (2–4 daily; 1hr–1hr 20min); Toulouse (5–7 daily; 50min–1hr 15min); Villefranche-de-Rouergue (Mon–Sat 2–3 daily; 1hr 45min–2hr 15min).

Montcuq to: Cahors (school term Mon–Sat 1–2 daily, school hols Wed & Sat 1 daily; 35–40min).

Najac to: Villefranche-de-Rouergue (Mon–Sat 1 daily; 30min).

Villefranche-de-Rouergue to: Cahors (Mon–Sat 1–2 daily; 1hr 10min–1hr 30min); Figeac (1–2 daily; 45min); Laguépie (school term Mon–Fri 1 daily; 45min); Montauban (Mon–Sat 2–3 daily; 1h 30min–2hr 20min); Najac (Mon–Sat 1 daily; 45min).

CONTEXTS

HISTORICAL FRAMEWORK

While France has existed in name since the tenth century, for much of its history the country has consisted of fiercely independent duchies, baronies and counties that, while they might have paid homage to the French king, were often a law unto themselves. One of these was the Duchy of Aquitaine and another the County of Toulouse. Their boundaries varied over the years as their fortunes ebbed and flowed, but between them they ruled over southwest France, including the areas now known as the *départements* of Dordogne and Lot.

THE BEGINNINGS

Primitive flint tools found in the Dordogne indicate a human presence dating back at least 400,000 years. However, the region's archeological treasure trove really gets going with the **Neanderthal** people, who arrived on the scene some 100,000 years ago. Despite their brutish image, evidence now suggests that Neanderthals were really quite sophisticated. They developed not only an increasingly elaborate range of stone tools but also complex burial rituals. This didn't, however, equip them to compete with the next wave of immigrants sweeping across Europe between 30,000 and 40,000 years ago, and the Neanderthals gradually died out.

Early archeologists named the newcomers **Cro-Magnon** after a rock-shelter near Les Eyzies where the first skeletons were identified. Now they are better known as *Homo sapiens sapiens* – in other words, our direct ancestors. While Cro-Magnons developed ever more sophisticated tools, they also began to scratch fertility symbols in the rock, made various pigments and then took the great leap into abstraction that led to drawing, painting and carving. The earliest evidence of **prehistoric art** dates from around 30,000 years ago, but reached its apogee during the **Magdalenian** era (17,000–10,000 years ago) – also named after a shelter in the Dordogne's Vézère valley. It was during this era that Cro-Magnon people covered the walls and ceilings of the region's caves with art of a quality that would not be seen again for several millennia (see box on p.208 for more on cave art).

Around 10,000 BC the all-important reindeer herds – the Cro-Magnons' one-stop source of meat, fat, skin, bone and sinew – began to move north as the climate became warmer and wetter. Over the next three thousand years these nomadic hunter-gatherers were gradually replaced by settled **farming and pastoral communities** who left hundreds of **dolmens** (megalithic stone tombs) scattered over the region. This Neolithic era in its turn made way for the great metal-working cultures, culminating in the Iron Age, from around 700 BC. About the same time **Celtic** people began to spread into the region from north and central Europe, establishing trade routes and building towns and hilltop fortresses. They were skilled manufacturers and had their own coinage, but instead of a cohesive entity, comprised individual, or loosely allied, clans continuously fighting amongst themselves. It was these disunited tribes that the Roman legions encountered when they arrived in what they called **Gaul** – roughly equivalent to modern France – in the second century BC.

THE ROMAN OCCUPATION

At first the **Romans** contented themselves with a colony along the Mediterranean coast, but in 59 BC the threat of a Germanic invasion and various Celtic uprisings prompted **Julius Caesar** to subjugate the rest of Gaul. It took him just eight years. By 56 BC he had pacified the southwest and the only real opposition came from a young Arvenian (modern-day Auvergne) chieftain called **Vercingetorix** who managed to rally a united Gaulish opposition in 52 BC. The Gauls had some initial victories, but in the end were no match for Caesar's disciplined armies. First Vercingetorix was taken back to Rome in chains in 52 BC and then a year later the Gauls were finally defeated at **Uxellodunum**, somewhere on the banks of either the Dordogne or Lot rivers.

The battle was one of the major turning points in the region's history. In 16 AD Emperor Augustus established the new Gallo-Roman province of **Aquitania**, stretching from Poitiers south to the Pyrenees. Its capital was Burdigala (Bordeaux), and regional administrative centres were set up in Vesunna (Périgueux) and Divona Cadurcorum (Cahors), each with its forum, amphitheatre, law courts and temples. During more than three centuries of peace – the **Pax Romana** – that followed, the Romans built roads, introduced new technologies, traded, planted vineyards and established an urbanized society administered by an educated, Latin-speaking elite. Gradually, too, Latin penetrated the rural areas, where it eventually fused with the local Celtic dialects to form two broad new language groups: the *langue d'oïl* (where "yes" is *oïl* – later, *oui*), spoken north of the Loire, and the *langue d'oc*, or **Occitan** (where "yes" is *oc*), to the south.

In the meantime, serious **disruptions** of the Pax Romana had begun in the third century AD. Oppressive aristocratic rule and an economic crisis turned the destitute peasantry into gangs of marauding brigands, who were particularly rampant in the southwest. But more devastating were the incursions across the Rhine frontier by various restless **Germanic tribes**, starting with the Alemanni and Franks, who pushed down as far as Spain, ravaging farmland and looting towns along the way. In response, urban centres such as Périgueux were hurriedly fortified while the nobles hot-footed it to their country villas, which became increasingly self-sufficient – economically, administratively and militarily.

The crunch came, however, in the fifth century when first the Vandals and then the **Visigoths** stormed through the region. For nearly a hundred years the Visigoths ruled a huge empire extending across southern France and into Spain, with its capital at Toulouse. But then they were pushed out in their turn by more invaders from the north.

THE FRANKS

By 500 AD the **Franks**, who gave their name to modern France, had become the dominant power in France. Their most celebrated and ruthless king, **Clovis**, consolidated his hold on northern France and drove the Visigoths out of the southwest in 507. But the **Merovingian** dynasty – as Clovis and his successors were called – failed to re-establish the same overarching authority as had the Romans. Aquitaine in particular displayed the first inklings of its independent streak as it became first a semi-autonomous duchy and then a kingdom from 781 to 877 (see below).

All this while **Christianity**, which had arrived from Rome in the early fourth century, was spreading slowly through France. Many of the early evangelizers of the southwest met a sticky end, though they were later commemorated in the abbeys and churches founded by the nascent Christian communities they left in their wake. Clovis himself embraced Christianity around 500 AD and devolved a great deal of everyday administration to increasingly powerful local bishops, such as those at Cahors.

The Merovingian empire began to disintegrate in the late seventh century, leaving the way clear for their chancellors, the Pepin family, to take control. One of their most dynamic scions, **Charles Martel**, defeated the Spanish Moors when they swept up through the southwest as far as Poitiers in 732. His grandson, **Charlemagne**, continued the expansionist policy of the **Carolingian** dynasty – so called for their penchant for the name Charles, or "Carolus" – to create an empire which eventually stretched from the Baltic to the Pyrenees.

To secure the allegiance of the southwest, in 781 Charlemagne created the nominally independent **kingdom** of Aquitaine – an area extending from the Loire to the Cévennes and from the Rhône to the Pyrenees – in the name of his infant son, the future King Louis the Pious. Within the kingdom, the Carolingians continued to administer through royally appointed bishops, now joined by a growing number of counts – of Quercy and Périgord, for example – who had been awarded territory in exchange for their loyalty.

While the Carolingnian empire dissolved into a long-drawn-out battle of succession following Charlemagne's death in 814, so the next wave of invaders was on its way from Scandinavia. The **Vikings** (also known as Normans, or Norsemen) had been raiding coastal areas for decades, but in 844 they penetrated deep inland along the Garonne, Dordogne, Isle and Lot rivers, plundering towns and churches. In the face of these destabilizing invasions the Carolingians were obliged to delegate ever more autonomy to the provincial governors until they eventually grew more powerful than the king. The last of the Carolingian kings was succeeded in 987 by Hugh Capet. In theory **Capetian** rule extended over the whole of France; in practice he had authority only over a small area near Paris. Nonetheless, Hugh Capet founded a dynasty that lasted until 1328.

THE MIDDLE AGES

Even as the Carolingian empire crumbled, the local aristocracy in the south began busily to jostle for power. During the tenth century Périgord was carved up into four **Baronies** (Beynac, Mareuil, Bourdeilles and Biron), while Quercy was divided between five powerful families – the Turenne, Gourdon, Cardaillac, Castelnau and St-Sulpice families. At the same time the counts of Poitou (based at Poitiers) and Toulouse were fighting for control of what was once again the **Duchy of Aquitaine**. The

former emerged victorious, thus creating a vast territory which by the twelfth century reached from the Loire to the Pyrenees. The Poitou counts also ushered in a period of relative peace, rapid economic growth and of renewed religious vigour which saw a wave of church building – leaving a legacy of lovely Romanesque churches that can be seen throughout the region to this day. At least some of this building activity was spurred – and financed – by the great procession of **pilgrims** passing along the route to Santiago de Compostela in Spain (see box).

Also wandering the southern highways and byways were the **troubadours**. Both poets and musicians, the troubadours flourished in the late twelfth century among the vibrant and cultured nobility of southern France. Their lyric poetry, written in Occitan, idealized courtly love and laid down codes of chivalry, whose influence eventually spread throughout Europe. The person who set it all off is generally held to be Guillaume IX, Duke of Aquitaine (1071–1126), whose court at Poitiers was regarded as one of the most civilized and sophisticated of its day.

Another famous troubadour was **Bertran de Born**, Viscount of Hautefort (c.1140–1212), who, among many others, wrote countless songs in praise of Guillaume's granddaughter. A woman of legendary beauty and intelligence,

---

THE WAY OF ST JAMES

According to the Bible, **St James the Apostle** was decapitated in Jerusalem in 44 AD. There is nothing to suggest how his remains came to be buried in northwest Spain, but in 820 it was declared that they had been discovered there, and during the fervent religious revival of the Middle Ages millions of pilgrims began flocking to his tomb in **Santiago de Compostela**. The route took on a life of its own: monasteries, churches and hospitals were founded and villages grew up along the way to cater to the pilgrims wearing their distinctive cockleshell badge.

The pilgrimage faded out during the sixteenth century, partly because of the wars sweeping France and partly because the cathedral canons lost the saint's remains; the relics were supposedly hidden to keep them out of the hands of Sir Francis Drake, who was then sniffing around Galicia, but later no one could remember where

they'd put them. By another "miracle" they were rediscovered by archeologists in 1879, declared by the pope to be the genuine article, and the pilgrimage revived, though on a far more modest scale.

In 1998 the whole system of paths and associated buildings was inscribed on the UNESCO World Heritage list and to walk the **chemin de St-Jacques** (Way of St James) – or at least some of it – is becoming increasingly popular once again, partly among those on a spiritual quest, but also simply as a walking holiday. Three of the four main routes – from Vézelay, Le Puy-en-Velay and Arles – have been waymarked as long-distance footpaths (*grands randonnées*, or GRs). Of these the GR654 from Vézelay and the GR65 from Le Puy pass through the Dordogne and Lot region; booklets outlining the routes are available in the Topo-guide series (see p.364 for more).

she married two kings and gave birth to three more, effectively ruled England for a time and died at the grand old age of eighty-two: **Eleanor of Aquitaine**. Eleanor inherited her father's domains in 1137 at the tender age of fifteen. The Capetian king, Louis VI, lost no time in marrying her off to his son and heir in Bordeaux's St-André Cathedral, but died just one week later, leaving the young couple King and Queen of France. **Louis VII** was no mean catch, but the marriage bore no heirs and in 1152 they were divorced, largely on Eleanor's instigation. In a matter of weeks she had married again, this time the handsome, charismatic and extremely ambitious **Henry of Anjou**, thus adding Anjou and Normandy in northwestern France to her possessions. This in itself was a disastrous blow to the Capetians, but it was compounded in 1154 when Henry succeeded to the English throne (as Henry II), meaning that almost half of France came under English rule. Much of it would remain so for the next three centuries.

With the major exception of **Richard the Lionheart** (Richard Cœur de Lion), Eleanor's third and favourite son, who plundered the region ruthlessly, the **English overlords** proved to be popular. For the most part they ruled indirectly and, by granting a large degree of independence to many of Aquitaine's rapidly growing towns, they bought the loyalty of their notoriously hot-blooded southern vassals. The economy flourished on the back of the Bordeaux wine trade and dozens of new towns, or *bastides*, were founded to accommodate the rapidly expanding population.

THE CATHAR CRUSADES

Over to the east of Aquitaine, meanwhile, the powerful **counts of Toulouse** were getting into hot water. From the mid-twelfth century on the so-called **Cathars** (also known as Albigensians) had won a great deal of support in the area, which extended as far as the Dordogne valley, by preaching that the material world was created by the Devil and the spiritual world by a benevolent God. They also believed in reincarnation and that the only way to escape the mortal coil was to lead a life of saintly self-denial. All of which completely undermined the role of the clergy. To put an end to such **heresy**, Pope Innocent III unleashed a

Crusade against the Cathars in 1209, starting off with a particularly murderous attack led by **Simon de Montfort** in which the entire population of the Mediterranean town of Béziers, estimated at 20,000 people, was slaughtered; the papal legate in charge of the assault is famously supposed to have proclaimed, "Kill them all. God will know his own."

A series of crusading armies, comprised largely of land-hungry northern nobles, then proceeded to rampage through the region on and off for the next twenty years. This was followed by an equally vicious **Inquisition** designed to mop up any remaining Cathars, which culminated in the siege of Montségur, in the eastern foothills of the Pyrenees, in 1244, when 200 people were burnt alive.

As a result of the Cathar Crusades, the French crown now held sway over the whole of southeastern France, including Toulouse. The new count of Toulouse was **Alphonse de Poitiers**, brother of the future Louis IX, whose lands stretched north through Quercy into Périgord, and west along the Garonne as far as Agen. Like his English neighbours, Alphonse started establishing a rash of *bastides* in order to impose his authority over his new domains.

THE HUNDRED YEARS' WAR

Though the English had lost their possessions north of the Loire by the mid-thirteenth century, thanks to their grip on Aquitaine they remained a perpetual thorn in the side of the French kings. There had been skirmishes throughout the century, followed by various peace treaties, one of which, in 1259, took Quercy and Périgord back into the English domain, but the spark that ignited the ruinous – and misnamed – **Hundred Years' War** (1337–1453) was a Capetian succession crisis. When the last of the line, Charles IV, died without heir in 1328, the English king, **Edward III**, leapt in to claim the throne of France for himself. Instead, Charles's cousin, **Philippe de Valois**, was chosen. Edward acquiesced for a time, but when Philippe began whittling away at English possessions in Aquitaine, Edward renewed his claim and embarked on war.

It started off badly for the French. Edward won an outright victory at **Crécy** in 1346 and seized the port of Calais as a permanent bridgehead. Then ten years later, his son, the

Black Prince, took the French king, Jean le Bon, prisoner at the Battle of Poitiers and established a capital at Bordeaux. To regain his liberty Jean was forced to sign the **Treaty of Brétigny** (1360) in which he ceded more than a quarter of his kingdom to the English. In exchange, Edward renounced his claim to the French throne.

The peace was short lived. Jean's successor, Charles V, waded in again and by 1377 the great military leader **Bertrand du Guesclin** had pushed the English back until they were reduced to a toehold in Bordeaux and a few other Atlantic ports. There they stayed until 1415 when Henry V came back with a vengeance to inflict another crushing defeat on the French army at **Agincourt**. In the treaty that followed, Henry was named heir to the French throne and it seemed that France was unravelling at the seams.

Just in the nick of time, however, **Jeanne d'Arc** (Joan of Arc) arrived on the scene. In 1429 she rallied the demoralized French troops, raised the English siege at Orléans and tipped the scales against the invaders. The English were slowly but surely driven back to their southwest heartland until even that was lost at the **Battle of Castillon** in 1453 (see p.186).

Apart from this last, no major battles of the Hundred Years' War were fought in southwest France, though most towns and castles were attacked at some point and many changed hands on numerous occasions, either by treaty or force, and by the end of the war farms and villages lay abandoned and roving bands of **brigands** terrorized the countryside. The population had been reduced by roughly a half to under 12 million, partly by warfare, but largely through famine and disease; during the fourteenth and fifteenth centuries millions died as the bubonic **plague** repeatedly swept through France.

Gradually the nightmare ended. Though the south now had to kow-tow to the hated northerners, Louis XI proved to be an astute ruler who allowed some of the privileges granted by the English to remain. The Bordelais smarted for a while, but were eventually brought round with the establishment of their own parliament in 1462. Trade – particularly the wine trade – began to revive, towns were rebuilt and land brought back into production.

THE WARS OF RELIGION

In the early sixteenth century the ideas, art and architecture of the **Renaissance** began to penetrate France as a result of an inconclusive military campaign in Italy. As elsewhere in Europe, the Renaissance had a profound influence on every aspect of life, engendering a new optimism and spirit of enquiry which appealed in particular to the new class of wealthy merchants. At the same time increased trade and better communications – including the invention of the printing press – helped disseminate ideas throughout Europe. Among them came the new **Protestant** message espoused by Martin Luther and John Calvin that the individual was responsible to God alone and not to the Church.

Such humanist ideas gained widespread adherence throughout France, but nowhere more so than in the southwest, where the Catholic clergy were closely linked to the oppressive feudal regime. The first Protestant (also known as **Huguenot**) enclaves to be established in the region were at Ste-Foy-le-Grand and Bergerac in the 1540s, followed soon after by Nérac, the fief of the **d'Albret** family (see p.325). As the Protestant faith took hold and Catholics became increasingly intolerant, the sporadic brutal attempts to stamp out Protestantism, such as a massacre in Cahors in 1560, erupted two years later into a series of bitter civil wars. Interspersed with ineffective truces and accords, the **Wars of Religion** lasted for the next thirty years.

The fighting was particularly vicious in the southwest, where whole towns opted for one side or the other – while the Protestants held Bergerac, Montauban and Figeac, for example, Sarlat and Périgueux remained staunchly Catholic – and Catholic and Protestant armies vied with each other in their savagery. By far the blackest event, however, was the **St Bartholomew's Day Massacre** in 1572, when some three thousand Protestants, gathered in Paris for the wedding of Marguerite de Valois, the sister of Henri III of France, to the Protestant **Henri d'Albret**, were slaughtered – a bloodbath repeated across France and countered by further Protestant reprisals.

By a twist of fate, however, Henri d'Albret – King of Navarre and leader of the Protestant army – became heir to the French throne when

Henri III's son died in 1584. Five years later, Henri III himself was dead, leaving a huge problem, since a Protestant could not occupy the throne of France. After trying to take it by force, Henri d'Albret eventually abjured his faith and became **Henri IV** of France. "Paris is worth a Mass," he is reputed to have said.

Once on the throne Henri IV set about reconstructing and reconciling the nation. By the **Edict of Nantes** of 1598 the Protestants were accorded freedom of conscience, freedom of worship in specified places, the right to attend the same schools and hold the same offices as Catholics, their own courts and the possession of a number of fortresses, including Montauban, as a guarantee against renewed attack.

Not surprisingly, the ructions didn't end there. Henri IV was assassinated by Catholic extremists in 1610 and conflict broke out again. Southern Protestants rebelled and several towns, such as Bergerac, were seized by the Catholics. Then in 1685 Louis XIII revoked the Edict of Nantes, forbade Protestant worship and set about trying to eliminate the faith completely. Orders were given for the destruction of Protestant churches and of the castles of its most fervent supporters. In response thousands of Protestants fled the southwest for the safety of the Netherlands, Germany and England.

THE STIRRINGS OF DISCONTENT

Once again the countryside lay in ruins and the cost of the wars and of rebuilding fell squarely on the peasants' shoulders. Ruinous taxes, a series of bad harvests, high prices and yet more outbreaks of the plague combined to push them over the edge in the late seventeenth century. There were **peasant rebellions** in Normandy and Brittany, but the worst of the "**Croquants'**" (yokels') uprisings broke out in the southwest in the late sixteenth century and rumbled on for two hundred years. The first major revolt occurred in the winter of 1594, when a number of towns and castles, including Monpazier, Excideuil and Puy-l'Évêque, were attacked. It was quickly and savagely put down by the allied forces of the local nobility, but the uprisings of May 1637 were altogether more serious. In the face of one tax demand too many, a **peasant army** 10,000 strong tried unsuccessfully to seize Périgueux but took Bergerac and then marched on Bordeaux. They were stopped, however, at Ste-Foy-la-Grande and the final show-

down took place soon after against 3400 royal troops at La Sauvetat-du-Dropt, south of Bergerac, leaving at least 1000 Croquants dead. The leaders were executed, one in Monpazier (see p.312), while the surviving rebels returned to the land for a while.

By the 1640s things were getting more complicated since the **aristocracy** themselves were also starting to protest, partly at the increasing tax demands, but mainly at the loss of privileges threatened by an increasingly centralized state. The **Fronde** (meaning a catapult or, more generally, a revolt), as the series of uprisings between 1648 and 1652 were known, were at their worst around Paris and Bordeaux, though other southwestern towns, such as Sarlat and Périgueux, also rebelled against royal authority. In Bordeaux the protests spilled over into a more widespread republican revolt which was only brought under control when the royal army was sent in again in 1653.

Things gradually settled down after 1661 as **Louis XIV** instigated major administrative and financial reform. At the same time, France was beginning to establish a **colonial empire** in North America, Africa, India and the Caribbean, and, as trade from these began to grow in the early eighteenth century, so Bordeaux and the other Atlantic ports prospered. Indeed, the late seventeenth and eighteenth centuries were golden years for Bordeaux and its hinterland. On the back of the colonial trade and a booming **wine trade** it grew to be the country's foremost port. Bordeaux town centre was almost completely rebuilt and intellectual life flourished under the leadership of Montesquieu (see p.101) and other liberal visionaries.

REVOLUTION

For the majority of people, however, little had changed. The gap between rich and poor grew ever wider as the clergy and aristocracy clung on to their privileges and the peasants were squeezed for higher taxes. Their general misery was exacerbated by a catastrophic harvest in 1788, followed by a particularly severe winter. Bread prices rocketed and on July 14, 1789, a mob stormed the **Bastille** in Paris, a hated symbol of the oppressive regime. As the **Revolution** spread, similar insurrections occurred throughout the country, accompanied by widespread peasant attacks on landowners' châteaux and the destruction of tax and rent records. In August the new National Assembly abolished the feudal rights and privileges of the nobility and then went on to nationalize church lands.

In these early stages the general population of the southwest supported the Revolution, as did the Bordeaux deputies to the Assembly, known as the **Girondins**. However, as the Parisian revolutionaries grew increasingly radical and proposed ever more centralization of power, the Girondins found themselves in bitter opposition. Towards the end of 1792, as the **First Republic** was being declared, they finally lost out to the extremists and in October the following year the **Terror** was unleashed as mass executions took place throughout France; estimates run to 3000 in Paris and 14,000 in the regions. Amongst the victims were the Girondin deputies, the last of whom were tracked down and killed in St-Émilion in 1794.

Though revolutionary bands wrought a fair amount of havoc in the southwest, looting and burning castles and churches, hacking at coats of arms and religious statuary, on the whole the region escaped fairly lightly; many aristocrats simply fled, and their possessions were sold off at knock-down prices. Among many administrative changes following the Revolution, one of the most significant was the creation of *départements* in 1790 to replace the old provinces. Thus began a process of national unification which continued in the following century with moves to stamp out Occitan and other regional dialects. So, gradually, did the traditionally independent southwest get drawn into mainstream France.

FROM NAPOLÉON I TO THE THIRD REPUBLIC

By the end of 1794 more moderate forces were in charge in Paris, but continuous infighting left the way open for **Napoléon Bonaparte**, who had made a name for himself as commander of the Revolutionary armies in Italy and Egypt, to seize power in a coup d'état in 1799. Napoléon quickly restored order and continued the process of centralization, replacing the power of local institutions by appointing a *préfet* to each *département* answerable only to the **Emperor**, as Napoléon declared himself in 1804. Nevertheless, the Dordogne and Lot *départements* supported the new regime by providing many military leaders – and more lowly troops – for Bonaparte's armies: the most notable

examples were Périgueux's Baron Pierre Daumesnil (see p.140) and Joachim Murat (1767–1815), the son of a village innkeeper born near Cahors, who was proclaimed King of Naples in reward for his numerous military successes. As elsewhere, however, it was the burden of the unceasing **Napoleonic wars** that cost the emperor his support. The economy of Bordeaux in particular and the southwest in general was hard hit when Napoléon banned commerce with Britain and Britain responded by blockading French ports in 1807.

So, few tears were shed in the region when Napoléon was finally defeated in 1815. The subsequent restoration of the **monarchy**, on the other hand, saw opinions divided along predictable lines: the aristocracy and the emerging *bourgeoisie* (the middle classes) rallied to the king, while the working population supported the uprising in 1848 – a shorter and less virulent reprise of the 1789 Revolution – which ended in the declaration of the **Second Republic**. The new government started off well by setting up national workshops to relieve unemployment and extending the vote to all adult males – an unprecedented move for its time. But in elections held later in 1848 the largely conservative vote of the newly enfranchised peasants was sufficient to outweigh the urban, working-class radicals. To everyone's surprise, Louis-Napoléon, nephew of the former emperor, romped home. In spite of his liberal reputation, he restricted the vote again, censored the press and pandered to the Catholic Church. In 1852, following a coup and further street fighting, he had himself proclaimed **Emperor Napoléon III**.

Like his uncle, Napoléon III pursued an expansionist military policy, both in France's colonial empire and in Europe. And like his uncle, too, it brought about his downfall: Napoléon III declared war on Prussia in 1870 and was quickly and roundly defeated by the far superior Prussian army. When Napoléon was taken prisoner the politicians in Paris – Cahors' Léon Gambetta among them (see p.274) – quickly proclaimed the **Third Republic**. Though it experienced a difficult birth, the Third Republic remained in power until 1940.

INTO THE TWENTIETH CENTURY

Napoléon was more successful on the economic front, however. From the 1850s on, France experienced rapid **industrial growth**, while foreign trade trebled. The effect on the Dordogne and Lot region, however, was mixed.

Bordeaux and the towns along the region's great rivers benefited most from the economic recovery. Bordeaux in particular prospered once again thanks to its colonial trade. Although the region had no coal or mineral resources to stimulate large-scale industrialization, beyond metalworking around Fumel, along the navigable rivers tanneries, paper mills and textile and glass industries were established. At the same time, agricultural areas within easy access of the rivers grew wealthy from exporting wheat, wine and tobacco. Many towns were given a facelift as their ramparts were torn down, wide avenues sliced through the cramped medieval quarters and a start was made on improving sanitation and water supply. Transportation was also modernized, although the **railways** came late to the Dordogne and Lot and were never very extensive. The region's first railway, the Bordeaux–Paris line, was completed in 1851, while the following year saw the opening of the **Canal latéral**, linking the Garonne with the Canal du Midi and thus the Mediterranean.

All this created pockets of economic growth, but the **rural areas** in between became increasingly marginalized. Rural industries began to dwindle in the face of competition from cheap manufactured goods and imports, and the railways simply provided the means for people to quit the country for the big cities.

But the biggest single crisis to hit the area's rural economy in the late nineteenth century was **phylloxera**. The parasite, which attacks the roots of vines, wiped out almost one third of the region's vineyards in the 1870s and 1880s. For a while growers tried all sorts of remedies, from flooding the fields to chemical fumigation, before it was discovered that vines in America, where phylloxera originated, were immune and that by grafting French vines on to American root-stock it was possible to produce resistant plants. The vineyards were slowly re-established, but over a much smaller area. In many areas farmers turned to alternatives, such as tobacco around Bergerac and sheep-rearing on the *causse* above Cahors.

THE WORLD WARS

Such problems paled into insignificance, however, when German troops marched into north-

ern France following the outbreak of **World War I** in 1914. The French government fled south to Bordeaux while thousands of southern men trekked north to lose their lives in the mud and horror of Verdun and the Somme battlefields. By the time the Germans were forced to surrender in 1918, France had 1.3 million dead, a quarter of whom were under 25 years of age, and three million had been wounded; every town and village in the Dordogne and Lot, as elsewhere in France, has its sad war memorial recording the loss of a generation of young men.

As a result, agricultural and industrial production declined and the birth-rate plummeted, although this was offset to some extent in the southwest by an influx of land-hungry refugees from Spain in the late nineteenth century and from Italy in the first decades of the twentieth. At the same time, however, Bordeaux's old-fashioned maritime industries were in terminal decline as the 1930s **Depression** hit home. The French government lurched from crisis to crisis while events across the border in Germany became increasingly menacing.

In April 1940, eight months after the outbreak of **World War II**, Hitler's western offensive began as he overran Belgium, Denmark and Holland. In June the French government retreated to Bordeaux again and millions of refugees poured south as Paris fell to the Germans. **Maréchal Pétain**, a conservative 84-year-old veteran of World War I, emerged from retirement to sign an armistice with Hitler and head the collaborationist **Vichy government**, based in the spa town of Vichy in the northern foothills of the Massif Central. France was now split in two. The Germans occupied the strategic regions north of the Loire and all along the Atlantic coast, including Bordeaux, while Vichy ostensibly governed the "Free Zone" comprising the majority of southern France; the frontier, with its customs points and guard posts, ran from the Pyrenees north through Langon and Castillon-la-Bataille to just south of Tours, and from there cut east to Geneva. Then, in 1942, German troops moved south to occupy the whole of France until they were driven out by Britain, America and their allies after 1944.

Resistance to the German occupation didn't really get going until 1943 when **General de Gaulle**, exiled leader of the "Free French", sent in **Jean Moulin** to unify the disparate and often ideologically opposed Resistance groups. Moulin was soon captured by the Gestapo and tortured to death by Klaus Barbie – the infamous "Butcher of Lyon", who was convicted as recently as 1987 for his war crimes – but the network Moulin established became increasingly effective. Its members provided information to the Allies, blew up train tracks, bridges and factories, as well as undertaking daring raids into enemy-held towns; the high, empty uplands of Dordogne and Lot *départements* afforded safe bases for many Resistance fighters. But for every action, the Germans hit back with savage **reprisals**. In May 1944 the SS Das Reich division, based at Montauban, set out to break the local resistance by massacring civilians and torching houses in some twenty towns and villages, of which the worst atrocities took place in Terrasson-la-Villedieu, Montpezat-de-Quercy, Mussidan and Frayssinet-le-Gélat.

Soon afterwards the Germans were being driven out, but the fighting didn't stop there. In the weeks following **liberation** thousands of **collaborators** were executed or publicly humiliated – women accused of consorting with the enemy had their heads shaved and were sometimes paraded naked through the streets – and the savagery got almost completely out of hand in the Dordogne. Not surprisingly, the issue of collaboration left deep scars in rural communities throughout the region, a bitterness which occasionally surfaces to this day in local disputes.

THE POSTWAR ERA

The main theme of the postwar years in the Dordogne and Lot, as in much of rural France, is one of **depopulation**. On average there are now 25 percent fewer people living on the land than at the end of the nineteenth century, rising to thirty percent or more in the worst-hit areas, such as parts of Lot-et-Garonne. Once again this has been partly offset by immigration, in this case by the *pieds noirs* (black feet) – French colonialists forced to flee Algeria after independence in 1962 – many of whom settled on farms in the southwest. Agricultural production has also been maintained thanks to a massive push towards mechanization and the amalgamation of small farms into larger, more efficient holdings – albeit often propped up by subsidies from the European Union.

Agriculture, including wine production, remains the backbone of the region's economy, but since the 1960s **tourism** has also become increasingly important. An enormous effort has gone into improving facilities and marketing the region, not just the honeypot attractions of Sarlat, Les Ezyies and the Dordogne valley châteaux, but also in the successful promotion of "green holidays", tempting people away from the Mediterranean and Atlantic coasts to discover all that the countryside has to offer. One of the largest such projects has been the reopening of the River Lot and the Canal latéral to navigation, but at a local level almost every town and village now puts on a programme of summer events to lure the tourists.

Ironically, the very backwardness of much of the Dordogne and Lot region is now proving to be one of its greatest assets. While its towns largely escaped the worst excesses of postwar modernization and have benefited from sensitive preservation schemes, its rural heartland continues to offer an unhurried, more traditional way of life which appeals as much to nostalgic Parisians as to the thousands of foreigners who flock into the region each year.

Since the 1960s many north Europeans – primarily British, but also increasing numbers of Dutch – have bought holiday-homes or settled permanently in the area. The French reaction to this invasion has been one of welcome, or at least tolerance, and not just because the newcomers restore the derelict farmhouses and pump money into the local economy. Even after all these centuries, there still exists a vague – and undoubtedly romantic – feeling among the resolutely independent, anti-Parisian southwesterners that they were better off under English rule, when at least the economy boomed and their forbears enjoyed a high degree of autonomy. Down the intervening years the region's strong sense of identity has been tested on many occasions, but has survived to resurface these days as a deep-burning pride in the land, its produce and its traditions.

BOOKS

There are few English-language history books specifically devoted to the Dordogne and Lot region, and a surprising dearth of novels, whether in English or in translation. A few of those that do exist – and are worth recommending – are detailed below, along with a number of general history books and classic texts which provide the background to events that have occurred in the region.

Publishers are given in the order of British publisher; American publisher, where both exist. Where books are published in one country only, UK, US or France follows the publisher's name. Books that are out of print are indicated by the abbreviation o/p.

HISTORY

Marc Bloch *Strange Defeat* (Norton). Moving personal study of the reasons for France's defeat in 1940 and subsequent caving-in to fascism. Found among the papers of this Sorbonne historian after his death at the hands of the Gestapo in 1942.

Alfred Cobban *A History of Modern France* (3 vols: 1715–99, 1799–1871 and 1871–1962; Penguin; Viking). Complete and very readable account of the main political, social and economic strands in French history from the death of Louis XIV to mid-de Gaulle.

Robert Cole *A Traveller's History of France* (Windrush Press, UK). Concise but enjoyable and informative romp through the essentials of French history up to the early 1990s.

Jonathan Fenby *France on the Brink* (Arcade Publishing). While France isn't perhaps quite as endangered as the title suggests, this provocative book takes a long, hard look at the problems facing contemporary France.

Christopher Hibbert *The Days of the French Revolution* (Penguin; Quill). Well-paced and entertaining narrative treatment by a master historian covering the salient events.

Johan Huizinga *The Waning of the Middle Ages* (Penguin; Dover). Primarily a study of the culture of the Burgundian and French courts – but a masterpiece that goes far beyond this, building up meticulous detail to re-create the whole life and mentality of the fourteenth and fifteenth centuries.

Colin Jones *The Cambridge Illustrated History of France* (Cambridge University Press). A political and social history of France from prehistoric times to the mid-1990s, concentrating on issues of regionalism, gender, race and class. Good illustrations and an easy, nonacademic writing style.

H. R. Kedward *In Search of the Maquis: Rural Resistance in South France 1942–44* (Clarendon Press, UK). Slightly dry style, but full of fascinating detail about the brave and often fatal struggle of the countless ordinary people across France who fought to drive the Germans from their country.

Emmanuel Le Roy Ladurie *Montaillou* (Penguin; Knopf). Village gossip and details of work and everyday life, all extracted by the Inquisition from Cathar peasants in the fourteenth century, and stored away until recently in the Vatican archives. Though academic and heavy-going in places, most of this book reads like a novel.

Marion Meade *Eleanor of Aquitaine* (Penguin USA, US). Highly accessible biography of one of the key characters in twelfth-century Europe. The author fleshes out the documented events until they read more like a historical novel.

Ian Ousby *Occupation: The Ordeal of France 1940–1944* (John Murray; Cooper Square Press). Somewhat revisionist 1997 account looking at how widespread collaboration was and why it took so long for the Resistance to get organized.

Stephen O'Shea *The Perfect Heresy* (Walker & Co). Lively but partisan nonacademic account of the history of the Cathars and the Catholic campaign mounted to wipe them out.

Simon Schama *Citizens* (Penguin; Vintage). Best-selling and highly tendentious revisionist history of the Revolution, which pretty well takes the line that the ideologues of the Revolution were a gang of fanatics who simply failed to see how good the *ancien régime* was. Well-written, racy and provocative.

Barbara Tuchman *A Distant Mirror* (Papermac; Ballantine). The history of the fourteenth century – plagues, wars, peasant uprisings and crusades – told through the life of a sympathetic French nobleman whose career took him through England, Italy and Byzantium and finally ended in a Turkish prison.

Paul Webster *Pétain's Crime: The Full Story of French Collaboration in the Holocaust* (Ivan R Dee). The fascinating and alarming story of the Vichy regime's more-than-willing collaboration with the Holocaust and the bravery of those, especially the Communist resistance in occupied France, who attempted to prevent it.

Alison Weir *Eleanor of Aquitaine* (Pimlico; Ballantine Books). A more scholarly account than Marion Meade's biography (see above), but still very readable. In telling Eleanor's tale, the author also gives a broad overview of twelfth-century French – and European – history.

Alexander Worth *France 1940–55* (Beacon Press, US, o/p). Extremely good and emotionally engaged portrayal of the taboo Occupation period in French history, followed by the Cold War and years of colonial struggle in which the same political tensions and heart-searchings were at play.

Theodore Zeldin *France 1848–1945* (Oxford University Press; o/p). Five thematic volumes on diverse French matters – all good reads.

Theodore Zeldin *The French* (Harvill; Kodansha). Urbane and witty survey of the French world view – chapter titles include "How to be chic" and "How to appreciate a grandmother".

TRAVEL, ART AND LITERATURE

Kenneth J. Conant *Carolingian and Romanesque Architecture, 800–1200* (Yale University Press). Good European study with a focus on Cluny and the Santiago de Compostela pilgrim route.

Joanne Harris *Chocolate* (Black Swan; Penguin USA). Set in the Garonne valley near Agen, this bittersweet bestseller gives little in the way of specific regional colour, but is worth

reading for its beautifully rendered view of life in claustrophobic, small-town rural France, albeit one wrapped inside a fairy-tale coating.

Mirabel Osler *The Elusive Truffle* (originally published as *A Spoon With Every Course*; Black Swan, UK). Part recipe book, part travelogue, Osler goes in search of the rapidly disappearing traditional cuisine of France, including the Périgord.

Christian Signol *La Rivière Espérance* (Presses Pocket, France). Set in the 1830s, this French novel – which was made into a hugely successful TV film – follows the adventures of a young sailor working the *gabares* which then plied the Dordogne. The nostalgic tale commemorates the end of an era as the railways relentlessly destroy the romanticized river life.

Ruth Silvestre *A House in the Sunflowers* & *A Harvest of Sunflowers* (Allison & Busby). These two books tell a gentle, engaging tale of restoring a tumbledown farmhouse in Lot-et-Garonne. Singer-actress Ruth Silvestre and her family are swept up into local life – the grape harvest, plum harvest, village fetes and gargantuan meals – thanks to their generous and exuberant neighbours, the Bertrands. Together they witness modern life gradually intrude into this deeply traditional corner of rural France.

Marguerite Smith *A House Among Vines* (Robert Hale, UK). In the 1970s Marguerite Smith found herself living alone with little money in a remote corner of southwest France. She describes her life and her neighbours – French and otherwise – with humour and compassion.

Freda White *Three Rivers of France* (Faber, o/p), *Ways of Aquitaine* (Faber, o/p). Freda White's classic books, written in the 1950s before tourism came along to the backwater communities that were her interest, are well worth getting hold of. They are evocative books, slipping in the history and culture painlessly, if not always too accurately, and still provide a valuable and vivid overview of the region.

GUIDES

Glynn Christian *Edible France* (Grub Street; Interlink). A guide to food rather than restaurants: regional produce, local specialities, markets and the best shops for buying goodies to bring back home.

Cicerone Walking Guides (Cicerone, UK). Neat, durable guides, with detailed route descriptions. Titles include *The Way of Saint James – A Walkers Guide* and *The Way of Saint James – A Cyclist's Guide*, both of which follow the route from Le Puy to Santiago (GR65).

Footpaths of Europe (Robertson-McCarta, UK). English-language versions of the Topo-guides (see below), covering the system of GR footpaths, illustrated with 1:50,000 colour maps.

Joy Law *Dordogne* (Pallas Athene, UK). Erudite and accessible thematic guide-cum-history text written by a long-time resident of the *département*, packed with interesting anecdotes and local colour.

Promenades et Randonnées (Comité Départemental du Tourisme du Lot, France). Series of guides detailing walks in Lot *département*, covering the Causse de Gramat, the Bouriane and southeast of the Célé valley, amongst other areas. The illustrated sketchmaps make it possible to follow the walks with a limited knowledge of French.

Alain Roussot (ed) *Discovering Périgord Prehistory* (Sud-Ouest, France). Translated into English, this guide provides a solid introduction to the prehistoric caves of the Périgord. It covers the most significant caves in chronological order, while the illustrations give a taste of what's on offer.

Jeanne Strang *Goose Fat and Garlic* (Kyle Cathie). Comprehensive cookbook covering the classics of southwestern cuisine, from *tourin* soup and scrambled eggs with truffles to *cassoulet* and *clafoutis*.

Paul Strang *Wines of South-west France* (Kyle Cathie). A bit dated now (1996), but still by far the best of the English-language guides to the region's wines. In addition to the history of viticulture and brief reviews of recommended producers in all the wine-producing areas from Figeac to Bergerac (excluding the Bordeaux vineyards), the book gives a glimpse into local culture and traditions.

Topo-guides *Les Sentiers de Grande Randonnée* (FFRP-CNSGR, France). The best of the walking guides covering the long-distance paths, Topo-guides are widely available in France and not hard to follow with a working knowledge of French. In addition to the *Sentier de St-Jacques-de-Compostelle*, the series includes the *Gorges de l'Aveyron* and the *Traversée du Périgord*.

Paula Wolfert *The Cooking of South West France* (Grub Street; HarperCollins). Rigorously researched cookbook containing a mix of traditional and modern dishes from the southwest. The recipes are sometimes lengthy and a bit complicated, but they work. For the serious cook.

LANGUAGE

French can be a deceptively familiar language because of the number of words and structures it shares with English. Despite this, it's far from easy, though the bare essentials are not difficult to master and can make all the difference. Even just saying "Bonjour Madame/Monsieur" and then gesticulating will usually get you a smile and helpful service. People working in tourist offices, hotels and so on, almost always speak English and tend to use it when you're struggling to speak French – be grateful, not insulted.

FRENCH PRONUNCIATION

One easy rule to remember is that **consonants** at the ends of words are usually silent. *Pas plus tard* (not later) is thus pronounced "pa-plu-tarr". But when the following word begins with a vowel, you run the two together: *pas après* (not after) becomes "pazaprey".

Vowels are the hardest sounds to get right. Roughly:

a	as in h**a**t
e	as in g**e**t
é	between g**e**t and g**a**te
è	between g**e**t and g**u**t
eu	like the **u** in h**u**rt
i	as in mach**i**ne
o	as in h**o**t
o, au	as in **o**ver
ou	as in f**oo**d
u	as in a pursed-lip version of **u**se

More awkward are the **combinations** *in/im, en/em, an/am, on/om, un/um* at the ends of words, or followed by consonants other than *n* or *m*. Again, roughly:

in/im	like the **an** in **an**xious
an/am, en/em	like the **don** in **Don**caster when said with a nasal accent
on/om	like the **don** in **Don**caster said by someone with a heavy cold
un/um	like the **u** in **u**nderstand

Consonants are much as in English, except that: *ch* is always "sh", *c* is "s", *h* is silent, *th* is the same as "t", *ll* is like the "y" in yes, *w* is "v", and *r* is growled (or rolled).

LEARNING MATERIALS

Rough Guide French Phrasebook (Rough Guides). Mini dictionary-style phrasebook with both English–French and French–English sections, along with cultural tips for tricky situations and a menu reader.

Mini French Dictionary (Harrap/Prentice Hall). French–English and English–French, plus a brief grammar and pronunciation guide.

Breakthrough French (Pan; book and 2 cassettes). Excellent teach-yourself course.

French and English Slang Dictionary (Harrap/Prentice Hall); **Dictionary of Modern**

Colloquial French (Routledge). Both volumes are a bit large to carry, but they are the key to all you ever wanted to understand about the French vernacular.

Verbaid (Verbaid, Hawk House, Heath Lane, Farnham, Surrey GU9 0PR). CD-size laminated paper "verb wheel" giving you the tense endings for the regular verbs.

A Vous La France; Franc Extra; Franc-Parler (BBC Publications/EMC Publishing; each has a book and 2 cassettes). BBC radio courses, running from beginners' level to fairly advanced.

A BRIEF GUIDE TO SPEAKING FRENCH

BASIC WORDS AND PHRASES

French nouns are divided into masculine and feminine. This causes difficulties with adjectives, whose endings have to change to suit the gender of the nouns they qualify. If you know some grammar, you will know what to do. If not, stick to the masculine form, which is the simplest – it's what we have done in this glossary.

today	*aujourd'hui*	that one	*celà*
yesterday	*hier*	open	*ouvert*
tomorrow	*demain*	closed	*fermé*
in the morning	*le matin*	big	*grand*
in the afternoon	*l'après-midi*	small	*petit*
in the evening	*le soir*	more	*plus*
now	*maintenant*	less	*moins*
later	*plus tard*	a little	*un peu*
at one o'clock	*à une heure*	a lot	*beaucoup*
at three o'clock	*à trois heures*	cheap	*bon marché*
at ten-thirty	*à dix heures et demie*	expensive	*cher*
at midday	*à midi*	good	*bon*
man	*un homme*	bad	*mauvais*
woman	*une femme*	hot	*chaud*
here	*ici*	cold	*froid*
there	*là*	with	*avec*
this one	*ceci*	without	*sans*

NUMBERS

1	*un*	15	*quinze*	80	*quatre-vingts*
2	*deux*	16	*seize*	90	*quatre-vingt-dix*
3	*trois*	17	*dix-sept*	95	*quatre-vingt-quinze*
4	*quatre*	18	*dix-huit*	100	*cent*
5	*cinq*	19	*dix-neuf*	101	*cent-et-un*
6	*six*	20	*vingt*	200	*deux cents*
7	*sept*	21	*vingt-et-un*	300	*trois cents*
8	*huit*	22	*vingt-deux*	500	*cinq cents*
9	*neuf*	30	*trente*	1000	*mille*
10	*dix*	40	*quarante*	2000	*deux milles*
11	*onze*	50	*cinquante*	5000	*cinq milles*
12	*douze*	60	*soixante*	1,000,000	*un million*
13	*treize*	70	*soixante-dix*		
14	*quatorze*	75	*soixante-quinze*		

DAYS AND DATES

January	*janvier*	November	*novembre*
February	*février*	December	*décembre*
March	*mars*		
April	*avril*	Sunday	*dimanche*
May	*mai*	Monday	*lundi*
June	*juin*	Tuesday	*mardi*
July	*juillet*	Wednesday	*mercredi*
August	*août*	Thursday	*jeudi*
September	*septembre*	Friday	*vendredi*
October	*octobre*	Saturday	*samedi*

August 1	*le premier août*	November 23	*le vingt-trois novembre*
March 2	*le deux mars*	2002	*deux mille deux*
July 14	*le quatorze juillet*		

TALKING TO PEOPLE

When addressing people you should always use *Monsieur* for a man, *Madame* for a woman, *Mademoiselle* for a young woman or girl. Plain *bonjour* by itself is not enough. This isn't as formal as it seems, and it has its uses when you've forgotten someone's name or want to attract someone's attention.

Excuse me	*Pardon*	please	*s'il vous plaît*
Do you speak English?	*Parlez-vous anglais?*	thank you	*merci*
How do you say it in French?	*Comment ça se dit en français?*	hello	*bonjour*
		goodbye	*au revoir*
What's your name?	*Comment vous appelez-vous?*	good morning /afternoon	*bonjour*
My name is . . .	*Je m'appelle . . .*	good evening	*bonsoir*
I'm	*Je suis*	good night	*bonne nuit*
English	*anglais[e]*	How are you?	*Comment allez-vous?/ Ça va?*
Irish	*irlandais[e]*		
Scottish	*écossais[e]/*	Fine, thanks	*Très bien, merci*
Welsh	*gallois[e]*	I don't know	*Je ne sais pas*
American	*américain[e]*	Let's go	*Allons-y*
Canadian	*canadien[ne]/*	See you tomorrow	*A demain*
Australian	*australien[ne]/*	See you soon	*A bientôt*
a New Zealander	*néo-zélandais[e]*	Sorry	*Pardon, Madame/ Je m'ex-*
yes	*oui*		
no	*non*		*cuse*
I understand	*Je comprends*	Leave me alone (aggressive)	*Fichez-moi la paix!*
I don't understand	*Je ne comprends pas*		
Can you speak slower?	*S'il vous plaît, parlez moins vite*	Please help me	*Aidez-moi, s'il vous plaît*
OK/agreed	*d'accord*		

FINDING THE WAY

bus	*autobus/bus/car*	on foot	*à pied*
bus station	*gare routière*	Where are you going?	*Vous allez où?*
bus stop	*arrêt*	I'm going to . . .	*Je vais à . . .*
car	*voiture*	I want to get off at	*Je voudrais descendre*
train/taxi/ferry	*train/taxi/ferry*	the road to	*à la route pour . . .*
boat	*bâteau*	near	*près/pas loin*
plane	*avion*	far	*loin*
train station	*gare (SNCF)*	left	*à gauche*
platform	*quai*	right	*à droite*
What time does it leave?	*Il part à quelle heure?*	straight on	*tout droit*
What time does it arrive?	*Il arrive à quelle heure?*	on the other side of	*à l'autre côté de*
a ticket to . . .	*un billet pour . . .*	on the corner of	*à l'angle de*
single ticket	*aller simple*	next to	*à côté de*
return ticket	*aller retour*	behind	*derrière*
validate your ticket	*compostez votre billet*	in front of	*devant*
valid for	*valable pour*	before	*avant*
ticket office	*vente de billets*	after	*après*
how many kilometres?	*combien de kilomètres?*	under	*sous*
how many hours?	*combien d'heures?*	to cross	*traverser*
hitchhiking	*autostop*	bridge	*pont*

QUESTIONS AND REQUESTS

The simplest way of asking a question is to start with *s'il vous plaît* (please), then name the thing you want in an interrogative tone of voice. For example:

Where is there a bakery?	*S'il vous plaît, la boulangerie?*	Question words	
Which way is it to the Eiffel Tower?	*S'il vous plaît, la route pour la tour Eiffel?*	where?	*où?*
		how?	*comment?*
		how many/how much?	*combien?*
Similarly with requests:		when?	*quand?*
		why?	*pourquoi?*
Can we have a room for two?	*S'il vous plaît, une chambre pour deux?*	at what time?	*à quelle heure?*
Can I have a kilo of oranges?	*S'il vous plaît, un kilo d'oranges?*	what is/which is?	*quel est?*

ACCOMMODATION

a room for one/ two people	*une chambre pour une/ deux personnes*	sheets	*draps*
a double bed	*un lit double*	blankets	*couvertures*
a room with a shower	*une chambre avec douche*	quiet	*calme*
		noisy	*bruyant*
a room with a bath	*une chambre avec salle de bain*	hot water	*eau chaude*
		cold water	*eau froide*
for one/two/three nights	*pour une/deux/trois nuits*	Is breakfast included?	*Est-ce que le petit déjeuner est compris?*
Can I see it?	*Je peux la voir?*	I would like breakfast	*Je voudrais prendre le petit déjeuner*
a room on the courtyard	*une chambre sur la cour*	I don't want breakfast	*Je ne veux pas de petit déjeuner*
a room over the street	*une chambre sur la rue*		
first floor	*premier étage*	Can we camp here?	*On peut camper ici?*
second floor	*deuxième étage*	campsite	*un camping/terrain de camping*
with a view	*avec vue*		
key	*clef*	tent	*une tente*
to iron	*repasser*	tent space	*un emplacement*
do laundry	*faire la lessive*	youth hostel	*auberge de jeunesse*

CARS

service station	*garage*	put air in the tyres	*gonfler les pneus*
service	*service*	battery	*batterie*
to park the car	*garer la voiture*	the battery is dead	*la batterie est morte*
car park	*un parking*	plugs	*bougies*
no parking	*défense de stationner/*	to break down	*tomber en panne*
	stationnement interdit	gas can	*bidon*
gas station	*poste d'essence*	insurance	*assurance*
fuel	*essence*	green card	*carte verte*
(to) fill it up	*faire le plein*	traffic lights	*feux*
oil	*huile*	red light	*feu rouge*
air line	*ligne à air*	green light	*feu vert*

HEALTH MATTERS

doctor	*médecin*	stomach ache	*mal à l'estomac*
I don't feel well	*Je ne me sens pas bien*	period	*règles*
medicines	*médicaments*	pain	*douleur*
prescription	*ordonnance*	it hurts	*ça fait mal*
I feel sick	*Je suis malade*	chemist	*pharmacie*
I have a headache	*J'ai mal à la tête*	hospital	*hôpital*

OTHER NEEDS

bakery	*boulangerie*	bank	*banque*
food shop	*alimentation*	money	*argent*
supermarket	*supermarché*	toilets	*toilettes*
to eat	*manger*	police	*police*
to drink	*boire*	telephone	*téléphone*
camping gas	*camping gaz*	cinema	*cinéma*
tobacconist	*tabac*	theatre	*théâtre*
stamps	*timbres*	to reserve/book	*réserver*

GLOSSARY

Below are terms you'll either come across in the *Guide* or encounter on your travels.

FRENCH TERMS

ABRI Prehistoric rock-shelter.

APPELLATION (Appellation d'Origine Contrôlée; AOC) Wine classification indicating that the wine meets strict requirements regarding its provenance and methods of production.

ABBAYE Abbey.

AUBERGE Country inn, usually offering accommodation.

AUTOROUTE Motorway.

BASTIDE New town founded in the thirteenth and fourteenth centuries, built on a grid plan around an arcaded market square.

BOULES Popular French game played with steel balls (see p.56).

CABANE, BORIE or **GARIOTTE** Dry-stone hut, probably used by shepherds.

CAUSSE Limestone plateau extending from Dordogne *département* south through Lot and into Aveyron.

CHAI Barn or storehouse in which wines are aged.

CHAMBRES D'HÔTE Bed-and-breakfast accommodation in a private house.

CHARTREUSE One-storey building typical of the Bordeaux wine region, slightly raised up and built on top of a half-buried *chai*; also a Carthusian monastery.

CHÂTEAU Castle, mansion, stately home.

CHÂTEAU FORT Castle built for a specifically military purpose.

COLLÉGIALE Church which shelters a community of priests.

COLOMBAGE Traditional building style consisting of a timber frame filled with earth and straw or bricks.

COMMUNE The basic administrative region, each under a mayor (very occasionally, a mayoress).

DÉGUSTATION Tasting (wine or food).

DÉPARTEMENT Mid-level administrative unit run by a local council – the equivalent of a county in Britain.

DOLMEN Neolithic stone structure, generally held to be a tomb, consisting of two or more upright slabs supporting a horizontal stone.

DONJON Castle keep.

ÉGLISE Church.

FALAISE Cliff.

FERME AUBERGE Farm licensed to provide meals in which the majority of the produce must come from the farm itself.

FOIRE Large market held once or twice monthly in some country towns.

FOUILLE Archeological excavation.

GABARE or **GABARRE** Traditional wooden boat used to transport goods on the Dordogne and Lot rivers up until the late nineteenth century.

GAVAGE Process of force-feeding ducks and geese to make foie gras.

GISEMENT Deposit, stratified layers of an archeological excavation.

GOUFFRE Limestone chasm or sink-hole.

GROTTE Cave.

HALLE(S) Covered market.

HÔTEL Hotel, but also an aristocratic town house or mansion.

LAUZE Small limestone slabs, a traditional roof covering in the Périgord.

NAVETTE Shuttle-bus, for example connecting a town with its airport.

OCCITAN Language (and associated culture) formerly spoken throughout most of south and southwest France.

PISÉ Traditional Périgordin floor made out of small limestone slabs inserted upright into a bed of clay or lime.

PÉTANQUE Southern version of the game *boules* (see p.56).

PIGEONNIER Dovecote, often built on stilts and used to collect droppings for fertilizer.

PORTE Gateway.

RETABLE Altarpiece.

SENESCHAL Chief administrator and justice in medieval times, the representative of the king.

TABLE D'HÔTE Meals served to residents of a *chambres d'hôte*.

TOUR Tower.

VERSION ORIGINALE (*v.o.*) film shown in its original language and subtitled in French.

ARCHITECTURAL TERMS

AMBULATORY Passage round the outer edge of the choir of a church.

APSE Semicircular or polygonal termination at the east end of a church.

BAROQUE High Renaissance period of art and architecture, distinguished by extreme ornateness.

CHEVET East end of a church.

CLASSICAL Architectural style incorporating Greek and Roman elements: pillars, domes, colonnades, etc, at its height in France in the seventeenth century and revived in the nineteenth century as **Neoclassical**.

FRESCO Painting in watercolour on a wall or ceiling while the plaster is still wet.

GALLO-ROMAN Period of Roman occupation of Gaul (1st century BC to 4th century AD).

FLAMBOYANT Very ornate form of Gothic.

GOTHIC Architectural style prevalent from the twelfth to sixteenth centuries, characterized by pointed arches and ribbed vaulting.

MACHICOLATIONS Parapet on a castle, fortified church, gateway etc. with openings for dropping stones and so forth on attackers.

MEROVINGIAN Dynasty (and art, etc), ruling France and parts of Germany from the sixth to mid-eighth centuries.

NARTHEX Entrance hall of church.

NAVE Main body of a church.

RENAISSANCE Architectural and artistic style developed in fifteenth-century Italy and imported to France in the sixteenth century by François I.

ROMANESQUE Early medieval architecture distinguished by squat, rounded forms and naive sculpture, called *Roman* in French (not to be confused with *Romain* – Roman).

STUCCO Plaster used to embellish ceilings, etc.

TRANSEPT Transverse arms of a church, perpendicular to the nave.

TYMPANUM Sculpted semi-circular panel above the door of a Romanesque church.

REGIONAL NAMES

AQUITAINE Originally a Roman administrative region extending from Poitiers and Limoges south to the Pyrenees. It later became a Duchy, which, at its apogee in the twelfth century, covered roughly the same area, though it fluctuated enormously. In the 1960s the name was resurrected with the creation of regional administrative units. Modern-day Aquitaine is based around Bordeaux and comprises the *départements* of Dordogne, Gironde and Lot-et-Garonne, amongst others.

GASCONY The region to the west and south of the River Garonne, named after a Celtic tribe (the Vascons). In the early tenth century it became an independent duchy but was soon subsumed into the duchy of Aquitaine, though still retained its own identity.

GUYENNE A corruption of the name "Aquitaine" originating during the period of English rule. Prior to the Revolution, the province of Guyenne extended from Gironde to Aveyron. Nowadays it is occasionally used to refer to an area roughly encompassing Entre-Deux-Mers and St-Émilion, although there is no strict demarcation.

QUERCY Former province roughly equivalent to the modern *département* of the Lot and the north part of the Tarn-et-Garonne. The latter is often referred to as Bas-Quercy, while Haut-Quercy comprises the Lot's northern region.

PÉRIGORD The confines of Périgord have changed little since pre-Roman times, when it was the home of the Gaulish tribe, the *Petrocori*. In the eighth century Périgord became a county, and then a province of France until the name was officially changed to Dordogne when *départements* were created in 1790 (each *département* was named after its principal river). However, Périgord is still used frequently, especially in tourist literature. These days it is often subdivided into Périgord Vert (Green Périgord; the *département*'s northern sector); Périgord Blanc (White; the central strip along the Isle valley including Périgueux); Périgord Pourpre (Purple; the southwest corner around Bergerac); Périgord Noir (Black; the southeast, including Sarlat and the Vézère valley).

MIDI-PYRÉNÉES The modern administrative region to the east of Aquitaine, based on Toulouse and incorporating the *départements* of Lot, Tarn-et-Garonne and Aveyron, amongst others.

INDEX

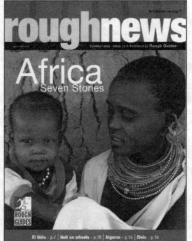

ROUGH GUIDES: Mini Guides, Travel Specials and Phrasebooks

MINI GUIDES

Antigua
Bangkok
Barbados
Beijing
Big Island of Hawaii
Boston
Brussels
Budapest
Cape Town
Copenhagen
Dublin
Edinburgh

Florence
Honolulu
Ibiza & Formentera
Jerusalem
Las Vegas
Lisbon
London Restaurants
Madeira
Madrid
Malta & Gozo
Maui
Melbourne
Menorca

Montreal
New Orleans

Paris
Rome
Seattle
St Lucia
Sydney
Tenerife
Tokyo
Toronto
Vancouver

TRAVEL SPECIALS

First-Time Asia
First-Time Europe
Women Travel

PHRASEBOOKS

Czech
Dutch
Egyptian Arabic
European
French
German
Greek

Hindi & Urdu
Hungarian
Indonesian
Italian
Japanese
Mandarin
  Chinese
Mexican
  Spanish
Polish
Portuguese
Russian
Spanish
Swahili
Thai
Turkish
Vietnamese

AVAILABLE AT ALL GOOD BOOKSHOPS

ROUGH GUIDES:
Reference and Music CDs

REFERENCE

Blues:
  100 Essential CDs
Classical Music
Classical:
  100 Essential CDs
Country Music
Country:
  100 Essential CDs
Drum'n'bass
House Music
Hip Hop
Irish Music
Jazz

Music USA
Opera
Opera:
  100 Essential CDs
Reggae
Reggae:
  100 Essential CDs
Rock
Rock:
  100 Essential CDs

Soul:
  100 Essential CDs
Techno
World Music

World Music:
  100 Essential CDs
English Football
European Football
Internet
Money Online
Shopping Online
Travel Health

ROUGH GUIDE MUSIC CDs

Music of the Andes
Australian Aboriginal
Bluegrass
Brazilian Music
Cajun & Zydeco
Music of Cape Verde
Classic Jazz
Music of
  Colombia
Cuban Music
Eastern Europe

Music of Egypt
English Roots Music
Flamenco
Music of Greece
Hip Hop
India & Pakistan
Irish Music
Music of Jamaica
Music of Japan
Kenya & Tanzania
Marrabenta
  Mozambique
Native American
North African
Music of Portugal
Reggae
Salsa
Samba
Scottish Music
South African Music
Music of Spain
Sufi Music
Tango

Tex-Mex
West African Music
World Music
World Music Vol 2
Music of Zimbabwe

NO FLIES ON YOU!

THE ROUGH GUIDE TO
TRAVEL HEALTH:
PLANNING YOUR TRIP
WORLDWIDE
UK£5.00, US$7.95

DON'T GET BITTEN BY
THE WRONG TRAVEL BUG

Will you have enough stories to tell your grandchildren?

©2000 Yahoo! Inc.

Yahoo! Travel

DO YOU
YAHOO!
?